Nabil EL-Sahli

SYSTEMS CONSTRUCTION AND
A MATHEMATICAL AND LOGICAL FR

THE McGRAW-HILL INTERNATIONAL SERIES IN SOFTWARE ENGINEERING

Consulting Editor

Professor D. Ince
The Open University

Other titles in this series

Portable Modula-2 Programming – Woodman, Griffiths, Souter and Davies
SSADM: A Practical Approach – Ashworth and Goodland
Software Engineering: Analysis and Design – Easteal and Davies
Introduction to Compiling Techniques: A First Course Using ANSI C, LEX and YACC – Bennett
An Introduction to Program Design – Sargent
Object Oriented Databases: Applications in Software Engineering – Brown
Object Oriented Software Engineering with C^{++} – Ince
Expert Database Systems: A Gentle Introduction – Beynon-Davies
Practical Formal Methods with VDM – Andrews and Ince
SSADM Version 4: A Users Guide – Eva
A Structured Approach to Systems Analysis – Heap, Stanway and Windsor
Software Engineering Environments – Brown, Earl and McDermid
Software Project Management – Ince, Sharp and Woodman
Introduction to VDM – Woodman and Heal
Rapid Information Systems Development – Bell and Wood-Harper

SYSTEMS CONSTRUCTION AND ANALYSIS: A MATHEMATICAL AND LOGICAL FRAMEWORK

Norman Fenton
and
Gillian Hill
Professor of Computing Science and Lecturer
City University
London

McGRAW-HILL BOOK COMPANY

London · New York · St Louis · San Francisco · Auckland
Bogotá · Caracas · Hamburg · Lisbon · Madrid · Mexico
Milan · Montreal · New Delhi · Panama · Paris · San Juan
São Paulo · Singapore · Sydney · Tokyo · Toronto

Published by
McGRAW-HILL Book Company Europe
SHOPPENHANGERS ROAD · MAIDENHEAD · BERKSHIRE SL6 2QL · ENGLAND
TELEPHONE 0628 23432; FAX 0628 770224

British Library Cataloguing in Publication Data
Fenton, Norman E.
Systems Construction and Analysis: Mathematical and Logical Framework
I. Title II. Hill, Gillian Ann Foard
004.2
ISBN 0-07-707431-9

Library of Congress Cataloging-in-Publication Data
Fenton, Norman E.
Systems construction and analysis: a mathematical and logical framework / Norman Fenton and Gillian Hill.
p. cm. –
(The McGraw-Hill international series in software engineering)
Includes bibliographical references and index.
ISBN 0-07-707431-9
1. System design. 2. System analysis. I. Hill, Gillian. II. Title. III. Series.
QA76.9.S88F5 1992 005.1′2–dc20 92-1487CIP

12345 CUP 9543

Typeset by Norman Fenton and Gillian Hill and printed and bound in Great Britain at the University Press, Cambridge.

To
Naomi and Nicole
and to
Barry
Graham and Anne
Lesley and Russ
Robert and Sue

CONTENTS

FOREWORD

When I was an undergraduate in the late 1960s the foundations of computer science which we studied consisted mainly of formal languages and automata theory, recursion theory and a bit of modern algebra. We did not study logic until the last year and even then it was an optional course.

Today our undergraduate programmes are pervaded by logic, 'applied' logic and discrete mathematics while formal languages, automata and recursion theory are relegated to a relative backwater of the subject. In my own department, the first-year student can look forward to spending half his or her time on set theory, propositional and first-order logic, tableaux proofs, specification and verification of programs, abstract data types and more. Of course, some of this material is interwoven with their programming courses. This is because programming, and much of computer science besides, may be seen to have its practical foundations in applied logic and discrete mathematics.

Thus, this new mathematics pervades much of the undergraduate programme and, moreover, some of the old material is still useful. (In how many different guises do we find finite automata or regular languages playing a role?)

As teachers, one of our main problems has been the identification of appropriate textbooks for our undergraduate students. In a fast-changing subject, this has been extremely difficult and many of us have resorted to producing our own 'student notes'. The subject now has reached a level of maturity and stability that is encouraging the production of these standard texts. I am very gratified to see that Norman Fenton and Gillian Hill have put together what can only be called a comprehensive and lively presentation of the requisite material—'old' theory and new. There is enough of substance here to keep the energetic student busy for a good part of his or her formal education (and, perhaps, long after). The examples are interesting and illustrative. There are threads through the material which bring coherence and structure to what in other hands might have been a simply presented 'set' of topics.

I am confident that future readers will enjoy reading this interesting, challenging and essential material. I also hope that they enjoy Spurs always overcoming Arsenal as much as I did!

Professor Tom Maibaum
Head of Department of Computing
Imperial College
London

PREFACE

This is the first book to bring together a formal approach to the construction of systems with a more pragmatic approach to their analysis. By working within a formal theoretical framework we are able to reason about the construction of systems; by providing mathematical techniques for analysis we are able to make quantitative assessments of the systems that we construct.

Our book is a textbook and is based on teaching material that has been subjected to an iterative process of trying out, testing and changing over the last six years. Our courses have been taught in computer science, business computing and electrical engineering departments; they have ranged from part-time and full-time MSc courses to undergraduate courses and short courses for industrial companies. The background of our students has been equally wide ranging: from postgraduate degrees in philosophy and mathematics to industrial experience with no previous training in mathematics.

We have written our book for full-time and part-time students as well as for those who are developing application systems in industry. After providing the mathematical foundations in Part I, we present in Part II the theoretical framework for the formal construction of systems, and the analytical techniques for measurement in Part III. Our approach is not constrained by traditional boundaries between disciplines; instead, we emphasize the links between the well-established disciplines of mathematics, logic and engineering. By presenting the fundamental concepts and theories that we currently need for system development, we aim to provide a theoretical framework for system development that will support an increase in the reliability of the application systems that our society is so dependent on.

Our unifying approach brings together under one cover: material that has been previously accessible only to the most dedicated academic theoreticians; with introductory topics that have been presented (but only at a more shallow level) in many textbooks on discrete mathematics. This enables us to build on the fundamental ideas of logic and mathematics and show how they can be applied to the industrial practice of system development. We have presented in detail applications of logic and mathematics to the construction of systems that have previously appeared only in research papers or in specialist textbooks. Other applications are given a new treatment within our theoretical framework so that they meet the current demands for systems engineering and measurement applications.

We provide a gentle introduction to the discrete mathematics and formal systems before giving a serious exposition of mathematical logic that emphasizes the link between theories in formal languages and their models. The theory of universal algebras, the λ-calculus and fixed-point theory contribute to the formal framework required for the specification of abstract data types as the primitive objects in a system. The major programming paradigms are linked to the approaches to specification. Programs are verified by the axiomatic method and graph models are used to identify program structure. The topics of algorithmic complexity, coding theory and measurement theory are provided with a rigorous foundation; probability theory is viewed from an axiomatic approach and provides a natural and powerful application of set theory.

Our textbook has been designed for a wide range of applied courses in discrete mathematics, programming, software engineering, business computing, data communications, database design, intelligent knowledge-based systems, information systems and digital control systems. We have taken the view that it is more valuable to present the theoretical framework for the wide range of existing application systems in the familiar languages of logic and mathematics. A deep understanding of the concepts involved is more important than skills that may be dependent on the transient nature of the popularity of specific notations and methods. We nevertheless include an introduction to both the theoretical foundation and the notation of VDM and Z as the currently most used and widely accepted approaches to specification of systems.

Because we have watched students gain an understanding of new, and sometimes difficult, concepts as they work through well-designed exercises, we have included a large number of well-tested exercises throughout our book. Many examples are given to help students work independently, and selected solutions are also provided after the last chapter in the book. Our experience of teaching students with widely differing backgrounds has also led us to star the more difficult sections in the text as an indication that they can be omitted at a first reading. We give suggestions for further reading at the end of each chapter and provide a bibliography at the end of the book. A separate booklet for teachers provides advice on structuring the material for courses of different levels, as well as solutions to the remaining exercises in the book, supplementary exercises and examination questions.

ACKNOWLEDGEMENTS

We thank Reem Bahgat, Bernie Cohen, David Dodson, Sylvia Jennings, Bev Littlewood, Ann Mitchell, Judith Secker, Robin Whitty and Roland How Tai Yah for making detailed comments on specific chapters in the book, and helping to improve them significantly. Numerous other people have influenced the contents and presentation. These include Charles Cohen, Bob Dickerson, Haya Freedman, Peter Mellor, Richard Mitchell, David Till, Peter Osmon, Peter Vamos and the South Bank METKIT team. We would also like to thank Stuart Green and Terry Stanley who drew to our attention some points of error.

The major influence on the book, however, has been made by the many students who over the years have both praised and objected to our course material and laboured over the exercises in tutorials. Their thoughtful criticisms have helped us to clarify our presentation and to correct many mistakes.

We are grateful to Andrew Ware of McGraw-Hill who both encouraged us and guided us through the series of deadlines that finally resulted in publication. We produced the manuscript in camera-ready form using LaTeX, and are indebted to Mike Piff for providing us with the LaTeX macros that presented the ordered solutions to the selected exercises at the end of the book. We used Mike Spivey's macros for printing the Z schemas.

We have gained from each other in the task of co-operating to present so many important concepts and applications within an integrated theoretical framework. For support and inspiration we give special thanks to our families.

Part I

Mathematical Foundations

Chapter 1

INTRODUCTION

An understanding of the mathematical nature of complex systems is vital to progress in the broad subject that is called information technology. This book provides the mathematical framework that we believe to be essential for the construction and analysis of such systems. We have two main objectives in our introductory chapter.

The first objective is to identify and explain those concepts that underpin the construction and analysis of systems. We show, in Sec. 1.1, that the concept of a model is closely linked with the process of abstraction and that both are essential tools for dealing with complexity. We use these concepts to discuss systems in detail in Sec. 1.2.

Our second objective in this chapter is to plan the route that leads to the main topics we have chosen to present in this book. The importance of these topics is highlighted as we describe the nature of the mathematical modelling process in Sec. 1.3. Since the mathematical framework that we provide in Part I of the book is to support the industrial process of system construction (in Part II) and system analysis (in Part III), we discuss these activities in Secs 1.4 and 1.5 respectively.

1.1 MODELS

There are two quite different, but related, ways in which the word *model* is used in modern mathematics and both play a central role in this book. One, the abstract model, is familiar in everyday life as well as traditional mathematics, and is used for the analysis of existing systems. The other, the concrete model, comes from modern mathematical logic, and is the key to the mathematical framework that we provide for system construction.

1.1.1 Abstract models

We are all aware of how useful it is to use diagrams and miniature scale versions to analyse or explain the main features of some complicated object or system. If we want to determine how far we have to travel to get to work we could use a scale map of the relevant geographical area which singles out the names and relative positions of a few key streets from the real-world urban sprawl. To explain why Denmark and Australia have different daylight hours we could use a globe and point out on it where these countries are. A child wanting to drive will play with a toy car that may even be big enough to sit in and steer.

Diagrams and toys like these are *models* of physical objects and systems. They *abstract* away from those details of the real world that are not relevant. We use traditional mathematical models in the same way.

Example 1.1 A collection of differential equations as a model of a nuclear reactor system highlights the system's thermodynamic properties and could be used to analyse its stability under specific environmental conditions.

Example 1.2 An algebraic equation as a model of the UK economy highlights certain relationships between key economic factors and could be used to determine the current inflation rate.

By using abstract models we simplify what are in reality detailed and complex objects or systems. We can then use the models to analyse certain properties of these existing objects or systems, which would be difficult or impossible to do directly.

Example 1.3 A *simulation* by a computer program is another means of providing an abstract model of a complex system. We can simulate the main features of an existing train system, like the passenger numbers and movements, to gain an understanding of how and where congestion is occurring.

Exercise 1.1 Explain why a set of graphs of a person's life functions, like blood pressure, pulse and temperature against time, may be viewed as an abstract model of the person. What could this model be used for?

1.1.2 Concrete models

Here the use of the word model is opposite from the previous use in that it refers to a more concrete rather than more abstract representation of an object or system. The notion of a concrete model is formalized in the domain of mathematical logic, as we shall show in Chapters 3 to 6, but it has a simple real-world analogy. Suppose that, rather than wishing to analyse an existing object or system, we want to construct a new one. For example, we may want to build a new office complex. Then during the design phase we will produce architectural drawings and plans of the proposed complex, and possibly even a miniature version. These will help us guide our design and subsequent construction. The final, real office complex can be thought of as a model of the plans or of the miniature; rather than taking away detail, it adds it.

In this book we build concrete models of systems by adding 'mathematical details' that represent, or model, the properties of the system. We have to work quite hard in order to construct this stricter notion of a model because we need to understand the mathematical concepts that are involved. The reward for this effort is that we can argue whether the properties of the system hold within the model. We build concrete models within formal systems and use the power of the mathematical model to help us construct and analyse application systems.

In mathematical logic, the formal system for which we are trying to find a concrete model is generally a collection of strings of symbols. The model is a specific mathematical structure in which the strings are given meaning. For example, the string $a \square b$ could be given the meaning $2 + 3$ in normal arithmetic (which is the model). Thus a model represents the strings by adding detail rather than removing it. We shall see in this book that systems can be described in formal languages and then modelled by mathematical structures. The advantage of this type of modelling is that we can use the rules of mathematics to reason formally about the system behaviour.

Exercise 1.2 Suppose you wish to buy a radio and you list a set of requirements that you want satisfied, such as 'maximum weight 20 g, FM *and* AM, and cost $\leq$ £15'. Assuming you find a radio that satisfies these requirements, what can you say about the relationship between the radio and the set of requirements?

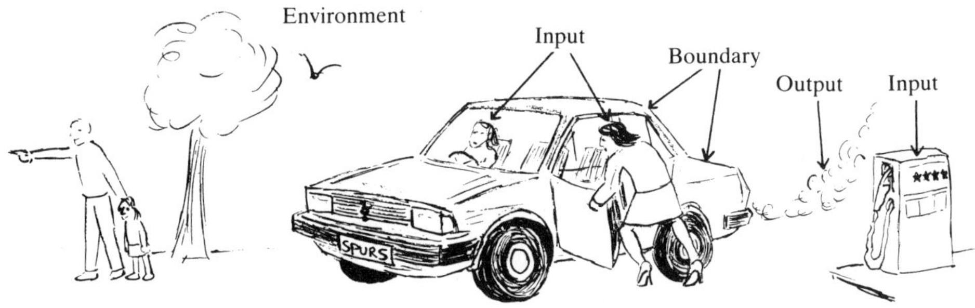

Figure 1.1 Key features of a system.

1.2 SYSTEMS

1.2.1 What is a system?

Most people have some intuitive understanding of what we mean by a system. Before attempting a formal definition, it is worth considering some examples of recognizable systems from everyday life.

Example 1.4 A car is a system that provides transport for people and objects between physical locations (Fig. 1.1). The system has numerous inputs, like petrol, oil and pre-journey passengers and driver, and numerous outputs like exhaust fumes, steam and post-journey passengers and driver. It is made up of many different types of components that are linked by often complicated relationships. Some components are large like the engine, the petrol tank and wheels, while some are small like nuts, bolts and wires. Size does not necessarily imply complexity, however. The carburettor is usually considered to be more complex than the bonnet, even though it is much smaller.

Example 1.5 A company payroll system is responsible for paying employees their correct salary each week or month. The system does this by processing information it receives about employees and outputting salary cheques and pay slips. This system is made up of lots of physical components which include people, paper and possibly also computers and printers. However, it may also include components, like the 'pension fund', which are conceptual.

Example 1.6 The London Underground is a more complex system of transport than the car. It has a multitude of physical components like trains, drivers, tracks, stations and signals, as well as conceptual components like routes and timetables. The major input to the system is passengers' money, while its major outputs, other than diesel fumes and smoke, are frustrated and weary passengers.

Example 1.7 A human being is a biological system. The components include flesh, blood and hair, or, at a lower level, protein molecules and water. In addition to these physical components, humans have conceptual components like intelligence, strength and ambition. Inputs include air and food, while outputs include speech and perspiration.

From the diversity of systems we identify some important common properties and from these construct a formal definition of a system:

1 Systems are made up of components, some of which are physical and some of which are conceptual. Conceptual components are those that do not correspond to a physical object in the real world.

2 Systems receive inputs and transform these into outputs.

3 Systems exist within an *environment*; the inputs come from the environment and the outputs are deposited within it. However, only those entities that interact with the system are considered as part of the environment. The 'moon' and 'Mickey Mouse' are clearly outside the payroll system, but we would not wish to consider either as being part of its environment. Systems therefore have a *boundary* which divides things inside the system from those in its environment, although it is not always clear where the boundary lies. In the case of the car we can see a physical boundary made of metal but it is more difficult to determine the boundary of the payroll system.

4 All systems seem to exhibit behaviour in the sense of being seen to fulfil some specific *purpose* which makes us view the system as a whole. The system purpose appears to depend on particular *viewpoints*. For example, from the viewpoint of its management or even the Government, the purpose of the London Underground system may be to make a profit; the viewpoint of its passengers may be for it to provide a fast, cheap and reliable means of getting around London. When there are conflicting viewpoints such as these it is impossible for the system behaviour to be universally acceptable.

Exercise 1.3 Contrast the purpose of a car from the viewpoints of the driver, a passenger and a pedestrian.

Definition 1.1 System A system is an assembly of components, connected together in an organized way, and separated from its environment by a boundary. This organized assembly has an observable purpose which is characterized in terms of how it transforms inputs from the environment into outputs to the environment.

In Fig. 1.2, we model general properties of systems by emphasizing the systems' inputs and outputs to the exclusion of all other details. Where a system has no inputs or outputs it is said to be *closed*. In practice closed systems, which are like mysterious, impregnable black boxes, are rare. Even a security system, which is intended to *appear* closed, must allow inputs from certain privileged users. Unfortunately, many computer systems, from the viewpoint of too many people, *appear* to be closed systems. Normally, this is because of poor design of the user interface, so potential users are excluded because they do not understand how to place input and receive output. An important task of systems designers and analysts is to construct systems that are as open as possible. This task has often been neglected in the past.

Exercise 1.4 For each of Examples 1.4 to 1.7 choose a specific viewpoint and, from this viewpoint, describe briefly:

(a) the purpose of the system,

(b) some system components,

(c) the system boundary,

(d) the key system inputs and outputs.

Exercise 1.5 A programming language compiler is a system. Identify its purpose and key inputs and outputs.

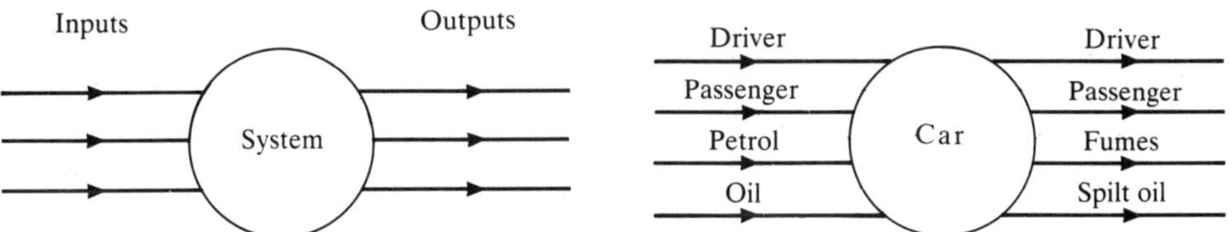

Figure 1.2 Simple diagrammatic models of systems.

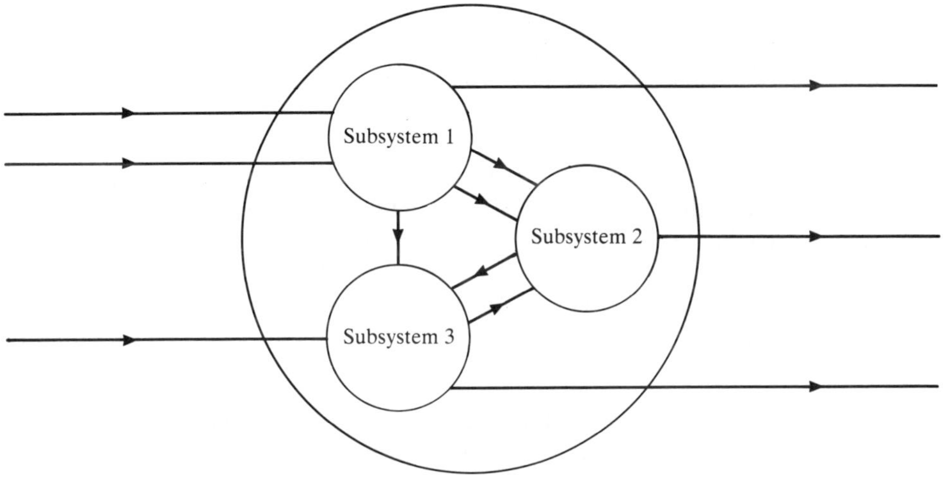

(*a*)

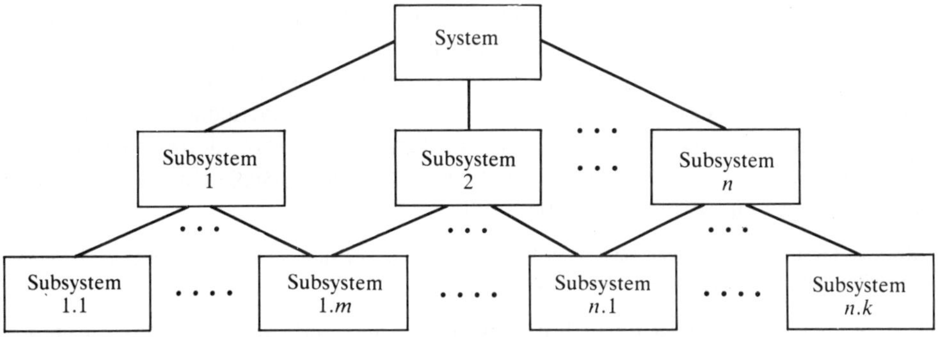

(*b*)

Figure 1.3 Subsystems.

1.2.2 Subsystems and system decomposition

A *subsystem*, as shown in Fig. 1.3(a), is a system in its own right that is contained within some other system. This recursive structure of a system is seen within our mathematical framework to be a fundamentally important property. We define recursive structures formally in Chapter 7.

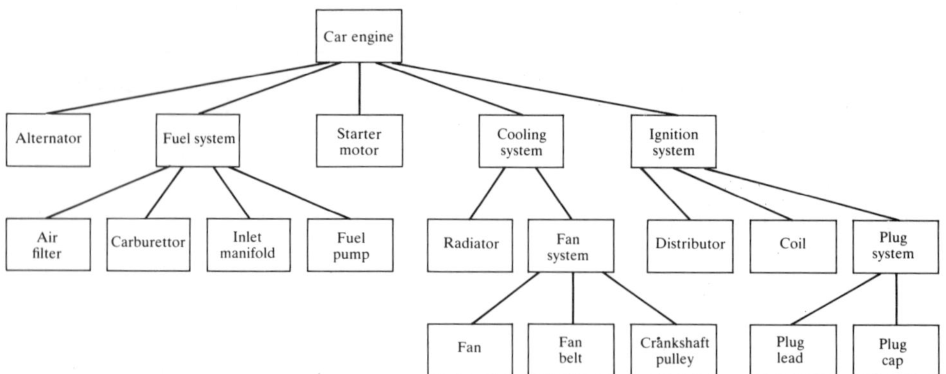

Figure 1.4 The system decomposition of a car engine.

> **Example 1.8** A subsystem should not be confused with a system component, even though sometimes these overlap. Hair and intelligence are both components of a human being but we would not wish to consider either as being subsystems. On the other hand, the heart is a component that *is* a subsystem since it has an identifiable purpose, inputs and outputs, boundary and environment. Examples of subsystems in this case that are *not* components are the digestive and respiratory systems.

Most real systems are so complex that the only way we can understand them is to understand their recursive structure by thinking in terms of their simpler, interconnected subsystems. If these subsystems are themselves too complex we again think in terms of *their* subsystems. We could repeat this process of looking for simpler subsystems within subsystems as many times as necessary. The process, called *top-down system decomposition*, is illustrated in Fig. 1.3(b) and gives rise to the notion of *levels of abstraction* as shown. It is the only known means of analysing complex systems.

Figure 1.4 illustrates the top-down system decomposition for a car engine. The appropriate level of system decomposition will depend on a particular viewpoint. For a mechanic who has only to change the alternator, the first level decomposition may be sufficient. For an engineer trying to improve a car's sluggish performance a much more detailed decomposition will be required.

> **Exercise 1.6** For each of Examples 1.4 to 1.7, identify some key subsystems from a chosen viewpoint. Explain briefly how these subsystems interact with each other.

Most of the important issues in both systems design and analysis involve a choice of system decomposition: which subsystems and their interconnections do we choose and which models are appropriate? The choice is largely determined by particular viewpoints, and in practice we may need a number of different system decompositions to represent these different viewpoints and to gain information about the structure of the system.

> **Example 1.9** The London Underground system is decomposed by its management into its separate lines. Thus, for example, the Central line and Northern line are viewed as distinct subsystems, and are given their own management structure and decision making authority. They have a large degree of autonomy regarding finance,

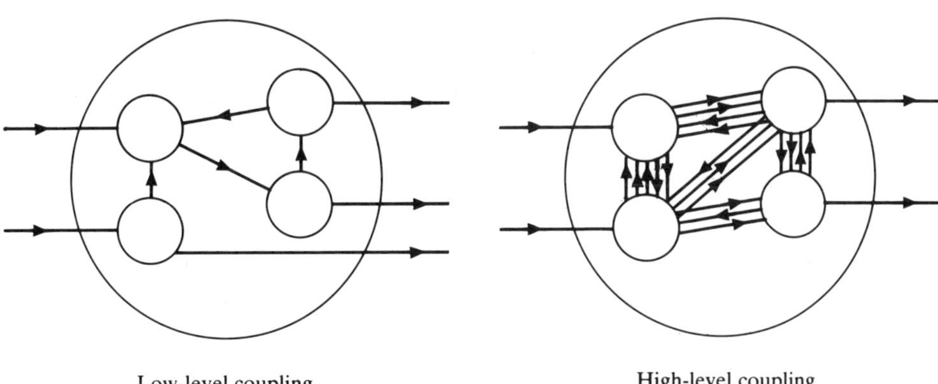

Figure 1.5 Coupling.

staffing policy, pay settlements and even maintenance. However, it is unlikely that this particular system decomposition is most helpful from the passenger viewpoint. Passengers would probably prefer to think of a decomposition of the entire system in terms of subsystems like the booking system, trains and the maintenance system. They may even be alarmed to learn that these are run differently according to different lines.

Despite the inevitable dependence on particular viewpoints, there are some general principles about effective system decomposition.

Principle 1.1 Subsystems should be highly cohesive.

This means that subsystems should be relatively 'single-minded'; each should have one clear purpose or function. As a consequence, interaction within each subsystem should be stronger than with other subsystems.

Example 1.10 Think of a university as a system of education. From the viewpoint of staffing, consider the decomposition into: teaching, administration, maintenance and cleaning. At this (high) level of abstraction, these are fairly cohesive subsystems. Each performs a relatively specific task in the overall context of the university system. Contrast this with the decomposition of staff into 26 groups according to the first letter of their surname. Any cohesion in the resulting 26 subsystems is purely coincidental.

Principle 1.2 Subsystems should be loosely coupled.

The level of interaction between subsystem components is often referred to as the level of coupling in a system, and is illustrated in Fig. 1.5. No matter how cohesive our subsystems are, any sensible system decomposition will require certain interactions between different subsystems. We should, however, aim for reasonably low levels of coupling.

In Example 1.10 we might have chosen an initial subsystem decomposition which included 'undergraduate teaching' and 'postgraduate teaching'. In most universities this would be a poor choice of decomposition since these two subsystems are far too closely coupled, even though individually they are reasonably cohesive. This illustrates the difficulty of getting the right balance between high cohesion and low coupling.

There are a number of practical ways in which we can minimize the level of coupling. For example, we should remove unnecessary inputs and outputs between subsystems. We should also ensure that the times at which processes are performed in one subsystem are not dictated by another. Another way to minimize the level of coupling is to use *standards*, which, for example, provide precise specifications for the interface of systems and subsystems. When a subsystem is constructed according to a known standard this can minimize the need for co-ordination and back-checking.

Communicating systems The coupling between subsystems may be a major characteristic of a system. The system designer must then consider how best to achieve the necessary interactions. This problem, of *communicating* systems and processes, is one of the most challenging tasks facing modern designers. Broadly speaking, there are two ways to achieve communication: *synchronously* or *asynchronously*.

Example 1.11 As in Example 1.10, a university system has separated the teaching staff from the administration staff. However, these subsystems are not entirely decoupled. Suppose that a lecturer, Jane, wishes to interview some applicants for a new research post. Peter from administration has the formal responsibility of co-ordinating interviews and ensuring that the relevant administration people are also there. In one way or another Jane and Peter must communicate to find an appropriate date for the interviews. Jane could get her diary out and telephone Peter. This type of communication is called *synchronous*, because it can only work if the actions of both parties are synchronized. Peter must be in his office, ready to receive the call, and must also have all the relevant information to hand. A radically different type of communication is where Jane sends a memo to Peter listing all the dates when she is free for the interviews. This memo eventually goes into Peter's in-tray where he can deal with it in his own time. Eventually he can send a return memo to Jane proposing a specific date. This type of communication is called *asynchronous*.

The normal physical analogy of synchronous communication is a handshake, while for asynchronous communication it is a buffer. From the viewpoint of the party seeking to initiate a communication, synchronous communication is preferable. However, in practice it is rare to be able to construct subsystem communications that are truly synchronous, and we have to be satisfied with asynchronous communication. We shall examine mathematical models of communicating systems in Secs 9.4 and 13.5.

States of a system In transforming its inputs into outputs a system may enter a number of different internal *states*. The particular states in which a system finds itself will generally influence the output for any given input.

Example 1.12 At a high level of abstraction we might think of the car as having a small number of states like 'engine working' and 'engine not working'; at a lower level of abstraction there will be an infinite number of states corresponding, for example, to the infinite possible adjustments to the engine tuning. In all of these cases the particular internal states will affect what output is produced for given inputs. For example, depending on the type and amount of petrol that is input, the internal states will affect how much carbon dioxide is emitted. Certain types of inputs may also cause internal states to change. For example, if the car is driven after water, instead of petrol, is poured into the tank, then the internal state of 'engine working' will soon change to 'engine not working'.

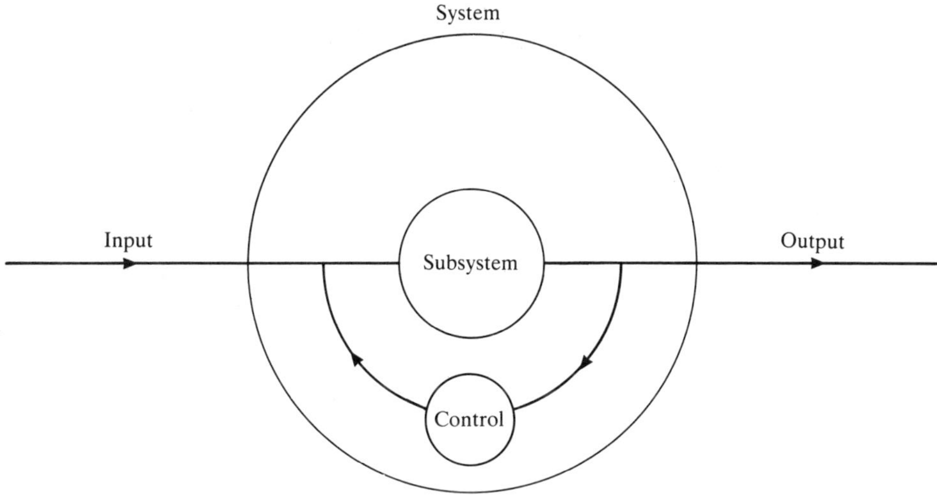

Figure 1.6 Control mechanism.

Being able to model the various states of a system is the key component of a class of specification methods, which include VDM and Z, that we shall describe in Chapter 10. The notion of verification, which we shall describe in Chapter 12, is also dependent on being able to model the changes in system states which occur for given inputs.

Control mechanisms In order for systems to function effectively, including being able to adapt to a changing environment and unexpected inputs, they generally require some kind of *control mechanisms* as shown in Fig. 1.6. These monitor external behaviour, providing feedback and enforcing changes to the system states where necessary. Some control mechanisms are themselves subsystems, while others are external entities in the system environment.

Example 1.13 Many mammals have a built-in control mechanism to help them survive the winter months; they grow extra fur.

Example 1.14 The maintenance department of the London Underground is an internal control subsystem.

Example 1.15 Local council planning departments act as external control mechanisms for building companies.

Ideally, systems should be built with the necessary control mechanisms to *prevent* the build-up of problems. Building regulations and standards are examples of such control mechanisms. However, where problems cannot be prevented, their effects need to be detected as quickly as possible so that their seriousness can be limited. Control mechanisms used specifically for this purpose are often called feedback mechanisms. However, *all* control mechanisms should provide feedback in order to be useful.

An important component of most control mechanisms is *measurement*. In fact, some of the most effective practical control mechanisms are measuring instruments. A thermostat in a central heating system, which measures the water temperature and switches off the heating element when it exceeds 50^0C, provides a good example. The

Figure 1.7 Discrete and continuous.

central role of measurement in the construction and analysis of systems has been recognized by engineers for many years. It may be of some surprise, therefore, for you to learn that measurement has been almost totally ignored in the construction and analysis of modern computer software systems. The lack of a rigorous approach to measurement in software engineering has been criticized by many professional engineers. To counter this and to emphasize its key role we have devoted Chapter 17 to a description of measurement theory.

1.2.3 Discrete and continuous systems

A discrete object is informally thought of as one that is 'made up of distinct parts' as shown in Fig. 1.7. We might wish to think of this book as being a discrete object if we think of its components as being the individual pages. Discrete does not necessarily mean finite. The collection of whole positive numbers 1,2,3,4,... is a discrete object, because all its components are distinct, but there is an infinite number of them.

Continuous objects are ones that are not discrete. Informally they are 'without interruption and abrupt changes'. An example is a line drawn with a pencil without interruption. The individual components of the line exist but cannot be separated.

> **Example 1.16** The most common example used to contrast discrete and continuous objects is a digital clock (discrete) compared with an analogue clock (continuous). We have to think of the components in each case as the collection of possible times that can be displayed. In the digital case there are just a finite number, corresponding to each of the 8640 minutes in a day. The collection of possible times in the analogue case is continuous.

Whether or not an object is discrete depends both on your particular viewpoint of it and also on the level of abstraction.

> **Example 1.17** Compare a compact disc player with a traditional record player. Most people accept that the CD player is discrete because the sound it produces is encoded as a discrete set of signals on the disc; these are 'read' by a laser. In contrast, the sound produced by the record player is encoded as a continuous groove on the record; this is 'read' by a stylus in direct contact. However, at a much more abstract level we could think of both these objects as being discrete, since they both may be either ON or OFF. Conversely, at a lower level, both objects can be thought of as continuous, since ultimately they produce sound waves that are continuous.

Example 1.17 illustrates the pragmatic approach we shall take to defining discrete systems and models. The CD player is discrete in contrast to the record player *at the most interesting and relevant level of abstraction*, namely when we consider how it produces sound. This is what is crucial.

> **Example 1.18** The digital computer is often presented as an example of a discrete system. However, at its lowest level this system produces electrical pulses that

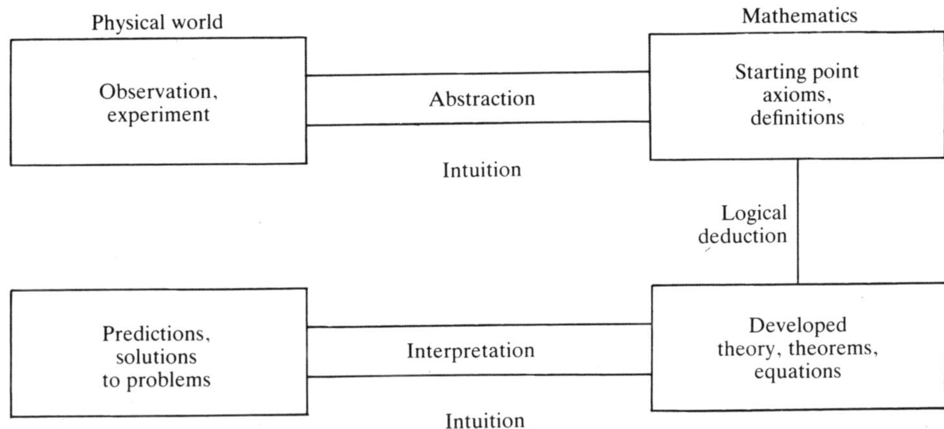

Figure 1.8 The mathematical modelling process.

are continuous. So why does everybody accept that a computer is a discrete system whereas, say, a human is not? The answer again is that, from all the most interesting and relevant viewpoints and levels of abstraction, the computer is discrete. It has a discrete set of internal states, is made up of a discrete set of components and it processes inputs by treating them as discrete objects.

Exercise 1.7 For each of the systems described in Examples 1.4 to 1.7 choose a fixed viewpoint and level of abstraction and state whether the system is discrete or continuous.

Many of the most useful and interesting models necessary for the construction and analysis of modern complex systems happen to be mathematical models that are discrete at all reasonable levels of abstraction. Discrete mathematics is about the study of such models. Traditionally, systems engineers were equipped only with knowledge of continuous mathematics, embodied by such topics as the differential and integral calculus and the solution of differential equations. While these kinds of models will continue to be important in many applications, we have deliberately omitted them from this book. They are more than adequately dealt with elsewhere.

1.3 MATHEMATICAL MODELLING

1.3.1 Problem solving

The construction and analysis of systems is a special case of *problem solving*. We have made it clear that the use of mathematical models will help us to solve these kinds of problems, and we adopt the well-accepted mathematical modelling process that is shown in Fig. 1.8.

Intuition is vital in the choice of where to begin the work of problem solving and also in finding the possible areas of application for a developed mathematical theory. We can think of intuition as the major link between the physical world and the abstract world of mathematics. First the link must be made when the axioms and definitions that form the starting point of the mathematical work are abstracted from nature.

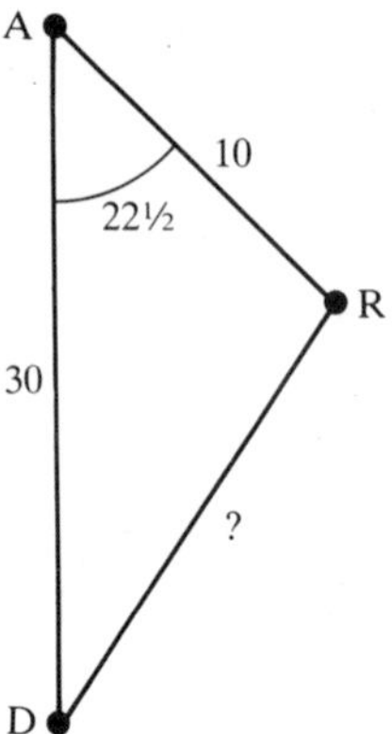

Figure 1.9 Geometric model.

Later, after logical deduction produces a developed theory, intuition is again required when the mathematical theory is matched against the problems of the environment.

We begin the presentation of a formal system in Chapter 3 and then extend the system, until it is sufficiently powerful to reason about complex systems, in the next three chapters. Because it deals with formal objects, a formal system is removed from the application system that we wish to construct and analyse. We cannot make mathematical bridges between formal and informal objects; instead we use our intuition to bridge the gap.

Accuracy of the problem solution will depend on both the accuracy of the abstract modelling process and the accuracy of the interpretation from the theory in the model to the predicted solution. In general these may be *subjective*. However, *inside* the model the transformations are completely objective, being determined by the axioms of the theory and the accepted logical proof rules.

Example 1.19 An aeroplane is 30 miles due north of its destination when it is forced to travel 10 miles SSE (because of strong cross winds) before returning to an optimal flight path. Our problem is to calculate the total distance actually travelled.

Experience of typical school maths would naturally direct us to the geometrical modelling process, and arrive at a model like that in Fig. 1.9. We calculate the length of the line DR using Euclidean geometry. This involves a transformation to another model in which equations using sin, cos, ... are developed. Tables can be used to make the necessary calculations.

Inside the model, the correctness of the solution is objectively determined by the axioms of geometry, trigonometry and the appropriate use of the tables. However, accuracy of the solution of the real-world problem is dependent on:

(a) whether the interpretation that gives $22\frac{1}{2}^{0}$ for SSE, for example, was appropriate;

(b) how realistically Euclidean geometry's axioms model the real world.

Where relatively small distances are involved, accuracy is reasonable (but not good). Inaccuracies occur because the axioms of Euclidean geometry do not accurately capture the curvature of the world.

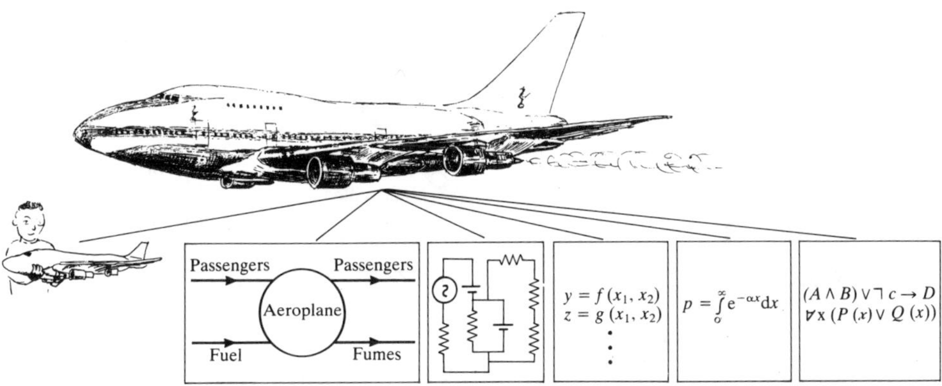

Figure 1.10 Different models representing different viewpoints of the same system.

This example highlights the power of abstraction in the mathematical modelling process. The model of Fig. 1.9 is appropriate for many different problems, since there is no explicit reference to either an aeroplane or strong winds.

We can construct concrete mathematical models and reason about them formally and objectively. This ability is what gives mathematical models the power over informal abstract models. It is why engineers in every classical discipline use mathematical models, in preference to rough design drawings or scale miniatures, in order to reason formally about the consequences of their designs.

1.3.2 Modelling systems

A single complex system can have many radically different types of models, as illustrated in Fig. 1.10. Each of the models focuses on particular features. Thus, the miniature scale model might be used to assess the aeroplane's stability in simulation, the differential equations to assess its aerodynamic properties, the probability model to assess its likelihood of failure-free operation and the logical model to assess whether there are any conflicting commands that the pilot can issue.

If we wished to construct a new aeroplane, then it is likely that we would first develop models like those of Fig. 1.10 to specify our requirements and help in the design stage. In this case the completed aeroplane is analogous to a concrete model for the stated requirements.

Just as a single complex system can have many different types of models, so it can have many similar models, but at different levels of abstraction. Just which level of abstraction is appropriate is largely determined by the viewpoint.

Example 1.20 Consider a typical route map of a city train system as shown in Fig. 1.11. The map is a model of the system. It emphasizes train routes while totally ignoring other features of the system like ticketing, timetabling, management and financing. It even ignores any notion of geographical scale. From the viewpoint of a passenger who wants to know which trains to catch to get from Spursville to Tottingham, the model is at an *appropriate level of abstraction* since it contains sufficient information for this. However, the model is too abstract for a passenger who also wants to know how long the journey is likely to take. It needs the added

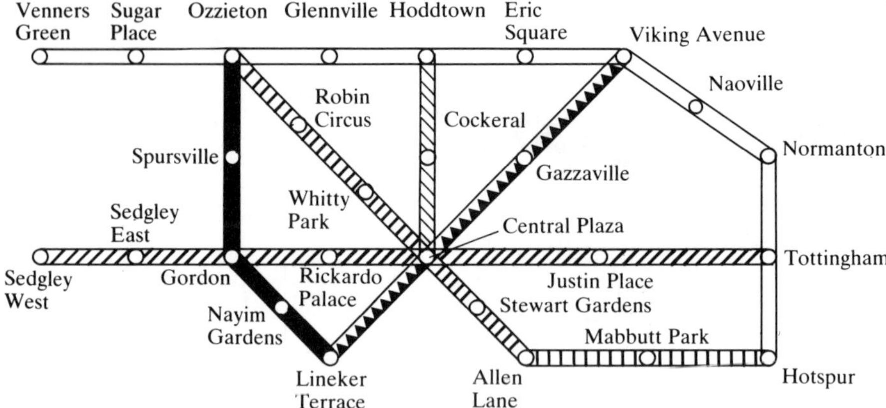

Figure 1.11 A model of a city train system.

detail of journey times between stations. For a maintenance engineer who needs to perform regular work to the electrical points throughout the tunnels, a far lower level of abstraction, like a full-scale map identifying the location of all electrical points, would be necessary.

Certain types of mathematical models for systems are the key components of this book. You may need the full range of them in constructing and analysing a single complex system.

Example 1.21 By way of motivation for the main topics in the book, we take as an example an underground railway system for a city. We can model the train network using *graph theory*; together with *linear algebra*, we can use this model to solve problems relating to optimal routing and layout. The most basic type of model of the system is a *function*, which is a rule that would be used to model the system's cost effectiveness given various funding scenarios.

The system will certainly contain safety-critical components, like signalling, which may need to be computer controlled. The specification and construction of the relevant hardware and software requires the use of models within *mathematical logic*, together with the techniques of deduction in a formal system. Only then can we have reasonable confidence in the correctness of such systems.

Clearly there must be various types of management subsystems, and many of these will be modelled by systems of *relations*. Only once these are understood can we build subsystems such as the maintenance control system and the payroll system. We need a structured approach to specify these systems and implement them in an appropriate *model of computation*.

Special kinds of models, like CSP and Petri nets, are required for constructing and analysing the problems of *concurrent subsystems and processes*, within the system. For example, different trains will need to use the same track, and we need to model the appropriate communications. We also need to identify potential problems like deadlock.

The system will require various means of communication, for example a system enabling drivers to talk to a central controller and an emergency communication system enabling secret codes between different managers and controllers to shut down all or parts of the network. *Coding theory* provides the necessary communication systems.

Finally, we shall need to provide rigorous, quantitative assessment of the system. We can use the models of *algorithmic efficiency* to analyse the time and memory efficiency of the various computerized subsystems that we construct. We use the theory and models of *probability* to assess the likelihood of individual component failure. More generally, we use *measurement theory* to guide our selection and use of data that we obtain from the system.

Exercise 1.8 For the system in Example 1.4 list three different types of models, and for each describe how the models may need to be changed to reflect different levels of abstraction.

1.4 SYSTEM CONSTRUCTION

The construction of systems normally takes place in distinct stages. We summarize the activities taking place in each main stage as those of: requirements capture, specification, design and implementation, and examine them in turn. There are many different views about the relative effort that should be spent on these activities, and the relationships between them, in order to develop a system in an optimal way. In software development the so-called waterfall model of development has traditionally been adopted for large systems. In this model, each phase must be completed entirely before the next can begin, and so the implemented system is delivered all in one go at the very end of the development process. A drawback of this approach is that user feedback comes too late to influence the specification and design. Consequently, alternative development models are now commonly used. These include:

1 *Rapid prototyping*, in which a rough and ready implementation is first constructed for user feedback, more or less directly from the specification. This allows appropriate changes to be made to the specification, before a refined version of the system is properly designed and implemented, replacing the prototype.

2 *Evolutionary development*, in which, after specification, parts of the system are designed and implemented sequentially in order of importance. A system is delivered incrementally to the user who is continually involved in providing feedback to the developers.

Until relatively recently software construction differed from other engineering disciplines in that mathematical models were not used in the development process. This made it difficult to move from phase to phase with any great confidence in the evolving system development. For example, there were no means of reasoning that the design satisfied the specification, because neither of these was expressed in a sufficiently formal language. However, the use of logic and mathematics has provided the necessary formal framework within which systems can be constructed and reasoned about. In principle, such a formal approach can complement any of the more traditional development approaches. However, there are now so many different formal methods, some of which have a radically different view of the software development process, that we discuss these separately.

1.4.1 Stages of system construction

Requirements analysis The construction of a new system normally starts with a *requirements capture phase*. In practice this is performed by *systems analysis*, since most 'new' systems to be built are in fact evolutions of some existing system which is believed to be inadequate. For example, a computerized payroll system will invariably be replacing a manual system; even a revolutionary new system of transport is replacing some existing system of transport. Thus a starting point for requirements capture is sometimes an analysis of the existing system, or the wider system into which the new system has to fit.

This phase consists of gathering information about the problem. It should involve detailed discussion with the customer who is requiring the construction of the system and who usually has expert knowledge of the application domain.

Specification As a result of the capturing of requirements a *specification* must be produced that states precisely what the new system must do. This is the statement of the problem that we have to solve. The specification should include details of the functional requirements, as well as any performance requirements such as how fast, efficient or reliable the system must be. It should exclude, unless absolutely necessary, any statements that constrain *how* the system is to be built.

> **Example 1.22** A constraint specifying that a particular programming language must be used because 'this is the only one that the system analyst has heard of' is not acceptable. However, a constraint specifying that the final physical system must not exceed a particular weight is acceptable if the system is an on-board spacecraft computer.

Design Once the specification is agreed the system *design* phase can begin. In this phase we consider *how* to construct the system according to the specification. There are no universally agreed methods of design, but traditionally a top-down approach, based on system decomposition, as discussed in Sec. 1.2.2, has been adopted. Thus, design proceeds through various stages of decreasing abstraction with more and more detail being added. With this approach, it is important to get the right balance between high cohesion and low coupling.

Implementation Implementation is the phase of turning a system design into a working system. In civil engineering this is the construction phase where actual building materials are used for the first time. If we were constructing a bridge, we would not begin this phase until our designs are sufficiently detailed that we would know with some degree of confidence that we could implement them and that the bridge would satisfy its specification. That we can reach such a phase is a result of centuries of bridge-building experience which ensures that modern bridges very rarely crash. A key component of this experience is the set of appropriate mathematical models which enable us to reason formally about all key aspects of bridge designs and to predict likely behaviour under different environmental conditions.

In software engineering, implementation corresponds to the activity of writing program code in a language that can be compiled and run on the target computer. The traditional lack of mathematical models in the earlier phases of specification and design unfortunately lead more often than not to the bridge analogy of a crash when the

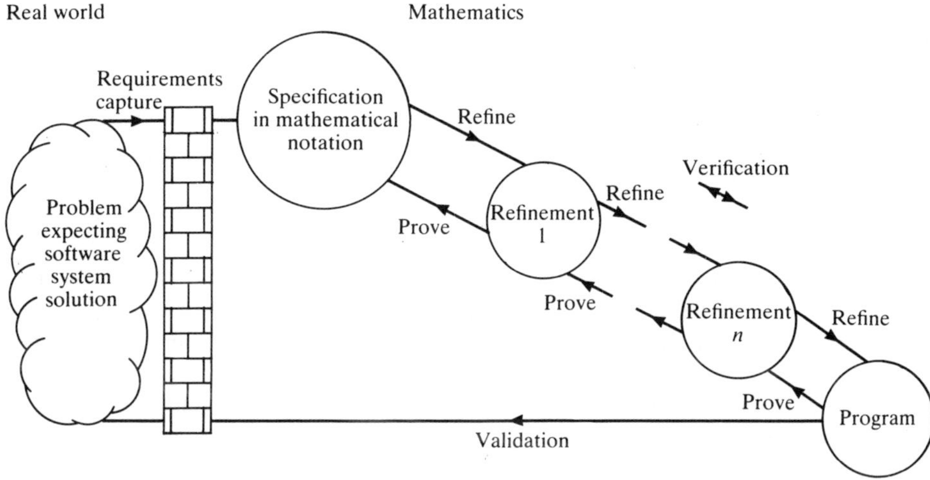

Figure 1.12 Formal verification of software systems.

program is run. Such crashes are even more likely when, as is quite common, the specification and design phases are blurred or even bypassed altogether.

1.4.2 Formal methods for system construction

The dissatisfaction experienced by users with software systems that failed to meet their requirements was an important symptom of the software crisis in the 1960s. As a reaction to the demands to increase software reliability, the software community has recently turned to a more formal approach to system construction. This is seen to be crucial, especially given the increasing use of software in systems with critical safety or financial requirements.

Example 1.23 The new family of European Airbus aircraft (A320) are genuinely 'fly-by-wire', meaning that all flight control functions are totally dependent on computers and the software that drives them. The aircraft have a formal reliability requirement which is: probability 10^{-9} of failure per flight.

At its most rigorous level, as illustrated in Fig. 1.12, formal software development involves the construction of increasingly detailed mathematical models of the required system. We start with the specification in an appropriate formal language and end with an executable program. Clearly the requirements capture and analysis must remain informal and based on the language of the client or customer. However, the activity of formalizing the specification has the advantage of providing a contractual basis for the development of the system. The introduction of formal languages has introduced the activity of verifying the correctness of a system during its construction. At each stage of development mathematical proofs are required to ensure correctness of the refinement. Chapter 12 describes a typical approach to such correctness proofs.

By a formal language we mean a language with a precisely defined syntax, or structure, and a precisely defined semantics, or meaning. We explain the relationship between formal languages and formal systems for reasoning in Part I of the book in order to provide the foundation for their subsequent applications. We present the activity of specification in terms of building theories about a system. In Chapter 10 we describe the most important approaches to formal specification. The concept of an abstract data type relates data to the operations on that data and underpins the specification of the structure of systems. We present the algebraic framework for this concept in Chapter 8. Logic provides the framework for reasoning about the properties of systems and ensuring that formal specifications are correctly refined throughout the design and implementation steps of development.

The concept of abstract data type has also influenced the design phase where the *object-oriented* design method focuses on abstracting the data in a system and representing it by 'objects'. This method uses a bottom-up method of constructing a system from objects and contrasts with the traditional top-down decomposition of a system according to its functions. Programming languages have been designed with structuring mechanisms, such as modules or packages, that represent objects. These mechanisms implement the design concept of information hiding, a means of reducing coupling between components, that is central to the modularity of systems. The different styles of programming languages are based on the different models of computation that are identified in Chapter 11.

We stress that formal methods alone will not guarantee the reliability of software systems. There is no way of guaranteeing that we can bridge the gap between the informal real-world requirements and the formal specification. Moreover, correctness proofs are themselves difficult and more prone to errors as they are used on larger systems. For these and other reasons, systems with high reliability requirements, like the A320 aircraft, have used formal methods *in conjunction* with other novel development techniques like *fault tolerant design*, whereby certain parts of the system are replicated by different design teams. However, despite the limitations identified, formal methods offer the possibility of reasoning about the behaviour of systems before we use them, and an improved chance of getting the system right first time.

Exercise 1.9 Explain how formal methods could be used in a software development project even if either the rapid prototyping or evolutionary development approach are being used.

1.5 SYSTEMS ANALYSIS

Because the construction of new systems involves the analysis of existing systems, systems analysis and construction are parallel activities. The analysis of the structure of systems is discussed in Chapter 13, which also includes a discussion of the analysis of such properties as deadlock and liveness, and some formal approaches to static analysis of software and structural testing. Chapters 14 and 17 lay the foundations for the quantitative assessment of systems. We now identify the activities of validation and verification and maintenance as dependent on sound systems analysis techniques.

1.5.1 Validation and verification

Whether our system is a program to add up a list of numbers or a computerized flight control system for a fly-by-wire aircraft, we want to make sure that we have obtained the 'right solution'. The general collection of techniques concerned with this kind of quality assurance are called *validation and verification*. It is assumed that these take place throughout the system development process. The following informal distinction is normally made:

Verification: are we building the system right?

Validation: are we building the right system?

We have already seen the most sophisticated notion of verification in the context of formal development. This is synonymous with proofs of correctness of each refinement stage, starting from the formal specification.

More generally, verification is also used to describe any technique concerned with assuring the internal accuracy and consistency between the products of the evolving system. In the case of software development this can involve many techniques far removed from a correctness proof. For example, it could involve checking that accepted design rules have not been violated, that the data types have been checked for consistency or that every program path can be executed. Internal design reviews and audits, where the development team informally justify the consistency of their own designs, is a well-used form of verification.

If we carry out verification without any errors we can be confident that, if our initial assumptions were reasonable, then we have a proper solution to our original problem as described by its specification. Unfortunately we know that most real-world problems are difficult to model. Moreover, we may not be able to interpret our results properly in the real world. Thus verification on its own may produce a system that is internally consistent, and can even be proved to be so mathematically, but is not the system required.

Consequently, verification must be complemented by validation which is the task of assuring that the formal solution is the one that is relevant to the 'real world'. Validation involves observation, experimentation and measurement.

Example 1.24 Much traditional software quality assurance revolves around a validation procedure called *black box testing*. In this, the system builders will try out a range of mostly random inputs, checking that the outputs are what they expect. When they are satisfied that their understanding of the clients' specification has been accurately modelled by the program, they will invite the clients to perform their own black box testing. This might involve:

(a) *observation* in the form of viewing the user interface,

(b) *experimentation* in the form of setting up a sample database and trying out various inputs to it,

(c) *measurement* in the form of recording sample response times.

Unfortunately validation in the form of black box program testing has often been approached in an *ad hoc* and unscientific manner. Some more formal approaches to program testing are discussed in Chapter 13.

1.5.2 Maintenance

Traditionally, maintenance has been viewed as the distinct phase of the system development life cycle which follows implementation and operation. During operation, failures or potential failures of the system will be observed. These failures are caused by faults in the system. Not all faults lead to failures, but even apparently minor ones can be catastrophic when they do.

Example 1.25 A NASA probe to Venus was lost in 1973. This system failure was caused by a fault in the software navigational code, which was written in FORTRAN.

A statement which should have read 'DO 3I=1,3', meaning perform statement 3 three times, was erroneously coded as the syntactically correct statement 'DO 3I = 1.3' which assigns the value 1.3 to the variable 'DO 3I'.

Maintenance is the activity of changing parts of the system by finding and removing such faults. In reality maintenance can take place at any time during system development; rigorous validation and verification reveals faults, which can potentially lead to system failures, throughout the construction process. Thus maintenance is either *corrective*, meaning that we change the system by eliminating a fault that leads to a known failure, or *perfective*, meaning that we change the system by eliminating a fault that we feel can potentially lead to a system failure. Sometimes, as in the case of Example 1.25, corrective maintenance cannot recover the system.

The ability to perform maintenance properly is dependent on the ease with which we can analyse the system and locate faults. A properly documented and well-structured system, constructed according to the kinds of techniques already discussed, is crucial for this ability. Without it maintenance will be a costly and error-prone activity which is just as likely to introduce new faults as remove existing ones.

1.6 SUMMARY

In this chapter we have shown how the mathematical modelling process underpins the activities of system construction and analysis. With appropriate models we are able to reason about the structure and properties of systems and to predict their behaviour. The mathematical models that we identify as appropriate are discrete as opposed to continuous, and are possibly less familiar to systems engineers.

The linked concepts of abstraction and a model are essential for laying the foundation for system construction and analysis. Intuition is vital in capturing the properties of an application system, and mathematical experience is required to reason about the system within the model.

We have planned a route through the stages of system construction and analysis, indicating how the theoretical framework that we establish in Parts II and III can be applied in the industrial process of system development. Formal languages and formal systems for reasoning together provide the framework within which we can construct and verify systems. We see the activities of constructing and analysing systems as closely linked and proceeding in parallel. The theoretical framework that we establish for system analysis is therefore complimentary to that for system construction.

FURTHER READING

For a more detailed account of some of the systems concepts introduced in this chapter, see Walker (1988) and Pressman (1988). For a detailed discussion of the distinction between abstract and concrete models, see Turski and Maibaum (1987). For further discussion of the role of formal models in system specification, see the book by Cohen, Harwood and Jackson (1986).

Chapter 2

DISCRETE MATHS FUNDAMENTALS

In this chapter we introduce some of the key foundational topics required for the construction and analysis of discrete systems. We view sets in Sec. 2.1 as the basic building blocks of discrete mathematics. Relations are introduced in Sec. 2.2 as special types of sets, and functions are presented in Sec. 2.3 as special types of relations. Graph theory in Sec. 2.4 is also shown to be based on the concept of relations. The key concepts in linear algebra are presented in Sec. 2.5, and finally techniques of counting that provide rules for computing permutations and combinations are described in Sec. 2.6.

2.1 SETS

2.1.1 Collections of objects

Consider the following collections of objects:

1 The numbers 2 and -2.

2 The numbers 1,2,3,4 and 7.

3 All syntactically correct Pascal programs.

4 All solutions to the equation $x^2 - 4 = 0$.

5 All positive whole numbers: 1,2,3,4,5, etc.

6 All real numbers corresponding to points on a line.

7 All positive whole numbers greater than 7.

8 All real number solutions to the equation $x^2 + 4 = 0$.

9 All people who ever dined at the same table as Napolean Bonaparte.

10 The books contained in the British Library on 1 April 1992.

11 The number 69, the person Norman Fenton and the book that Norman Fenton last read.

These collections do not appear to have much in common. Some are finite, like 1, some are infinite, like 5, while one, 8, contains no objects at all. Some of the infinite sets are discrete (in the sense of Sec. 1.2.3), like 5, while others are continuous, like 6. Some are collections of numbers, while others are collections of people, programs or books. One, 11, contains a mixture of these. Some list all their objects explicitly, like 2, while others only describe their objects implicitly, like 4.

For some of the collections, like 7, we can easily determine whether a given object is in the collection or not, even though the collection is infinite. For others, like 9, we have no means of determining this, even though the collection is finite.

However, what these collections of objects have in common is that they all appear to be uniquely defined. An object is either in the collection or not, even though it might be difficult or impossible to determine which objects are in each collection. Contrast this with the following collection of objects:

All great books in the British Library on 1 April 1992.

This does not describe a unique collection of objects since it is based on subjective criteria. Whether or not *Systems Construction and Analysis* by Fenton and Hill is in this collection is very much a matter of personal taste. In contrast, whether or not it is in collection 10 can be objectively determined by consulting appropriate records.

In the light of these observations we provide the following broad definition:

Definition 2.1 Set A set is a uniquely defined collection of objects. The objects that make up the set are called members or elements of the set.

Although this definition allows us to assert that all the collections listed on page 23 are sets, it is only an informal definition. It will be sufficient for our needs, but we shall see in Sec. 2.1.6 that it can lead to some unfortunate consequences.

2.1.2 Set notation

When we list the elements of a set we use the braces $\{$ and $\}$ as delimiters, so that, for example, $S = \{1, 2, 3, 4, 7\}$ both names and explicitly describes the collection 2 on page 23.

Definition 2.2 Set containment When an element x belongs to a set S we say x is contained in S and write $x \in S$. When x does not belong to S we write $x \notin S$.

Example 2.1 $2 \in \{1, 2, 3, 4\}$ but $5 \notin \{1, 2, 3, 4\}$.

When we wish to describe a set implicitly in terms of some property that each member must satisfy, we write $S = \{x : x \text{ satisfies some property } P\}$ to specify S as the set of elements that satisfy the property P. In Chapter 5 we will use the predicate calculus to describe formally what we mean by a 'property P'.

Example 2.2 $S = \{x : x \text{ is a syntactically correct Pascal program}\}$ is the collection 3 on page 23.

Our set notation enables us to express sets themselves as elements of sets.

Example 2.3 $S = \{\{\text{USA, UK}\}, \{\text{UK, Ireland}\}, \{\text{USA, Israel}\}, \ldots\}$ is the set of international extradition treaties between sets of two countries.

The concept of *type* is fundamental in computing and is an application of set theory. The type declaration 'a: A' means that 'a' is defined by the *behaviour* of type 'A'. In Chapter 10 we present an abstract data type as one or more sets *together* with operations on the elements of those sets.

Example 2.4 Any variable that is used in a program in some languages must be declared to be of a particular type. The compiler prevents programming errors by checking that the operations applied to a variable are appropriate to its pre-declared type. The Pascal declaration:

```
type   percentage = 0..100;
variable   mark: percentage;
```

specifies that the type 'percentage' is the set of whole numbers $\{0, 1, 2, \ldots, 100\}$. The variable declaration asserts that any value assigned to 'mark' must be in $\{0, 1, 2, \ldots, 100\}$, or equivalently that mark $\in$ percentage.

Exercise 2.1 Use the notation of set theory to describe the meaning of the following declaration in Pascal. Provide an example of two distinct, valid assignments for the variable 'division'.

```
type soccerclubs = (Spurs, Arsenal, Chelsea, West Ham, Liverpool);
      league = set of soccerclubs;
variable division: league;
```

Exercise 2.2 Identify two sets, from the list on page 23, that contain exactly the same objects.

Set membership is the key to equality between sets. Neither the order of the elements, nor the number of repetitions of a specific element, matter.

Definition 2.3 Set equality The sets A and B are equal, written $A = B$, if every element of A is in B and every element of B is in A.

Example 2.5 $\{1, 1, 2, 3, 4, 4, 4\} = \{1, 2, 3, 4\} = \{2, 1, 4, 3\}$

Exercise 2.3 Which of the following sets are equal?
$\{1, 1, 1, 2, 2, 3, 3, 4, 5\}, \{1, 2, 2, 2, 2, 3, 4\}, \{1, 2, 3, 4, 5\}, \{2, 1, 3, 4, 5\}, \{4, 3, 2, 1\}$

We refer to the following sets by name only in the rest of the book:

$\{\}$	the empty set that does not contain any elements
$\mathbb{N}$	the natural numbers $\{0, 1, 2, 3, \ldots\}$
$\mathbb{N}^+$	the positive natural numbers $\{1, 2, 3, \ldots\}$
$\mathbb{Z}$	the integers $\{0, 1, -1, 2, -2, 3, -3, \ldots\}$
$\mathbb{Q}$	the rational numbers of the form a/b where $a, b \in \mathbb{Z}$ and $b \neq 0$
$\mathbb{R}$	the real numbers that correspond to the set of points on a line extending infinitely from 0 in both directions (this is the set of all decimal numbers)

There are many circumstances where we do need to distinguish repeated elements in a set.

Example 2.6 Suppose that the set of political parties running in an election contest is $S = \{$Labour, Conservative, Liberal, Green$\}$. We know that this is the same set as $S' = \{$Labour, Green, Conservative, Labour, Labour, Conservative, Liberal$\}$. However, suppose that S' represented the results of asking seven different people who they were going to vote for in the election. Then S' represents the results of an opinion poll. In this situation it would be very unwise to ignore the number of repetitions of each element. It is precisely these numbers that help us predict the results of the election.

To model problems like this we generalize the concept of a set.

Definition 2.4 Multiset A multiset is a collection of objects whose members need not be distinct. The number of repetitions of each distinct element is called its multiplicity.

Exercise 2.4 Let $A = \{1, 1, 2, 3, 3, 3\}$ and $B = \{1, 2, 2, 2, 3, 3\}$. What can you say about these collections when viewed: (a) as sets and (b) as multisets?

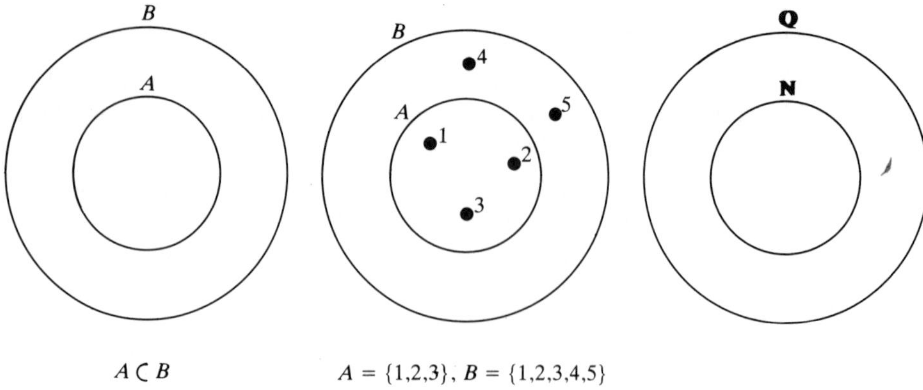

Figure 2.1 Venn diagram illustrating subsets.

2.1.3 Subsets and supersets

Definition 2.5 Subset and superset The set A is a subset of the set B if every element of A is also an element of B. We write this as $A \subseteq B$, and also say that B is a superset of A.

Definition 2.6 Proper subset If $A \subseteq B$ and, in addition, B is not equal to A (in which case it must contain at least one element that is not in A) then we say that A is a proper subset of B. We write this as $A \subset B$.

Example 2.7 For any set A we have $A \subseteq A$.

Example 2.8 $\mathbb{N}^+ \subset \mathbb{N}$, since $0 \in \mathbb{N}$ but $0 \notin \mathbb{N}^+$.

Example 2.9 For any set A we have $\{\} \subseteq A$; the empty set is a subset of any set.

Exercise 2.5 For each of the sets $\mathbb{N}$, $\mathbb{N}^+$, $\mathbb{R}$, $\mathbb{Q}$, determine which sets are subsets of which.

Exercise 2.6 Suppose A and B are sets. Show that $A = B$ if and only if $A \subseteq B$ and $B \subseteq A$. You need to show *both* that if $A = B$ then $A \subseteq B$ and $B \subseteq A$, and also that if $A \subseteq B$ and $B \subseteq A$ then $A = B$, using Definition 2.3.

In Fig. 2.1 we describe sets and subsets using a diagrammatic notation called *Venn diagrams*.

Exercise 2.7 Draw a single Venn diagram that captures all the subset hierarchies of the sets $\mathbb{N}$, $\mathbb{N}^+$, $\mathbb{Z}$, $\mathbb{Q}$, $\mathbb{R}$.

Example 2.10 The set of *prime numbers* is an important subset of $\mathbb{N}$. A natural number $m \neq 1$ is said to be prime if its only divisors are ± 1 and $\pm m$. The first few prime numbers are $2, 3, 5, 7, 11, 13, 17, 19, 23, 29, \ldots$. The real importance of prime numbers is that every natural number is a product of prime numbers. For example, $60 = 2 \times 2 \times 3 \times 5$. In general, every number m may be written as $m = p_1^{m_1} p_2^{m_2} \cdots p_k^{m_k}$ for some prime p_i's. Moreover, it can be shown, by the *fundamental theorem of arithmetic*, that this decomposition into primes is unique.

Exercise 2.8 Show that 2 is the only even prime number.

Exercise 2.9 Determine the prime decomposition of the numbers: 10, 48, 72, 113, 240.

We now consider sets that contain every possible subset of some specified set. For example, the set $S = \{\{\}, \{1\}, \{2\}, \{3\}, \{1,2\}\{1,3\}, \{2,3\}, \{1,2,3\}\}$ contains every possible subset of $\{1,2,3\}$.

Definition 2.7 Power set Let A be a set. Then the power set of A, written $\mathscr{P}(A)$, is the set that consists of every subset of A.

Exercise 2.10 Determine $\mathscr{P}(\{1,2,3,4\})$.

2.1.4 Operations on sets

Suppose that as a result of council expenditure cuts, Wanstead and Aldersbrook social service staff (which already have a number of personnel in common) are to merge into a single organization. Suppose that $A = \{$Julie, Fred, Jim, Betty$\}$ is the set of Wanstead staff and that $B = \{$Fred, Betty, Alan, Naomi$\}$ is the set of Aldersbrook staff. Then the new merged organization consists of the set of staff, C, which is the *union* of the sets A and B. Specifically, it is the new set $C = \{$ Julie, Fred, Jim, Betty, Alan, Naomi$\}$.

Definition 2.8 Union The union of two sets A and B, written $A \cup B$, is the set of elements that are in either A or B or both. Thus $x \in A \cup B$ if and only if $x \in A$ or $x \in B$.

Next consider the case where, instead of merging, the social services create an extra department consisting of those people who are in both the Wanstead and Aldersbrook social services. Then the new department is the set of staff, D, which is the *intersection* of the sets A and B. Specifically, this is the new set $D = \{$Fred, Betty$\}$.

Definition 2.9 Intersection The intersection of two sets A and B, written $A \cap B$, is the set of elements that are in both A and B. Thus $x \in A \cap B$ if and only if $x \in A$ and $x \in B$.

In the case where $A \cap B = \{\}$, we say that the sets A and B are *disjoint*.

Example 2.11 Let A be the set of even integers and B be the set of odd integers. Then A and B are disjoint and $A \cup B = \mathbb{Z}$.

Next, suppose we are interested in the special problems of Wanstead social services, and we want to consult only with those personnel who work full time for Wanstead. Then we are interested in forming the *difference* of A and B which is $E = \{$Julie, Jim$\}$.

Definition 2.10 Difference The difference of set A and set B, written $A \setminus B$, is the set of elements that are in A but not in B. Thus $x \in A \setminus B$ if and only if $x \in A$ and $x \notin B$. We also say that $A \setminus B$ is the relative complement of B with respect to A.

Exercise 2.11 For the social service departments represented by the sets A and B above, determine $B \setminus A$.

When we constructed the set C as the union of the sets representing the social services departments, we lost the information that Betty and Fred work in *both* departments. This is because repetition is not explicitly in sets. It is often important to construct set unions that keep the members of the respective sets separate. The merged department could be the set

$$F = \{(0, \text{Julie}), (0, \text{Fred}), (0, \text{Jim}), (0, \text{Betty}), (1, \text{Fred}), (1, \text{Betty}), (1, \text{Alan}), (1, \text{Naomi})\}$$

which is the *sum* or *disjoint union*. By using this notation, the two occurrences of Betty and Fred are clearly distinguished.

Definition 2.11 Disjoint union The disjoint union of sets A and B is the set

$$A + B = \{(0, x) : x \in A\} \cup \{(1, y) : y \in B\}$$

Exercise 2.12 What can you say about the operation $+$ when two sets A and B are disjoint?

Suppose that all sets that we wish to consider in a specific context are subsets of some set U. For example, if we are concerned with sets that consist of people then U might be the set of all people. In such circumstances we define:

Definition 2.12 Complement The complement of a set A, written $\overline{A}$, is the set $U \setminus A$.

2.1.5 Rules about operations

We have identified operations on sets that enable us to construct new sets. Now let us consider operations on numbers as elements of sets. We are all familiar with the operations of addition and multiplication, and we know that for any numbers a and b, $a + b = b + a$ and $a \times b = b \times a$. This property of operations is called commutativity.

Just as the set operations $\cup$ and $\cap$ are defined on *pairs* of sets, so these numerical operations are defined on pairs of numbers. So what happens if we want to add or multiply more than two numbers? We just perform the operations a pair at a time. Thus $6 + 2 + 3 = (6 + 2) + 3 = 8 + 3 = 11$. Alternatively, we could have computed $6 + 2 + 3 = 6 + (2 + 3) = 6 + 5 = 11$.

In general, it does not matter in what order we perform addition, because for any numbers a, b, c we have $(a + b) + c = a + (b + c)$. This property of numbers is called associativity, and it is the reason why we can write the expression $6 + 2 + 3$ without ambiguity. Multiplication of numbers is also associative. However, we have to be much more careful when we combine addition and multiplication. For example, the expression $6 + 2 \times 3$ is ambiguous without brackets to indicate the *priority* of the operations, since $(6 + 2) \times 3 \neq 6 + (2 \times 3)$. Thus, in general,

$$a + (b \times c) \neq (a + b) \times (a + c)$$

However, we do have the following general property for combining addition and multiplication:

$$a \times (b + c) = (a \times b) + (a \times c)$$

Formally we say that multiplication distributes over addition. Addition does not distribute over multiplication.

So what has all this to do with the set operations? It turns out that there are important analogies between the set operations $\cup$ and $\cap$ and the operations $+$ and $\times$ for numbers. These general properties, and others, are shown in Fig. 2.2. Union and intersection are both associative, meaning that we can unambiguously compute the union and intersection of an arbitrary number of sets. Interestingly, unlike $+$ and $\times$, union and intersection do distribute over each other.

All of these set rules can be described using Venn diagrams. An example is given in Fig 2.3.

Exercise 2.13 Use Venn diagrams to illustrate the other rules in Fig. 2.2.

Exercise 2.14 Duality property Show that, with the exception of the first and third lines, if you replace every occurrence of $\cup$ by $\cap$ and $\cap$ by $\cup$ in the left-hand column of Fig. 2.2, you end up with precisely the set of properties in the middle column.

$A \cup \{\} = A$	$A \cap \{\} = \{\}$	identity
$A \cup A = A$	$A \cap A = A$	idempotence
$A \cup \overline{A} = U$	$A \cap \overline{A} = \{\}$	complements
$A \cup B = B \cup A$	$A \cap B = B \cap A$	commutative
$(A \cup B) \cup C = A \cup (B \cup C)$	$(A \cap B) \cap C = A \cap (B \cap C)$	associative
$A \cup (B \cap C) = (A \cup B) \cap (A \cup C)$	$A \cap (B \cup C) = (A \cap B) \cup (A \cap C)$	distributive
$\overline{A \cup B} = \overline{A} \cap \overline{B}$	$\overline{A \cap B} = \overline{A} \cup \overline{B}$	De Morgan

Figure 2.2 Rules for set operations.

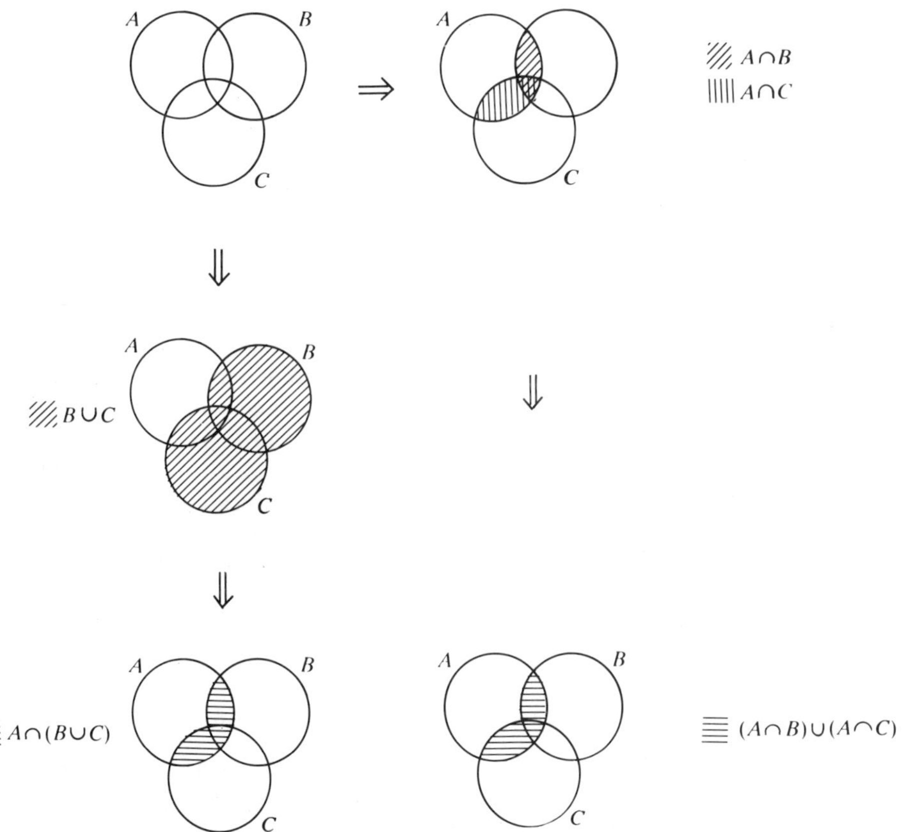

Figure 2.3 Venn diagrams illustrating $A \cap (B \cup C) = (A \cap B) \cup (A \cap C)$.

2.1.6 Paradoxes in set theory

We said that our definition of sets was informal. It would be more accurate to call it naïve. If we assume, as we have done, that *any* uniquely defined collection of objects is a set then we can arrive at logical inconsistencies, which are called paradoxes. These are statements that are apparently both true and false at the same time.

Example 2.12 Russell's paradox Since we have seen examples of sets that contain sets it is perfectly reasonable to ask: 'is $S \in S$?' or 'is S a member of itself?' Most sets are not members of themselves, so let us consider $T = \{S; S \text{ is a set such that } S \notin S\}$. So T consists of all sets that are not members of themselves. Now we ask: 'is $T \in T$?' Well, if $T \in T$ then T is a member of itself and so T is not a member of T. Thus $T \in T$ implies that $T \notin T$. On the other hand, it $T \notin T$, then our definition of T leads us to deduce that T is a member of T. Thus $T \notin T$ implies that $T \in T$. We have arrived at a contradiction. The problem is that our naïve definition of sets allows us to create sets that are very strange – normally they are too large (see also Exercise 2.15). In practice we are never interested in such sets, but they are a problem from a theoretical viewpoint. When mathematicians, at the turn of the last century, discovered these problems, they avoided them by proposing various *axiomatic approaches* to set theory. Because these approaches restrict the kind of sets that can be constructed, so that T above is not a set at all, they lead to an elimination of paradoxes.

Exercise 2.15 Universal set paradox* For any *well-defined* set S, it can be shown that $\mathscr{P}(S) \notin S$. Deduce that the existence of a universal set S, which contains every set, leads to contradictions.

2.1.7 Cartesian products

We now present an important method for building new sets from old sets. To motivate this discussion, think about a typical 'A to Z' road atlas of a major city. This will consist of a number of pages of maps, like the one shown in Fig. 2.4, and an index of road names or sites. A particular road or site on a given page is located by reference to the particular square in which it appears. Each square is represented by a 'pair' of numbers (x, y), where x represents the horizontal position and y represents the vertical position. For example, Hampton Road is located by the pair (2,4). Note that the pairs (x, y) are *ordered* in the sense that (x, y) is different from (y, x). Certainly (2,4) does not represent the same square as (4,2). The set of squares (locations) on a given page may be viewed as a set of 20 pairs, $S = \{(x, y) : x \in \{1, 2, 3, 4, 5\} \text{ and } y \in \{1, 2, 3, 4\}\}$, called the *Cartesian product* of the set $\{1, 2, 3, 4, 5\}$ and the set $\{1, 2, 3, 4\}$.

Definition 2.13 Cartesian product If A and B are sets, then the Cartesian product of A and B, written $A \times B$, is the set $A \times B = \{(x, y) : x \in A \text{ and } y \in B\}$.

Exercise 2.16 A telephone directory may be viewed as a subset of the set $A \times B$ where A is the set of all names and addresses and B is the set of all phone numbers. Show that $A \times B \neq B \times A$.

Example 2.13 The two-dimensional plane (Cartesian plane), as used in high school geometry, is simply the Cartesian product $\mathbb{R} \times \mathbb{R}$. It is normally represented diagrammatically as shown in Fig. 2.5 where an element $(x, y) \in \mathbb{R} \times \mathbb{R}$ is represented by the point lying at distance x horizontally from the vertical axis and distance y vertically from the horizontal axis.

Example 2.14 The rational numbers $\mathbb{Q}$ may be thought of as the set $\mathbb{Z} \times (\mathbb{Z} \setminus \{0\})$. We just associate each rational a/b with the pair (a, b).

Exercise 2.17 Suppose $A = \{\text{Anna, Leonie, Mary}\}$ is the set of women registered with a dating agency and $B = \{\text{John, Fred, Ben, Bert}\}$ is the set of men registered. Write out in full the set of potential dates, namely the set $A \times B$.

Using our 'A to Z' road atlas we now generalize the Cartesian product of sets. Rather than the pair (a, b), it is more accurate to think of each location in the A to Z as consisting of a triple (n, a, b) where n represents the page number and (a, b) the location on page n. Thus if our A to Z has 30 pages of maps, the set of locations may be viewed as the set of 600 triples, $S = \{(x, y, z) : x \in \{1, 2, \ldots, 30\}, y \in \{1, 2, 3, 4, 5\}, z \in \{1, 2, 3, 4\}\}$.

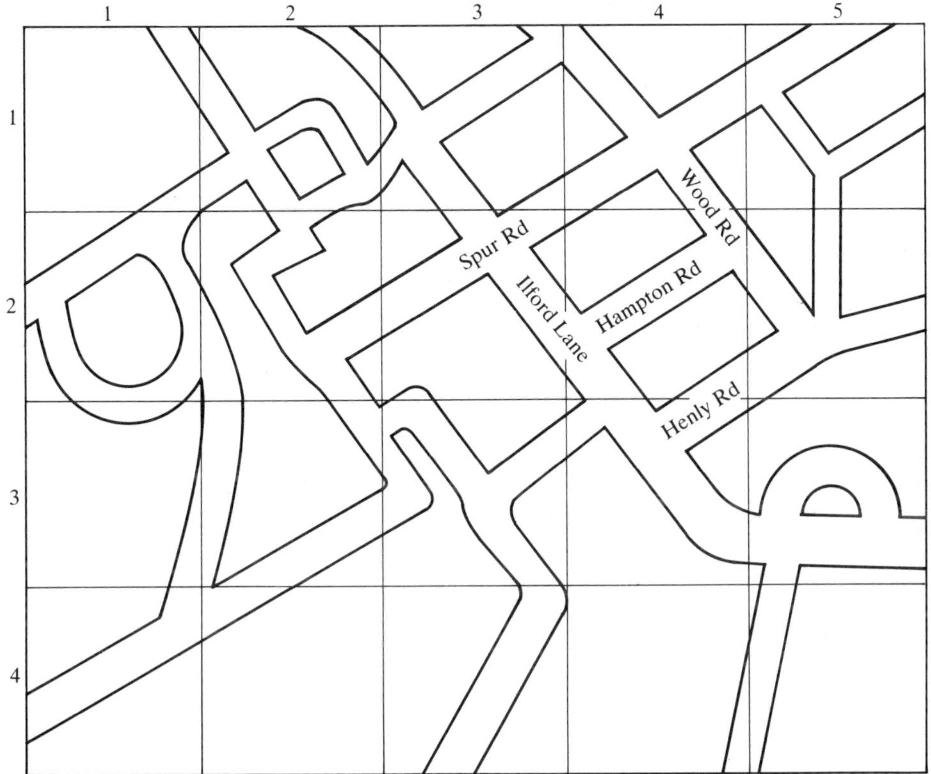

Figure 2.4 'A to Z' road map.

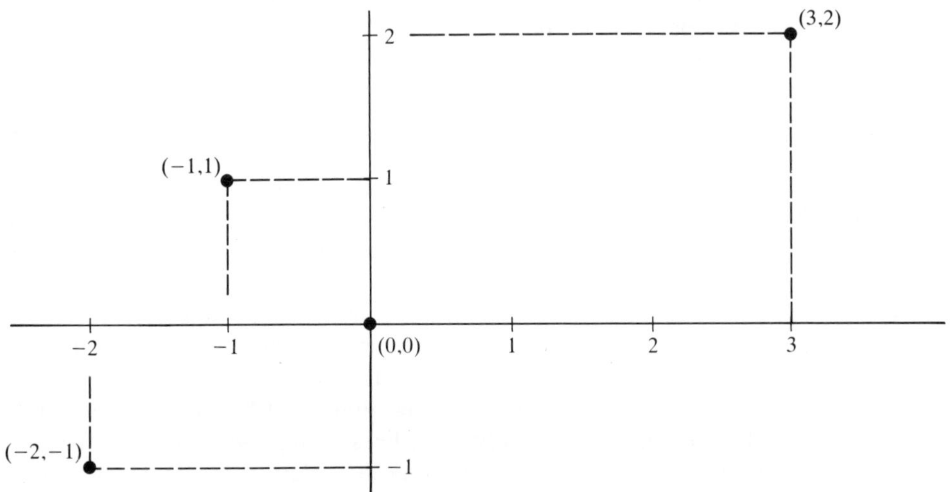

Figure 2.5 Cartesian plane.

Definition 2.14 Direct product The direct product of n sets $A_1, \ldots, A_n$ is the set $A_1 \times \cdots \times A_n = \{(a_1, \ldots, a_n) : a_i \in A_i \text{ for each } i = 1, \ldots, n\}$.

Example 2.15 A *record type* in a programming language like Pascal may be viewed as the direct product of a number of other types. Thus the declaration

```
type
  team = (Spurs, Arsenal, West Ham, Chelsea);
  stadium = (Wembley, Hillsborough, Villa Park);
  match = record
            teaml : team;
            team2 : team;
            venue : stadium
          end;
variable
  cup-semi-final : match;
```

means that *match* is the direct product team × team × stadium. A possible value for the variable *cup-semi-final* is the triple (Spurs, Arsenal, Wembley).

Exercise 2.18 In Example 2.15, identify six other triples that are values for the record structure. Assuming that it is not meaningful for teams to play themselves, identify a possible weakness in the type specification. Finally, identify six elements that belong to the set (team × team) × stadium and six elements that belong to the set team × (team × stadium). Are these sets equal?

2.2 RELATIONS

Let us think about our dating agency in Exercise 2.17. The Cartesian product $A \times B$ is an exhaustive list of all possible dates between a woman and a man. In practice, however, information about each individual person will ensure that certain dates are not possible. For example, suppose Anna specifies that she cannot date a smoker; then, if Bert is a smoker, the pair (Anna, Bert) is not a viable date. In practice, the set of viable dates will therefore be a subset of $A \times B$.

We now give a rule that explicitly describes the elements of this subset of $A \times B$. We represent the set of viable dates by a picture consisting of blobs and lines, as shown in Fig. 2.6(a). The blobs represent the people and a line between person a and person b represents the fact that it is feasible for a and b to date. Thus Anna can date all men except Bert, while Mary cannot date anybody. The resulting set of ordered pairs is an example of a relation that we could name *compatibility*. Since A and B are disjoint we call it a relation from A to B.

Now suppose that the dating agency has a party and invites all its clients along. They mingle freely and talk to each other. At the end of the evening every person is discreetly asked which other people they 'like'. The result of this survey may be represented by the picture in Fig. 2.6(b). We now think in terms of a single set C of people. We need to use arrows instead of just lines to represent order in the new relation *likes*, since we see, for example, that Anna likes Bert even though Bert does not like Anna. We could also represent the results of this survey by listing all the ordered pairs (a, b) for which a likes b. The relation *likes* on the people in the set C forms a subset of $C \times C$.

Definition 2.15 Relation Let $S_1, \ldots, S_n$ be sets where $n \geq 1$. A relation on $S_1, \ldots, S_n$ is a subset of $S_1 \times \cdots \times S_n$.

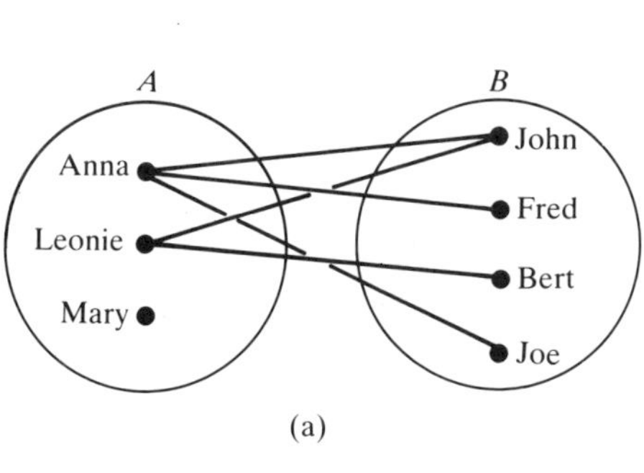

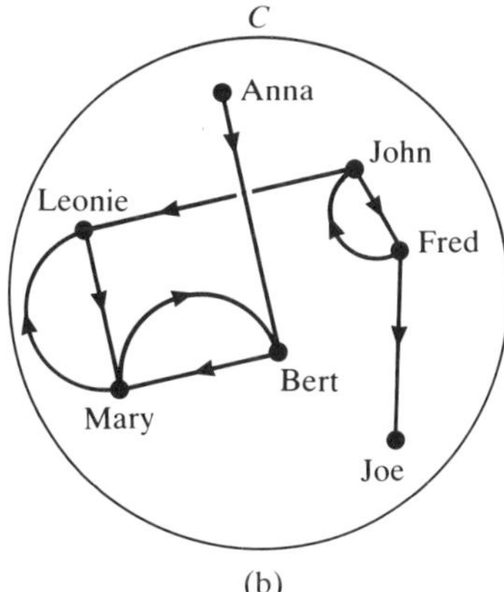

Figure 2.6 Relation representing viable dates.

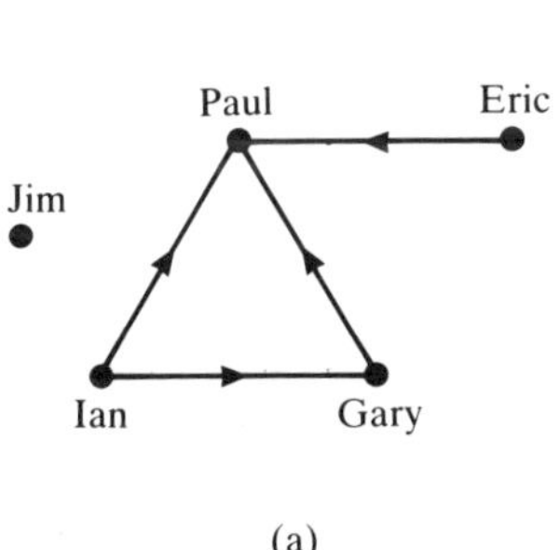

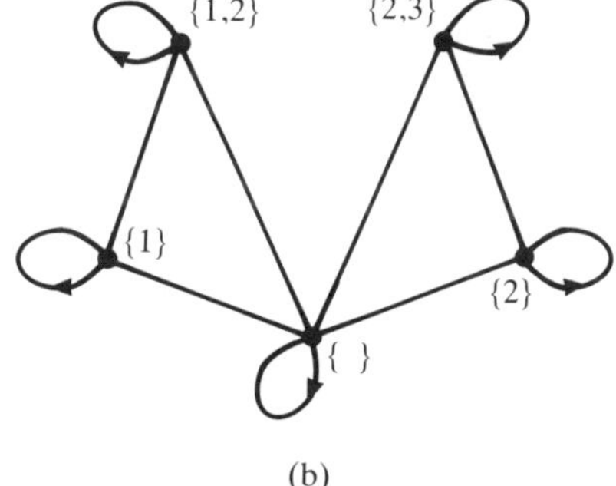

Figure 2.7 Graphical representation of binary relations.

In the case where $n = 2$ we speak about a *binary* relation. Thus each of the relations *compatability* and *likes* described in the dating example are binary relations. In the case where $S_1 = \cdots = S_n = S$, we talk about a relation *over* the set S. Thus *likes* is a binary relation over the set C of people.

Example 2.16 Using our convention for representing binary relations by 'blobs and arrows' type figures, Fig. 2.7(a) represents the relation $R(x, y)$ that denotes 'y is a better player than x'. The underlying set of players is $S = \{$Jim, Ian, Gary, Eric, Paul$\}$. Thus Paul is a better player than all the others except for Jim who is not comparable with anybody. Gary is better than Ian, while Eric is not comparable with Ian or Gary.

Exercise 2.19 Figure 2.7(b) represents the relationship of subset inclusion over a set of sets. If $S = \{1, 2, 3\}$, draw the relation representing subset inclusion over the set $\mathscr{P}(S)$.

Example 2.17 Consider a set of people C. The relation $R_2(x, y)$ denoting 'x is taller than y' is a binary relation over C. Some pairs that are in this relation are illustrated in Fig. 2.8. The relation $R_1(x)$ that denotes 'x is tall' is a unary relation over C; it is a subset of C. Figure 2.8 also gives an example of a *ternary* relation

Relation R_1: $(x, y) \in R_1$ if 'x is taller than y'.
Relation R_2: $x \in R_2$ if 'x is tall'.
Relation R_3: $(x, y) \in R_3$ if 'x is much taller than y'.
Relation R_4: $(x, y, z) \in R_4$ if 'x is higher than y if sitting on z's shoulders'.

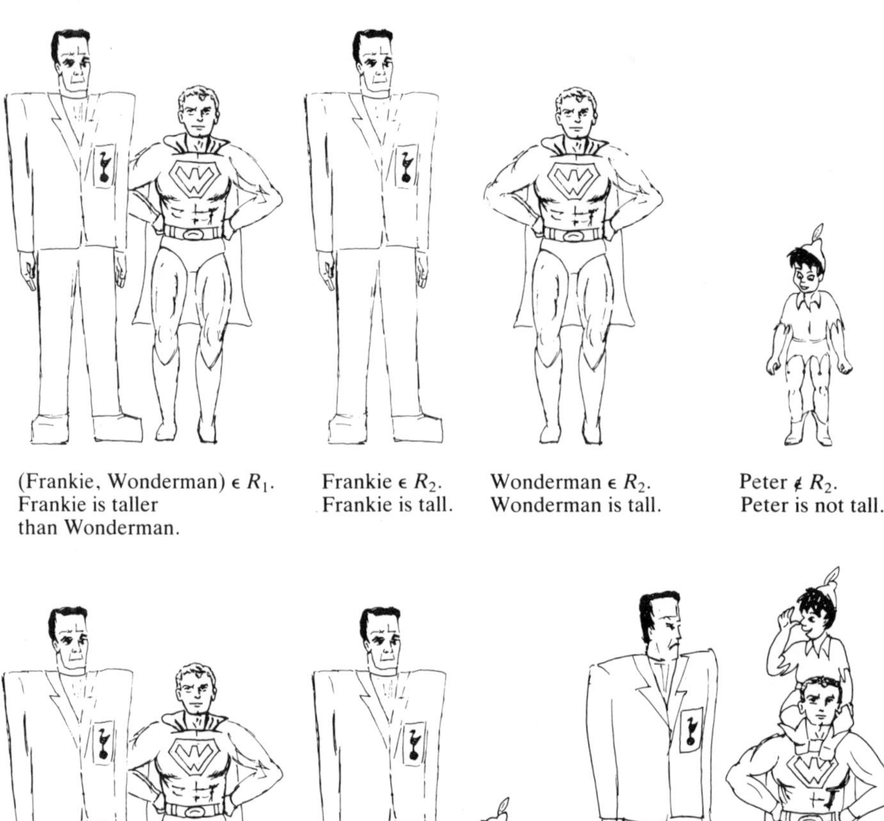

(Frankie, Wonderman) $\in R_1$. Frankie is taller than Wonderman.

Frankie $\in R_2$. Frankie is tall.

Wonderman $\in R_2$. Wonderman is tall.

Peter $\notin R_2$. Peter is not tall.

(Frankie, Wonderman) $\notin R_3$. Frankie is not much taller than Wonderman.

(Frankie, Peter) $\in R_3$. Frankie is much taller than Peter.

(Peter, Frankie, Wonderman) $\in R_4$. Peter is higher than Frankie if sitting on Wonderman's shoulders.

Figure 2.8 Some relations.

R_4 over C. Specifically, $(x, y, z) \in R_4$ when x is higher than y when sitting on z's shoulders. We shall use this particular set of relations to illustrate an important principle in the theory of measurement in Chapter 17.

Exercise 2.20 In Example 2.15 the direct product team $\times$ team $\times$ stadium represented the set of all possible matches between two teams at a given stadium. Write down explicitly a subset of this direct product that might represent the relation 'FA Cup semi-finals'.

Example 2.18 Operations as relations The binary operations '+' and '×' defined on $\mathbb{R}$ may be viewed as ternary relations. For example, '+' $\subset \mathbb{R} \times \mathbb{R} \times \mathbb{R}$ where $(x, y, z) \in$ '+' if $x + y = z$. Similarly, the binary operations $\cup, \cap$ defined on sets of sets are ternary relations. Not all operations are binary. The complement operation '‾' defined on sets is unary in the sense that it operates on single sets rather than pairs of sets. It follows that a unary operation like this may be viewed as a binary relation '‾' $\subseteq S \times S$ where $(A, B) \in$ '‾' if $\overline{A} = B$ where S is a family of sets.

Exercise 2.21 Explain how the operations $\cup$ and $\cap$ may be viewed as ternary relations. Also, give an example of a unary operation defined on $\mathbb{R}$ and explain how this may be viewed as a binary relation.

Example 2.19 Sometimes it is convenient to represent a finite relation by listing all its elements in a box. Suppose, for example, that we want to describe the relation of students attending certain courses given by certain lecturers. Specifically our relation A is a subset of students × courses × lecturers where $(x, y, z) \in A$ precisely when student x attends course y given by lecturer z. We can represent this as a box by:

Student	Course	Lecturer
Naomi	Maths	Norman
Joe	Computing	Norman
Naomi	Computing	Gillian
Anna	Statistics	Peter

2.2.1 Relations in a database

Suppose a faculty provides lecture courses in various subjects for various years of a degree programme. For example, Discrete Maths is taught in years 1 and 2 on the BSc degree programme to different numbers of students for the two years. Particular subjects are the responsibility of one or more lecturers, who may be drawn from different departments. Lecturers from the same department may have offices in different locations.

The collection of information describing the faculty's teaching is an example of what is often called a database. It could be represented as the single 7-ary relation

teaching $\subset$ Locations × People × Departments × Degrees × Courses × $\mathbb{N} \times \mathbb{N}$

as given in Table 2.1. Then, for example

(Building A, Norman, Maths, BSc, Discrete Maths, 2, 70) $\in$ *teaching*
(Building B, Gillian, Computing, BSc, Software Eng, 1, 90) $\notin$ *teaching*

The relation *teaching* can be viewed as a model of a particular view of the faculty's teaching system. However, as such it contains a lot of redundant information. For example, the information about a particular subject's years and student numbers is repeated for each different lecturer responsible for the subject. Similarly, the fact that Norman is in the Maths Department is modelled five times.

A better model represents a set of smaller relations as shown in Fig. 2.9. There is no redundant information here, and there are only 39 table entries compared with 70 in the original model. Think of the space saved in a large database with many different subjects, lecturers and types of degrees.

Any database system that is modelled as a set of relations in this way is called a relational database. There are numerous special purpose computer languages that

Table 2.1 The relation *teaching*

Location	Lecturer	Department	Degree	Subject	Year	Students
Building A	Norman	Maths	BSc	Software Eng	1	90
Building A	Norman	Maths	BSc	Software Eng	2	50
Building A	Norman	Maths	BSc	Software Eng	3	30
Building A	Norman	Maths	BSc	Discrete Maths	1	90
Building A	Norman	Maths	BSc	Discrete Maths	2	70
Building B	Peter	Maths	BSc	Software Eng	1	90
Building B	Peter	Maths	BSc	Software Eng	2	50
Building B	Peter	Maths	BSc	Software Eng	3	30
Building B	Gillian	Computing	BSc	Discrete Maths	1	90
Building B	Gillian	Computing	BSc	Discrete Maths	2	70

RELATION R_1

Location	Lecturer
Building A	Norman
Building B	Peter
Building B	Gillian

RELATION R_2

Lecturer	Department
Norman	Maths
Peter	Maths
Gillian	Computing

RELATION R_3

Course	Degree
Software Eng	BSc
Discrete Maths	BSc

RELATION R_4

Lecturer	Subject
Norman	Discrete Maths
Norman	Software Eng
Peter	Software Eng
Gillian	Discrete Maths

RELATION R_5

Subject	Year	Students
Software Eng	1	90
Software Eng	2	50
Software Eng	3	30
Discrete Maths	1	90
Discrete Maths	2	70

Figure 2.9 A set of simple relations that captures the same information as Table 2.1.

support the implementation and manipulation of such database systems. Once we have modelled a system as a set of relations (which is the hard part performed by a systems analyst) we can apply a number of mathematical operations to the relations themselves. We say that these operations 'query' the database for information.

Example 2.20 We now describe three important operations, illustrating these with reference to the relations $R_1, \ldots, R_5$ in Fig. 2.9.

(a) *Selection.* Consider the relation R_5. Suppose we want to find out about numbers of students in each year for one particular subject, say Discrete Maths. We form a new relation $R_5' \subseteq R_5$ which consists of only those tuples (rows) in R_5 for which the first entry is Discrete Maths. Thus R_5' is the relation:

Subject	Year	Students
Discrete Mathematics	1	90
Discrete Mathematics	2	70

We have defined a new relation that *selects* from an old one. A typical database query language would have a built-in operation for selection, so that we can create R_5' using a command like: R_5' = SELECT R_5 WHERE COURSE = 'DISCRETE MATHS'.

(b) *Projection.* Suppose now that we are only interested in the years in which

Discrete Maths is taught. Then we want to find a new relation $R_5'' \subset R_5'$ by selecting only the two columns Subject and Year of R_5'. The relation R_5' is then

Subject	Year
Discrete Mathematics	1
Discrete Mathematics	2

This particular operation is called *projection* and it would be implemented by a command like: $R_5'' =$ PROJECT R_5' OVER SUBJECT, YEAR.

(c) *Join.* Suppose we want to find out the number of students taught by which lecturers in each year. This information is certainly not contained in any one of the relations $R_1, \ldots, R_5$. The relation R_4 contains the information about which subjects are taught by which lecturers, and the relation R_5 contains the information about years and student numbers for each subject. Hence, if we concatenate tuples of R_4 and R_5 which have the same value in the Subject column then we will arrive at the new relation R_6 with the required information:

Lecturer	Subject	Year	Students
Norman	Software Eng	1	90
Norman	Software Eng	2	50
Norman	Software Eng	3	30
Norman	Discrete Maths	1	90
Norman	Discrete Maths	2	70
Peter	Software Eng	1	90
Peter	Software Eng	2	50
Peter	Software Eng	3	30
Gillian	Discrete Maths	1	90
Gillian	Discrete Maths	2	70

This *join* operation is implemented by: $R_6 =$ JOIN R_4 AND R_5 OVER SUBJECT.

Exercise 2.22 Write down the relation R_4' which would be produced by the statement: $R_4' =$ SELECT R_4 WHERE LECTURER = 'NORMAN'.

2.2.2 Special properties of binary relations

Let R be a binary relation over a set S. Then R is said to be:

Reflexive if $(x, x) \in R$ for each $x \in S$.

Symmetric if $(x, y) \in R$ implies $(y, x) \in R$ for each $x, y \in S$.

Transitive if $(x, y) \in R$ and $(y, z) \in R$ implies $(x, z) \in R$ for each $x, y, z \in S$.

Asymmetric if $(x, y) \in R$ implies $(y, x) \notin R$ for each $x, y \in S$.

Anti-symmetric if $(x, y) \in R$ and $(y, x) \in R$ implies $y = x$ for each $x, y \in S$.

Irreflexive if $(x, x) \notin R$ for each $x \in S$.

Negatively transitive if for any $x, y \in S$, $(x, y) \in R$ implies that for every $z \in S$ either $(x, z) \in R$ or $(z, y) \in R$.

Strongly complete if for any $x, y \in S$ either $(x, y) \in R$ or $(y, x) \in R$.

Example 2.21 Let S be a set of people. Then the following all define binary relations over S:

(a) $(x, y) \in$ *brother* if x is a brother of y. Then *brother* is transitive and irreflexive, but satisfies none of the other properties.

(b) $(x, y) \in$ *cousin* if x and y are first cousins. Then *cousin* is symmetric and irreflexive only.

(c) $(x, y) \in$ *same-parents* if x and y have the same parents. Then *same-parents* is reflexive, symmetric and transitive.

Exercise 2.23 Define $(x, y) \in$ *mother* if x is the mother of y. Which of the properties are satisfied by this relation?

Example 2.22 The relation $\{(0,0),(1,1),(2,2)\}$ on $\{0,1,2\}$ is both symmetric and anti-symmetric but is not asymmetric.

Example 2.23 Consider the relation '$\leq$' on $\mathbb{Z}$ defined by $(x, y) \in$ '$\leq$' if $x \leq y$. This is reflexive, transitive and strongly complete. Any relation that is strongly complete is also negatively transitive. The converse is not true. Consider, for example, the relation D 'properly divides' on the set $\{2,4,6,12\}$. This is negatively transitive, but is not strongly complete because neither $4D6$ nor $6D4$.

Exercise 2.24 For each of the binary relations '$<$', '$\leq$' and '$|$' (divides) over the set $\mathbb{Z}$, determine which of the various properties holds.

Definition 2.16 Modulo n relation Equivalence modulo n, written $\equiv_n$, for any $n \geq 0$, is a binary relation over $\mathbb{Z}$ defined by $x, y \in$ '$\equiv_n$' if $x - y$ is exactly divisible by n. We normally write this as $x \equiv_n y$ or $x = y \bmod n$.

Example 2.24 The relation $\equiv_{12}$ represents our understanding of time equivalence on a 12-hour clock. Thus, 15 hours after midnight is equivalent to 27 hours after midnight because $15 \equiv_{12} 27$. In fact both are equivalent to 3 mod 12, which is the hour that will be shown on the clock.

The relation $\equiv_n$ is reflexive, symmetric and transitive. Since the set of remainders upon division by n is the set $\mathbb{Z}_n = \{0, 1, 2, \ldots, n-1\}$, it follows that every integer is equivalent to exactly one element in $\mathbb{Z}_n$. Thus the relation $\equiv_n$ *partitions* the set $\mathbb{Z}$ into n subsets. For example, when $n = 12$ these are

$$\begin{array}{l}\{0, 12, -12, 24, -24, 36, -36, \ldots\} \\ \{1, 13, -11, 25, -23, 37, -35, \ldots\} \\ \quad\vdots \\ \{11, 23, -1, 35, -13, 47, -25, \ldots\}\end{array}$$

Definition 2.17 Modulo n addition and multiplication The sets $\mathbb{Z}_n$ have their own addition and multiplication operations defined by $a \oplus_n b = (a + b) \bmod n$ and $a \otimes_n b = (a \times b) \bmod n$.

For example, $3 \oplus_{12} 11 = 2$ which, in the context of Example 2.24, says that 11 hours after 3 o'clock is 2 o'clock. The special case $\mathbb{Z}_2$ is called the set of *binary numbers*. It contains just 0 and 1 and the arithmetic operations are binary addition and multiplication.

Definition 2.18 Equivalence relation A relation that is reflexive, symmetric and transitive is called an equivalence relation.

Example 2.25 The relation $\equiv_n$ (for each n) is an equivalence relation.

Table 2.2 Types of order relations

	Relation type				
Property that must be satisfied	Partial order	Strict partial order	Total order	Strict weak order	Strict order
Reflexive	√		√		
Transitive	√	√	√		√
Asymmetric		√		√	√
Antisymmetric	√		√		
Irreflexive		√			√
Negatively transitive				√	√
Strongly complete			√		

The equivalence relation $\equiv_n$ induces a partition of the set $\mathbb{Z}$ into disjoint subsets. In general, if $\sim$ is any equivalence relation over a set S then $\sim$ induces a partition in which elements that are equivalent with respect to $\sim$ are in the same subset.

Definition 2.19 Equivalence classes An equivalence relation $\sim$ on S partitions S into disjoint subsets called the equivalence classes of S with respect to $\sim$.

Example 2.26 There are just two equivalence classes of $\mathbb{Z}$ with respect to $\equiv_2$. These are $\{0, \pm 2, \pm 4, \pm 6, \ldots\}$ and $\{1, \pm 3, \pm 5, \pm 7, \ldots\}$.

Exercise 2.25 What are the equivalence classes of $\mathbb{Z}$ with respect to $\equiv_3$?

Exercise 2.26 Show that the relation *same-parents* defined in Example 2.21 is an equivalence relation. What are its equivalence classes?

2.2.3 Order relations

A number of important binary relations R intuitively express a notion of ordering in the sense that $(x, y) \in R$ precisely when y is 'bigger' or 'smaller' than x. Consider, for example, the binary relations over $\mathbb{Z}$:

'$<$' defined by: $(x, y) \in$'$<$' if $x < y$
'$\leq$' defined by: $(x, y) \in$ '$\leq$' if $x \leq y$
'$|$' defined by: $(x, y) \in$ '$|$' if $x \mid y$

and the binary relations over a set of sets:

'$\subset$' defined by: $(x, y) \in$ '$\subset$' if $x \subset y$
'$\subseteq$' defined by: $(x, y) \in$ '$\subseteq$' if $x \subseteq y$

Relations such as these are called *order* relations. There are five important classes of order relations, and the classification is according to the properties they satisfy. This information is summarized in Table 2.2. In general, if we want to talk about an arbitrary order relation we normally use the symbol $\preceq$ and write $x \preceq y$ instead of $(x, y) \in R$.

Example 2.27 The relation $\leq$ over $\mathbb{Z}$ is a total order.

Example 2.28 The relation $<$ over the set $\mathbb{Z}$ is a strict order. Transitivity, asymmetry and irreflexivity are all clear. To see that it is negatively transitive, suppose $x < y$. For any z we have to show that either $x < z$ or $z < y$. If $z = x$ then $z < y$.

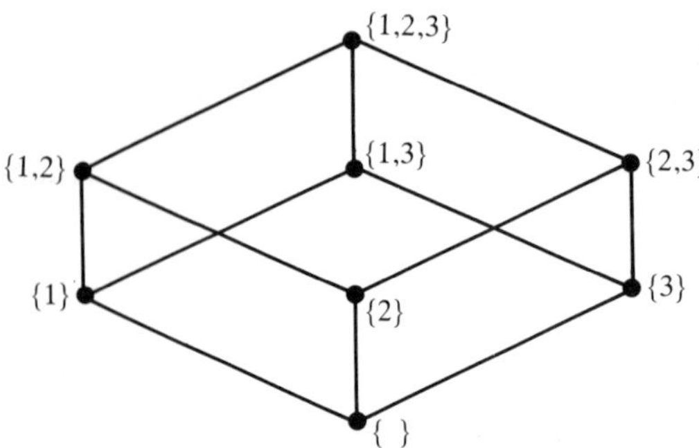

Figure 2.10 The poset $(\mathscr{P}(\{1,2,3\}), \subseteq)$.

If $x \neq z$ then either $z < x$ or $x < z$. If $z < x$ then we must also have $z < y$ since $<$ is transitive. Note that $<$ is not strongly complete since this would imply that for each x, $x < x$ must hold. Hence $<$ cannot be a total order.

Example 2.29 The relation $\subseteq$ over a collection of sets is a partial order. It is not in general a total order since we might have sets X and Y such that neither $X \subseteq Y$ nor $Y \subseteq X$.

Exercise 2.27 Give an example of a collection of sets for which $\subseteq$ is a total order.

Exercise 2.28 Show that the relation $|$ over $\mathbb{Z}$ is a partial order. Why is it not a total order?

Definition 2.20 Poset A poset (or partially ordered set) is a pair $(S, \preceq)$ where S is a set and $\preceq$ is a partial order over S.

Example 2.30 The pairs $(\mathbb{Z}, |)$ and $(\mathbb{Q}, \leq)$ are posets.

Exercise 2.29 Let A be any set. Show that the pair $(\mathscr{P}(A), \subseteq)$ is a poset.

2.2.4 Lattices*

Let us look more closely at posets of the form $(\mathscr{P}(A), \subseteq)$ where A is a set. Figure 2.10 illustrates this poset where $A = \{1,2,3\}$. We have removed the directions from each arrow since it is assumed that they all point from bottom to top, and we have also removed redundant arrows. Hence we have removed all 'loops' (since we know $\subseteq$ is reflexive), and all arrows that follow from transitivity of $\subseteq$, such as one from $\{\}$ to $\{1,2\}$.

Definition 2.21 Hasse diagram A diagram of a poset relation from which redundant lines have been removed is called a Hasse diagram.

Now let $(S, \preceq)$ be any poset, and let $x, y \in S$:

1 If there is an element $i \in S$ that satisfies

(a) $i \preceq x$ and $i \preceq y$ and

(b) if $i' \in S$ such that $i' \preceq x$ and $i' \preceq y$ then $i' \preceq i$

then i is called the *infimum* of x and y.

2 If there is an element $j \in S$ that satisfies

(a) $x \preceq j$ and $y \preceq j$ and

(b) if $j' \in S$ such that $x \preceq j'$ and $y \preceq j'$ then $j \preceq j'$

then j is called the *supremum* of x and y.

Example 2.31 In the poset $(\mathscr{P}(A), \subseteq)$ any two sets $X, Y \in \mathscr{P}(A)$ have an infimum, namely the set $X \cap Y$, and a supremum, namely the set $X \cup Y$.

Definition 2.22 Lattice Let $(S, \preceq)$ be a poset. Suppose that, for each $x, y \in S$, there is both an infimum and a supremum in S for x and y with respect to $\preceq$. Then $(S, \preceq)$ is called a lattice. Normally we write $x \sqcap y$ for the infimum of x and y and $x \sqcup y$ for the supremum of x and y.

Example 2.32 For any set A, $(\mathscr{P}(A), \subseteq)$ is a lattice, where for any two elements $x, y \in \mathscr{P}(A)$, $x \sqcap y$ is the element $x \cap y$ and $x \sqcup y$ is the element $x \cup y$.

Example 2.33 The poset $(\mathbb{Z}^+, |)$ is a lattice. For any two elements $x, y \in \mathbb{Z}^+$, $x \sqcap y$ is the greatest common divisor of x and y, and $x \sqcup y$ is the least common multiple of x and y.

Exercise 2.30 Draw the Hasse diagram for the poset $(\{1, 2, 3, 4, 5, 6\}, |)$. Deduce that this is not a lattice.

Exercise 2.31 Show that any poset $(S, \preceq)$, where $\preceq$ is a total order, must be a lattice.

Definition 2.23 Minimal and maximal elements Let $(S, \preceq)$ be a poset. An element x of S for which there is no other $y \in S$ satisfying $y \preceq x$ in S is called a minimal element. An element z of S for which there is no other $y \in S$ satisfying $z \preceq y$ is called a maximal element.

Example 2.34 The poset $(\mathbb{N}, \leq)$ has a minimal element, namely 0, but no maximal element.

Exercise 2.32 Identify the minimal and maximal elements of the poset of Exercise 2.30.

Definition 2.24 Bounded lattice If a lattice has minimal and maximal members, then it follows from the definition of infimum and supremum that these must be unique. Such a lattice is called a bounded lattice.

Example 2.35 For any set S, $(\mathscr{P}(S), \subseteq)$ is a bounded lattice. The minimal element is $\{\}$ and the maximal element is S.

Exercise 2.33 Let S be any finite subset of $\mathbb{N}$. Show that $(S, \leq)$ is a bounded lattice.

2.3 FUNCTIONS

2.3.1 Defining functions

Suppose that S is a set of people. Figure 2.11 illustrates the relation *age* from S to $\mathbb{N}$ which describes a person's age. Specifically $(a, n) \in age$ precisely when person a is n years old. The relation has two important properties:

1 Every element in S has an arrow coming out of it. This is because every person has an age.

2 No element of S has more than one arrow coming out of it. This is because age is *uniquely* defined. Each person has only one age (Hollywood actors excepted).

Definition 2.25 Function A function is a binary relation f between two sets A and B, such that

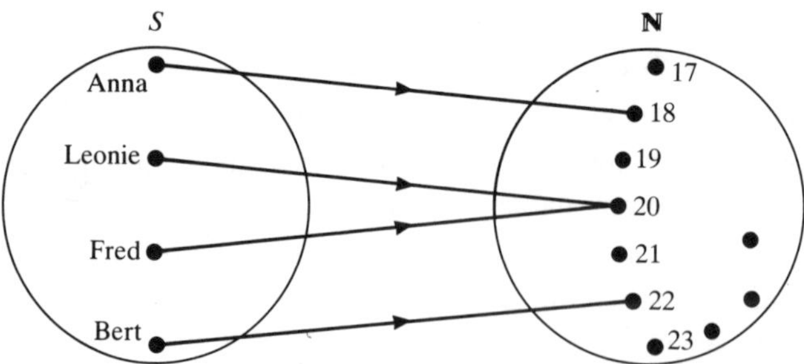

Figure 2.11 The relation *age*.

domain

(a) For each $x \in A$ there is some $y \in B$ such that $(x, y) \in f$.

(b) If $x \in A$ and $y, z \in B$ such that $(x, y) \in f$ and $(x, z) \in f$, then $y = z$.

A function is also called a *mapping*. We would not normally define the function *age* by listing every possible pair (X, n) where X is a person and n is that person's age. Rather, we would define some *rule* that told us how to compute a given person's age. For example, the rule might be simply to ask that person. The rule would be taken as the definition of the function. It does not explicitly list pairs (such a list could be infinite), but we could try to generate all the necessary pairs by applying the rule.

To reflect the view that a function between two sets A and B is a rule that assigns to each $a \in A$ a unique $b \in B$, we write $f : A \to B$. We say that A is the *domain* of f and B is the *codomain* of f.

If $a \in A$ and b is the unique element of B for which $(a, b) \in f$ then we write this as $f(a) = b$ or as $f : a \mapsto b$; in such an expression we call a the *argument* of f and b the *value* of the function for argument a. We also say that b is the *image* of a under f.

The *range* of f is $\{b : b \in B \text{ and } f(a) = b \text{ for some } a \in A\}$ and is the set of elements of B which are the image under f of some element in A.

Example 2.36 Consider the function *age*. The argument 'Anna' has value 18 under this function, so *age*(Anna) = 18. The domain of *age* is S, the set of all people. We could think of the codomain as $\mathbb{N}$. If it is known that nobody is older than 120 then the image of *age* is the set $\{0, 1, \ldots, 120\}$.

Clearly it is always the case that $f(A) \subseteq B$. When $f(A) = B$ we say that f is *surjective* (or *onto*). When no element of B is the image of more than one element of A we say that f is *injective* (or *one-to-one*). When f is both surjective and injective we say it is *bijective*. These ideas are illustrated in Fig. 2.12.

The following examples all view functions as rules.

Example 2.37 The award of points to a soccer team resulting from matches played in the English league system may be viewed as a function $f : M \to \mathbb{N}$ where M is the set of matches in which the team is involved. We define f by the rule:

$$f(m) = \begin{cases} 0 & \text{if match } m \text{ is lost} \\ 1 & \text{if match } m \text{ is drawn} \\ 3 & \text{if match } m \text{ is won} \end{cases}$$

Example 2.38 The functions that are common in high school mathematics are mostly of the form $f : \mathbb{R} \to \mathbb{R}$. The rules that characterize these functions may

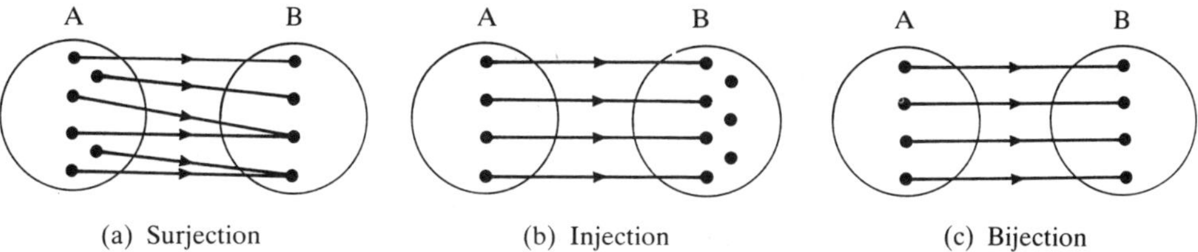

Figure 2.12 Types of functions: surjections, injection, bijections.

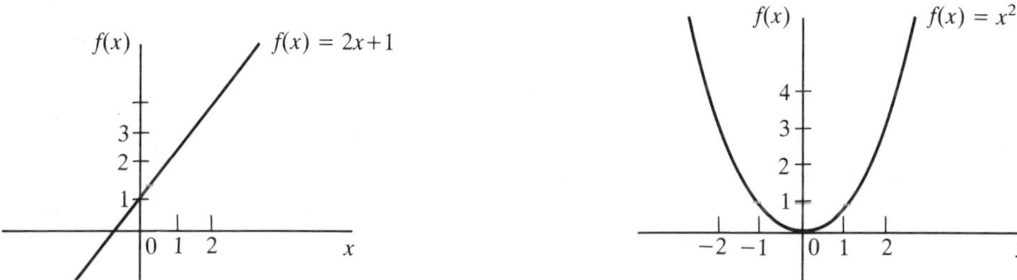

Figure 2.13 Real-valued functions represented as graphs.

often be described by simple mathematical expressions. For example, the rule that transforms a number into its square is characterized by the expression x^2. Thus the function *square* : $\mathbb{R} \to \mathbb{R}$ is defined by the rule $square(x) = x^2$ for each $x \in \mathbb{R}$. This is what is meant when people talk about 'the function x^2'. Similarly 'the function $2x + 1$' refers to the function f for which $f(x) = 2x + 1$ for each x, etc. We really need to be able to give a name to a function that clearly indicates what the rule of the function is. In Chapter 9 we tackle this issue in some depth.

In Figure 2.13 we draw graphs of functions where x is represented on the horizontal axis and $f(x)$ on the vertical axis.

Example 2.39 The rule for computing the circumference of a circle of radius r may be viewed as a function *circum* : $\mathbb{R} \to \mathbb{R}$ in which $circum(r) = 2\pi r$.

Example 2.40 The sex of people is a function *sex* : $\{\text{People}\} \to B$ where B is the set $\{\text{male, female}\}$. In this case the result of applying the function is *not* a number. This function is surjective but not injective.

Example 2.41 Operations as functions In Example 2.18 we noted that binary operations like '+' and '×' defined on real numbers are ternary relations. These specific relations can also be defined as the functions '+': $\mathbb{R} \times \mathbb{R} \to \mathbb{R}$ and '×': $\mathbb{R} \times \mathbb{R} \to \mathbb{R}$. Similarly, the operations $\cup, \cap$ on sets of sets can be defined as functions. In general, if $\square$ is a binary operation which is a function $\square : S \times S \to S$ then we would write $s_1 \square s_2$ instead of $\square(s_1, s_2)$ for the result of applying $\square$ to the pair (s_1, s_2). This is called *in-fix* as opposed to *pre-fix* notation. We shall see shortly that not all operations can be defined as functions.

Exercise 2.34 Explain how the binary operations $\cup, \cap$ defined on sets of sets may be viewed as functions. Also explain how the unary complement operation may be viewed as a function.

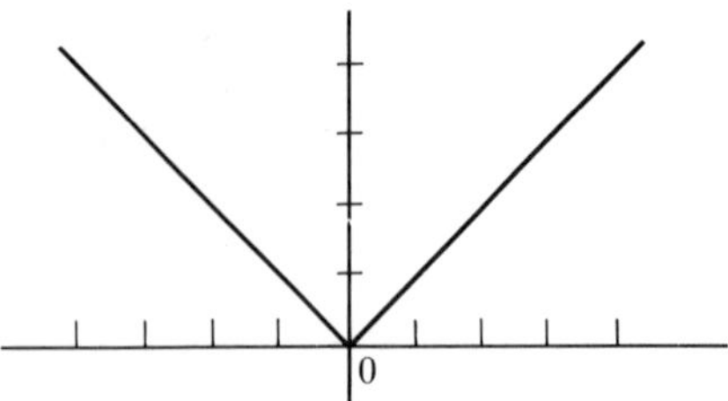

Figure 2.14 Absolute value function.

The crucial requirement of the definition of function is that every element in the domain gives rise to a *unique* element in the codomain.

Example 2.42 The rule that assigns to each positive number x the square root of x is not a function since positive numbers have two square roots. However, the rule *sqrt-set* : $\mathbb{R} \to \mathscr{P}(\mathbb{R})$ that assigns to each positive number its set of square roots *does* define a function.

Example 2.43 Consider a rule that assigns to each observed failure of a computer program an error that caused the failure. The rule *cause* : $\{\text{Program failures}\} \to \{\text{program errors}\}$ is not a function because some failures are caused by more than one error.

Exercise 2.35 Write a function that assigns to a real number its positive square root.

2.3.2 Unsmooth functions

High school mathematics can sometimes create the impression that interesting functions are precisely those whose graphs are nice curves, or those that can be described by simple formulae like that for the volume of a cylinder.

Unfortunately, many interesting, and quite simple, functions cannot be so described. Consider, for example, the function to compute the absolute value of a real number. Plotting the graph for this function in Fig. 2.14 illustrates its non-smoothness. If we want to describe the function explicitly, we normally write

$$abs(x) = \begin{cases} x & \text{if } x \geq 0 \\ -x & \text{otherwise} \end{cases}$$

In fact, many functions have to be expressed by dividing up the domain into separate classes and defining the function rule differently in each case. We have already seen this in Example 2.37. Such functions are commonly referred to as *conditional functions*, and there is an alternative notation for writing these:

$$abs(x) = (x \geq 0 \to x, -x)$$

Specifically this means that if $x \geq 0$ then map x to x, otherwise map x to $-x$.

Example 2.44 Consider the function $f : \mathbb{R} \times \mathbb{R} \to \mathbb{R}$ for which

$$f(x, y) = \begin{cases} x + y & \text{if } x > 0 \text{ and } y > 0 \\ 0 & \text{if } x = 0 \\ 0 & \text{if } y = 0 \\ -x - y & \text{otherwise} \end{cases}$$

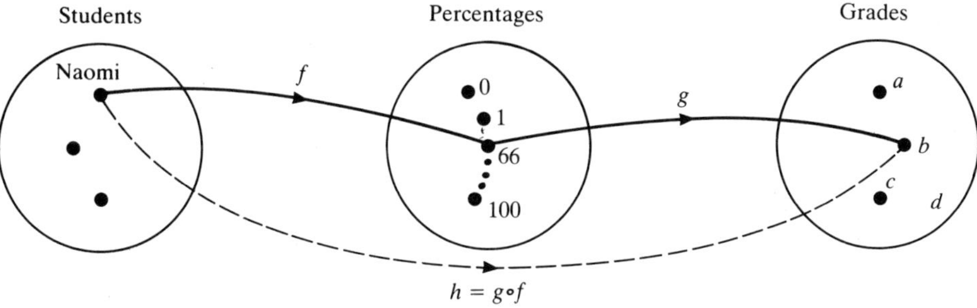

Figure 2.15 Function composition.

We may write this as $f(x, y) = (x > 0 \text{ and } y > 0 \rightarrow x + y,\ x = 0 \rightarrow 0,\ y = 0 \rightarrow 0,\ -x - y)$.

Exercise 2.36 Write down the function of Example 2.37 using the notation for conditional functions.

2.3.3 Function composition

In Fig. 2.15 we have a function $f : \text{Students} \rightarrow \{0, \ldots, 100\}$ representing exam results (in percentages) of a set of students. Also there is a function $g : \{0, \ldots, 100\} \rightarrow \{a, b, c, d\}$ which assigns to each percentage a grade a, b, c or d. Suppose g is defined by

$$g(n) = (70 \leq n \leq 100 \rightarrow a,\ 60 \leq n < 70 \rightarrow b,\ 50 \leq n < 60 \rightarrow c,\ 0 \leq n < 50 \ \rightarrow d)$$

If Naomi is one of the students and we want to know her *grade* rather than her percentage mark then we apply the function f to compute $f(\text{Naomi})$ and then apply the function g to compute $g(f(\text{Naomi}))$.

What we have done is to construct a new function h resulting from first applying f and then applying g. Thus, we have a function $h : \text{Students} \rightarrow \{a, b, c, d\}$ which computes students' grades. This particular means of constructing a new function from two old functions is called *function composition*.

In general, for functions f and g where $f : A \rightarrow B$ and $g : B \rightarrow C$, the *composition of* g and f, written $g \circ f$ is the function $h : A \rightarrow C$ defined by $h(a) = g(f(a))$ for each $a \in A$.

2.3.4 New functions from old

Just as complex systems are constructed from simple components so complex functions can be constructed from simple ones.

Example 2.45 The function $max_2 : \mathbb{R} \times \mathbb{R} \rightarrow \mathbb{R}$, to compute the maximum of two numbers, is defined by $max_2(x, y) = (x \geq y \rightarrow x, y)$. We can use this function to construct a function $max_3 : \mathbb{R} \times \mathbb{R} \times \mathbb{R} \rightarrow \mathbb{R}$ that computes the maximum of three numbers, and is defined by $max_3(x, y, z) = max_2(x, max_2(y, z))$.

Exercise 2.37 Write down the function to compute the maximum of four numbers in terms of the function max_3.

Example 2.46 Suppose we have the two simple functions *plus-one* (which adds one to each $x \in \mathbb{N}$) and *minus-one* (which subtracts one from each $x \in \mathbb{N}^+$). Then we can use these to define the addition function '+' for any natural numbers. Informally, to compute $a + b$ we keep adding one to a and subtracting one from b until $b = 0$. Formally, we have

$$a + b = (b = 0 \rightarrow a,\ \textit{plus-one}(a) + \textit{minus-one}(b))$$

This function definition is *recursive*, meaning it is defined in terms of itself, since '+' appears on both sides of the equation.

Similarly, we can now define multiplication of natural numbers in terms of the addition function. Informally, to compute $a \times b$ we keep adding a to itself and subtracting one from b until $b = 0$.

Exercise 2.38 Write down the formal recursive definition of the function '×' in terms of the functions '+' and *minus-one*.

These examples show how we construct new functions in terms of *specific* old functions. The following two examples are somewhat different:

Example 2.47 Suppose $\mathscr{F}$ is the set of all functions of the form $f : \mathbb{R} \rightarrow \mathbb{R}$. Suppose *add-functions* $: \mathscr{F} \rightarrow \mathscr{F}$ is defined by *add-functions* $(f, g) = h$ where $h(x) = f(x) + g(x)$. For example, if f is the function that adds one to its argument and g is the function that squares its argument then *add-functions* (f, g) is the function that maps x to $x + 1 + x^2$. So *add-functions* has a pair of functions as its argument and creates a new function in terms of these.

Example 2.48 Consider the function *composition* $: \mathscr{F}_1 \times \mathscr{F}_2 \rightarrow \mathscr{F}_3$ which is the operation defined in Sec. 2.3.3, where $\mathscr{F}_1$ is the set of functions from A to B, $\mathscr{F}_2$ is the set of functions from B to C and $\mathscr{F}_3$ is the set of functions from A to C. Specifically, if $f \in \mathscr{F}_1$ and $g \in \mathscr{F}_2$, *composition*$(f, g) = f \circ g$.

Functions such as *add-functions* and *composition*, whose domains and codomains are sets of functions, are called *higher order functions* or *functionals*.

Exercise 2.39 A number of classical rules of the differential calculus are in fact higher order functions. The derivative rule D, which, for example, maps the function $f(x) = x^2$ onto the function $f'(x) = 2x$, is a higher order function $D : F \rightarrow F$ where F is the set of all differentiable functions. Show how this particular higher order function is also used in the definition of the product rule, and show that the product rule is also a higher order function.

2.3.5 Partial functions

Not all functions need to be totally defined on their domain.

Definition 2.26 Partial function A partial function $f : A \nrightarrow B$ is defined exactly as a function except that there may be some elements $a \in A$ for which there is no b such that $(a, b) \in f$. Then f is undefined for a.

Example 2.49 Let $A = \{x, y, z\}$ and $B = \{u, v\}$. The relation $f = \{(x, u), (y, v)\}$ is a partial function $f : A \nrightarrow B$. It is undefined for $z \in A$.

Example 2.50 The reciprocal relation $f : \mathbb{R} \nrightarrow \mathbb{R}$ given by $f(x) = 1/x$ for each x is a partial function that is undefined for $x = 0$.

Exercise 2.40 Explain why the positive square root relation *pos-sqrt* $: \mathbb{R} \nrightarrow \mathbb{R}$ is only a partial function.

Example 2.51 Although all operations may be viewed as relations, we remarked that not all are functions. Consider the division operation on $\mathbb{R}$. This is a relation from $\mathbb{R} \times \mathbb{R}$ to $\mathbb{R}$. However, it is only a partial function because it is undefined for each pair $(r, 0)$.

Programs that fail to terminate for specific inputs are undefined for those inputs. This is an example of a *partially defined*, or incompletely defined, function. We shall see in Chapter 10 that loose or permissive specifications are based on partially defined functions.

If $f : A \nrightarrow B$ is a partial function, then the subset of A for which f is defined is called the *domain of* f. Clearly if A' is the domain of f then the relation $f' : A' \rightarrow B$ for which $f'(a) = f(a)$ for each $a \in A'$ is a function. It is called the *restriction of* f *to* A'. It is sometimes useful to transform a partial function into a total function in this way.

Example 2.52 The set of results of soccer matches played in a league may be viewed as a partial function $f : T \times T \nrightarrow \mathbb{N} \times \mathbb{N}$ where T is the set of teams. Specifically $f(a, b) = (n, m)$ where the home team a scores n goals against the away team b which scores m goals. For example, if Spurs win 3-1 away to Arsenal, then f(Arsenal, Spurs) $=$ (1,3). The mapping f is undefined when $a = b$ since teams do not play themselves. Thus f is undefined for the subset S of $T \times T$ where $S = \{(a, a); a \in T\}$. The partial function f has the set $(T \times T) \setminus S$ as its domain. The restriction of f is the total function $f' : (T \times T) \setminus S \rightarrow \mathbb{N} \times \mathbb{N}$.

We cannot always transform a partial function into a total function. In Example 2.52, suppose that some matches are abandoned due to bad weather and are never replayed. The problem now is that we do not know in advance which matches will be abandoned and so we do not know which values will be undefined. In Chapter 9 we shall describe a rigorous theory for dealing with partial functions.

2.3.6 Machines, algorithms and computability

Functions as simple machines A good way to think of a function $f : A \rightarrow B$ is as a very simple machine or system that has no internal states. The machine accepts certain types of inputs (namely elements from A), does some processing to A and then produces an output that is an element of B. At all times the same input leads to the same output. Contrast this with, say, a vending machine that outputs a drink upon input of two 10p's. When we input 10p the first time we get no output other than possibly some message asking for more money. However, when we input 10p the second time we get a drink. This is because the machine has internal states. The output is dependent on both the input and these internal states. Only by thinking of the input as being the set of all 'sequences of input actions' can we really think about such machines as functions.

However, machines in everyday life often break down or produce unexpected results. Even our simple vending machine will not always output a drink after we input two 10p's. This is because it might enter some unexpected internal state, like running out of liquid or jamming. We say that such an unreliable machine is *non-deterministic*. In contrast, a total function is always reliable and is like a simple *deterministic* machine that we shall define formally in Sec. 2.4.5.

Now consider a computer that executes a program which we believe is the implementation of some function. It may fail to reproduce the same outputs for given inputs for a variety of reasons. For example, some intermediate computation may have caused a data structure to become over full, resulting in an erroneous output during one particular execution, even though normally the program works properly for that input. Or the whole computer may malfunction because of an electrical fault beyond our control.

These examples illustrate that although many systems are *intended* to be deterministic, in practice they turn out to be non-deterministic. It is this undesirable non-determinism that infuriates us, but that must be understood and modelled. This will be explored further in Chapter 9.

Algorithms and computability Having considered a function as a special kind of machine, it is reasonable to ask whether we really can construct such special machines to implement every function. This question leads directly to the notion of *algorithm*, which is the necessary abstraction of the machines we are seeking. Informally, an algorithm is a precise set of instructions for transforming inputs to outputs. In Chapter 15 we shall show that there are many formal proposed definitions of algorithm, but that these are all believed to be equivalent. For example, an algorithm has been defined as *any terminating computer program written in language X*, where X is any programming language you have ever heard of. We can now rephrase our question as: 'Can every function be implemented by a terminating computer program?' We shall see, in Chapter 15, that the answer to this question is 'no'. Consequently, we define the *computable functions* to be those that can be defined by an algorithm; equivalently, they can be implemented by a terminating computer program.

2.3.7 Sequences

Sets are unstructured collections with no order defined on the elements. However, in many circumstances we *are* interested in the order.

Example 2.53 Suppose $\{1.2,\ 1.3,\ 1.3,\ 1.5,\ 1.8,\ 1.9\}$ is the set representing the numbers of unemployed people (in millions) in the United Kingdom in six consecutive months. The order here provides valuable trend information.

Example 2.54 The set $\{1.4,\ 1.41,\ 1.414, \ldots\}$ represents increasingly accurate decimal expansions of the number $\sqrt{2}$. Specifically, the nth element is the expansion of $\sqrt{2}$ to n decimal places.

Such ordered sets may be finite, as in Example 2.53, or infinite, as in Example 2.54. They are called *sequences*. In the case of a finite sequence of k elements from a set S we can think of the elements as being ordered by the numbers $1, 2, \ldots, k$.

Definition 2.27 Finite sequence A sequence of k elements from a set S is a function $s : \{1, 2, \ldots, k\} \rightarrow S$ that describes a rule for assigning order. Thus $s(i)$ is the ith element of the sequence. We normally use the notation $\langle s_1, s_2, \ldots, s_k \rangle$ to represent the sequence in which $s(i) = s_i$.

Thus, in Example 2.53, $s(i)$ is the ith month's unemployment figure.

Definition 2.28 Infinite sequence An infinite sequence of elements from a set S is a function $s : \mathbb{N}^+ \rightarrow S$.

Thus, in Example 2.54, $s(i)$ is the expansion of $\sqrt{2}$ to i decimal places.

As with any function we could describe the rule for assigning order explicitly by writing the sequence in full, such as $\langle 1, 4, 9, 16, 25, 36 \rangle$. However, this is impossible for infinite sequences, and even for most finite sequences we would normally prefer to use a formula, such as $s_n = n^2$ in this case, which we call the *general term of the sequence*.

Example 2.55 The sequence $\langle 1, -1, 1, -1, 1, -1, \ldots \rangle$ has the general term $s_n = (-1)^{n+1}$. The sequence $\langle 5, 8, 2, 4, 1, 9, 3, 5, 9, 1, \ldots \rangle$ has no obvious general term.

Exercise 2.41 What is the general term of the sequences: $\langle 5, 7, 9, 11, 13, 15, \ldots \rangle$, $\langle 2, 2, 2, 2, 2, \ldots \rangle$, $\langle 2, 5, 10, 17, 26, 37, \ldots \rangle$, $\langle$off, on, off, on, off, on, ...$\rangle$?

2.4 GRAPH THEORY

2.4.1 Directed graphs

In Sec. 2.2 we represented relations diagrammatically, using 'blobs' to represent objects and 'arrows' to represent relations between objects. 'Blobs and arrows' type pictures can be used to model a range of systems, as shown in Fig. 2.16. We call them directed graphs, or just digraphs. What Fig. 2.16 also illustrates is that in certain cases it is clear how we would model a real-world system as a digraph, while in other cases the modelling process is tricky. In this section we are more concerned with the properties of the formal mathematical model, namely the digraphs, than of the modelling processes. However, we will provide numerous examples of the latter which give an insight into the importance and usefulness of graphs as a mathematical model of complex systems.

Definition 2.29 Digraph Let V be a set of elements, called vertices. Let E be a subset of $V \times V$ whose elements are called arcs. Then the pair (V, E) is called a digraph.

Vertices are sometimes also called *nodes* or *blobs* and arcs are sometimes called *arrows* or *directed edges*. Thus a digraph is just a binary relation over a set whose elements are the 'blobs'. An arc (a, b) represents an arrow from blob a to blob b. We say that a is the tail of the arc and b is the head. When $a = b$ the arc is said to be a *loop*. Note that, as all our pictures so far confirm, both the head and tail of every arc is a blob.

It follows from Def. 2.29 that a digraph may be completely specified by just listing the sets V and E.

Example 2.56 The digraph of Fig. 2.17(a) may be equivalently specified by the listing $V = \{a, b, c, d, e\}$, $E = \{(c, b), (c, d), (c, e), (e, c), (e, b)\}$.

Exercise 2.42 Provide an equivalent specification of the digraph of Fig. 2.17(b) by listing V and E.

Example 2.57 Figure 2.18(a) is *not* a digraph, because there is an 'arc' with tail vertex a which has no vertex on its head. It cannot be specified as a subset of $\{a, b, c\}$, its set of vertices.

Exercise 2.43 Explain why Fig. 2.18(b) is not a digraph. (*Hint*: A digraph must be a binary relation over its set of vertices.)

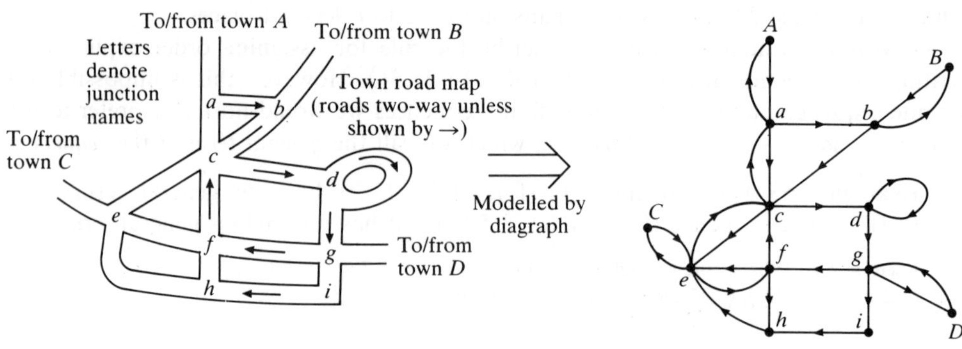

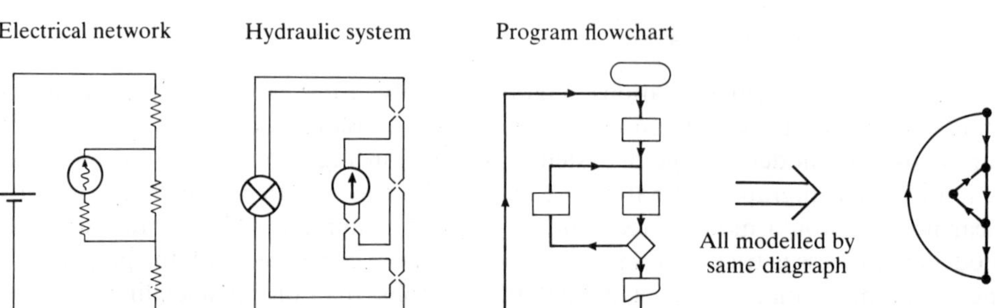

Figure 2.16 Modelling systems by 'blobs and arrows' type pictures.

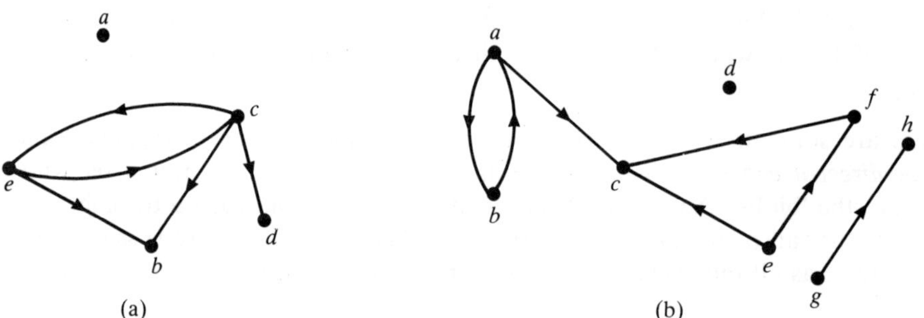

Figure 2.17 Digraphs.

Figure 2.18 'Pictures' that are not digraphs.

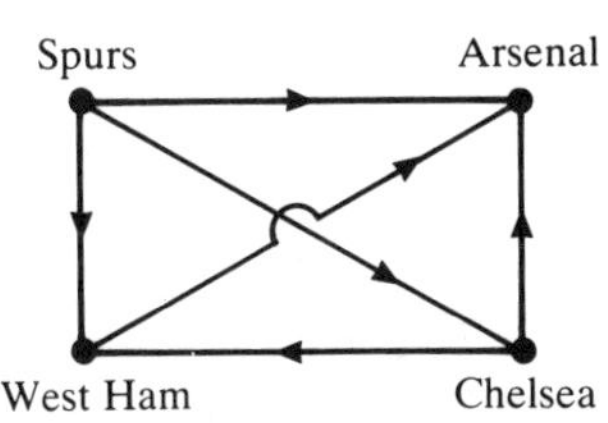

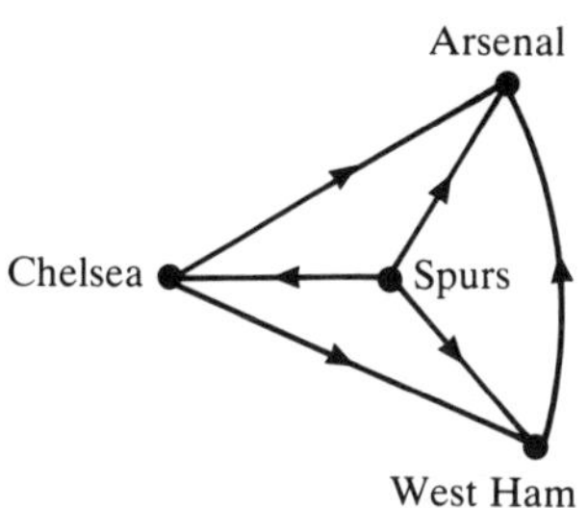

Figure 2.19 Different drawings of the same digraph.

It follows from Def. 2.29 that the particular way that we *draw* a digraph is unimportant; all that matters is knowing what the vertices are and which arcs join which vertices.

Example 2.58 Figure 2.19 shows two different drawings of the same digraph which describes the results of a round-robin tournament of four soccer teams, with an arc (a, b) representing the fact that team a beat team b. For example, Spurs beat Arsenal.

Figure 2.19 also confirms that we sometimes allow ourselves to draw digraphs in such a way that arcs may cross at points that are themselves not vertices. When we do this, as for the arc (West Ham, Arsenal) crossing (Spurs, Chelsea), we sometimes emphasize that the intersection is not a vertex by drawing a hump as shown. Such intersections are called *crossovers*. In many real-world situations there is a perfectly realistic analogy. For example, the crossover in a road system, where one road crosses another via a tunnel or an overpass, is not a junction. Similarly, on a printed circuit board, wires may cross at points that are not terminals. In many situations there is no option other than to draw a graph with crossovers. We shall return to this point in Sec. 2.4.5.

Definition 2.29 asserts that the set E is a subset of $V \times V$. Because of our definitions in Sec. 2.1, this means that for any two vertices a and b, a digraph cannot have more than one arc going from a to b; thus we do not allow 'multiple' arcs in digraphs. This is the reason why Fig. 2.18(b) is not a digraph. However, there are some systems for which we may wish to model multiple arcs, for example a road system like Fig. 2.20 which contains two one-way streets (in the same direction) linking the same two junctions. Consequently, just as we extended the notion of sets to multisets, we define a directed multigraph as a digraph whose arcs is a multiset of pairs of vertices.

Definition 2.30 Directed multigraph Let V be a set of vertices. Let E be a multiset of elements from $V \times V$. Then the pair (V, E) is called a directed multigraph.

Example 2.59 Figure 2.18(b) is a directed multigraph.

2.4.2 Undirected graphs

There are many systems that we wish to model diagrammatically as blobs and lines rather than blobs and arrows. These are systems in which we are interested in links between objects but for which the notion of direction of link is irrelevant or meaningless.

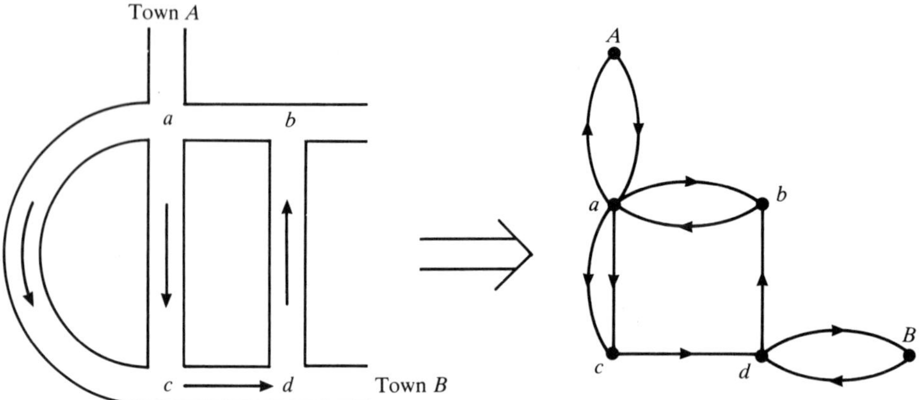

Figure 2.20 Directed multigraph modelling road system.

Consider the city train route map in Fig. 1.11 on page 16. The lines have no arrows because it is always assumed that all links are two-way.

Definition 2.31 Graph Let V be a set of elements, called vertices. Let E be a set of unordered pairs of these elements, called edges. Then the pair (V, E) is called a graph.

Informally we can think of a *graph* as a digraph with the arrows removed from the lines. To emphasize the distinction, we call the lines edges.

Strictly speaking, Def. 2.31 does not allow multiple edges. If we want multiple edges between vertices, then we speak about a *multigraph*:

Definition 2.32 Multigraph Let V be a set of elements, called vertices. Let E be a multiset of unordered pairs of these elements. Then the pair (V, E) is called a multigraph.

Examples of systems modelled by graphs and multigraphs are shown in Fig. 2.21.

Exercise 2.44 Show that a graph may be viewed as a special case of a digraph if each edge (a, b) is assumed to be bidirectional, that is corresponds to two arcs (a, b) and (b, a).

2.4.3 Basic concepts and definitions in graph theory

So as not to duplicate all definitions we restrict our attention to graphs. Unless otherwise stated, all definitions apply equally to digraphs with appropriate rewording.

Definition 2.33 Subgraph Let $G = (V, E)$ be a graph. A subgraph of G is a graph $G' = (V', E')$ for which $V' \subseteq V$ and $E' \subseteq E$.

Example 2.60 Figure 2.22(a) shows a graph together with four of its subgraphs, while Fig. 2.22(b) shows a digraph together with four of its subdigraphs.

Exercise 2.45 Give explicit specifications for all of the subgraphs in Fig. 2.22.

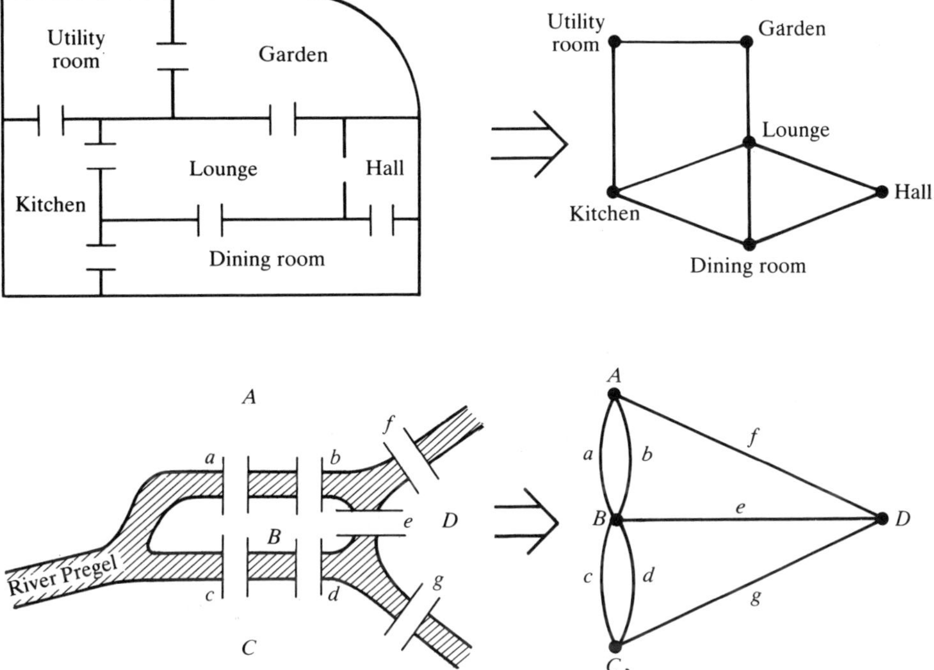

Figure 2.21 Modelling systems as graphs and multigraphs.

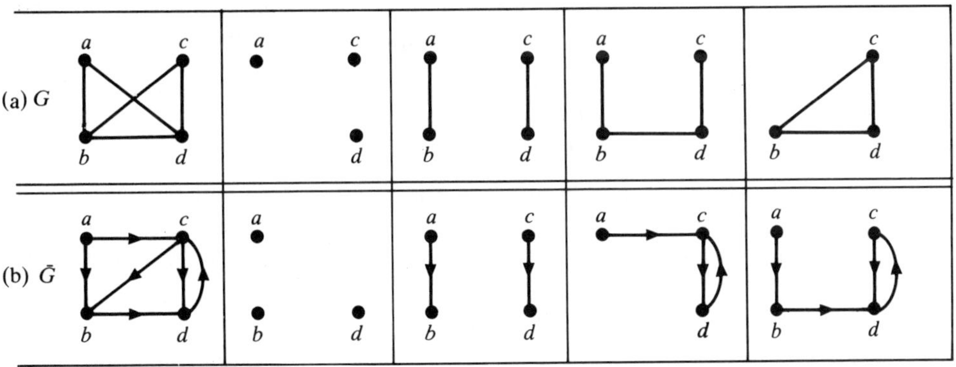

Figure 2.22 Subgraphs and subdigraphs.

Definition 2.34 Vertex degree For each vertex v of a graph G, the degree of v, written $\deg(v)$, is the number of edges meeting at v (with loops counting as two edges). For a digraph we also define the indegree of v, written $\mathrm{id}(v)$, as the number of arcs with head at v, and the outdegree of v written $\mathrm{od}(v)$ as the number of arcs with tail at v.

Example 2.61 In Fig. 2.22, $\deg(v) = 3$ in G and 2 in G_2. In $\overline{G}$, $\mathrm{od}(b) = 1$ and $\mathrm{id}(b) = 2$.

Exercise 2.46 For any vertex v of a digraph G, show that $\deg(v) = \mathrm{id}(v) + \mathrm{od}(v)$.

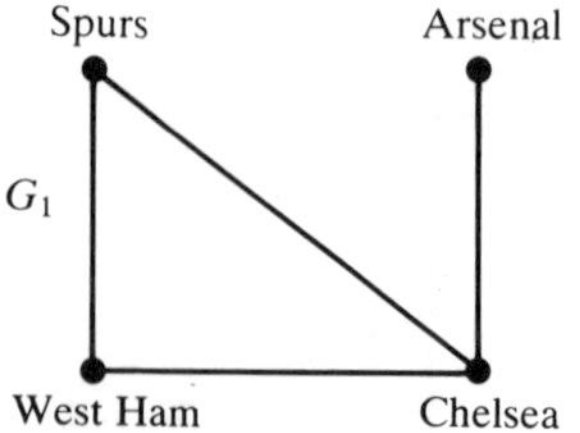

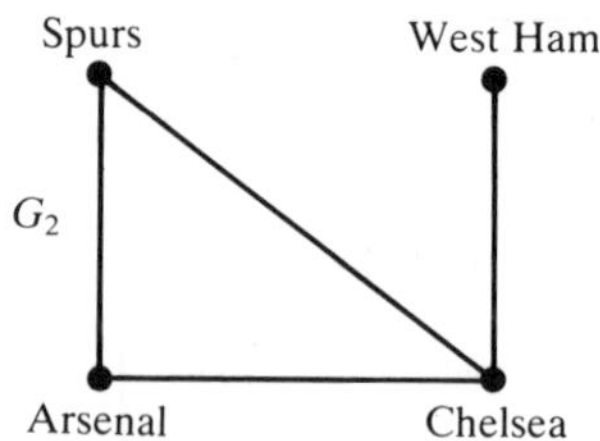

Figure 2.23 Different but isomorphic graphs 'drawn the same'.

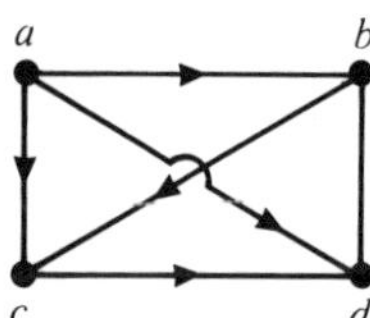

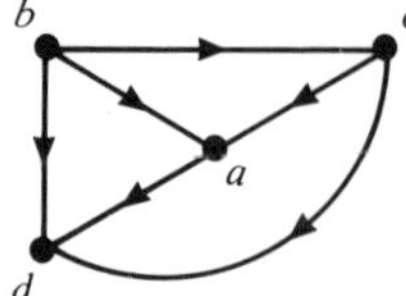

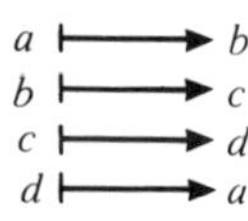

Figure 2.24 Different but isomorphic digraphs 'drawn differently'.

Exercise 2.47 'Handshaking' lemma Show that in any graph the sum of all the vertex degrees is equal to twice the number of edges.

We have seen, in Fig. 2.19, that two different pictures can represent exactly the same graph. Conversely, two very similar pictures can represent quite different graphs.

Example 2.62 The two graphs in Fig. 2.23 represent matches played between teams, so (a, b) is an edge precisely when teams a and b have already played each other. These graphs are not the same since, in G_1, Spurs have not played Arsenal, while in G_2 they have.

If, in Fig. 2.23, we relabel G_2 by interchanging Arsenal and West Ham, then we arrive at the same graph as G_1. Hence we say that these graphs are *isomorphic*.

Definition 2.35 Graph isomorphism Two graphs $G = (V, E)$ and $G' = (V', E')$ are isomorphic if G' can be obtained from G by relabelling the vertices. This means there is an injective function $f : V \to V'$ such that $(f(a), f(b)) \in E'$ if and only if $(a, b) \in E$.

Figure 2.24 shows two isomorphic digraphs. Note that in this case the graphs are also drawn differently. This shows why, in general, it is notoriously difficult to determine whether two graphs are isomorphic. However, it is easy to *check* whether a proposed vertex relabelling gives rise to an isomorphism.

In situations where we are not interested in labels on vertices, we can talk about an *unlabelled graph* G; this refers to a class of graphs, namely all those that are isomorphic to G.

2.4.4 Getting connected

In many applications of graph theory we are concerned with whether or not, or how, we can 'get from one vertex to another', for example whether it is possible to reach Wanstead from Woodford given that a particular road is closed, and if so what is the shortest route. We need the following definitions which are illustrated in Fig. 2.25.

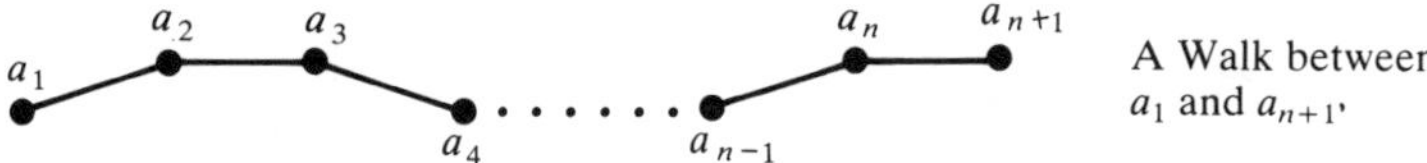

A Walk between a_1 and a_{n+1}.

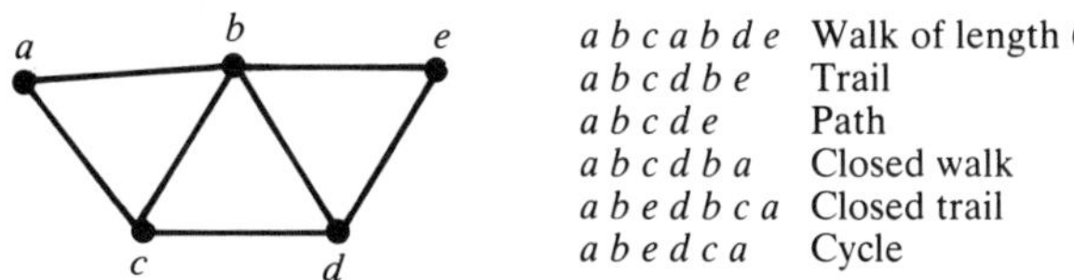

Figure 2.25 Walks, trails, etc.

Definition 2.36 Let G be a graph and let a_i be vertices of G ($i = 1, \ldots, n+1$). Then:

(a) A walk of length n between a_1 and a_{n+1} is a succession of n edges of G of the form $(a_1, a_2), (a_2, a_3), (a_2, a_3), \ldots, (a_n, a_{n+1})$ which is written in shorthand as $a_1 a_2 a_3 \cdots a_{n+1}$

(b) If all the edges (but not necessarily all the vertices) of a walk are different, then the walk is called a trail.

(c) If, in addition, all the vertices are different, then the trail is called a path.

(d) If $a_0 = a_{n+1}$ then the walk is called a closed walk.

(e) If all the edges of a closed walk are different then the walk is called a closed trail.

(f) If all the vertices except a_1 and a_{n+1} of a closed trail are different then the trail is called a cycle.

The following definition does not apply to digraphs.

Definition 2.37 Connected graph A graph G is connected if there is a path in G between any two vertices, and disconnected otherwise. Every disconnected graph can be split up into a number of connected subgraphs called components.

The following definition applies only to digraphs.

Definition 2.38 Connected, strongly connected digraph A digraph G is connected if its underlying graph is connected, and disconnected otherwise. It is strongly connected if there is a path between any two vertices.

Example 2.63 Consider the graphs of Fig. 2.26. Graph (a) is a disconnected graph consisting of four connected components. Digraph (b) is disconnected, while (c) is connected but not strongly connected. Digraph (d) is strongly connected.

Example 2.64 Bridges of Königsberg Simple properties of graphs often enable us to answer important and apparently difficult questions about the systems that they model. Figure 2.21 on page 53 shows a graph model of the bridges linking the various parts of the town of Königsberg. The townspeople were interested to know if it was possible to find a route by which they would cross each bridge exactly once

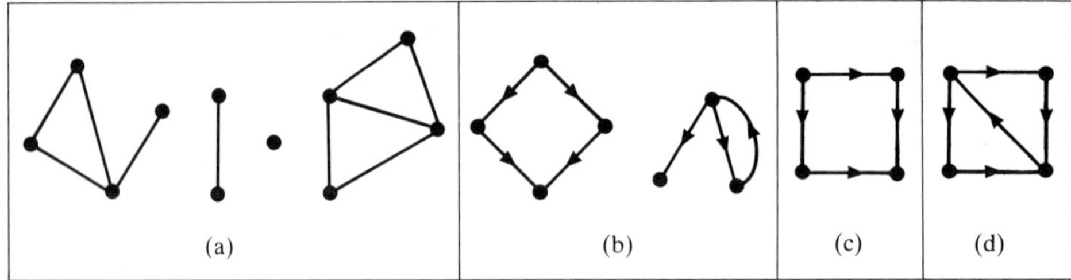

Figure 2.26 Graph components.

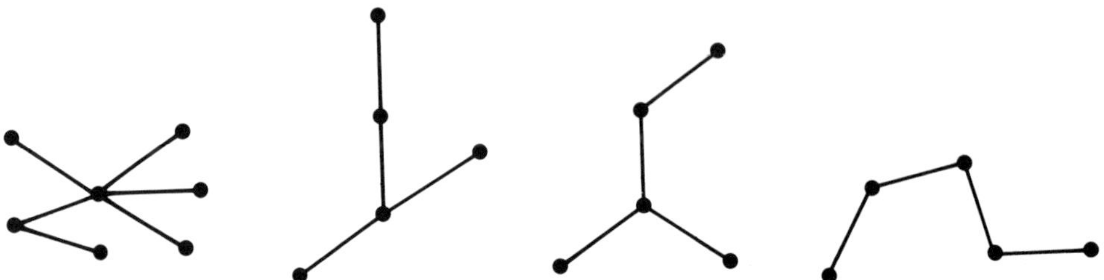

Figure 2.27 Different drawings of the same tree.

and return to the starting point. Nobody could find such a route, but it was not until Euler investigated the problem in 1736 that the impossibility of finding such a route was proved. The proof is based on the fact that the problem is equivalent to finding a closed trail of the associated graph which includes every edge. Euler showed that, in any graph with this property, all vertices must have even degree (alert readers should be able to prove this themselves, but it does not matter if you cannot). However, the graph in question has a vertex D of odd degree, 3.

2.4.5 Special types of graphs

Definition 2.39 Tree A tree is a connected graph that has no cycles.

Four examples of trees are shown in Fig. 2.29. In contrast to our intuitive understanding of trees in nature, these trees have no unique 'root' vertex from which all the other branches 'grow'. In fact, even if we draw trees to look like they do in nature we can take *any* vertex and call it the root. This is shown in Fig. 2.27, where each of the four graphs represents exactly the same tree. Trees arise as natural models in many areas of information technology and, fortunately, the real world that we are modelling normally suggests which vertex must be the root. Consider the systems being modelled in Fig. 2.29.

Sticking with an unfortunate, but widely accepted, convention in information technology we draw the trees 'upside down'. In each case we have a distinguished root node. Once this root node is appropriately labelled by an extra circle, we can dispense with the digraph in favour of the underlying graph.

Definition 2.40 Rooted tree A tree with a distinguished root node is called a rooted tree.

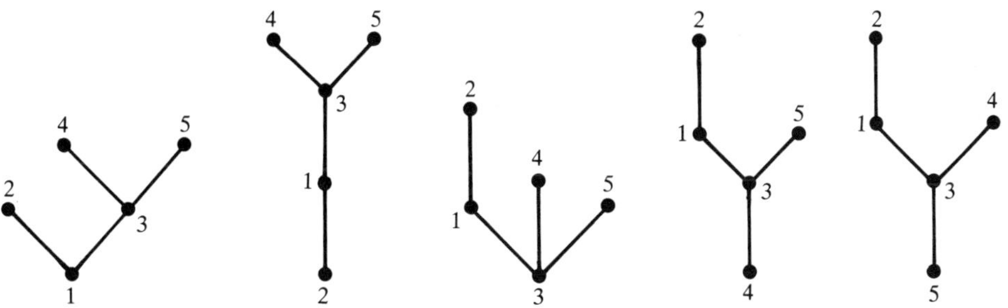

Figure 2.28 Various tree-type models.

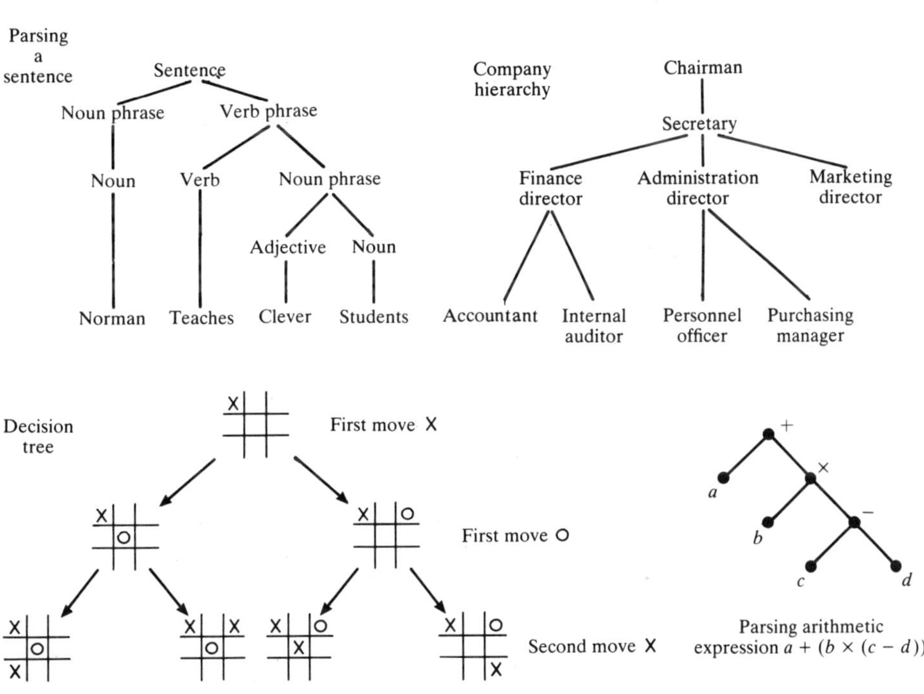

Figure 2.29 Trees.

Any tree can be built from the tree of one vertex by successively adding a new vertex and an edge joining any existing vertex to the new one. At each stage the number of vertices exceeds the number of edges by one. From this observation it follows that:

Theorem 2.1 A tree with n vertices has $n-1$ edges.

Since there are no cycles it also follows that:

Theorem 2.2 Any two vertices in a tree are connected by exactly one path.

A common problem of interest in graph theory is to find the smallest connected subgraph of a connected graph G. Suppose, for example, that the graph G in Fig. 2.30(a) represents a (two-way) road system in a town. Suppose that extensive road maintenance must be performed as soon as possible. Our problem is to leave open at all times the

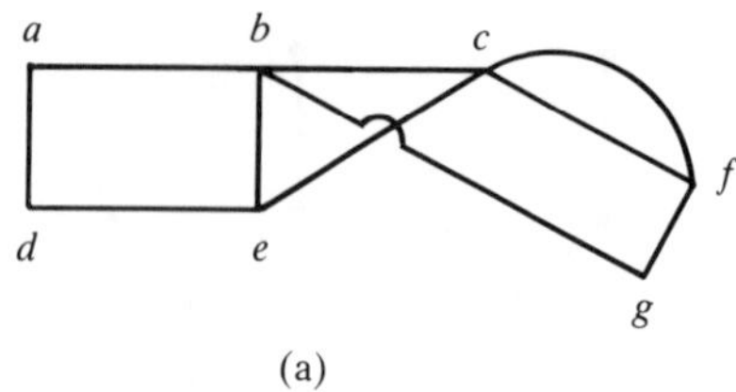

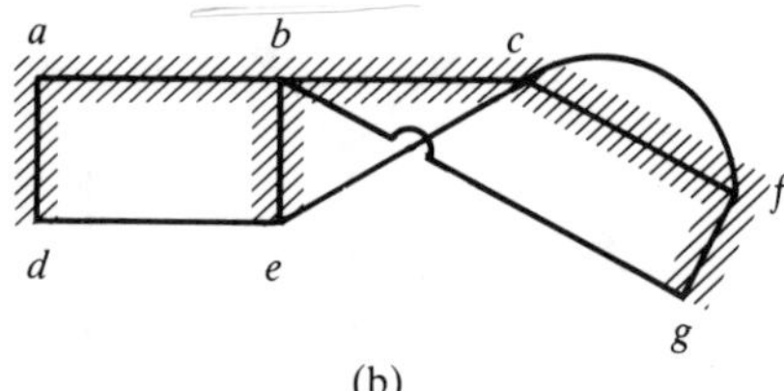

Figure 2.30 Spanning tree.

minimal number of roads such that any two points are still mutually accessible. Then we can perform maintenance on the closed roads. What we are looking for is a smallest connected subgraph. An example of one such subgraph is shown in Fig. 2.30(b). Note that this subgraph must be a tree.

Definition 2.41 Spanning tree Let G be a connected graph of n vertices. Then the smallest connected subgraph of G is a tree of n vertices, called a spanning tree of G.

Exercise 2.48 Draw three spanning trees for the graph of Fig. 2.30 that differ from the one shown in Fig. 2.30(b).

Once we have chosen a spanning tree T of G we can think of the edges of G as partitioned into two sets: those in T and those not. Thus in Fig. 2.30(b):

$$\begin{aligned} T &= \{(a,b),(b,c),(a,d),(b,e),(c,f),(f,g)\} \\ G \setminus T &= \{(d,e),(e,c),(b,g)\} \end{aligned}$$

The edges of $G \setminus T$ are called *chords*. For each chord x look at $T \cup \{x\}$. For example, look at the chord $x = (d,e)$ here. It is easy to see that $T \cup \{x\}$ contains a unique cycle, namely $(a,b)(b,e)(e,d)(d,a)$. The same is true for the other chords.

Theorem 2.3 Fundamental cycle If T is a spanning tree of G and if x is any chord then $T \cup \{x\}$ contains a unique cycle, which we call the fundamental cycle of T with respect to x.

Suppose G has n vertices and m edges. Since T has $n-1$ edges, there must be $m-(n-1)$ chords. Hence there must be $m-n+1$ fundamental cycles. This set of cycles plays a crucial role in network analysis, since a knowledge of these gives us all the important information about a graph in a concise form. We shall explore this application in Sec. 2.5.

Exercise 2.49 List all the fundamental cycles of the graph in Fig. 2.30(b).

Complete graphs We have seen that trees are connected graphs with a minimal number of edges. We now wish to consider a class of graphs at the other extreme—ones with a 'maximal' number of edges.

Definition 2.42 Complete graph A complete graph is a graph in which every two distinct vertices are joined by an edge. Up to isomorphism there is just one complete graph of n vertices for each n. This graph is called K_n.

The complete graphs K_n for $n = 1, \ldots, 5$ are shown in Fig. 2.31.

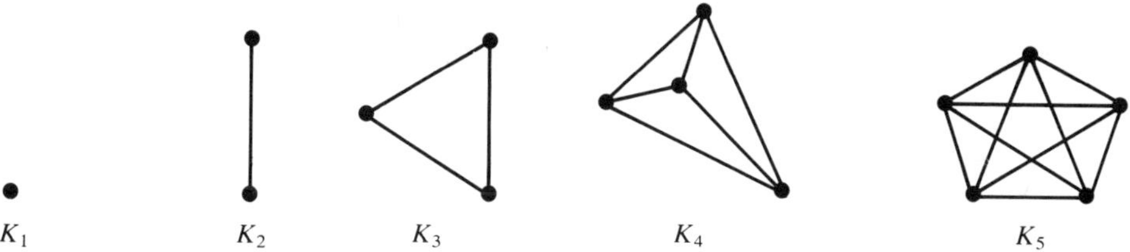

Figure 2.31 Complete graphs.

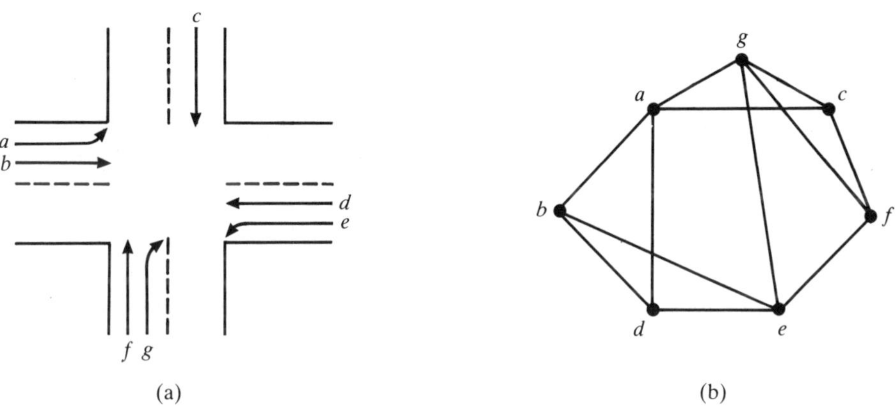

Figure 2.32 Compatibility graph modelling traffic junction.

Exercise 2.50 Draw the complete graph K_6.

Exercise 2.51 Show that each vertex in the complete graph K_n has degree $n-1$. Hence deduce, by the handshaking lemma of Exercise 2.47, that K_n has $(n/2)(n-1)$ edges.

Example 2.65 Complete graphs are particularly important in the study of so-called *compatibility* problems. Consider the traffic junction in Fig. 2.32(a). The labels $a, b, \ldots, g$ represent allowable traffic flows. The problem is to find a traffic light phasing that allows as much traffic to flow as possible at one time with minimal delay for those waiting. An appropriate graph model for solving this problem is the compatibility graph of Fig. 2.32(b). The vertices correspond to the traffic flows. Two vertices are joined precisely when they are 'compatible', meaning they may flow at the same time without possible collision. Thus a and e are compatible while a and f are not. In this model our problem reduces to finding subgraphs which are the biggest possible complete graphs, since all vertices of a complete graph are mutually compatible. It is easy to see that there is no subgraph of the form K_5, K_6 or K_7. The largest complete subgraph is a K_4 consisting of the vertices a, b, d, e. This leaves c, f, g, which between them form a complete graph K_3. It follows that we only need two phases for the traffic lights. In one phase lanes a, b, d, e can go while in the next phase lanes c, f, g go.

Exercise 2.52 Suppose an extra lane of traffic h is added to the junction of Fig. 2.32(a). Specifically h is a right turn next to lane c. Draw the resulting compatibility graph and propose an optimal traffic light phasing.

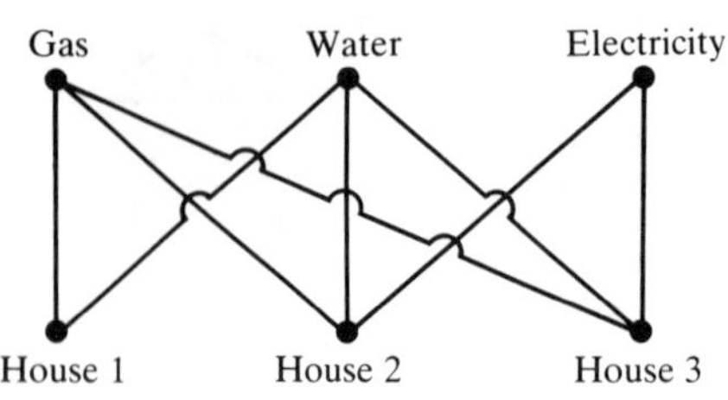

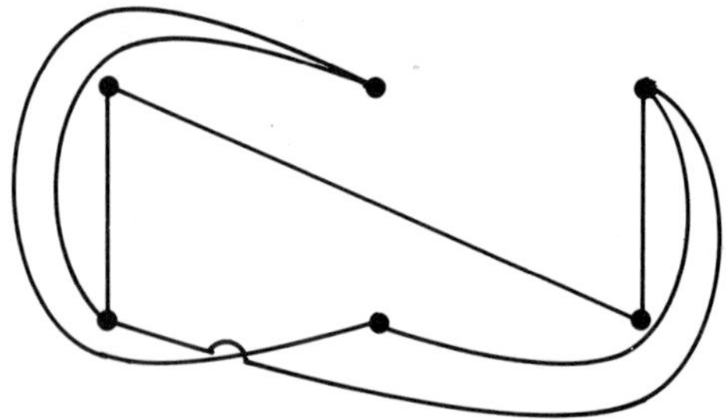

Figure 2.33 Utilities problem.

Planar graphs Consider the two drawings of the same graph in Fig. 2.19 on page 51. In (a) we have a crossover which can be avoided by drawing the graph as in (b). The question is whether we can always draw graphs in such a way that crossovers are avoided.

Exercise 2.53 Try drawing the complete graph K_5 without crossovers.

Example 2.66 A classic problem for motivating the study of planar graphs is the so-called *utilities problem* described in Fig. 2.33. Three houses have each to be connected to the three utilities supplies of gas, water and electricity. The problem is to make the connections in such a way that no supply lines cross. Thus we have to draw the graph without crossovers. While (b) is a better solution than (a) we still have one crossover. For reasons that do not concern us here this particular graph is referred to as $K_{3,3}$.

Definition 2.43 Planar graph A graph G is planar if it can be drawn in such a way that edges only intersect at a vertex of G, that is if it can be drawn without crossovers. Any such drawing is called a planar representation of G.

The graphs K_5 and $K_{3,3}$ are not planar. In fact they can be shown, in a certain sense, to be the smallest non-planar graphs. One of the most important theorems of graph theory asserts that a non-planar graph *must* 'contain' (in a certain well-defined sense) at least one of these two graphs as a subgraph. Thus, there is a general means of testing for planarity.

A major problem in modelling many types of complex systems, such as printed circuit boards, is to keep any necessary non-planarity down to a minimum, that is to have the minimum number of crossovers. There are many theorems that help achieve this in given practical situations. Another famous theorem concerned with planar graphs is:

Theorem 2.4 Four-colour theorem The vertices of any connected planar graph can be coloured with four colours in such a way that no two adjacent vertices are coloured the same.

Since a map of countries can be modelled by a planar graph as shown in Fig. 2.34, it follows that if we want to colour each country such that no bordering countries have the same colour, then four colours will always be sufficient. A proof of the four-colour theorem eluded mathematicians for many years. It was finally proved, with the help of computers, in 1976.

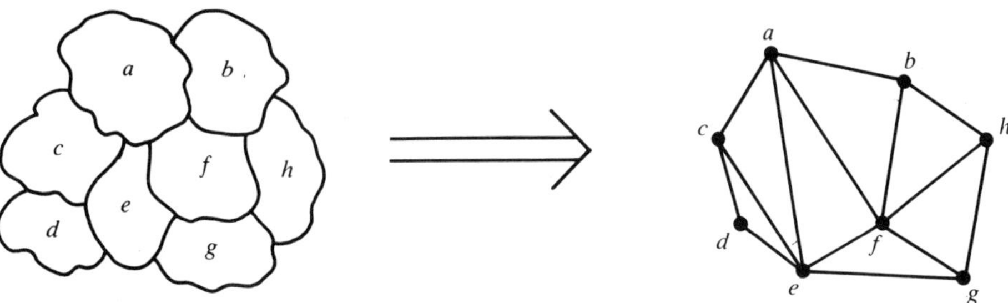

Figure 2.34 Map colouring.

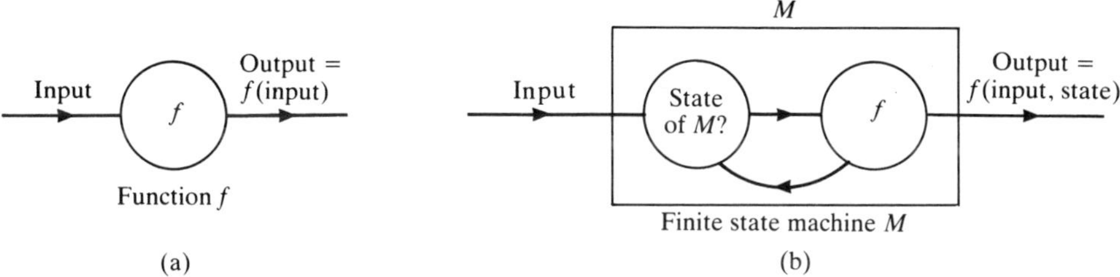

Figure 2.35 Functions and finite state machines.

Finite state machines We now want to consider an important generalization of the idea of a function, and show that it can be modelled by a special type of digraph. Figure 2.35(a) describes our understanding of a function as a black box system. We put some input into the black box and the output is dependent only on the input. There are no hidden internal states of the black box that can cause different outputs to be produced for the same inputs. However, we are also interested in systems whose output may be dependent on some internal state of the system, as illustrated in Fig. 2.35(b).

Example 2.67 When we pull the cord of a bathroom light switch we do not always get the same result. The result will be dependent on the current 'state' of the light. If the light is on, then pulling the cord results in the light going off. If the light is off, then pulling the cord results in the light going on.

Input	Old state	New state	Output
Pull cord	Light off	Light on	Light goes on
Pull cord	Light on	Light off	Light goes off

Example 2.67 is a *deterministic finite state machine*. Such a machine consists of a collection of inputs I, a collection of outputs O and a finite collection of states S. There is a *next-state* function $f : I \times S \to S$, where $f(i, s)$ is the next state of the machine when input i is received with the machine in state s. Also there is an *output* function $g : I \times S \to O$, where $g(i, s)$ is the output when i is received with the machine in state s. The functions f and g may be described by a table, like that above, called a state transition table. It is also normal to specify which of the states is the *initial* state for the machine. In Example 2.67 'light off' would be the initial state.

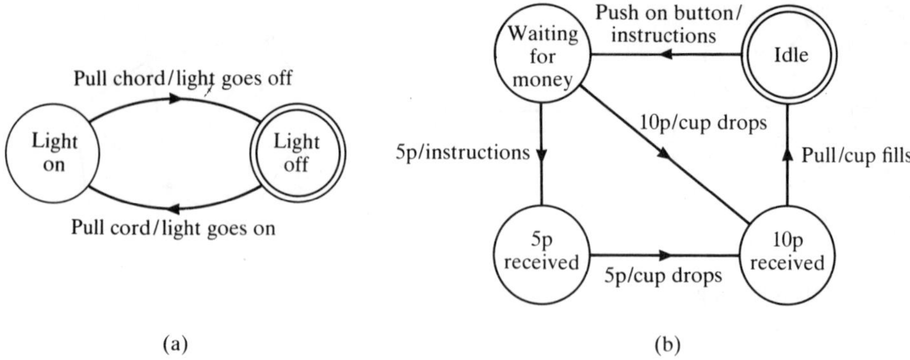

Figure 2.36 Modelling finite state machines as digraphs.

The machine is called deterministic because the function f always yields the same next state for the same pair (i, s). A non-deterministic finite state machine is one that may enter more than one state for the same pair (i, s). In other words, we would have the next state function $f : I \times S \rightarrow \mathscr{P}(S)$. In practice a real light switch system is non-deterministic. This is because every so often when we pull the cord in the 'light off' state the bulb will blow out and the output will be 'light goes off' rather than 'light goes on'.

Deterministic finite state machines may be represented as digraphs as shown in Fig. 2.36. The vertices correspond to the states, as can be seen from (a) which models the light switch system. The arcs represent the possible transitions between states, and these are labelled by the form 'i/o'; an arc from state s to state s' labelled i/o means that when the system is in state s the input i causes the next state to be s' with an output of o. The initial state is highlighted by encircling.

Figure 2.36(b) shows a more interesting system, namely a drinks dispenser. When an on button is pushed the machine issues some instructions and moves from its idle state to one of awaiting money. A drink may be obtained by inputting 10p, either with a single 10p coin or two 5p coins. As soon as the full 10p is input a cup drops. At this point the user pulls a handle and the cup fills.

Exercise 2.54

(a) Draw the state transition table for the drinks machine of Fig. 2.36(b).

(b) Refine the state transition table so that the drinks machine can cope with an erroneous coin input.

2.5 LINEAR ALGEBRA

Much of high school mathematics is concerned with two- and three-dimensional geometry. The points in the two-dimensional plane are represented as ordered pairs and in the three-dimensional space as ordered triples. In either case these points are commonly referred to as vectors. This kind of geometry has many important applications that go beyond the normal study of objects and their transformations in space. For example, since a linear equation in two unknowns is just a line and a linear equation in three unknowns is just a plane, it turns out that we can solve simultaneous linear equations purely geometrically. We just look at points of intersection of lines and planes.

Although there is no conceptual view of n-dimensional space when $n > 3$, we still have to solve linear equations in n unknowns, and other similar problems. Linear algebra is the natural extension of high school geometry into n dimensions which enables us to solve such problems. Vectors in n-dimensional space are just ordered n-tuples. We will consider some basic properties of vectors and their operations. Matrices are vectors of vectors, just like a sequence of simultaneous linear equations. We describe properties and operations on matrices, and present an illustration of their power in equation solving and computer graphics. We also describe how linear algebra, when combined with graph theory, can help to solve electrical circuit analysis problems.

2.5.1 Vectors

Suppose that we have a class of six students who are each awarded a mark for their mathematics course. The resulting set of marks would normally be represented as a sequence like $(63\ 71\ 34\ 69\ 45\ 60) \in \mathbb{R} \times \mathbb{R} \times \mathbb{R} \times \mathbb{R} \times \mathbb{R} \times \mathbb{R}$ (or $\mathbb{R}^6$). This sequence is a *vector* of dimension 6 over $\mathbb{R}$.

Definition 2.44 Vectors and scalars A vector $\boldsymbol{v}$ of dimension n over a set S is a member of S^n, and is denoted by $\boldsymbol{v} = (\boldsymbol{v}_1\ \boldsymbol{v}_2\ \cdots\ \boldsymbol{v}_n)$. The set S is referred to as the set of scalars.

Vectors may be written either in row form, as in Def. 2.44, or in column form. If $\boldsymbol{v}$ is a column vector then the *transpose* of $\boldsymbol{v}$, written $\boldsymbol{v}^{\mathrm{T}}$, is just the row version of $\boldsymbol{v}$, and vice versa.

Example 2.68 $(2\ 1\ -4)^{\mathrm{T}} = \begin{pmatrix} 2 \\ 1 \\ -4 \end{pmatrix}$ and $\begin{pmatrix} 5 \\ 1 \\ -4 \\ 3 \end{pmatrix}^{\mathrm{T}} = (5\ \ 1\ \ -4\ \ 3)$

Definition 2.45 Equality of vectors Two vectors are equal if they have identical components in each position.

Example 2.69 $(1\ \ 4\ \ 5\ \ 3) = (1\ \ 4\ \ 5\ \ 3)$ but $(1\ \ 4\ \ 5\ \ 3) \neq (1\ \ 4\ \ 3\ \ 5)$

Example 2.70 The declaration:

```
type  vector = array[1..6] of integer;
var   a:vector;
```

in the programming language Pascal specifies that vector is the set $\mathbb{Z}^6$ of six-dimensional vectors over $\mathbb{Z}$ and that $a \in$ vector. A subsequent assignment statement like 'a[3]:= 38' assigns the value of 38 to the third component of the vector. In Pascal each element of the vector must be initialized to some default value.

Example 2.71 Vectors to represent set membership Let $B = \{0, 1\}$. For a set $S = \{x_1, x_2, \ldots, x_n\}$ we can represent any subset A of S as a vector over B^n. Specifically the vector $(b_1\ b_2\ \cdots\ b_n)$ corresponds to that subset A of S for which $x_i \in A$ precisely when $b_i = 1$. Suppose that S is our set of six students a, b, c, d, e, f.

For any vectors $x, y, z \in \mathbb{R}^n$ and scalars $\alpha, \beta \in \mathbb{R}$:

$x + y = y + x$	vector addition is commutative
$(x + y) + z = x + (y + z)$	vector addition is associative
$x + 0 = x$	0 is additive identity
$x + (-1x) = 0$	additive inverses
$\alpha(x + y) = \alpha x + \alpha y$	scalar multiplication distributes over vector addition
$(\alpha\beta)x = \alpha(\beta x)$	scalar multiplication associative
$1x = x$	1 is identity for scalar multiplication
$0x = 0$	zero for scalar multiplication

Figure 2.37 Rules for algebraic operations on vectors.

Suppose $\{a, e, f\}$ is the subset of those who pass their computing exam and $\{a, c, e\}$ is the subset who pass their maths exam. Then

$$\{a, c, e\} \text{ is represented by } (1\ 0\ 1\ 1\ 0)$$
$$\{a, c, f\} \text{ is represented by } (1\ 0\ 1\ 0\ 1)$$

Exercise 2.55 Suppose every student except student b passes their electronics exam. Write the relevant Pascal program text for representing the set of students who fail electronics.

Operations on vectors There are two important operations on vectors that we shall consider.

Addition of vectors Suppose that v is a vector representing students' marks in the maths exam and w is a vector representing their marks in the computing exam. If we wanted to find the total combined marks we would add the vectors component-wise. Consequently we define: $v + w = (v_1 + w_1\ v_2 + w_2\ \cdots\ v_n + w_n)$.

Example 2.72 (63 71 34 69 45 60) + (51 68 45 65 27 56) = (114 139 79 134 72 116)

Clearly vector addition is only defined for vectors of the same dimension and when the underlying set of scalars has its own addition operation.

Scalar multiplication In many situations we may want to perform some rescaling of a set of students' marks. This might entail rescaling marks that are out of 80 as percentages or computing the average when the marks represent the sum of two exam marks. In either case we perform the rescaling by multiplying every component of the vector by a fixed scalar. Thus multiplication of the n-dimensional vector v over S by the scalar $\alpha \in S$ is defined by: $\alpha v = (\alpha v_1\ \alpha v_2\ \cdots\ \alpha v_n)$.

Example 2.73 To find the average of the students' exam marks in Example 2.72 we perform scalar multiplication by 0.5: 0.5 (114 139 79 134 72 116) = (57 69.5 39.5 67 36 58).

Clearly scalar multiplication is only defined when multiplication is defined in the underlying set of scalars.

Given the above two operations on vectors, it is easy to check the rules described in Fig. 2.37. The vector 0 denotes the *zero vector* $(0\ 0\ \cdots\ 0)$.

Dot product ('multiplying vectors') Suppose that we need to buy a number of differently priced items on a shopping expedition. We can think of our shopping list as consisting of two vectors. One vector, $\boldsymbol{v}$, represents the number of each item we have to buy. For example, if our items are apples, oranges and pears then $\boldsymbol{v} = (3 \quad 4 \quad 2)$ means that we have to buy 3 apples, 4 oranges and 2 pears. The other vector, $\boldsymbol{w}$, represents the price per item. For example, $\boldsymbol{w} = (20 \quad 40 \quad 25)$ means that apples are 30p each, oranges are 40p each and pears are 25p each. To compute the total cost of our shopping we perform an operation on the two vectors called the dot product '$\cdot$':

$$(3 \quad 4 \quad 2) \cdot \begin{pmatrix} 20 \\ 40 \\ 25 \end{pmatrix} = (3 \times 20) + (4 \times 40) + (2 \times 25) = 60 + 160 + 50 = 270$$

Thus our total cost is 270p. As a matter of convention we always assume that the dot product is applied to a row vector and a column vector (in that order).

Clearly the dot product is only defined on vectors of the same dimension, and where multiplication is defined for the underlying scalars.

Properties of the dot product

1 The dot product is commutative: $\boldsymbol{x} \cdot \boldsymbol{y} = \boldsymbol{y} \cdot \boldsymbol{x}$ for any vectors $\boldsymbol{x}, \boldsymbol{y}$.

2 The dot product is distributive over vector addition: $\boldsymbol{x} \cdot (\boldsymbol{y} + \boldsymbol{z}) = \boldsymbol{x} \cdot \boldsymbol{y} + \boldsymbol{x} \cdot \boldsymbol{z}$.

Exercise 2.56 Prove the two properties of the dot product and explain why the dot product is not in general associative.

Linear dependence and independence of vectors

Definition 2.46 Linear combination of vectors A linear combination of n vectors $\boldsymbol{x}_1, \ldots, \boldsymbol{x}_n$ is a vector $\boldsymbol{v}$ of the form $\boldsymbol{v} = a_1\boldsymbol{x}_1 + a_2\boldsymbol{x}_2 + \cdots + a_n\boldsymbol{x}_n$ where the a_i are scalars, not all of which are zero.

Example 2.74 Suppose $\boldsymbol{x} = (1 \ 2 \ -1)$, $\boldsymbol{y} = (-2 \ 0 \ 4)$, $\boldsymbol{z} = (4 \ 2 \ -7)$. Then the vector

$$\boldsymbol{v} = 3\boldsymbol{x} + \boldsymbol{y} - 2\boldsymbol{z} = 3(1 \ 2 \ 1) + (-2 \ 0 \ 4) - 2(4 \ 2 \ -7) = (-7 \ 10 \ -15)$$

is a *linear combination* of the vectors $\boldsymbol{x}, \boldsymbol{y}, \boldsymbol{z}$.

For the particular vectors $\boldsymbol{x}, \boldsymbol{y}, \boldsymbol{z}$ in Example 2.74, one linear combination is the zero vector, since $2\boldsymbol{x} - 3\boldsymbol{y} + 2\boldsymbol{z} = \boldsymbol{0}$. Whenever the zero vector is a linear combination of a specific set of vectors it follows that each of the vectors is in turn a linear combination of the others.

Example 2.75 Since $2\boldsymbol{x} - 3\boldsymbol{y} + 2\boldsymbol{z} = \boldsymbol{0}$ it follows that $\boldsymbol{x} = (3/2)\boldsymbol{y} - \boldsymbol{z}$.

Exercise 2.57 Express $\boldsymbol{y}$ as a linear combination of $\boldsymbol{x}$ and $\boldsymbol{z}$.

Definition 2.47 Linear dependence and independence If it is possible to express the zero vector as a linear combination of a given set of vectors, then the set of vectors is linearly dependent. Otherwise the set of vectors is linearly independent.

Definition 2.48 Basis sets Any linearly independent set of n vectors of n-dimensions is said to be a basis set.

Example 2.76 The set of vectors $e_1 = (1\ 0\ 0)$, $e_2 = (0\ 1\ 0)$, $e_3 = (0\ 0\ 1)$ from $\mathbb{R}^3$ are linearly independent and hence a basis set for $\mathbb{R}^3$. Basis sets play a crucial role in linear algebra. This is because, for a fixed dimension n, any vector can be expressed as a linear combination of the basis vectors. In $\mathbb{R}^3$, any vector, say $(a\ b\ c)$, can be written as $(a\ b\ c) = ae_1 + be_2 + ce_3$. The vectors e_1, e_2, e_3 may be viewed as the x, y and z axes in three-dimensional space.

Exercise 2.58 Show that any subset of a set of linearly independent vectors must itself be linearly independent.

2.5.2 Matrices

Just as we noted how it was often necessary to consider arrays of numbers, it is often equally necessary to think in terms of arrays of arrays.

Example 2.77 Suppose we want to monitor the progress each term of our class of six students in the subjects: maths, computing and electronics. For each subject we have an array of six marks corresponding to each student each term. Then each term we could represent the class achievements as an array of three arrays. Specifically, we would represent this as

$$\left(\begin{pmatrix}50\\60\\55\\40\\70\\30\end{pmatrix}\begin{pmatrix}45\\70\\50\\60\\65\\40\end{pmatrix}\begin{pmatrix}50\\70\\60\\55\\65\\40\end{pmatrix}\right) \quad \text{which is normally written as} \quad \begin{pmatrix}50 & 45 & 50\\60 & 70 & 70\\55 & 50 & 60\\40 & 60 & 55\\70 & 65 & 65\\30 & 40 & 40\end{pmatrix}$$

The six rows by three columns array on the right is called a (6×3) matrix. In this case the rows correspond to specific students, e.g. row 1 is student a, etc., and the columns correspond to specific subjects, e.g. column 1 is mathematics, etc. In general, when we talk about the (i, j) element of a matrix we mean the entry in the ith row and jth column. Thus the (4,3) entry above is 55; this is the electronics mark of student d.

Definition 2.49 Matrix An $(m \times n)$ matrix over a set S is a rectangular array of elements of S arranged in m rows and n columns.

Example 2.78 Vectors are special case of matrices. An $(m \times 1)$ matrix is just a column vector of dimension m, while a $(1 \times n)$ matrix is a row vector of dimension n. A (1×1) matrix is simply an element of S, that is a scalar.

Just as we sometimes want to turn a column vector $\mathbf{v}$ into a row vector by taking its transpose $\mathbf{v}^{\mathrm{T}}$, so we sometimes want to turn an $(m \times n)$ matrix $\mathbf{A}$ into an $(n \times m)$ matrix. To do so we just transpose all the n columns of $\mathbf{A}$ into rows, so that we turn the matrix on its side. Again the resulting matrix is called the *transpose* of $\mathbf{A}$ and is written $\mathbf{A}^{\mathrm{T}}$.

Example 2.79 $$\begin{pmatrix}5 & 3\\30 & -9\\-4 & 18\end{pmatrix}^{\mathrm{T}} = \begin{pmatrix}5 & 30 & -4\\3 & -9 & 18\end{pmatrix}$$

If the number of rows in a matrix is the same as the number of columns, we call the matrix a *square* matrix. If $\mathbf{A}$ is a square matrix for which $\mathbf{A}^T = \mathbf{A}$, we say that $\mathbf{A}$ is a *symmetric* matrix.

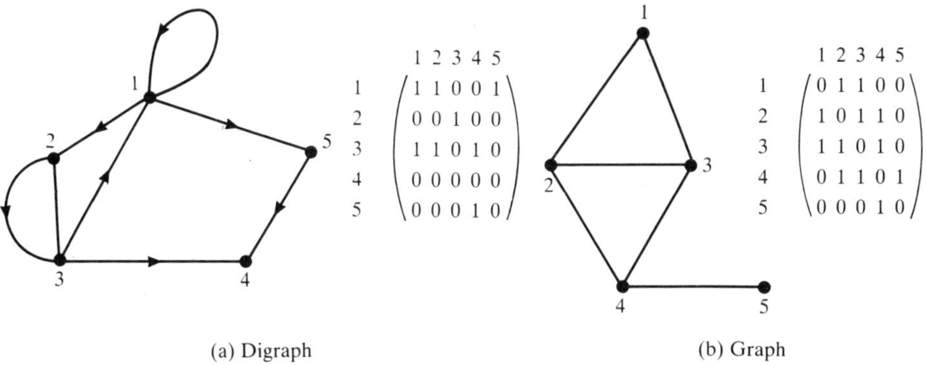

Figure 2.38 Adjacency matrices.

Example 2.80 $\begin{pmatrix} 2 & 5 \\ 5 & 3 \end{pmatrix}$ is a (2×2) square matrix which is symmetric.

For any n there is a special square $(n \times n)$ matrix called the *identity matrix* I (or I_n if we need to make the dimension n explicit). This matrix consists of 0's everywhere except on the main diagonal where all the entries are 1. Thus

$$\mathbf{I}_1 = (1),\ \mathbf{I}_2 = \begin{pmatrix} 1 & 0 \\ 0 & 1 \end{pmatrix},\ \mathbf{I}_3 = \begin{pmatrix} 1 & 0 & 0 \\ 0 & 1 & 0 \\ 0 & 0 & 1 \end{pmatrix},\ \mathbf{I}_4 = \begin{pmatrix} 1 & 0 & 0 & 0 \\ 0 & 1 & 0 & 0 \\ 0 & 0 & 1 & 0 \\ 0 & 0 & 0 & 1 \end{pmatrix},\ \text{etc.}$$

Another special matrix (or more specifically family of matrices) is the zero matrix, denoted **0**, which consists entirely of 0's.

Example 2.81 Adjacency matrices We have seen how arrays can be used to represent sets. Matrices may be used to represent digraphs and graphs, and hence also binary relations. Figure 2.38 illustrates the *adjacency matrix* of both a digraph (in (a)) and a graph (in (b)). In each case the adjacency matrix is a square matrix whose rows and columns are both considered to be 'labelled' by the vertices of the graph (in any fixed order). In each case the ijth entry of the matrix is defined to be 1 if there is an edge from vertex i to vertex j and 0 otherwise. The adjacency matrix of a graph (but not a digraph) is always symmetric since we assume that edges are bidirectional.

Exercise 2.59 Construct the adjacency matrices for the graphs of Fig. 2.21.

Exercise 2.60 Incidence matrices An alternative matrix representation of a graph G is the *incidence matrix*. In this case the rows of the matrix are again labelled by the vertices of G, but the columns are labelled by the edges of G. The ijth entry of the graph is 1 if vertex i is incident with edge j and 0 otherwise. Construct the incidence matrices for the graphs of Fig. 2.21.

Example 2.82 Fundamental cycle incidence matrix Suppose G is a connected graph. We remarked in Sec. 2.4.5 that knowledge of the set of fundamental cycles of G told us everything about G. We can in fact use a matrix representation as shown in Fig. 2.39. The rows of the matrix are labelled by the edges of the spanning tree T, and the columns are labelled by the remaining edges $E \setminus T$. For each edge $j \in E \setminus T$ we consider the fundamental cycle of $T \cup \{j\}$. For example, the fundamental cycle

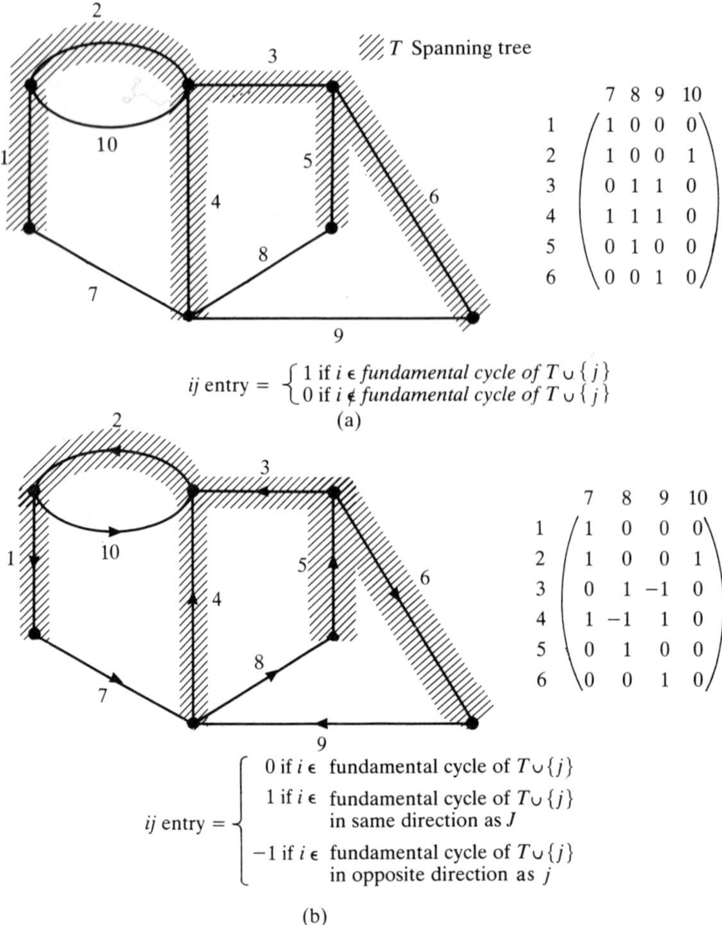

Figure 2.39 Fundamental cycle incidence matrices.

of $T \cup \{8\}$ is $(4, 3, 5, 8)$. To form the column of the matrix labelled by j we simply put 1's in rows labelled by edges that are in this fundamental cycle and 0's otherwise. Thus in the column labelled by 8, the rows labelled by 3,4,5 contain 1's.

In the case of a digraph the only difference is that we think about the direction of j in its fundamental cycle. For example, consider the same cycle in (b). Here the edges 3 and 5 are in the same direction as the edge 8, but the edge 4 is opposite. Consequently we put 1's in the rows labelled by 3 and 5, but a -1 in the row labelled by 4.

Operations on matrices Just as we considered a number of algebraic type operations on vectors, so we want to consider analogous ones for matrices.

Since matrices are simply arrays of arrays, the definition of matrix addition and scalar multiplication is the obvious extension of their definition for vectors.

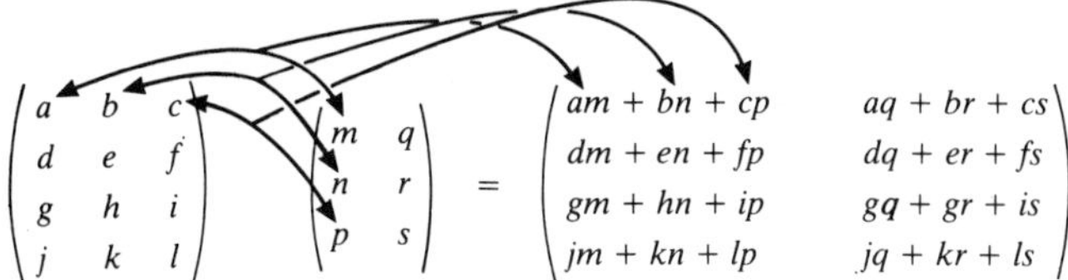

Figure 2.40 Matrix multiplication.

Matrix addition Suppose **A** and **B** are two $(n \times m)$ matrices. Then the matrix $\mathbf{A} + \mathbf{B}$ is an $(n \times m)$ matrix formed by component-wise addition of **A** and **B**.

Example 2.83

$$\begin{pmatrix} 2 & 7 & -5 \\ 1 & 0 & 3 \end{pmatrix} + \begin{pmatrix} 4 & -2 & 3 \\ 2 & 5 & -7 \end{pmatrix} = \begin{pmatrix} 6 & 5 & -2 \\ 3 & 5 & -4 \end{pmatrix}$$

Matrix scalar multiplication Suppose **A** is an $(n \times m)$ matrix and α is a scalar. Then the matrix $\alpha\mathbf{A}$ is an $(n \times m)$ matrix formed by multiplying each component of **A** by α.

Example 2.84

$$5\begin{pmatrix} 2 & 7 & -5 \\ 1 & 0 & 3 \end{pmatrix} = \begin{pmatrix} 10 & 35 & -25 \\ 5 & 0 & 15 \end{pmatrix}$$

Exercise 2.61 Rules of algebraic operations for matrices Consider the list of rules in Fig. 2.37 on page 64 which hold for vectors with respect to the operations of addition and scalar multiplication. Show that exactly the same set of rules hold for matrices.

Matrix multiplication Suppose that **A** is an $(n \times k)$ matrix and **B** is a $(k \times m)$ matrix. Then the matrix **AB** is the $(n \times m)$ matrix whose ijth entry is the dot product of the ith row of **A** and the jth column of **B**. This is illustrated in Fig. 2.40.

Example 2.85 Suppose

$$\mathbf{A} = \begin{pmatrix} 2 & 3 \\ 1 & 0 \end{pmatrix} \text{ and } \mathbf{B} = \begin{pmatrix} 4 & 1 \\ 2 & 5 \end{pmatrix}$$

Then

$$\mathbf{AB} = \begin{pmatrix} 2 & 3 \\ 1 & 0 \end{pmatrix}\begin{pmatrix} 4 & 1 \\ 2 & 5 \end{pmatrix} = \begin{pmatrix} 14 & 17 \\ 4 & 1 \end{pmatrix}$$

while

$$\mathbf{BA} = \begin{pmatrix} 4 & 1 \\ 2 & 5 \end{pmatrix}\begin{pmatrix} 2 & 3 \\ 1 & 0 \end{pmatrix} = \begin{pmatrix} 9 & 12 \\ 9 & 6 \end{pmatrix}$$

Thus even for square matrices **A** and **B**, we find that **AB** is not always the same as **BA**. Hence matrix multiplication is an example of a mathematical operation that is not commutative. However, the following properties do hold for matrix multiplication:

1 $\mathbf{A}(\mathbf{B} + \mathbf{C}) = \mathbf{AB} + \mathbf{AC}$, so matrix multiplication is distributive over matrix addition.

2 Assuming **A** is a square $(n \times n)$ matrix, then $\mathbf{A0} = \mathbf{0A} = \mathbf{0}$ and $\mathbf{AI} = \mathbf{IA} = \mathbf{A}$.

It is also worth noting that some square matrices **A** have a multiplicative inverse, that is a matrix **B** such that $\mathbf{AB} = \mathbf{BA} = \mathbf{I}$.

Example 2.86 Consider the matrix

$$\mathbf{A} = \begin{pmatrix} 5 & 2 & 2 \\ 2 & 3 & 4 \\ 3 & 2 & 1 \end{pmatrix}$$

Note that

$$\begin{pmatrix} 5 & 2 & 2 \\ 2 & 3 & 4 \\ 3 & 2 & 1 \end{pmatrix} \begin{pmatrix} 1/3 & -2/15 & -2/15 \\ -2/3 & 1/15 & 16/15 \\ 1/3 & 4/15 & -11/15 \end{pmatrix} = \begin{pmatrix} 1 & 0 & 0 \\ 0 & 1 & 0 \\ 0 & 0 & 1 \end{pmatrix}$$
$$= \begin{pmatrix} 1/3 & -2/15 & -2/15 \\ -2/3 & 1/15 & 16/15 \\ 1/3 & 4/15 & -11/15 \end{pmatrix} \begin{pmatrix} 5 & 2 & 2 \\ 2 & 3 & 4 \\ 3 & 2 & 1 \end{pmatrix}$$

whence the matrix

$$\mathbf{B} = \begin{pmatrix} 1/3 & -2/15 & -2/15 \\ -2/3 & 1/15 & 16/15 \\ 1/3 & 4/15 & -11/15 \end{pmatrix}$$

is a multiplicative inverse of **A**. We normally express this by writing $\mathbf{B} = \mathbf{A}^{-1}$.

Example 2.87 Matrix operations in computer graphics A two-dimensional 'picture' may be specified as a collection of two-dimensional vectors (coordinates) corresponding to points in the plane. For example, in Fig. 2.41 the triangle is specified by its three endpoints $(1\ 1), (1\ 2)$ and $(2\ 1)$. To translate, scale or rotate the picture we simply apply a relevant matrix operation to the vectors. Rotation and scaling are matrix multiplications, while translation is matrix addition. To treat all three transformations in a uniform manner, we extend the picture coordinates into homogeneous coordinates. This means that each vector $(x\ y)$ is expressed as $(x\ y\ 1)$. Then each of the two-dimensional transformations is equivalent to multiplication by a (3×3) matrix. Specifically the point $(x\ y\ 1)$ is transformed to the point $(x'\ y'\ 1)$ where

$$\begin{pmatrix} x' \\ y' \\ 1 \end{pmatrix} = \begin{pmatrix} a & b & 0 \\ c & d & 0 \\ e & f & 1 \end{pmatrix} \begin{pmatrix} x \\ y \\ 1 \end{pmatrix}$$

where a and d control scaling, a, b, c and d control rotation, and e and f control translation.

Exercise 2.62 What matrix would you use to translate the picture in Fig. 2.41 4 units along the x axis and 5 units along the y axis? What matrix would rotate the picture 45^0 around the origin?

Using matrices to solve linear equations Consider a set of simultaneous equations in three unknowns:

$$\begin{aligned} 5x_1 &+ 2x_2 + 2x_3 = 3 \\ 2x_1 &+ 3x_2 + 4x_3 = 15 \\ 3x_1 &+ 2x_2 + x_3 = 5 \end{aligned}$$

where, for example, the unknown x_i's are the unit costs of three different commodities and the equations express known information about total cost of various sums of the commodities. The system of equations is called *linear* because each equation expresses a linear combination of the variables. Our task is to find a solution for the system of

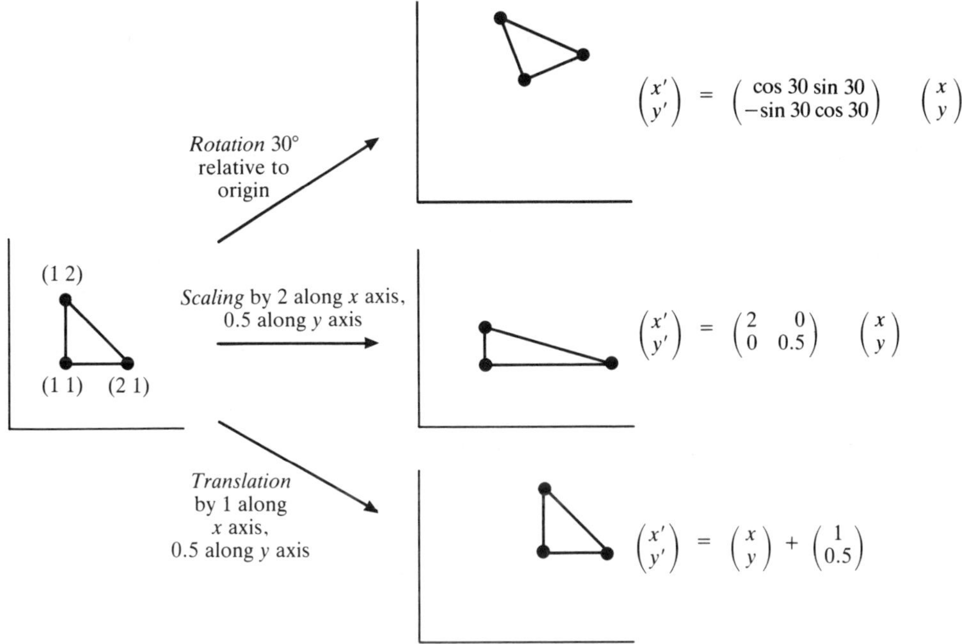

Figure 2.41 Matrix operations in computer graphics.

equations. This means finding values of x_1, x_2 and x_3 that satisfy all the equations. Solving systems of linear equations (which in general may have many variables) is one of the most common problems in science since it turns out that many complex systems may be modelled by a set of linear equations. Matrix algebra is an invaluable tool for solving such equations.

First note that, using matrix multiplication, the above system may be written in matrix form as

$$\begin{pmatrix} 5 & 2 & 2 \\ 2 & 3 & 4 \\ 3 & 2 & 1 \end{pmatrix} \begin{pmatrix} x_1 \\ x_2 \\ x_3 \end{pmatrix} = \begin{pmatrix} 3 \\ 15 \\ 5 \end{pmatrix}$$

which has the form $\mathbf{A}\boldsymbol{x} = \boldsymbol{b}$. It turns out that we can solve systems of linear equations by studying and manipulating the matrix $\mathbf{A}$ which models the system. It is beyond the scope of this introductory chapter to provide any details of this, but we can give a flavour of this important work.

Example 2.88 The matrix $\mathbf{A}$ of the system of equations above is the same as matrix $\mathbf{A}$ in Example 2.86. We know that this matrix has an inverse, namely

$$\mathbf{A}^{-1} = \begin{pmatrix} 1/3 & -2/15 & -2/15 \\ -2/3 & 1/15 & 16/15 \\ 1/3 & 4/15 & -11/15 \end{pmatrix}$$

However, then it follows that since $\mathbf{A}\boldsymbol{x} = \boldsymbol{b}$, we must have $\mathbf{A}^{-1}\boldsymbol{b} = \mathbf{A}^{-1}\mathbf{A}\boldsymbol{x} = \mathbf{I}\boldsymbol{x} = \boldsymbol{x}$, that is:

$$\begin{pmatrix} 1/3 & -2/15 & -2/15 \\ -2/3 & 1/15 & 16/15 \\ 1/3 & 4/15 & -11/15 \end{pmatrix} \begin{pmatrix} 3 \\ 15 \\ 5 \end{pmatrix} = \begin{pmatrix} -5/3 \\ 47 \\ 4/3 \end{pmatrix} = \begin{pmatrix} x_1 \\ x_2 \\ x_3 \end{pmatrix}$$

Hence we have solved the system of equations, since this means that $x_1 = -5/3$, $x_2 = 47$ and $x_3 = 4/3$.

Example 2.88 provides a general procedure for solving systems of linear equations providing that we can compute the inverse of the matrix **A**. There are numerous techniques for doing this. When the inverse exists the solution of the corresponding system of equations is unique.

However, not all square matrices have an inverse. In fact a matrix has an inverse if and only if the rows of the matrix form a linearly independent set of vectors. When the rows are lincarly dependent the corresponding system of linear equations will generally have either no solution at all or an infinite number of solutions.

Example 2.89 Consider the system of equations:

$$\begin{aligned} x + 3y &= 5 \\ 2x + 6y &= 6 \end{aligned}$$

which written equivalently is

$$\begin{pmatrix} 1 & 3 \\ 2 & 6 \end{pmatrix} \begin{pmatrix} x \\ y \end{pmatrix} = \begin{pmatrix} 5 \\ 6 \end{pmatrix}$$

The rows are linearly dependent (just multiply the first row by the scalar 2 to get the second row). There is no solution at all because the equations are inconsistent; $2x + 6y$ cannot be equal to both 10 and 6. However, if we change the system slightly:

$$\begin{pmatrix} 1 & 3 \\ 2 & 6 \end{pmatrix} \begin{pmatrix} x \\ y \end{pmatrix} = \begin{pmatrix} 5 \\ 10 \end{pmatrix}$$

we get an infinite set of solutions. Just take any value for x, say α, and take $y = (5 - \alpha)/3$. For example, $x = 2, y = 1$ is one such solution.

Electrical circuit analysis using graphs and matrices In Fig. 2.21 on page 53 we illustrated how to represent electrical networks as graphs. Consider now the example in Fig. 2.42. Note that the circuit's electrical elements (which are labelled) are represented in the graph G by edges and the circuit's junctions are represented in G by vertices. The assumption is that we are only concerned with two-terminal elements. We are interested in three attributes of each element α, namely *current* i_α, *voltage* v_α and *resistance* r_α. In general some of these will be known and some will be unknown. However, by Ohm's law we know that

$$v_\alpha = r_\alpha i_\alpha$$

Now since current and voltage have direction, we have to turn G into a digraph. We can choose any orientation we like. If the current in element a happens to be 3 A in the direction chosen then we assert that $i_a = 3$; if it happens to be 3 A in the opposite direction, then we simply assert that $i_a = -3$, etc.

Having chosen a spanning tree T of G we form the fundamental cycle incidence matrix **M** as described in Fig. 2.39. We can now express the so-called Kirchhoff laws using matrix algebra.

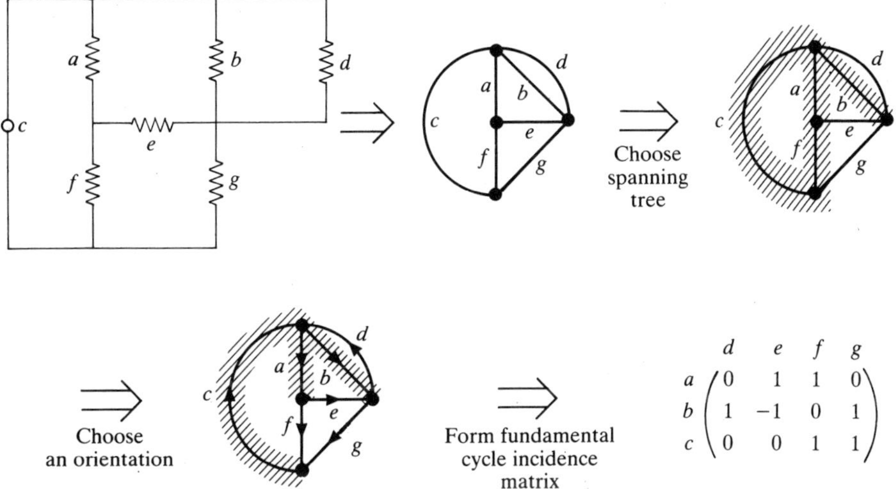

Figure 2.42 Analysing circuits by the fundamental cycle incidence matrix.

The current law This asserts that

$$\begin{pmatrix} i_a \\ i_b \\ i_c \end{pmatrix} = \mathbf{M} \begin{pmatrix} i_d \\ i_e \\ i_f \\ i_g \end{pmatrix}$$

Using T to denote the spanning tree edges and C to denote the cord edges, we can express this more concisely as

$$\boldsymbol{i}_T = \mathbf{M}\boldsymbol{i}_C \tag{2.1}$$

The voltage law This asserts that

$$\boldsymbol{v}_C = -\mathbf{M}^T \boldsymbol{v}_T \tag{2.2}$$

Now, by Ohm's law, we deduce that

$$\begin{pmatrix} v_a \\ v_b \\ v_c \end{pmatrix} = \begin{pmatrix} r_a & 0 & 0 \\ 0 & r_b & 0 \\ 0 & 0 & r_c \end{pmatrix} \begin{pmatrix} i_a \\ i_b \\ i_c \end{pmatrix} \quad \text{so that } \boldsymbol{v}_T = \mathbf{R}_T \boldsymbol{i}_T$$

whence by (2.1)

$$\boldsymbol{v}_T = \mathbf{R}_T \mathbf{M} \boldsymbol{i}_C \tag{2.3}$$

Finally, by substituting (2.3) into (2.2) we get

$$\boldsymbol{v}_C = -\mathbf{M}^T \mathbf{R}_T \mathbf{M} \boldsymbol{i}_C \tag{2.4}$$

The significance of Eqs (2.1), (2.3) and (2.4) is that all the network unknowns can be determined by knowing the cord currents. Thus given a circuit to analyse, we just construct its graph and choose a spanning tree for which (if possible) the chord currents are known.

Exercise 2.63 Suppose that in Fig. 2.42 we know that

$$i_d = 3, i_e = -2, i_f = 1, i_g = 2 \text{ and } r_a = 1, r_b = 5, r_c = 2$$

Determine the current, voltage and resistance of all the elements in the circuit.

2.6 FUNDAMENTAL PRINCIPLES OF COUNTING

In this section we consider techniques that enable us to count the number of objects in a finite set. You may think you already know everything about counting from junior school. But beware: in many situations your intuitive counting skills will not be sufficient. For example, if you know the rules for forming variable names in a particular programming language, can you compute the number of distinct possible names that are allowed? The branch of mathematics that deals with counting is innocuously called *enumeration*, which is in turn the basis for a branch of discrete mathematics called combinatorics. Enumeration lies at the heart of discrete mathematics. In the construction and analysis of complex systems, enumeration enables us to compare different design options, evaluate the efficiency of specific problem solutions, compute probabilities of system failures and predict the amount of resources required to implement a system.

2.6.1 Counting rules

Our study of enumeration begins with two basic principles (called rules) of counting which are 'known intuitively' to everybody. Many enumeration problems may ultimately be decomposed into problems which are solved by these principles.

Rule 2.1 Rule of sum If a task can be performed in n_1 distinct ways, while a second task can be performed in n_2 distinct ways, and the tasks cannot be performed simultaneously, then performing either task can be accomplished in any of $n_1 + n_2$ distinct ways.

Example 2.90 A library has 4 different books on algebra and 5 on calculus. By the rule of sum a student can select among $4 + 5 = 9$ books in order to learn about algebra or calculus.

Example 2.91 The rule can be extended beyond two tasks as long as no pair of them can occur simultaneously. If the other maths books in the library of Example 2.90 consist of 10 different books on geometry and 6 on discrete maths, a student can select any one of the $5 + 4 + 10 + 6 = 25$ books to learn some mathematics.

Suppose now that an administrator assigns 12 employees to 2 committees; committee A (5 members) is to investigate possible favourable results from an expansion, while committee B (7 members) will scrutinize possible unfavourable repercussions. Should the administrator decide to speak to just one committee member before making a decision, then by rule of sum there are 12 members who can be called for input. However, in order to be unbiased the administrator decides to speak with a member of committee A on Thursday and a member of committee B on Friday. There are 5×7 ways in which this can be done. This is an example of the following 'rule of product'.

Rule 2.2 Rule of product If a procedure can be broken down into first and second stages, and if there are n_1 possible outcomes for the first stage and n_2 for the second, then the total procedure can be carried out, in the designated order, in $n_1 \times n_2$ ways.

Example 2.92 A class of 30 students will eventually be graded and there will be a prize for the best student and another for the second best. The number of different possible selections for the prizes is 30×29. The rule of product extends to any number of stages. If there is also a prize for the third best student, then the number of different possible selections for the prizes is $30 \times 29 \times 28$.

Example 2.93 At times we need both rules. In certain versions of the programming language BASIC, a variable name consists of a single letter or a single letter followed by a single decimal digit. By the product rule there are $26 \times 10 = 260$ two-character variables. Since there are also 26 one-character variables the rule of sum implies that there are $26 + 260 = 286$ possible variable names in all.

Exercise 2.64 How many strings of length 4 can be constructed from the 'alphabet' $A = \{a, b, c, d\}$ which begin with a and end in either a or d?

Exercise 2.65 In how many ways can four letters of the word BRIDGE be arranged in a row, if no letter is repeated?

Exercise 2.66 In a class of 30 boys, one prize is awarded for Latin, another for French and a third for mathematics. In how many ways can the recipients be chosen?

Exercise 2.67 Variables in a certain programming language may be up to three characters in length. The first character must be a letter of the alphabet while the last (if there are more than one) must be a decimal digit. What is the total number of distinct variables?

Exercise 2.68 Five letters of the word SHILLING are arranged in a row. Find the number of ways in which this can be done, when the first letter is I and the last is L,

(a) if no letter may be repeated,

(b) if each letter may occur as many times as it does in SHILLING.

Exercise 2.69 How many numbers greater than 5000 can be formed using some or all of the digits 7, 6, 5, 4, 3, without repetition?

2.6.2 Permutations

Suppose that in a class of 10 students, 5 are to be chosen and seated in a row for a photograph. How many such arrangements are possible? The key word is *arrangement*, emphasizing the importance of *order*. If the students are called A,B,C,D, ...,I,J then (B,C,E,F,I) and (C,E,F,I,B) are two *different* arrangements, even though they involve the same set of students. The question is answered by rule of product applied to the number of ways of filling positions:

Position 1	Position 2	Position 3	Position 4	Position 5
10	9	8	7	6

Total $= 10 \times 9 \times 8 \times 7 \times 6 = 30\,240$ possible arrangements.

If there were to be a full class photograph (with 10 students in a row) then there are $10 \times 9 \times 8 \times 7 \times 6 \times 5 \times 4 \times 3 \times 2 \times 1$ possible arrangements.

Definition 2.50 Factorial For an integer $n \geq 1$, 'n factorial', denoted $n!$, is defined by $n! = n \times (n-1) \times (n-2) \times \cdots \times 3 \times 2 \times 1$.

Thus $1! = 1,\ 2! = 2 \times 1 = 2,\ 3! = 3 \times 2 \times 1 = 6, \ldots$.

Exercise 2.70 Show that, in general, $n! = (n+1)!/(n+1)$.

The sequence

$$3! = \frac{4!}{4},\ 2! = \frac{3!}{3},\ 1! = \frac{2!}{2}$$

leads us to define, for completeness: $0! = 1!/1 = 1$.

Example 2.94 A travelling salesman has the following problem. He has to visit n cities, starting and ending at the same one. Since he wishes to minimize the distance he has to drive, he is only interested in planning a route that involves visiting each other city once. How many different possible routes are there? Solution: we label the cities as $1, 2, \ldots, n$. He has to start and end at city 1. There are then $n-1$ ways to choose the second city to visit, $n-2$ ways to visit the third city, etc. By the rule of product there are $(n-1)!$ different routes.

Definition 2.51 Permutation Given a selection of n objects, any arrangement of these objects is called a permutation of the collection.

Example 2.95 There are 6 permutations of the letters A,B,C, namely the 6 ordered triples (A,B,C),(A,C,B),(B,C,A),(B,A,C),(C,B,A),(C,A,B). If we are only interested in arranging two letters at a time there are 6 permutations of *size 2* from the collection, namely the ordered pairs (A,B),(B,A),(A,C),(C,A),(B,C),(C,B).

In general, if there are n objects and r is an integer such that $1 \leq r \leq n$ then the *number of permutations of size r for the n objects* is

$$\underset{\text{position 1}}{n} \times \underset{\text{position 2}}{(n-1)} \times \underset{\text{position 3}}{(n-2)} \times \underset{\cdots}{\cdots} \times \underset{\text{position } r}{(n-r+1)}$$

Exercise 2.71 Show that

$$10 \times 9 \times 8 \times 7 \times 6 = \frac{10 \times 9 \times 8 \times 7 \times 6 \times 5 \times 4 \times 3 \times 2 \times 1}{5 \times 4 \times 3 \times 2 \times 1} = \frac{10!}{5!}$$

From Exercise 2.71, it should be clear that the number of permutations of size r from n objects is equal to

$$\frac{n \times (n-1) \times \cdots \times (n-r+1) \times (n-r) \times (n-r-1) \times \cdots \times 3 \times 2 \times 1}{(n-r) \times (n-r-1) \times \cdots \times 3 \times 2 \times 1} = \frac{n!}{(n-r)!} \triangleq P(n,r)$$

Here the notation $\triangleq$ denotes 'is defined by'.

Many problems in combinatorial or statistical analysis rely on 'taking a sample of objects from some population.' We will show that the key approaches to enumeration can all be viewed in this context.

Suppose we have n objects and that for some integer r we wish to choose r of these objects one after the other for our sample. If, as above, we assume order is important then there are still two relevant approaches that are different:

1 *Repetition is not allowed* ('sampling without replacement'). In this case only $1 \leq r \leq n$ is meaningful and the number of different samples of size r is just $P(n,r)$. We have just determined this above.

2 *Repetition is allowed* ('sampling with replacement'). In this case, *for any r* there are n^r different samples. This again follows by applying the rule of product r times to obtain

$$\underbrace{n \times n \times n \times \cdots \times n}_{r \text{ times}}$$

as the number of different samples of size r from n objects.

Example 2.96 We are to select three cards, noting them in order, from a pack of 52. If cards are not replaced then there are $P(52,3) = 52!/49! = 132\,600$ different selections, whereas with replacement there are $52^3 = 140\,608$ selections.

Example 2.97 The number of permutations of the letters of the word COMPUTER is 8! If only four of the letters are used, the number of permutations (of size 4) is $P(8,4) = 8!/(8-4)! = 8!/4! = 1680$. If repetitions are allowed, the number of possible four-letter sequences is $8^4 = 4096$. The number of 12-letter sequences is 8^{12}.

Example 2.98 A computer word consists of a string of eight 0's or 1's. How many distinct words are there? It is just the number of samples of size 8 from a population of size 2 (with replacement) $= 2^8 = 256$.

Example 2.99 In contrast to the previous example the number of permutations of the word BALL is not 4! (24) but 12. This is because there are not four distinct letters to permute. If the two L's were distinguishable as L_1, L_2 then there would be 4! permutations. However, to each permutation for which the L's are indistinguishable there corresponds a pair of permutations with distinct L's. For example,

$$BALL = \begin{cases} BAL_1L_2 \\ BAL_2L_1 \end{cases} \qquad LBAL = \begin{cases} L_1BAL_2 \\ L_2BAL_1 \end{cases}$$

Hence the solution is $4!/2 = 12$.

Example 2.100 How many permutations are there of the letters in PEPPER? Again if we could distinguish three P's and two E's then there would be 6! However, to each permutation in which letters are indistinguishable there now corresponds (3!)(2!) permutations where we can distinguish between the letters. For example,

$$PEPPER = \begin{cases} P_1E_1P_2P_3E_2R \\ P_2E_1P_1P_3E_2R \\ P_3E_1P_1P_2E_2R \\ \vdots \end{cases}$$

Hence the solution is $6!/(3!2!) = (6 \times 5 \times 4)/2 = 60$.

Examples 2.99 and 2.100 naturally lead us to:

Theorem 2.5 If there are n objects with n_1 of first type, n_2 of second type, ...,n_r of the rth type where $n_1 + n_2 + n_3 + \cdots + n_r = n$, then there are

$$\frac{n!}{n_1!n_2!\cdots n_r!}$$

permutations of the given objects.

Example 2.101 There are $10!/(4!3!1!1!1!)$ permutations of the letters in MASSASAUGA.

2.6.3 Combinations

Let us return to our theme of selecting a sample of size r from a population of size n. We have seen two ways to interpret this. Suppose now that from a class of ten students we wish to select three as representatives for the course board committee. Certainly this involves sampling without replacement. However, the formula of permutations is not appropriate since we would not wish to distinguish the ordered triple (B,E,F) from (F,E,B), say. In short, *order is now not important*. In this case each sample or selection or combination of three students with no reference to order corresponds to 3! permutations. That is:

$$\begin{aligned}(3!) \times \text{(number of combinations of size 3 from 10)} \\ &= \text{number of permutations of size 3 from 10} \\ &= P(10,3) = 10!/7!\end{aligned}$$

Therefore, if we have n distinct objects, each *combination* of r of these objects (with no reference to order) corresponds to $r!$ permutations of size r from n.

We can now use this fact to calculate the number of *combinations* of size r from n using the number of *permutations* of size r from n.

Theorem 2.6 The number of combinations of size r from n denoted $C(n,r)$ or $\binom{n}{r}$ satisfies the formula $r!\ C(n,r) = P(n,r)$.

Thus

$$C(n,r) = \frac{P(n,r)}{r!} = \frac{n!}{r!(n-r)!}$$

where $r = 0, 1, 2, \ldots, n$. So the above theorem gives us a *formula* for the number of combinations.

Example 2.102 In a certain exam the students must answer four out of the seven questions. The total number of different ways to answer the exam is thus

$$C(7,4) = \frac{7!}{3!4!} = \frac{7 \times 6 \times 5}{3 \times 2 \times 1} = 35 \text{ ways}$$

Exercise 2.72 Show that $C(n,n) = 1$ and that $C(n,r) = C(n, n-r)$.

Example 2.103 If the students must answer three questions out of five in section A and two out of four in section B, then section A can be completed in $\binom{5}{3}$ ways and section B in $\binom{4}{2}$ ways. By the rule of product the exam can be completed in $\binom{5}{3}\binom{4}{2}$ ways.

The binomial theorem We now apply our work on combinations to expand $(x+y)^n$ by the binomial expansion using the $\binom{n}{r}$ notation. Since $(x+y)$ is the sum of *two* numbers, it is known as the *binomial* expansion. We begin by stating the binomial expansion as the *binomial theorem* and then ask you to give an informal proof in the form of an intuitive explanation.

Theorem 2.7 Binomial If $x, y \in \mathbb{R}$ and $n \in \mathbb{N}$, then $(x+y)^n$ is equal to:
$$\binom{n}{0}x^n y^0 + \binom{n}{1}x^{n-1}y^1 + \binom{n}{2}x^{n-2}y^2 + \cdots + \binom{n}{i}x^{n-i}y^i + \cdots + \binom{n}{n-1}x^1 y^{n-1} + \binom{n}{n}x^0 y^n$$

Exercise 2.73 In Theorem 2.7 we are using our notation for combinations to find a *general* formula for $(x+y)^n$. Give the expansions for $n = 0, \ldots, 4$ and find a pattern for the general form of the coefficients of $(x+y)^n$. This pattern is called *Pascal's triangle*.

Exercise 2.74 Now consider the expansion of

$$\underbrace{(x+y)(x+y)\cdots(x+y)}_{n \text{ factors}}$$

First suppose that $n = 4$ and see how the product is formed. Use the product rule to find out how many ways there are of forming the terms x^3y and x^2y^2. Generalize this to show that the coefficient of $x^{n-i}y^i (0 \leq i \leq n)$ is the number of ways we can select i y's from i of the n factors and then $(n-i)$ x's from the remaining $n-i$ factors.

Exercise 2.75 Use the results of Exercise 2.73 and Exercise 2.74 to give an informal proof of Theorem 2.7.

Corollary 2.1 For any integer $n > 0$: $\binom{n}{0} + \binom{n}{1} + \binom{n}{2} + \cdots + \binom{n}{n} = 2^n$.

PROOF Apply the binomial theorem to the case where $x = 1, y = 1$ to get $(1+1)^n$ on the left-hand side of the equation. On the right-hand side of the equation we get

$$\binom{n}{0} + \binom{n}{1} + \binom{n}{2} + \cdots + \binom{n}{n}$$

2.6.4 Applying the counting rules

We have been concerned with the problem of finding the number of different ways of choosing a sample of size r from n distinct objects. The solution to this problem depends on whether the *ordering* of the sample is important; that is we need to *choose* between ordered selection and non-ordered selection when we choose our sample of size r from n distinct objects. The algorithm that we use to solve our problem, which involves choosing, will itself contain a choice construct. A solution to the problem can be expressed by the following algorithm:

To choose a sample of size r from n distinct objects:

If order matters then consider *arrangements*

  if choice is *with replacement*, so that repetition is allowed, then choose in n^r ways
  else use *permutations* and choose in $n!/(n-r)!$ ways
else use *combinations* and choose in $n!/(r!(n-r)!)$ ways.

Exercise 2.76 In how many ways can a party of eight persons arrange themselves:

(a) in a row of eight chairs,

(b) around a circular table?

Exercise 2.77 How many different signals, each consisting of eight flags hung in a vertical line, can be formed from four identical red flags, two identical blue flags and two identical white flags?

Exercise 2.78 How many numbers between 1000 and 3000 can be formed from the digits 1, 2, 3, 4, 5, if repetition of digits is:

(a) allowed,

(b) not allowed?

Exercise 2.79 A student has to answer eight out of ten questions in an exam.

(a) How many choices are available?

(b) How many choices are available if the first three must be answered?

(c) How many choices are available if at least four out of the first five questions must be answered?

Exercise 2.80 In how many ways can ten pearls be arranged in a necklace?

Exercise 2.81 Ten guests are invited to the theatre. In how many ways can the guests be arranged in a row of ten seats in the stalls if the only constraint is that two of the guests are newly married and must sit together?

Exercise 2.82 How many positive integers with three different digits are greater than 700?

Exercise 2.83 If repetition is not permitted how many different three-digit numbers can be formed from the digits 2, 3, 5 and 7? How many numbers do not end in a 3? (You could consider how many numbers *do* end in a 3.)

Exercise 2.84 Four women and their best friends sit on a park bench. In how many ways can they be arranged if:

(a) there is no restriction,

(b) each woman wants to sit next to her best friend?

Exercise 2.85 In how many ways can five trade union officials, four members of the board of British Rail and three members of ACAS sit at a round negotiating table if all those people representing the same organization must sit together?

Exercise 2.86 A team of six runners is to be chosen to run for their county. The runners are to be chosen from three local athletics clubs. Each local club has a team of eight runners and from each of these local clubs two runners are to be chosen. In how many ways can the team of six runners be chosen?

Exercise 2.87 A king is placed on the bottom left-hand square of an 8×8 chess board and is to move to the top right-hand corner square. If it can move one square at a time up or to the right only, how many possible paths does it have to choose from?

Exercise 2.88 Consider four groups of students. There are six students in each group, and all the students belonging to the same group wear the same coloured jumpers. Group colours are amber, blue, charcoal and dark grey. The groups are called A, B, C and D. Each student within a group has a number on his or her jumper, from 1 to 6 (no students with the same coloured jumper have the same number). In how many ways can the following groups be formed in the coffee bar:

(a) a group of five students, all wearing the same coloured jumpers,

(b) a group of five students in which two students have the same number on their jumpers and three students have different numbers on their jumpers?

Exercise 2.89 Five cards are selected at random from a standard deck of 52 cards. In how many ways can the following hands be chosen:

(a) a hand consisting of exactly one pair of cards,

(b) a hand containing two pairs (and one odd card),

(c) a hand containing two cards of one suit and three cards of another suit,

(d) a hand containing three cards of one suit, but the other two do not form a pair,

(e) a hand consisting of five cards all of the same suit?

2.7 SUMMARY

In this chapter we have introduced some of the key foundational topics of discrete mathematics, on which the rest of this book hinges. We have emphasized the central role played by the concept of sets. Functions, relations and graphs are all defined in terms of sets, while linear algebra has been presented in a set-theoretic manner. Even the techniques of counting are dependent on identifying elements of sets.

FURTHER READING

Although our presentation has been self-contained, it has been necessarily brief in places in order to cover such a sizeable area of mathematics. There are many books that are entirely devoted to one or more of the topics in this chapter, and you may like to refer to one or more of these for more detailed coverage. The books of Ince (1988), Kalmanson (1986), Kolman and Busby (1987), Levy (1980), Prather (1976), Skvarcius and Robinson (1986), Stanat and McAllister (1977) and Tremblay and Manohar (1975) all cover most of the fundamental topics (especially sets, functions, relations and counting) in some detail. Grimaldi (1985) also covers graph theory and its applications well but, for a really thorough and entertaining introduction to graph theory, Wilson and Watkins' book (1990) is highly recommended. Lipschutz (1974) provides a thorough introduction to linear algebra. Also highly recommended as background material is the book by Stewart and Tall (1977) which provides an excellent introduction to the foundations of mathematics.

Chapter 3

THE CALCULUS OF PROPOSITIONAL LOGIC

In this chapter we introduce the concept of a logical calculus as a formal language with rules for reasoning in that language. We begin our development of a simple logical calculus as the essential starting point for the task of expressing the formal construction and analysis of any system. We show how logic and mathematics are intertwined, and construct in Sec. 3.2 the simple calculus of propositions. Because this calculus is so simple (too simple to be really useful when we work with complex systems), the well-formed formulae of the calculus can be evaluated in a simple way by the assignment of truth-values. We give rules about the structure and meaning of formulae in the calculus, which is itself modelled by an algebraic structure, before we use the propositional calculus to model English sentences in Sec. 3.3.

Logical formulae are joined by logical connectives and the important connectives for implication and equivalence are introduced in Sec. 3.4. These enable us to express the logical axioms for the propositional calculus in Sec. 3.5. Applications are featured throughout. The hard work of building our calculus brings its reward in Chapter 4, when we introduce rules for reasoning within the calculus and carry out proofs within a system of formal deduction.

3.1 A LOGICAL CALCULUS*

Before describing the construction of a calculus in mathematical logic, we summarize the development of logic and identify its relationship with mathematics. The long-term interaction between these two disciplines has now been extended by the demands of the new discipline of computer science for a formal framework of logic and mathematics. If you are impatient to get to grips with using the calculus, you can omit this section initially. Return to it when you need to see the motivation for working within formal logic, as we do in the later chapters of the book.

3.1.1 Logic is needed for mathematics

Mathematics is the study of properties of mathematical structures. Such structures will be studied extensively in Chapter 8. In order to reason about such structures we use *mathematical logic*, which consists of its own 'calculus' for building and reasoning about mathematical structures. We shall see that logic itself is treated according to mathematical rules; so we see that logic and mathematics are intertwined. The interaction between logic and mathematics has stimulated progress in both disciplines. In particular, the major advances in logic seem to have come from developments in mathematics. The study of mathematical structures and the development of universal algebras led to the study of classical model theory in logic. Over the last 30 years this historical partnership has been further stimulated by a third (immature) discipline—computer science. The urgent demands for a sound theoretical framework for the construction of software systems have led to interaction and rich research between the trio: logic, mathematics and computer science.

Before we introduce a logical calculus, we should explain how logic has developed as a subject. The science of formal logic can be seen as a highly developed branch of applied mathematics, concerned with the mathematical analysis of the structure of deductive argument. However, logic also has a 'pure' side, when logical systems based on sets of axioms (as formal rules) are studied for their own interest—just as structures are studied for their own sake in pure mathematics. Work in 'pure' logic is increasingly applied to the theoretical framework that is required for the construction and analysis of complex systems. Logical rules of inference provide the basis for the process of verification that is described in Sec. 1.2. A logic for reasoning about programs is used to verify the correctness of algorithms in Chapter 12.

In its widest sense, logic is the theoretical study of the structure of reasoning in all its possible forms. It is a very varied discipline. The logicians of the nineteenth century were concerned with 'judgements', or acts of assertion, which are backed by adequate grounds for maintaining what is asserted. A judgement in logic was defined as a thought or belief in the mind, which could be discussed once it was put into words, and then was termed a proposition. The process of deriving one judgement or proposition from another, or from others, was the act of inference, and logic was the systematic study of the general conditions of valid inference.

Recently logic has been studied increasingly as a formal system. The main object of discussion is no longer the act of judgement, but the sentence or verbal statement which can be considered purely by itself without being related to the mind of a person. With the use of a formalized language, the inexactness and irregularities of structure and expression in colloquial or literary English are avoided. Adopting a formalized language means adopting a particular system or theory of logical analysis. The formal system of logic, therefore, lacks reference to meaning and achieves versatility. It can correctly judge a chain of reasoning, particularly mathematical reasoning, solely on the basis of the form, or structure, and not the content of the sequence of statements that make up the chain.

Formal logic is concerned more with how we should reason rather than with how we actually do reason, and is directly relevant to mathematics. Every development of mathematics uses logic. It follows, however, that logic itself, as the systematic study of a structure, can be treated mathematically to form mathematical logic (symbolic logic). Thus we can treat mathematically the logic that we use in the study of mathematics! To avoid a paradox, the logic to be studied can be treated separately from the logic we are using to study it. The logic to be studied can be expressed in the object language, since the language, including its logic, is an object of study, while the logic used to carry out the study can take place in another language, the observer's language or the meta-language. We need to distinguish clearly between the object language and the observer's logic.

3.1.2 Constructing a calculus

In order to construct and analyse discrete systems we need to construct many calculi.

We begin by defining a calculus informally as a general concept, and then define a logical calculus as a particular instance of a calculus.

Definition 3.1 Calculus A calculus is both a language to describe objects and a set of rules for building those objects.

A calculus in mathematical logic builds mathematical objects and provides logical rules for reasoning *about* those mathematical objects. A *logical* calculus adds rules that enable objects in other calculi to be reasoned about. Essentially a calculus consists of a set of special symbols including *variables, constants* and *operations*, together with a set of rules that tell us which strings of these symbols are allowed. This set of rules is sometimes referred to as the *syntax*. The strings that are allowed in logical languages are called well-formed formulae, or wffs, to indicate that they are syntactically correct formulae.

Example 3.1 The calculus of the integers includes variables $x, y, z, \ldots$, constants (,) ,0, 1,... and operations $+, -, \times$ (but not $\div$). Note that '$x + 2$', '-1','$(x \times z) + 2$' and '$x - (2 \times y)$' are permissible strings in the language but '$+ - 3x\times$' is not.

Example 3.2 The differential calculus includes an infinite list of variables $x, y, x_1, y_2, \ldots$, constants including $2, \pi, e, \ldots$ and operations like 'd/dx', 'd^2/dx^2'. Strings of symbols in the differential calculus include '$2y$', 'd/dx($2+x$)', 'e d^2/dx^2' and '($x+y$) d/dx'. The string 'd/dx($x^2 + y$)' is permissible, because it is syntactically correct, but 'e d^2/dx^{2}' is not.

A calculus may be viewed as a notation with symbols and rules for building formulae that will capture the special properties of the application, or problem, domain that is being described.

Exercise 3.1 Give an informal description of some strings that are generated by the set of syntax rules that belong to the calculus of words in the English language.

Exercise 3.2 Give some of the syntactic rules for building programs as the sentences of the language Pascal. How are the phrases that are *not* well formed detected in a programming system?

We shall give the rules for generating the valid strings of formal languages in Chapter 7.

3.1.3 A meta-level calculus

We have defined a calculus as a language and a set of rules for building formulae, and have talked about examples of calculi in different application domains. In order to *reason* about the objects in these application domains, however, we need the power of a *logical* calculus that will both include the languages of any example application calculus that we need to construct and help us to reason *about* the application domain.

Example 3.3 If we have a rule in the calculus of the integers that states that $a + 0 = a$ for any integer, we need a logical rule that allows us to deduce that $3 + 0 = 3$ for the constant integer 3.

You could think of a logical calculus as sitting 'above' all the calculi that describe numbers, sentences and programs; logic gives us a language to 'talk about' these objects and to deduce useful properties about them. We use logic to keep our descriptions of problem domains orderly and precise. From the height of an abstract meta-level, logic presides over the concrete objects that are described in some object-level language.

In summary, a logical calculus provides a precise description of the problem domain. For this we need some basic formulae, called *axioms*, which express properties that we accept must hold without needing to prove them. Next we need some *rules* for deducing further properties, which we call *theorems*, about the problem domain. Our deductions are made from the axioms, which we take as our agreed starting point. Finally, we choose a *mathematical model* or *structure* to represent the application domain to which our well-formed formulae refer. We want to ensure that our calculus does represent the application domain! Clearly the task of constructing a calculus to describe a complex system in the real world is a major task. It is the topic underlying the majority of chapters in this book. In this chapter we embark on the early stages of this task and lay the foundations for an axiomatic approach to constructing systems.

Axioms First we identify a set of axioms, or *postulates*, which are usually wffs of the calculus and which we *assume* to be true. Axioms can usually be given independently and without reference to other wffs in the calculus.

Example 3.4 Four of the axioms for the calculus of the integers are familiar to us:

$$\begin{aligned} a+(b+c) &= (a+b)+c \\ a+b &= b+a \\ a+0 &= a \\ a+(-a) &= 0 \end{aligned}$$

where it is assumed that a, b, c are any integers.

Example 3.5 We could take the following statements as axioms of the differential calculus:

$$\begin{aligned} \frac{\mathrm{d}}{\mathrm{d}x}x &= 1 \\ \frac{\mathrm{d}}{\mathrm{d}x}(\mathscr{F}(x)\mathscr{G}(x)) &= \left(\frac{\mathrm{d}}{\mathrm{d}x}\mathscr{F}(x)\right)\mathscr{G}(x) + \left(\frac{\mathrm{d}}{\mathrm{d}x}\mathscr{G}(x)\right)\mathscr{F}(x) \end{aligned}$$

The differential calculus also of course includes all the axioms listed in Example 3.4. Thus the axioms for the differential calculus may be thought of as forming an *extension* of the axioms for the calculus of the integers. Similarly, the axioms for the real numbers will include, or extend, that of the rationals, which in turn includes those of the integers. *All* of these calculi in turn include the axioms of the logical calculus which we are going to study. Clearly our choice of axioms is vitally important to the trust that we place in the calculus that is built on the axioms.

Rules of inference We need rules of inference in our logical calculus in order to make the deductions that we need from the assumed axioms. If we state the rules of inference precisely *and* keep to them, we increase our confidence in the mathematical and logical systems that we build.

Example 3.6 We can use the four axioms for the integers, given in Example 3.4, to deduce that 'if an integer x satisfies $a+x=a$ for any one integer a, then $x=0$'. An informal proof involves subtracting from both sides of the equation, but we need the four axioms to formally justify the last three steps of the following formal proof:

If	$a + x = a$
then	$(-a) + (a + x) = (-a) + a = 0$
that is	$((-a) + a) + x = 0$
that is	$0 + x = 0$
that is	$x = 0$

Exercise 3.3 Explain how the four axioms are used in each step of the proof.

The axioms are used as equations that are asserted to be true. They are used as patterns in which we can replace the variable symbols that stand for *any* integer by a particular integer, which in this case is represented by x. The rule that allows us to replace the symbol a in the axiom $a+0=a$ to get $x+0=x$ is the rule of *substitution*. This rule will allow us to replace x by the constant integer to obtain $3+0=3$. Another rule of inference that we used was the *rule of equivalence* that allowed us to replace the formula $(-a)+a$ by the equivalent formula 0 according to the axioms $x+(-x)=0$ and $x+y=y+x$.

The inference rules that we have just stated informally belong to *equational logic* which is itself part of the more general first-order logic that we present in the next three chapters. You probably felt that our example proof made a lot of work out of a trivial deduction. We gain from confidence in a firm foundation for our proof system, however, as we carry out deductions that are hundreds of lines long.

Our choice of axioms and rules can be made intuitively to suit the problem domain. By using an infinite set of logical axioms we shall see in Chapter 4 that we can manage to reason with only one inference rule: *modus ponens*. Alternatively, we can work without any logical axioms if we use several rules of inference.

Definition 3.2 Axiomatic system A language with formal rules of syntax, a set of axioms and a set of rules of inference is a formal axiomatic system.

Theories In any axiomatic system the deductions made from the axioms by means of the rules of inference are called *theorems*. The collection of axioms and theorems derived from them are called *theories* and describe a particular application.

Example 3.7 The assertion that we proved in Example 3.6 is a theorem that belongs to the theory of the integers. Our theorem was deduced from the non-logical axioms about the domain of the integers.

Definition 3.3 Theory The collection of all the theorems deduced from the set of axioms, Γ, is called the theory determined by Γ. (The Greek letter Γ is pronounced 'gamma'.)

Example 3.8 The axiom of extension is an axiom of set theory and states that 'two sets are equal if and only if they have the same elements'. In Exercise 2.6 you were asked to prove a theorem about sets, using the axiom of extension and the definition of the subset relation.

Exercise 3.4 Another axiom of set theory is the axiom of pairing. This states that 'for any two sets there exists a set that they both belong to'. From this axiom and the definition of set union deduce the theorem that 'for any two sets there exists the union of these two sets'.

Formally set theory is the set of consequences of the sentences that form the axioms for set theory and provides a starting point for the mathematical theories of algebra and analysis. A stronger assertion is that mathematics itself can be *embedded* in set theory.

Mathematical theories are based on formal objects that are without meaning. In contrast, scientific theories are based on abstractions of the observations about some part of the real world; they are constructed *as* the observations are made. When we build theories about complex systems we need to understand the ways in which both mathematical and scientific theories are built. The task of writing specifications for discrete systems is the task of building theories about discrete systems! When we build a theory we abstract from the real world and move into the real world of mathematics and logic, as illustrated in Sec. 1.3.

Models Having constructed a calculus with formal rules for building wffs and formal rules for deducing theorems from axioms, we must make sure that we can *interpret* our theorems in some mathematical domain that represents the application. This involves assigning a meaning, called a *semantics*, first to each of the symbols and then to each of the theorems in our calculus.

Example 3.9 Consider the axioms in Example 3.4. These statements will all be true statements if we interpret them in a model that consists of the set of integers with functions representing the operations of $+$ and $-$. The theorems deduced from the axioms will also be true in this model.

Definition 3.4 Logical model If every theorem in the theory determined by some axiom system, Γ, is a true statement in the mathematical domain, we say that the assignment of meanings constitutes a logical model for that theory.

The notion of truth is very difficult to pin down in the real world, however. We shall have to rely on a simplified notion of truth in our mathematical domain.

The importance of a model for a theory is that if the model is constructed correctly, so that it *satisfies* a theory, the model can be used to validate the construction of some discrete system as a possible solution to a real-world problem. The elements of the model may be numbers, sets or functions that 'stand for' the objects described in the syntax. Model theory matured as a branch of mathematical logic that connected formal languages with their interpretations. It brought together the results of logic with those of universal algebra. Now the construction of algebraic models and set-theoretic models underlies our formal methods for constructing discrete systems.

When we model a theory by sets and functions we build a model that is more concrete than the abstract theory it represents. This is the usual meaning of the word 'model' when we use mathematics and logic as the framework for building systems. Unfortunately this differs from the use of the word 'model' in Chapter 1 where a model is more abstract than the object it models, because the modelling process omits unnecessary detail.

Example 3.10 A theory about the social services includes theorems about the merging of centres into a single organization. In Sec. 2.1, sets are used to *model* the collections of people. Clearly, the operation of set union 'satisfies' the merging of the Wanstead and Aldersbrook staff which already have a number of personnel in common.

Exercise 3.5 An axiom for the theory about the social services might be, 'there exists at least one member of staff in each social service centre'. Otherwise the centre itself does not exist. Write another axiom for the theory.

Exercise 3.6 Two centres each have a member of staff called Betty. How would you model the merging of these centres by a set operation?

The axiomatic approach The formal approach of describing a theory about some application domain by making deductions from a set of axioms has matured within the disciplines of logic and mathematics. The importance of the axiomatic approach is now recognized within the immature discipline of computer science. By changing the traditional presentation of logic (as we do in this book), computer scientists and engineers are now able to apply the concepts and the techniques of logic to the construction and analysis of systems.

As we shall see in Part II of this book, the axiomatic approach is becoming a very popular way of defining abstract data types in the specification of software systems. If a model is not required, the approach is proof-theoretic; with the use of a model an algebraic or set-based approach is chosen. We also use the axiomatic approach in Part III when we present the theory of probability, which plays a part in the analysis of complex systems, and the theory of measurement.

Example 3.11 A classical example of a system of axioms is Euclidean geometry in which the special symbols are the variables, $p_1, p_2, \ldots$ for points and $l_1, l_2, \ldots$ for lines. The relation 'lies on' between points and lines is symbolized by $\in$. The relation between lines of 'being parallel' is symbolized by $\|$. The rules of syntax tell us that '$p_1 \in l_1$' and '$l_1 \parallel l_2$' are wffs but neither '$\in p_l$' nor '$p_1 \parallel p_2$' are wffs. One of the axioms is

$$\forall p_1, p_2\ [p_1 \neq p_2 \rightarrow \exists! l_1\ (p_1 \in l_1 \wedge p_2 \in l_1)]$$

This states that 'for any two points, which are not equal, there is exactly one line on which both points lie'. The symbols $\rightarrow$, $\wedge$ are all symbols in the propositional calculus, which we present in this chapter, and $\forall$ and $\exists!$ are symbols in the predicate calculus, which we present in Chapter 5.

The most controversial of the five Euclidean axioms is the last one,

$$\forall p_1, l_1\ [p_1 \notin l_1 \rightarrow \exists\ ! l_2\ (p_1 \in l_2 \wedge l_1 \parallel l_2)]$$

This states that 'through any point outside a given line there can be drawn only one line parallel to the given line'.

The fifth axiom is not (as was believed for centuries) a consequence of the other axioms. An equally respectable (but different) geometry, called non-Euclidean, may be derived if this axiom is dropped. This different geometry plays a prominent role in the theory of relativity. In short, since the resulting theories are different it is up to us to find appropriate models for them. We saw in Example 1.19 that although we can model the real-world geometry by Euclidean geometry we lose some accuracy.

3.2 THE CALCULUS OF PROPOSITIONS

It is very difficult to make a general logic that satisfies the needs of every application. For instance, reasoning in formal mathematical languages is very different from reasoning in informal natural languages. Because of the varying demands on logic, many different forms of logic have been developed. Initially we consider a simple form of logical calculus that builds propositions, or statements, in the English language. Later we shall work with the predicate calculus which is sufficiently powerful to express the proofs that we need to undertake in mathematics.

Our language of logic will be a formal language in order that we can build with it and make deductions as we build. This means that our language will not be a *natural* language and that we shall lose much of the expressiveness and ambiguity that we enjoy in everyday speech. As we move from the English language to our formal language we shall be restricted in what we can express, but we shall gain in the security of being able to use a precise language for our reasoning. Once we have made our proof in the formal language, we can translate back into the more expressive natural language that we use for communication. An important advantage of formal languages is that we can automate the manipulations that we make as we reason in them.

3.2.1 Propositions

We now consider a calculus as a system within which we can build and manipulate propositions in both English as well as mathematics. Our calculus uses symbols like $p, q, \ldots, \wedge, \vee, \ldots$ in order to represent propositions like 'It is cold and it is damp' as $p \wedge q$.

In order to define what we mean by a proposition we exclude from our language sentences that are questions or commands. We call the sentences that remain *statements*.

Definition 3.5 Proposition A proposition is a statement that is either true or false but not both.

We speak of the *truth-value* of a proposition as being true or false.

Definition 3.6 Truth-value The function truth-value: {propositions}→{true, false} assigns a unique truth-value to every proposition.

Example 3.12 These are 'true' propositions:

2+3=5
Bombay is in India
Spurs won the FA cup in 1991

Example 3.13 These are 'false' propositions:

$10 > 87$
The ink on this page is blue
Arsenal play entertaining soccer

Example 3.14 These are accepted as propositions:

n is an even integer
She is attractive
$x + y > 7$

They are called *open* statements, since in each case whether they are true or false depends on the value of *n*, She, *x* and *y*.

Example 3.15 These are not propositions:

Well done!
How did you score that goal?

Some surprising propositions Some of the statements that we accept as propositions may seem surprising. Any statement that is grammatically correct can be given as a proposition. We define a proposition as a grammatical English sentence that can be put in place of '*x*' in the open statement, 'is it true that *x*', so as to give a grammatical English question. We therefore only make a syntactic restriction and do not question the *meaning* of the statement. Since we are only using a two-valued logic, any statement that is not true in a real-life domain is given the value false. Consequently, the statement

If Winston Churchill is not Prime Minister then he is Prime Minister

is a proposition which cannot be true (whoever is Prime Minister) and is therefore false — even though it does not make sense in everyday English.

Additional complications arise when some sentences appear to be propositions but are *not* because an assignment of *truth-value* leads to a contradiction. Consider the sentence

This sentence is false

This sentence cannot be a proposition because if it is true then it is false! However, if it is false then it is true! In either case it is *both* true and false. The problem with this sentence is that it 'talks about itself'. It is the *recursive* structure of the sentence that is to blame. Such sentences are called *paradoxes* and are not accepted as propositions.

There are other sentences in which the assignment of a truth-value may be subjective or impossible to determine correctly. For example,

Gary is a better player than Pele

It rained in the place that is now called Lambeth on 2 March 11658 BC

Such sentences *are* considered to be propositions, because we can give a truth-value once and for all without a fear of contradiction. Of course changing our assumptions may lead to radically different logical consequences. The underlying truth or falsity of a sentence depends on assumptions that cannot be verified by pure reasoning in a formal system.

Even if we do not know whether Gary is a better player than Pele (or even if we do not know who they are), we do know that the sentence

Gary is a better player than Pele `or` Gary is *not* a better player than Pele

is true. The truth of a proposition can sometimes be determined from its structure alone, without knowing whether its constituents are true or false. The sentence above is an instance of the abstract proposition 'p or (not p)' and this proposition is true, regardless of whether p is a true or false proposition.

Exercise 3.7 Are the following sentences propositions?

(a) I am going on holiday.

(b) $x > y$

(c) Either you like dancing or you do not.

(d) Are you coming?

(e) If Fred is the goalkeeper he is not the goalkeeper.

(f) Spurs will win the cup in 2001.

Building propositions The beauty of mathematical logic is that propositions are stripped of any meaning and only given a *value* true or false. Once the proposition p is given a truth-value, true say, it remains forever true and it is up to us to deduce what we can from this. Propositions can be built up from other propositions through the use of logical operations, such as `and`, `or`, `not`. For example, from the propositions

roses are red

violets are blue

we can form new propositions, called *compound* propositions,

roses are red `and` violets are blue

roses are red `or` violets are blue

roses are `not` red

3.2.2 Building well-formed formulae

Depending on the truth-value of the original propositions, we would expect to be able to determine the truth-value of the compound propositions. We shall see in the next section that the calculus of propositional logic allows us to do this. We introduce the notation for the calculus informally and extend it later in the chapter, as we develop the need for more ways of building propositions. The symbols that represent the operations to build compound propositions in the logic are called *connectives*.

Initially we require the following *logical* symbols whose meanings are fixed:

- Connectives $\neg, \wedge, \vee$
- Punctuation symbols (,), and ,
- Constant symbols T and F

The *non-logical* symbols complete the definition of the language:

- An infinite set of variables $p, q, r, \ldots$

The wffs of this calculus are defined by the following rules for construction:

1 Every propositional variable or T or F is a wff.

2 If x and y are wffs then so are $(\neg x)$, $(x \wedge y)$, $(x \vee y)$.

In these rules x and y are variables in the language that we use to 'talk about' the propositional calculus. We allow the outer brackets round a wff to be dropped so that the wff $(\neg p)$ simplifies to $\neg p$.

Example 3.16 The formulae $F \wedge \neg q$, $(p \wedge q) \vee (p \wedge q)$ are wffs in the propositional calculus, but $p\neg q$, $pq\wedge$, (p) and $\wedge T \neg r$ are not wffs.

Definition 3.7 Compound proposition Any wff of the propositional calculus which consists of more than just a single propositional variable is called a compound proposition.

p	$\neg p$
T	F
F	T

p	q	$p \wedge q$
T	T	T
T	F	F
F	T	F
F	F	F

p	q	$p \vee q$
T	T	T
T	F	T
F	T	T
F	F	F

Figure 3.1 Truth tables for basic connectives.

3.2.3 Calculating truth-values for propositions

We have introduced a formal notation which allows us to build wffs by abstracting away from the detail of what propositions mean. We only interpret propositions by the values true or false. Now we must ensure that we have a clear rule to help us determine whether *compound* propositions are true or false. Sometimes it is difficult to assign a truth-value to an English sentence because of the way it is formed. We shall need to be careful in Sec. 3.3 when we translate English sentences into our logical calculus. Clearly we shall lose expressiveness. However, it is more important that we gain precision and lose ambiguity. We must insist in our calculus that the following rule is kept as we build propositions.

> **Rule 3.1 Truth-functionality** The truth-value of a compound proposition is uniquely determined by the truth-value of its constituent parts.

The symbols that we use for building propositions are truth-functional connectives. The following simple method for assigning truth-values to propositions follows the rule of truth-functionality.

Truth-values for basic connectives The simple semantics of the propositional calculus is summarized by drawing *truth tables*. Rules express the assignment of truth-values by the function defined in Def. 3.6. The truth-values are abbreviated by the constant symbols T and F. We give the truth tables for the connectives $\neg$, $\wedge$ and $\vee$ in Fig. 3.1.

From the truth table for $\neg$ we can read the rule that 'if p is T then $\neg p$ is F'. The symbol p denotes any simple or compound proposition in the calculus. In the truth table for $\wedge$ we have the rule that 'if p is T and q is F then $p \wedge q$ is F'. The logical connectives, $\vee$ and $\wedge$, are often called *disjunction* and *conjunction* respectively.

> **Example 3.17** If p, q are of type Boolean in a Pascal program, the declaration p, q: *boolean* appears in the type definition at the beginning of the program. The above tables will define the meaning of the Pascal operations *not, and, or.*

The connective $\vee$ corresponds to '*inclusive or*', meaning that the 'or both' case is included. We say that both *disjuncts* can be true. In our informal English language we use the connective 'or' sometimes to include the 'or both' case and sometimes to exclude it. We rely on the general context to convey our meaning. If we are offered pork or lamb for dinner we *usually* understand that we cannot have both. However, if we are offered salt or pepper we frequently take both! We do not usually need to give an exclusive meaning to our use of 'or' in English because of the incompatibility of the two propositions. For example, in the English statement

> This number is odd or this number is even

we find that it is impossible for both propositions to be true. We do not seem to have an English connective that imposes the exclusive meaning on 'or'. We shall see in Sec. 3.4.1 that in logic we *can* express the exclusive meaning by using another logical connective. This connective is mainly used for mathematics rather than English language sentences, however.

Truth-values for compound propositions We can use the truth tables for $\neg$, $\wedge$ and $\vee$ to build truth tables that allow us to compute the truth-value, or the semantics, of any wff of propositional logic. Once a truth-value is given to the symbols that denote the simple propositions, we can use truth tables to give a meaning of true or false to each wff of the calculus.

Example 3.18 Consider the wff, $(p \wedge q) \vee (\neg r)$. This is in the form $A \vee B$, which we can determine from the $\vee$ table if we know how to determine the truth-values of A and B. Now the truth of A comes straight from the $\wedge$ table and the truth of B from the $\neg$ table. We can therefore draw the truth table:

p	q	r	$(p \wedge q)$	$\vee$	$\neg r$
T	T	T	T	T	F
T	T	F	T	T	T
T	F	T	F	F	F
T	F	F	F	T	T
F	T	T	F	F	F
F	T	F	F	T	T
F	F	T	F	F	F
F	F	F	F	T	T

Compound propositions are given names P, Q,... to distinguish them from single propositional variables. More usefully, parameterized names like $P(p, q, r)$, where P is a compound statement involving the propositional variables p, q, r, are given. We say that $P(p, q, r)$ is a *three-place proposition* to make it clear that there are 'holes' in P to be filled by three propositional variables.

Example 3.19 We might refer to $\neg(p \wedge q)$ as $P(p, q)$ and $(\neg p) \vee (\neg q)$ as $Q(p, q)$. The truth tables of these two compound propositions are identical:

p	q	$\neg$	$(p \wedge q)$	$(\neg p)$	$\vee$	$(\neg q)$
T	T	F	T	F	F	F
T	F	T	F	F	T	T
F	T	T	F	T	T	F
F	F	T	F	T	T	T

We now define a notion of equivalence between propositions that is at a *meta-level* to the calculus itself.

Definition 3.8 Equivalence Two propositions $P(p, q, \ldots)$, $Q(p, q, \ldots)$ are said to be equivalent if they have identical truth tables. We write $P \equiv Q$ if P is equivalent to Q.

It follows from Example 3.19 that $P(p,q) \equiv Q(p,q)$ where $P(p,q)$ and $Q(p,q)$ are as defined. It is important to understand that $\equiv$ 'talks about' compound propositions and is not itself a connective in the calculus.

Exercise 3.8 By drawing truth tables, demonstrate that the following equivalences hold:

$$\begin{aligned} p \wedge q &\equiv q \wedge p \\ p \vee q &\equiv q \vee p \\ \neg(p \wedge q) &\equiv \neg p \vee \neg q \\ p \wedge p &\equiv p \\ \neg(p \vee q) &\equiv \neg p \wedge \neg q \end{aligned}$$

The equivalences $p \wedge q \equiv q \wedge p$ and $p \vee q \equiv q \vee p$ demonstrate that the property of *commutativity* holds for the connectives $\wedge$ and $\vee$.

The size of truth tables Clearly truth tables provide a very simple method for showing that compound propositions are equivalent. However, as propositions of increasing complexity are constructed, the truth table method decreases in efficiency. If a compound statement P has n propositional variables called $p_1, p_2, \ldots, p_n$ then the truth table of $P(p_1, \ldots, p_n)$ has 2^n rows.

Exercise 3.9 Use the principles for counting, in Sec. 2.6, to explain why a truth table for a proposition with n variables has 2^n rows.

Exercise 3.10 Use the method of truth tables to demonstrate that two six-place propositions, called $P(p,q,r,s,t,u)$ and $Q(p,q,r,s,t,u)$, and constructed by you, are not equivalent.

Exercise 3.11 Prove that disjunction has the 'inclusive' meaning by showing that $p \vee q \equiv (p \wedge \neg q) \vee (\neg p \wedge q) \vee (p \wedge q)$ but that $p \vee q \not\equiv (p \wedge \neg q) \vee (\neg p \wedge q) \vee (p \wedge q) \vee (\neg p \wedge \neg q)$.

Tautologies and contradictions Now consider the two special propositions $\neg p \vee p$ and $\neg p \wedge p$,

p	$\neg p$	$\vee$	p	$\neg p$	$\wedge$	p
T	F	T	T	F	F	T
F	T	T	F	T	F	F

The truth-value of the first is always T, the second always F; that is

$$\neg p \vee p \equiv T, \quad \neg p \wedge p \equiv F$$

We see that some propositions will *always* be given the value F in a truth table—simply because of their structure.

Definition 3.9 Tautology A proposition that always has T as its truth-value is called a tautology.

Definition 3.10 Contradiction A proposition that always has F as its truth-value is a contradiction.

Since the propositional variables are actually irrelevant, the constant symbols T, F may be used respectively to denote any tautology or contradiction.

3.2.4 Rules in the calculus

By using rules in the syntax of our calculus we can write simpler wffs. By providing semantic rules of equivalence that are based on an algebraic structure we can work within a convenient model and then translate our results back into the real-world domain.

Syntactic rules of precedence Brackets are used in compound propositions to describe explicitly an order of evaluation. We evaluate *inside* the brackets first. If we make syntactic rules about the precedence of the logical connectives we can drop some of the brackets in wffs.

Rule 3.2 Brackets outside whole wffs can be dropped.

Rule 3.3 The connective $\neg$ has precedence over $\wedge$ and $\vee$.

Example 3.20 The wff $(\neg p) \wedge (\neg q)$ can be written as $\neg p \wedge \neg q$.

Example 3.21 The wff $\neg p \wedge q$ is the same as $(\neg p) \wedge q$ but is different from $\neg(p \wedge q)$.

Exercise 3.12 Show that $\neg p \wedge q$ is *not* equivalent to $\neg(p \wedge q)$.

Rule 3.4 The connectives $\wedge$ and $\vee$ are equal in precedence.

A wff like $p \wedge q \vee r$ is genuinely ambiguous without brackets. It could be $(p \wedge q) \vee r$ or $p \wedge (q \vee r)$.

Exercise 3.13 Use truth tables to check that $(p \wedge q) \vee r$ is not equivalent to $p \wedge (q \vee r)$.

We could drop more brackets by saying that $\wedge$ has higher precedence than $\vee$. However, there is no agreement on this in the literature and we feel it is clearer to keep the brackets in order to make the meaning explicit.

Exercise 3.14 Show that $(p \wedge q) \wedge r \equiv p \wedge (q \wedge r)$.

From the exercise we see that the statement $p \wedge q \wedge r$ is unambiguous. Similarly $(p \vee q) \vee r \equiv p \vee (q \vee r)$, so that we may write $p \vee q \vee r$ without fear of ambiguity. We see in Sec. 3.2.4 that the equivalences that we have just described depend on a property that holds in many algebraic systems and is called the property of *associativity*. We already know from Sec. 2.1 that set union and intersection are associative.

Rule 3.5 All connectives have a higher precedence than the meta-level symbol $\equiv$.

Exercise 3.15 Use the rules of precedence to simplify $(((\neg r) \wedge (\neg q)) \vee (p))$. At each stage state which rule you are using.

We can use the propositional calculus to represent English statements in symbolic form and then determine their truth-values. We give further examples in Sec. 3.3.

Example 3.22 Suppose that

p represents the statement 'Ossie is tall'.
q represents the statement 'Ossie is handsome'.
r represents the statement 'Ossie is a great player'.

Then the statement 'Ossie is neither tall nor handsome but he is a great player' may be represented by the compound proposition $(\neg p \wedge \neg q) \wedge r$ which can be written as $\neg p \wedge \neg q \wedge r$. Suppose that we assign truth-values to p, q and r in the following way: p is F, q is F, r is T. Then the truth-value of $\neg p \wedge \neg q \wedge r$ is T.

1.	$p \vee p$	$\equiv$	p	$p \wedge p$	$\equiv$	p	(idempotent)
2.	$p \vee q$	$\equiv$	$q \vee p$	$p \wedge q$	$\equiv$	$q \wedge p$	(commutative)
3.	$(p \vee q) \vee r$	$\equiv$	$p \vee (q \vee r)$				
	$(p \wedge q) \wedge r$	$\equiv$	$p \wedge (q \wedge r)$				(associative)
4.	$p \vee (q \wedge r)$	$\equiv$	$(p \vee q) \wedge (p \vee r)$				
	$p \wedge (q \vee r)$	$\equiv$	$(p \wedge q) \vee (p \wedge r)$				(distributive)
5.	$\neg(p \vee q)$	$\equiv$	$\neg p \wedge \neg q$	$\neg(p \wedge q)$	$\equiv$	$\neg p \vee \neg q$	(De Morgan)
6.	$p \vee F$	$\equiv$	p	$p \wedge T$	$\equiv$	p	
	$p \vee T$	$\equiv$	T	$p \wedge F$	$\equiv$	F	(identity)
7.	$p \vee \neg p$	$\equiv$	T	$p \wedge \neg p$	$\equiv$	F	
	$\neg\neg p$	$\equiv$	p				
	$\neg T$	$\equiv$	F	$\neg F$	$\equiv$	T	(complement)
8.	$p \wedge (p \vee q)$	$\equiv$	p				
	$p \vee (p \wedge q)$	$\equiv$	p				(absorption)

Figure 3.2 Rules of the algebra of propositions.

Algebraic rules for propositions We now consider the semantics of the propositional calculus as a simple algebraic structure. We shall see in Chapter 8 that an algebra is formed from a set of elements together with a set of operations on those elements. For this algebra the elements p, q, r belong to the set of propositions and $\neg, \wedge, \vee$ represent the operations on this set. Within this structure we use the symbol $\equiv$ to represent equivalence between propositions that have the same truth-value. The rules of the algebra of propositions are given in Fig. 3.2. Some of these rules have already been proved in Exercise 3.8 using truth tables. The algebraic structure of the propositional calculus is identical to that of the algebra of sets. In fact they are both examples of a more abstract algebra that is known as a *Boolean algebra* and will be presented in Sec. 8.1. Theorems may be proved entirely by algebraic manipulation in this algebra and then applied both to the propositional calculus and to set algebra. Truth tables (for the propositional calculus) and Venn diagrams (for the set algebra) then merely demonstrate the theorems that are proved algebraically. The importance of the Boolean algebra is that it provides a *model* for working with the propositional calculus.

Exercise 3.16 The algebra of propositions and the algebra of sets, as summarized in Sec. 2.1, have analogous rules. Show this by writing down the sets, as the elements, and the operations on sets that form the algebra of sets, next to the corresponding laws of the algebra of propositions.

The analogy that we have shown also means that problems in the algebra of propositions can be demonstrated in the algebra of sets and then translated back into the logical symbols of the propositional calculus.

Exercise 3.17 Demonstrate the distributive law for propositions by using Venn diagrams of the corresponding sets and set operations.

3.3 MODELLING ENGLISH SENTENCES

We need to be able to put English sentences into formal languages so that we can manipulate logical expressions and make deductions from them. For example, specifications for systems that are written in English may be ambiguous; we need to represent these precisely in a formal language. Work on the formalization of natural languages is also important in expert systems with user dialogues, knowledge representation (using

Prolog) and speech input and output devices. We only touch the surface of the topic of analysing English sentences in logic. Our aim is to contrast a formal language with a natural language and to develop the skill of moving between them. This is an essential skill for the formal specification of application systems in the real world. We build propositions by abstracting away from their meaning and only interpret them by the values true and false. It is often difficult to assign a truth-value to an English sentence because of the way it depends on the truth of its parts. We need a clear rule to help us determine whether a compound proposition is true or false.

3.3.1 Analysing English sentences

English sentences need to be *analysed* before they are translated into the formal calculus. The logical analysis of complex sentences in the English language requires an initial analysis of the structure of the sentence. The combination of short sentences to form longer sentences can be seen to be made by only a few 'combinators' in the English language. Other ways of building sentences can, in some informal sense, be shown to 'mean' the same as sentences built by these few basic 'combinators'. The analysis of English sentences consists of finding those sentences that are built in the chosen simple ways. We can express the *constituent* sentences from which complex sentences are constructed by marking them with square brackets.

Example 3.23 [John bowled the ball] and [David hit the ball to the boundary]. The constituent sentences are combined by 'and' into the complex sentence.

We showed on page 91 that propositions can be built through the use of logical operations such as `and`. Later we gave the truth table for the connective $\wedge$ in the propositional calculus. In English, words such as 'and' that are used to build sentences are called sentence functors. If they also have truth tables they are called *truth functors*. To translate a complex English sentence with more than one functor we start with the truth functor of largest scope, as shown by the overall sentence structure. We then work inwards to the truth functors of smaller scope. We analyse the sentence into constituent sentences, marked with square brackets, and separated by a truth functor. Finally we translate the truth functors into connectives and denote the propositions by variables.

3.3.2 Truth functors

The truth functors most commonly used in English are those symbolized by the propositional logic connectives, $\neg, \wedge$ and $\vee$:

- `not` for negation
- `and` for conjunction
- `or` for 'either or' or 'both'
- `arrow` sometimes called material implication (introduced in Sec. 3.4.5)

Some English sentences are easily represented in the propositional calculus because they have constituents that are sentences.

Example 3.24 [I shall get a century] or [I shall be out for a duck]. This expresses two constituent sentences built by 'or'. As we pointed out on page 92, if we accept a 'weak' inclusive meaning for 'or', we define it by the truth table for $\vee$. Otherwise we assert that 'I get both a century and a duck' must be false and we take a 'strong' meaning for 'or' that will be defined in Sec. 3.4 by the truth table for $\oplus$, the connective for 'exclusive or'.

In some sentences 'or' has a meaning that is closer to 'and' and should be translated to $\wedge$ rather than $\vee$.

Example 3.25 The sentence 'The mechanic can mend motor bikes or he can mend cars' is built by the truth functor 'or' and should be translated by $\wedge$.

Some sentences are easy to analyse but require work in defining a truth table for the truth functor.

Example 3.26 The sentence 'The batsman hit the ball but the fielder caught it' has constituents that are sentences, and is analysed as follows:

[The batsman hit the ball] but [the fielder caught it]

This sentence is obviously constructed by 'but' which does have a truth table and therefore is a truth functor. The truth table for 'but' has the same meaning as that for another truth functor!

Not every way of building an English sentence is by a truth functor, however. Sometimes the truth-value of the constituent sentences may not determine the truth-value of the whole sentence.

Example 3.27 The sentence 'I know that black is white' is constructed by the sentence functor 'I know that'. This functor is *not* a truth functor, however, because it only has a *partial* truth table. Since 'black is white' is false the second row of the table is false. For a true sentence the first row of the table must be left blank. Some truths are not known!

This last example contrasts with our narrower view, given in Sec. 3.2, of defining propositions in the formal calculus. In our formal language we cut through the subtleties of English sentences and only use a two-valued logic. If the sentence is not false it is true!

The negation truth functor is expressed by 'It is not true that' and precedes an English sentence.

Example 3.28 The negation of 'I am an egg producer' is 'It is not true that I am an egg producer', which is symbolized by

$\neg$ I am an egg producer

3.3.3 Paraphrasing English sentences

The analysis of a sentence into constituent sentences will often produce more constituent sentences if we *paraphrase* a sentence, or replace it by another sentence that means the same thing.

Example 3.29 The sentence 'She regretted not having argued more' can be paraphrased as

She regretted that [she did not argue more]

Paraphrasing is useful for simplifying sentences involving negation.

Example 3.30 The sentence 'It isn't as if Margaret needs the support' can be paraphrased as

¬ Margaret needs the support

Example 3.31 The negation of 'Some people like eating snails' is

¬ Some people like eating snails

The negation connective is placed at the outermost scope and negates the whole sentence. The sense of ¬ in this sentence can be expressed by 'No one likes eating snails', or even better by 'Everyone dislikes eating snails'.

Paraphrasing is not always accurate, however, and may change the truth-value of a sentence.

Example 3.32 The sentence 'He didn't touch anything' usually paraphrases the meaning of

¬ He touched something

in logic. The sentence 'He didn't touch anything' implies that some male person is being observed. In fact, if there is *no* male person the sentence shows referential failure and is used improperly. However, in logic,

He touched something

is false if there is no male person to be referred to by 'he' and it follows that

¬ He touched something

is then true!

These apparent inaccuracies are due to the differences between a two-valued formal calculus of logic and an expressive but complex natural spoken language.

3.3.4 Truth functionality

We have seen that it may be difficult to decide on a truth-value for an English sentence because of the way the truth of the sentence depends on the truth of the parts. We have to be careful in the way we build compound propositions in our calculus from such sentences.

Example 3.33 The sentence 'Mike is a wonderful guitarist' cannot be rewritten for translation by a compound proposition as

[Mike is wonderful and Mike is a guitarist]

This is because the meaning of 'wonderful' must be attached to the noun guitarist. This sentence must be represented by a simple proposition in the calculus.

Example 3.34 The sentence 'Sue is a beautiful woman' can be rephrased to give the compound sentence

[Sue is beautiful and Sue is a woman]

This is because 'beautiful' is not used *restrictively* and can be separated from the noun woman.

In the logical calculus we avoid the problems that compound English sentences give us, by requiring that Rule 3.1 is satisfied. By keeping Rule 3.1 we ensure precision and lack of ambiguity in our logical calculus. This is more important in our work on formal systems than the extra expressiveness that we leave behind as we move into our formal language.

We have given examples where rephrasing is used to introduce a compound sentence. Rephrasing is sometimes necessary to allow a translation of a truth functor into a logical connective. For example, if the word 'and' occurs between adjectives we can rephrase the sentence to allow a translation by $\wedge$.

Example 3.35 The sentence 'Your attitude is both hurtful and extreme' is rephrased to give

[Your attitude is hurtful $\wedge$ your attitude is extreme]

Sometimes rephrasing will give the wrong meaning, however.

Example 3.36 The sentence 'I like large and juicy steaks' is not translated in logic by

[I like large steaks $\wedge$ I like juicy steaks]

Exercise 3.18 Analyse the following compound sentences into constituent sentences:

(a) The post was delivered but I received no letters.

(b) I saw the tram coming but I couldn't run to catch it.

(c) The wind blew several trees down but only one blocked the road.

(d) I like coffee but my husband likes tea.

Now let p, q stand for the constituent sentences. Construct a truth table for the expression 'p but q'. Which basic logical truth functor expresses the sense of the English language truth functor 'but'?

Exercise 3.19 Write down a negation of each of the following English sentences. Then write down the negation of each sentence as a proposition:

(a) The man has grey eyes.

(b) $x \leq y$, where x and y are integers.

(c) The temperature is over 80°C.

(d) It is not sunny.

Exercise 3.20 Show by means of a truth table that $\neg\neg p \equiv p$ and also that $\neg\neg\neg p \equiv \neg p$. What can we infer about $\underbrace{\neg \ldots \neg p}_{n \text{ times}}$, where n is a positive integer?

How can we relate this to the repeated complement of a set?

Exercise 3.21 Replace the propositional variable in the one-place proposition 'It is not true that p' by a true proposition. Is the resulting proposition true or false?

Exercise 3.22 Are the 'holes' or free occurrences of p in

Since she swears that p we can believe that p

correctly filled by

Since she swears that she was at work, we can believe that she is innocent?

Exercise 3.23 Give the truth-values of the following sentences in logic:

(a) The King of Japan is bald.

(b) The King of Japan is not bald.

(c) $\neg$ The King of Japan is bald.

Exercise 3.24 Rephrase the following English sentences as propositions joined by the logical connectives $\wedge, \vee$ and $\neg$ where necessary:

(a) I am not a Frenchman.

(b) There will be a firm wages policy or we shall see vast unemployment. (Suppose both are true. Is the proposition true?)

(c) Neither I nor my husband speak Russian.

(d) He is a rich man or a liar.

(e) The athlete can run the 500 metres sprint or he can run the 400 metres hurdles race.

(f) We'll go to the park today unless it rains.

(g) Although it was cold she ran in her shorts.

(h) The work is simple but time-consuming.

(i) My daughter wants a brown and white kitten.

(j) He laughs often and loudly.

(k) She didn't say anything.

(l) Peter is a brilliant violinist.

(m) I hardly think she will get to college in that old car.

(n) George Washington never told a lie.

(o) Margaret is a clever woman.

Identify those solutions that you feel are difficult to rephrase accurately.

3.4 FURTHER CONNECTIVES

3.4.1 The 'exclusive or' connective

We have already noted that although in the English language 'or' can have either the meaning of the 'inclusive or' or the meaning of the 'exclusive or', in logic the connective $\vee$ corresponds to the notion of 'inclusive or'. If we do wish to denote the 'exclusive or' to represent 'Fred eats breakfast or lunch (but not both)' then we *can* do so using the logical connectives we already have. In fact, p 'exclusive or' q, meaning 'p or q but not both' may be represented by

$$(p \vee q) \wedge \neg(p \wedge q)$$

or equivalently as we see in the next section by

$$(p \wedge \neg q) \vee (\neg p \wedge q)$$

In this section we introduce a special connective symbol, $\oplus$, as a shorthand for 'exclusive or' and define $\oplus$ by the truth table:

p	q	$p \oplus q$
T	T	F
T	F	T
F	T	T
F	F	F

Within the algebra of propositions we then have the additional equivalence

$$\begin{aligned} p \oplus q &\equiv (p \vee q) \wedge \neg(p \wedge q) \\ &\equiv (p \wedge \neg q) \vee (\neg p \wedge q) \end{aligned}$$

The 'exclusive or' connective is not really intended for English statements, however, since as we have noted their meaning is usually clear from the context. The symbol $\oplus$ is equivalent to the *addition modulo two* operation defined in Example 2.16 with 0 replaced by F and 1 by T. We have already seen that the algebraic structure of the propositional calculus is known as a Boolean algebra.

Exercise 3.25 Find out whether $\oplus$ is commutative and associative.

3.4.2 The 'either not or not' connective

Here we introduce the connective $|$, called the Schaeffer stroke, and defined by the truth table:

p	q	$p \mid q$
T	T	F
T	F	T
F	T	T
F	F	T

The compound proposition is 'either not-p or not-q' where 'or' is used in the inclusive sense. Equivalently $p \mid q$ means 'not(p and q)', so that

$$p \mid q \equiv \neg(p \wedge q) \equiv \neg p \vee \neg q$$

giving

$$p \vee q \equiv \neg p \mid \neg q$$

Exercise 3.26 Find out whether $|$ is commutative and associative.

3.4.3 The 'neither nor' connective

The compound proposition 'neither p nor q' is written as $p \downarrow q$. This connective is the negation of the connective 'or' and can be defined by the algebraic equivalence $p \downarrow q \equiv \neg(p \vee q)$.

Exercise 3.27 Draw the truth table for the connective $\downarrow$.

Exercise 3.28 Find out whether $\downarrow$ is commutative and associative.

Exercise 3.29 Show that *within* the formal logical calculus, the propositions that represent the sentences 'It is neither funny nor sad' and 'It is not either funny or sad' are equivalent. Is there a notion of formal equivalence between these sentences in the English language?

3.4.4 Complete sets of connectives

We now see that the various rules for the algebra of propositions enable us to construct new propositions from old, as well as to simplify propositions.

Example 3.37 The connective $\wedge$ can in fact be constructed from $\neg, \vee$:

$$p \wedge q \equiv \neg(\neg p \vee \neg q)$$

This can of course be shown by truth tables. However, it follows (algebraically) by the rules of Sec. 3.2.4 that

$$\begin{aligned} p \wedge q &\equiv \neg\neg(p \wedge q) && \text{(complement)} \\ &\equiv \neg(\neg p \vee \neg q) && \text{(De Morgan)} \end{aligned}$$

It seems we could 'get by' in the calculus by just using two connectives $\neg, \vee$. We can build wffs that have the connective $\wedge$ from wffs that only have the connectives $\neg$ or $\vee$. This leads us to ask the question, 'Which of the connectives we have defined are redundant?'; that is 'Is there a subset of the connectives consisting of elements from which the remaining connectives can be constructed?' In answer to these questions we have just shown that $\neg$ and $\vee$ are *sufficient* for the construction of $\wedge$.

Exercise 3.30 Show that $\neg$ and $\wedge$ are also sufficient for the construction of $\vee$.

Definition 3.11 Complete sets of connectives A set of connectives that is sufficient to build up the complete propositional calculus is a complete set of connectives.

The set $\{\wedge, \vee, \neg\}$ is complete but its completeness can be narrowed down. The sets $\{\wedge, \neg\}$ and $\{\vee, \neg\}$ are complete sets of connectives. If we reduce the set $\{\wedge, \vee, \neg\}$ by removing $\neg$, however, we find that $\{\wedge, \vee\}$ is not a complete set of connectives. Could we get by using just one connective? The answer is 'yes', but not any of $\{\vee, \wedge, \neg\}$.

It is easily seen that

$$\begin{aligned} \neg p &\equiv p \mid p \\ p \wedge q &\equiv (p \mid q) \mid (p \mid q) \end{aligned}$$

Hence $\{ \mid \}$ is complete since $\{\neg, \wedge\}$ is a complete set of connectives.

Exercise 3.31 Show that $\{ \mid \}$ can be defined as complete because $\{\neg, \vee\}$ can be simulated using only $\{ \mid \}$.

Exercise 3.32 Show that $\downarrow$ can also generate wffs that use only the connectives $\{\neg, \vee, \wedge\}$. Construct an argument for completeness of $\{ \downarrow \}$.

We saw on page 96 that the algebra of propositions and the algebra of sets are both examples of a more abstract algebra. We now show how this abstract algebra—the Boolean algebra—also underlies simple two-valued systems called switching systems. The completeness of $\mid$ enables a complex switching system to be designed from only one type of basic component.

Example 3.38 A *binary device* is a switch, usually electronic, that accepts a finite number of 'inputs' and produces a finite number of 'outputs' where each of the inputs and outputs have only two possible values. These two values are usually given as 1 and 0, representing high voltage and low voltage, but we could equally as well think of them as T and F. Thus any wff of propositional calculus may be viewed as a binary device. The circuits in digital computers are binary devices which are built up from simple devices called *logic gates*. We can view logic gates as logical operations: in fact logic gates are the physical implementation of the logical connectives in the more abstract domain of the logical calculus. Therefore a device that implements the `not` operation is both defined in Fig. 3.3 by its truth table and represented by its logic gate. This device is called a NOT-gate and takes a single input of high (or low) voltage and outputs a voltage that is the complement of its input.

The type of diagram used to represent the NOT-gate is known as a logic diagram and is frequently used by system designers. By working from the truth tables for the propositional connectives we give in Fig. 3.4 the logic diagrams for the gates that implement the connectives, $\wedge$, $\vee$, $\downarrow$ and $\mid$. From the appropriate basic devices we then construct in Fig. 3.5 a physical device to implement the $\oplus$ connective

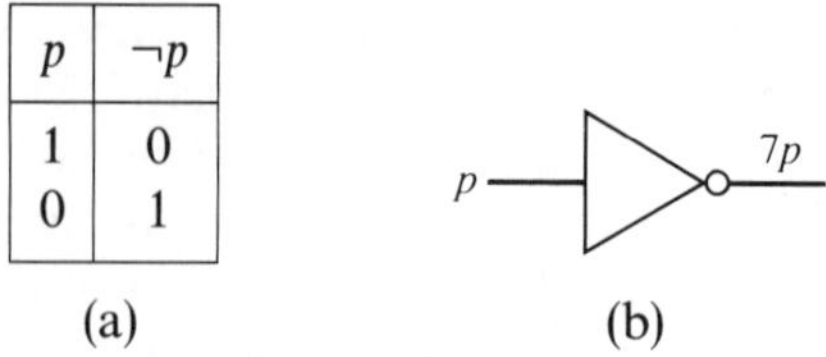

Figure 3.3 Truth table definition and logic gate for the not operation.

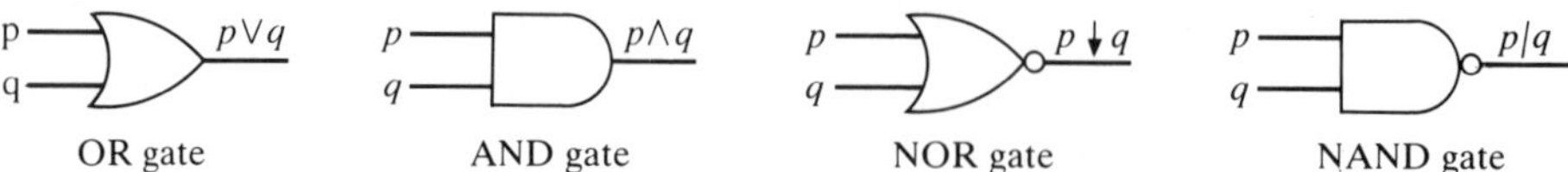

Figure 3.4 Logic gates to implement the connectives $\wedge$, $\vee$, $\downarrow$ and $\mid$.

(representing 'exclusive or') as a binary 1-bit adder. We base our construction on the algebraic equivalence

$$p \oplus q \equiv (p \vee q) \wedge \neg(p \wedge q)$$

The implementation of a binary device by composing logic gates is called a *combinatorial network*. Using the algebra of the propositional calculus we can show combinatorial networks to be equivalent and we can simplify their construction. The network in Fig. 3.6 implements $(p \wedge \neg q) \vee (p \wedge \neg q \wedge r)$. However, by the absorption law this proposition is equivalent to $p \wedge \neg q$. The network in Fig. 3.6 is therefore equivalent to the simpler network in Fig. 3.7. The importance of the completeness of $\{ \mid \}$, which is implemented by a NAND-gate, should now be evident. One can implement *all* the combinatorial networks using just a single type of gate. For example, to implement the gate for the $\oplus$ connective we use the equivalence, $p \oplus q \equiv (p \vee q) \wedge \neg(p \wedge q)$ again and note that

$$\begin{aligned}
(p \vee q) \wedge \neg(p \wedge q) &\equiv (p \vee q) \wedge p \mid q \\
&\equiv \neg(\neg p \wedge \neg q) \wedge p \mid q \\
&\equiv (\neg p \mid \neg q) \wedge p \mid q \\
&\equiv ((p \mid p) \mid (q \mid q)) \wedge p \mid q \\
&\equiv (((p \mid p) \mid (q \mid q)) \mid (p \mid q)) \mid (((p \mid p) \mid (q \mid q)) \mid (p \mid q))
\end{aligned}$$

The compound proposition $p \oplus q$, defining Boolean addition, can therefore be implemented, as in Fig. 3.8, by a network that is constructed from only one type of gate: a NAND-gate. This can be made easier if we can use n-input NAND-gates rather than the two-input NAND-gates that we have introduced in this example.

We have introduced an application of the algebra of propositions to the construction of digital computer circuits. We have raised questions of whether a solution that only uses one type of device is better than a solution that uses *fewer* devices of different types. A more important question, which has been investigated, is whether there is a systematic procedure for finding some minimal, or 'best', solution.

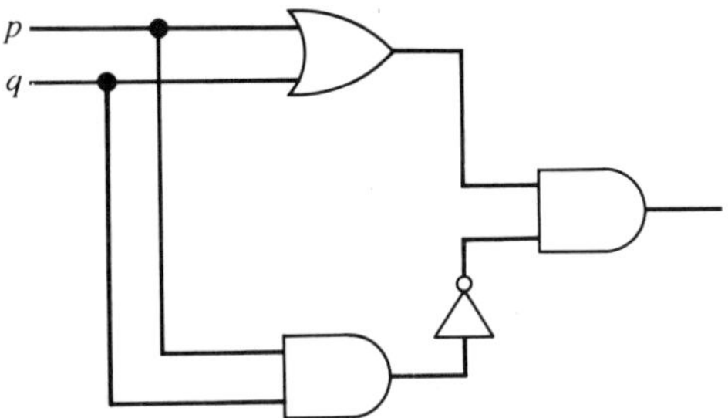

Figure 3.5 Implementation of the connective ⊕.

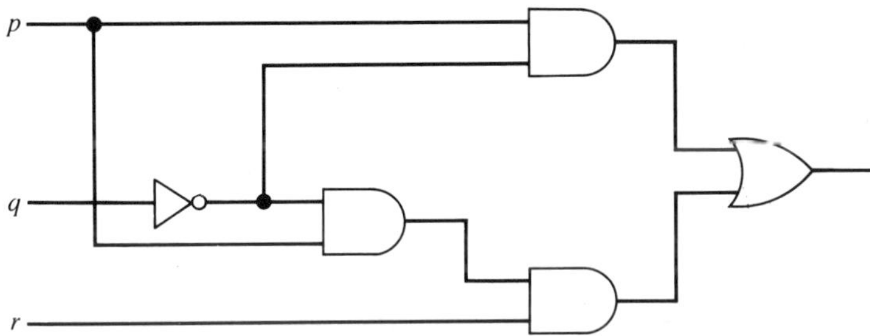

Figure 3.6 Network to implement $(p \wedge \neg q) \vee (p \wedge \neg q \wedge r)$.

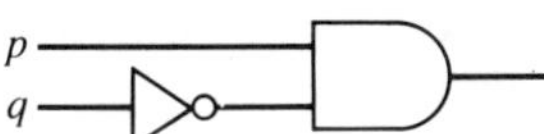

Figure 3.7 Network to implement $p \wedge \neg q$.

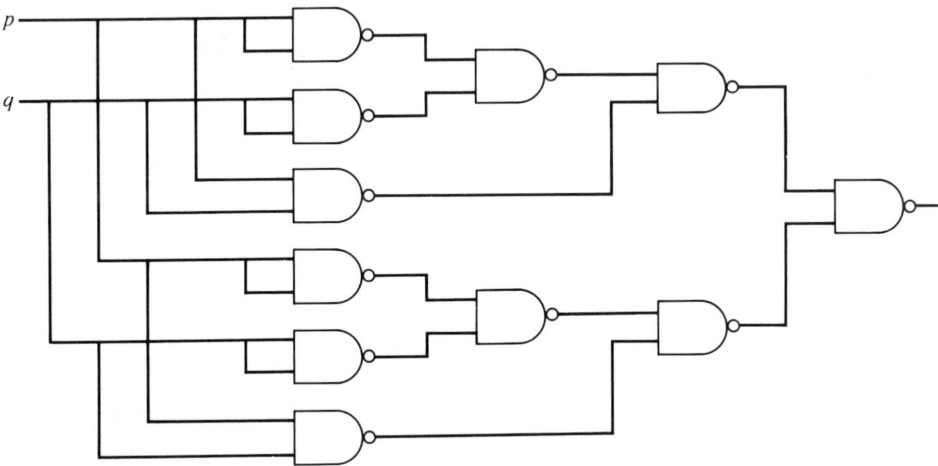

Figure 3.8 Network of NAND-gates.

3.4.5 The implication connective in the propositional calculus

Formal languages allow us to escape from the ambiguities of natural language, but as we have seen they have a sharply limited degree of expressiveness. Our next logical connective is very important for carrying out proofs in the mathematical world. We should not be concerned that no English expression gives the meaning of this logical connective *exactly*. We use the formal definition given by a truth table to give a meaning to the connective.

The definition of $\rightarrow$ in the propositional calculus Many statements in mathematics are of the form 'if p then q' or 'p implies q'. We need to represent these statements in our calculus. The logical connective for implication is symbolized by $\rightarrow$, called 'arrow' or the conditional symbol. The truth table for $\rightarrow$ is defined by:

p	q	$p \rightarrow q$
T	T	T
T	F	F
F	T	T
F	F	T

The definition of the conditional symbol, $\rightarrow$, is therefore that $p \rightarrow q$ (read as p arrow q) is true in all cases where p is false. The only case when $p \rightarrow q$ is defined to be false is when p is true and q is false.

We show in Sec. 3.4.6 that there are many kinds of implication, or 'if p then q', statements in English with overlapping meanings. The meaning of $\rightarrow$ is a restricted form of ordinary implication called *material* implication. Each form of implication shares a common strand, however, and it is this strand that provides the meaning of $\rightarrow$. The common strand of meaning for the implication $p \rightarrow q$ to hold is that q is asserted to be true whenever p is true. However, this means that $p \wedge \neg q$ is *excluded* when $p \rightarrow p$ is asserted; that is $\neg(p \wedge \neg q)$ is asserted and this is taken to be the meaning of $\rightarrow$.

Definition 3.12 The meaning of $\rightarrow$ The meaning of the conditional symbol, $\rightarrow$, is given by the equivalences, $\neg(p \wedge \neg q) \equiv \neg p \vee q \equiv p \rightarrow q$.

Exercise 3.33 Demonstrate by truth tables that the previous equivalences hold.

From the equivalence for $p \rightarrow q$ we see that $\rightarrow$ has only been introduced for convenience since it can be defined in terms of $\{\neg, \wedge\}$ and $\{\neg, \vee\}$.

Exercise 3.34 Show that $\{\neg, \rightarrow\}$ is complete.

Exercise 3.35 Show that

	$p \rightarrow q$	$\not\equiv$	$q \rightarrow p$	(the converse)
and	$p \rightarrow q$	$\not\equiv$	$\neg p \rightarrow \neg q$	(the inverse)
but	$p \rightarrow q$	$\equiv$	$\neg q \rightarrow \neg p$	(the contrapositive)

We shall use the converse, inverse and contrapositive of $p \rightarrow q$ in our work on proof methods in Chapter 4.

Exercise 3.36 Show that $p \rightarrow (q \rightarrow p)$ is a tautology. This means that if p is true it is implied by *any* proposition q.

Exercise 3.37 Show that any false proposition implies that any other proposition is true; that is $(p \wedge \neg p) \rightarrow q$, which is in the form $F \rightarrow q$, where q is any proposition.

This means that $\neg p \rightarrow q$ where q is any proposition. If we take $p = q$ in the proposition $\neg p \rightarrow q$ we get the proposition $\neg p \rightarrow p$ which is counter-intuitive! This emphasizes the fact that $\rightarrow$ does not symbolize ordinary implication. We do not use a proposition of the form $\neg p \rightarrow p$ in everyday conversation! It would be considered nonsense.

Recall that our rule of truth functionality, on page 92, eliminates ambiguity in meaning as we build wffs in our formal calculus. A further convincing argument for the truth table for $\rightarrow$ is that it yields the validity of the tautology

If $A \wedge B$ is true then B is true

in *all* cases (which it would not if it were defined in any other way). Try it out.

A	B	$(A \wedge B)$	$\rightarrow$	B
T	T	T	T	T
T	F	F	T	F
F	T	F	T	T
F	F	F	T	F

Example 3.39 The anti-symmetric property of a binary relation R over a set S was defined in Sec. 2.2. We can now define this formally as

$$(x, y) \in R \wedge (y, x) \in R \rightarrow x = y \text{ for each } x,\ y \in S$$

If R is the relation $<$ over the set $\mathbb{Z}$, then $x < y \wedge y < x$ is false and $x = y$ is either true or false. Therefore $<$ is anti-symmetric.

Exercise 3.38 Draw graphs to represent the following binary relations over $\{x, y, z\}$:

(a) $xRy \wedge yRz \rightarrow xRz$

(b) $xRy \wedge y \not R z \rightarrow xRz$

(c) $xRy \wedge y \not R z \rightarrow x \not R z$

where $x \not R y$ represents $(x, y) \notin R$. Which of these graphs represents a transitive relation? Use the formal definition of the connective for implication to confirm your result.

We give the following syntactic rule for the precedence of the connective $\rightarrow$.

Rule 3.6 The connectives $\wedge$ and $\vee$ have a higher precedence than $\rightarrow$.

Exercise 3.39 Use the rules of precedence to simplify $(((\neg p) \wedge r) \rightarrow q)$. At each stage state which rule you are using.

3.4.6 Conditional sentences in the English language

This subsection can be omitted by those who accept the definition that we have given for $\rightarrow$ in our formal calculus of propositions. Our intention has been to delay the introduction of $\rightarrow$ until our readers have become sufficiently aware of the contrast between the formality of logic and the expressiveness of English, to accept a precise truth-functional definition for $\rightarrow$.

We now provide some English sentences that do demonstrate the truth-functional meaning of material implication that is symbolized by $\rightarrow$. At the risk of confusing our readers, we also present English conditional sentences that are definitely not truth-functional. Our aim is to emphasize the need for precise rules for building wffs and assigning truth-values, at the risk of losing expressiveness in our calculus. First we repeat the truth table definition for $\rightarrow$ as the conditional symbol for implication:

p	q	$p \rightarrow q$
T	T	T
T	F	F
F	T	T
F	F	T

There is no exact way of expressing $p \rightarrow q$ in ordinary English but the following sentences can usually be expressed with this connective:

'if p then q', 'if p, q', 'q if p', 'p only if q', 'q provided p'

We only discuss the first two English equivalents of $\rightarrow$.

Definition 3.13 Conditional sentence When 'If ... then' connects English sentences we call the whole sentence a conditional sentence, the first constituent sentence the 'antecedent' and the second the 'consequent'.

For 'If ... then' to be truth-functional it must express material implication which is the meaning of $\rightarrow$. We can show this by finding English conditional sentences that correspond to the rows of the truth table for $\rightarrow$.

Row 1. 'If Winston Churchill is Prime Minister, then he is an MP.' (Suppose that Winston Churchill *is* the Prime Minister and consequently an MP.) This conditional sentence is *true* with both the antecedent and the consequent true.

Row 2. 'If Winston Churchill is Prime Minister, then he is not an MP.' This is a false conditional with a true antecedent and a false consequent. We cannot argue for it to be true!

Row 3. 'If Winston Churchill is not an MP then he is not the Chancellor of the Exchequer.' This is *true* with a false antecedent and a true consequent.

Row 4. 'If Winston Churchill is not an MP then he is not Prime Minister.' This is *true* with both the antecedent and the consequent false.

Exercise 3.40 Write more conditional sentences that have the same truth-value as each row of the truth table for $\rightarrow$.

Loss of truth-functionality We have shown that 'If ... then' can be truth-functional and express material implication. Now we give two reasons why 'If ... then' may not be truth-functional.

The first is that in logic if p is false then $p \rightarrow q$ is true. In an English conditional, however, p being false may not be enough to make 'If p then q' true.

Exercise 3.41 Give the truth-value of the following material implication:

[Winston Churchill is not Prime Minister $\rightarrow$ Winston Churchill is Prime Minister]

This sentence is of the form $\neg p \rightarrow p$ which was discussed on page 107 as counter-intuitive. We could also consider the following sentence as counter-intuitive:

If Gillian is not the lecturer then she is the lecturer

Example 3.40 We have already argued in Sec. 3.2 that the following English conditional sentence is false:

If Winston Churchill is not Prime Minister then he is Prime Minister

The second is that in logic if q is true then $p \to q$ is true. In English the truth of q may not be enough to make 'If p then q' true.

Exercise 3.42 Give the truth-value of the following material implication:

[Food is cheaper in London than in Hull $\to$ more people live in London than in Hull]

Example 3.41 The sentence 'If food is cheaper in London than in Hull, then more people live in London than in Hull' is false. Even though more people do live in London than in Hull, it is not just *because* food is cheaper in London than in Hull! We cannot argue that this sentence is true in English.

We have given two reasons for the loss of truth-functionality for some conditional statements. They show that when we move away from material implication, which is the definition of $\to$, we lose truth-functionality. There are many kinds of conditional statement in English, however, and each asserts a different kind of implication. We give the following as examples.

Causal implication In the following conditional statement 'If a lump of ice is put into hot water, the ice melts', the form of implication is *causal*. The translation into logic is

[Lump of ice is put into hot water $\to$ lump of ice melts]

The proposition is true if the ice is *not* put into water. It is only false if the ice *is* put into hot water but does not melt.

Exercise 3.43 Identify a previous example as one of causal implication and explain why the sentence is false.

Logical implication The conditional statement 'If all men are mortal and Socrates is a man, then Socrates is mortal' involves reasoning and is presented as a logical argument in Chapter 5.

Definitional implication In the statement 'If grandfather is bald, then grandfather has no hair' the form of implication is definitional and can be translated as

[Grandfather is bald $\to$ grandfather has no hair]

We consider this sentence to be false if grandfather is bald *and* has long hair!

Intentional implication The statement 'If $2 + 1 = 5$ then I will jump in the river' describes an intention that is not true. However, the proposition

[$2 + 1 = 5 \to$ I will jump in the river]

is true because the antecedent is false!

Material implication To complete the types of conditional sentence, we give another example of the implication that *is* represented by $\to$. The statement 'You will get paid provided you do some work' is translated as

[You do some work $\to$ you will get paid]

Translating conditional sentences into logic Once the analysis of English sentences and their translation into logic has been mastered, the notion of algebraic equivalence in the formal model of the calculus can be exploited. By translating conditional sentences we also prepare for making proofs in the calculus. If we do not translate correctly we are unlikely to be able to carry out our proofs correctly.

There are some sentences that use 'if' but should not be translated by $\rightarrow$ in the propositional calculus.

Example 3.42 The English sentence 'The team was energetic, if a little tense' translates to

[The team was energetic $\wedge$ the team was a little tense]

in the propositional calculus.

Example 3.43 Are the symbolic expressions for the following sentences equivalent?

(a) If it is sunny and my homework is done, I am going out.

(b) If it is sunny, then, if my homework is done, I am going out.

As suggested in Sec. 3.3, we work from the truth functor of largest scope inwards where more than one truth functor is used in an English sentence. Then sentence (a) has the structure

[It is sunny and my homework is done $\rightarrow$ I am going out]

Analysing the next largest constituent sentence gives the structure

[[It is sunny] $\wedge$ [my homework is done] $\rightarrow$ I am going out]

Now let
p: 'it is sunny'
q: 'my homework is done'
r: 'I am going out'

Then sentence (a) may be symbolized by $(p \wedge q) \rightarrow r$. In sentence (b) the truth functor of largest scope is 'If ... then'. The truth functor for the constituent sentence is 'If ...'. Therefore sentence (b) has the structure

[It is sunny] $\rightarrow$ [[my homework is done $\rightarrow$ I am going out]]

which is symbolized by $p \rightarrow (q \rightarrow r)$.

Now	$(p \wedge q) \rightarrow r$	$\equiv$	$\neg(p \wedge q) \vee r$	since $A \rightarrow B \equiv \neg A \vee B$
		$\equiv$	$\neg p \vee \neg q \vee r$	by De Morgan
but	$p \rightarrow (q \rightarrow r)$	$\equiv$	$\neg p \vee (q \rightarrow r)$	since $A \rightarrow B \equiv \neg A \vee B$
		$\equiv$	$\neg p \vee (\neg q \vee r)$	
		$\equiv$	$\neg p \vee \neg q \vee r$	by the associative law

So they are equivalent!

By stating in Sec. 3.2.4 that $\rightarrow$ has a lower precedence than $\wedge$ we allow the brackets in $(p \wedge q) \rightarrow r$ to be dropped. Informally we say that $\wedge$ 'applies to as little as possible'!

We presented syntactic rules of precedence in Sec. 3.2.4. There is no agreement in the literature on the rules of precedence when $\rightarrow$ is used repeatedly, however. Some authors use association to the right so that $p \rightarrow q \rightarrow r$ stands for $p \rightarrow (q \rightarrow r)$. Others use association to the left giving $(p \rightarrow q) \rightarrow r$.

Exercise 3.44 Show that the symbolic expressions for the following sentences are equivalent in the propositional calculus:

(a) If it is raining then I shall get wet.

(b) It is not raining or I shall get wet.

(c) I shall not get wet if it is not raining.

Example 3.44 Analyse the sentence 'If Charlie cycles home then Charlie is late for supper if his tyre is punctured'. The overall form is 'if p then q' and the connective of largest scope is $\rightarrow$. We have the structure

[Charlie cycles home $\rightarrow$ Charlie is late for supper if his tyre is punctured]

Now we find the next largest constituent sentence which has no connective symbol in it. This is

Charlie is late for supper if his tyre is punctured

and has the form 'q if p'. The logical connective is $\rightarrow$ and gives the form $p \rightarrow q$. The correct analysis is then

[Charlie cycles home $\rightarrow$[Charlie's tyre is punctured $\rightarrow$ Charlie is late for supper]]

Many of the problems in this section have concerned the translation of English sentences, many of which are ambiguous, into the precise language of logic. This translation is part of the modelling process described in Fig. 1.8.

Exercise 3.45 Draw the particular modelling diagram for the translation of the previous example sentence 'If Charlie cycles home then Charlie is late for supper if his tyre is punctured'. Show that $p \rightarrow (r \rightarrow q) \equiv (p \wedge r) \rightarrow q$.

Add this result to your diagram. Can we deduce that the natural language sentences represented by these formal sentences are equivalent? Discuss the advantages and disadvantages encountered by moving into the setting of formal logic.

3.4.7 The meta-level connective $\Rightarrow$

We have seen that we should not interpret $p \rightarrow q$ as

'p causes q'
'q results from p'
'p is sufficient for q'
'q is a necessary condition for p'

since these are assertions that link p and q by some cause. This is much stronger than the situation we have with $p \rightarrow q$ and we shall work with this later. We shall introduce the notation $p \Rightarrow q$ to represent the *assertion*, made at a meta-level to the propositional calculus, that

'p is sufficient for q'

This is the notation that is often used to represent a theorem in mathematics. If we do have a cause and effect relationship then of course we can deduce the weaker relationship $\rightarrow$ between p and q.

Exercise 3.46 Let x be any natural number. Give the truth-value of 'x is prime $\Rightarrow$ the only divisors of x are 1 and x itself'. Consider the cases when

(a) $x = 6$

(b) $x = 11$

Exercise 3.47 Give the truth-value of 'for any integer x, x is odd $\rightarrow$ x is not divisible by 2'. Consider the cases when

(a) $x = 3$

(b) $x = 6$

Exercise 3.48 Give the truth-value of 'If $A \subseteq B$ and $a \in A$ then $a \in B$', when

$$A = \{1, 2, 3\}$$
$$B = \{3, 4, 5\}$$

for *each* element in A. Can we write this as an assertion using $\Rightarrow$?

3.4.8 The connective for equivalence

The final logical connective we introduce represents the notion of equivalence between propositions *within* the propositional calculus. The symbol $\leftrightarrow$ is called the biconditional symbol. Thus 'p is equivalent to q' or 'p if and only if q' or 'p iff q' or 'p implies and is implied by q' or 'p precisely if q' or 'p just if q' are *all* denoted by $p \leftrightarrow q$.

The truth table is defined by:

p	q	$p \leftrightarrow q$
T	T	T
T	F	F
F	T	F
F	F	T

We see that $p \leftrightarrow q$ is T precisely when p and q have the same truth-value.

Exercise 3.49 Show that if $p \leftrightarrow q$ is true then $p \rightarrow q$ and $q \rightarrow p$ are both true. Conversely, show that if $p \rightarrow q$ and $q \rightarrow p$ are both true then $p \leftrightarrow q$ is true; that is show that $(p \leftrightarrow q) \equiv (p \rightarrow q) \wedge (q \rightarrow p)$.

Equivalence can be thought of as 'double implication' or 'implication both ways'. Although $\leftrightarrow$ is derived from $\rightarrow$ and $\{\neg, \rightarrow\}$ is a complete set of connectives, we must be careful not to assume that $\{\neg, \leftrightarrow\}$ is complete. There are only two connectives that when added to $\neg$ do *not* form a complete set. These are $\oplus$ and $\leftrightarrow$.

The following syntactic rule compares the precedence of the connectives $\rightarrow$ and $\leftrightarrow$.

Rule 3.7 The connective $\rightarrow$ has a higher precedence than $\leftrightarrow$.

Exercise 3.50 Use the rules of precedence to simplify $((\neg(\neg q) \wedge (p \rightarrow r)) \leftrightarrow (\neg((\neg r) \vee q)))$. At each stage state which rule you are using.

Exercise 3.51 Define $\leftrightarrow$ in terms of $\oplus$ and any other connective.

Exercise 3.52 Show that $\{\wedge, \leftrightarrow, \oplus\}$ is a complete set of connectives, but that no proper subset is complete.

Since $\leftrightarrow$ is derived from the symbol $\rightarrow$ for implication, we must emphasize that $\leftrightarrow$ is also simply a logical connective. In connecting p and q by $\leftrightarrow$ we allow that p and q may have any of the possible combinations of the truth-values true or false. This enables us to differentiate between the logical connective $\leftrightarrow$ and the mathematical symbol $\equiv$. In connecting two propositions by $\equiv$, we automatically exclude the two cases where the propositions differ in truth-value, that is the *assertion* that

$p \equiv q$ means the same as truth-value: $(p \leftrightarrow q) \mapsto$ true

(Here we use the symbol $\mapsto$ to denote the assignment by the truth-value function of a truth-value to a *specific* proposition.) We forget the second and third lines of the above truth table. We have already seen, for example, that $p \equiv \neg\neg p$.

This distinction highlights the need for a language to *talk about* propositions and the propositional calculus *over and above* the formal language of the propositional calculus itself. It also highlights the difference between a *proposition* that *may* be either true or false and an *assertion* that states that a proposition is true or false. The symbol $\equiv$ is part of a meta-language for the propositional calculus and is described as a *meta-symbol*.

In summary we make the connection between the meta-symbol, $\equiv$, and the logical symbol, $\leftrightarrow$, which is *within* our language. If P, Q are any (compound) propositions then $P \equiv Q$ is the same as saying that $P \leftrightarrow Q$ is a tautology.

Exercise 3.53 Show that $(p \rightarrow q) \equiv (\neg p \vee q)$ and hence that $(p \rightarrow q) \leftrightarrow (\neg p \vee q)$ is a tautology.

3.4.9 A short cut to truth tables

Truth tables provide a general method for deciding whether or not a wff is a tautology. For wffs that have hundreds of propositional symbols, however, the method becomes too cumbersome. Methods that reduce the work involved are particularly useful in the design of automated theorem provers. We introduce these methods by suggesting a short cut to using truth tables that involves some additional reasoning at a meta-level to the calculus.

Exercise 3.54 Draw a truth table to show that $\neg(p \wedge q) \not\equiv \neg p \wedge \neg q$. Identify the one row in the table that is required to show that these two wffs are not equivalent.

Let $P(p, q, r)$ be the wff $p \vee (q \wedge r) \leftrightarrow (p \vee q) \wedge (p \vee r)$.

Exercise 3.55 Draw the truth table with eight rows that demonstrates that $P(p, q, r)$ is a tautology.

We can avoid drawing all eight rows of the previous table by working selectively from the first line in which p is true and $P(p, q, r)$ is true. Now assume that p is false and in the second row assume q is also false. Then again the wff is true. Then assume q is true and r is true, noting that q and r are symmetric in the wff.

Exercise 3.56 Draw out only the rows in the truth table for the previous exercise that have been specified in the previous argument. Enter only those values that have been used in the argument.

Exercise 3.57 Reason that $p \rightarrow (q \rightarrow p)$ is a tautology without drawing a full truth table, but entering only those values that are required. In addition repeat this exercise for the wff $p \wedge (q \vee r) \leftrightarrow (p \wedge q) \vee (p \wedge r)$.

Exercise 3.58 Reason that $(p \rightarrow (q \rightarrow r)) \rightarrow ((p \rightarrow q) \rightarrow (p \rightarrow r))$ is a tautology without using all eight rows of the truth table.

Exercise 3.59 Reason that $(\neg q \rightarrow \neg p) \rightarrow ((\neg q \rightarrow p) \rightarrow q)$ is a tautology without drawing a full truth table.

Exercise 3.60 Reason that $((p \wedge q) \rightarrow r) \rightarrow s) \rightarrow ((p \rightarrow r) \rightarrow s)$ is a tautology without using all 16 rows of the truth table.

3.5 LOGICAL AXIOMS FOR THE PROPOSITIONAL CALCULUS

We have put a lot of effort into building a collection of tautologies within our propositional calculus that always have the value T in the truth table. You may have been wondering whether there is some effective procedure for generating all the tautologies in a logic. The answer is 'yes'! If we define a suitable subset of wffs as logical axioms, we can then generate from the wffs all the tautologies of the propositional calculus. No information about an application is required. We shall see in Chapter 4 how the tautologies are generated from the logical axioms in an axiom deduction system. The logical axioms are themselves a subset of the tautologies and can be written down without reference to any other wff in the language of the propositional calculus.

Logical axioms describe the *kind* of logic that is used to describe some application domain. They do not describe objects in the application domain, however. We shall see in later chapters that this is done by *non-logical axioms* that express, in both logical and non-logical symbols, the properties of the objects and operations of a particular application. The *theory* of the application is built by deductions from the non-logical axioms.

The logical axioms for the propositional calculus are

1 $p \to (q \to p)$

2 $p \to (q \to r) \to (p \to q) \to (p \to r)$

3 $(\neg q \to \neg p) \to ((\neg q \to p) \to q)$

We can give intuitive 'meanings' for these axioms. The first axiom could be interpreted as meaning 'if p holds, then p is implied by some other proposition that we may choose to call q'. This would seem to be a sensible starting point for reasoning in any logic.

Exercise 3.61 Give intuitive meanings for the logical axioms 2 and 3.

We have given the logical axioms in a rather restricted form, however, as referring only to the propositions p, q and r. A more powerful presentation would be to generalize over *all* wffs and to present the logical axioms as axiom *schema*:

Axiom 1 $\quad A \to (B \to A)$
Axiom 2 $\quad (A \to (B \to C)) \to ((A \to B) \to (A \to C))$
Axiom 3 $\quad (\neg B \to \neg A) \to ((\neg B \to A) \to B)$

where A, B and C can be replaced by any wff.

Exercise 3.62 Produce an *instance* of an axiom schema by replacing A by $\neg p \wedge q$, B by $p \vee r$ and C by $\neg q$ in the second schema.

Now we have an infinitely large set of axioms for our calculus. We have given the logical axioms in terms only of the connective $\to$. A formal presentation of the propositional calculus would state the axiom schema initially in this form, and then proceed to derive all the tautologies in terms of the rest of the logical connectives from these axiom schema. Our own approach has been to begin at a less abstract level, with the more intuitively obvious connectives. We have delayed the definition of the logical axioms in terms of $\rightarrow$ until our readers are (we hope) aware of the advantages of taking a formal syntactic approach that is without real meaning!

Exercise 3.63 Rewrite the first axiom scheme in terms of the connectives $\neg$ and $\vee$, and prove that the resulting wff is a tautology.

Since $\{\neg, \rightarrow\}$ is complete we are clearly able to express the axiom schema in terms of any other logical connectives.

3.6 SUMMARY

At the beginning of this chapter we identified the axiomatic approach as one that is useful for the construction and analysis of discrete systems. Because the mathematical concepts that underlie the building of complex systems are very abstract and difficult to understand, we have chosen to concentrate on studying the structure of the *sentences* that express the axioms rather than on the meaning of the sentences. This we believe to be a sensible choice! The syntactic approach to studying axioms and theorems as concrete sentences helps us to *begin* to understand the abstract meanings of these sentences. Patience is needed at this stage—it takes time and effort to acquire the ability to work with abstract concepts.

We define an axiomatic system as a formal language with a set of axioms and a set of rules of inference. We have made progress with the first two ingredients, but leave the definition of the inference rules and the proof of theorems until the next chapter. Our formal language is the language of sentences, precisely defined as propositions. Within our calculus we gave carefully defined syntactic rules for building propositions. The semantics for the language is the simple assignment of a unique truth-value to each proposition. The wffs of the calculus are constructed by the propositional connectives and the semantics of each connective is defined by its truth table. An important rule within the calculus is that the meaning of all the propositions that we construct is truth-functional.

Our intuitive approach emphasizes the contrast between the precision and lack of ambiguity of a formal language and the expressiveness of a natural language. We have encouraged movement *in to* the formal system in order to gain experience in manipulating expressions according to formal rules of equivalence; also we have encouraged movement *out of* the formal system in order to interpret results in a natural language. An axiomatic system should be a familiar tool that helps us to understand abstract concepts and to put our understanding to practical use. For a tool to be useful we need to stay in command of it. If formal logic appears only to be some meaningless activity within which we manipulate symbols, we are not in command of it and cannot comprehend how it can be used as a powerful tool.

Our approach has been to present the simplest logical connectives at the beginning of the chapter and to develop experience in both translating and manipulating wffs built from these connectives. To our 'experienced' reader we then introduce the connective $\rightarrow$ and finally the logical axioms for the calculus. We shall build on the connective $\rightarrow$ in Chapter 4 by defining inference rules that enable theorems to be deduced from the axioms. Our calculus is too simple, however, and we need to develop the predicate calculus in Chapter 5 before we can be confident about understanding and reasoning about the systems that we discussed in Chapter 1.

3.7 FURTHER EXERCISES

Exercise 3.64 Show that the following equivalences hold and deduce that $\{ \mid \}$ is complete:

(a) $\neg p \equiv p \mid p$

(b) $p \vee q \equiv (p \mid p) \mid (q \mid q)$

(c) $p \wedge q \equiv (p \mid q) \mid (p \mid q)$

Exercise 3.65 For each of the following, find equivalent expressions that use only the $\downarrow$ connective:

(a) $\neg p$

(b) $p \vee q$

(c) $p \wedge q$

Exercise 3.66 Give the sets of operations within the algebra of sets that are complete.

Exercise 3.67 Show that $(p \leftrightarrow q) \rightarrow (q \leftrightarrow p)$ and $(p \leftrightarrow q) \wedge (q \leftrightarrow r) \rightarrow (p \leftrightarrow r)$ are also tautologies.

Exercise 3.68 Show that $p \rightarrow q \equiv \neg p \vee q$.

Exercise 3.69 Use the propositional calculus to represent the following statement in symbolic form: 'I shall pay the poll tax if I am asked to and I haven't spent all my money'.

Exercise 3.70 Use a truth table to determine whether $(p \rightarrow q) \wedge (q \rightarrow r) \leftrightarrow (p \rightarrow r)$ is a tautology.

Exercise 3.71 By Exercise 3.68 we have seen that $\rightarrow$ can be expressed in terms of $\vee$ and $\neg$. Find a way of expressing $\oplus$ using

(a) only $\wedge, \vee$ and $\neg$

(b) only $\vee$ and $\neg$

Exercise 3.72 For each of the following expressions, use identities to find equivalent expressions that use only $\vee$ and $\neg$ and are as simple as possible:

(a) $(p \wedge q) \vee \neg p$

(b) $(p \rightarrow (q \vee \neg r)) \wedge \neg p \wedge q$

(c) $\neg p \wedge \neg q \wedge (\neg r \rightarrow p)$

Exercise 3.73 Which of the following is a negation of the statement 'Some people like applied mathematics'?

(a) Some people dislike applied mathematics.

(b) Everybody dislikes applied mathematics.

(c) Some people like pure mathematics.

(d) Everybody likes applied mathematics.

Exercise 3.74 Which of the following logical expressions is equivalent to $(p \vee q) \wedge (p \vee \neg q)$?

(a) $p \wedge q$

(b) $p \vee q$

(c) p

(d) q

Exercise 3.75 Show that $\leftrightarrow$ is self-transitive; that is $[(p \leftrightarrow q) \leftrightarrow (q \leftrightarrow r)] \leftrightarrow (p \leftrightarrow r)$.

Exercise 3.76 A woman who was captured by a crowd of football enthusiasts was promised her freedom if she could determine with a single 'yes' or 'no' question the colour of their team's shirts. She knew the colour was either black or white. Unfortunately, the crowd contained only two kinds of individuals: liars, who invariably gave the wrong answer to any question they were asked, and truth-tellers, who invariably gave the right answer.

How did the 'victim' save herself?

Exercise 3.77 Write in English the inverse, converse and contrapositive for the statement 'If you run, then you will catch the bus'. Which of these are *not* equivalent to the original statement?

Exercise 3.78 Use the propositional calculus to represent the following statement in symbolic form: 'We shall swim, provided we can find a shady beach, only if the sun shines.'

FURTHER READING

The logical analysis of sentences is presented in more detail in the book by Hodges (1977). A comprehensive treatment of logic for information theory is given in Galton (1990). The book by Enderton (1972) is a classic which treats the subject of mathematical logic at a greater depth than we do.

Chapter 4

PROOF

In this chapter we build on our formal language of propositions, in which a subset of the wffs are logical axioms, by defining rules of inference that enable us to deduce theorems formally from the logical axioms. Because the formal process of proof by logical deduction seems far removed from the informal style of mathematical proof used in Chapter 2, we begin by presenting some informal proofs before we trace the development of formal deductive systems in logic. The emergence of computer science as a discipline has stimulated the formalization and automation of proof systems, and we introduce the logical system of proof by natural deduction as an appropriate foundation for our work in constructing systems.

As in Chapter 3 we follow an order of presentation that is more intuitive than the classical presentation. We begin with a semantic notion of proof, in Sec. 4.2, that is based on the truth-values of propositions and introduce the meta-level symbol, $\models$, which we call the 'semantic turnstile'. This semantic notion of entailment is based on the assignment of truth-values to propositions and the algebraic notion of equivalence, introduced in Chapter 3. A deductive notion of proof that is not based on truth-values is introduced in Sec. 4.3. The syntactic process of deduction is symbolized by $\vdash$ and called the 'consequence relation' or 'turnstile'. We show that the traditional axiomatic style of proof, based on logical axioms, requires only one inference rule: *modus ponens*. The converse of this inference rule is the important theorem *about* a logical calculus, called the deduction theorem. No axioms are assumed for our natural deduction proof system; instead two sets of inference rules define the logical connectives. Finally, we show that we can move between the syntactic consequence relation for the derivation of proofs and the semantic consequence relation that depends on the truth-values of the premises and conclusion of an argument. We explain that this movement is possible because propositional logic has the property of completeness.

4.1 INFORMAL PROOFS IN MATHEMATICS

A mathematician usually 'proves' a theorem informally by arguing, in some natural language, that the theorem is true. The argument is usually given in distinct stages, to someone else, with the aim of convincing the other person that the *assertion* of the theorem is true. The notion that an assertion is *true* is also usually informal and refers to some particular problem.

Example 4.1 A theorem asserts that 'If x is an even integer then x^2 is an even integer'. The proof argues informally that the theorem is true:

'Suppose x is an even integer. Then there is some integer k such that $x = 2k$. By squaring we get $x^2 = 4k^2 = 2(2k^2)$. But this is in the form of an even integer. Therefore x^2 is even.'

In the argument, English is used as a *meta-language* to justify the assertion about mathematics, which is itself studied in an *object language*.

Many mathematicians will introduce some logical notation to make their proof shorter and also to explicitly state a theorem as an assertion. We introduced the notation $p \Rightarrow q$ in Sec. 3.4.7 to express the *assertion* that $p \rightarrow q$ is always a true proposition. Mathematicians use $\Rightarrow$ to express the causal relationship in mathematical theorems.

Example 4.2 The theorem $a \mid b \ \wedge \ b \mid c \Rightarrow a \mid c$, where $\mid$ means 'divides', is in number theory. An informal proof argues: '$a \mid b$ means that there is some number n such that $an = b$. Similarly, $b \mid c$ means there is some number m such that $bm = c$. Substituting for b gives $anm = c$. Therefore, a divides c.'

These informal arguments short cut the formal axiomatic approach which starts by assuming the primitive definitions and axioms of number theory. We do the same when we pay the milk bill. In this chapter, however, we want to establish a formal deductive calculus with inference rules that will mirror the informal proofs given by mathematicians. The advantage of a formal proof system is that it can be automated. The power of a formal proof system is that it is purely symbolic and does not require a notion of meaning from some application domain. The formal system *abstracts* over the detail of different application domains; the non-logical symbols and the non-logical axioms express the properties of the application.

There are limitations to our formal approach, however! Any axiomatic theory relies on the assumed definitions and axioms. If these do not hold, even though our reasoning is valid, we cannot assert that our conclusions hold. The notion of 'truth' is elusive! We have to rely in the end on our intuitions and observations to guide us in accepting 'true' assumptions.

4.2 SEMANTIC CONSEQUENCE

An informal argument that a theorem in mathematics is true begins by assuming the truth of the premises of the theorem and then, by arguing in distinct stages, demonstrates 'therefore' that the conclusion of the theorem is true. In order to mirror this informal process in our formal language we need some meta-level symbol to represent the *process* of arguing in distinct stages from a set of premises that are true, in order to reach a true conclusion as a *consequence* of the argument. Before defining a symbol for the result of the process of arguing that a proof is true, we develop a notion of *satisfaction* for a proposition.

Definition 4.1 Satisfaction The function truth-value is said to satisfy a proposition if it assigns the value 'true' to that proposition.

The function truth-value was defined over the set of *all* propositions in Def. 3.6. It is an *extension* of the function that assigns truth-values to the simple propositions. In a truth table, every row represents a truth-value function from the set of propositional symbols to the set $\{T, F\}$ as abbreviations for the set {true, false}.

Example 4.3 In the truth table for $\rightarrow$, if truth-value(p) $= T$ and truth-value(q) $= F$ then truth-value($p \rightarrow q$) $= F$. Otherwise truth-value($p \rightarrow q$) $= T$ and *satisfies* the compound proposition $p \rightarrow q$.

Exercise 4.1 Which rows in the truth table for the connective $\rightarrow$ satisfy the proposition $p \rightarrow q$?

Now we define, at a meta-level to the propositional calculus, a symbol to represent the informal argument that a conclusion follows from a set of premises if the assumption that the premises are true guarantees that the conclusion is true.

Definition 4.2 Semantic consequence The proposition P is a semantic consequence of the set of propositions, Γ, if and only if every truth assignment for the propositions in Γ and for P which satisfies every member of Γ also satisfies P. We write $\Gamma \models P$, and call the symbol $\models$ the 'semantic turnstile'.

The notation $\Gamma \models P$ can also be read as 'Γ semantically entails P', or 'Γ tautologically implies P'.

The assignment of the value true or false to a proposition by the truth-value function is an *interpretation* of that proposition by the value true or false. An interpretation that makes the proposition true is also called a *model* for that proposition. We can then say that $\Gamma \models P$ if and only if every model of Γ is also a model of P. The notion of a model that we use is the more concrete mathematical model that we introduced in Chapter 3.

Example 4.4 If Γ is $\emptyset$ we write $\models P$ and say that P is a tautology. So $\models p \vee \neg p$, since $P(p)$ is satisfied by *all* truth assignments.

Example 4.5 If no truth assignment satisfies Γ then it is vacuously true that P is satisfied. So $\{p, \neg p\} \models q$. Here $\Gamma = \{p, \neg p\}$ and P is $P(q)$.

Example 4.6 $\{p, p \rightarrow q\} \models q$. Only one truth-value assignment satisfies both p and $p \rightarrow q$. This is the row in the truth table when both p and q are true. Clearly this also satisfies q.

Exercise 4.2 Decide whether the following expressions of semantic entailment hold:

(a) $\neg p,\ q \vee p \models q$

(b) $p \wedge q \models p \vee q$

(c) $p \vee q \models p \wedge q$

(d) $\models p \rightarrow (p \vee q)$

Our new meta-level notation for semantic consequence can now be used to define the meta-level symbol, $\equiv$, that we introduced in Sec. 3.2.4. Recall that $P \equiv Q$ when $P \leftrightarrow Q$ is a tautology. Therefore $P \equiv Q$ iff $\models P \leftrightarrow Q$.

It is important to keep the concepts represented by these three symbols distinct:

$P \leftrightarrow Q$	is a proposition within the propositional calculus that may be true or false.
$P \equiv Q$	is an assertion at a meta-level that $P \leftrightarrow Q$ is always true.
$P \models Q$	is an assertion that Q is a semantic consequence of the singleton set $\{P\}$ (we can write $P \models Q$ instead of $\{P\} \models Q$).

Exercise 4.3 Let P be $p \rightarrow q$ and Q be $\neg p \vee q$. Argue that if $P \models Q$ and $Q \models P$ then $P \equiv Q$. Also argue that if $P \equiv Q$ then $P \models Q$ and $Q \models P$.

Exercise 4.4 Provide a counter-example to the assertion that if $P \models Q$ then $Q \models P$.

4.2.1 The rule of equivalence

You should by now be able to argue confidently that if $P \equiv Q$ then $P \models Q$ and $Q \models P$. The semantically based notion of equivalence that depends on the truth-value of propositions provides us with our first rule of inference. We have already used the rule implicitly, but now state it explicitly.

> **Rule 4.1 Rule of equivalence** At any stage of an argument we can replace any proposition by an equivalent proposition.

By definition this means that within any compound proposition we can replace any proposition by an equivalent one. For example, within a compound proposition $p \rightarrow q$ can be replaced by $\neg p \vee q$.

This rule justifies the modelling process that we presented in Fig. 1.8. We can move into the most convenient system for working and making deductions, and then finally interpret our results back to the physical world. We prefer not to call this rule the 'rule of substitution' because the name is more appropriate for a rule that we introduce in Chapter 5.

Example 4.7 We use the rule of equivalence to argue that when $((p \rightarrow q) \vee (p \rightarrow r)) \rightarrow (q \vee r)$ is the proposition $P(p, q, r)$ and $p \vee q \vee r$ is the proposition $Q(p, q, r)$ then $P \models Q$.

Now $((p \rightarrow q) \vee (p \rightarrow r)) \rightarrow (q \vee r)$

$\equiv$	$((\neg p \vee q) \vee (\neg p \vee r)) \rightarrow (q \vee r)$	since $p \rightarrow q \equiv \neg p \vee q$
$\equiv$	$((\neg p \vee \neg p) \vee (q \vee r)) \rightarrow (q \vee r)$	by the commutative and associative laws
$\equiv$	$(\neg p \vee (q \vee r)) \rightarrow (q \vee r)$	since $\neg p \vee \neg p \equiv \neg p$
$\equiv$	$\neg(\neg p \vee (q \vee r)) \vee (q \vee r)$	since $p \rightarrow q \equiv \neg p \vee q$
$\equiv$	$(p \wedge \neg(q \vee r)) \vee (q \vee r)$	by De Morgan
$\equiv$	$(p \vee (q \vee r)) \wedge (\neg(q \vee r) \vee (q \vee r))$	by the distributive law
$\equiv$	$(p \vee q \vee r) \wedge T$	by the law of complement
$\equiv$	$p \vee q \vee r$	by the law of identity

We have used the rule of equivalence at *each* step in the argument to show that

$$((p \rightarrow q) \vee (p \rightarrow r)) \rightarrow (q \vee r) \equiv p \vee q \vee r$$

We could have demonstrated the equivalence by drawing a large truth table. Since this equivalence holds, not only does $P \models Q$ but also $Q \models P$.

The method of carrying out a proof in stages will be used in the syntactic style of proof by natural deduction.

4.3 A DEDUCTIVE PROOF CALCULUS

The notion of semantic consequence depends on truth tables. A more useful calculus for formal proofs enables a deductive process of reasoning to take place purely by the syntactic manipulation of symbols. In this section we present a deductive calculus that is independent of interpretation by some model and amenable to automation. The formal derivation of a mathematical proof is presented as an array of wffs.

Definition 4.3 Formal deduction The deduction of the wff Q from a set of wffs Γ is a finite sequence of wffs ending in Q that record how Q was derived from Γ by rules of inference. Each wff in the finite sequence is either:

(a) a member of Γ that may be a non-logical axiom,

(b) a member of the set of logical axioms or

(c) a consequence of applying an inference rule to one or more of the wffs that occur earlier in the sequence.

A formal deductive system is an essential part of any logical calculus. For the propositional calculus, the axioms and the rules of the calculus contain only propositions. The *presentation* of the axioms and the rules varies, however. In an axiomatic system, first suggested by Hilbert in 1925, there is only one inference rule, the axioms are of central importance and the rules for forming the logical connectives are defined in terms of axioms. In a natural deduction system, suggested by Gentzen in 1935, the inference rules are of central importance and the logical connectives are defined in terms of these rules. Gentzen suggested his system, in which no axioms are assumed, because it had more in common with the style of deduction that was used by mathematicians.

At a meta-level to the calculus of propositions, with axioms and rules, there are the theorems and relations that 'talk about' the calculus. We have already defined the semantic turnstile, $\models$, in Sec. 4.2, as talking about a relationship of semantic consequence between propositions. The relationship of formal deduction between propositions is described by the syntactic turnstile, $\vdash$, and is called a *consequence relation*. This relation is used to talk about the axiomatic and natural deduction systems for propositional logic. It is important to note that we remain within the propositional calculus throughout this chapter. The relation $\vdash$ has also been developed into its own 'turnstile calculus' that relates sets and formulae in a more general logic. The turnstile calculus is itself given an axiomatic and natural deduction presentation, and uses a notation that is more complicated than we require here.

Other systems for presenting logical deduction, which we do not describe, are the sequent calculus and intuitionistic logic and each of these can be used to present the propositional calculus or the more general turnstile calculus. Intuitionistic logic is not presented in this book, but is likely to be very important in future developments in the specification of discrete systems. Of particular interest is the constructive type theory of Martin-Löf (1984), which builds on the constructive approach of intuitionism. Martin-Löf has created a philosophy of mathematics with a formal set of rules that is based on sets as data structures and proofs as programs. We discuss the relationships between constructive type theory and programming in Chapter 11.

4.3.1 The syntactic turnstile $\vdash$

This symbol represents a consequence relation between the premises of a formal deduction and the consequence.

Definition 4.4 Consequence relation In a formal deduction when a proposition Q is a consequence of a finite set of other propositions, Γ, we say that Q is related to Γ by the consequence relation and write $\Gamma \vdash Q$.

The symbol $\vdash$ is also called just 'turnstile' or the 'derivability relation'.

It is important to note the change from $\models$ to $\vdash$. The horizontal bar added to form $\models$ identifies it as a *semantic* assertion concerning truth. The symbol $\vdash$ merely asserts that a deduction is made.

Definition 4.5 Deduction of a theorem We write $P_1, \ldots, P_n \vdash Q$ to mean that Q is derivable from the premises $P_1, \ldots, P_n$ by rules of inference. If $\Gamma = \{P_1, \ldots, P_n\}$

then $\Gamma \vdash Q$ says that Q is derivable as a theorem from Γ. If the deduction of Q from Γ is made, we can assert that Q follows as a theorem.

Definition 4.6 Assertion of a theorem If $\Gamma = \{P_1, \ldots, P_n\}$ the formula $\Gamma \Rightarrow Q$ asserts that the theorem Q is true.

The distinction is sometimes made between a derivation $\Gamma \vdash Q$ and the *proof* $\vdash Q$ which is a derivation from an empty premise.

4.3.2 An axiomatic system

We identified the set of logical axioms as axiom schema for the propositional calculus in Sec. 3.5. Clearly each logical axiom is derivable from the empty premise. We write $\vdash_{\text{Ax}}$ to identify the consequence relation for the axiomatic system of deduction.

Example 4.8 The proof $\vdash_{\text{Ax}} A \to (B \to A)$ holds within the formal propositional calculus.

Exercise 4.5 Express the proofs that the other two axiom schema are derivable from the empty premise.

From the set of logical axioms, built from the connective $\to$, the theorems of the propositional calculus that define the remaining logical connectives can be derived. The rules about the propositional connectives are therefore built into the infinite set of axioms that are expressed by the axiom schema. In an axiomatic proof system only one *inference* rule is required to reduce the theorems of the system from the infinite set of logical axioms.

4.3.3 *Modus ponens*

An axiomatic proof system for the propositional calculus has *modus ponens* as its only rule for deducing all the wffs of the calculus from the logical axiom schema. We can say that all the wffs are *generated* from the axiom schema by *modus ponens*. The rule asserts that if A and if also $A \to B$ then we may deduce B. We symbolize this as

$$\frac{\begin{array}{c} A \\ A \to B \end{array}}{B}$$

where A and B are any wffs. We shall use this presentation for all our rules of inference. The symbol under the horizontal line represents the consequence of the vertical list of symbols above the line. The *form* of the propositional symbols gives the meaning of the rule which is also called the rule of *detachment*.

Example 4.9 We derive the tautology $p \to p$ from the axiom schema of page 114. We can replace A, B and C by any wff. It is difficult to see how we apply *modus ponens* to derive $p \to p$ from the first or third axiom schema. The second schema is more useful to us!

1 In Axiom 2 we substitute p for C, p for A and $p \to p$ for B. This gives

$$p \to ((p \to p) \to p)) \to ((p \to (p \to p)) \to (p \to p))$$

2 Now substitute in Axiom 1 as in step 1 but only for A and B to get

$$p \to ((p \to p) \to p)$$

3 Now use *modus ponens* on steps 1 and 2 as premises to get $(p \to (p \to p)) \to (p \to p)$ as a conclusion.

4 Now substitute p for A and for B in Axiom 1 to get $p \to (p \to p)$.

5 Using *modus ponens* on steps 3 and 4 now gives the conclusion $p \to p$.

Therefore we write $\vdash_{Ax} p \to p$.

The problem with the axiomatic system of deduction is that the axioms do not appear to be natural. We have given the axiom schema of implication. From this schema we can derive axioms about the connectives $\wedge$ and $\vee$. Some of these are: $A \wedge A \to A$, $A \to (B \to A \wedge B)$ and $A \to (A \vee B)$.

We also need to make clear in our deduction which wffs belong to the set of axioms called Ax and which belong to the non-logical set of wffs called Γ.

Definition 4.7 Theorem The theorems of Γ are those wffs that can be formally deduced from $\Gamma \cup \text{Ax}$. We write $\Gamma \vdash Q$ when Q is a theorem of Γ.

It is important to understand that an axiom system is defined by its set of axioms and its set of inference rules. In one axiom system, Ax_1, we may have $\Gamma \vdash_{\text{Ax}_1} Q$. If Γ is added to the set of axioms in a second axiom system, Ax_2, however, we would then have $\vdash_{\text{Ax}_2} Q$, giving Q as a tautology.

Modus ponens was originally used within the axiomatic system with only axioms as the premises. We shall see within the natural deduction system that the rule has been generalized to have any wffs as premises. In the following example A and B are any propositions and A and $A \to B$ are statements that we have either assumed or deduced from inference rules.

Example 4.10 We take as our premises

'If Gary plays well then the team plays well.'

'Gary is playing well.'

By *modus ponens* we may deduce that

'The team is playing well.'

We have made the formal deduction, $p, p \to q \vdash q$ where

p: 'Gary plays well.'
q: 'The team plays well.'

using *modus ponens* as the only inference rule.

4.3.4 The deduction theorem

Before we introduce a system of deduction that is more natural than the axiomatic system, we introduce a theorem, from classical logic, that 'talks about' a logic and will be very useful to us in carrying out our derivations of theorems within the logic.

Theorem 4.1 The deduction theorem If Γ, $A \vdash B$ then $\Gamma \vdash A \to B$.

This meta-level theorem is essentially the converse of *modus ponens* and asserts that the theorem $A \to B$ in the logic can be deduced if B is a consequence of the set $\Gamma \cup A$. We use $\vdash$ within the theorem to indicate that $\vdash$ is at a meta-level to any specific system of deduction.

In Example 4.10 we deduced that 'The team is playing well' from the premise that 'Gary is playing well'. In symbols,

$$p,\ p \rightarrow q \vdash q$$

We eliminated the arrow when we obtained our conclusion. Now by the deduction theorem we can bring the premise, p, to the right of the turnstile and gain as a consequence the theorem $p \rightarrow q$. The set Γ in the theorem is $\{p \rightarrow q\}$. We obtain $p \rightarrow q \vdash p \rightarrow q$ as an obvious deduction.

We have gone in the opposite direction from *modus ponens* and introduced an arrow on the right of $\vdash$. Our consequence is now a theorem. The *assertion* that the theorem 'If Gary plays well then the team plays well' is true will be represented by $p \Rightarrow q$. The movement between *modus ponens* and its converse, the deduction theorem, can be symbolized by presenting the two rules themselves as part of a rule, but using two horizontal lines to indicate that the movement is upwards as well as downwards. We write

$$\frac{P \vdash Q}{\vdash P \rightarrow Q}$$

Notice that the turnstile is now used *within* a meta-level rule. The set Γ is allowed to contain any wff of the propositional calculus that may or may not be a non-logical axiom. It is also important to re-emphasize that A and B stand for *any* wffs and that logical reasoning does not take into account any knowledge of the problem domain.

Exercise 4.6 Make a derivation of your own in the formal system using both *modus ponens* and the deduction theorem.

Exercise 4.7 Go back to Example 4.6 and convince yourself that this is a justification for the result of *modus ponens*.

Exercise 4.8 Draw the truth table for $A \wedge (A \rightarrow B) \rightarrow B$. If $A \rightarrow B$ is false what is the truth-value of B?

4.3.5 A natural deduction system

We now discuss a deduction system that does not assume any wffs as axioms but relies on rules of inference to define the logical connectives of the propositional calculus. Each connective is defined by two inference rules:

An introduction rule that shows how a proposition containing the connective can be inferred.

An elimination rule that shows which consequence can be made from a proposition containing the connective.

The system, suggested by the logician Gentzen in 1935, makes the idea of assumptions in a proof more explicit and is closer to the form of deduction used in mathematical proofs than the axiomatic system that was used by Hilbert in the 1920s. We write $\vdash_{ND}$ to express the consequence relation in a natural deduction system.

To compensate for the lack of logical axioms we are allowed to introduce a wff as a hypothesis to the argument at any stage in the deduction. These extra hypotheses are represented by *assumptions* and are distinguished from the hypotheses on which the original *premises* for the deduction depend. It is important to organize a derivation in a natural deduction system so that the hypotheses that a formula depends on are clearly identified. Hypotheses that are assumed during a derivation have an area of *scope* and must only be used within this area. Although the logical axioms are not assumed in the natural deduction system, the non-logical axioms, that describe the application, are clearly important since they are assumed to belong to the hypotheses of the proof.

Rules of introduction and elimination In the rules that follow, A and B denote any propositions (possibly compound):

$$\frac{\begin{array}{c}A\\B\end{array}}{A \wedge B} \qquad (\wedge\text{-introduction})$$

$$\frac{A \wedge B}{A} \qquad \frac{A \wedge B}{B} \qquad (\wedge\text{-elimination})$$

$$\frac{A}{A \vee B} \qquad \frac{B}{A \vee B} \qquad (\vee\text{-introduction})$$

$$\frac{A \vee B; \quad \Gamma,\ A \vdash C; \quad \Gamma,\ B \vdash C}{C} \qquad (\vee\text{-elimination})$$

where A and B are assumptions. We separate by ; the hypotheses that require separate proofs. The $\vee$-elimination rule models case analysis for informal arguments.

$$\frac{\Gamma,\ A \ \vdash \ B}{\Gamma \ \vdash \ A \rightarrow B} \qquad (\rightarrow\text{-introduction})$$

where A is an assumption. The $\rightarrow$-introduction rule is expressed by the deduction theorem

$$\frac{A \qquad A \rightarrow B}{B} \qquad (\rightarrow\text{-elimination})$$

The $\rightarrow$-elimination rule is generalized *modus ponens*,

$$\frac{\Gamma,\ A \vdash B; \qquad \Gamma,\ A \vdash \neg B}{\neg A} \qquad (\neg\text{-introduction})$$

where A is an assumption. The $\neg$-introduction rule is sometimes called RAA or *reductio ad absurdum*.

$$\frac{\neg\neg A}{A} \qquad (\neg\text{-elimination})$$

The rules that we have given for $\neg$-introduction and $\neg\neg$-elimination are together equivalent to the following pair of rules for $\neg$-elimination and $\neg$-introduction. In some presentations of a natural deduction system these alternative rules are presented.

The alternative $\neg$-elimination rule is

$$\frac{\Gamma \vdash \neg A; \qquad \Gamma \vdash A}{\Gamma \vdash B}$$

The alternative $\neg$-introduction rule is

$$\frac{A,\ \Gamma \vdash \neg A}{\Gamma \vdash \neg A} \qquad \frac{\neg A,\ \Gamma \vdash A}{\Gamma \vdash A}$$

Example derivations When carrying out our syntactic derivations within a natural deduction system we need to record each stage in the derivation clearly, noting both the rule that we use and the lines in the derivation to which each rule applies. By working methodically we can see both 'where we have come from' and 'where we have to go'. Essentially we just match the patterns of symbols in the derivation with the grammatical patterns of the rules and pick the rule that helps us to get to the conclusion. Finding a path from the premises to the conclusion involves finding a *strategy*, and is a skill that requires practice. To construct a derivation we need to work backwards from the conclusion, selecting the appropriate rule at each stage. If the deduction is not clearly recorded it can be a confusing activity, and also frustrating if early stages are worked through incorrectly and the conclusion cannot be reached! Many of our exercises are purely syntactic derivations in which the skill of choosing the appropriate rules is required. The rest involve translating English sentences into the propositional calculus in order to make deductions. These examples will re-enforce the work of Chapter 3.

Example 4.11 Show that $p \wedge r,\ p \wedge q \rightarrow r, q \wedge s \vdash_{\text{ND}} r$. We number each stage in the derivation and explain the use of the inference rule on the right-hand side of each formula as it is derived. This information is not part of the derivation but is given to help both in making the derivation and in reaching it.

We begin by listing all the premises. Our experience with the rule of *modus ponens* tells us that if we can derive $p \wedge q$ then with $p \wedge q \rightarrow r$ we can reach the conclusion r. It looks as though the $\rightarrow$-elimination rule could be our final stage in the derivation. In order to prepare for this stage all we have to do is to derive $p \wedge q$. By working *backwards* from the conclusion our strategy is becoming clear. We describe the derivation as though it was all clear at the beginning—sometimes many attempts have been made before the final strategy is worked out.

Derivation

1.	$p \wedge r$	premise
2.	$p \wedge q \rightarrow r$	premise
3.	$q \wedge s$	premise
4.	p	$\wedge$-elimination on 1
5.	q	$\wedge$-elimination on 3
6.	$p \wedge q$	$\wedge$-introduction on 3,4
7.	r	$\rightarrow$-elimination (*modus ponens*) on 2,5

end

Our next example requires the use of the deduction theorem. In order to derive a proposition in the form $A \rightarrow B$ we need to *assume* A and then proceed to derive B. If we can do this by the rule of $\rightarrow$-introduction (which represents the deduction theorem) we can claim that the conclusion $A \rightarrow B$ holds. We must make clear in our derivation that A is only assumed and is not a premise—it can only be used for a derivation *within the scope* of the $\rightarrow$-introduction rule. When an assumption is used by the rule that called for it, we say it is *discharged* and we move back out of its area of scope. Variables in block-structured programming languages have areas of scope outside which they must not be used; similarly assumptions in formal derivations must not be used outside their area of scope. The scope for each assumption is shown by opening and closing the brackets, {, and , }. In the $\rightarrow$-introduction rule all the derivations and assumptions, apart from A, that are in scope are in Γ.

Example 4.12 Show that $p \rightarrow q,\ q \rightarrow r \vdash_{ND} p \rightarrow r$.

Derivation

1.	$p \rightarrow q$	premise
2.	$q \rightarrow r$	premise
3.	$\{p$	assumption
4.	q	$\rightarrow$-elimination (*modus ponens*) on 1,3
5.	$r\}$	$\rightarrow$-elimination on 2,4
6.	$p \rightarrow r$	$\rightarrow$-introduction on 3,4,5

end

The derivation that we have just made in Example 4.12 is one that may be useful in later derivations. It expresses the transitivity of the conditional connective. In some systems it is presented as an inference rule itself, and is called the chain rule (or the rule of syllogism).

Rule 4.2 Chain rule For any propositions A, B and C,

$$\frac{\begin{array}{ccc} A & \rightarrow & B \\ B & \rightarrow & C \end{array}}{\begin{array}{ccc} A & \rightarrow & C \end{array}}$$

Once we have made a derivation in our system we want to be able to introduce it into further derivations and take advantage of the work we have already done. Either we refer to the derivation in Example 4.12 as the chain rule or we give it explicitly—in either case we should explain the substitutions that we make when we use it.

Our next derivation is of another rule that is used for inference in other systems.

Example 4.13 Show that $p \rightarrow q,\ \neg q \vdash_{ND} \neg p$.

Derivation

1.	$p \rightarrow q$	premise
2.	$\neg q$	premise
3.	$\{p$	assumption
4.	$q\}$	$\rightarrow$-elimination on 1,3
5.	$\neg p$	$\neg$-introduction on 2,3,4

end

Our previous derivations have proceeded directly from the hypothesis to the conclusion. In Example 4.13, however, we have taken an *indirect* route because none of our 'direct' rules seemed to be of any help to us. The method we have used is called *proof by contradiction* (or *reductio ad absurdum*). We assumed the negation of the conclusion that we wished to derive and then, within the scope of this assumption, produced a contradiction to a premise. The contradiction could of course be to a derivation from a premise. The $\neg$-introduction rule ends the scope of the assumption by discharging it, and, in order to avoid the contradiction, introduces instead the negation of the assumption. This is, of course, the conclusion that we first wanted.

The derivation in Example 4.13 is often called *modus tollens* and is presented as an inference rule in some formal systems.

Rule 4.3 ***Modus tollens*** For any propositions A, B we have the inference rule

$$\frac{\begin{array}{l}A \rightarrow B\\ \neg B\end{array}}{\neg A}$$

Modus tollens is applied in automated deduction where it is known as the inference rule of *resolution*.

Our next example uses the previous derivation of *modus tollens*. We refer to it as a derived rule. Alternatively we could introduce a previous result in later derivations by giving it explicitly as a *lemma* before the derivation in which it is used. A final, but least attractive, alternative is to include the complete text of a previously worked derivation as it is required.

Example 4.14 Show that $\neg p \rightarrow q,\ r \rightarrow \neg q,\ r \vdash_{\text{ND}} p$.

With some practice and a good eye for matching patterns, it will become obvious that in this example the conclusion p is the negation of the antecedent of the first hypothesis. This is just right for using *modus tollens*.

Derivation

1. $\neg p \rightarrow q$ premise
2. $r \rightarrow \neg q$ premise
3. r premise
4. $\neg q$ $\rightarrow$-elimination on 2
5. p derived rule of *modus tollens* on 1,4

end

Our next example derivation uses the rule for $\vee$-elimination. Intuitively we begin with the hypothesis that we can make derivations from either A or B but we do not know which. If we can derive C, whether we assume A or we assume B, then we can confidently proceed to use our derivation of C. Having achieved this we need to discharge the assumptions that we made in order to derive C.

Example 4.15 Show that $(p \wedge q) \vee (\neg p \wedge q) \vdash_{\text{ND}} q$.

Derivation

1. $(p \wedge q) \vee (\neg p \wedge q)$ premise
2. $\{p \wedge q$ assumption
3. q $\wedge$-elimination on 2
4. $\{\neg p \wedge q$ assumption
5. $q\}\}$ $\wedge$-elimination on 4
6. q $\vee$-elimination on 2,5

end

We use the scoping brackets to indicate the scope of each of our two assumptions that lead to the derivation of q. The scope of these assumptions ends when the assumptions are discharged before the rule for $\vee$-elimination is used in line 6.

4.4 LINKING THE SEMANTIC AND SYNTACTIC TURNSTILES

We have been careful to differentiate between the semantic notion of consequence based on satisfaction, which was introduced in Sec. 4.2, and the purely syntactic notion of deduction which we used in Sec. 4.3. The symbol $\models$ expresses a relation between propositions that is based on their truth-values; the symbol $\vdash$ similarly expresses a relation of consequence but is based on a view of propositions that strips them of any meaning. We can picture $\vdash$ sitting in an abstract world 'above' $\models$ and far away from the real world of values and meanings. When using $\vdash$ we distance ourselves from the detail of concrete models and interpretations—it is easier to manipulate symbols and not bother about what the symbols represent. The retreat into an abstract world of formal symbols brings the reward of being able to solve general problems that apply to many apparently different concrete parts of real-world experience. Clearly, however, we must have confidence that our formal deduction system, which uses $\vdash$, really does mirror our reasoning about truth-values that is based on $\models$.

4.4.1 Soundness and completeness

Fortunately two important theorems in mathematical logic reassure us (at a meta-level) that our deduction system for the propositional calculus is both *sound* and *complete*. Intuitively this means that $\vdash$ mirrors $\models$ and also that $\models$ mirrors $\vdash$. We present the theory but do not go into any detail about the proofs. It is important to note that we are now considering the soundness of a *deduction* rather than the soundness of the inference of some argument when the premises are true.

Theorem 4.2 Soundness theorem If $\Gamma \vdash Q$ then $\Gamma \models Q$.

This theorem reassures us that in our formal deduction system we will not derive a false conclusion from a set of true premises. Our next theorem reassures us that any informal reasoning that we make based on the satisfaction of sentences can be carried out within our formal deductive system.

Theorem 4.3 Completeness theorem If $\Gamma \models Q$ then $\Gamma \vdash Q$.

The completeness theorem, proved by Gödel in 1930, is the converse of the soundness theorem and is a much deeper result. These theorems tell us that we can confidently move between the semantic and syntactic worlds of mathematical logic. In particular, we can use the rich results that we built up in Chapter 3 concerning equivalences between propositions. We have already argued in Sec. 4.2 that if $P \equiv Q$ then $P \models Q$ and $Q \models P$. Now by the completeness theorem we can call on the rule of equivalence, stated on page 121, to help us in our final derivations. We choose to refer to the rule of equivalence at the stage that it is used in a derivation and to state the equivalences explicitly. Alternatively, we could state the equivalences as a lemma at the beginning of a derivation and short cut the reference to the general rule of equivalence. We prefer to extend the set of inference rules for natural deduction by extra rules that we derive within the formal system.

Example 4.16 Consider the hypotheses:

'If pigs fly or Arsenal play entertaining football then Margaret Thatcher is a man.'

'If Margaret Thatcher is a man then Gary is not a great player. But Gary is a great player.'

From these hypotheses deduce that

'Arsenal do not play entertaining football.'

First we represent the argument in symbolic form. Let:

p: 'pigs fly'
a: 'Arsenal play entertaining football'
m: 'Margaret Thatcher is a man'
g: 'Gary is a great player'

We show that $(p \vee a) \rightarrow m\ ,\ (m \rightarrow \neg g) \wedge g \vdash_{\mathrm{ND}} \neg a$.

Derivation

1. $(p \vee a) \rightarrow m$ — premise
2. $(m \rightarrow \neg g) \wedge g$ — premise
3. $m \rightarrow \neg g$ — $\wedge$-elimination on 2
4. $(p \vee a) \rightarrow \neg g$ — the derived chain rule on 1,3
5. g — $\wedge$-elimination on 2
6. $\neg(p \vee a)$ — the derived rule of *modus tollens* on 4,5
7. $\neg p \wedge \neg a$ — the rule of equivalence (by De Morgan) on 6
8. $\neg a$ — $\wedge$-elimination on 7

end

Exercise 4.9 Show that $(q \vee s) \wedge \neg r, (p \rightarrow r) \wedge s \vdash_{\mathrm{ND}} \neg p$ by using our formal inference rules.

Exercise 4.10 Show that $p \rightarrow q, \neg r \rightarrow \neg q, \neg r \vdash_{\mathrm{ND}} \neg p$ by using formal deduction.

Exercise 4.11 By representing the following argument symbolically in the propositional calculus show that the following deduction is correct:

'If Margaret travels on the tube then Margaret is not early. Margaret travels on the tube if Margaret does not cycle to work. Therefore Margaret cycles to work if it is not raining and Margaret is early.'

Exercise 4.12 By representing the following argument symbolically in the propositional calculus carry out the following deduction formally:

'If George saves money then he feels rich. If George's mortgage repayment increases then he doesn't feel rich. George's salary does not increase but his mortgage repayment does. Therefore George does not save money.'

Exercise 4.13 By 'translating' the following argument into symbolic form show that the following deduction can be made in a formal system:

' If I do not work hard I will sleep. If I am worried I will not sleep. Therefore, if I am worried I will work hard.'

4.4.2 Back in the semantic world

Our new confidence in moving between the semantic and syntactic worlds of propositional logic will be increased if we now investigate the underlying semantics of the chain rule, derived in Example 4.12, and *modus tollens*, derived in Example 4.13.

Exercise 4.14 Justify the chain rule by showing that

$$\models ((A \rightarrow B) \wedge (B \rightarrow C)) \rightarrow (A \rightarrow C)$$

Exercise 4.15 Justify *modus tollens* by reference to the truth table for $p \rightarrow q$.

Exercise 4.16 Draw the truth tables for the propositions

$$p \wedge (p \rightarrow q) \rightarrow q \text{ and } (p \rightarrow q) \wedge (\neg q \rightarrow \neg p)$$

Explain how these truth tables justify two of our rules of inference.

Exercise 4.17 The rule of *modus tollens* is based on the equivalence between $p \to q$ and the contrapositive proposition $\neg q \to \neg p$. Is the contrapositive of $p \to q$ equivalent to:

(a) the converse of $p \to q$,

(b) the inverse of $p \to q$?

Exercise 4.18 Justify *modus ponens* as the rule for $\to$-elimination by using the truth table for $p \to q$. Find a row that corresponds to both p and $p \to q$ being true. What is the value for q?

In an informal argument we say that a statement is *valid* if it is true under any interpretation. A tautology is valid, therefore, because every line of a truth table assigns the value true to it.

Definition 4.8 Valid argument An argument is said to be valid if there is no possible situation in which its premises are all true and its conclusion is not true.

The inference rule *modus tollens* can be phrased as the following principle in logic:

Rule 4.4 The falsehood of a conclusion of a valid argument implies the falsehood of a hypothesis.

Exercise 4.19 Consider the *valid* statement 'All equiangular triangles are isosceles'. Represent this in the symbolic form $p \to q$. The proposition q then represents the conclusion of the valid statement and p the hypothesis. Is the converse of this proposition true? State a principle in logic that expresses this result in a form similar to the principle above.

If you have difficulty with deriving the conclusion of an argument from its premises, in some formal deductive calculus, it is sensible to check whether there is an interpretation in which the premises are all true but the conclusion is false. If you do find such an interpretation you have found a counter-example to the validity of the argument. This explains why the derivation was so difficult. It is important always to keep the syntactic and semantic worlds of logic in touch with each other.

4.5 SUMMARY

In this chapter we have presented the proof of a theorem in some non-logical application domain as the formal process of logical deduction. A calculus for deduction is constructed within which the process of formal reasoning is carried out purely by the syntactic manipulation of symbols. The relation between the premises of a formal deduction and the consequence of the deduction is symbolized by the syntactic turnstile, $\vdash$. We have presented derivations within a natural deduction system. Because the system for deduction within the propositional calculus is both sound and complete, the syntactic notion of deduction, represented by $\vdash$, is mirrored by the semantic notion of entailment, represented by $\models$. This means that we are able to use the algebraic notion of equivalence, established in Chapter 3, to help us in our derivations.

4.6 FURTHER EXERCISES

Exercise 4.20 The statement 'If I understand football then I support Spurs' is logically equivalent to one of the following statements. Select which one.

(a) I support Spurs or I do not understand football.

(b) If I support Spurs then I really understand football.

(c) I support Spurs or I understand football.

(d) I do not like football or I support Spurs.

(e) I understand football and I support Spurs.

Exercise 4.21 Use the formalism of the propositional calculus to represent the following assertions:

(a) If Spurs win the league or the cup then Norman is very happy.

(b) It is a bad year if Spurs do not win the league.

Assuming the above two assertions as hypotheses derive the statement:

If Norman is unhappy then it is a bad year and Spurs do not win the cup.

Exercise 4.22 Consider the following premises:

(a) If Gillian drives to work then she gets to work late, if the traffic is heavy.

(b) Gillian does not leave work early if she gets to work late and she has a lot of scripts to mark.

(c) If Gillian's classes are too large then she has a lot of scripts to mark and she does not leave work early.

First represent these premises in logical notation. Then further suppose that Gillian drives to work and suppose also that the traffic is heavy. Prove that Gillian gets to work late.

Finally, using the previous premises prove the statement:

If Gillian gets to work late and leaves work early then her classes are not too large.

Exercise 4.23 Translate the following argument into symbolic form and test its validity:

If 6 is even, then 2 does not divide 7
either 5 is not prime or 2 divides 7
but 5 is prime

Therefore 6 is odd

If the argument is valid, formally derive its conclusion in a natural deduction system.

Exercise 4.24 Translate into symbolic form and test the validity of the following argument:

If I work, I cannot study
either I work, or I pass Maths
I passed Mathematics

Therefore, I studied

If the argument is valid, formally derive its conclusion in a natural deduction system.

Exercise 4.25 Translate into symbolic form and test the validity of the following argument:

If I work, I cannot study
either I study, or I pass Maths
I worked

Therefore I passed Maths

If the argument is valid, formally derive its conclusion in a natural deduction system.

Exercise 4.26 Use a truth table to deduce whether the following argument is valid. You should explain your results carefully.

$$(p \rightarrow q) \vee p \models q$$

FURTHER READING

As for Chapter 3 we recommend the books by Enderton (1972) and Galton (1990). These books provide a treatment of proof that is in greater depth. A similar style of proof by natural deduction is used in Woodcock and Loomes (1988). A thorough presentation of the fundamental ideas of intuitionistic mathematics and the formalization of intuitionistic logic, that uses both a natural deduction system and the sequent calculus, is given by Michael Dummett (1980). Michael Beeson (1984) shows how the constructive approach of intuitionism has led to the development of constructive type theories and how Martin-Löf's rules for types actually define a formal system. Beeson explains how the existence of the computer makes it possible to manipulate symbols on the scale that is required for reasoning about large systems.

Chapter 5

THE CALCULUS OF PREDICATE LOGIC

We have introduced our proof system of natural deduction within the simple calculus of propositions. Such a simple calculus is, however, unable to model many deductions that we feel are correct at an intuitive level. In this chapter we develop a more powerful calculus within which we can prove the correctness of the systems that we construct and analyse. We introduce a predicate in Sec. 5.1 as a way of describing the properties of objects and relations between objects.

The semantics of the language of predicates, given in Sec. 5.2, is based on the construction of mathematical models, and is more appropriate for the interpretation of application domains in the real world than the simple semantics of truth tables. The power of predicate logic is gained by the introduction of quantification over some domain of interpretation. The individual quantifiers that bind variables in a predicate are introduced in Sec. 5.3.

An aim of this chapter is to give both a theoretical understanding of the calculus and the experience at a more practical level of writing mathematical statements in the calculus. We provide a foundation for the later chapters of the specification of complex systems. The work of specifying systems involves building theories about systems. The predicate calculus provides the logical framework for specification.

5.1 PREDICATES

5.1.1 The need for increased power of expression

We have seen in the propositional calculus that all propositions are either true or false. We have distinguished between the proposition p and the assertion that p is true by saying that an assertion 'talks about' the truth of a proposition. We shall now see that the language of propositional calculus is not sufficiently powerful to make all the assertions (and hence all the inferences) that are needed in mathematics.

Consider the following argument:

All mothers are female
Gillian is a mother

Gillian is female

The two premises, or assumptions, are separated from the conclusion by a horizontal line.

Any attempt to represent (let alone prove) this argument using just propositional calculus is doomed to failure. The assertions talk about the truth of distinct propositions and we would have to represent the argument symbolically by

$$\frac{\begin{array}{c}P\\Q\end{array}}{R}$$

It is obvious that we cannot prove this argument by deriving R from P and Q. Our symbolic representation of the argument in the propositional calculus has failed to express that P is a statement about a *class* of individuals whereas Q concerns a *specific* individual. It has also failed to capture the notion that both Q and R are statements about the particular individual named Gillian. It seems that our language of propositions is too coarsely grained to express the meanings of the statements in this argument. We need to describe properties about *an* individual and also properties about *all* individuals.

We have already provided the foundations for extending the propositional calculus to form the more expressive language that we require. In Chapter 2, we defined a relation as a way of describing properties of single objects or as rules between more than one object. We also described objects symbolically, as the elements of sets, and saw a relation as a rule over these sets. These fundamental ideas from mathematics help us to build a powerful logic with a finer grain than the propositional calculus.

5.1.2 Predicates as templates

In Chapter 3 we saw that in mathematics we need to make assertions like

'$x = 3$'	'$x \geq y$'
'$x - y = z$'	'$x + y = z$'
'y is a divisor of 10'	'x is prime'

The assertion '$x = 3$' means 'there is some integer that has the value 3'. Although these assertions are accepted as simple propositions, they are called open statements since they may be true or false depending on values assigned to the variables. Once values are assigned they become propositions or closed sentences. We could form the following propositions by assigning values to x and y:

'$4 = 3$'	'$3 \geq 3$'
'$5 + 7 = 13$'	'$5 + 7 = 12$'
'4 is a divisor of 10'	'13 is prime'

Similar assertions occur in everyday English. For example,

'He is small'	(x is small)
'This person is a female'	(x is female)
'She lives in a city'	(x lives in y)
'He is her husband'	(x is the husband of y)

Both our assertions in mathematics and our assertions in English have been presented in a pattern, or *template*, which expresses the property of an object, or objects, but avoids any detail that is irrelevant to the structure of the assertion.

If we remove the variable that represents the object in the assertion 'x is small', we are left with the template '____ is small'. The hole in the template represents a *place* that could be filled by any other variable symbol, by a proper name such as 'Jack', or by a constant symbol, c, to stand for some individual. For example, the symbol c might be used to refer to the person named 'Jill' *constantly* throughout a logical argument.

We add this simple way of defining the property of some object to the propositional calculus and say that the property is denoted by a predicate.

The logical analysis of sentences into objects and properties precedes the translation of sentences into the predicate calculus. This is merely an extension, providing more detail, of the logical analysis of sentences that we made in Chapter 3 before translating the sentences into the propositional calculus.

Example 5.1 The logical analysis of the open statement 'This person is a female' is the predicate ' ___ is female' with x as the variable that represents the object *and* fills the hole in the predicate. The hole could be filled by: 'Jack' to form a proposition that is probably false; by the constant symbol c to name, or stand for, 'Jill' to form a true proposition; or by any other constant or variable symbol.

Example 5.2 The open statement 'Each student voted for the president' is logically analysed as consisting of the predicate 'Each student voted for ___ ' with the unique object that fills the hole in the predicate described by 'the president'. We cannot, however, pick out a unique individual object from the description 'Each student'. The intention of the description is to identify 'many' students, and this must also be expressed precisely within our logical calculus.

The concept of a predicate provides a very powerful abstraction for ascribing properties to objects and clearly adds a finer grain of expression to the propositional calculus. The hole in the predicate is filled by the names of arguments to the predicate. Initially we consider *unary* predicates that have only one argument.

Definition 5.1 Unary predicate A unary predicate is part of any statement that assigns a property to an object. A predicate is denoted by a predicate letter together with the place for an argument. The argument place is also called a place holder and must be filled by a name or a description of a unique individual object.

Exercise 5.1 Analyse the following statements into predicates and suggest alternative names that could fill the placeholder. Discuss the truth-values of the resulting propositions.

(a) 'y is a divisor of 10'

(b) 'x is prime'

(c) 'Jill writes books'

(d) 'Everybody likes Neil'

(e) 'No one finds logic difficult'

Relations between objects can be logically analysed in a similar way to properties of a unique individual object. Relations between n objects are fully described in Chapter 2. The aim of this chapter is to present relations in a logical language by predicates with enough holes for each object in the relation. We shall therefore extend our concept of a predicate to an *n-place predicate* in order to express n-ary relations between objects.

Example 5.3 The open statement '$x = y$' represents the binary relation '=' between objects named by the variables x and y. This can be analysed by the two-place, or binary, predicate ' ___ = ...'. Because the relation is symmetric the order of the objects is irrelevant. We distinguish the argument places from each other. We could, however, fill the two argument places by the same name, to give the true proposition $2 = 2$.

Example 5.4 The open statement 'He is her husband' represents a binary relation and can be analysed as consisting of a binary predicate with the argument places filled by names of people. This relation is clearly not symmetric. We express it by the predicate '____ is the husband of ...'. If we had not distinguished between the two places we would have implied that the same name *had* to be put in each of the argument places. This would have resulted in closed statements such as 'Sam is the husband of Sam'. Instead the names 'Sam' and 'Sarah' could fill the places and form a true proposition.

Exercise 5.2 Analyse the following statements into predicates and suggest alternative names that could fill the placeholder. Discuss the truth-values of the resulting propositions.

(a) '$x \geq 3$'

(b) 'xy'

(c) '$x + y = z$'

(d) 'She lives in a city'

5.1.3 The notation for predicates in the calculus

We have used the concept of a predicate to represent the unary relation of an individual object having a property, as well as the n-ary relation between more than one individual object. In fact, predicate logic can be used to describe and reason about parts of the world that are viewed as relational structures.

Within the predicate calculus we avoid the cumbersome notation of writing out predicates in full, by denoting each property or relation by a *predicate letter* and using a mathematical notation for the arguments of a predicate. The place for the name of the object, as the argument, follows the name of the predicate and is parenthesized. Some predicates that we have already used in Chapter 2 are sufficiently important to warrant special notation. Examples include the use of '=' in assertions of the form 'x is equal to y', and '>' to assert 'x is greater than y'. We will use these whenever convenient, but in general predicates will be denoted by capital letters. In addition to the letters that give names to the predicates in our language, we need letters to denote the names that appear in the list of arguments to the predicate. For example,

'x is a female'	might be denoted by	female(x) or $\mathscr{F}(x)$
'x hates y'	might be denoted by	hates(x, y) or $\mathscr{H}(x, y)$
'$x + y = z$'	might be denoted by	sum(x, y, z) or $\mathscr{S}(x, y, z)$
'$x = y$'	might be denoted by	equals(x, y) or $\mathscr{E}(x, y)$

Examples of predicates occurring in Pascal programs are those statements that follow reserved words *while, if* and *until*.

When a symbol, such as $\mathscr{F}, \mathscr{H}, \mathscr{S}, \mathscr{E}$ or =, denotes a specific predicate, it is called a *predicate constant*. A variable that appears in the parenthesized list of names is called an *individual variable*.

Definition 5.2 n-place predicate An n-place predicate, or an n-ary predicate, expresses a property or a relation between n objects and is denoted by $\mathscr{P}(t)$ where t is a list of n names of objects. The arity of the predicate determines the number of places in the predicate and is sometimes denoted by $\mathscr{P}^n(t)$.

When the notation describing a particular application system in the predicate calculus is established, the arity of the number of arguments in the predicate must be determined by definition. The notation allows $\mathscr{P}^1, \mathscr{P}^2, \ldots$ all to occur in the same system without risk of ambiguity.

In addition to the letters $x, y, z, \ldots$, which represent the list of variable names for the objects to the predicates, we need a list of letters $a, b, c, \ldots$ to denote the proper names of objects.

Definition 5.3 Individual constants The letters $a, b, c, \ldots$ are the individual constants that refer to individuals of some kind in the calculus. Each letter is a constant because it is used for the same individual in a particular interpretation.

Example 5.5 Let a denote 'Harry' and b denote 'Sarah'. Then $\mathscr{H}(a, b)$ denotes 'Harry hates Sarah' and $\mathscr{H}(b, a)$ denotes 'Sarah hates Harry'. Let $\mathscr{D}(x)$ denote 'x is a doctor'. The compound assertion that 'Sarah is a doctor whom Harry hates' is denoted by $\mathscr{D}(b) \wedge \mathscr{H}(a, b)$.

Exercise 5.3 Use the predicates above to express the following assertions:

(a) '$2 = 5$'

(b) 'Sam is a female'

(c) 'The sum of 0 added to 4 is 4'

(d) '$2 + 5 = 9$'

(e) 'Sam hates the female Liz'

5.2 THE SEMANTICS OF PREDICATE LOGIC

We have provided a finer grain of expression by adding predicates to the propositional calculus. Now we provide a semantics for the more expressive predicate calculus. A truth-value function expressed the semantics of the propositional calculus by assigning a truth-value to each proposition. A predicate does not have a truth-value, however. It merely expresses a property, or relation, and leaves a place corresponding to each argument of the predicate. Only when the argument place is filled by an object can a truth-value be assigned to the resulting proposition. The formation of a *closed* proposition from an *open* predicate is made by *interpreting* the letters that denote the arguments to the predicate by the objects in the application domain that give meaning to the predicate.

Example 5.6 The predicate $\mathscr{H}(a, b)$ represents a true assertion if the letter a is interpreted by the object 'Henry' and b by the object 'Sarah'. It is also true if a is interpreted by 'Sarah' and b by 'Henry'. If a is interpreted by 'Sally', $\mathscr{H}(a, b)$ is false. Clearly, however, $\mathscr{H}(4, 7)$ has no sensible meaning, so we must formally express the domain of objects for which the predicate $\mathscr{H}(x, y)$ makes sense.

The notion of a variable is precisely defined in logic as a syntactic object that is either *free* or *bound*. A variable is free in some context, such as an open predicate, and within this context other syntactic variables may be substituted. We have seen in Example 5.6 that we need to make a choice of how to interpret the free variables as elements in the domain of interpretation. In the open predicate $\mathscr{H}(x, y)$ both x and y are free. We shall see that once a variable is bound there is no possibility of substitution or interpretation. A variable can be bound by instantiating it by a value or by using quantification, which we describe in Sec. 5.3, to bind the variable to a meaning. We shall draw an analogy between the bound and free variables in logic and those in programs.

5.2.1 Interpretation

To give meaning to a predicate, the values of the individual variables are drawn from sets that contain the elements that interpret the symbols for the variables. The elements of these sets represent the objects that have the properties specified by the predicate.

Example 5.7 In discussing the predicate '$<(x, y)$' it would be meaningless to assign anything other than numbers to the variables, thus avoiding the possibility of assertions like 'green $<$ 3'. We usually write this predicate in infix form as $x < y$.

The set of values that interpret the individual constants and variable letters of the predicate calculus must be specified in advance. This is analogous to the notion of strong typing in Pascal.

Definition 5.4 Interpretation The assignment of semantic values, or objects, from a set, or structure, to a predicate defines an interpretation for the predicate expression.

In order to define the set for the interpretation of a predicate expression we change the predicate notation slightly and write $\mathscr{P}(x_1, \ldots, x_n)$ to express the order of the variables that are arguments to the predicate.

Definition 5.5 Domain of interpretation The predicate $\mathscr{P}(x_1, \ldots, x_n)$ has as its domain of interpretation, or universe of discourse, the set $D = D_1 \times D_2 \times \cdots \times D_n$.

Example 5.8 The predicate constant '$<(x, y)$' may have domain $\mathbb{Z} \times \mathbb{Z}$ or $\mathbb{R} \times \mathbb{R}$ but not $\mathbb{C} \times \mathbb{C}$ or $\{\text{men}\} \times \{\text{men}\}$. Possible interpretations of the predicate are $<(4, 2)$ and $<(5, 10)$.

Clearly all the order relations in Chapter 2 can be expressed as predicates given suitable interpretations.

Example 5.9 The predicate constant $\mathscr{F}(x)$ that denotes 'x is a female' may have domain {earth inhabitants} or {English names}. A possible interpretation is $\mathscr{F}$(Sally).

Example 5.10 The predicate constant $\mathscr{S}(x, y, z)$ that denotes '$x + y = z$' may have domain $\mathbb{Z} \times \mathbb{Z} \times \mathbb{Z}$ or $\mathbb{Z} \times \mathbb{Z} \times \mathbb{R}$ (but not $\mathbb{R} \times \mathbb{R} \times \mathbb{Z}$). A possible interpretation that is true in either of these domains is $\mathscr{S}(4, 2, 6)$. The interpretation $\mathscr{S}(2, 4, 5)$ is false.

Example 5.11 The predicate constant $\mathscr{H}(x, y)$ that denotes 'x hates y' may have domain $\{\text{men}\} \times \{\text{women}\}$ or $\{\text{people}\} \times \{\text{animals}\}$. A possible interpretation is $\mathscr{H}$(Sally, Fred), where Fred is the name of a snake.

Example 5.12 The predicate constant $\in(x, y)$, written in infix form as an arbitrary relation $x \in y$, may have domain $\mathbb{Z} \times \mathscr{P}(\mathbb{Z})$. A possible interpretation that is true is $\in(3, \{1, 2, 3\})$. The interpretation $\in(4, \{5, 6\})$ is false.

In the propositional calculus we defined a truth-value function to interpret the variable propositions by the values true or false. We abbreviate these values by T and F in truth tables. In the predicate calculus we define a function that gives meaning to the symbols that we have added to the propositional calculus.

Definition 5.6 Interpretation function The interpretation function, I, establishes a correspondence between the symbols of the predicate language and the domain of interpretation, D.

The individual constants correspond to names of objects, so $I(a)$ where a is a constant is an element of D.

Example 5.13 For the predicate $\mathscr{F}(a)$, $I(a) =$ Sally where Sally $\in$ {English names}.

Definition 5.7 Interpretation of a unary predicate constant A unary predicate constant describes a property that each element in the domain D may or may not have. It is interpreted as a subset of the interpretation domain. We have $I(\mathscr{P}) \subseteq D$.

Example 5.14 For the predicate $\mathscr{F}(x)$ we have $I(\mathscr{F}) \subseteq$ {English names}. The names not in $I(\mathscr{F})$ are the names of people who are not female.

Definition 5.8 Interpretation of an *n*-ary predicate constant An n-ary predicate constant is interpreted by the set of all ordered n-tuples that define the relation on the interpretation domain. We have $I(\mathscr{P}) \subseteq D = D_1 \times \cdots \times D_n$.

Example 5.15 For the predicate $\mathscr{S}(x, y, z)$ that denotes '$x + y = z$' we could have, $I(\mathscr{S}) \subseteq \mathbb{Z} \times \mathbb{Z} \times \mathbb{Z}$ or $I(\mathscr{S}) \subseteq \mathbb{Z} \times \mathbb{Z} \times \mathbb{R}$ as possible interpretations.

5.2.2 Satisfaction and validity

In our examples we have given interpretations of predicates that are either true or false, depending on the elements, that we choose from the domain of interpretation. If the elements in the domain give an interpretation of a predicate that is true, we say they *satisfy* the predicate. If the predicate is true for any choice of elements, we can say that the predicate is *valid*.

Example 5.16 The following predicates are satisfied by some domains:

$\mathscr{S}(x, y, z)$: '$x + y = z$' is satisfiable in $\mathbb{Z} \times \mathbb{Z} \times \mathbb{Z}$ and $(2, 3, 5)$ satisfies $\mathscr{S}$
$\mathscr{P}(x, y)$: '$x = y + \frac{1}{2}$' is satisfiable in $\mathbb{Q}$ but is not satisfiable in $\mathbb{N}$

Definition 5.9 Satisfaction of a predicate If the interpretation of a predicate $\mathscr{P}(x_1, \ldots, x_n)$ is true for some choice $(d_1, \ldots, d_n) \in D_1 \times \cdots \times D_n$, then we say that $\mathscr{P}$ is satisfiable in $D = D_1 \times \cdots \times D_n$ and that $\mathscr{P}$ is satisfied by the tuple $(d_1, \ldots, d_n) \in D$.

Definition 5.10 Validity of a predicate If the interpretation of a predicate $\mathscr{P}(x_1, \ldots, x_n)$ is true for every choice $(d_1, \ldots, d_n) \in D_1 \times \cdots \times D_n$, then we say that $\mathscr{P}$ is valid in $D = D_1 \times \cdots \times D_n$. Predicates that are valid in all domains of interpretation are just said to be valid.

Definition 5.11 Model An interpretation, I, which is true for every element of a given domain, D, is called a model for D.

This definition of a model corresponds to the concept of a concrete model that was introduced in Chapter 1.

Example 5.17 The predicate $\mathscr{P}(x)$ that denotes '$x \geq 0$' is valid in $\mathbb{N}$ but not valid in $\mathbb{Z}$.

Example 5.18 The predicate $\mathscr{P}(x)$ that denotes '$x = x$' is valid in all domains, and is therefore a valid predicate.

Exercise 5.4 Describe interpretations that satisfy the following predicates:

(a) $\mathscr{L}$: 'x lives in y'

(b) $\mathscr{P}$: 'x is prime'

(c) $\mathscr{T}$: 'x is taller than y'

(d) $\mathscr{D}$: 'x divides y'

(e) $\mathscr{V}$: 'x voted for y'

Identify those domains of interpretation within which the predicates are valid.

The tautologies of propositional logic are valid because they are true for every interpretation of the constituent propositions. Truth tables demonstrate the validity of tautologies. The extension of validity to the predicate calculus is much harder, however, because we have to consider all possible interpretations of the symbols in the predicate expressions. Whereas the truth table method enables us to *decide* in a finite amount of time whether a proposition is valid, we have no analogous decision procedure in the predicate calculus where the domains of interpretation may be infinite.

5.2.3 Instantiation

We have seen that by the interpretation of all its variables an n-place predicate becomes a proposition, which is a closed predicate expression or a zero-place predicate. By assigning a value to only one of the variables of an n-place predicate, $\mathscr{P}(x_1, \ldots, x_n)$, an $(n-1)$-place predicate is formed.

Example 5.19 The predicate $\mathscr{S}(x, y, z)$ denoting '$x + y = z$' becomes a two-place predicate by assigning to z the value 5. We then have the predicate $\mathscr{S}'(x, y)$ which denotes $x + y = 5$.

Exercise 5.5 The predicate $\mathscr{C}(x, y)$ denoting '$x + y = y + x$' describes the property of commutativity for addition on the integers. By interpretation form a one-place predicate $\mathscr{C}'(x)$.

Exercise 5.6 Let the assertion 'x is a friend of y' be denoted by the predicate $\mathscr{F}(x, y)$. Define a suitable domain for this predicate and use the predicate to express the assertion 'Sam is a friend of Sarah's'.

Definition 5.12 Instantiation of a variable The assignment of a value to a variable in a predicate expression is called instantiating a variable.

Instantiation is a way of *binding* a variable that was free, by giving it a meaning. Once a free variable is captured by the binding there is no other way of interpreting it.

Exercise 5.7 In the predicate $\mathscr{V}(x, y)$, which denotes 'x voted for y' over the domain $\{\text{adults}\} \times \{\text{adults}\}$, the variables x and y are free. Give an instantiation for y and form a one-place predicate expression. Then give an instantiation for this one-place expression.

Binding the free variables in a predicate expression by instantiation gives the predicates a meaning and forms a proposition. A bound variable can no longer be instantiated. There is another very different method of binding variables in order to turn predicates into propositions. This method involves the key concepts of predicate calculus which give it power over the propositional calculus, namely *quantification*.

5.3 QUANTIFICATION

By adding the concept of a predicate to the propositional calculus we are able to express formally the assertions 'Gillian is a mother' and 'Gillian is a female'. However, we are still unable to express the assertion that 'all mothers are female'. The word 'all' is important because it gives a particular property to all the individuals in the domain {mothers}.

By rewriting the sentence we obtain 'For every x, if x is a mother then x is female', where the symbol x links the parts of the proposition together. We could, of course, choose the symbol y instead of x to do the linking for us. The linking symbol is a bound variable.

We also need to extend our calculus to enable us to express statements such as 'Some women are mothers' and 'There is only one integer that when added to 5 produces 5 as a result'. The technique of quantification applied to predicates describes the instantiation that is required in order to express such statements.

5.3.1 Universal quantification

We begin with a formal notation for expressing statements such as 'Every house has a door' and 'All students work hard'.

Definition 5.13 Universal quantification If $\mathscr{P}(x)$ is a unary predicate then the assertion 'For all x, $\mathscr{P}(x)$' meaning 'For all values of x, the assertion $\mathscr{P}(x)$ is true' is a statement that is universally quantified. The symbol, $\forall$, is the universal quantifier, and we write the assertion as $\forall x\ \mathscr{P}(x)$.

The free variable x in $\mathscr{P}(x)$, which fills the argument place of P, becomes *bound* by the quantifier $\forall$. Although x is not actually given a value, it is captured by the symbol $\forall$ into the 'meaning' of the predicate. The variable that is bound is said to be within the *scope* of the quantifier.

An alternative notation for universal quantification is

$$\forall\ \mathscr{P}(\ \underline{\quad}\ )$$

which explicitly shows the binding structure of the quantifier to the argument places.

This notation demonstrates that there is no need for the argument places to be filled by variables. It follows that the choice of symbols for the bound variables is unimportant. The notation does make clear, however, the scope of the binding by the quantification. Any variable that is not bound is a free variable in the predicate.

Example 5.20 In the expression $\underline{\forall x}\,\mathscr{M}(x)\wedge\mathscr{P}(x)$ the scope of $\forall x$ is the *first* predicate $\mathscr{M}(x)$ to which it is applied, so that the x in $\mathscr{P}(x)$ is free. To capture the free x in $\mathscr{P}(x)$ we write $\forall x\ [\mathscr{M}(x) \wedge \mathscr{P}(x)]$. We have used square brackets around a compound predicate expression that is quantified in order to improve the clarity of the notation. If the expression is complex we alternate the round and square brackets beginning from inside the expression.

Exercise 5.8 Use the notation for quantification that explicitly shows the binding structure in $\forall x\ \mathscr{M}(x)\wedge \forall y\ \mathscr{P}(x,y)$. Are there any free variables in the expression?

The bound occurrences of a variable are really just 'marks of connection' that link or bind a variable to its meaning. Variables are merely place holders that mark a position.

Example 5.21 The assertion that 'not every natural number is equal to 4' is $\neg\forall x\ (x = 4)$ and is true. This expression has only one meaning. The assertion $x = 4$ has many possible meanings depending on the value of the free occurrence of x.

Exercise 5.9 Use the predicate $\mathscr{V}(x, y)$, denoting 'x voted for y', to express the assertion that 'everyone voted for Donald Duck'.

If the predicate $\mathscr{P}(x)$ is true for every possible value of x, then $\forall x\ \mathscr{P}(x)$ is defined to be true; otherwise $\forall x\ \mathscr{P}(x)$ is false. Thus if the domain of interpretation is D, the assertion $\forall x\ \mathscr{P}(x)$ is true precisely when P is valid in D.

Quantification binds variables to form closed expressions that are propositions. A predicate that is closed by quantification therefore has a truth value.

Example 5.22 $\forall x\ (x < x + 1)$ meaning 'for all x, x is less than $x + 1$' is denoted by $\forall x\ \mathscr{P}(x)$ where $\mathscr{P}(x)$ denotes '$x < x + 1$'. Consider $\mathscr{P}(-3)$ as an example. Assuming the domain $\mathbb{Z}$, the proposition $\forall x\ \mathscr{P}(x)$ is true.

Example 5.23 $\forall x(x < 2^{32})$ is false if the domain is $\mathbb{Z}$, but true if the domain is the type *integer* in Pascal on the VAX 750.

Example 5.24 $\forall i(A[i] \geq 0)$ is true where $D = \{1, \ldots, 50\}$ and A is an array of 50 natural numbers. The following formula in the predicate calculus asserts that this array is sorted in non-decreasing order: $\forall i\ [(1 \leq i) \wedge (i < 50) \rightarrow A[i] \leq A[i + 1]]$.

Example 5.25 The proposition $\forall x\ \forall y\ (x + y > x)$ means 'for all x and y, $x + y$ is greater than x' and is true if $D = \mathbb{N}^+$ but false if $D = \mathbb{N}$ since $0 + 0 \not> 0$.

Exercise 5.10 Suppose $D = \{1, 2, \ldots, 100\}$ and that 'A = array[1 ... 100] of integer' is a Pascal declaration.

(a) Express in logical notation the fact that each entry of A is equal to 69.

(b) Write the Pascal code that makes the above condition true.

5.3.2 Existential quantification

We have used the symbol $\forall$ to capture the idea of quantification over *all* values in a domain of interpretation. Now we use quantification to assert that there is *at least one* element in the domain for which a predicate is true. We are then able to express the assertion that 'Mary has a grandfather' by rewriting it in the form 'There is an x such that x is the grandfather of Mary'.

Definition 5.14 Existential quantification If $\mathscr{P}(x)$ is a unary predicate, the assertion 'For some x, $\mathscr{P}(x)$' meaning 'There exists a value of x for which the assertion $\mathscr{P}(x)$ is true' is a statement that is existentially quantified. The symbol $\exists$ is the existential quantifier and we write $\exists x\ \mathscr{P}(x)$.

We define the proposition $\exists x\ \mathscr{P}(x)$ with domain D to be true if there is at least one element $d \in D$ for which $\mathscr{P}(d)$ is true and false otherwise. Thus the assertion $\exists x\ \mathscr{P}(x)$ is true in D precisely when $\mathscr{P}(x)$ is satisfiable in D.

Example 5.26 The truth of the assertion $x = 5y$ depends on the choices of both x and y. The truth of $\exists y\ (x = 6y)$ depends on x but not on y. It is true if $x = 12$ and $D = \mathbb{Z}$, but false if $x = 2$ and $D = \mathbb{Z}$. We restate the assertion as 'x is divisible by 6'. The assertion $\exists x\ (x = 5y)$ depends on y but not on x. It is true if $y \in \mathbb{Z}$ and $D = \mathbb{Z}$ but false if $D = \{1, 2, 3, 4\}$.

Example 5.27 The meaning of $\exists x\ (x < x + 1)$ is 'There exists an x such that x is less than $x + 1$' and is true if $D = \mathbb{Z}$.

Example 5.28 $\exists x\ (x = x + 1)$ is false if $D = \mathbb{Z}$ because there is no largest integer.

Exercise 5.11 Use the predicate $\mathscr{L}(x, y)$ denoting 'x laughed at y' to express the assertion that 'someone laughed at Charlie Chaplin'.

Exercise 5.12 Let $D = \{\text{houseowners}\}$ and let Julie, Dave, Ann, Bill, Henry $\in D$. The following predicates are defined over D:

$\mathscr{S}(x, y, z)$: 'x lives next door to y and z lives opposite x and y'
$\mathscr{M}(x, y)$: 'x and y have the same milkperson'

Consider the statement $\exists x\ \exists y\ \mathscr{S}(x, y, z) \wedge \mathscr{M}(x, z)$.

(a) Identify those variables that are not free.

(b) Identify those variables that are free.

(d) Explain why some variables are not free.

(e) Instantiate the free variables by suitable values and interpret the resulting proposition in English.

5.3.3 Existential quantification for uniqueness

Although we have used $\exists$ to capture the meaning of the assertion 'Mary has a grandfather' we have only captured the meaning that Mary has at least one grandfather. In order to assert that Mary has *only* one grandfather, we extend the predicate calculus by a third symbol for quantification.

Definition 5.15 Existential quantification for uniqueness The symbol $\exists!$ asserts that there is one and only one element of the domain of interpretation that makes a predicate true. The assertion $\exists! x\ \mathscr{P}(x)$ means 'There exists a unique x for which $\mathscr{P}(x)$ is true'.

The assertion $\exists! x\ \mathscr{P}(x)$ is true in D when there is exactly one $x \in D$ for which $\mathscr{P}(x)$ is true.

Example 5.29 $\exists! x\ (x < 1)$ is true if $D = \mathbb{N}$, but false if $D = \mathbb{Z}$.

Note that for any predicate $\mathscr{P}$ the proposition $\exists! x\ \mathscr{P}(x) \rightarrow \exists x\ \mathscr{P}(x)$ is true.

Exercise 5.13 Express in the predicate calculus the assertion that 'Bill is married to only one woman'.

Exercise 5.14 Assume that the arithmetic predicates, $=$ and $<$, and operations $+$, $-$ and $\times$ have been defined in the usual way. Write the following statement in the formal notation of the predicate calculus: 'There is a real number y such that for every real number x the sum $x + y$ is positive'.

Exercise 5.15 Write in English the inverse, converse and contrapositive for the statement 'If I do problems in mathematics, then I will enjoy mathematics more'. Which of these is equivalent to the original statement?

Exercise 5.16 By defining appropriate predicates, express the following sentences in predicate logic and give their truth-values:

(a) The King of Japan is bald

(b) The King of Japan is not bald

(c) $\neg$ the King of Japan is bald

You should obtain the same truth-values that were correct for the same exercise in Sec. 3.3.

5.3.4 Binding variables in a program

The concept of a bound variable was first used in logic but there are many familiar examples of binding a variable in mathematics. One occurs when the Greek letter Σ is used to define the sum of the numbers $f(i)$ obtained by letting i vary from 1 through to n, where f is any function over $\mathbb{N}$. We write

$$\sum_{i=1}^{n} f(i) = f(1) + f(2) + \cdots + f(n)$$

where i is bound by the summation and the expression $f(i)$ is the scope of the binding. For example, $\sum_{i=1}^{n} i^2 = 1^2 + 2^2 + \cdots + n^2$.

Exercise 5.17 Use the notation for summation to express the binomial theorem that is given on page 78.

The concept of free and bound variables has been applied to the semantics of programs. We shall see in Chapter 11 that the binding of a variable in an environment is fundamental to declarative languages. In procedural programming languages, such as Pascal, the concept of a variable is more complex than in logic. A Pascal variable has both a name and a value which can be changed.

Pascal variables are free within an area of scope. They are bound to a *meaning* when they are declared. The text within which the variable can be used is called the *scope* of the variable and may be the whole program or an inner block of the program. When we run a Pascal program all the bound variables are given an actual value by the execution of the assignment statements in the program. The program state is changed by assignment in a way that cannot be reversed. When a variable is declared, however, the binding only lasts while the control of the program is within those blocks within which the variable can be used. As soon as a particular binding is out of scope, the variable may resume a meaning it was given in some outer block.

Exercise 5.18 In this fragment of a Pascal program, the names of program variables and constants are bound to their meanings by declarations:

```
const   i=2;
type    age=10 ... 100;
var     personsage: age;

begin
        personsage := 10;
        personsage := personsage + i
end;
```

(a) Record all the declarations that give the Pascal identifiers a meaning. These declarations are *definitions* in the program. What are the meanings?

(b) Record all the *commands* in this program fragment.

(c) Contrast the effect that definitions and commands have on the computational state of a program.

(d) Binding is a localized association of an identifier to a value established by a definition. What is the name for the region of text over which binding is effective?

(e) In part (a) you have made a record of identifier bindings. This is called an *environment*. In part (b) you recorded the effect of assignments. This is called the *store*. The computational state of a program in Pascal consists of both a store and an environment. Expressions, definitions and commands are all interpreted relative to a complete state. Their 'outputs' differ. Using the example program fragment to illustrate your answer, describe the 'output' for expressions, commands and definitions relative to a complete state.

(f) Draw the binding arrows from the occurrences of names (or Pascal identifiers) that are being *used* in the program to the occurrences where they are being *bound*.

It is useful to compare the use of free and bound variables in a Pascal program with the concept of free and bound variables as they were originally defined in the predicate calculus. We say that the occurrence of a name that is being used in a program is an *applied* occurrence; the occurrence of a name that is being bound is a *binding* occurrence.

Example 5.30 In a Pascal program the declaration

```
type month = 1 ...12;
var thismonth: month;
```

gives 'thismonth' as a binding occurrence where 'thismonth' is being defined and 'month' as an applied occurrence where 'month' is being used in a definition.

It seems that we could manage without names in a Pascal program and just use arrows to show where values are given. Unfortunately we would then suffer from the loss of readability.

We can now identify the *free* identifiers in a program construct as those identifiers that are not bound in the construct. Identifiers are *bound* in the block of text where they are declared but are *free* in any inner blocks of text.

Exercise 5.19 Consider the binding that takes place in the following part of a program:

```
var
        temp: tableindex;
begin
        temp := x;
        x := y;
        y := temp
end;
```

In the above fragment of a Pascal program, draw in 'binding arrows' from the applied occurrence of each identifier to its binding occurrence. Which of the identifiers x, y, i, 'temp', 'tableindex' are free?

Exercise 5.20 Identify the free identifiers in the following fragment of a Pascal program and explain why the remaining identifiers are not free:

```
type
    index = 1 ...maxindex;
    aword=array[index] of char;
var
    word: aword;
    i: index;
begin
     while i < maxindex
     do
        begin
            read(firstcharacter);
            word[i] := firstcharacter;
            i := i + 1
        end
end
```

5.3.5 The domain of interpretation

We have now identified four ways of binding the free variables in a predicate: one is by instantiation and the remaining three are by quantification. The meaning of a predicate is given by interpretation in a domain which should be specified outside a quantified assertion. This is preferable to including the domain within the quantified assertion by writing $\forall x \in D.\mathscr{P}(x)$.

Example 5.31 The assertion that 'every integer is less than 2^{32}' should be written 'if $D = \mathbb{Z}$ then $\forall x\,(x < 2^{32})$', rather than $\forall x \in \mathbb{Z}\;\; x < 2^{32}$. If $D = Q$ the assertion would be written $\forall x\,(x \in \mathbb{Z} \rightarrow x < 2^{32})$.

If the domain of interpretation is finite, we can express the quantifiers $\forall, \exists, \exists!$ in terms of the propositional calculus. However, for a large finite domain this is impractical and for an infinite one it is impossible.

Example 5.32 Let $D = \{a, b, c\}$. Then

$$\begin{aligned}
\forall x\; \mathscr{P}(x) &\equiv \mathscr{P}(a) \wedge \mathscr{P}(b) \wedge \mathscr{P}(c) \\
\exists x\; \mathscr{P}(x) &\equiv \mathscr{P}(a) \vee \mathscr{P}(b) \vee \mathscr{P}(c) \\
\exists! x\; \mathscr{P}(x) &\equiv (\mathscr{P}(a) \wedge \neg\mathscr{P}(b) \wedge \neg\mathscr{P}(c)) \\
&\quad \vee(\mathscr{P}(b) \wedge \neg\mathscr{P}(a) \wedge \neg\mathscr{P}(c)) \\
&\quad \vee(\mathscr{P}(c) \wedge \neg\mathscr{P}(a) \wedge \neg\mathscr{P}(b))
\end{aligned}$$

In a quantified expression there may be argument places that remain free, waiting to be bound by instantiation or by further quantification to give meaning to the predicate.

Example 5.33 The predicate $\exists y\; \mathscr{P}(x, y, z)$ has two free variables x and z. If $D = \{a, b, c\}$ then $\exists y\; \mathscr{P}(x, y, z) \equiv \mathscr{P}(x, a, z) \vee \mathscr{P}(x, b, z) \vee \mathscr{P}(x, c, z)$.

The syntax of predicate logic will allow the formation of meaningless predicate expressions that quantify over variables that are not free. We give simple equivalences to reduce these expressions to ones that have meaning. If y does not occur as an individual variable in $\mathscr{P}(x_1, \ldots, x_n)$ then the assertions $\forall y\; \mathscr{P}(x_1, \ldots, x_n)$ and $\exists y\; \mathscr{P}(x_1, \ldots, x_n)$ are both equivalent to $\mathscr{P}(x_1, \ldots, x_n)$, since none of the x_i's are bound by the quantification. As a special case, if $\mathscr{P}$ is a proposition then the truth-value of $\exists x\; \mathscr{P}$ or $\forall x\; \mathscr{P}$ is equal to the truth-value of $\mathscr{P}$ since $\exists x\; \mathscr{P} \equiv \forall x\; \mathscr{P} \equiv \mathscr{P}$.

The domain must not be empty The semantics of the predicate calculus is based on the construction of a domain of interpretation which contains those objects for which a predicate makes sense. Quantification can then take place over those variables. A predicate is satisfied if there are some objects in the domain for which it makes sense; a predicate is valid if it makes sense for all objects in the domain. The meaning of a predicate is therefore characterized by those objects for that it makes sense.

Suppose there are no such objects, however. Many people might feel that they belong to the domain of 'perfect people', but they are unlikely to satisfy all the properties demanded by the predicate for 'x is perfect'. We consider that such a domain is artificial since we cannot construct it, and exclude such domains from the semantics of the predicate calculus. However, within philosophical logic the fact that universal quantification does *not* imply that there are objects that can be quantified over has been a difficult problem. Clearly, in the construction and analysis of complex systems, it is essential that the domain of interpretation is stated before predicates are defined.

Quantification over a subset of the domain We aim to represent the *meaning* of an English sentence when we translate it into the predicate calculus. The translation is not a mechanical activity, and we identify two patterns of translation that are easily confused. They are illustrated by examples that allow the quantification to range over some elements that belong to a particular subset of a domain. In order to express our example argument on page 135 we need to translate 'All mothers are female'. We should also be able to translate 'Some men are fathers'.

Example 5.34 Let $D = \{\text{living things}\}$ and let

$\mathscr{S}(x)$ denote 'x is a student'
$\mathscr{P}(x)$ denote 'x is poor'

The assertion that 'All students are poor' means 'Whatever value we choose for x, if x is a student then x is poor'. The translation is $\forall x\ [\mathscr{S}(x) \rightarrow \mathscr{P}(x)]$.

The assertion that 'Some students are poor' expresses the fact that there is at least one student in our domain of interpretation. This can be phrased intuitively as 'There is a student and the student is poor', and can be translated as $\exists x[\mathscr{S}(x) \wedge \mathscr{P}(x)\ ]$.

We have illustrated two patterns for quantifying over a subset of the domain of interpretation. The first asserts that everything in a certain category has some property, and its translation has the pattern

$$\forall x\ [\ldots \rightarrow \ldots]$$

The second asserts that there is some object or objects in the category having the property, and is translated as

$$\exists x\ [\ldots \wedge \ldots]$$

These patterns describe the universal quantifier applied to a conjunction between predicates and the existential quantifier applied to a conditional expression between predicates. We should explore the result of applying $\forall$ to $\wedge$ and $\exists$ to $\rightarrow$ in expressions of compound predicates.

Example 5.35 Using the notation of Example 5.34, we see that the assertion

$$\forall x\ [\mathscr{S}(x) \wedge \mathscr{P}(x)]$$

is a translation of the assertion that 'Everything is a student and is poor'. This is a much stronger assertion than the sentence in Example 5.34 asserting that 'All students are poor'.

Similarly, the assertion

$$\exists x\ [\mathscr{S}(x) \rightarrow \mathscr{P}(x)]$$

is translated as 'There is something which is poor, if it is a student' and is a much weaker assertion than the sentence, in Example 5.34, that 'Some students are poor'.

The pattern

$$\forall x\ [\ldots \wedge \ldots]$$

is usually too strong because it asserts that each object in the domain of interpretation has both of the properties that are quantified over. In order to translate 'All mothers are female' we want to say that 'Those people who are mothers are female'. The assertion that 'every person is both a mother and female' is much stronger!

The pattern

$$\exists x\ [\ldots \rightarrow \ldots]$$

is usually too weak because it asserts that some objects either lack the property denoted by the first predicate or have the property denoted by the second predicate. In order to translate 'Some men are fathers', we want to say that 'There is at least one man and that man is a father'. The assertion that 'There is a father, if that person is a man' is much weaker!

Exercise 5.21 Represent the assertions 'All fathers are male' and 'Some women are sisters' in the predicate calculus.

Example 5.36 We now express the more complicated assertion, 'Students like grants'. Let $D = \{\text{people}\}$ and define the predicates:

$\mathcal{S}(x)$: 'x is a student'
$\mathcal{G}(x)$: 'x is a grant'
$\mathcal{L}(x, y)$: 'x likes y'

We must capture the meaning 'if a person is a student and there is something that is a grant, then that person likes the grant'. We write, $\forall x\ \forall y\ [(\mathcal{S}(x) \wedge \mathcal{G}(y)) \rightarrow \mathcal{L}(x, y)]$. This expression is true if there are no students and no grants!

Exercise 5.22 Use the predicate calculus to express the meaning of the assertion 'There is a student who likes every lecturer'.

The notational convention of relativizing quantifiers is sometimes used to abbreviate those sentences in predicate logic that quantify over particular subsets of the domain of interpretation.

Definition 5.16 Relativized quantifier For any unary predicate constant symbols $\mathcal{P}$ and $\mathcal{F}$:

(a) $\forall x\ \mathcal{P}\ \mathcal{F}(x)$ stands for $\forall x\ [\mathcal{P}(x) \rightarrow \mathcal{F}(x)]$,

(b) $\exists x\ \mathcal{P}\ \mathcal{F}(x)$ stands for $\exists x\ [\mathcal{P}(x) \wedge \mathcal{F}(x)]$.

5.3.6 Relating the quantifiers by order

If more than one quantifier is applied to a predicate, the order in which the variables are bound is the same as the order in the quantifier list. For example, $\forall x\ \exists y\ \mathcal{P}(x, y)$ denotes $\forall x\ [\exists y\ \mathcal{P}(x, y)]$. The *binding* order can profoundly affect the *meaning* of an assertion. The assertion $\forall x\ \exists y\ P(x, y)$ can be paraphrased informally as

> 'No matter what value of x is chosen, a value of y can be found such that $P(x, y)$ holds'

In contrast, the assertion $\exists y\ \forall x\ P(x, y)$ can be paraphrased as

> 'There is at least one value for y that can be chosen so that no matter what value is chosen for x, then $P(x, y)$ holds'

Example 5.37 Let $D = \{\text{married people}\}$ and let $\mathcal{M}(x, y)$ be the predicate denoting 'x is married to y'. Then $\forall x\ \exists y\ \mathcal{M}(x, y)$ is true, but $\exists y\ \forall x\ \mathcal{M}(x, y)$ is false (unless $D = \{\text{Sultan}\} \cup \{\text{wives in harem}\}$) .

Example 5.38 Let $D = \mathbb{Z}$ and let $\mathcal{A}(x, y)$: '$x + y = 0$'. Then $\forall x\ \exists y\ \mathcal{A}(x, y)$ meaning 'every integer has an additive inverse' is true, but $\exists y\ \forall x\ \mathcal{A}(x, y)$ meaning 'there exists a number which when added to any number gives 0' is false.

Example 5.39 Let $D = \mathbb{Z}$ and let $\mathscr{S}(x, y, z)$: '$x + y = z$'. Then $\forall x\ \forall y\ \exists! z\ \mathscr{S}(x, y, z)$ meaning 'every pair of integers has a unique sum' is true, but $\forall x\ \exists! z\ \forall y\ \mathscr{S}(x, y, z)$ meaning 'for every x there is a unique z which is the sum of x plus any number y' is false.

Exercise 5.23 Use 'everyday English' to explain the meaning of the propositions $\forall x\ \exists y\ \mathscr{S}(x, y)$ and $\exists y\ \forall x\ \mathscr{S}(x, y)$. If the domain is $\mathbb{Z}$, is $\exists y\ \forall x\ (x.y = x)$ true?

Exercise 5.24 Let the domain of interpretation be the set of all people that have lived and let $\mathscr{F}(x, y)$ denote 'x is the father of y'. Use everyday English to explain the meaning of the propositions $\forall x\ \exists y\ \mathscr{F}(x, y)$ and $\exists y\ \forall x\ \mathscr{F}(x, y)$. State whether these assertions are true or false.

Exercise 5.25 If the domain of interpretation is $\mathbb{Z}$, state the meaning of the assertion $\exists x\ \forall y\ (x.y = x)$ informally and say whether it is true or false.

We use equivalence between propositions to state where the order of individual bound variables *can* be changed without affecting the meaning:

$$\begin{aligned} \forall x\ \forall y\ \mathscr{P}(x, y) &\equiv \forall y\ \forall x\ \mathscr{P}(x, y) \\ \exists x\ \exists y\ \mathscr{P}(x, y) &\equiv \exists y\ \exists x\ \mathscr{P}(x, y) \end{aligned}$$

Exercise 5.26 Let $\mathscr{P}(x, y)$ denote the predicate '$x + y = 0$'. Given that the domain of interpretation is $\mathbb{Z}$, which of the following describes the fact that every integer has an additive inverse? Which is the strongest and which is the weakest of these assertions?

(a) $\exists x\ \forall y\ \mathscr{P}(x, y)$

(b) $\forall x\ \forall y\ \mathscr{P}(x, y)$

(c) $\exists x\ \exists y\ \mathscr{P}(x, y)$

(d) $\forall x\ \exists y\ \mathscr{P}(x, y)$

5.3.7 Equivalences between quantifiers

The notion of equivalence within the predicate calculus is, as in the propositional calculus, at a meta-level to the formal system. Assertions in English will often be represented by different but equivalent expressions in the predicate calculus.

Our first basic equivalence means that the existential quantifier can be expressed in terms of the universal quantifier. We have

$$\neg\forall x\ \mathscr{P}(x) \equiv \exists x\ \neg\mathscr{P}(x)$$

We can argue intuitively that this equivalence holds:

> 'Since $\forall x\ \mathscr{P}(x)$ is true when $\mathscr{P}(x)$ is true for *every* object in the domain of interpretation, it must be that $\neg\forall x\ \mathscr{P}(x)$ is true when $\mathscr{P}(x)$ is *not* true for every interpretation of x. However, that is so when $\mathscr{P}(x)$ is false for some x. Therefore $\neg\mathscr{P}(x)$ is true for some x, and we have $\exists x\ \neg\mathscr{P}(x)$.'

It follows that $\forall x\ \mathscr{P}(x) \equiv \neg\exists x\ \neg\mathscr{P}(x)$ because:

> 'Since $\mathscr{P}(x)$ is true for all x, it must be that there is no x for which $\mathscr{P}(x)$ is false.'

A further equivalence states $\forall x\ \neg\mathscr{P}(x) \equiv \neg\exists x\ \mathscr{P}(x)$:

> 'Since $\mathscr{P}(x)$ is false for all x, it must be that there is no x for which $\mathscr{P}(x)$ is true.'

It follows that $\neg\forall x\ \neg\mathscr{P}(x) \equiv \exists x\ \mathscr{P}(x)$ because:

> 'Since $\mathscr{P}(x)$ is not false for all x, it must be that there is at least one x for which $\mathscr{P}(x)$ is true.'

These equivalences imply that $\exists$ is redundant if we have $\forall$.

Exercise 5.27 Use the rules of equivalence to write $\exists x[\mathscr{S}(x) \wedge \mathscr{P}(x)\ ]$ in a language of predicates in which only the symbols $\forall, \rightarrow$ and $\neg$ are used.

Clearly $\exists x\ \mathscr{S}(x)$ is more readable than $\neg\forall x\ \neg\mathscr{S}(x)$ and we usually use it for that reason. Using a minimal set of connectives detracts from the readability of the notation.

The following equivalences involve compound quantified assertions:

$$\begin{array}{rcll} \forall x\ \mathscr{P}(x) \wedge \forall x\ \mathscr{Q}(x) & \equiv & \forall x\ [\mathscr{P}(x) \wedge \mathscr{Q}(x)] & (\text{ not true for } \vee) \\ \exists x\ \mathscr{P}(x) \vee \exists x\ \mathscr{Q}(x) & \equiv & \exists x\ [\mathscr{P}(x) \vee \mathscr{Q}(x)] & (\text{ not true for } \wedge\ ) \end{array}$$

Example 5.40 To see that $\exists x\ P(x) \wedge \exists x\ \mathscr{Q}(x) \not\equiv \exists x\ [\mathscr{P}(x) \wedge \mathscr{Q}(x)]$ consider the case where $D = \mathbb{Z}$ and

$\mathscr{P}(x)$: '$x = 2$'

$\mathscr{Q}(x)$: '$x = 3$'

Clearly $\exists x\ \mathscr{P}(x)$ is true, and $\exists x\ \mathscr{Q}(x)$ is true so $\exists x\ P(x) \wedge \exists x\ Q(x)$ is true. However, $\exists x\ [\mathscr{P}(x) \wedge \mathscr{Q}(x)]$ is false since there is *no* integer that is equal to both 2 and 3.

Exercise 5.28 Show that the following equivalence holds:

$$\neg\forall x\ [\mathscr{P}(x) \rightarrow \mathscr{Q}(x)] \equiv \exists x\ [\mathscr{P}(x) \wedge \neg\mathscr{Q}(x)]$$

5.3.8 Modelling mathematics in the calculus

We have already seen in Chapter 2 that there are a number of ways of defining sets. Whereas finite sets can be defined explicitly, by enumerating the elements, for large sets this is inconvenient and for infinite sets it is impossible. Many important sets have all their elements characterized by a particular predicate.

Example 5.41 If the domain of interpretation is $\mathbb{Z}$, then the set of natural numbers is characterized by the fact that each of its members is greater than or equal to 0. Thus $\mathbb{N}$ is precisely that subset of $\mathbb{Z}$ whose elements x satisfy the predicate $x \geq 0$. We can write $\mathbb{N} = \{x : x \geq 0\}$. If the domain were $\mathbb{Q}$, however, this would not be a correct description of $\mathbb{N}$.

In general, if the domain is D and $\mathscr{P}$ is a 1-ary predicate then the set $S = \{x : \mathscr{P}(x)\}$ is the set of elements x of D for which $\mathscr{P}(x)$ is true. The statement that there *exists* a set whose elements are exactly those elements x of S for which $\mathscr{P}(x)$ holds is the axiom of comprehension in set theory. It is therefore necessary to have a set already in order to specify the set S uniquely.

Example 5.42 If $D = \mathbb{Z}$ then the set E of even integers may be described by $E = \{x : \exists y\ (x = 2y)\}$.

Exercise 5.29 Describe the following sets in 'everyday English':

(a) $\{p/q : p \geq 0 \wedge q > 0\}$ where $D = \mathbb{Z}$

(b) $\{(x, y) : 0 \leq x \leq 1 \wedge 0 \leq y \leq 1\}$ where $D = \mathbb{R} \times \mathbb{R}$

Exercise 5.30 Translate the following into symbolic notation:

(a) The set of all numbers between 1 and 2 inclusive

(b) The set of all points in the plane whose distance from the origin does not exceed 2 and whose coordinates are rational numbers

(c) The set of all irrational numbers

An important use of the predicate calculus is to formalize mathematical statements about the elements of sets.

Example 5.43 Let $D = \mathbb{Z}$ and assume the definition of the predicates:

$\mathscr{N}(x)$: 'x is a non-negative integer'
$\mathscr{E}(x)$: 'x is even'
$\mathscr{O}(x)$: 'x is odd'
$\mathscr{P}(x)$: 'x is prime'
$\mathscr{M}(x, y, z)$: '$x.y = z$'

We translate into the predicate calculus the following informal mathematical statements:

'There exists an even integer'	$\exists x \; \mathscr{E}(x)$
'Every integer is even or odd'	$\forall x \; [\mathscr{E}(x) \vee \mathscr{O}(x)]$
'All prime integers are non-negative'	$\forall x \; [\mathscr{P}(x) \rightarrow \mathscr{N}(x)]$
'The only even prime is two'	$\forall x \; [(\mathscr{E}(x) \wedge \mathscr{P}(x)) \rightarrow x = 2]$
'There is one and only one even prime'	$\exists! x \; [\mathscr{E}(x) \wedge \mathscr{P}(x)]$
'Not all integers are odd'	$\neg\forall x \; \mathscr{O}(x)$ or $\exists x \; \neg\mathscr{O}(x)$
'Not all primes are odd'	$\neg\forall x \; [\mathscr{P}(x) \rightarrow \mathscr{O}(x)]$ or $\exists x \; [\mathscr{P}(x) \wedge \neg\mathscr{O}(x)]$
'If $x = 0$, then $xy = x$ for all values of y'	$\forall x \; [x = 0 \rightarrow \forall y \; \mathscr{M}(x, y, x)]$
'If $x.y = x$ for every y, then $x = 0$'	$\forall x \; [\forall y \; \mathscr{M}(x, y, x) \rightarrow x = 0]$
'If $x.y \neq x$ for some y, then $x \neq 0$'	$\forall x[\exists y \; \neg\mathscr{M}(x, y, x) \rightarrow \neg(x = 0)]$

5.4 SUMMARY

In this chapter, we have presented a logical calculus that is sufficiently powerful for use in both the construction and analysis of complex systems. The calculus is constructed by adding predicates and the technique of quantification to the propositional calculus. After presenting the syntax and semantics of the predicate calculus at a theoretical level we have illustrated its expressiveness by writing mathematical statements formally as predicates. In Chapter 7 the language of predicates will be extended to a first-order language that is appropriate for the expression of theories about systems. The predicate calculus therefore underpins the activity of building theories in order to specify systems. The extra inference rules that must be added to the calculus are presented in Chapter 6, and complete the deduction system for reasoning about complex systems. We shall see in Chapter 10 that some specification approaches are based on the predicate calculus whereas others use equational logic, as a subset of predicate logic, and the concept of an algebra for specification.

5.5 FURTHER EXERCISES

Exercise 5.31 Determine the truth-value of the following propositions. The domain is the set $\mathbb{R}$.

(a) $\forall x \; (x < x + 5)$

(b) $\exists x \; (x \in \mathbb{Q} \wedge x = 8\frac{1}{2})$

(c) $\exists x \; (x \in \mathbb{Q} \wedge x = 3.172 \vee x = 5)$

(d) $\exists! x \; ((x > 100) \wedge (x \leq 101))$

(e) $\forall x\ \exists y\ (x < y)$

(f) $\forall x\ \exists y\ (x > y)$

(g) $\exists x\ \forall y\ (x > y)$

(h) $\forall x\ \exists y\ (x.y = 0)$

(i) $\forall x\ \exists! y\ (x.y = 0)$

(j) $\forall x\ \exists y\ (x.y = 1)$

(k) $\exists y\ \forall x\ (x.y = x)$

(l) $\exists x\ (x = 5 \wedge x \neq x)$

Exercise 5.32 Let

$\mathscr{S}(x, y, z)$ denote the predicate '$x + y = z$
$\mathscr{P}(x, y, z)$ denote '$x.y = z$'
$\mathscr{L}(x, y)$ denote '$x < y$'

where $+$, $.$ and $<$ are the usual arithmetic operators. Assuming that the domain is $\mathbb{N}$, use these predicates to express in symbolic notation the following assertions:

(a) For every x and y, there is a z such that $x + y = z$.

(b) No x is less than 0.

(c) For all $x, x + 0 = x$.

(d) For all $x, x.y = y$ for all y.

(e) There is an x such that $x.y = y$ for all y.

What are the truth-values of these assertions?

Exercise 5.33 Assuming that the domain is $\mathbb{N}$, for each of the following assertions find a predicate $\mathscr{P}$ that makes the implication false:

(a) $\forall x \exists! y\ \mathscr{P}(x, y) \rightarrow \exists! y\ \forall x \mathscr{P}(x, y)$

(b) $\exists! y\ \forall x \mathscr{P}(x, y) \rightarrow \forall x \exists! y\ \mathscr{P}(x, y)$

Exercise 5.34 Find a domain of interpretation for which the following propositions are true. In each case choose the domain to be as large as possible a subset of $\mathbb{Z}$.

(a) $\forall x\ (x > 3)$

(b) $\forall x (x = 3)$

(c) $\forall x\ \exists y\ (x + y = 3)$

(d) $\exists y\ \forall x\ (x + y < 0)$

Exercise 5.35 Identify the constructs that give the predicate calculus greater expressive power than the propositional calculus.

Exercise 5.36 Suppose that over the domain $\mathbb{Z}$ the predicate $\mathscr{P}(x, y)$ denotes '$y^2 = x$'. Which of the following assertions states that the square of every integer is an integer? Describe the meaning of each of these assertions and state whether they are true or false.

(a) $\exists x\ \forall y\ \mathscr{P}(x, y)$

(b) $\forall y\ \exists x\ \mathscr{P}(x, y)$

(c) $\forall x\ \exists y\ \mathscr{P}(x, y)$

(d) $\exists y\ \forall x\ \mathscr{P}(x, y)$

(e) $\forall x\ \forall y\ \mathscr{P}(x, y)$

Exercise 5.37 Use equivalences in the predicate calculus to reduce the negation of $\exists x\ [\mathscr{P}(x) \wedge \forall y\ \mathscr{Q}(x, y)]$ to a form in which any 'not' connective operates on a simple predicate expression (and not on a quantified predicate expression).

Exercise 5.38 Use the predicate calculus to express the assertion that 'every non-zero rational has a multiplicative inverse'. Be careful to choose your domain so that quantification of variables takes place over the whole domain.

Exercise 5.39 Show on a Venn diagram the set of prime numbers in the domain of natural numbers. Let

$\mathscr{P}(x)$ denote 'x is a prime number'
$\mathscr{O}(x)$ denote 'x is an odd number'

Express the following assertions in the predicate calculus:

(a) '2 is a prime number'
(b) '4 is not prime'
(c) '5 and 11 are both prime'
(d) 'Neither 8 nor 10 are prime'
(e) 'Some numbers are not prime'
(f) 'If x is prime then x is odd'

Now express the negation of these assertions first in English and then in the predicate calculus. You may give more than one answer but should present the simplest form finally in the predicate calculus.

FURTHER READING

Again Enderton (1972) and Galton (1990) are recommended for their comprehensive treatment of mathematical logic and the predicate calculus.

Chapter 6

PROOF WITHIN PREDICATE LOGIC

In this chapter we extend the system of natural deduction for the propositional calculus, which we presented in Chapter 4, to the predicate calculus, by adding inference rules for each of the quantifiers. We also use the direct method of proof in the domain of mathematics in Sec. 6.1, and identify logical implication as a stronger notion of implication before proving necessary and sufficient conditions between propositions. In Sec. 6.2 we use the indirect methods of proof by contraposition and by contradiction. After introducing the principle of induction we use the proof method of mathematical induction in Sec. 6.3 and show how induction is used to define sets and sequences. Finally we give inductive definitions of the well-formed formulae of the propositional and predicate calculi.

6.1 DIRECT METHODS OF PROOF

The direct method of proof was used in the deduction system that we constructed in Chapter 4. We begin by extending this system in order to make deductions within the predicate calculus.

6.1.1 The need for more proof rules

At the beginning of Sec. 5.1 we observed that we could not formally represent (let alone prove) the argument

All mothers are female
Gillian is a mother

Gillian is female

Now we can represent the argument using the following predicates:

$\mathscr{M}(x)$: 'x is a mother'
$\mathscr{F}(x)$: 'x is female'
g: 'Gillian'

The predicates $\mathscr{M}(x)$ and $\mathscr{F}(x)$ are defined over the domain of interpretation, $D = \{\text{people}\}$. The constant symbol, g, names the object Gillian in that domain. The argument is then written as

$$\frac{\begin{array}{c}\forall x\ [\mathscr{M}(x) \rightarrow \mathscr{F}(x)] \\ \mathscr{M}(g)\end{array}}{\mathscr{F}(g)}$$

In order to be able to *prove* such inferences we need to add more inference rules to the natural deduction system presented in Chapter 4.

6.1.2 Proof rules for quantifiers

We need to add four more rules: two for the universal quantifier and two for the existential quantifier. In this chapter we assume that derivations are made within the natural deduction system constructed in Chapter 4, and therefore write $\vdash$ rather than $\vdash_{ND}$.

Universal instantiation (UI) rule (or the $\forall$-elimination rule) From the assertion $\forall x\, \mathscr{A}(x)$ where $\mathscr{A}$ is a predicate over D, we may infer $\mathscr{A}(t)$ where t is any *arbitrary* element of D. That is,

$$\frac{\forall x\ \mathscr{A}(x)}{\mathscr{A}(t)}$$

giving $\forall x\ \mathscr{A}(x) \vdash\ \mathscr{A}(t)$.

An expression that refers to any one element in D is called an arbitrary term. A particular element could be referred to by a proper name, such as Joe, or by an individual constant such as a.

To eliminate a universal quantifier we could use a specific element instead of an arbitrary element. In our example argument we need to use a specific element from the domain of all people in order to prove that Gillian is female. The use of a specific element of D provides a *weaker* rule for universal instantiation. If we used a *stronger* rule and if the names of the elements in D are $a_1, a_2, \ldots, a_n$ we can infer

$$\mathscr{P}(a_1) \wedge \mathscr{P}(a_2) \wedge \cdots \wedge \mathscr{P}(a_n)$$

Here each a_i is an individual constant symbol that names an element in D. For an infinite domain, however, we would need an infinitely long formula. To overcome this problem we have introduced the idea of the arbitrary element in our domain and use the name t to denote the arbitrary term.

The previous argument is proved by the following sequence of deductions:

Derivation

1.	$\forall x\ [\mathscr{M}(x) \rightarrow\ \mathscr{F}(x)]$	premise
2.	$\mathscr{M}(g)$	premise
3.	$\mathscr{M}(g)\ \rightarrow \mathscr{F}(g)$	UI with g/x on 1
4.	$\mathscr{F}(g)$	MP on 2,3

end

We add a comment to our formal derivation to explain that in using the universal instantiation rule the variable x is replaced by the constant symbol g that refers to Gillian as an element in D. We write g/x to represent the substitution of x by g.

Universal generalization (UG) rule (or the $\forall$-introduction rule) If the assertion $\mathscr{A}(a)$ is true and a is a name that can refer to *any* element in D then $\forall x\ \mathscr{A}(x)$ may be inferred:

$$\frac{\mathscr{A}(a)}{\forall x\ \mathscr{A}(x)}$$

To *introduce* a universal quantifier the predicate must involve a name that is completely general and has not already been used in the derivation to refer to a particular element in D. We ensure that it *does not matter* which individual is referred to by a, by requiring that a does *not* occur in either the premises or the assumptions that are in the current scope of the derivation.

Whereas we need a general name, in the syntax of our language, in order to introduce $\forall$, we can name either a general element or a specific element in D to eliminate $\forall$.

Existential instantiation (EI) rule (or the $\exists$-elimination rule) From the assertion $\exists x\ \mathscr{A}(x)$ we may infer $\mathscr{A}(a)$ for *some* element $a \in D$. Here we choose the name a to stand for some specific and as yet unnamed object in the domain:

$$\frac{\exists x\ \mathscr{A}(x)}{\mathscr{A}(a)}$$

We choose the individual constant a as a dummy name to instantiate the bound variable x. The hypothesis states that *something* has the property denoted by $\mathscr{A}(\underline{\quad})$, we just give it the name a. We must ensure that the individual constant that we choose has not already been used in either the predicate $\mathscr{A}(\underline{\quad})$, in a premise or in the assumptions that are in the current scope of the derivation.

Existential generalization (EG) rule (or the $\exists$-introduction rule) If the assertion $\mathscr{A}(t)$ is true, where t is an arbitrary term in the domain D, then D must be non-empty. If that is so we can infer that there is at least one object for which $\mathscr{A}$ holds and we can assert $\exists x\ \mathscr{A}(x)$:

$$\frac{\mathscr{A}(t)}{\exists x\ \mathscr{A}(x)}$$

Example 6.1 The following example is indicative of the kind of argument that is used in a knowledge-based system. The domain of interpretation is {footballers}. We have the following 'facts' that we take as premises for our deduction:

1. The England team wins providing it contains at least one brilliant player.
2. Every Spurs player is brilliant.
3. Fred plays for Spurs.

A 'query' to this 'knowledge-based' system might be something like

'If it is known that Fred is playing for England, will England win?'

We make the following definitions

$\mathscr{P}(x)$:	'x plays for England'	
$\mathscr{B}(x)$:	'x is brilliant'	
$\mathscr{S}(x)$:	'x plays for Spurs'	
$\mathscr{E}$:	'England win'	(proposition)
f :	'Fred'	(individual constant)

We have as premises:

$$\exists x\ [\mathscr{B}(x) \wedge \mathscr{P}(x)] \rightarrow \mathscr{E},\ \forall x\ [\mathscr{S}(x) \rightarrow \mathscr{B}(x)] \text{ and } \mathscr{S}(f)$$

We have to prove that $\mathscr{P}(f) \rightarrow \mathscr{E}$. We express our deduction as

$$\exists x\ [\mathscr{B}(x) \wedge \mathscr{P}(x)] \rightarrow \mathscr{E},\ \forall x\ [\mathscr{S}(x) \rightarrow \mathscr{B}(x)],\ \mathscr{S}(f) \vdash \mathscr{P}(f) \rightarrow \mathscr{E}$$

In our derivation we use the $\rightarrow$-introduction rule that represents the deduction theorem.

Derivation

1.	$\exists x\ [\mathscr{B}(x) \wedge \mathscr{P}(x)] \rightarrow \mathscr{E}$	premise
2.	$\forall x\ [\mathscr{S}(x) \rightarrow \mathscr{B}(x)]$	premise
3.	$\mathscr{S}(f)$	premise
4.	$\{\ \mathscr{P}(f)$	assumption
5.	$\mathscr{S}(f) \rightarrow \mathscr{B}(f)$	UI with f/x on 2
6.	$\mathscr{B}(f)$	MP on 3,5
7.	$\mathscr{B}(f) \wedge \mathscr{P}(f)$	$\wedge$-introduction on 4,6
8.	$\exists x\ [\mathscr{B}(x) \wedge \mathscr{P}(x)]$	EG with x/f on 7
9.	$\mathscr{E}\}$	MP on 8,1
10.	$\mathscr{P}(f) \rightarrow \mathscr{E}$	$\rightarrow$-introduction on 4 to 9

end

Recall that this proof is a purely syntactic process of deduction. It does not depend on the meaning of the proposition $\mathscr{E}$.

Exercise 6.1 Let $D = \{\text{people}\}$ be the domain of interpretation. Consider the predicates

$\mathscr{S}(x)$: 'x is a student'
$\mathscr{C}(x)$: 'x likes coffee'

Express the following assertions in the predicate calculus:

(a) 'Some students like coffee.'

(b) 'All students dislike coffee.'

Use the laws of the algebra of propositions to show that the negation of the first assertion, expressed in the predicate calculus, is equivalent to the second assertion, also expressed in the predicate calculus.

Exercise 6.2 Formally deduce that $\exists x\ [\mathscr{P}(x) \wedge \mathscr{Q}(x)] \vdash [\exists x\ \mathscr{P}(x) \wedge \exists x\ \mathscr{Q}(x)]$.

Exercise 6.3 By representing the following argument symbolically in the predicate calculus show that the following deduction is correct

'Every hardworking student is successful. All successful students are rich. Therefore, every hardworking student is rich.'

Exercise 6.4 Translate into symbolic form and use the inference rules of a formal deduction system to test the validity of the following argument:

Some married women are mothers
Some mothers are in employment

Therefore, some married women are in employment

Exercise 6.5 Consider the following assumptions:

(a) Joe is a student who enjoys working hard.

(b) Every student hates exams.

(c) If there is anybody who hates exams but enjoys working hard then the world is a funny place.

By choosing appropriate predicates, propositions and constants, prove formally 'that the world is a funny place'.

Exercise 6.6 Let $D = \{\text{fish}\}$ be the domain of interpretation. Let $\mathscr{A}(x)$ denote the predicate 'x likes swimming'. Using this domain and predicate define symbolically and explain in your own words the following proof rules in the predicate calculus: universal instantiation; universal generalization; existential instantiation; and existential generalization.

Exercise 6.7 Assume that 'all students are hardworking' and that 'Ronald is a student'. By using rules of inference in a formal argument deduce that 'some students are hardworking'.

Exercise 6.8 Use formal deduction to find out if $\forall x\ \mathscr{P}(x) \rightarrow \exists x\ \mathscr{P}(x)$ holds.

Exercise 6.9 Use formal deduction to find out if $\forall x\ [\mathscr{A}(x) \rightarrow \mathscr{B}(x)] \rightarrow [\exists x\ \mathscr{A}(x) \rightarrow \exists x\ \mathscr{B}(x)]$ holds.

Exercise 6.10 Prove that $\forall x\ [\mathcal{P}(x) \rightarrow \mathcal{Q}(x)] \rightarrow [\forall x\ \mathcal{P}(x) \rightarrow \forall x\ \mathcal{Q}(x)]$.

Exercise 6.11 Use the inference rules of our formal deduction system in an attempt to prove the following equivalence: $\exists x\ [\mathcal{P}(x) \wedge \mathcal{Q}(x)] \equiv [\exists x\ \mathcal{P}(x) \wedge \exists x\ \mathcal{Q}(x)]$. What conclusions can you make?

Exercise 6.12 Show that $\exists x\ [\mathcal{P}(x) \rightarrow \mathcal{Q}(x)] \rightarrow [\exists x\ \mathcal{P}(x) \rightarrow \exists x\ \mathcal{Q}(x)]$ is not valid by constructing a counter-example.

Exercise 6.13 Prove that $\forall x\ [\mathcal{P}(x) \wedge \mathcal{Q}] \vdash \forall x\ \mathcal{P}(x) \wedge \mathcal{Q}$, where $\mathcal{Q}$ is a proposition and does not contain any free variables.

Exercise 6.14 Prove that $\exists x\ [\mathcal{P}(x) \rightarrow \mathcal{Q}(x)] \rightarrow [\forall x\ \mathcal{P}(x) \rightarrow \exists x\ \mathcal{Q}(x)]$. Compare this assertion with that of Exercise 6.12 and note that the counter-example to Exercise 6.12 no longer holds.

Exercise 6.15 Consider the following assumptions:

(a) Charlie is an engineer and likes logic.

(b) All engineers like parties.

(c) If there is anybody who likes parties and likes logic then life is sometimes dull.

Prove formally that 'life is sometimes dull'.

6.1.3 Direct proof

We have seen that many of the statements we wish to prove are of the form $A \rightarrow B$. A *direct* proof of the statement $A \rightarrow B$ shows that the truth of B follows logically from the truth of A; that is we use inference rules to get through the steps of the deduction in the style of natural deduction and show that $A \vdash B$ as in Sec. 4.3. We now give a further example of a direct proof that uses some definitions and theorems from the calculus of the integers.

Example 6.2 We gave an informal proof at the beginning of Chapter 4 that 'If x is an even integer then x^2 is an even integer'. Here we give a formal proof in our deductive system. We let $D = \mathbb{Z}$ and assume that the predicate $\mathcal{E}(x)$ denotes 'x is even'. We have to show that

$$\vdash \forall x\ [\mathcal{E}(x) \rightarrow \mathcal{E}(x^2)]$$

Derivation

1.	$\mathcal{E}(n)$	premise where n is any element in $\mathbb{Z}$
2.	$\exists m\ (n = 2m)$	from 1, using the definition of an even integer $m \in \mathbb{Z}$
3.	$n = 2c$	from 2, using EI with c/m for some $c \in \mathbb{Z}$
4.	$n^2 = (2c)^2$	squaring both sides
5.	$n^2 = 4c^2$	by algebraic equivalences
6.	$n^2 = 2(2c^2)$	by algebraic equivalences
7.	$\exists m\ (n^2 = 2m)$	from 6, using EG with m/c
8.	$\mathcal{E}(n^2)$	from 6, using the definition of an even integer
9.	$\mathcal{E}(n) \rightarrow \mathcal{E}(n^2)$	from 1 and 8, using $\rightarrow$-introduction
10.	$\forall x\ [\mathcal{E}(x) \rightarrow \mathcal{E}(x^2)]$	from 9, using UG with x/n

end

6.1.4 Necessary and sufficient conditions

We have already seen in Sec. 3.4.7 that a typical theorem in mathematics has the form $P \Rightarrow Q$, where P and Q are *assertions* and $P \Rightarrow Q$ denotes the *assertion* that P implies Q. The operator $\Rightarrow$ is at a meta-level to the propositional connective for implication, $\rightarrow$, because it 'speaks' about $\rightarrow$, asserting that $P \rightarrow Q$ is true. We first met this notion of 'a logic applied to logic' in Sec. 3.4.8 where the symbol $\equiv$ was at a meta-level to the propositional connective $\leftrightarrow$. In connecting P and Q by $\Rightarrow$ we exclude the case where $P \rightarrow Q$ is false, and only consider $P \Rightarrow Q$ as a *valid* statement. We may *use* $\Rightarrow$ to indicate cause and effect, whereas we have seen that $\rightarrow$ is not strong enough to express causality. The advantage of $\rightarrow$, however, is that it is *truth-functional*, as we require in the propositional calculus. This means that the truth-value of $P \rightarrow Q$ is uniquely determined by the truth-values of P and Q. This enables us to build compound propositions with security in our calculus.

We can define the meaning of $\Rightarrow$ by expressing the logical connective $\rightarrow$ in the predicate calculus. Recall that $\forall x \ \mathscr{P}(x)$ is a statement whose truth-values can be worked out provided that we have a definition of the domain of interpretation.

Example 6.3 Let $D = \mathbb{N}$ and assume the predicates

$\mathscr{P}(x)$: '$x \in \{2, 4, 6\}$

$\mathscr{Q}(x)$: 'x is even'

Then $\forall x \ [\mathscr{P}(x) \rightarrow \mathscr{Q}(x)]$ is true and $\mathscr{P}(x) \rightarrow \mathscr{Q}(x)$ is a tautology with $\mathscr{P}$ and $\mathscr{Q}$ defined over D.

We now have a stronger notion of implication and represent this by the symbol $\Rightarrow$.

Definition 6.1 Logical implication If $\mathscr{P}(x)$ and $Q(x)$ are predicates with domain D and $\forall x \ [\mathscr{P}(x) \rightarrow \mathscr{Q}(x)]$ then $\mathscr{P}(x) \Rightarrow \mathscr{Q}(x)$, meaning that $\mathscr{P}(x)$ logically implies $\mathscr{Q}(x)$ or $\mathscr{Q}(x)$ is a logical consequence of $\mathscr{P}(x)$. $\mathscr{P}(x)$ logically implies $\mathscr{Q}(x)$ if and only if $\mathscr{P}(x) \rightarrow \mathscr{Q}(x)$ is logically valid.

We now introduce the concept of necessary and sufficient conditions which play an important part in mathematical proof and are based on the notion of logical implication.

Definition 6.2 Sufficient condition The assertion that $P \Rightarrow Q$ is true means that P is a sufficient condition for Q. We say that the truth of P is sufficient to ensure the truth of Q.

Definition 6.3 Necessary condition The assertion $Q \Rightarrow P$ is the converse of the assertion $P \Rightarrow Q$ and means that P is a necessary condition for Q. If Q is true we say that it necessarily follows that P is true.

Clearly, if $Q \Rightarrow P$ we can also say that the truth of Q is sufficient to ensure the truth of P. Recall that we showed in Exercise 4.19 that the converse of a proposition does not necessarily follow from the proposition itself.

Definition 6.4 Necessary and sufficient conditions The assertion $P \Leftrightarrow Q$ means that P is necessary and sufficient for Q. We write $P \Leftrightarrow Q \equiv P \Rightarrow Q \wedge Q \Rightarrow P$.

We can clarify the meaning of necessary and sufficient conditions by using the analogy between the algebra of sets and the algebra of propositions. If we take the algebra of sets as a model for our logic of propositions we can draw Venn diagrams to represent the assertions in the algebra of propositions.

Exercise 6.16 Consider the sets P, Q and R in the universal set U. Now assume the following propositions concerning the membership of some element $x \in U$ to these sets:

$$\begin{array}{ll} p: & x \in P \\ q: & x \in Q \\ r: & x \in R \end{array}$$

We have the true propositions $p \Rightarrow q$ and $r \Rightarrow q$ and the false proposition $p \wedge r$.

(a) Draw the Venn diagram to represent these assertions about the sets P, Q and R. The fact that the proposition $p \wedge r$ is false is represented by the statement in set theory that $P \cap R = \emptyset$.

(b) Is p the only proposition that is sufficient for q? If not, the other proposition may be true only when p is false.

(c) Is it necessary for p to be true in order that q is true?

(d) Is q a necessary condition for p?

(e) Is q a sufficient condition for r?

For the propositions p and q above, if p is to be a necessary *and* sufficient condition for q we require that $p \Leftrightarrow q \equiv p \Rightarrow q \wedge q \Rightarrow p$. In our model of sets this requirement is that $P = Q$.

To prove $P \Leftrightarrow Q$ involves proving:

$$\begin{array}{ll} \text{either} & (P \Rightarrow Q) \wedge (Q \Rightarrow P) \\ \text{or} & (P \Rightarrow Q) \wedge (\neg P \Rightarrow \neg Q) \\ \text{or} & (P \Leftrightarrow Q_1 \Leftrightarrow Q_2 \Leftrightarrow, \ldots, \Leftrightarrow Q) \end{array}$$

As an alternative notation for 'P is necessary and sufficient for Q' we can write

'Q holds *if and only if* P holds' which abbreviates to 'Q *iff* P'

where

'Q holds if P holds' is equivalent to 'P is sufficient for Q' or $P \Rightarrow Q$
'Q holds only if P holds' is equivalent to 'P is necessary for Q' or $Q \Rightarrow P$

Exercise 6.17 Suppose A and B are sets. Show that $A = B$ iff $A \subseteq B$ and $B \subseteq A$, using the definitions for set equality and the subset relation given in Sec. 2.1.

6.2 INDIRECT METHODS OF PROOF

Sometimes it is easier to prove an assertion that is different from the one we really want but equivalent to it within the logical calculus. By the rule of equivalence on page 121 we can turn an indirect proof into a direct proof by adding one more stage in the deductive process. An example of this style of proof is proof by contraposition. Our second example of an indirect proof method has been used to prove theorems for which no direct proof has been successful—this is the method of proof by contradiction.

6.2.1 Proof by contraposition

This indirect method of proving $A \rightarrow B$ is a direct proof of the equivalent proposition $\neg B \rightarrow \neg A$; that is we assume $\neg B$ and deduce $\neg A$. This allows us to conclude $A \rightarrow B$. We symbolize this as an inference rule by

$$\frac{\begin{array}{c}\neg B \\ \neg A\end{array}}{A \rightarrow B}$$

The inference rule, *modus tollens*, derived in Example 4.13, is based on this equivalence. We also established in Exercise 4.19 that if $A \to B$ is valid and B is true this does not imply that A is true.

Example 6.4 We prove that 'If the integer x^2 is even then x is even' by an indirect proof. Let $D = \mathbb{Z}$ and assume the predicates

$\mathscr{E}(x)$: 'x is even'
$\mathscr{O}(x)$: 'x is odd'

We carry out the formal derivation $\vdash \forall x\ [\mathscr{E}(x^2) \to \mathscr{E}(x)]$ and then conclude that $\mathscr{E}(x^2) \Rightarrow \mathscr{E}(x)$. We assume initially that n is any element in $\mathbb{Z}$ and that the conclusion that we need to derive is false. Each of these assumptions is indicated by a scoping bracket.

Derivation

1.	$\{\ \{\ \neg\mathscr{E}(n)$	assumption
2.	$\mathscr{O}(n)$	by definition of an even integer from 1
3.	$\exists m\ (n = 2m + 1)$	by definition of an odd integer from 2
4.	$n = 2c + 1$	EI with c/m for some $c \in \mathbb{Z}$ on 3
5.	$n^2 = (2c+1)^2 = 2(2c^2 + 2c) + 1$	by algebraic equivalence
6.	$\exists y\ (n^2 = 2y + 1)$	EG with y/c from 5
7.	$\mathscr{O}(n^2)$	by definition of an odd integer from 6
8.	$\neg\mathscr{E}(n^2)\}$	by definition of an even integer from 7
9.	$\mathscr{E}(n^2) \to \mathscr{E}(n)\}$	contraposition on 1,8
10.	$\forall x\ [\mathscr{E}(x^2) \to \mathscr{E}(x)]$	UG with x/n on 9

end

Therefore we conclude that $\mathscr{E}(x^2) \Rightarrow \mathscr{E}(x)$ by the indirect proof method of contraposition.

Exercise 6.18 Prove directly that 'If the integer x^2 is even then x is even'. This is more difficult than an indirect proof.

We can now use our examples above of direct and indirect proofs to prove that 'x is an even integer' is a necessary condition *and* sufficient condition for 'x^2 is an even integer'.

Example 6.5 We show that 'For every integer x, x is even iff x^2 is even'. By universal generalization it is enough to show that this is true for *any* $x \in \mathbb{Z}$. However, we have already done this in Example 6.2 and Example 6.4. Therefore 'x is even' $\Rightarrow$ 'x^2 is even' and 'x^2 is even' $\Rightarrow$ 'x is even' and so 'x is even' $\Leftrightarrow$ 'x^2 is even' as required.

6.2.2 Proof by contradiction

This second method of indirect proof is sometimes called *reductio ad absurdum.* In order to prove a conclusion, we make an initial assumption that the conclusion is false. Then to demonstrate that our assumption cannot hold, we try to derive a contradiction or an 'absurdity'. For example, we might derive some proposition and its negation as a contradiction in the form $T \wedge \neg T$. We have already presented the method as the inference rule for $\neg$-introduction in Sec. 4.3 where it was used in Example 4.13.

The only similarity between our two indirect proof methods is that each makes an initial assumption of the negation of the conclusion of an argument. Our reason for giving a detailed treatment of these rules in this chapter is that they are more difficult to use than the other inference rules. Similarly the $\rightarrow$ connective is less intuitively obvious and required a detailed treatment in Chapter 3.

Exercise 6.19 The method of proof by contradiction is based on the equivalence between $A \rightarrow B$ and $(A \wedge \neg B) \rightarrow F$. Demonstrate this equivalence using truth tables, and argue that if $(A \wedge \neg B) \rightarrow F$ is T then $A \rightarrow B$ is T.

Example 6.6 We prove that 'If n is a prime number different from 2 then n is odd'. Let $D = \mathbb{N}$ and assume the predicates:

$\mathscr{E}(x)$: 'x is even'
$\mathscr{O}(x)$: 'x is odd'
$\mathscr{P}(x)$: 'x is prime'
$\mathscr{D}(x, y)$: 'x is a divisor of y'

We carry out the formal derivation $\vdash \forall x\ [(\mathscr{P}(x) \wedge x \neq 2) \rightarrow \mathscr{O}(x)]$ and then conclude that $(\mathscr{P}(x) \wedge x \neq 2) \Rightarrow \mathscr{O}(x)$. We shall introduce $\forall$ and assume $\mathscr{P}(n) \wedge n \neq 2$ where n is any element in $\mathbb{N}$. Following the method of proof by contradiction we assume initially that $\mathscr{O}(n)$ is F.

Derivation

1.	$\{\mathscr{P}(n) \wedge n \neq 2$	assumption
2.	$\{\neg\mathscr{O}(n)$	assumption where n is the same name as in 1
3.	$\mathscr{E}(n)$	by definition from 2
4.	$\exists\ m(n = 2m)$	by definition from 3
5.	$\mathscr{P}(n)$	$\wedge$-elimination on 1
6.	$n \neq 2$	$\wedge$-elimination on 1
7.	$D(2, n)$	by definition '2 is a divisor of n' from 4
8.	$\neg\mathscr{P}(n)\}$	since the only divisors of a prime are 1 or the prime itself and $n \neq 2$ from 6
9.	$\mathscr{O}(n)\}$	$\neg$-introduction on 2,5,8
10.	$\mathscr{P}(n) \wedge n \neq 2 \rightarrow \mathscr{O}(n)$	$\rightarrow$ -introduction on 1,9
11.	$\forall x\ [(\mathscr{P}(x) \wedge x \neq 2) \rightarrow \mathscr{O}(x)]$	UG with x/n on 10

end

Proof by contradiction is *not* a constructive proof method, however. Using the proof we may prove that something exists without showing how to find it. The underlying assumption is the law of the excluded middle which asserts that a proposition is either true or false and holds in classical mathematics. In constructive mathematics this assumption is not allowed, and a proof of a proposition in the form $\exists x\ \mathscr{A}(x)$ is only accepted if x can be found explicitly.

Proof by contradiction must be differentiated from the previous method of proof by contraposition. They are similar only in their initial assumption of $\neg B$ when attempting to prove $A \rightarrow B$.

Exercise 6.20 Use an indirect method of proof to show that $p \rightarrow q \vdash \neg(p \wedge \neg q)$.

Exercise 6.21 Use proof by contradiction and the rules of inference in a natural deduction system to prove the following argument:

> 'If the Prime Minister were able and willing to prevent unemployment he or she would do so. If the Prime Minister were unable to prevent unemployment he or she would be ineffective; if he or she were unwilling to prevent unemployment he or she would be uncaring. The Prime Minister does not prevent unemployment. If the Prime Minister exists he or she is neither ineffective nor uncaring. Therefore the Prime Minister does not exist'.

Exercise 6.22 Show that $\neg(t \wedge \neg p) \rightarrow q,\ s \wedge p \vdash \neg(p \rightarrow \neg q)$ by an indirect proof.

6.3 PROOF BY INDUCTION

The method of proof by induction depends on an important property of the set of natural numbers. With $\mathbb{N}$ as the domain of interpretation, this powerful method allows us to prove assertions of the form $\forall n\ \mathscr{P}(n)$ where $\mathscr{P}$ is a predicate constant.

The basis for the proof method is the *principle of mathematical induction*. We express the principle in terms of an arbitrary predicate $\mathscr{P}(\ \_\_\_\ )$ that asserts some property of a natural number. We let n name an arbitrary natural number and we make the following assertions:

1 $\mathscr{P}(0)$ is true.

2 If $\mathscr{P}(n)$ is assumed to be true then $\mathscr{P}(n+1)$ is also true.

If these assertions hold, the principle of mathematical induction allows us to conclude that $\mathscr{P}(n)$ is true for all natural numbers. The first assertion is called the basis and the second the inductive step for the proof. We give the following intuitive argument that the principle of induction holds:

> 'By the inductive step and the basis step we have $\mathscr{P}(0) \rightarrow \mathscr{P}(1)$, as well as $\mathscr{P}(0)$. Therefore, by *modus ponens* we conclude that all of $\mathscr{P}(0), \mathscr{P}(1), \mathscr{P}(2), \mathscr{P}(3), \ldots$ are true; that is $\forall n\ \mathscr{P}(n)$ is true.'

Principle 6.1 Simple induction If $\mathscr{P}(n)$ asserts a property about any $n \in \mathbb{N}$ then

$$[\mathscr{P}(0)\ \wedge \forall n\ (\mathscr{P}(n) \rightarrow \mathscr{P}(n+1))] \rightarrow \forall n\ \mathscr{P}(n)$$

PROOF We use the indirect method of proof by contradiction and assume that $\mathscr{P}(0)\ \wedge \forall n\ (\mathscr{P}(n) \rightarrow \mathscr{P}(n+1))$ is true but $\forall n\ \mathscr{P}(n)$ is false. Therefore $\neg\forall n\ \mathscr{P}(n)$ is true and $\exists n\ \neg\mathscr{P}(n)$ is true.

Now let n_0 be the least n for which $\mathscr{P}(n)$ is false. Since we know $\mathscr{P}(0)$ is true, then $n_0 \neq 0$, so $n_0 - 1 \in \mathbb{N}$. By minimality of n_0, $\mathscr{P}(n_0 - 1)$ is true. From our premise we know that $\mathscr{P}(n_0 - 1) \rightarrow \mathscr{P}(n_0)$, and by *modus ponens* we conclude $\mathscr{P}(n_0)$ is true. However, this contradicts our assumption that $\mathscr{P}(n_0)$ is false. Therefore, by the method of proof by contradiction we conclude that $\forall n\ \mathscr{P}(n)$ is true.

The principle of simple induction yields the following proof method that $\forall n\ \mathscr{P}(n)$ is true:

Basis step. Prove $\mathscr{P}(0)$.

Inductive step. Assume $\mathscr{P}(n)$ for some arbitrary n and show that $\mathscr{P}(n+1)$ follows.

We then conclude that $\forall n\ \mathscr{P}(n)$ is true.

Proof by induction may also be used to prove a property for all integers $n \geq m$ where m is some constant that is different from 0. In this case the basis of the induction is $\mathscr{P}(m)$ instead of $\mathscr{P}(0)$ and we have *relativized* the domain of the natural numbers for induction to be restricted to those greater than m. The concept of relativization was previously presented in Sec. 5.3 on page 150.

Example 6.7 Let $\mathscr{P}(n)$ be 'the sum of the first n natural numbers is equal to $n(n+1)/2$'. We prove by mathematical induction that for every $n \in \mathbb{N}$, $\sum_{i=0}^{n} i = n(n+1)/2$.

PROOF

Basis step. Prove $\mathscr{P}(0)$, the assertion that $\sum_{i=0}^{0} i = 0(0+1)/2$. Since $0 = 0, \mathscr{P}(0)$ is true.

Inductive step. Assume $\mathscr{P}(n)$, the assertion $\sum_{i=0}^{n} i = n(n+1)/2$. Then deduce $\mathscr{P}(n+1)$ from $\mathscr{P}(n)$. $\mathscr{P}(n+1)$ is the assertion $\sum_{i=0}^{n+1} i = (n+1)(n+2)/2$. Now,

$$\begin{aligned}\sum_{i=0}^{n+1} i &= 0+1+2+\cdots+n+(n+1)\\ &= (\sum_{i=0}^{n} i)+(n+1)\\ &= n(n+1)/2+(n+1) \quad \text{by the inductive assumption}\\ &= (n+1)(n/2+1)\\ &= (n+1)(n+2)/2\end{aligned}$$

So $\mathscr{P}(n+1)$ is true when $\mathscr{P}(n)$ is assumed and $\mathscr{P}(0)$ has also been proved true. Therefore $\mathscr{P}(n)$ is proved by induction.

Example 6.8 Let $\mathscr{P}(n)$ be the predicate 'every set S having n elements has 2^n distinct subsets'. We prove $\forall n\ \mathscr{P}(n)$ by mathematical induction.

PROOF

Basis step. Prove $\mathscr{P}(0)$, the assertion 'every set S having 0 elements has $2^0 = 1$ distinct subsets'. Clearly $\mathscr{P}(0)$ is true since the only set with 0 elements is the empty set, $\emptyset$, whose (unique) subset is itself, $\emptyset$.

Inductive step. Assume $\mathscr{P}(n)$, the assertion that $\mathscr{P}(n)$ is true for every set having n elements. Then deduce $\mathscr{P}(n+1)$ from $\mathscr{P}(n)$. $\mathscr{P}(n+1)$ is the assertion 'every set having $(n+1)$ elements has 2^{n+1} distinct subsets'.

Let $S = \{a_1, \ldots, a_n, a_{n+1}\}$ be a set of $n+1$ *distinct* elements. Also let $S' = \{a_1, \ldots, a_n\}$, so that $S = S' \cup \{a_{n+1}\}$. Certainly every subset of S' is also a subset of S, and by the inductive hypothesis there are 2^n of these. Now every subset of S is either one of these or is formed from one of these by adding a_{n+1}. Thus there are 2^n subsets of S which do not contain a_{n+1} and 2^n subsets of S which do. By the Rule of Sum in Sec. 2.6 there are $2^n + 2^n$ subsets of S in all. Now $2^n + 2^n = 2.2^n = 2^{n+1}$ as required.

So $\mathscr{P}(0)$ is true and $\mathscr{P}(n+1)$ is true when $\mathscr{P}(n)$ is assumed. Therefore $\forall n\ \mathscr{P}(n)$ is proved true by induction.

Exercise 6.23 Prove by induction that for every natural number $n \geq 1$,

$$1.1! + 2.2! + \cdots + n.n! = (n+1)! - 1$$

Exercise 6.24 Prove by induction that $\sum_{i=1}^{n} 2^{i-1} = 2^n - 1$ for every $n \geq 1$.

Exercise 6.25 Let $\mathscr{P}(n)$ be the predicate over $\mathbb{N}$: '$4^n + 1$ is divisible by 3'. Assume that $\mathscr{P}(n)$ is true and show that $\mathscr{P}(n+1)$ is also true. Does this prove that 4^n+1 is divisible by 3 for all natural numbers?

Exercise 6.26 Prove by induction that $n! > 2^n$ for every n where $n > 3$.

Exercise 6.27 Prove by induction that $2^n \geq 2n+1$ where $n \in \mathbb{Z}^+$ and $n \geq 3$. Explain why your proof will fail for $n \geq 0$.

Exercise 6.28 Prove by induction that $P(n)$ is $\sum_{k=0}^{n} \binom{n}{k} = 2^n$.

The inductive definition of sets of numbers We have introduced the principle of simple induction as the basis for proof by induction. The principle also provides a method for deciding whether a given set of integers contains all the positive integers. In fact the induction principle is an axiom schema for the theories of the non-negative integers, strings, trees, lists, sets and other structures that are fundamental to the construction of systems. We begin with examples of how unstructured sets of integers can be generated by inductive definitions. The generation of the strings of formal languages by induction will be presented in Chapter 7 and the theories of some inductively defined structures will be presented as specifications in Chapter 10.

In Sec. 5.3 we gave a method for characterizing infinite sets by a particular predicate. For many sets, however, the construction of defining predicates will be difficult.

Example 6.9 In order to define the set of Pascal programs, we need to think of a predicate that describes the construction of a Pascal program from the set of valid expressions in the Pascal language. Such a predicate would need to be a specification of the syntax of Pascal as well as of the set $\mathbb{N}$, in order to define the set of arithmetic expressions in Pascal.

A definition of the set $\mathbb{N}$ is based on the principle of induction which expresses the property that each natural number can be constructed by the successor function operating on zero. Conventionally we write 2 for the number succ(succ(zero)) and think of building 3 by adding 1 to 2 and so on.

We now generalize the principle of induction to construct other infinite sets whose elements can be generated by some building operation on the basic elements of the set. We then use our definition to construct $\mathbb{N}$ and other infinite sets of numbers. The sets that can be generated by induction are called *inductive sets* and are fundamentally important in the mathematical framework for discrete systems.

Definition 6.5 Inductive definition of a set An inductive definition for a set S consists of three clauses:

Basis clause which establishes that certain elements are in S. These are the building blocks for S and ensure that $S \neq \emptyset$.

Inductive clause which establishes ways of combining elements of S to generate new elements of S.

Extremal clause which asserts that unless an element can be shown to be a member of S by applying the basis clause and the inductive clause a finite number of times then the element is not in S. The set S is then the smallest set that is closed (or formed) by the two rules.

Example 6.10 Suppose $D = \mathbb{Q}$. An inductive definition of $\mathbb{N}$ is:

1 $0 \in \mathbb{N}$

2 $n \in \mathbb{N} \rightarrow n+1 \in \mathbb{N}$

3 Unless an element can be shown to be a member of $\mathbb{N}$ by applying the basis clause and the inductive clause a finite number of times then the element is not in $\mathbb{N}$.

Note the importance of the extremal clause. Without it we could not assert that $\frac{1}{2} \notin \mathbb{N}$, since the first two clauses alone only tell us that certain elements are in $\mathbb{N}$. We must ensure that these are the *only* elements in $\mathbb{N}$.

Example 6.11 Suppose $D = \mathbb{Q}$. An inductive definition of E, the set of even integers is:

1 $0 \in E$

2 $n \in E \rightarrow (n+2) \in E \wedge -(n+2) \in E$

3 Unless an element can be shown to be a member of E by applying the basis clause and the inductive clause a finite number of times then the element is not in E.

In this definition the extremal clause asserts that $1, 3, \frac{1}{4}, -\frac{1}{4} \notin E$ because we cannot build $1, 3, \frac{1}{4}, -\frac{1}{4}$ using the basis and inductive clauses.

Exercise 6.29 Give an inductive definition of the set of odd integers. You may assume that $\mathbb{Z}$ together with the usual arithmetic operations has already been defined.

Exercise 6.30 Inductively define the set of natural numbers that are powers of 2.

Exercise 6.31 Give an inductive definition of the set of integers that are multiples of 7. You may assume that $\mathbb{Z}$, together with the usual arithmetic operations, has already been defined.

The principle of strong induction is a variation of the principle of simple induction. When strong induction is used in a proof the inductive step assumes $\mathscr{P}(k)$ for all $k \leq n$ rather than just $\mathscr{P}(n)$, in order to infer $\mathscr{P}(n+1)$.

Principle 6.2 Strong induction If $\mathscr{P}(n)$ asserts a property about any $n \in \mathbb{N}$ and we assume that:

(a) $\mathscr{P}(0)$ is true and

(b) if $\mathscr{P}(0), \mathscr{P}(1), \ldots, \mathscr{P}(n)$ are all true then $\mathscr{P}(n+1)$ is also true,

then we may conclude $\forall n\ \mathscr{P}(n)$.

As for simple induction we may alter the basis step to prove $\mathscr{P}(n)$ is true for integers $n \geq m$.

The principle of strong induction can be used to verify the definition of a sequence. We saw in Sec. 2.3.7 that it is not always the case that there will be an obvious explicit formula for the nth term of a sequence. For example, the first few terms in a well-known sequence are: $1, 1, 2, 3, 5, 8, 13, 21, 34, 55, \ldots$. It is not immediately obvious, however, what the nth term is.

If we know the first term of a sequence and if in addition we can generate the $(n+1)$th term from the nth, for any n, then the sequence is defined for every n.

Example 6.12 The sequence $3, 6, 9, 12, \ldots$ is defined by noting that $a_1 = 3$ and $a_{n+1} = 3 + a_n$ for each n.

Example 6.13 The first few terms $1, 1, 2, 3, 5, 8, 13, 21, 34, 55, \ldots$ belong to the Fibonacci sequence. We see that for each $n > 2$, $a_n = a_{n-1} + a_{n-2}$. If we also observe that $a_1 = 1$ and $a_2 = 1$ then these three equations will uniquely determine every term in the sequence.

We have defined the Fibonacci sequence in Example 6.13 by a *recurrence system*. The first equation is called a *recurrence equation* and the second and third give the *boundary conditions*. These equations are analogous to the inductive and basis steps respectively of the principle of strong induction. In general a recurrence system will involve boundary conditions and a recurrence equation in which a_n is specified as a function of $a_1, a_2, \ldots, a_{n-1}$. The definition of a recurrence system is also called a recurrence relation. We saw in Sec. 2.3.7 that a sequence is defined by a function. In fact sequences that are defined in terms of a recurrence equation are defined by *recursive* functions.

Example 6.14 $1, 2, 3, \ldots$ has the recurrence system

$$\begin{array}{ll} a_1 = 1 & \text{(boundary conditions)} \\ a_n = a_{n-1} + 1 \text{ for } n > 1 & \text{(recurrence equation)} \end{array}$$

In general the *solution* of recurrence systems, which involves finding an *explicit* formula for a_n, is a difficult problem.

Example 6.15 Here we represent some common sequences:

$$\begin{array}{ll} 1, 2, 3, \ldots & \{n\} \\ 6, 7, 8, \ldots & \{n+5\} \\ 2, 4, 6, 8, \ldots & \{2n\} \\ 1, 2, 4, 8, \ldots & \{2^{n-1}\} \\ 1, 1+2, 1+2+3, \ldots & \{(n(n+1))/2\} \end{array}$$

We have given explicit formulae for the nth term of some common sequences in Example 6.15. By choosing the appropriate principle of induction we can verify that our intuitions for the explicit formulae of recurrence systems are correct.

Example 6.16 We have the recurrence system

$$\begin{aligned} a_1 &= 1 \\ a_n &= 1 + a_1 + a_2 + \cdots + a_{n-1} \text{ for } n > 1 \end{aligned}$$

Our intuitions are guided by the first few values,

$$a_1 = 1,\ a_2 = 2,\ a_3 = 4,\ a_4 = 8$$

and we guess that $a_n = 2^{n-1}$ for all $n \geq 1$.

We verify the formula for a_n by strong induction. Let $\mathscr{P}(n)$ be the assertion $a_n = 2^{n-1}$.

PROOF

Basis step. $\mathscr{P}(1)$ is $a_1 = 1 = 2^{1-1}$ and is true.

Inductive step. For $n \geq 1$, we suppose that $a_1 = 2^{1-1}$, $a_2 = 2^{2-1}$, $a_3 = 2^{3-1}$, $\cdots$, $a_n = 2^{n-1}$. We need to prove that $a_{n+1} = 1 + 2^0 + 2^1 + \cdots + 2^{n-1}$. We have already proved by simple induction in Exercise 6.24, however, that $2^0 + 2^1 + \cdots + 2^{n-1} = 2^{n-1}$. Therefore $a_{n+1} = 2^n = 2^{(n+1)-1}$.

From the assumption that $\mathscr{P}(0), \mathscr{P}(1), \ldots, \mathscr{P}(n)$ are all true, we have shown that $\mathscr{P}(n+1)$ is true. Therefore by strong induction we have proved that $a_n = 2^{n-1}$ for all $n \geq 1$

Exercise 6.32 Give the recurrence system definitions for the sequences in Example 6.15.

Exercise 6.33 Write down the next term and give the recurrence system definition for the following sequences:

(a) $5, 7, 9, 11, \ldots$

(b) $4, 6, 9, 13, \ldots$

Give the formula for the nth term and use simple induction to prove from the recurrence system definition that your explicit definition of the nth term is correct.

Exercise 6.34 Use the principle of strong induction to show that if the following recursive function is defined:

$$f(1) = 3,\ f(2) = 5 \text{ and } f(n+1) = 3f(n) - 2f(n-1) \text{ for } n \geq 2$$

then $f(n) = 2^n + 1$ for all positive integers n.

6.4 SUMMARY

In this chapter we have continued to build on the greater expressive power of the predicate calculus, which, as we have seen, is constructed as a refinement of the propositional calculus. We have extended thc natural deduction system of the propositional calculus in order to make deductions about quantified assertions. By giving examples of proofs in mathematics, we have compared direct and indirect methods of proof and have introduced the proof of necessary and sufficient conditions. Induction is fundamental to our work of constructing and analysing complex systems, and we have defined the principles of both simple and strong induction. The definitions of sets and sequences have been verified by induction. We shall build on the inductive method in Chapter 7 when we use structural induction to define the syntactic rules for formal languages. Structures that are built by induction will be specified in Chapter 10 and represented by programming paradigms in Chapter 11.

FURTHER READING

The books by Galton (1990) and Enderton (1972) provide a detailed treatment of proof rules for predicate logic. The importance of induction in programming is shown in Bornat (1987), and the application of structural induction in software engineering is demonstrated in the books by Jones (1986) and Cohen, Harwood and Jackson (1986).

Chapter 7

FORMAL LANGUAGES

The theoretical framework that we present for the construction and analysis of systems depends on formal languages and formal deductive systems. In previous chapters we have presented many examples that use formal languages; in this chapter we define the structure of formal languages by induction and identify the string as our first example of a mathematical structure that is recursive. Whereas formal language theory is traditionally concerned only with the syntactic rules that build the strings that are permissible in a formal language, we also discuss the semantic rules that provide meanings for these strings. We therefore view a language as the pair (syntax, semantics).

This is a pivotal chapter for two reasons: it generalizes the simple mathematical concept of a set to the recursive structure of a string that is built from a set of symbols. It also generalizes the formal languages of the propositional and predicate calculi to the first-order languages of logic. These languages are sufficiently powerful to express theories about the properties of the objects (that are often recursively structured) in some application system. When we construct a theory, within a formal system, about some application system, we specify our perception of that application system, and convince ourselves that our theory is internally consistent by making deductions within the formal system. Often, however, we want to make a link with another formal system by building a mathematical model in which we can interpret or give a value to the objects in the statements of our theory. The formal link is made between the two mathematical systems: the formal language with its apparatus for deduction and the mathematical structure (which in this sense provides a concrete model) that gives an interpretation for the formal language. The possibility for making a bridge between a formal language and its structure is the key to working within a formal framework when we construct and analyse systems. If we construct a formal mathematical model we present the meaning of the theory by interpretation in the model—this is a model-based semantics. We may be satisfied to use the deductive system for our formal language, however, and present the meaning of the theory by the statements that are deduced from the axioms—this is a proof-theoretic semantics. These possibilities will be presented in Chapter 10.

We continue to link the syntax and semantics of formal languages when we show, in Sec. 7.3, that a parse tree models the recursive structure of languages abstractly and explain how the semantics of a simple language can be based directly on the syntax of the language. The rules for structuring languages can also be presented formally as production rules that belong to the grammar of the language. We classify formal grammars in Sec. 7.4 and identify the class of machines that recognize the languages produced by each type of grammar. As examples of different grammars, we give detailed definitions of the simple language of regular expressions, as well as of a subset of the Pascal programming language.

7.1 THE STRUCTURE OF FORMAL LANGUAGES

7.1.1 Defining a formal language

We have already given many examples that have been written in a formal language. A language is *formal* if it is defined by a precise set of rules that enable us to decide, in a finite amount of time, whether some finite string of symbols, or some sentence formed from strings, is permitted in that language.

The rules are expressed in some meta-language, which can be either a natural language (which is an informal language) or some other formal language. The rules that specify which strings or sentences are allowed in a particular language are *syntactic* rules that describe the structure, or the syntax, of the language. We can think of these rules as specifying the language's grammar. Only those strings or sentences that are correctly formed will be given a meaning by the *semantic* rules of the language. We have already seen how the syntactically correct wffs of the predicate calculus are given a meaning, within a formal system of logic, by interpreting them in some mathematical structure.

Example 7.1 A formal language can be built from the symbols @ and * according to the following rule:

> The only strings permitted are those that are finite strings of zero or more @ symbols followed by between one and three * symbols, or a string of one or more @ symbols with no * symbols following.

The following strings will be accepted in this language:

@ * * * @@ * * @@@*
@@@@@@
@@
**

The rule will not permit the strings:

@@ * * * * * @@ * * * **
* * * * *
*@@ * *@@ * *@@

The fact that the string ** is itself part of the string * * @@ indicates that in some way a string could be described as a recursive structure. The rules that specify the syntactic structure of the language enable us to test a string to see if it is acceptable and also to generate all the strings that form the language.

Exercise 7.1 The following strings are allowed in a formal language L:

bbbbca
baaaaaaabcb
abc
aaabbbbbcccccccccccc
bca

The following strings are not allowed in L:

accccc
bbbbbbc
ab
abaaa...

Identify a set of symbols used in L and *suggest* a rule for the syntactic structure of L.

Clearly, in order to be certain about the complete set of symbols that are used in a language we need an exhaustive list of *all* the strings that are permissible. An exhaustive list of permissible strings would also enable us to decide on the precise syntactic rules for the language. We can present a formal language either by listing all its permissible strings or by specifying the set of basic symbols and the set of rules that both define the permissible strings *and* say how the strings can be generated.

Definition 7.1 Formal language A formal language is constructed from a set of symbols, called its alphabet, and a set of rules, called its syntax. The rules specify, in some meta-language, how the symbols are put together to form the strings of the language and how the strings are put together to form the phrases and sentences of the language.

We shall use several different meta-languages to express the structure of formal languages and identify *how* the symbols and strings of the language are combined. Initially we give inductive definitions, in the style of Def. 6.5, and identify this form of induction as structural induction. Later we use a meta-language to present the syntax of formal languages by a grammar. With the structure of the syntax identified we are then able to define the semantics of a simple formal language.

7.1.2 Structural induction

We have given many examples in previous chapters of programs written in the formal language of Pascal. Programs are 'sentences' in Pascal, and are formed from several kinds of phrases: identifiers and numerals are built into expressions, and expressions are combined with identifiers to form statements that are conditional, repetition or assignment statements.

Clearly the set of rules that specify the Pascal language are more complex than the single informal rule that we used to describe the simple language in Example 7.1. However, these languages have in common the property of being recursive structures.

Example 7.2 In Example 7.1 the string ** is part of the string * * @@ and also part of the string @@ * *. The rule that stated which strings are permitted in this simple language did not specify *how* the strings could be constructed, however. The string * * @@ is a finite sequence of symbols that are *juxtaposed* or put together. It could be built by adding the symbol * as a *pre-fix* to *@@, by adding the symbol @ as a *suffix* to * * @ or by juxtaposing ** and @@ to form the *concatenation* of these two strings.

Theories of strings vary in the definitions that they give for building strings. Strings formed by concatenating two strings are directly recursive structures with strings nested inside strings. Strings built by the *post-fix* operation of adding a symbol as a suffix to a string are structurally similar to the sequences defined in Sec. 6.2 by recurrence systems. Sequences are not *directly* recursive structures with sequences nested inside sequences; they are defined by recursive functions and are constructed *in only one way* by adding the next term to the end of a sequence.

The structure of Pascal programs can be directly recursive: conditional statements can be nested inside conditional statements and expressions can be formed from expressions.

Example 7.3 In the set of valid integer expressions in Pascal the following expressions are valid: $16*3-4, (6+2)*3, ((+6-100)*33), 45$ div $5, 8$ mod 2 and $(49-5)$. The following expressions would not be accepted by a Pascal compiler: $151+, 2*$, $62-, 9$ mod, $39(+, 6-+2$, div $*1$ and (2. The valid expression 62 is nested inside the valid expression $62+3$.

Clearly there are several ways of building the set of valid integer expressions. When we built the set $\mathbb{N}$ by induction in Def. 6.5 each new natural number was generated simply by adding 1 to the previous natural number. In order to define the generation of structures that can be combined in more than one way we use *structural induction*. The extra structure of integer expressions in Pascal is reflected by adding the ways of combining these expressions to the inductive clause of the definition.

Example 7.4 The alphabet for the language of valid integer expressions in Pascal is

$$A = \{0, 1, 2, 3, 4, 5, 6, 7, 8, 9\}$$

The set A^+ is defined as the set of all non-empty integer expressions:

$$A^+ = \{0, 1, \ldots, 12, 123, \ldots, 59, \ldots\}$$

The elements of A^+ are the building blocks for the set $\mathscr{E}$ of integer expressions. We define $\mathscr{E}$ by structural induction, using Def. 6.5.

Basis clause. $\forall x\ [x \in A^+ \rightarrow x \in \mathscr{E}]$

Inductive clause. If $x, y \in \mathscr{E}$ then the following are all elements in $\mathscr{E}$: (x), $+x$, $-x$, $x+y, x-y$, $x*y$, x div y and x mod y.

Extremal clause. Unless an element can be shown to be a member of $\mathscr{E}$ by applying the basis clause and the extremal clause a finite number of times then that element is not in $\mathscr{E}$.

In Sec. 7.4 we shall give an alternative definition of Pascal expressions using the Backus Naur form of meta-language.

In future we shall not write the extremal clause of a definition by structural induction in full because it always has the same form. This clause is important, however, in expressing the closure of the defined set.

We have given examples of simple formal languages generated by juxtaposing symbols to form strings. We have also used structural induction to define a small part of the Pascal syntax. Now we should put these ideas together and give an inductive definition for a string as the basic structure for the more complex formal languages that are built from phrases and sentences.

We begin with a definition of strings that are built in at most one way by a pre-fix operation in which a symbol is added at the beginning of a possibly empty string. Strings are defined over some alphabet A, which usually consists of a finite set of characters. A possible language is the set of all strings over a fixed alphabet A, that is denoted by A^*, and includes the empty string Λ.

Example 7.5 If $A = \{a\}$, then $A^* = \{\Lambda, a, aa, aaa, \ldots\}$.

Exercise 7.2 If $A = \{0, 1\}$ describe A^*.

Definition 7.2 String with pre-fix operation For an alphabet A, the set of all non-empty strings over A is denoted by A^+. It is defined as follows by structural induction:

Basis clause. $\forall x\ [x \in A \rightarrow x \in A^+]$

Inductive clause. $x \in A \wedge y \in A^+ \rightarrow xy \in A^+$

Extremal clause. ...

Sometimes the pre-fix operation is denoted by the binary operation symbol '.' to form $u.x$, where u is a character and x is a string. We use juxtaposition to show the results of the pre-fix operation and identify in our definition those sets to which u and x belong.

Strings are often defined as being constructed by the binary operation of *concatenation* that juxtaposes two strings together. This operation is commonly used to join lists, which are also important recursive structures, and is denoted either by '.' or '*'. The inductive definitions that we write in this section give the actual values of the strings that are composed and are written by juxtaposing strings and characters.

Example 7.6 If $x * y$ denotes concatenation between strings then $ab * cba = abcba$ and $\Lambda * ab = ab$. If $x.y$ denotes the pre-fix operation on strings then $a.bba = abba$.

Exercise 7.3 Give a definition by structural induction of a string with the concatenation operation. Base your definition on Def. 7.2 but use concatenation as the only way of building new strings.

We shall see in Chapter 8 that the set A^* that is formed by adding the empty string Λ to the set A^+ is an important algebraic structure. In Chapter 10 we shall specify a string as an important abstract data type.

Exercise 7.4 If $A = \{a, b\}$ and strings are built only by concatenation give some of the elements in A^*. Decide whether the operation of concatenation, denoted by $*$, is associative and commutative.

7.2 FIRST-ORDER LANGUAGES

In this section we define the formal languages of propositions and of predicates by induction and then extend our definition to all first-order logical languages. A first-order language contains the language of the predicate calculus, but in addition expresses the construction of terms by functions. Terms are the expressions that describe objects in some application domain and predicates describe the properties of these objects. We can think of the terms as the nouns and pronouns of the language and the predicates as well-formed formulae, or wffs, that are either true or false. Axioms describe the basic properties about objects in a formal system and rules of inference enable theorems to be deduced. We present the notion of a first-order theory to express the properties of some application and the construction of a model (which is concrete in the sense that it adds mathematical detail) for the interpretation of the statements of the theory.

7.2.1 Inductive definition of the predicate calculus

We begin with an inductive definition of the language of the propositional calculus. We saw in Sec. 3.2 that the permissible strings in this language are wffs, and that only these are interpreted by truth-values.

Definition 7.3 Wffs of the propositional calculus The set $\mathscr{P}$ of wffs of the propositional calculus is defined inductively. We assume that P is the set of propositional variables.

Basis clause. $\forall p\ [p \in P \rightarrow p \in \mathscr{P}]$

Inductive clause. If $A, B \in \mathscr{P}$ then the following are all elements in $\mathscr{P}$: (A), $A \wedge B$, $A \vee B$, $\neg A$, $A \rightarrow B$ and $A \leftrightarrow B$.

Extremal clause. ...

It is harder to give an inductive definition of wffs of the pure predicate calculus, because this calculus has been refined in order to model mathematical proofs. First we need to define a set of basic formulae. These are analogous to the set of propositional variables that we built from the basis clause of the inductive definition for wffs of the propositional calculus. We define the set $\mathscr{A}$ of *atomic formulae* that are wffs without connective or quantifier symbols, and build from these the remaining wffs of the predicate calculus by our inductive clause.

In order to define the set $\mathscr{A}$ we look back to Sec. 5.1 where we denoted an n-ary predicate by $\mathscr{P}^n(t)$ where t is a list of n names of objects. As an example of a *simple* unary predicate, which can be derived from $\mathscr{F}(a)$ or $\mathscr{F}(x)$ by replacing the individual constant name a or variable name x by the argument place '____', we wrote $\mathscr{F}(\_\_\_\_)$. The argument place was not part of the formal notation, however. We now use such simple unary predicates as the building blocks for the quantified expressions in the predicate calculus. The n-ary predicates are the building blocks for the expressions that are built by the logical connectives, and, together with the simple unary predicates, form the set of atomic formulae, $\mathscr{A}$. We use upper-case Greek letters, such as Φ and Ψ, to generalize over all atomic formulae rather than referring to a particular example.

Definition 7.4 Wffs of the predicate calculus Let $\mathscr{A}$ be the set of atomic formulae that contains expressions of the form $\mathscr{P}^n(t)$, where $\mathscr{P}$ is a predicate constant and t is a list of n names, and $\mathscr{F}(\_\_\_\_)$, where $\mathscr{F}$ is a predicate constant. We define the set $\mathscr{W}$ of wffs of the predicate calculus inductively as follows:

Basis clause. $\forall \Phi\ [\Phi \in \mathscr{A} \rightarrow \Phi \in \mathscr{W}]$

Inductive clause.

1 If $A, B \in \mathscr{W}$ then the following are all elements in $\mathscr{W}$: (A), $A \wedge B$, $A \vee B$, $\neg A$, $A \rightarrow B$ and $A \leftrightarrow B$.

2 If $\Phi(\_\_\_\_) \in A$ and x is a variable not in $\Phi(\_\_\_\_)$ then $\forall x\ \Phi(x)$ and $\exists x\ \Phi(x)$ are in $\mathscr{W}$.

Extremal clause. ...

Inductive definition of a first-order language In Chapter 5 we defined a non-empty set of predicate constants in the pure predicate language so that expressions can be built that describe the properties of objects in some application domain. We now generalize this pure language of predicates in order to build expressions that denote the objects themselves. By generalizing to a pattern for all *first-order* languages we can define languages that contain both the logical symbols of the predicate calculus, whose meanings are fixed, and the non-logical symbols, whose meanings denote objects in some application domain. We shall use first-order languages in many of the later chapters of this book.

Building terms in a first-order language Our generalized first-order language includes a set, which may be empty, of n-place function symbols $f, g, h, \ldots$ for each n. The actual objects in a problem domain are represented by expressions called *terms* that are built by induction from the individual constant and variable symbols of the language. The terms are built as strings of symbols that denote the application of functions to the objects in the domain.

Definition 7.5 Inductive definition of the terms of a first-order language A term is an expression that denotes objects. Let $\mathscr{S}$ be the set of simple terms that contains the individual constant symbols $a, b, c, \ldots$ and the variable symbols $x, y, z, \ldots$. We define the set $\mathscr{T}$ of terms of a first-order language as follows:

Basis clause. $\forall s\ [s \in \mathscr{S} \rightarrow s \in \mathscr{T}]$

Inductive clause. If $t_1, t_2, \ldots, t_n$ are terms where $n \geq 1$ and f is a function of arity n, then the string $f(t_1, t_2, \ldots, t_n)$ is a term.

Extremal clause. ...

The introduction of functions allows the internal logical structure of an object to be represented. Within the pure predicate calculus we were unable to represent the *uniqueness* of an object.

Example 7.7 In the predicate calculus we would analyse the sentence 'Sue's father is a teacher' by denoting the object 'Sue's father' by an individual constant symbol such as a (where (a) is in maths mode as a). Then we could represent the sentence by $\mathscr{T}(a)$ where $\mathscr{T}(x)$ denotes 'x is a teacher'. We cannot remove the name 'Sue' from $\mathscr{T}(a)$, however, because there is no component 'Sue' that can be separated from the component 'father' in the object denoted by a (where (a) is in maths mode as a). Also, we cannot express the fact that Sue has only one father.

Example 7.8 In order to express the sentence 'Bob's mother is a dentist' in a first-order language we need to paraphrase the sentence as 'For some x, x is Bob's mother and x is a dentist'. The three components of the sentence can then be represented in the pure predicate calculus by using the following symbols:

$\mathscr{M}(x, y)$: 'x is y's mother'
$\mathscr{D}(x)$: 'x is a dentist'
b : 'Bob'

The sentence is then expressed as the assertion $\exists x\ [\mathscr{M}(x, b) \wedge \mathscr{D}(x)]$. The use of predicates does not convey the precise meaning, however, because the assertion also represents the sentence 'Some of Bob's mothers are dentists'.

We need to use a function to represent the uniqueness of Bob's mother. The function symbol m with one argument place forms a complex term when an individual constant or a previously constructed term is put in the argument place. So if we choose $m(a)$ to denote the term 'Bob's mother' we can now write $D(m(a))$ to denote 'Bob's mother is a dentist'.

Exercise 7.5 Let

$f(x)$: 'the father of x'
$m(x)$: 'the mother of x'
c: 'Charlie'

Write the four terms that represent the grandparents of Charlie and identify them in English.

Exercise 7.6 If a denotes zero and s is the symbol for the successor function build the set of terms that represents the natural numbers.

Exercise 7.7 In a first-order language there are function symbols f and g of arity 2. The predicate symbol q is binary, whereas the predicate symbol p is ternary or three-place. Explain why some of the following are not wffs:

(a) $p(a, x, f(a, x))$

(b) $q(g(b, x), y, z)$

(c) $\neg\vee$

(d) $(p(a, x, f(a, x)) \wedge (\exists y\ (q(g(b, x), y))))$

(e) $\forall x(p(a, x, f(a, x)) \wedge (\exists y\ (q(g(b, x), y)))$

We are now able to define an expression in a first-order language as either a wff or a term. Both x and $\mathscr{P}(f(x, y), g(x))$ are therefore expressions. The symbol for equality, $=$, is sometimes defined as a logical symbol in a first-order language. Alternatively it is defined as one of the predicate symbols and so is described as a non-logical or *extralogical* symbol. In order to provide a uniform notation the constant symbols are also called zero-place function symbols.

7.2.2 Theories in first-order languages

In a first-order language we have defined some non-logical symbols that we can use for the description of some application system. Just as we choose some of the symbols and strings that are available to us in a programming language when we write a program, we can choose some of the symbols from our first-order language to write a theory about an application system. Using Defs 3.2 and 3.3 we can now define a language for a theory as belonging to the language of a formal axiomatic system.

Definition 7.6 Language of a first-order theory Let a formal axiomatic system, FS, be the pair $(L_{\mathrm{FS}}, \vdash_{\mathrm{FS}})$ where L_{FS} is the first-order language and $\vdash_{\mathrm{FS}}$ is the consequence relation of the formal system. Then L_T is called the language of the first-order theory T and is chosen to describe the objects and properties of some application.

Here are examples of languages that are used to express first-order theories.

A theory of arithmetic We begin by choosing some non-logical symbols to describe the properties and numbers and use these to introduce a simple theory of arithmetic in a first-order language. In Sec. 5.3 we used existential quantifiers in the predicate calculus to express assertions about numbers. In order to express general properties, such as the commutativity of operations on numbers, however, we need to quantify over numbers that are represented by terms. Using a first-order language we are able to express general arithmetical statements as axioms, and use rules of inference to deduce the theorems of arithmetic that we presented in Chapter 2 and use freely in mathematics. The collection of all the theorems deduced from the axioms of arithmetic is, according to Def. 3.3, the *first-order theory of arithmetic*.

This theory provided the stimulus for the development of first-order logic but also revealed the limitations of the axiomatic approach. In 1931 Gödel showed that it is not possible to construct an axiom system that completely axiomatizes the theory of arithmetic. For our purposes only a fragment of the theory is needed as an example of a first-order theory that expresses the properties of an application domain. We present further theories as specifications of abstract data types, such as strings and lists, in Chapter 10, and show how the activity of specification is one of building theories about application systems.

In the first-order language of arithmetic there is a symbol for equality $=$, a two-place predicate symbol $<$, a constant symbol 0, a one-place function symbol s that names the successor function and a two-place function symbol $+$. The symbols denote their usual mathematical meanings in arithmetic. We use the pure logical notation in order to emphasize the structure of the first-order language.

The name for the natural number 2 is the term $s(s(0))$, while the name for 3 is the term $s(s(s(0)))$. We write $+(s(s(0)), s(s(s(0))))$ as the term that denotes the natural number 5, which we know is the arithmetic sum of 2 and 3.

Mathematicians use the logic symbols of a first-order language freely and write expressions using the relation $<$ and the operation $+$ in infix form. When we are working within logic, however, it is important to use the pure logic notation in the pre-fix form and to avoid using the purely intuitive steps that we need to make freely in mathematics. It is particularly important when we work with first-order theories of complex systems not to make compromises that interfere with the logical understanding of assertions.

Exercise 7.8 Using the first-order language of arithmetic write an atomic formula over terms to denote the relation between numbers, $1 < 2$. Use this atomic formula to write a wff that denotes the mathematical assertion $1 < 2 \wedge 0 < 1 \rightarrow 1 + 0 < 2$.

Arithmetic is concerned with operations like addition and multiplication defined on numbers, and we defined the general properties of these operations in Chapter 2. Within a first-order theory of arithmetic are the subtheories of the successor function, of addition and of multiplication. We present a fragment of the theory of arithmetic and begin by giving the three axioms for the successor function:

Axiom S1. $\forall x\ [\neg s(x) = 0]$

Axiom S2. $\forall x \forall y\ [s(x) = s(y) \rightarrow x = y]$

Axiom S3. $[\mathscr{P}(0) \wedge \forall x(\mathscr{P}(x) \rightarrow \mathscr{P}(s(x)))] \rightarrow \forall x\ \mathscr{P}(x)$

Axiom S1 states that the number zero is not the successor of any number; while Axiom S2 asserts that the successor function is one-to-one. Axiom S3 is, of course, the principle of mathematical induction that we gave in Def. 6.1. The theory of addition is axiomatized by the following two axioms:

Axiom A1. $\forall x\ [x + 0 = x]$

Axiom A2. $\forall x \forall y\ [x + s(y) = s(x + y)]$

From these axioms for addition the theorems for addition can be derived. In particular, we can deduce theorems that express the commutative and associative properties of addition.

Example 7.9 We deduce from the axioms that $1 + 1 = 2$. We express the statement in our first-order language as $s(0) + s(0) = s(s(0))$ and show that this statement is a consequence of the axioms and therefore a theorem.

Derivation

1.	$s(0) + s(0) = s(s(0) + 0)$	A2 with $s(0)/x,\ 0/y$
2.	$s(0) + 0 = s(0)$	A1 with $s(0)/x$
3.	$s(s(0) + 0) = s(s(0))$	s-introduction on 2
4.	$s(0) + s(0) = s(s(0))$	transitivity of $=$ on 1,3

end

We have used the property of transitivity for the identity relation, $=$, in step 4. This would be given formally by the first-order theory of identity, which we do not give in detail here.

Exercise 7.9 Use the first-order language of arithmetic and the axioms for addition to deduce the theorem 1+2=3.

We have made these derivations within our formal deduction system and without a notion of interpretation by some model—later we consider a formal structure for interpreting the symbols of our first-order language.

A theory about sets We can use predicate logic as a meta-mathematical language to talk about sentences in the language of set theory. For the language of our first-order theory we choose the following non-logical symbols:

- The equality symbol $=$
- The two-place predicate symbol $\in$
- The function symbol $\emptyset$ as a constant
- The variable symbols $u, v, w, \ldots$

The domain of interpretation for our theory is the set of all sets. The symbol $\in$ is interpreted by the relation 'is a member of' and $\emptyset$ is interpreted by the empty set.

Exercise 7.10 Give examples of terms, atomic formulae and wffs in the language of set theory. In particular express the assertion that 'no set is a member of itself'.

Example 7.10 The assertion that 'there is no set of which every set is a member' can be translated into the language of set theory in the following stages:

$\neg$ [There is a set of which every set is a member]
$\neg\exists v$ [Every set is a member of v]
$\neg\exists v\ \forall w\ \in (w, v)$

Exercise 7.11 Write the final assertion in Example 7.10 using the universal quantifier instead of the existential quantifier. This should be syntactically correct but will not be very readable.

We have developed a formal first-order language that can be used to study the mathematical theories of numbers and sets, and illustrates the intertwining between the disciplines of logic and mathematics. Our own motivation is to present formal logic as an essential tool for the analysis and formalization of the patterns of thought that are needed for reasoning about the behaviour of complex systems. Formal languages with added rules for reasoning provide us with the formal systems that are the subject matter of this book.

7.2.3 Models for first-order theories

From the language of a first-order system we have selected non-logical symbols to include in the languages of first-order theories. By making deductions from axioms we construct the set of formulae that constitute a theory and express the properties of an application. In this way we can represent the semantics of our application. The consequence relation, $\vdash$, will enable us to check that our theory is internally consistent. It is always important to remember that our theory is a formal object that expresses our informal ideas about some application system. Although we can verify the properties *within* our formal axiomatic system, we are unable to check the process of building a formal theory as our perception of some application system. The stage of moving from an informal picture of some application domain to formalizing the properties of that domain in a formal system is difficult and one that cannot itself be formalized.

7.2.4 A model is a mathematical structure

We now have a purely syntactic axiomatic system, within which we can write theories about application systems. It may be that we wish to construct for our axiomatic system a formal *model* in which we can interpret, or give value to, the terms and formulae of our theory. Clearly we can only represent the objects in an application domain by *mathematical* objects in our formal model. We therefore connect our syntactic axiomatic system with some mathematical structure in order to gain the extra power of being able to reason and make proofs within a mathematical model. The ability to move from the syntactic world of deduction, symbolized by $\vdash$, to the semantic world of entailment and satisfaction in a model, symbolized by $\models$, was discussed for the propositional calculus in Chapter 4. We defined the satisfaction and validity of a predicate in Sec. 5.2.2 and defined a model for a predicate in Def. 5.11. The choice of a suitable model for a first-order theory is an important task in the formal construction of systems. Usually there are many possible models, and the most useful is, in some sense, the smallest or simplest model. We often say that the model is a mathematical structure that *realizes* a theory.

Clearly within an axiomatic system every possible model must interpret the logical symbols in the way we have specified in Chapters 3 and 5. The models will vary in the interpretation that they give to the non-logical symbols, however.

Example 7.11 We consider a model for the fragment of the first-order theory of arithmetic, called $\mathscr{A}$, that was given in Sec. 7.2.2. The terms of the language of the theory, $L_{\mathscr{A}}$, are interpreted by objects in the domain $D = \mathbb{N}$. The one-place function symbol, s, is interpreted by a function that adds 1 to a natural number. The two-place predicate symbol, $<$, and the two-place function symbol, $+$, are interpreted by the infix relation $<$ and the infix binary operation $+$ respectively. The domain D and the interpretations of the predicate and function symbol together form a *structure*, which models the theory of arithmetic. We write the structure as $\mathscr{N}_{\mathscr{A}} = (\mathbb{N}, 0, s, <, +)$ and represent the interpretation of the terms and wffs of the theory A by the structure $\mathscr{N}_{\text{A}}$ in Fig. 7.1.

Exercise 7.12 Interpret the wff $<(0, s(0)) \wedge <(+(s(0), s(0)), s(0))$ informally in the structure $\mathscr{N}_{\mathscr{A}}$.

Exercise 7.13 In the language L_T for a theory T, there is one two-place predicate symbol $\mathscr{P}$ and a list of variable symbols $x, y, z, \ldots$. The formula $\exists x\ \forall y\ (\mathscr{P}(x, y))$ is interpreted in the following two structures:

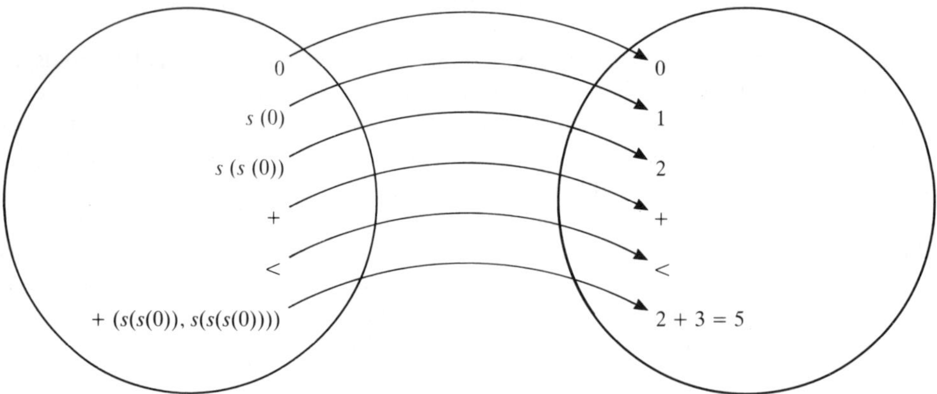

Figure 7.1 Interpretation of terms and wffs by a structure.

(a) $D = \mathbb{N}$ and the symbol $\mathscr{P}$ is interpreted by the binary relation $\leq$ on $\mathbb{N}$.

(b) $D = \{\text{giraffes}\}$ and $\mathscr{P}$ denotes the binary relation 'has a longer neck'.

Give the different interpretations of the formula in English and state their truth-values in the two different structures.

An interpretation for a closed formula is said to be a *model* for that formula only if the formula is true in that interpretation. If we can find at least one model the formula is said to be *consistent*.

Example 7.12 The formula $\exists x\ \forall y\ (\mathscr{P}(x, y))$ is consistent because it has the model given in Exercise 7.13(a).

We have seen that a structure for the language of a first-order theory is a *function* that tells us what collection of objects we can quantify over and what the symbols of the language denote. If we want to construct mathematical structures to give a semantics to the sentences of a theory, we are going to be interested in those structures where the sentences are all true. This is exactly what is meant when a structure is defined as a model for a theory.

Definition 7.7 Model of a theory Let T be a theory in a first-order language L_T. A structure $\mathscr{S}$ for T is a model for T if all the sentences of T are true in $\mathscr{S}$.

Example 7.13 Consider the language of set theory given in Sec. 7.2.2 and the sentence $\exists x\ \forall y\ \neg(\in (y, x))$. The structure $(\mathbb{N}, <)$ in which the symbol $\in$ is interpreted by the relation 'less than' is a model for the sentence. The interpretation is 'there is a natural number such that no natural number is smaller'.

When a predicate of a first-order language is interpreted formally it is sufficient to give the predicate a meaning by saying what *set* of objects are related in the interpretation. The structure, as a function, therefore assigns a set to a predicate symbol rather than a named relation.

Example 7.14 The language L_T has a two-place predicate constant symbol $\mathscr{H}$. A model for the theory T is the structure $\mathscr{A}$ that consists of $D = \mathbb{N}$ and the set $A \subseteq D \times D$ which consists of all the pairs (n, m) of natural numbers for which $n < m$. The theory T contains the sentence $\forall x \forall y\ \mathscr{H}(x, y)$. This sentence is interpreted by $\mathscr{A}$ as 'for any pair (n, m) of natural numbers $(n, m) \in A$'.

7.2.5 Formal interpretation

You probably realized that we only presented an intuitive picture of the interpretation of terms and wffs by the diagram in Fig. 7.1. When we work with large theories that describe complex systems we need to understand precisely how the terms and wffs can be realized by objects and truth-values in a mathematical structure. We therefore formalize the interpretation for first-order languages by extending Def. 5.6 to deal with the interpretation of terms as well as predicates and individual constants. In a theory we reason by deduction using $\vdash$, but in a model, as a mathematical structure, we use $\models$ and assert that the wffs of our theory are *satisfied* when they are true in a certain interpretation.

We have seen that a structure is formally defined as a function, which includes the domain of interpretation, and by interpretation assigns the objects in the domain to the symbols of a first-order language. A *value* is therefore given to the symbols of a language by the interpretation of terms and wffs. For this reason the structure for interpretation is sometimes called a *valuation system*. We denote the interpretation function by I.

Definition 7.8 Interpretation for a first-order language A structure for the interpretation of a first-order language L_{FS} in a formal system FS consists of:

1 A non-empty set D, the domain of interpretation.

2 A function I from the predicate, function and constant symbols of L_{FS} such that

(a) for each predicate symbol $\mathscr{P}$ of arity n, $I(\mathscr{P}) \subseteq D^n$,

(b) for each function symbol f of arity n, $I(f) : D^n \to D$,

(c) for each individual constant symbol c, $I(c) \in D$.

A structure interprets the terms of a first-order language by extending the function I to the function I^*. Thus predicate symbols of arity n are interpreted as n-ary predicates of D, function symbols of arity n as n-ary functions over D and constant symbols as individuals in D.

Example 7.15 We interpret the term $s(0)$ in the theory $L_{\mathscr{A}}$, given in Sec. 7.2.2. The structure is $\mathscr{N}_S = (\mathbb{N}, 0, \mathbf{s})$ where $\mathbf{s}$ is the successor function on $\mathbb{N}$. We have $D = \mathbb{N}$ and $I(0) = 0 \in \mathbb{N}$. Here the symbol 0 in the term $s(0)$ is interpreted to, or realized by, the number zero. The term $s(0)$ is just a string in the first-order language and the symbol s is interpreted by a function $I(s) : \mathbb{N} \to \mathbb{N}$. This function can then be *applied* to the element in D that is called $I(0)$. (Here we have the name $I(0)$ for the natural number that is also called zero in the domain of interpretation. They just happen to be two different names for the same number.)

Example 7.16 The result of applying the function $I(s)$ to $I(0)$ is $I(s)[I(0)]$, and it is this object in D that realizes the term $s(0)$. Using the extended function we write $I^*(s(0)) = I(s)[I(0)]$.

In general we have the familiar pattern of recursion for the function that interprets a term in a first-order language. We should expect this since we gave an inductive definition of the set $\mathscr{T}$ of terms in a first-order language in Def. 7.5. The set $\mathscr{S}$ of simple terms formed the basis for the induction. Elements from the same set terminate the

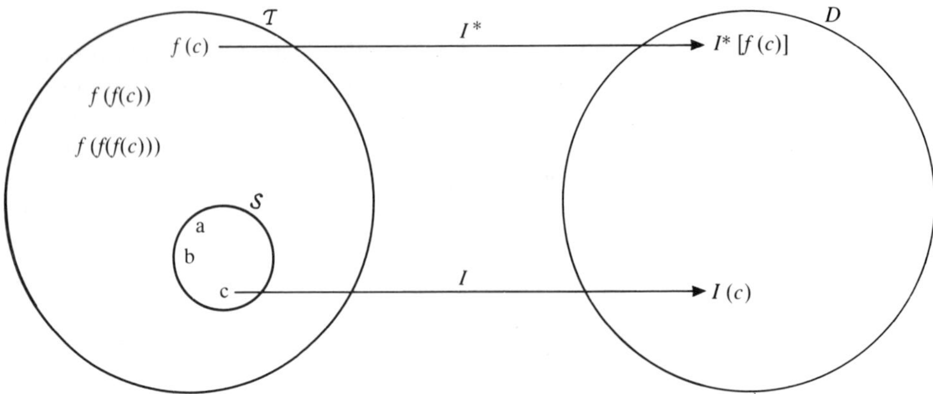

Figure 7.2 Interpretation of terms in $\mathcal{T}$ by the function I^* in a structure.

recursion when the terms built by the inductive clause are interpreted by the extended function I^*. The constant symbols in $\mathcal{S}$ are simply function symbols of arity 0.

We represent the interpretation of the terms in $\mathcal{T}$ by the objects in D, the domain of interpretation, in Fig. 7.2.

Definition 7.9 The interpretation of a term by a structure Let a structure for a language L_{FS} in a formal system FS consist of a domain D and interpretation function I that is defined on the set of simple terms $\mathcal{S}$. Then the term $f(t_1,\ldots,t_n)$, where f is an n-place function symbol and $t_1,\ldots,t_n$ are terms, is interpreted by the extension of I, called I^*, in the following way:

$$\begin{aligned} I^*(f(t_1,\ldots,t_n)) &= I(f)[I^*(t_1),\ldots,I^*(t_n)] \\ I^*(c) &= I(c) \text{ where } c \text{ is a constant symbol in } \mathcal{S} \end{aligned}$$

In order to interpret a term, therefore, we take the outermost symbol of the term, which is f in the general term, and interpret that to a function $I(f)$. This function is then *applied* to the results of interpreting each of the n terms $t_1,\ldots,t_n$ by objects in the domain D. The recursive interpretation of the syntactic string of symbols terminates when the interpretation function I is applied to a constant symbol in $\mathcal{S}$.

Exercise 7.14 Interpret the term $s(s(s(0)))$ in the theory $L_{\mathcal{A}}$, given in Sec. 7.2.2, in the structure $\mathcal{N}_s = (\mathbb{N}, 0, \mathbf{s})$. As in Example 7.2.5 **s** is the successor function on $\mathbb{N}$.

We have now built a mathematical structure for the interpretation of sentences in a first-order language of logic. The key point of this structure is to provide a definition of truth for the formal language and, based on this, the concept of a model for a theory. The structure is a *model* for a theory in a first-order language if all the sentences of a theory are true in the structure. This concept of a model is an example of a concrete model because it adds mathematical detail in the modelling process. These ideas belong to model theory and have influenced the formal approaches to system construction.

Model theory developed from bringing together the results of work with universal algebras with those from work in mathematical logic. We shall present mathematical structures as algebras in Chapter 8, and shall then build on both the framework of model theory and algebraic theory in Chapter 10 when we discuss the formal specifications.

In this section we have considered the syntax and semantics of the first-order languages of logic. We present next an approach to providing a meaning for formal languages that is closely linked to the syntactic structure of the language. This approach to semantics has proved to be useful for describing and designing the formal languages that are used for programming systems. It has also influenced the formal approaches to specifying systems.

7.3 SYNTAX DIRECTED SEMANTICS

Formal language theory is concerned only with the syntactic rules for generating the permissible strings in a formal language. We wish to discuss the semantics of formal languages, as well as their syntax, because we believe that providing a formal definition of the semantics presents a greater challenge in the construction of complex systems. We give a simple example of a syntax directed approach to describing the meaning of a formal language. This structured approach has been used to provide a denotational semantics for programming languages and has also influenced both the design of programming languages and the formal specification of systems.

7.3.1 Syntactic structure

Many formal languages are so complex that a structured approach is essential if they are to be both understood and used properly. The meaning of a formal language can be usefully described by basing it on the syntactic description of the language. This involves the important idea that each syntactic unit of a language, such as a string, phrase or sentence, has a meaning that can be based on its syntactic structure. The meaning of a composite syntactic structure is identified as a meaning of its components. This important property is described as the property of *compositionality* .

The advantage of a syntax directed approach to semantics is that the meaning of a language is mirrored by its syntactic structure. As a result, any component can be replaced by a component with the same meaning without changing the meaning of the whole composite structure.

As an example we give the semantics of the simple language of binary numerals. The alphabet for the language is $A = \{0, 1\}$. The meaning of each binary numeral is given by a natural number. For example, the number 5 is *denoted* by the binary numeral '0101'. The syntax of the language of binary numerals is defined by structural induction.

Definition 7.10 The language of binary numerals Let $\mathscr{B}$ denote the set of binary numerals over the alphabet $\{0, 1\}$. Then $\mathscr{B}$ is defined inductively as follows:

Basis clause. The characters '0' and '1' are in $\mathscr{B}$.

Inductive clause. If $B \in \mathscr{B}$ then B with a '0' or '1' appended to the right of it is also in $\mathscr{B}$.

Extremal clause. ...

The extremal clause ensures that $\mathscr{B}$ is the *smallest* set that can be built according to the basis and inductive clauses of the definition.

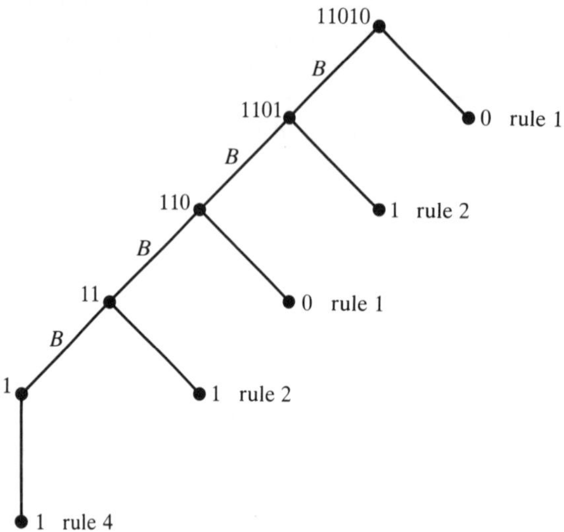

Figure 7.3 Parse tree for '11010'.

7.3.2 Parsing

The inductive definition has specified not only the criteria for a binary numeral to be accepted as an element of $\mathscr{B}$ but has also identified how a binary numeral can be analysed into its component parts. This description of the structural composition of a binary numeral is called its *phrase structure* and can be represented abstractly by a tree diagram that we call a *parse tree*. This diagrammatic representation of the phrase structure of the text in some language is called a model (in the abstract sense), and the process of constructing the tree by analysing the structure of the text is called *parsing*. We have already seen a simple example of parsing in Sec. 2.4. The parsing of a program is an important stage in the syntactic analysis of programs that is carried out by compilers.

Example 7.17 The phrase structure of the binary numeral '11010' is represented in Fig. 7.3 by its parse tree. The analysis of the string is carried out by parsing '11010' as an element of $\mathscr{B}$ and labelling the node at the root of the tree by B. By the inductive clause, '1101' with '0' appended to the right is also in $\mathscr{B}$, so we label the node that is the left child of the root again by B, while the right child is a leaf node labelled by '0'. Parsing '1101' gives, by the inductive clause again, '110' with '1' appended to the right, so we add another node as a left child of '1101', labelled by B, and a right child labelled by '1'. Similarly '110' is parsed to give '11' with '0' appended to the right. Finally, by the basis clause, '1' and '1' are both in $\mathscr{B}$ and so form leaves of the tree.

Exercise 7.15 Parse the binary numeral '01100' by using the inductive definition and draw its parse tree.

We can express the syntactic structure of $\mathscr{B}$ by a meta-language which is more formal than the language we used for our inductive definitions. The basis and inductive clauses of structural induction are represented by *production rules* which are written recursively.

Definition 7.11 Production rules for binary numerals Let $\mathscr{B}$ be the set of valid binary numerals over the alphabet $A = \{0,1\}$. Each $B \in \mathscr{B}$ is formed by the following set of production rules:

$$\begin{aligned} P \;=\; \{&1.\;\; B \longrightarrow B\text{'0'} \\ &2.\;\; B \longrightarrow B\text{'1'} \\ &3.\;\; B \longrightarrow \text{'0'} \\ &4.\;\; B \longrightarrow \text{'1'}\} \end{aligned}$$

Exercise 7.16 Draw the parse tree for the binary numeral '0010' and indicate at each level of the parse tree which production rule has been used.

7.3.3 Semantics

Production rules define the *grammar* of a language. We now base a specification of the meaning of each binary numeral on the syntactic structure of $\mathscr{B}$. The semantics of every binary numeral is *denoted* by a number, and is specified in the following definition:

Definition 7.12 The semantics of the binary numerals This is defined by the following rules:

1 The binary numerals '0' and '1' denote numbers 0 and 1.

2 If B is a binary numeral that denotes number n then

(a) B'0' denotes $n \times 2 + 0$,

(b) B'1' denotes $n \times 2 + 1$.

Example 7.18 To give the semantics of '11010' we use the parse tree in Fig. 7.3. We begin with the leaf at the left of the tree and give the semantics for that binary numeral. Then we work our way up the parse tree, giving the *denotations* for the binary numerals that belong to the structure of '11010' as we go. At each stage we give the rule that we have used.

'1'	denotes 1	rule 1
'11'	denotes $(1) \times 2 + 1$	rule 2b
'110'	denotes $((1) \times 2 + 1) \times 2 + 0$	rule 2a
'1101'	denotes $(((1) \times 2 + 1) \times 2 + 0) \times 2 + 1$	rule 2b
'11010'	denotes $((((1) \times 2 + 1) \times 2 + 0) \times 2 + 1) \times 2 + 0$	rule 2a
	$= 26$	

We can represent the denotational method for giving a semantics to binary numerals by labelling the parse tree for the numeral. This tree represents the phrase structure of the binary numeral and we can label each node in the tree by the number that is denoted by the phrase at that node. We therefore climb up the tree labelling the nodes with their denotations as we go. The semantics for '11010' is given in Fig. 7.4.

7.3.4 The denotational semantic approach

Our example of basing the semantics of binary numerals on their syntactic structure belongs to the denotational approach for specifying the semantics of languages. This structural approach has been used for a long time in logic and the study of linguistics and has been applied to the analysis of natural languages. Denotational descriptions

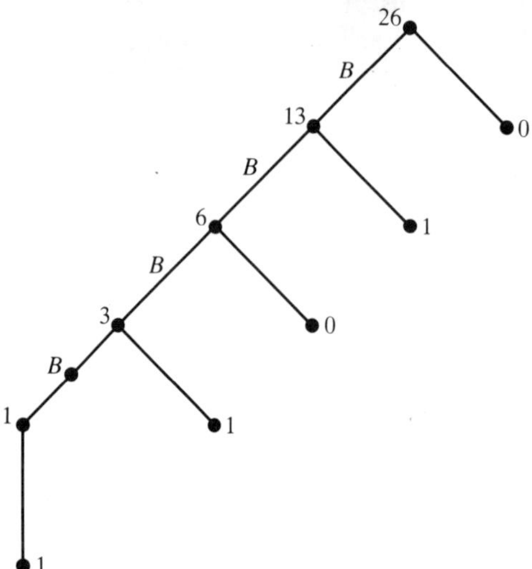

Figure 7.4 The semantics of '11010'.

have been written for programming languages, and have influenced the demand for simple languages that have the meaning of composite structures expressed in terms of the meaning of their parts. Such well-designed programming languages aid the programmer in the task of constructing correct programs.

Another approach to defining the semantics of programming languages is the more abstract *axiomatic* approach that was used by Hoare to define Pascal. We use the axiomatic approach in Chapter 12 when we construct a logical proof system to verify the correctness of algorithms. Finally, a further approach is the *operational* approach that is used to specify the semantics of programming languages, and is particularly appropriate for the specification of the programs that compile these languages. We shall see some examples of the semantics of program structure defined operationally in Chapter 13.

☆7.4 A HIERARCHY OF FORMAL LANGUAGES

In this section we concentrate on describing the structure of formal languages by meta-languages that are themselves formal. We present a definition of a grammar that expresses the generation of the well-formed strings of a language by recursive production rules. Using the definition of a grammar we are then able to classify formal languages according to the complexity of their structure. Four classes of grammars are identified and each is equivalent to the abstract machine that will recognize or accept the strings produced by that class of grammar. The languages of regular expressions are produced by the simplest class of grammars—we define this type of language inductively and build the set of strings that are denoted by regular expressions. A more complex grammar is required to produce the well-formed statements of a Pascal program, and we use the Backus Naur Formalism, BNF, as the meta-language to define arithmetic expressions in Pascal.

7.4.1 A formal description of language syntax

We have already noted that the early work on formal language theory focused on the syntax of languages. In fact the application of this early work to compiler design and development has been one of the most successful uses of a formal mathematical approach to solving problems that are fundamental to programming. Now that this work is formalized and well understood, attention has moved to solving further difficult problems such as specifying the semantics of programming languages and of complex systems.

The rules that express the structure of a language are defined by a *grammar*. A useful notation for both producing and analysing the structure of the phrases in a language is that used to define a *phrase structure* grammar. With this notation we can classify formal languages into four types according to their complexity.

Definition 7.13 A phrase structure grammar A phrase structure grammar is an ordered 4-tuple $G = (V_t, V_n, P, S)$ where

- V_t is the set of terminal symbols,
- V_n is the set of non-terminal symbols,
- P is a set of generating rules defining how members of V_t and V_n can be combined,
- S is a member of V_n called the start symbol.

We also define $V = V_t \cup V_n$.

Example 7.19 In Sec. 7.3 we defined the rules for producing the binary numerals. Using the notation for a phrase structure grammar we would denote the syntax of binary numerals by $G = (\{0, 1\}, \{B\}, P, B)$. The production rules are given by P in Def. 7.11.

The phrase structure of a language is represented by a parse tree, and the creation of the tree structure demonstrates the way that a particular grammar generates the phrases of the language. The tree that is created for a particular string or sentence shows the hierarchical relationships between the phrases that are defined by the grammar.

Exercise 7.17 The parse tree for the structure of '11010' is 'unbalanced to the left'. The grammar is called a left-linear grammar. What form would the production rules take if they represented an 'unbalanced tree to the right'? We would have to work from the *rightmost* character first when specifying the meaning. Our grammar would then be a right-linear grammar. Suggest why this set of production rules might be less satisfactory.

7.4.2 Classifying grammars

The four types of grammar that we classify belong to the *Chomsky hierarchy*. They are classified according to the restrictions that their production rules impose on the structure of the strings that they produce. We present the main features of these grammars and identify the abstract machine that will recognize the strings that are produced by each of these types of grammars.

The Chomsky hierarchy The most complicated and expressive languages are the natural languages, and these have so far resisted attempts to be formalized. They are intended for communication between people and contain ambiguities that are too difficult to resolve for communication with machines. For example, the statement 'fruit flies like a banana' has two possible meanings; the question of whether a fruit fly exists is a semantic question.

The most complicated languages that can be recognized by a machine are defined by the simplest set of production rules and are defined by the type 0 grammars. The simplest languages are defined by the most restrictive production rules and are defined by the type 3 grammars. We base our classification on Def. 7.13 and use the notation defined on page 174 for the sets A^* and A^+.

Type 0 grammars The production rules for these unrestricted grammars are of the form $\alpha \to \beta$ where $\alpha \in V_N^+$ and $\beta \in V^*$. Therefore α is a non-empty string of non-terminals and β is a possibly empty string of terminals or non-terminals in the closure of V.

These rules are so relaxed that they will allow a string to be produced that is shorter than the variable (non-terminal) string it is made from. This makes the process of analysing a string to see if it belongs to the grammar quite complicated.

Every language defined by a type 0 grammar is a 'recursively enumerable set of its sentences'. Its structure can be recognized by a Turing machine. We shall see, in Chapter 15, that this is equivalent to asserting that we can always find a computer program to recognize its structure.

Type 1 grammars The production rules for these grammars are of the form $\alpha_1 A \alpha_2 \to \alpha_1 \beta \alpha_2$ where $\beta \in V^+$, $A \in V_N$, $\alpha_1, \alpha_2 \in V^*$. The rules are more restrictive than those for type 0 grammars because they specify that each string produced must be at least as long as the string it is made from. The string β cannot be an empty string and only replaces the variable A if it is surrounded by, or *in the context* of, α_1 and α_2. We write α_1 ___ α_2 to indicate the place that β fills.

Languages defined by type 1 grammars are called 'context-sensitive' languages and are recursive sets. While many features of programming languages are context-sensitive, type 1 grammars are not always used for them because they are hard to analyse. For example, inconsistencies in the Pascal language are due to the incomplete and imprecise specification of its syntax. The structure of type 1 grammars cannot be modelled by a parse tree but can be recognized by an abstract machine called a linear bounded automaton. More details on the abstract automata that recognize formal languages are given in Hopcroft and Ullman (1979).

Example 7.20 In a Pascal program the information about typing is contextual information that should be specified in a type 1 grammar. The following fragment of a Pascal program should then be found incorrect:

```
const i = 32;
begin
      i := i + 1;
end.
```

Type 2 grammars The production rules for these grammars are of the form $A \to \alpha$, where $A \in V_N$ and $\alpha \in V^+$. These grammars enforce the restriction that there is a single non-terminal symbol on the left side of each of the production rules. This restriction means that the structure of the grammar can be modelled by a parse tree. Type 2 grammars are called 'context-free' and formalize the process of parsing for programming languages. They describe arithmetic expressions and block structure.

The equivalent machine to a context-free grammar is a push-down automaton with a stack to implement the recursion required in recognizing the languages. We shall describe a subset of the Pascal language using a type 2 grammar and shall also illustrate the parsing process.

Type 3 grammars The production rules for these grammars are the most restrictive of the grammars in the hierarchy and are of the form

$$\begin{array}{lll} A & \rightarrow & B\alpha \\ A & \rightarrow & \alpha \end{array} \qquad \text{where } A, B \in V_{\mathrm{N}} \text{ and } \alpha \in V_{\mathrm{T}}$$

Languages defined by type 3 grammars are called 'regular expressions' and are the simplest type of language in the hierarchy. Only a simple abstract machine is required to recognize the structure of these languages. The type 3 or regular grammars are equivalent to the finite state machines or automata that are defined in Sec 2.4. We shall describe the languages of regular expressions in more detail on page 194. Their importance in programming is that the initial analysis of the text of a program that is made by the compiler, and called lexical analysis, is based on regular grammars and can be modelled by the finite state machine.

The syntax of arithmetic expressions in Pascal We present a subset of the Pascal language that is defined by a type 2 grammar and illustrate the process of parsing that is carried out by the compiler. The phase of syntax analysis, based on a type 2 grammar, follows the phase of lexical analysis, that is based on a type 3 grammar.

We use the BNF notation as a meta-language for expressing the syntax of a context-free language. In this notation all non-terminal symbols are placed within angle brackets on the left-hand side of the production symbol ::=. If more than one production has the same left-hand side, we list the left-hand side once, and then on the same line list all the right-hand sides separated by vertical bars. The start symbol of the phrase structure grammar notation is replaced by the non-terminal that represents the 'most structured' phrase or sentence in the language. In our example grammar this is the phrase *expression*.

Grammar 7.1 Arithmetic expressions in Pascal The syntax of arithmetic expressions in Pascal is defined in BNF by the following rules:

1. ⟨expression⟩ ::= ⟨term⟩ | ⟨expression⟩⟨addop⟩⟨term⟩
2. ⟨term⟩ ::= ⟨factor⟩ | ⟨term⟩⟨multop⟩⟨factor⟩
3. ⟨factor⟩ ::= ⟨identifier⟩ | ⟨literal⟩ | (⟨expression⟩)
4. ⟨identifier⟩ ::= *a* | *b* | *c* ··· | *z*
5. ⟨literal⟩ ::= 0 | 1 | 2 ··· | 9
6. ⟨addop⟩ ::= + | - | or
7. ⟨multop⟩ ::= * | / | div | mod | and

The brackets round the non-terminal ⟨expression⟩ in the rule for a factor are valid symbols in the language.

The BNF meta-language specifies not only the syntactic structures of a type 2 language but also tells us which strings of characters are well-formed program texts. As a description of a grammar it provides more detail, and in this sense is more concrete, than a meta-language that merely lists the syntactic structures that are available in the language. The specification of a *concrete syntax* is required for the analysis of the text of a program by a compiler because the recognition of grammatically correct sentences in the program must terminate with the construction of a unique parse tree. Detail, such as brackets round expressions, is added to the concrete syntax to ensure that parsing terminates.

The description of the concrete details about the strings of symbols in the program text merely *abbreviate* the actual structure of a program, however. These concrete details are not needed to determine the semantics of a programming language. The specification of an *abstract syntax* is needed to describe the structure of a program as a tree and to determine its semantics as in Sec. 7.3. We use the concrete syntax for Pascal expressions given by Grammar 7.1 before we express the simpler abstract syntax by trees.

Example 7.21 Using Grammar 7.1, the phrase structure of the expression $c+d/2$ is recognized as consisting of the component parts ⟨expression⟩⟨addop⟩⟨term⟩ where the term is $d/2$. The expression therefore has a structure that is composed from the simpler phrase structure $d/2$.

In Sec. 7.3.2 we constructed a parse tree to represent the phrase structure of a binary numeral. The tree is a hierarchy of non-terminal symbols, positioned at the internal nodes of the tree, and terminal symbols that form the strings of the language, as the leaves of the tree. The parsing process for a Pascal program can be either a *bottom-up* or a *top-down* process:

- Bottom-up parsing starts with the leaves of the parse tree and works up towards the root, trying to combine the neighbouring terminal symbols to form non-terminal phrase structures. When the entire text is identified as belonging to the non-terminal ⟨program⟩, the parsing of the complete Pascal program terminates.
- Top-down parsing starts with the root of the parse tree and works down towards the leaves. It assumes a valid program text and looks for the non-terminals that belong to the non-terminals of the rule of the higher level in the grammar. The recursion terminates with the construction of the complete parse tree.

Example 7.22 In order to recognize $f * g$ as an expression by a bottom-up parsing process we begin with Rule 7 of Grammar 7.1 which identifies $*$ as belonging to the non-terminal ⟨multop⟩. By Rule 4, f and g belong to the non-terminal ⟨identifier⟩. In order to use Rule 2 which defines ⟨multop⟩ in terms of ⟨term⟩, we must first use Rule 3 to define the identifier g as the phrase structure ⟨factor⟩. For Rule 2 we also need to define f by the non-terminal⟨term⟩. Finally by Rule 1 we define a term as belonging to the non-terminal ⟨expression⟩. The parse tree that has been constructed is given in Fig. 7.5.

The process of top-down parsing for the expression $f * g$ begins with Rule 1 of Grammar 7.1. Since there is no $+, -$ or *or* in the expression, we use Rule 2 and look for the non-terminals that belong to ⟨term⟩. Now we find the appropriate non-terminal for $*$ and work downwards from Rule 2 to find the terminal symbols that complete the structure of the parse tree for $f * g$.

Exercise 7.18 Work through the complete top-down parsing process to construct the parse tree for $f * g$.

Exercise 7.19 Identify the sequence of rules of Grammar 7.1 that are used to recognize $a + b * c$ as an expression when parsing is both bottom-up and top-down.

Exercise 7.20 Use Grammar 7.1 to draw the parse trees for the expressions $a + b * c$ and $(b + 2) * d$.

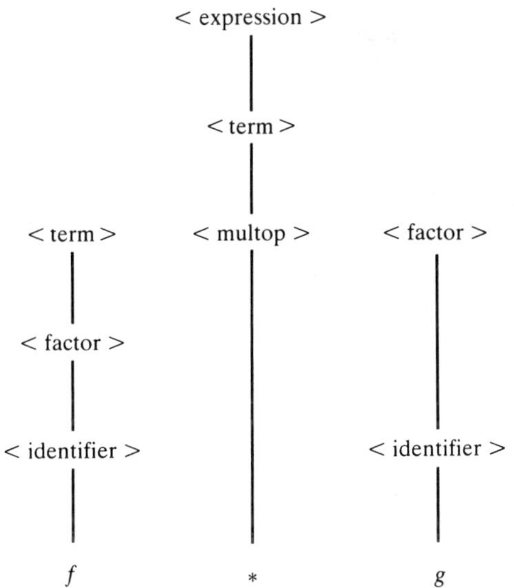

Figure 7.5 Parse tree for the expression $f * g$.

The concrete syntax of Grammar 7.1 provides enough levels of structure to ensure that $*$ takes precedence over $+$ by binding more tightly. The operator $+$ associates to the left. Because $*$ has a higher precedence, it is evaluated to form the term before $+$ is evaluated to form the expression.

Exercise 7.21 Use Grammar 7.1 to draw the parse trees for $a * (b + c)$ and $a * b + c$.

Operators of higher precedence will be replaced by non-terminals that are closer to the leaves of the parse tree. By specifying the precedence of the operators Grammar 7.1 ensures that the language is free from ambiguity. Any ambiguity in the syntax would allow two different meanings for an expression, so that parsing would no longer terminate with the construction of a unique tree.

Example 7.23 The sentence 'I talked to a policeman in my pyjamas' will have two possible parse trees.

Definition 7.14 Ambiguity A formal language is ambiguous if and only if it contains a sentence whose syntax is represented by two or more distinct parse trees.

Exercise 7.22 The expressions $a - b - c$ and $a - (b - c)$ have different meanings. Draw their respective parse trees.

By changing Rule 1 in Grammar 7.1 we can make it ambiguous:

Rule 1′. ⟨expression⟩::=⟨term⟩ | ⟨expression⟩⟨addop⟩⟨expression⟩

Exercise 7.23 Using Rule 1′ in Grammar 7.1 instead of Rule 1, draw the two different parse trees that are produced for the expression $a - b - c$.

Exercise 7.24 Using the complete set of rules in Grammar 7.1 draw the parse tree for the Pascal expression m mod $n + r$.

Next we change Rule 2 of Grammar 7.1 to the rule:

Rule 2′. ⟨term⟩::=⟨factor⟩ | ⟨term⟩⟨multop⟩⟨expression⟩

Exercise 7.25 Explain the problem that using Rule 2′ instead of Rule 2 of Grammar 7.1 introduces, and demonstrate its effect on the parsing process by parsing the expression $d * 29 + a$.

Next we define a further rule to replace Rule 1 of Grammar 7.1:

Rule 1″. ⟨expression⟩ ::= ⟨term⟩ | ⟨expression⟩⟨addop⟩⟨term⟩
| ⟨expression⟩⟨multop⟩⟨term⟩

Exercise 7.26 Explain the problem that using Rule 1″ instead of Rule 1 of Grammar 7.1 introduces. Demonstrate its effect on the parsing process by parsing the expression $r + p$ div c. Explain the effect that the changed rule has on the precedence of the operators in a Pascal expression.

A BNF definition that adequately specifies the structure of an expression in Pascal, but allows ambiguity, is called an *abstract syntax* definition. Each tree generated for a string, that is defined from a concrete syntax, identifies a tree for that string in some abstract definition. The ambiguity allowed in the abstract syntax definition is removed by adding extra details in the concrete syntax.

Exercise 7.27 Identify the concrete parse tree for $a - b - c$, drawn in Exercise 7.22, with its abstract parse tree, which has the same structure and was drawn in Exercise 7.23.

If, in Def. 7.11, we had allowed the production rule $B \to BB$ instead of the rules $B \to B0$ and $B \to B1$ we would have produced the strings BBB. By associativity we have $BBB = B(BB) = (BB)B$ for these strings.

Exercise 7.28 Draw trees to represent the expressions $B(BB)$ and $(BB)B$.

The trees show the *different* structures of the expression BBB. This information is the true meaning of the expression and is captured by the *abstract syntax*. In the concrete syntax the string BBB abbreviates the trees and requires the addition of brackets to differentiate between the two possible structures.

The building blocks of an abstract syntax are words, or tokens, rather than terminal symbols. The lexical analyser of a compiler builds tokens from the program text and passes these on to the syntax analyser.

Example 7.24 Examples of tokens that are constructed from the text of a Pascal program are 'begin', 'end', 'integer', 'I', ';', 'j', ':=' and '+'. Comments and formatting characters are ignored.

The stage of lexical analysis is based on a type 3 grammar and the identifiers of programming languages are called regular sets.

Regular expressions Regular sets are the type 3 languages that are denoted by regular expressions. We described regular sets informally at the beginning of this chapter as possibly infinite sets of finite strings over some finite alphabet, A, and used the notation A^*. Now we define the class of regular expressions by induction and base the definition on the class of regular sets. We make no distinction between the alphabet $A = \{a, b\}$ and the language A, which consists of strings a and b each of length 1. Neither does our notation distinguish between a symbol that belongs to an alphabet and the same symbol when it is used to denote a regular expression. The context in which the symbols are used should make the distinction clear.

Definition 7.15 Regular expressions Let $A = \{a_1, a_2, \ldots, a_n\}$ be some finite alphabet. Then

Basis clause. For each a_i in A, a_i is a regular expression.

Inductive clause.

1 If E, F are regular expressions, so is $(E + F)$.

2 If E, F are regular expressions, so is (EF).

3 If E is a regular expression, so is E^*.

Extremal clause. ...

The *meaning* of this definition is based on the following definition of the class of regular sets.

Definition 7.16 Regular sets If E, F are regular expressions for the two sets E, F then

1 $\emptyset$ is a regular expression and denotes the empty set $\{\}$.

2 Λ is a regular expression (for the concatenation of empty strings) and denotes the set $\{\Lambda\}$.

3 $E + F$ is the regular expression for the set $E \cup F$.

4 EF is the regular expression for the set $E \times F$.

5 E^* is the regular expression for the set E^*.

The following regular sets are denoted by the regular expressions:

1 $E^* = E^0 \cup E^1 \cup E^2 \cup \cdots$

2 $E^i = E \times E^{i-1}$ for $i > 0$

3 E^0 is defined as $\{\Lambda\}$.

Definition 7.17 Kleene closure The Kleene closure (or just closure) of the set E is the set E^*.

The meaning of this definition is that E^* denotes *exactly* the set of strings constructed by concatenating the set E of symbols from the alphabet A.

We define the regular *expression* E^0 to be the 'concatenation of empty strings' and write E^0 as Λ to denote the regular *set* $\{\Lambda\}$. The concatenation of a regular expression, E, with Λ gives E. We need both Λ and $\emptyset$ as regular expressions due to the definition of concatenation for regular expressions. We require ΛE to denote

$$\{\Lambda\} \times \{E\} = \{\Lambda E\} = \{E\}$$

By contrast $E\emptyset$ denotes $\{E\} \times \{\} = \{\}$ for any set E.

We can omit many brackets from regular expressions by saying that $*$ has a higher precedence than concatenation or $+$ and that concatenation has a higher precedence than $+$. Therefore $((0(1^*)) + 0)$ may be written as $01^* + 0$. Both $((EF)G)$ and $(E(FG))$ are regular expressions for the same set $E \times F \times G$.

Example 7.25 Let $A = \{a, b, c, d\}$. If $S = \{ab, cb\}$ and $T = \{b, cab\}$ then

$$\begin{aligned} S \cup T &= \{ab, cb, b, cab\} \\ S \times T &= \{abb, abcab, cbb, cbcab\} \\ S^* &= S^0 \cup S^1 \cup S^2 \cup \cdots \\ &= \{\Lambda\} \cup \{ab, cb\} \cup \{abab, abcb, cbab, cbcb\} \cup \cdots\} \\ &= \{\Lambda, ab, cb, abab, abcb, cbab, cbcb, \cdots\} \end{aligned}$$

By Def. 7.17, E^* denotes the infinite set of finite strings that are not limited to a specific length and include the empty string, Λ. It is useful to have a notation for regular expressions that denote a finite set of strings that are limited to a specific length. As an example, we say that the regular expression E_5^* denotes the set of strings that includes the empty string and, if E is a regular set, is limited to a length of five instances of E: that is E_5^* denotes the set $E_5^* = E^0 \cup E^1 \cup E^2 \cup \cdots \cup E^5$.

Definition 7.18 Positive closure The positive closure of E is denoted by E^+ and excludes the empty string.

We may therefore abbreviate EE^* by E^+.

Exercise 7.29 Using the sets defined in Example 7.25 give the *set* that is denoted by the regular expressions $S + T$ and T_2^*.

Exercise 7.30 Using the sets defined in Example 7.25 and the definition of a regular expression, give the *regular expression* that denotes the regular set T.

Example 7.26 00 is a regular expression that denotes $\{00\}$.

Exercise 7.31 Let $E = \{10, 1\}$ and $F = \{011, 11\}$. Give the set of strings that is denoted by the regular expression EF.

Example 7.27 The regular set $\{01, 11\}^* = \{\Lambda, 01, 11, 0101, 0111, 1101, 1111, \ldots\}$

Example 7.28 Let $A = \{0, 1\}$; then 0 and 1 are regular expressions and $(0 + 1)^*0$ denotes the set of all finite binary sequences that terminate in 0. This is $\{0, 10, 00, 110, 010, \ldots\}$. We show that $(0 + 1)^*0$ denotes

$$\begin{aligned}
(\{0\} \cup \{1\})^* &= (\{0, 1\})^* \times \{0\} \\
&= (\{0, 1\}^0 \cup \{0, 1\}^1 \cup \{0, 1\}^2 \cup \{0, 1\}^3 \cup \cdots) \times \{0\} \\
&= (\{\Lambda\} \cup \{0, 1\} \cup (\{00, 01, 10, 11\} \cup \cdots) \times \{0\}) \\
&= \{\Lambda, 0, 1, 00, 01, 10, 11, \ldots\} \times \{0\} \\
&= \{\Lambda 0, 00, 10, 000, 010, \ldots\} \\
&= \{0, 00, 10, 000, 010, \ldots\}
\end{aligned}$$

Note that 0 follows the empty sequence in the set denoted by $(0 + 1)^*0$.

Example 7.29 Let the finite alphabet be the set of all the letters in our alphabet for the English language. Then $(A + B + \cdots + X + Y + Z)^*(SON + TON)$ denotes the set of all the strings of letters that end in SON or TON. The shortest strings of letters in the set are of length three.

Example 7.30 ALGOL identifiers, which are upper- or lower-case letters followed by any string of letters or digits, with no limit on length, may be expressed as (letter)(letter + digit)*, where

(letter)	stands for	$(A + B + C + \cdots + Y + Z + a + b + \ldots + y + z)$
(digit)	stands for	$(0 + 1 + \cdots + 8 + 9)$

Example 7.31 Let $A = \{0, 1\}$; then $(01)^*$ is the regular expression for the set that is the union of the set denoted by $0(10)^*1$ with the null string. First we show that

$0(10)^*1 + \Lambda$ denotes

$$\begin{aligned}
&\{0\} \times \{10\}^* \times \{1\} \cup \{\Lambda\}\\
&\quad = \{0\} \times (\{10\}^0 \cup \{10\}^1 \cup \{10\}^2 \cup \{10\}^3 \cup \cdots) \times \{1\} \cup \{\Lambda\}\\
&\quad = (\{0\} \times (\{\Lambda\} \cup \{10\} \cup (\{10\} \times \{10\}) \cup (\{10\} \times \{10\}^2) \cup \cdots)) \times \{1\} \cup \{\Lambda\}\\
&\quad = (\{0\} \times (\{\Lambda\} \cup \{10\} \cup \{1010\} \cup \{101010\} \cup \cdots)) \times \{1\} \cup \{\Lambda\}\\
&\quad = (\{0\} \times \{\Lambda, 10, 1010, 101010, \cdots\}) \times \{1\} \cup \{\Lambda\}\\
&\quad = \{0\Lambda, 010, 01010, 0101010, \ldots\} \times \{1\} \cup \{\Lambda\}\\
&\quad = \{0, 010, 01010, 0101010, \ldots\} \times \{1\} \cup \{\Lambda\}\\
&\quad = \{01, 0101, 010101, 01010101, \ldots\} \cup \{\Lambda\}\\
&\quad = \{\Lambda, 01, 0101, 010101, 01010101, \ldots\}
\end{aligned}$$

Then we show that $(01)^*$ denotes

$$\begin{aligned}
&\{01\}^0 \cup \{01\}^1 \cup \{01\}^2 \cup \{01\}^3 \cup \cdots\\
&\quad = \{\Lambda\} \cup \{01\} \cup \{01\} \times \{01\} \cup \{01\} \times \{01\} \times \{01\} \cup \cdots\\
&\quad = \{\Lambda\} \cup \{01\} \cup \{0101\} \cup \{010101\} \cup \cdots\\
&\quad = \{\Lambda, 01, 0101, 010101, \ldots\}
\end{aligned}$$

So both $(01)^*$ and $0(10)^*1 + \Lambda$ denote the same sets.

Exercise 7.32 Derive the sets of strings that are denoted by the following regular expressions:

(a) 1^*
(b) 01^*
(c) $0^*0 + 1$
(d) $1(01)^*0$
(e) $00^*11^*22^*$
(f) $0^+1^+2^+$
(g) $(00)^*$

Exercise 7.33 Give the regular expression for the set of Boolean sequences that are exactly one character in length. You should first give the set of possible strings. Then use the definitions of regular sets and regular expressions to derive precisely the required regular expression.

Exercise 7.34 Give the regular expression for the set of Boolean sequences that are exactly two characters long.

In Sec. 2.6 we calculated the number of ways that strings of a particular length could be formed from a set of characters. Now we use our inductive definitions to build some of these strings. The rule of sum expresses the property of the + operation that is analogous to the operation + between regular expressions. The $\times$ operation in the product rule is analogous to concatenation between regular expressions.

Exercise 7.35 Define the regular expression for the names of variables in a programming language that may be *up* to two characters in length. The first character is a letter of the alphabet while the second is either a letter of the alphabet or a decimal digit.

Exercise 7.36 Define the regular expression for the strings of length four that can be constructed from the alphabet $A = \{a, b, c, d\}$ that begin with a and end with d. You already know how many there are from Sec. 2.6.

Exercise 7.37 Define the regular expression for the names of variables in a programming language that may be *up* to three characters in length. The first character is a letter of the alphabet, while the last (if there are more than one) must be a decimal digit. Again you already know how many there are.

Exercise 7.38 Define a regular expression for integer identifiers in FORTRAN. These are limited to a length of six and may only begin with the letters I–N.

Exercise 7.39 Give a verbal description of the set of strings that are denoted by the regular expression $(A + B + \cdots + X + Y + Z)^*(LAND + ES)$ and give some example strings from the set.

We now return to using the BNF notation and the notation of phrase structure grammars, given by Def. 7.13, for formal languages. First we show that we can define the language of regular expressions more concisely using the BNF meta-language:

$$\begin{array}{rcl} a & ::= & a_1 \mid a_2 \mid \cdots a_n \\ E & ::= & a \mid (EE) \mid (E+E) \mid E^* \end{array}$$

Next we show that a specific type 2 grammar, defined on page 190, can be expressed in phrase structure form as $G = (V_t, V_n, P, S)$ where

$$\begin{array}{rcl} V_n & = & \{S\} \\ V_t & = & \{0, 1\} \\ P & = & \{S \rightarrow 0S1,\ S \rightarrow 01\} \\ S & = & S \end{array}$$

The language of this type 2 grammar is $L = \{0^n 1^n \mid n \geq 1\}$. We can generate the strings of L directly from the production rules in the following way:

$$S \rightarrow 0S1 \rightarrow 00S11 \rightarrow 000S111 \rightarrow 00001111$$

We used the first rule to produce strings from the start symbol, S, and the second rule to produce the last of the strings. This pattern builds the solution set of strings by set union from the start symbol. We choose Λ as the start symbol and rearrange the derivation to display the production of the set of strings that correspond to the start symbol as:

$$\begin{array}{l} \Lambda \\ \Lambda \cup \{\underline{01}\} \\ \{0\underline{01}1\} \cup \{\underline{01}\} \\ \{\underline{00011}1,\ 0\underline{01}1\} \cup \{\underline{01}\} \\ \vdots \\ 0T1 \cup \{01\} \end{array}$$

Here T is a variable to represent all those strings of the form $0t1$, where t is part of T. The motivation for this final example is to introduce the concept of a fixed-point solution for a recursive definition such as the production rule in a grammar. Fixed-point solutions will be presented in detail in Chapter 9.

The rule P can also be written in BNF as $\langle E \rangle ::= 0\langle E \rangle 1 \mid 01$. Now from this rule we have produced the regular set denoted by $0T1 \cup \{01\}$. We can name the regular set as $E = 0T1 \cup \{01\}$ or more compactly as $E = \Phi(T)$, where $\Phi(T) = 0T1 \cup \{01\}$. Our grammar then tells us that the regular set E, generated by the regular expression E, is a fixed point of the function Φ so that $\Phi(E) = E$.

7.5 SUMMARY

In this chapter we have focused on both the syntax and semantics of formal languages. The syntactic structure has been presented at increasing levels of formality. We introduced a string, informally as our first example of a recursively defined structure, and then defined a string by structural induction. Other recursively defined structures will be specified formally as abstract data types in Chapter 10.

Inductive definitions were also used to define the wffs of the languages of propositions and of predicates. These languages of mathematical logic were then generalized to first-order languages, with logical symbols that have a fixed meaning and non-logical symbols that describe both the objects of application systems and their properties. A first-order language, together with a formal consequence relation for the derivation of theorems from non-logical axioms, provides a formal linguistic system within which we can construct and analyse our application systems.

Because a formal system provides both a formal language and a framework for deduction we can reason about the theories that we build. In Chapter 12 we verify the correctness of algorithms by working within a formal axiomatic system. We must remember, however, that formal objects are removed from our informal perceptions of application systems so that we cannot make mathematical links between the objects of formal systems and the informally described objects in an application domain. If we need to link with the syntactic part of a formal system we can construct a formal structure, as a function, that interprets the terms and wffs of a first-order theory by a set of values. In this way we build a bridge between the construction of wffs and the derivation of a theory, and the assignment of truth-values to wffs by a structure for a theory. Those structures that satisfy the sentences of a theory are the models for that theory.

In logic, structures provide interpretation and we focus on predicates to express formal relations between objects. Model theory itself developed from mathematical logic and the theory of universal algebras, however. The structures that we have used to interpret the symbols of first-order theories are just the same as the algebraic structures that we shall present in Chapter 8. In the theory of universal algebras, the algebra is a function from the terms that are built from names in the signature, as the syntactic component, to the elements in the carrier set, which is the analogue of the domain of interpretation in a structure. If we divide the domain of interpretation into subsets we can give interpretations for objects of different *sorts*. This gives us the increased power of being able to write many-sorted theories about application systems, as we illustrate in Chapter 10. We lay the foundation for this extension in Chapter 8 when we build many-sorted algebras by dividing the carrier set into subsets.

Non-logical axioms express the basic properties of an application domain and further properties are derived to form the theory of the application. By giving values to the terms of a theory, through interpretation, we provide a semantics for the theory. An important approach to the semantics of formal languages provides compositionality by basing the semantics on the syntactic structure of the language. The meaning of a language construct is denoted by the meaning of the syntactic components of the construct. This denotational approach to semantics has influenced both specification and programming language design.

We have characterized the syntactic structure of formal languages and used a formal meta-language to present a hierarchy of formal grammars. The production rules of grammars are analogous to the inductive definitions of theories that are expressed as specifications in Chapter 10. The BNF meta-language is used to present both the concrete and abstract syntax of a subset of Pascal, and parsing represents the abstract syntax by representing the structure of a language. The simple language of regular expressions is defined by induction and the regular sets are derived in examples. Finally we presented regular sets as the solution of fixed point equations as a motivation for the detailed work on fixed points in Chapter 9.

FURTHER READING

A detailed treatment of the structure of formal languages and the Chomsky hierarchy is given in the book by Hopcroft and Ullman (1979). First-order languages and their interpretation by structures is presented in Enderton (1972) and in Turski and Maibaum (1987). For the semantics of languages with an emphasis on denotational semantics we recommend Schmidt (1986) and Tennent (1981).

Chapter 8

ALGEBRAS

In this chapter we are concerned with the properties of structures that are built from sets and the functions that are defined on the sets. Our aim is to define formally an *abstract algebraic structure* as a structure that consists of a syntactic part, called a *signature*, and a set of axioms that express the properties of the structure. A concrete model for an algebraic structure is called an *algebra*. There are many interesting abstract algebraic structures that give rise to different classes of algebras.

Our motivation for introducing the concept of an abstract algebraic structure is to provide the mathematical framework required for Chapter 10 when we present the algebraic approach to the specification of abstract data types. We begin in Sec. 8.1 by considering the properties of sets and functions that we have presented in earlier chapters. Then we construct classical algebras from sets with only one *sort* of element, and finally construct many-sorted algebras in preparation for the theory of universal algebras that we present in Sec. 8.2.

One of the most important concepts in algebraic theory is that of functions between algebras that preserve the abstract structure of the algebras. Such structure-preserving functions are called *homomorphisms*. We can use *category theory*, the abstract theory that arose from universal algebra, to express the general properties of homomorphisms between algebras. This abstract theory is introduced in Sec. 8.3, and we show how it enables us to select representative algebras from a given class.

8.1 CLASSICAL ALGEBRAS

The simplest types of algebras are those with a single set and single function. We discuss these first. We then consider algebras with one set and many functions and finally algebras with many sets and many functions; the latter are called many-sorted algebras. Most of the important general principles about algebras, including the notion of homomorphisms, can be gauged from examples of the one-set, one-function case.

8.1.1 One-set, one-function algebras

We begin by thinking about the set of real numbers $\mathbb{R}$ and the addition function '+' defined on $\mathbb{R}$. The first important property to note about this function is that it is *closed*. This means that if you add two real numbers a and b together you get another real number, which by convention we write in infix notation as $a+b$ rather than $+(a, b)$. One of several important properties of +, which we noted in Sec. 2.3, is commutativity; another is associativity.

The pair $(\mathbb{R}, +)$, that is the set $\mathbb{R}$ together with the function + defined on $\mathbb{R}$, is an example of an *algebra*. The second column of Table 8.1 (you can ignore the last

Table 8.1 One-set, one-function algebras

1.	$(\mathbb{Q}, +)$	Commutative group	Identity 0 Inverse $(-x)$ for each x
2.	$(\mathbb{Z}_2, \oplus_2)$	Commutative group	Identity 0 0 inverse is 0, 1 inverse is 1
3.	$(M_2, +)$	Commutative group	Identity is zero matrix $\mathbf{0}$ Inverse $(-\mathbf{A})$ for each matrix $\mathbf{A}$
4.	$(\mathbb{R}^4, +)$	Commutative group	Identity is zero vector $\boldsymbol{0}$ Inverse $(-\boldsymbol{x})$ for each vector x
5.	$(\mathscr{P}(X), \cup)$	Commutative group	Identity $\{\}$ Inverse $\overline{A}$ (complement in X) for each set A
6.	$(\mathrm{Bij}(X), \circ)$	Non-commutative group	Since $f \circ g \neq g \circ f$ in general Identity is identity mapping id_X Inverse f^{-1} for each bijection f
7.	$(\mathbb{N}, +)$	Commutative monoid	Identity 0 but no inverses
8.	$(\mathbb{R}, \times)$	Commutative monoid	Identity 1 but no inverse for 0
9.	$(M_2, \times)$	Non-commutative monoid	Since $A \times B \neq B \times A$ in general Identity I_2 but no inverses in general
10.	$(A^*, conc)$	Non-commutative monoid	Identity is empty string <>
11.	$(A^+, conc)$	Semi-group	No identity

two columns for the moment) lists a number of other familiar algebras. These are constructed from specific sets with specific named functions. We clarify some of the notation of Table 8.1 by referring to the numbered examples:

2. The set $\mathbb{Z}_2$ is the set of integers modulo 2, and $\oplus_2$ is the 'mod 2' addition function as defined in Sec. 2.2.

3, 9. The set M_2 is the set of (2×2) matrices over $\mathbb{R}$; the functions $+$ and $\times$ respectively refer here to matrix addition and multiplication as defined in Sec. 2.5.2.

4. The set $\mathbb{R}^4$ is the set of four-dimensional vectors over $\mathbb{R}$ and $+$ here refers to the function of vector addition as defined in Sec. 2.5.1.

5. $\mathscr{P}(X)$ is the power set of some fixed set X.

6. $\mathrm{Bij}(X)$ is the set of all bijections of a fixed set X, and the function $\circ$ is just function composition.

10, 11. A^* and A^+ are sets of finite strings from the alphabet A. With *conc*, the concatenation function, these are defined in Chapter 7.

As an abstract view of each of the algebras in Table 8.1 we think in terms of a pair $(S, \square)$. Here S is a set name, which we call a *sort*, and $\square$ is the name of a function over S, which in each case has the form $\square : S \times S \rightarrow S$ (meaning that it is a closed, binary operation over S). We say that $S \times S \rightarrow S$ is the *arity* of $\square$. The pair $\Sigma = (S, \square)$ is called a *signature*. A Σ-*algebra* is any structure in which we give S and $\square$ actual values; thus S is mapped to a specific set A, called a *carrier set* for S, and $\Box$ is mapped to a specific function $f : A \times A \to A$ which has the same arity as $\Box$. Thus, in the sense of Chapters 4 and 7, it is a concrete model of Σ. All of the examples in Table 8.1 are, of course, Σ-algebras.

Example 8.1 The pair $(\mathrm{Bij}(\{1,2\}), \circ)$ is a Σ-algebra where $\mathrm{Bij}(\{1,2\})$ is the carrier set of sort S and the function $\circ : \mathrm{Bij}(\{1,2\}) \times \mathrm{Bij}(\{1,2\}) \to \mathrm{Bij}(\{1,2\})$ is the interpretation of $\Box$.

Exercise 8.1 Show that $(\mathbb{Z}, +)$ is a Σ-algebra.

Example 8.2 Let X be the set of propositions $\{p, q, p \vee q\}$. The pair $(X, \wedge)$ is *not* a Σ-algebra. This is because it is not closed with respect to $\wedge$, and so $\wedge$ does not have arity $X \times X \to X$. To see this, just note that $p \wedge q \notin X$. However, let us define $\mathrm{Prop}(X)$ to be the set of all propositions that can be generated recursively from X by the usual propositional connectives. Then $(\mathrm{Prop}(X), \wedge)$ *is* a Σ-algebra and so is $(\mathrm{Prop}(X), \vee)$.

The algebra $(\mathbb{R}, +)$, as well as each of the examples 1 to 5 of Fig. 8.1, all satisfy the following properties with respect to their function $\Box$:

$$\begin{array}{lll} \text{(a)} & x \Box y = y \Box x & \text{commutative} \\ \text{(b)} & x \Box (y \Box z) = (x \Box y) \Box z & \text{associative} \\ \text{(c)} & \exists e\ (e \Box x = x \Box e = x) & \text{identity element} \\ \text{(d)} & \forall x \exists y\ (x \Box y = y \Box x = e) & \text{inverses} \end{array} \tag{8.1}$$

where the variables x, y and z are assumed to be universally quantified in each case.

The signature $(S, \Box)$, together with the above set of properties, is our first example of an *abstract algebraic structure*. Any algebra with this signature that satisfies the four properties (8.1) is called a *commutative group*.

Justification of why examples 1 to 5 of Table 8.1 are commutative groups is given in the fourth column. In Sec. 2.5 we have already established these properties for examples 3 and 4.

Example 8.3 Consider the pair $(\mathbb{Z}_2^3, \oplus_2)$, that is the set of all three-dimensional vectors over $\mathbb{Z}_2$, together with the modulo 2 addition function $\oplus_2$ defined component-wise. For example, we have $(0\ 1\ 1) \oplus_2 (1\ 1\ 0) = (1\ 0\ 1)$. This is a finite, commutative group with eight elements. The function is clearly commutative and associative—we already showed this in Sec. 2.5.1. We also saw that it has an identity, namely the zero vector $\mathbf{0} = (0\ 0\ 0)$; when we add $\mathbf{0}$ to any other $\boldsymbol{x} \in \mathbb{Z}_2^3$ we get $\boldsymbol{x}$. For example, $(0\ 0\ 0) \oplus_2 (0\ 1\ 1) = (0\ 1\ 1)$. Finally we note that every member $\boldsymbol{x} \in \mathbb{Z}_2^3$ has an inverse, namely $\boldsymbol{x}$ itself, since, for example, $(0\ 1\ 1) \oplus_2 (0\ 1\ 1) = (0\ 0\ 0)$.

Example 8.4 Zero group Consider the set $\mathbb{Z}_1$ with the modulo 1 addition function $\oplus_1$. This set contains just one element, 0, and the operator $\oplus_1$ is defined explicitly by $0 \oplus_1 0 = 0$. The pair $(\mathbb{Z}_1, \oplus_1)$ is a group, called the *zero* group.

Exercise 8.2 Show that the pair $(\mathbb{Z}_3^2, \oplus_3)$, that is the set of all two-dimensional vectors over $\mathbb{Z}_3$, together with the modulo 3 addition operation $\oplus_3$, is a commutative group. Deduce that for any natural numbers k and n, the pair $(\mathbb{Z}_k^n, \oplus_k)$ is a commutative group.

If we drop the first property (commutativity) in (8.1) we get a different abstract algebraic structure, which gives rise to a broader class of algebras. Specifically, any algebra with the signature $(S, \Box)$ that satisfies properties (b), (c) and (d) of (8.1) is called a *group*. Obviously any commutative group is a group, but the converse is not true. Example 6 of Table 8.1 is a non-commutative group.

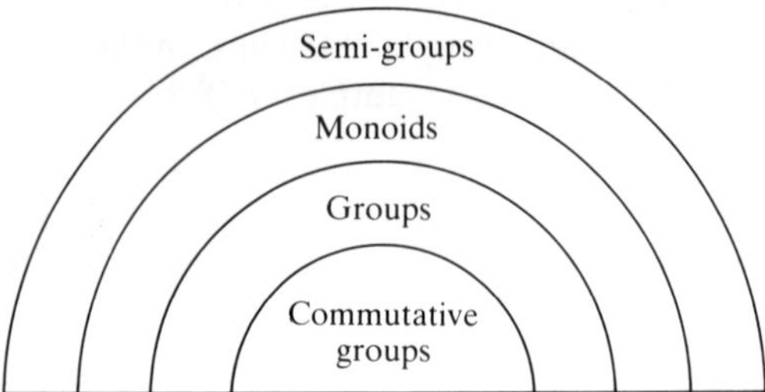

Figure 8.1 Relationship between groups, monoids and semi-groups.

Exercise 8.3 Let $X = \{1, 2, 3\}$. Let f and $g : X \to X$ be defined by

$$f(1) = 2,\ f(2) = 3,\ f(3) = 1 \text{ and } g(1) = 3,\ g(2) = 2,\ g(3) = 1$$

Clearly $f, g \in \text{Bij}(X)$. Show that $f \circ g \neq g \circ f$ and hence deduce that $(\text{Bij}(X), \circ)$ is a non-commutative group.

If we further restrict the class of properties (8.1) we get other important classes of algebras:

Definition 8.1 Monoid Any algebra with the signature $(S, \Box)$ that satisfies properties (b) and (c) of (8.1) is called a monoid.

Definition 8.2 Semi-group Any algebra with the signature $(S, \Box)$ that satisfies property (b) of (8.1) is called a semi-group.

Examples 7 and 8 of Table 8.1 are commutative monoids which are not groups while 9 and 10 are non-commutative monoids which are not groups. We shall use the property of a monoid for the definition of *fields* in Sec. 8.1.2.

The only property we expect to hold for the operator $\Box$ in a semi-group is associativity. Example 11 is a semi-group which is not a monoid (and hence also not a group). Semi-groups illustrate that we can have interesting algebras that have no identity element. The relationship between groups, monoids and semi-groups is illustrated in Fig. 8.1.

Example 8.5 Let $\mathbb{R}^* = \mathbb{R} \setminus \{0\}$. The pair $(\mathbb{R}^*, \times)$ *is* a group. We know that it is commutative and associative. Its identity is 1, since each $a \in \mathbb{R}$ except $a = 0$, a has an inverse, namely $1/a$.

Example 8.6 For any $n \in \mathbb{N}$, the pair $(\mathbb{Z}_n, \otimes_n)$, where $\otimes_n$ is modulo n multiplication, is a monoid with identity element 1. It cannot be a group for any n because 0 cannot have an inverse. However, if n is prime, then any element *except* 0 has an inverse. For example, in $\mathbb{Z}_5$, the inverse of 2 is 3 since $2 \otimes_5 3 = 1$ and the inverse of 3 is 2 for the same reason.

The general case follows from a well-known result in number theory. This asserts that for any prime p, if $0 < a < p$ then we can find integers n, m such that $na = 1 + mp$ and hence $n \otimes_p a = 1$.

Exercise 8.4 Show that $(\mathbb{Z}, \times)$ is a commutative monoid which is not a group.

(Σ, E)-algebras We began by looking at examples of algebras and searching for common properties of these. Then we worked in the opposite direction: we started with a given signature Σ and listed a set of properties E. We wanted to know which algebras satisfied E. Any Σ-algebra satisfying all the properties is called a (Σ, E)-*algebra*.

Example 8.7 Let E be the set of properties (b),(c) and (d) of (8.1). Then the (Σ, E)-algebras are precisely groups. The reason why mathematicians were interested in these properties is that they are the minimum properties required of a set S (with binary function operation $\Box$) in order for us to solve equations over the set that have the form

$$a \Box x = b \tag{8.2}$$

where x is unknown. To see this we note that a has an inverse, so there is some element a' for which $a' \Box a = e$ where e is the identity element. Now from (8.2) we deduce that

$$a' \Box (a \Box x) = a' \Box b \tag{8.3}$$

However, by associativity, $a' \Box (a \Box x) = (a' \Box a) \Box x = e \Box x = x$, with the last two equalities following from the property of the identity element e. Now it follows from (8.3) that $x = a' \Box b$ is a solution to our equation.

Sub-algebras Consider the Σ-algebras $(\mathbb{Q}, +)$ and $(\mathbb{Z}, +)$. These are both groups, but $\mathbb{Z}$ is a subset of $\mathbb{Q}$ and the function $+$ of $\mathbb{Q}$, when restricted to $\mathbb{Z}$, is the same as the function $+$ of $\mathbb{Z}$. Consequently, we say that $(\mathbb{Z}, +)$ is a *subgroup* of $(\mathbb{Q}, +)$.

Example 8.8 Consider the group $(\mathbb{Z}_2^3, \oplus_2)$ described in Example 8.3. Consider the following two subsets of $\mathbb{Z}_2^3$:

$$E = \{(0\ 0\ 0), (1\ 1\ 0), (1\ 0\ 1), (0\ 1\ 1)\} \text{ and } F = \{(1\ 0\ 0), (0\ 1\ 0), (0\ 0\ 1), (1\ 1\ 1)\}$$

E is the subset with an even number of 1's and F is the subset with an odd number of 1's. The pair $(E, \oplus_2)$ is a group, and hence a subgroup of $(\mathbb{Z}_2^3, \oplus_2)$, but $(F, \oplus_2)$ is not, because it does not have an identity element.

In general, suppose we have a signature $\Sigma = (S, \Box)$ and a set of properties E. Let $(S_1, \Box_1)$ be a particular (Σ, E)-algebra. Then if $X \subseteq S_1$ such that $(X, \Box_1)$ is itself a (Σ, E)-algebra, we say that $(X, \Box_1)$ is a *sub-algebra* of $(S_1, \Box_1)$.

Example 8.9 Let $2\mathbb{N}$ denote the set of even natural numbers. Then $(2\mathbb{N}, +)$ is a submonoid of $(\mathbb{N}, +)$.

Example 8.10 $(\mathbb{Z}^+, +)$ is a subgroup of $(\mathbb{R}^+, +)$ but not of the group $(\mathbb{R}^+, \times)$ because the functions are different.

Exercise 8.5 Show that $(\mathbb{Z}, +)$ is a subgroup of $(\mathbb{R}, +)$ and that $(\mathbb{Z}, \times)$ is a submonoid of $(\mathbb{R}, \times)$.

In Chapter 16 we use the following concept about groups and their subgroups:

Definition 8.3 Coset Suppose $(G, \Box)$ is a group with subgroup $(H, \Box)$. For any $x \in G$, the coset $x \Box H$ is the set $\{x \Box h : h \in H\}$.

Example 8.11 Consider the group $(\mathbb{N}_2^3, \oplus_2)$ and its subgroup $(E, \oplus_2)$ as described in Example 8.8. Here $(0\ 1\ 0) \oplus E = \{(0\ 1\ 0), (1\ 0\ 0), (1\ 1\ 1), (0\ 0\ 1)\}$, whence the coset $(0\ 1\ 0) \oplus E = F$.

Homomorphisms It is often the case that different (Σ, E)-algebras have structural similarities over and above that of having the same signature and satisfying the same properties. These structural similarities are highlighted by functions between the algebras that 'preserve' the functions of the algebras.

Example 8.12 Consider the two groups $(M_2, +)$ and $(\mathbb{R}^4, +)$ in Fig. 8.1 and the function $f : M_2 \rightarrow \mathbb{R}^4$ defined by

$$f(\begin{pmatrix} a & b \\ c & d \end{pmatrix}) = (a\ b\ c\ d) \text{ for each } a, b, c, d \in \mathbb{R}$$

This function has two very important properties. First, for any two matrices $A, B \in M_2$, $f(A + B) = f(A) + f(B)$ since

$$\begin{aligned} f(\begin{pmatrix} a & b \\ c & d \end{pmatrix} + \begin{pmatrix} a' & b' \\ c' & d' \end{pmatrix}) &= f(\begin{pmatrix} a+a' & b+b' \\ c+d' & d+d' \end{pmatrix}) \\ &= (a+a'\ b+b'\ c+c'\ d+d') \\ &= (a\ b\ c\ d) + (a'\ b'\ c'\ d') \\ &= f(\begin{pmatrix} a & b \\ c & d \end{pmatrix}) + f(\begin{pmatrix} a' & b' \\ c' & d' \end{pmatrix}) \end{aligned}$$

This is what we mean by f preserving the group functions. We can think of f mapping the function $+$ in M_2 to the function $+$ in $\mathbb{R}^4$. Second, f preserves the identities, since

$$f(\begin{pmatrix} 0 & 0 \\ 0 & 0 \end{pmatrix}) = (0\,0\,0\,0)$$

A function like f, which preserves group functions and identities, is called a *group homomorphism*. In general, suppose that $(S_1, \Box_1)$ and $(S_2, \Box_2)$ are two particular (Σ, E)-algebras and that $f : S_1 \rightarrow S_2$. Then we say that f preserves the functions if

$$f(x \Box_1 y) = f(x) \Box_2 f(y) \text{ for each } x, y \in S_1$$

If S_1 has an identity e_1 and S_2 has an identity e_2, then we say that f preserves the identities if $f(e_1) = e_2$.

Definition 8.4 (Σ, E)-algebra homomorphism If f preserves functions and identities (where these exist) we say that f is a (Σ, E)-algebra homomorphism.

In the case where f is surjective we also call it an *epimorphism*, while if it is injective we call it an *endomorphism*.

Definition 8.5 Isomorphism If f is both injective and surjective, we call f an isomorphism. Whenever it is possible to find an isomorphism between algebras we say that the algebras themselves are isomorphic.

Example 8.13 The function f in Example 8.12 is an isomorphism. Thus $(M_2, +)$ and $(\mathbb{R}^4, +)$ are isomorphic groups. We write $(M_2, +) \cong (\mathbb{R}^4, +)$ or, more simply, $M_2 \cong \mathbb{R}^4$.

Exercise 8.6 Show that the function $g : M_2 \rightarrow \mathbb{R}^4$ defined by

$$g(\begin{pmatrix} a & b \\ c & d \end{pmatrix}) = (\mid a \mid +1\ \ b\ c\ d) \text{ for each } a, b, c, d \in \mathbb{R}$$

is not a group homomorphism.

The following four examples concerning group homomorphisms will be needed in Sec. 8.3:

Example 8.14 Consider any two groups $(G, \Box)$ and $(G', \Box')$, where the latter has identity e'. There is always a trivial homomorphism $f : G \to G'$ in which $f(x) = e'$ for each $x \in G$.

Example 8.15 Every group $(G, \Box)$ for which G has just one element (namely the identity element) must be isomorphic to the zero group of Example 8.4. Thus when we talk about *the* zero group $(G_0, \Box)$ we mean any one of these isomorphic groups. For any group $(G, \Box)$ there is exactly one homomorphism $f : G_0 \to G$, namely the trivial homomorphism of Example 8.14.

Example 8.16 The group $(2\mathbb{Z}, +)$ is a (proper) subgroup of $(\mathbb{Z}, +)$, but the two groups are isomorphic, since the homomorphism $f : \mathbb{Z} \to 2\mathbb{Z}$ defined by $f(n) = 2\times n$ for each n is a bijection. In fact, for any m, $(m\mathbb{Z}, +) \cong (\mathbb{Z}, +)$.

Example 8.17 For each n there is exactly one non-trivial homomorphism from $(\mathbb{Z}, +)$ to $(\mathbb{Z}_n, \oplus_n)$. This is the function f defined by $f(m) = m \bmod n$ for each m. There is no non-trivial homomorphism from $(\mathbb{Z}_n, \oplus_n)$ to $(\mathbb{Z}, +)$.

Quotient algebras Think about the group $(\mathbb{Z}, +)$. In Sec. 2.2 we saw that the relation $\sim_3$ over $\mathbb{Z}$ defined by $a \sim_3 b$ if $a = b \bmod 3$ is an equivalence relation. It partitions $\mathbb{Z}$ into three sets:

$\{0, \pm3, \pm6, \pm9, ...\}$ which we will call [0]
$\{1, 4, -2, 7, -5, 10, -8, ...\}$ which we will call [1]
$\{2, 5, -1, 8, -4, 11, -7, ...\}$ which we will call [2]

The elements 0,1 and 2 are called the *canonical* or *representative* elements from their respective equivalence classes [0], [1] and [2] with respect to $\sim_3$. The set $\{[0], [1], [2]\}$ of equivalences classes of $\sim_3$ is denoted by $\mathbb{Z}/(\sim_3)$ to represent the fact that it is the set $\mathbb{Z}$ with the relation $\sim_3$ 'factored out'. The relation $\sim_3$ also gives rise to the modulo 3 addition function $\oplus_3$ which we can apply to $\mathbb{Z}/(\sim_3)$. Specifically, we define $\oplus_3$ on the canonical elements by

$$[0] \oplus_3 [1] = [0],\ [0] \oplus_3 [2] = [2],\ [1] \oplus_3 [2] = [0],\ \text{etc.}$$

It follows that the pair $(\mathbb{Z}/(\sim_3), \oplus_3)$ is a group, called the *quotient group of* $\mathbb{Z}$ *with respect to* $\sim_3$. In fact, it is clear that this group is isomorphic to the group $(\mathbb{Z}_3, \oplus_3)$ (the integers modulo 3).

In general, let $(S, \Box)$ be any specific (Σ, E)-algebra. If $\sim$ is an equivalence relation over S, let $S/\sim$ denote the set of equivalence classes of S with respect to $\sim$. Thus we write $[a] \in S/\sim$ to mean that $[a]$ is the equivalence class that contains the element $a \in S$.

We can define a function $\Box' : (S/\sim) \times (S/\sim) \to (S/\sim)$ by adapting $\Box$ as follows:

$$[a]\Box'[b] = [a\Box b] \text{ for any } [a], [b] \in S/\sim$$

It follows that $((S/\sim), \Box')$ is itself a (Σ, E)-algebra, called the *quotient algebra of S with respect to* $\sim$.

8.1.2 One-set, many-function algebras

In Sec. 8.1.1 we singled out a specific function for each of the sets we considered. In some cases, like that of the concatenation function over the set A^* of strings over an alphabet A, the function we selected was the *only* obvious one. However, in other cases we could have chosen different functions. Consequently, in this section we want to think of algebras in a more general sense as consisting of a set together with one or *more* functions. We want to examine the properties of the sets in terms of the way the various functions interact.

Example 8.18 The set $\mathbb{R}$ has two obvious function operations, namely $+$ and $\times$. Although we have noted the properties of the individual algebras $(\mathbb{R}, +)$ and $(\mathbb{R}, \times)$, we now want to think in terms of an algebra $(\mathbb{R}, \{+, \times\})$ and its properties. For example, we know that $\times$ distributes over $+$, that is $a \times (b+c) = (a \times b) + (a \times c)$, but that $+$ does not distribute over $\times$. We know that every non-zero element a of $\mathbb{R}$ has an inverse (namely $1/a$) with respect to the function $\times$, but this inverse is different to the inverse of a with respect to $+$.

Example 8.19 The set M_2 also has two binary functions $+$ and $\times$, as defined in Sec. 2.5.2. Again we saw there that $\times$ distributes over $+$ but not vice versa. We also saw that in this case the non-zero elements do not all have inverses with respect to $\times$.

Exercise 8.7 Consider the set $\mathbb{Z}$ and its two functions $+$ and $\times$. What can you say about distributivity in this case? Do all the non-zero elements have an inverse with respect to $\times$?

Example 8.20 Let P be any set of propositions. Consider the set Prop(P) (as described in Example 8.2) of all propositions generated from P, together with the functions $\vee$ and $\wedge$. In this case $\vee$ distributes over $\wedge$ and vice versa (as we showed in Sec. 3.2). Also if $p \in \text{Prop}(P)$ then the inverse of p with respect to $\vee$ is the same as its inverse with respect to $\wedge$, namely $\neg p$.

Exercise 8.8 Show that the set $\mathscr{P}(X)$ (where X is any set) together with the functions $\cup$ and $\cap$ have analogous properties to those of $(\text{Prop}(P), \{\vee, \wedge\})$ which are stated in Example 8.20.

Each of the examples and exercises from Example 8.18 to Exercise 8.8 consists of a set together with two binary functions. Let us think in terms of a signature $\Sigma = (S, \{\square, \circ\})$ consisting of a sort S and the names of two functions $\square$ and $\circ$, where each has arity $S \times S \to S$. Each of the specific examples just described is a Σ-algebra, since each is a (concrete) model for Σ. For example, $(\mathbb{Z}, \{+, \times\})$ is a Σ-algebra where $\mathbb{Z}$ is the carrier set of sort S and $+, \times$ are the functions representing the names $\square, \circ$ respectively.

Now let us list some properties that hold for some of the Σ-algebras we have seen:

(a) S, together with $\square$, is a commutative group.

(b) S, together with $\circ$, is a group.

(c) S, together with $\circ$, is a monoid.

(d) The operator $\circ$ distributes over $\square$.

(e) The operator $\square$ distributes over $\circ$.

(f) Every element of S (which is not the identity with respect to $\square$) has an inverse with respect to $\circ$.

(g) For every $a \in S$ the inverse of a with respect to $\square$ is the same as the inverse with respect to $\circ$.

As for one-function algebras, if E is any set of properties that are defined for some signature Σ, any Σ-algebra that satisfies E is called a (Σ, E)-algebra.

Example 8.21 Rings For Σ defined above, let E be the set of properties (a), (c) and (d). Then any (Σ, E)-algebra is called a *ring*. Each of the examples and exercises from Example 8.18 to Exercise 8.8 describe rings. However, the Σ-algebra $(\mathbb{N}, \{+, \times\})$ is not a ring because $\mathbb{N}$ has no inverses in general with respect to $+$. Thus property 1 is not satisfied. It does not help to change round the roles of $+$ and $\times$, because the same is true of $\times$.

Example 8.22 Fields If E is the set of properties (a), (c), (d) and (f), then any (Σ, E)-algebra is called a *field*. The Σ-algebras $(\mathbb{R}, \{+, \times\})$, $(\text{Prop}(P), \{\vee, \wedge\})$ (for some set of propositions P) and $(\mathscr{P}(X), \cup, \cap)$ (for some set X) are all fields. In a field we can perform all the normal arithmetic operations except division by 'zero'.

Exercise 8.9 Show that $(\mathbb{Q}, \{+, \times\})$ is a field.

Exercise 8.10 Let p be any prime number. Show that $(\mathbb{N}_p, \{\oplus_p, \otimes_p\})$ is a field. (*Hint*: Just refer to Example 8.6.) This particular field is important for Chapter 16.

Example 8.23 Boolean algebras If E is the set of properties (a), (b), (d), (e), (f) and (g), then any (Σ, E)-algebra is called a *Boolean algebra*. For any set of propositions P, the Σ-algebra $(\text{Prop}(P), \{\vee, \wedge\})$ is a Boolean algebra and so is $(\mathscr{P}(X), \cup, \cap)$ for each set X. A more usual description of Boolean algebras will be given in Example 8.25.

Although so far we have only spoken about *binary* functions (those of arity $S \times S \to S$) we have implicitly been using *unary* functions, that is functions of arity $S \to S$. Consider, for example, a group, say $(\mathbb{Z}, +)$. The group properties infer that each element of $\mathbb{Z}$ has an inverse with respect to $+$. Specifically the inverse of a is $-a$. However, then we have a unary function $inv : \mathbb{Z} \to \mathbb{Z}$ defined by $inv(a) = -a$. The group properties also infer the existence of a specific (constant) element of $\mathbb{Z}$, namely the identity element 0. We can think of such mandatory constants as being 'nullary' functions, having arity $\to S$. Thus, $0 :\to \mathbb{Z}$. In general, such a function $const :\to S$ simply asserts the existence of a specific member of S called *const*.

What we have shown is that we do not need to restrict all our functions to be of the same arity. By allowing algebras to have functions of varying arity we can present a more explicit signature definition for specific types of algebras.

Example 8.24 For groups we can refine the signature to be $\Sigma = (S, \{\Box, inv, e\})$ where the arity of the function names is given by:

$$\begin{array}{rrl} \Box : & S \times S & \to S \\ inv : & S & \to S \\ e : & & \to S \end{array}$$

Comparing this with our previous definition of the signature for groups, we have added explicit function names *inv* and *e*. This enables us to present the properties of a commutative group as:

(a)	$x \Box y = y \Box x$	commutativity
(b)	$x \Box (y \Box z) = (x \Box y) \Box z$	associative
(c)	$e \Box x = x \Box e = x$	identity element
(d)	$x \Box inv(x) = inv(x) \Box x = e$	inverses

If you compare these with the properties (8.1) listed on page 203 you will see that the existential quantifiers in (c) and (d) have been removed. Properties like these are called *equational axioms*. In Sec. 8.1.3 we shall define these formally and show why it is so useful to be able to express properties in this form.

Example 8.25 A more explicit, and more usual, definition of the signature for Boolean algebras is given by $\Sigma = (S, \{\Box, \circ, inv, e_1, e_2\})$ where the arity of the function names is given by:

$$\begin{array}{rrl} \Box, \circ : & S \times S \to & S \\ inv : & S \to & S \\ e_1, e_2 : & \to & S \end{array}$$

The properties are normally expressed as:

$\Box$ commutative and associative	$\circ$ commutative and associative
$x \circ (y \Box z) = (x \circ y) \Box (x \circ z)$	$x \Box (y \circ z) = (x \Box y) \circ (x \Box z)$
$x \Box e_1 = x$	$x \circ e_2 = x$
$x \Box inv(x) = e_1$	$x \circ inv(x) = e_2$

Now we see that, for any set of propositions P, the set Prop(P), together with the functions $\vee, \wedge, \neg, T$ and F, is a Boolean algebra; we just take

$$S = \text{Prop}(P),\ \Box = \vee,\ \circ = \wedge,\ inv = \neg,\ e_1 = T,\ e_2 = F$$

We would normally refer to this Boolean algebra as $(\text{Prop}(P), \{\vee, \wedge, \neg, T, F\})$.

Exercise 8.11 Show that, for any non-empty set X, $(\mathscr{P}(X), \{\cup, \cap, ^-, \{\}, X\})$ is a Boolean algebra in the sense of Example 8.25.

Example 8.26 We can now make precise the natural relationship between the calculus of propositions Prop(P) and the calculus of sets $\mathscr{P}(X)$ which was discussed in Exercise 3.17 on page 96. For any P and any X these are both Boolean algebras. Moreover, we can always find a Boolean algebra homomorphism that maps $\vee$ to $\cup$, $\wedge$ to $\cap$, T to $\{\}$ and F to X.

Example 8.27 The algebra Bool It seems reasonable to ask if there is a smallest Boolean algebra. The answer is 'yes', up to isomorphism. We just take the set of propositions $P = \{T, F\}$. Then Prop(P) $= P$ since any proposition we can generate from T and F is equivalent to either T or F. The specific Boolean algebra that results, namely $(\{T, F\}, \{\vee, \wedge, \neg, T, F\})$, is normally referred to as Bool.

Exercise 8.12 Let X be any set with just one element. Show that the Boolean algebra $(\mathscr{P}(X), \{\cup, \cap, ^-, \{\}, X\})$ is isomorphic to Bool.

8.1.3 Many-sorted algebras

So far we have only constructed algebras with one carrier set to give values to the symbols of a single sort. We often wish to think of an algebra as consisting of a number of different carrier sets and functions defined over these, however. Hence we wish to make a further generalization from the previous sections. We have already seen a number of examples of such algebras earlier in the book.

Example 8.28 In Sec. 2.4 we defined finite state machines. Any particular finite state machine consists of three sets: a set of *states*, a set of *inputs* and a set of *outputs*. There are two functions: a next-state function of arity *states* $\times$ *inputs* $\rightarrow$ *states* and an output function of arity *states* $\times$ *inputs* $\rightarrow$ *outputs*. Additionally there is a special state, namely the *initial* state. It follows that we can think of a finite state machine as an algebra whose signature $\Sigma = (\{S, I, O\}, \{f, g, s_0\})$, where the arity of the function names is given by:

$$\begin{array}{lll} f : S \times I & \rightarrow S & \text{(next-state function name)} \\ g : S \times I & \rightarrow O & \text{(output function name)} \\ s_0 : & \rightarrow S & \text{(initial state name)} \end{array}$$

Example 8.29 Think about the set of (2×2) matrices M_2 over $\mathbb{R}$ (the set of scalars). In Sec. 2.5.2 we defined operations on matrices. As well as the matrix addition function $+_M : M_2 \times M_2 \rightarrow M_2$, we defined the important operation of *scalar multiplication*. Specifically, scalar multiplication is a function $\bullet : \mathbb{R} \times M_2 \rightarrow M_2$. The set of scalars, in this case $\mathbb{R}$, is a field as defined in Example 8.22. Thus it has its own functions $+, \times : \mathbb{R} \times \mathbb{R} \rightarrow \mathbb{R}$, as well as the constant function 1 which is the identity with respect to $\times$. Similarly, think about the set of matrices or vectors of any fixed dimension over $\mathbb{R}$ or over a different set of scalars like $\mathbb{Q}$. In each case both addition and scalar multiplication are defined, and the set of scalars is a field.

What all these examples have in common is that they are Σ-algebras with

$$\Sigma = (\{S, V\}, \{+, \times, 1, \Box, \circ\})$$

where S, V are the sorts (normally called the *scalars* and *vectors* respectively) and $+, \times, 1, \Box$ and $\circ$ are function names of arity:

$$\begin{array}{rlll} + : & S \times S & \rightarrow & S & \text{`addition of scalars'} \\ \times : & S \times S & \rightarrow & S & \text{`multiplication of scalars'} \\ 1 : & & \rightarrow & S & \text{`scalar multiplicative identity'} \\ \Box : & V \times V & \rightarrow & V & \text{`vector addition'} \\ \circ : & S \times V & \rightarrow & V & \text{`multiplication by scalars'} \end{array}$$

Thus, for example, $(\{\mathbb{R}, M_2\}\{+, \times, 1, +_M, \bullet\})$ is a Σ-algebra in which the sort S of scalars is interpreted as $\mathbb{R}$, the sort V of vectors is interpreted as M_2, the function names $+$, $\times$, 1 are intepreted as $+$, $\times$, 1 (in $\mathbb{R}$), $\Box$ is interpreted as $+_M$ and $\circ$ is interpreted as $\bullet$.

The Σ-algebras of Example 8.29 all satisfy the following properties with respect to their signature $\Sigma = (\{S, V\}, \{+, \times, 1, \Box, \circ\})$:

(a) $(S, +)$ is a commutative group.
(b) $(S, \times)$ is a monoid with identity 1.
(c) if $s \neq 1$ then s has an inverse with respect to $\circ$.
(d) $s \circ (x \Box y) = (s \circ x) \Box (s \circ y)$
(e) $(s_1 \times s_2) \circ x = s_1 \circ (s_2 \circ x)$
(f) $1 \circ x = x$

where $s, s_1, s_2 \in S$ and $x, y \in V$. Properties (a) to (c) simply assert that the signature $(S, \{+, \times, 1\})$ satisfies the field properties defined in Example 8.22.

Definition 8.6 Vector space Any algebra with the signature $\Sigma = (\{S, V\}, \{+, \times, 1, \Box, \circ,\})$ that satisfies all the properties listed above is called a vector space.

Thus we can think of the set M_2 as a vector space with $\mathbb{R}$ being the carrier set of sort S (the scalars), M_2 being the carrier set of sort V (the vectors) and the functions matrix addition representing $\Box$ and scalar multiplication representing $\circ$.

Exercise 8.13 Show how the set of three-dimensional vectors over $\mathbb{Q}$ may be regarded as a vector space.

Extending algebras The definition of vector space was built on the earlier definitions of commutative groups and monoids. It is very important to be able to define algebras that are extensions of previously defined algebras in this way. When we do this we need to be able to relax our notation a little, so that we do not have to repeat all the details of the signature and properties of the algebra we are extending.

Example 8.30 Given that the signature and properties for fields had already been defined, it would have been acceptable to define a vector space as a (Σ, E)-algebra where $\Sigma = (\{S, V\}, \{\Box, \circ\})$ and where S is a field (meaning $(S, \{+, \times, 1\})$ satisfies the field properties defined in Example 8.22. The set E of properties is then:

(a) $s \circ (x \Box y) = (s \circ x) \Box (s \circ y)$

(b) $(s_1 \times s_2) \circ x = s_1 \circ (s_2 \circ x)$

(c) $1 \circ x = x$

Properties (b) and (c) of course *use* the field signature which is already defined.

In Example 8.30 we can think of the definition of vector spaces as *including* the definition of a field as one of its sorts. Sometimes we would like to include, in the same way, specific algebras. A very common algebra that we would like to include in definitions of new algebras is the algebra Bool described in Example 8.27:

Example 8.31 In Sec. 2.1 we said that if you declared a variable x to have type *integer* in Pascal then this was the same as saying that the value of x can be any member of $\mathbb{Z}$. This is not strictly true. There are an infinite number of integers, but a computer must have a maximum size integer it can recognize. Thus the type *integer* cannot be the same as the set $\mathbb{Z}$. It must be a *finite* set that is an 'approximation' to $\mathbb{Z}$, with similar operations and properties. Our task is to define an algebra that is such an approximation.

Our algebra must have a constant term *max* which corresponds to the maximum size integer that can be handled. We shall also need a constant term 'undefined', $\perp$, together with appropriate functions that handle overflow. We want to be able to test whether a given number exceeds *max*; to do this we need to have a function $>: S \times S :\rightarrow$ Bool which returns the value T or F. Therefore, we want to include the set Bool as one of our sorts. The signature for the extended algebra might be something like $\Sigma = (\{S, Bool\}, \{+, \times, >, 0, 1, max, \perp\})$ where the arity of the functions is given by:

$$\begin{aligned} +, \times &: S \times S \rightarrow S \\ 0, 1, max, \perp &: \quad\quad \rightarrow S \\ > &: S \times S \rightarrow Bool \end{aligned}$$

The properties to be satisfied would include:

$$\begin{aligned}
&a + b = b + a \\
&a \times b = b \times a \\
&\ldots \\
&a + \perp = \perp \\
&a \times \perp = \perp \\
&a > max \rightarrow a = \perp \\
&a + b > max \rightarrow a + b = \perp \\
&\ldots
\end{aligned}$$

8.2 UNIVERSAL ALGEBRAS

We now show how all the classical algebras of Sec. 8.1 can be presented as examples of a completely general theory of algebras. It is called the theory of universal algebras to emphasize that it subsumes the most general types of algebras that we considered in Sec. 8.1. We have already presented many of the concepts informally. We now provide the formal definitions, using many of the concepts of Chapter 7.

One of the most important concepts that we wish to formalize is that of properties, or axioms, to be satisfied by algebras. To do this we first consider the terms that can be generated from Σ. It turns out that the allowable properties are equations involving these terms. These are called equational axioms. We then provide the formal definition of Σ-algebras that satisfy the properties. Finally, we define the important class of finitely generated algebras and show how, for a given Σ, these can all be constructed from the set of Σ-terms.

8.2.1 Signatures, terms and algebras

Definition 8.7 Signature A signature $\Sigma = (\mathscr{S}, \mathscr{F})$ is a pair consisting of a set $\mathscr{S}$ whose members s_i are called sorts, and a set of function names $\mathscr{F}$. The function names each have an arity over $\mathscr{S}$, written in the form $f : s_i \times \cdots \times s_j \rightarrow s_k$. Any function name f with arity $f :\rightarrow s_k$ is said to be a constant of sort s_k. If $\mathscr{S}$ contains more than one sort, then the signature is said to be many-sorted.

For purposes of illustration we now define formally three specific signatures which we shall refer to by name only throughout the examples in this section:

(a) $\Sigma_0 = (\mathscr{S}, \mathscr{F})$ where $\mathscr{S} = \{S, I, O\}$ and $\mathscr{F} = \{f, g, s_0\}$ and the function arities are:

$$\begin{aligned}
f &: S \times I \rightarrow S \\
g &: S \times I \rightarrow O \\
s_0 &: \quad\quad\;\; \rightarrow S
\end{aligned}$$

This is the signature we used in defining finite state machines. Note that s_0 is a constant of sort S.

(b) $\Sigma_1 = (\mathscr{S}, \mathscr{F})$ where $\mathscr{S} = \{s\}$, $\mathscr{F} = \{\Box, inv, e\}$ and function arities are:

$$\begin{aligned}
f &: S \times S \rightarrow S \\
g &: \quad\quad\; S \rightarrow S \\
e &: \quad\quad\quad\; \rightarrow S
\end{aligned}$$

This is the signature for groups we described in Example 8.24.

(c) $\Sigma_2 = (\mathscr{S}, \mathscr{F})$ is the same as Σ_1 except that $\mathscr{F}$ contains an extra constant e' of sort S. Think of this as the signature for groups that contains at least one non-identity element (all groups except the zero group).

Definition 8.8 Σ-algebra For a signature $\Sigma = (\mathscr{S}, \mathscr{F})$, a Σ-algebra $\mathscr{A}$ is a pair $(\mathscr{A}_{\mathscr{S}}, \mathscr{A}_{\mathscr{F}})$ which is a model for Σ. This means that for each sort $S \in \mathscr{S}$ there is a set $A_s \in \mathscr{A}_{\mathscr{S}}$ (called a carrier set), and for each $f \in \mathscr{F}$ of arity $s_i \times \cdots \times s_j \to s_k$ there is a function $A_f \in \mathscr{A}_{\mathscr{F}}$ of arity $A_{s_i} \times \cdots \times A_{s_j} \to A_{s_k}$.

Example 8.32 Consider the finite state machine of Fig. 2.36(a) on page 62. This is a Σ_0-algebra in which the sort S is mapped to the carrier set of states {LIGHT OFF, LIGHT ON}, the sort I is mapped to the carrier set of inputs {PULL CORD}, the sort O is mapped to the carrier set of outputs {LIGHT GOES ON, LIGHT GOES OFF}, the function name f is mapped to the next-state function, the function name g is mapped to the output function and the constant name s_0 is mapped to the state LIGHT OFF.

Example 8.33 $(\mathbb{Z}, \{+, -, 0\})$ is a Σ_1-algebra. The carrier set for S is $\mathbb{Z}$, and the function names $\Box, inv, e$ are represented by the actual functions $+, -, 0$.

Exercise 8.14 Show that $(\mathbb{Z}, \{+, -, 0, 1\})$ is a Σ_2-algebra.

Our next task is to define the set of terms of a signature. As we saw in Chapter 7 these are the expressions that can be generated inductively from the constant and function names. In this context, Definition 7.5 on page 177 gives us:

Definition 8.9 The set of Σ-terms The set T_Σ of Σ-terms is defined inductively by:

Basis clause. Any constant name $f :\to s$ in $\mathscr{F}$ is in T_Σ and is of sort s.

Inductive clause. If $f \in \mathscr{F}$ has arity $f : s_i \times \cdots \times s_j \to s_k$ and if $t_i, \ldots, t_j$ are terms in T_Σ with sorts $s_i, \ldots, s_j$ respectively, then the expression $f(t_i, \ldots, t_j)$ is in T_Σ and has sort S_k.

Extremal clause. Unless an element can be shown to be in T_Σ by applying the basis and inductive clauses a finite number of times the element is not in T_Σ.

Example 8.34 We use the inductive definition to determine the Σ_1-terms. First, note that the only constant term is e. Using the function names $\Box$ and inv we get the terms

$$e,\ e\Box e,\ (e\Box e)\Box e, \ldots,\ inv(e),\ inv(inv(e)),\ inv(e)\Box e,\ inv(inv(e)\Box e), \ldots$$

(where we are using infix, as opposed to pre-fix, notation for $\Box$). Expressions like $\Box e$ and $inv(e, e)$ are *not* terms because they cannot be generated by the basis and inductive clauses of Def. 8.9.

Exercise 8.15 List some of the terms of T_{Σ_2}.

Example 8.35 Consider the signature Σ_0. There is just one constant term s_0 and this has sort S. Because of the arity of the function names f and g there is no way of creating any new terms. This is because both these function names require a term of sort I, in addition to a term of sort S. Since there are no constants of sort I we cannot, therefore, generate any new terms from the inductive definition.

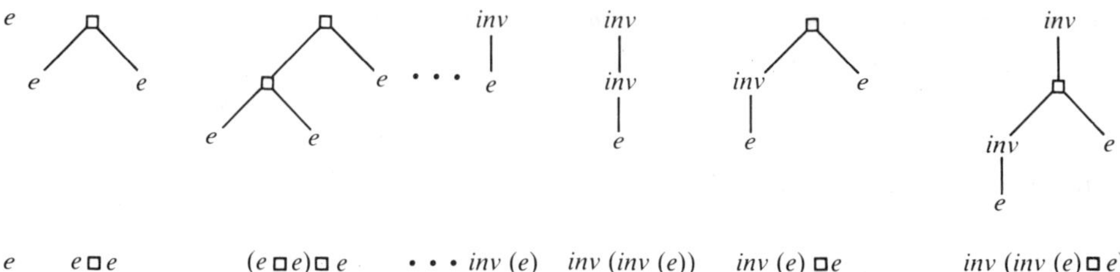

Figure 8.2 Presenting terms as trees.

The set of terms T_Σ is itself a very important Σ-algebra, called the *word algebra*. For each $S \in \mathscr{S}$ we take the carrier set of sort S in T_Σ to be the set of terms of sort S. For each $f \in \mathscr{F}$, the function representing the name f is the construction of a Σ-term using f from simpler Σ-terms of the right sort. This is like forming strings in the syntax, rather than function application.

Example 8.36 We consider the algebra T_{Σ_1}:

$$T_{\Sigma_1} = \{e,\ e\Box e,\ (e\Box e)\Box e, \ldots,\ inv(e),\ inv(inv(e)),\ inv(e)\Box e,\ inv(inv(e)\Box e), \ldots\}$$

In Fig. 8.2 we present these terms as trees (as in Chapter 7) rather than strings to emphasize how they are constructed from the inductive definition. This is like an abstract syntax whereas the strings are a concrete syntax. The function in T_{Σ_1} that corresponds to the name $\Box$ is $f : T_{\Sigma_1} \times T_{\Sigma_1} \to T_{\Sigma_1}$, defined by

$$f(e,e) = e\Box e,\ f(e\Box e, e) = (e\Box e)\Box e,\ f(e, inv(e)) = e\Box inv(e), \ldots$$

Exercise 8.16 What is the function corresponding to the name *inv* in the Σ_1-algebra T_{Σ_1}?

Example 8.37 Consider the signature $\Sigma = (S, \{\circ, a, b, c\})$ with a binary function name and three constant names:

$$\begin{aligned} \circ &: S \times S \to S \\ a, b, c &: \quad\quad\;\; \to S \end{aligned}$$

The distinct Σ-terms are:

$a,\ b,\ c$
$(a \circ a),\ (b \circ b),\ (c \circ c),\ (a \circ b),\ (b \circ a),\ (a \circ c),\ (c \circ a),\ (b \circ c),\ (c \circ b), \ldots$
$((a \circ (a \circ a)),\ ((a \circ a) \circ a),\ ((a \circ a) \circ b),\ (a \circ (a \circ b)),\ (a \circ (b \circ c)),\ ((a \circ b) \circ c)), \ldots$
...

Note that $(a \circ b)$ is a different term from $(b \circ a)$, that $((a \circ b) \circ c)$ is a different term from $(a \circ (b \circ c))$, etc. One way to think of T_Σ is as represented by the set of all binary trees (meaning that each node of the tree has outdegree 0 or 2) whose leaves are from the set $\{a, b, c\}$. This is illustrated in Fig. 8.3. We shall use this example again when we discuss quotient algebras; we will then be able to construct strings, multisets and sets over $\{a, b, c\}$. Hence we will show how some of the basic mathematical structures introduced in Chapter 2 can be constructed as algebras.

Given a Σ-algebra $\mathscr{A}$ and a Σ-term of sort S, we can talk about the interpretation of t in $\mathscr{A}$, written $I^*(t)$, by appealing to Def. 7.9 on page 184. This is the value in A_S which is the result of applying the various functions that occur in t.

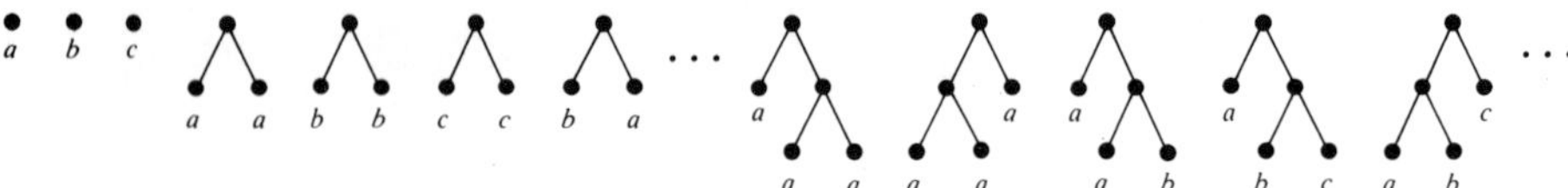

Figure 8.3 Representing T_Σ by binary trees over the set $\{a, b, c\}$.

Example 8.38 Consider the Σ_2-algebra $\mathscr{A} = (\mathbb{Z}, \{+, -, 0, 1\})$. What is the interpretation of the Σ_2-term $t = inv(e)\Box inv(e')$? We know that the constant e is mapped to 0 and e' to 1. The function names $\Box$ and inv are mapped to $+$ and $-$ respectively. Thus $I^*(t) = (-0) + (-1) = -1$.

Exercise 8.17 Consider the T_{Σ_2}-term $t = inv(e'\Box e')$. Compute $I^*(t)$ in $(\mathbb{Z}, \{+, -, 0, 1\})$.

Definition 8.10 The set of Σ-terms with variables Let X be a set of variable names where each is associated with one of the sorts in $\mathscr{S}$. Then the set $T_\Sigma(X)$ of Σ-terms with variables is defined exactly as the set T_Σ in Def. 8.9, except that in addition each of the variables is a term.

To make clear the distinction between terms in T_Σ that are not in $T_\Sigma(X)$ we shall refer to terms without variables as *ground terms*.

Example 8.39 Σ_0 has three sorts S, I, O. Let $X = \{x_1, x_2, \ldots, y_1, y_2, \ldots, z_1, z_2, \ldots\}$ be a set of variable names where the x_i's have sort S, the y_i's have sort I and the z_i's have sort O. Then $T_{\Sigma_0}(X)$ contains the terms

$$\begin{array}{rl} s_0, x_1, x_2, \ldots & \text{of sort } S \\ y_1, y_2, \ldots & \text{of sort } I \\ z_1, z_2, \ldots & \text{of sort } O \\ f(s_0, y_2), f(f(x_1, y_3), y_3), \ldots & \text{of sort } S \\ g(s_0, y_3), g(f(f(x_1, y_3), y_3), y_3), \ldots & \text{of sort } O \\ \ldots & \ldots \end{array}$$

Only s_0 is a ground term.

Exercise 8.18 Write down some terms in $T_{\Sigma_1}(X)$.

8.2.2 Equational logic and algebras

Our next task is to formalize the notion of an axiom and what it means to say that an axiom 'holds' in a given algebra. In fact, we are going to restrict our axioms to be *equations*. In doing so we are defining a subset of first-order logic, called *equational logic*.

Essentially, an equation is just a pair of terms. If Σ is a signature and t and t' are Σ-terms of the same sort, then the pair $\langle t, t' \rangle$ is a Σ-equation, which we would write as $t = t'$.

Example 8.40 The following are all Σ_1-equations:

$$\begin{array}{rcl} x\Box y & = & y\Box x \\ x\Box(y\Box z) & = & (x\Box y)\Box z \\ x\Box inv(x) & = & e \\ x\Box e & = & x \end{array}$$

They are also all Σ_2-equations. In fact, these equations are the properties for a commutative group listed in (8.1) on page 203.

Definition 8.11 Σ-algebra satisfying an equation A Σ-equation $t = t'$ containing variables X is satisfied by a Σ-algebra $\mathscr{A}$ if, for any assignment of the variables of X in the equation, the interpretations $I^*(t)$ and $I^*(t')$ are equal in $\mathscr{A}$.

Example 8.41 The Σ_1-equation $x\Box y = y\Box x$ is satisfied by any commutative group.

Definition 8.12 Abstract algebraic structure Any pair (Σ, E) where E is a set of Σ-equations is called an abstract algebraic structure.

It has been claimed that an abstract data type, defined as a collection of data and operations defined on that data, is an abstract algebraic structure. We shall return to this point in Chapter 10.

Definition 8.13 (Σ, E)-algebra Let (Σ, E) be an abstract algebraic structure. Any Σ-algebra that satisfies all the axioms in E is called a (Σ, E)-algebra.

Thus a (Σ, E)-algebra is a (concrete) model for the abstract algebraic structure (Σ, E).

Example 8.42 If $E = \{\}$ (the set of axioms is empty) then every Σ-algebra is a (Σ, E)-algebra. In particular, the word algebra T_Σ is a $(\Sigma, \{\})$-algebra.

Example 8.43 The Σ_1-algebra $(\mathbb{Z}, \{+, -, 0\})$ satisfies all of the axioms E in Example 8.40 and hence is a (Σ_1, E)-algebra.

Exercise 8.19 Show that the Σ_2-algebra $(\mathbb{Z}, \{+, -, 0, 1\})$ satisfies all the axioms E in Example 8.40 and is thus a (Σ_2, E)-algebra. Explain why the Σ_1-algebra $(\mathbb{Z}, \{+, -, 27\})$ is not a (Σ_1, E)-algebra.

In order to link the above ideas with Chapters 3 to 6, we now consider what it means to say that an equation eq follows from a set of equations E. As in Chapter 4, we can give two definitions of this. One definition is semantic in nature while the other is syntactic, although again they turn out to be equivalent. We begin with the semantic definition:

Definition 8.14 Semantic consequence A Σ-equation eq is a consequence of a set of Σ equations E if any (Σ, E)-algebra also satisfies eq; that is eq holds in all (Σ, E)-algebras. We write $E \models eq$ to denote that eq is a consequence of E.

The definition of $\models$ therefore refers to algebras.

Example 8.44 Let E be the group axioms. These are all Σ_1-equations. Let eq be the Σ_1-equation $e\Box e = e$. Then $E \models eq$.

Next, we use a purely syntactic definition that does not mention algebras at all but is merely concerned with manipulating equations as strings of symbols. This syntactic definition is based on the following five rules of inference in equational deduction (in which t, t', t_i, t'_i, u_i are all terms and $t(u_1, \ldots, u_n)$ is the n-ary term which results from substituting, for each i, each occurrence of the ith variable of t with u_i).

Rule 1 Instance Suppose t, t' jointly contain n variables. Then

$$\frac{t = t'}{t(u_1, \ldots, u_n) = t'(u_1, \ldots, u_n)}$$

Rule 2 Substitution Suppose u contains m variables. Then

$$\frac{t_1 = t'_1, \ldots, t_m = t'_m}{u(t_1, \ldots, t_m) = u(t'_1, \ldots, t'_m)}$$

Rule 3 Transitivity $$\frac{t = t' \qquad t' = t''}{t = t''}$$

Rule 4 Symmetry $$\frac{t = t'}{t' = t}$$

Rule 5 Reflexivity $$\frac{}{t = t}$$

We write $E \vdash_1 eq$ to express the deduction of eq from E in one step.

Example 8.45 With E and eq as in Example 8.44 we have $E \vdash_1 eq$. This is because E contains the equation $e \Box x = x$. Using the term e, we infer $e \Box e = e$ (this is eq) from Rule 1.

Our next task is to define $E \vdash eq$; that is we define formally what we mean by eq being deducible from E, where we allow any finite number of sequences of inferences. There are a number of ways that we can make this definition formal. We choose one that motivates the theory of fixed points in Chapter 9.

Let $f(E) = E \cup \{eq : E \vdash_1 eq\}$; that is $f(E)$ is the set of equations deducible in one step from E. In general $f(E)$ is infinite. The set $f(f(E))$ is the set of equations deducible from E in at most two steps. In fact, we have an infinite ascending sequence of sets of equations: $E \subseteq f(E) \subseteq f(f(E)) \subseteq \cdots \subseteq f^i(E) \subseteq \cdots$. If we take the union of this sequence we get the set of *all* equations deducible from E in a *finite* number of steps. This is the set $E^* = \cup_{i=0}^{i=\infty}\{f^i(E)\}$, which we call the *closure* of the set E. Clearly we have $E \subseteq E^*$ and $f(E^*) = E^*$. Thus E^* is a *fixed point* of the function f. In fact, it can be shown that E^* is the smallest fixed point of f that includes E. This means that an equation $eq \in E^*$ iff either $eq \in E$ or eq is deduced in one step from equations already in E^*.

Definition 8.15 Deduction of a Σ-equation The equation eq is deducible from E precisely when $eq \in E^*$.

From Def. 8.15 and from Chapter 4, we can deduce that

$$E \vdash eq \text{ iff } E \models eq$$

The notion of the closure E^* of E will be used in Chapter 10. If $E = E^*$ we say that the set of equations E is closed. For example, if E is empty then it is certainly closed. We will define a *theory* for Σ as an abstract algebraic structure (Σ, E) where E is closed. This will also be called a *theory presentation*. The simplest theory, where $E = \{\}$, is said to be *anarchic* because it obeys no laws at all, and is just a starting point for a theory presentation; as we saw in Example 8.42, it is satisfied by every Σ-algebra. In general, a theory is said to be *satisfiable* if it has at least one model, that is at least one (Σ, E)-algebra.

Having provided a completely general and formal definition of algebras, our next task is to develop the theory that enables us to construct specific (Σ, E)-algebras for a given abstract algebraic structure (Σ, E). This construction is of fundamental importance in computer science, because it represents the realization of an abstract data type specification by a module in a program; the algebra is a concrete model for the implementation of an abstract data type. The aim of the rest of the chapter is to construct a (Σ, E)-algebra, which is representative of all (Σ, E)-algebras for a given algebraic structure (Σ, E). Computer scientists would regard such an algebra as the semantic definition of the abstract data type that is described by its signature and set of axioms. We characterize abstract data types and give their algebraic specifications in Chapter 10.

8.2.3 Finitely generated algebras

In this section we will show that a very large and important class of (Σ, E)-algebras, namely the so-called finitely generated algebras, can be generated from the term algebra. Specifically we will show that every finitely generated algebra is isomorphic to a quotient structure of the term algebra.

We shall assume the many-sorted notions of *homomorphism* and *sub-algebra* as the natural extension of the one-sorted notions described in Sec. 8.1.1. The formal definitions of these are straightforward and intuitive, but too long to include here.

Consider again the signatures Σ_1 and Σ_2. We have noted that these are both signatures for groups. The difference is that any group that is a Σ_2-algebra must have a constant which is different from the identity element. The group $(\mathbb{Z}, \{+, -, 0, 1\})$ is an example of a Σ_2-algebra. Think about the Σ_2 ground terms and their interpretation in $(\mathbb{Z}, \{+, -, 0, 1\})$. For example, the interpretation function I^* maps:

$$\begin{array}{rcl} e & \mapsto & 0 \\ e' & \mapsto & 1 \\ inv(e') & \mapsto & -1 \\ e'\Box e' & \mapsto & 1+1=2 \\ inv(e'\Box e') & \mapsto & -(1+1)=-2 \\ e'\Box(e'\Box e') & \mapsto & 1+(1+1)=3 \\ \ldots & \ldots & \ldots \end{array}$$

Exercise 8.20 Write down a Σ_2 ground term whose interpretation is -4.

It is not difficult to see that *every* element of $\mathbb{Z}$ is the interpretation of some Σ_2 ground term. So the whole algebra can be 'generated', by structural induction, from the signature's constants and functions alone. This is *not* true when we think of $(\mathbb{Z}, \{+, -, 0\})$ as a Σ_1-algebra. In that case the only terms we can generate are from e. For example, e, $e\Box e$, $inv(e)$, $inv(e)\Box e, \ldots$. Since e is mapped to 0, the interpretation of each of these terms is 0; for example, $i(e\Box e) = 0 + 0 = 0$.

These observations lead us to define a very important restriction on Σ-algebras:

Definition 8.16 Finitely generated algebra A Σ-algebra $\mathscr{A}$ is finitely generated, or null-generated, if the interpretation function I^*, which maps terms in T_Σ to elements of the carrier set(s) of $\mathscr{A}$, is surjective.

Example 8.46 It is now clear that $(\mathbb{Z}, \{+, -, 0, 1\})$ is a finitely generated Σ_2-algebra, but is not a finitely generated Σ_1-algebra. The only finitely generated Σ_1-algebra (up to isomorphism) is the zero group, described in Example 8.4.

Exercise 8.21 Show that, for each n, the group $\mathbb{Z}_n$ with binary function $\oplus_n$ is a finitely generated Σ_2-algebra.

Example 8.47 Let E be the group axioms. It can be shown that the only finitely generated (Σ_2, E)-algebras (up to isomorphism) are the group $(\mathbb{Z}, +)$ and the groups $(\mathbb{Z}_n, \oplus_n)$ for each $n \in \mathbb{N}$.

Now let $\mathscr{A}$ be a finitely generated Σ-algebra. Then each element of $\mathscr{A}$ is the interpretation of some term of T_Σ. In general, several terms may give rise to the same interpretation. For example, $((e'\Box e')\Box e')$, $e'\Box(e'\Box e')$ and $inv(inv(e')\Box(e'\Box e'))$ all give rise to the interpretation '3' in the Σ_2-algebra $(\mathbb{Z}, \{+,-,0,1\})$. It follows that we can define an equivalence relation $\sim$ on T_Σ by

$$t \sim t' \text{ iff } I^*(t) = I^*(t')$$

where i is the interpretation function.

Example 8.48 For T_{Σ_2}, with the interpretation in $(\mathbb{Z}, \{+,-,0,1\})$, we have equivalence classes:

$[e]$	$= \{e,\ g(e),\ e\Box e,\ inv(e\Box e), \ldots\}$	(all interpreted as 0)
$[e']$	$= \{e',\ e\Box e',\ inv(inv(e'),\ (e\Box e)\Box e'), \ldots\}$	(all interpreted as 1)
$[e'\Box e']$	$= \{e'\Box e',\ e\Box(e'\Box e'),\ inv(inv(e'\Box e')), \ldots\}$	(all interpreted as 2)
...	...	...

Since every element of $\mathscr{A}$ is in exactly one of these equivalence classes it follows that the resulting quotient algebra $(T_\Sigma/\sim)$ is isomorphic to $\mathscr{A}$. This presents an informal proof of the important theorem:

Theorem 8.1 Every finitely generated Σ-algebra is isomorphic to a quotient structure of T_Σ.

Example 8.49 The group $(\mathbb{Z}_3, \oplus_3)$ is a finitely generated Σ_2-algebra. Every Σ_2 term is interpreted as either 0,1 or 2. Thus the interpretation function induces a partition of T_{Σ_2} into just three equivalence classes $[e]$, $[e']$ and $[e'\Box e']$. This is a much coarser partition than that induced by $\mathbb{Z}$ in Example 8.48. This might lead us to say that $\mathbb{Z}$ is a 'finer' Σ_2-algebra than $\mathbb{Z}_3$. In the next section we will show formally that $\mathbb{Z}$ is the 'finest' finitely generated Σ_2-algebra.

Now let E be a set of Σ-equations. We then form an important quotient algebra of T_Σ using E. We define an equivalence relation $\sim_E$ over T_Σ by: $t \sim_E t'$ iff $E \models t = t'$. We write T_Σ/E for the quotient algebra $T_\Sigma/\sim_E$. The following examples of this technique build on Example 8.37 on page 215 and enable us to 'construct' trees, strings, multisets and sets:

Example 8.50 We take Σ to be the signature in Example 8.37, with a single binary function name $\circ$ and three constant names a, b, c. We want to consider each of the four quotient algebras T_Σ/E_i where, for $i = 0, 1, 2, 3$:

(a) $E_0 = \{\}$
(b) $E_1 = \{(x \circ (y \circ z)) = ((x \circ y) \circ z)\}$ (associativity)
(c) $E_2 = E_1 \cup \{(x \circ y) = (y \circ x)\}$ (associativity and commutativity)
(d) $E_3 = E_2 \cup \{(x \circ x) = x\}$ (associativity, commutativity and idempotence)

We consider each algebra T_Σ/E_i in turn:

(a) For E_0 there are no equations and so $T_\Sigma/E_0 = T_\Sigma$ which is the algebra already described in Example 8.37 and Fig. 8.3. We view its elements as binary trees over $\{a \circ b \circ c\}$.

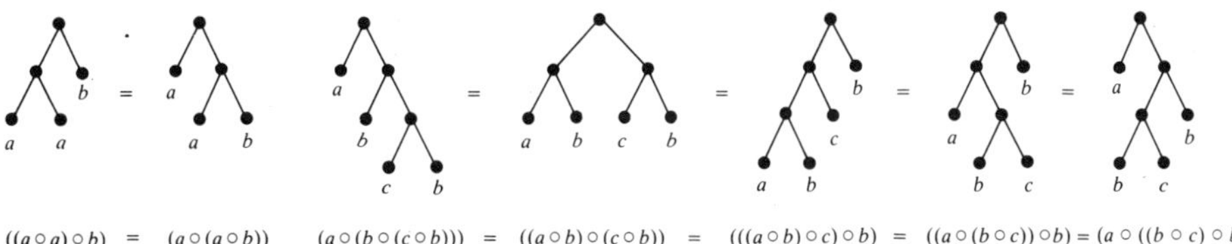

Figure 8.4 The algebra T_Σ/E_1.

(b) For E_1 certain terms are made equal by definition of the quotient structure. For example, $((a \circ a) \circ b) = (a \circ (a \circ b))$ in T_Σ/E_1 since $((a \circ a) \circ b) \sim_E (a \circ (a \circ b))$. Similarly, $(a \circ (b \circ c)) = ((a \circ b) \circ c)$, etc. We illustrate this in Fig. 8.4. Note, however, that $(a \circ b) \neq (b \circ a)$ and $(a \circ (b \circ c)) \neq (b \circ (a \circ c))$, etc. It follows that the elements of the algebra T_Σ/E_1 may be viewed as strings over $\{a \circ b \circ c\}$ in the sense of Chapter 7. For example, we can view the string $\langle a, b, c\rangle$ as the representative for each of $(a \circ (b \circ c))$ and $((a \circ b) \circ c)$. Similarly, the string $\langle a, b, c, b\rangle$ is the representative for each of $(a \circ (b \circ (c \circ b)))$, $((a \circ b) \circ (c \circ b))$, $(((a \circ b) \circ c) \circ b)$, $(a \circ ((b \circ c) \circ b))$ and $((a \circ (b \circ c)) \circ b)$.

(c) For E_2 still more terms are made equal by definition of the quotient structure. For example, we now have $(a \circ b) = (b \circ a)$, and $((a \circ b) \circ a) = (a \circ (b \circ a)) = (a \circ (a \circ b)) = ((a \circ a) \circ b))$ in T_Σ/E_2. Note, however, that $((a \circ b) \circ b) \neq ((a \circ a) \circ b)$. It follows that the elements of T_Σ/E_2 may be viewed as multisets over $\{a, b, c\}$. For example, we can view the multiset $\{a, b, a\}$ as the representative for each of $(a \circ (b \circ a))$, $((a \circ b) \circ a)$, $((a \circ a) \circ b)$, $(a \circ (a \circ b))$, $(b \circ (a \circ a))$, $((b \circ a) \circ a)$.

(d) For E_3 the elements of T_Σ/E_3 may be viewed as sets over $\{a, b, c\}$. For example, the set $\{a, b\}$ is the representative for all the equivalent terms $(a \circ b)$, $(b \circ a)$, $(a \circ (b \circ a))$, $((a \circ b) \circ a)$, $(a \circ (b \circ b))$, etc.

In the next section we will show that, for each i, the algebra T_Σ/E_i is the 'finest' finitely generated (Σ, E_i)-algebra.

Exercise 8.22 In the algebra T_Σ/E_2 of Example 8.50 write down all the terms that are equivalent to $((a \circ b) \circ (b \circ c))$.

Finitely generated algebras, which are especially important in computing, have useful properties. We have just seen that we can construct them from equivalence classes of the word algebra, a result that we shall use in Sec. 8.3. Also, since every element is generated from a fixed set of constants and functions, we can prove properties about these algebras by the principle of structural induction, introduced in Chapter 6.

8.3 CATEGORY THEORY

Having achieved the goal of constructing (Σ, E)-algebras by using the term algebra, we now turn our attention to the goal of choosing representative algebras of a given structure. To do this we need to introduce the elements of *category theory*.

For many years mathematicians and scientists studied homomorphisms in many different types of algebras independently. Category theory provides a framework, which is independent of any particular algebra, for describing general principles and theorems

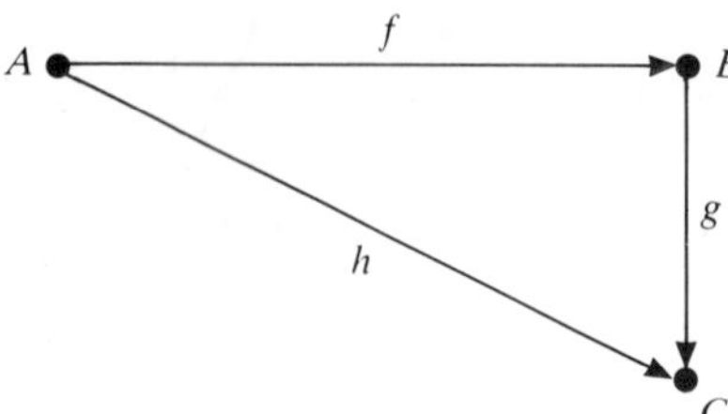

Figure 8.5 Commutative diagram.

about homomorphisms. It thus abstracts out the properties of homomorphisms and ignores the details of particular algebras.

We will introduce the basic definitions of category theory and then concentrate on one particular topic, namely initial and final elements of categories. We will then show how initial and final elements are used to define representative algebras of a given class.

8.3.1 Defining categories

Our search for general properties of homomorphisms is motivated by an example.

Example 8.51 A very simple abstract algebraic structure is (Σ, E) where $\Sigma = (S, \{\})$ and $E = \{\}$. Thus the signature has just one sort and no function names, and the set of axioms is empty. In short there is no structure at all.

Question: What are the (Σ, E)-algebras in this case?
Answer: Any *set* is a (Σ, E)-algebra.
Question: What are the (Σ, E)-homomorphisms?
Answer: Any *function* between two sets.

So we have a collection of objects; these are just sets. For each pair of objects A, B we have a set of homomorphisms $M(A, B)$ from A to B. These are just the functions from A to B.

For each $f : A \to B$ and $g : B \to C$ we can find $h : A \to C$ such that $h = g \circ f$. This is just function composition. The relationship between f, g and h is summarized by a *commutative diagram* in Fig. 8.5.

There are two other key properties of the set of homomorphisms in Example 8.51, and it is these that characterize any *category*.

Definition 8.17 Category A category $\mathscr{C}$ is a collection of objects, and for each pair of objects A, B there is a set of morphisms which we denote as $M(A, B)$. Composition of morphisms is defined, and the following two properties hold:

Property 1 (associativity). For any morphisms $f : A \to B$, $g : B \to C$, $h : C \to D$ we have $h \circ (g \circ f) = (h \circ g) \circ f$.

Property 2 (identities). For each object A there is an identity morphism $i_A : A \to A$ such that if $f : A \to B$ is any morphism, then $f \circ i_A = i_B \circ f = f$.

Example 8.52 Let $\mathscr{C}$ be the class of all groups and for each pair of groups A, B, let $M(A, B)$ be the set of all group homomorphisms. Then $\mathscr{C}$ is a category. The same is true if we replace 'groups' by 'monoids', 'rings', 'fields', 'vector spaces', etc.

In fact, any class of (Σ, E)-algebras and their (Σ, E)-homomorphisms, that is their structure preserving functions, yields a category.

Example 8.53 Any poset $(S, \preceq)$ (defined in Sec. 2.2) may be viewed as a category. The objects are the elements of S. For each pair of elements $A, B \in S$, the set of morphisms $M(A, B)$ is defined to contain exactly one element if $A \preceq B$ and is empty otherwise. In this case the composition operation exists because $\preceq$ is transitive. Property 1 is satisfied since if f, g and h exist as specified then it follows that $A \preceq D$ and hence that there is exactly one morphism $A \rightarrow D$. Property 2 is satisfied since for each $A \in S$, $A \preceq A$.

Exercise 8.23 Show that categories may themselves be viewed as abstract algebraic structures by defining an appropriate signature and set of axioms.

8.3.2 Initial and terminal objects

We wish to single out a property of categories that has great significance to the kind of algebraic structures in which we are most interested.

Consider the category of finitely generated (Σ_2, E)-algebras where Σ_2 is the signature for groups with a non-identity constant and E is the set of group axioms. We noted in Example 8.47 that, up to isomorphism, the only finitely generated (Σ_2, E)-algebras are the infinite group $\mathbb{Z}$ and the finite groups $\mathbb{Z}_n$ for each n. In Example 8.17 we also noted that there is exactly one (Σ_2, E)-morphism from $\mathbb{Z}$ to $\mathbb{Z}_n$. Because of this property we say that the group $\mathbb{Z}$ is an *initial* object in the category of (Σ_2, E)-algebras. This is the formal idea of it being the 'finest' in the sense discussed in Sec. 8.2.3 and Example 8.49.

Definition 8.18 Initial object An object I in a category $\mathscr{C}$ is said to be initial if, for any object X of $\mathscr{C}$, there is exactly one morphism $f : I \rightarrow X$.

Example 8.54 Initial objects do not always exist. Consider the category of Example 8.53. In particular, consider the poset $(\{2, 3, 6\}, |)$. This has two minimal elements 2 and 3 since both of these divide 6, but neither divides the other. It follows that no element can be initial in this category since there are just two morphisms—one from 2 to 6 and one from 3 to 6. In general, only posets with a unique minimal element have an initial object (namely the minimal element).

Example 8.55 It follows from Example 8.14 that the zero group is the initial object in the category of groups.

Example 8.56 In Example 8.50 we constructed algebras of the form T_Σ/E where E is a set of equations. It turns out that, for any (Σ, E), the algebra T_Σ/E is initial in the category of finitely generated (Σ, E)-algebras. Let $\mathscr{A}$ be such an algebra. Then, by Def. 8.16, the interpretation function is a surjective Σ-homomorphism from $T_\Sigma \rightarrow \mathscr{A}$. This function can then be extended in such a way that we obtain a function from $T_\Sigma/E \rightarrow \mathscr{A}$ that is a (Σ, E)-homomorphism. It follows that T_Σ is an initial algebra in this category.

Thus, for each E_i in Example 8.50 on page 220, the algebra T_Σ/E_i is initial. In the algebraic approach to specification this class of initial algebras is crucial, particularly in the light of the following theorem.

Theorem 8.2 If a category has an initial object then any two initial objects are isomorphic. Thus initial objects are unique up to isomorphism.

PROOF Let I, I' be two initial objects in $\mathscr{C}$. Since I is initial there is a unique $f : I \to I'$, and since I' is initial there is a unique $g : I' \to I$. However, $g \circ f : I \to I$. Again using the initiality of I, the identity morphism $i_I : I \to I$ must be equal to $g \circ f$. Hence $g \circ f = i_I$ and by a similar argument $f \circ g = i_{I'}$. It therefore follows that f (and also g) is an isomorphism.

There are analogous definitions and results for *terminal* objects.

Definition 8.19 Terminal object An object T in a category $\mathscr{C}$ is said to be terminal if for any object X of $\mathscr{C}$ there is exactly one morphism $f : X \to T$.

In the case of finitely generated algebras, we saw that initial objects impose the 'finest' partition on T_Σ. It turns out that final objects impose the 'coarsest' partition.

Example 8.57 In the category of finitely generated Boolean algebras, the two-element algebra Bool, described in Example 8.27, is a terminal object.

Example 8.58 In the category of groups, the zero group is a terminal object. Hence it is both an initial and terminal object in this category.

Exercise 8.24 Show that if a category has two terminal objects then they must be isomorphic.

8.3.3 Defining representative algebras

A central problem in the algebraic approach to specification is the following: we have an abstract algebraic structure (Σ, E). From the set of all finitely generated (Σ, E)-algebras, can we choose one that is 'most representative' and therefore somehow characterizes (Σ, E)? We shall see, in Chapter 10, that this is what computer scientists require when they define the semantics of an abstract data type specified by (Σ, E).

Example 8.59 In Example 8.31 on page 212 we attempted to define the signature and axioms of a particular algebra which was a finite approximation of $\mathbb{Z}$. We wanted to be able to construct such an algebra and to use it as a data type in a programming language. We are not interested in every such algebra; we just want one that is most representative.

The results of Sec. 8.3.2 suggest two approaches that we could take to defining representative algebras: we could take the initial or terminal algebras when these exist. Both approaches are used, and both have their advantages and disadvantages.

Example 8.60 Using the initial approach we can construct the data types: *binary tree, string, multiset* and *set* by using the algebras T_Σ/E_i of Example 8.50. Thus, for example, T_Σ/E_1, which is initial among all finitely generated (Σ, E_1)-algebras, may be viewed as the definition of strings over $\{a, b, c\}$. The initiality of T_Σ/E_1 means that, alone out of all the (Σ, E_1)-algebras, T_Σ/E_1 contains no 'junk' (there are no elements that do not correspond to an equivalence class of ground terms) and no 'confusion' (any two distinct equivalence classes of terms are interpreted differently).

Example 8.60 illustrates the algebraic approach to specification, which we describe in Chapter 10. Note that we have defined the data type in a finite way. For example, for the algebra T_Σ/E_1, which defines all strings over $\{a, b, c\}$, the signature Σ has just one binary function name and three constant names; the set E_1 has just one equation. The ability to construct initial algebras in this finite way is crucial for practical applications.

The idea of no 'junk' and no 'confusion' in the initial algebra may be considered advantageous. However, to avoid unnecessary redundancy, in some situations we may *want* to have 'confusion' in the sense that we may want to force two distinct equivalence classes of terms to be equal. For this reason it is sometimes preferable to choose the terminal algebra, if it exists, as this gives the least redundancy of terms.

The initial algebra only satisfies the axioms of E and their logical consequences; it does not satisfy any additional properties. The major advantages of using the initial algebra is that it is known that if all axioms of E are equational then an initial algebra always exists. Also, it can be shown that every finitely generated (Σ, E)-algebra is a quotient structure of the initial algebra. We can prove this for the example of the category of finitely generated (Σ_2, E)-algebras.

Example 8.61 We have seen that for every n the group $\mathbb{Z}_n$ is isomorphic to $\mathbb{Z}/\sim$, where $\sim$ is the equivalence relation over $\mathbb{Z}$ defined by $x \sim y$ if $x = y \bmod n$. Hence $\mathbb{Z}_n$ is a quotient group of $\mathbb{Z}$ which we know is the initial algebra. However, these are the only (Σ_2, E)-algebras.

In a sense, the ideal situation is when the initial and terminal algebras are one and the same, as in the case of the category of groups. Here the zero group is both initial and terminal. The following example is more interesting:

Example 8.62 The algebra Bool is both initial and terminal in the category of finitely generated Boolean algebras.

Definition 8.20 Monomorphic algebraic structure An abstract algebraic structure (Σ, E) is said to be monomorphic if the initial and terminal (Σ, E)-algebras exist and are isomorphic.

Example 8.63 If we keep adding axioms to E we can sometimes force (Σ, E) to be monomorphic. If we add the axiom $e' \Box e' = e$ to the abstract algebraic structure (Σ_2, E), then this ensures that any (Σ_2, E)-algebra has exactly two elements. Up to isomorphism, there is just one such algebra, namely $\mathbb{Z}_2$, which is of course both initial and terminal.

8.4 SUMMARY

The classical notion of an algebra is of one or more sets, together with one or more functions defined over these sets. We have shown how the theory of universal algebra provides a general framework for describing the classical algebras, including groups, rings, vector spaces and Boolean algebras. The theory also provides the framework for the algebraic approach to specifications that we shall present in Chapter 10.

In the universal algebra approach we start with an abstract algebraic structure (Σ, E). The signature Σ, which could be viewed as the syntax, specifies a number of sorts and a number of function names whose arity is given in terms of the sorts. The set E of axioms derived from Σ could be viewed as the semantics. In most cases we restrict our interest to the case where E is a set of equations. A (Σ, E)-algebra is a concrete model $\mathscr{A}$ for an abstract algebraic structure (Σ, E). This means that $\mathscr{A}$ consists of one or more sets and functions that correspond to the sorts and function names of Σ, in such a way that the axioms of E are all satisfied in $\mathscr{A}$. Different classes of classical algebras (groups, rings, etc.) are characterized by the particular choice of (Σ, E). Abstract data types may be represented by particular algebraic structures (Σ, E); in this case any (Σ, E)-algebra is an implementation (also called a realization) of that data type.

For any abstract algebraic structure (Σ, E), we can form a special (Σ, E)-algebra, called the word algebra, which is generated from the constants and functions of Σ. Then every finitely generated (Σ, E)-algebra $\mathscr{A}$ is a quotient structure of the word algebra. This means that $\mathscr{A}$ partitions the word algebra into equivalence classes such that every element of $\mathscr{A}$ corresponds to exactly one of these equivalence classes. It follows that we can generate all the useful (Σ, E)-algebras by just considering the word algebra. Where (Σ, E) represents an abstract data type, this gives us a practical means of constructing implementations for it.

A (Σ, E)-homomorphism is a structure preserving function between (Σ, E)-algebras. The set of all (Σ, E)-algebras for a given (Σ, E), together with all homomorphisms between these algebras, is an example of a category. In many cases such a category will possess an initial object, meaning an algebra $\mathscr{A}$ that induces the finest partition of the word algebra. The algebra $\mathscr{A}$ may be considered to be representative of all (Σ, E)-algebras. Where (Σ, E) represents an abstract data type, the initial algebra can be regarded as the specification of the initial semantics of the abstract data type.

FURTHER READING

For a very thorough introduction to classical algebras, Cohn (1974) is highly recommended. The theory of universal algebras is explained in depth in Birkhoff and Lipton (1974), while Bauer and Wossner's book (1982) gives a good account of initial and terminal algebras.

Chapter 9

THE CALCULUS OF FUNCTIONS

In Chapter 2 we defined a *function* as a relation between each element in some predefined domain set and a unique element in some defined codomain set. We also described how we could think of functions as rules. While adequate for much conventional mathematics, this definition is rather restrictive for the practical construction of functions, which is our objective in this chapter. To this end we wish to extend our notion of functions so that:

1 We have an effective means of naming and talking about functions.

2 We can allow the domain of the function to vary while the rule remains the same.

3 We can deal with partial functions as if they were functions.

4 We know when we can construct recursive functions.

The importance of points 1 and 2 are discussed in Sec. 9.1. We resolve these issues by defining a calculus of functions called the λ-calculus. This calculus is based on the idea of recursion and is described in Sec. 9.2. In Sec. 9.3, with the help of the λ-calculus notation, we describe a theory of fixed points which enables us to resolve issues 3 and 4. By thinking of functions as expressions in the λ-calculus we pave the way for implementing them as programs. In Sec. 9.4 we describe how to apply the λ-calculus and fixed point theory to the definition and construction of interactive processes.

9.1 EXTENDING OUR NOTION OF A FUNCTION

9.1.1 Defining, naming and referring to functions

We begin by considering some examples that highlight the problems we have when we use the notation of Chapter 2 for defining, naming and referring to functions.

Example 9.1 The function $f : \mathbb{Z} \to \mathbb{Z}$ defined by the rule $f(x) = x^2$ for each x is the set $\{(0,0),(1,1),(-1,1),(2,4),(-2,4),(3,9),(-3,9),(4,16),\ldots\}$. The rule only gives an implicit definition of f while the set of all pairs gives an explicit definition. Suppose we want a precise mathematical means of expressing the assertion: 'f applied to 2 is equal to 4'. Using the notation of Sec. 2.3 we would write this as '$(2,4) \in f$', '$f(2) = 4$', or as '$f : 2 \mapsto 4$'. However, these are only meaningful in the context of our having provided a separate definition of the rule for f. On the other hand, the notation '$2^2 = 4$' fails to capture the assertion precisely since it makes no mention of f at all. The problem is that naming functions does not describe meaning. It would not help even if we give f a descriptive name, say *square*.

Example 9.2 Suppose we want to assert that the function f (of Example 9.1) is always greater than the function $g : \mathbb{Z} \rightarrow \mathbb{Z}$ defined by the rule $g(x) = x - 1$. We could write '$f > g$' but again this is only meaningful in the context of our separate definitions of the rules for f and g. What is commonly used instead is the expression '$x^2 > x - 1$'. This is unsatisfactory since the expression x^2 is meant to represent some *value* in $\mathbb{Z}$, and not a function. So the variable x would have to be bound by a universal quantifier, and even then we have failed to make explicit the domain of interpretation.

Example 9.3 When we talk about the 'function' $\pi \times r^2 \times h$ to compute the *volume of a cylinder* we do not specify its domain or codomain as these are assumed to be known from the context. We know that π is constant and that r, h can vary. The problem is that sometimes we might want to keep h constant and only allow r to vary. Do we have a different function? If we do, then how do we refer to it?

The problems of defining, naming and referring to functions are especially important when it comes to higher order functions, whose arguments are themselves functions.

Example 9.4 Suppose we wish to define a function *square* : $\mathscr{F} \rightarrow \mathscr{F}$, where $\mathscr{F}$ is the set of all functions $f : \mathbb{R} \rightarrow \mathbb{R}$. The rule is that *square* maps a function f to the function that is the square of f. Suppose, for example, that f is the function defined by the rule $f(x) = x + 3$; then $square(f) = g$ where $g(x) = (x + 3)^2$. In general we would define $square(f) = g$ where $g(x) = f(x)^2$. This kind of definition is rather awkward and it creates more problems when talking about *square* than we saw for the functions in Examples 9.1 and 9.3.

Exercise 9.1 Let $\mathscr{F}$ be the set of all functions with domain and codomain equal to $\mathbb{R}$. How would you define a function *multiply* : $\mathscr{F} \times \mathscr{F} \rightarrow \mathscr{F}$ which, for two functions f and g, returns the function that is the product of the values of f and g.

What is evident from these examples is that our notation does not enable us to define higher order functions in a way that we can refer to them conveniently. Because higher order functions are the basis of functional programming languages, we will provide a solution to this problem.

9.1.2 Polymorphic functions

Consider again the function $f : \mathbb{Z} \rightarrow \mathbb{Z}$ of Example 9.1 defined by the rule $f(x) = x^2$. The domain of f is $\mathbb{Z}$. Thus, even though the expression x^2 is well defined for each $x \in \mathbb{R}$, the value $f(x)$ is undefined for a number like $x = \frac{1}{2}$ which is not in the domain of f. Rather, we have to define a new function $f' : \mathbb{R} \rightarrow \mathbb{R}$ where $f'(x) = x^2$ for each $x \in \mathbb{R}$, even though it is defined by the same rule as f. This seems to be a waste of time. Ideally, the rule $f(x) = x^2$ should define a function for any domain in which x^2 is meaningful, but our notation does not allow this.

Our definition of a function forces us to specify the domain in advance. To apply the same rule to different domains we have to define a new function in each case. To get round this problem we will have to extend our notion of function to allow for functions with different (or unspecified) domains. Such functions are called *polymorphic*. In functional programming languages, polymorphism is a notational device that allows functions to have parameters of any type.

Example 9.5 For any set S the *identity* function is defined by $i_S : S \to S$ where $i_S(x) = x$ for each $x \in S$. Although the rule defining each identity function is the same, each different set S leads to a different function. Suppose then that we wish to make some statement about, or perform some operation on, identity functions in general. We might, for example, wish to assert that 'the composition of the identity function with itself is the identity function'. Although this is true for each identity function, we have no convenient way of making this assertion; we need to make a separate assertion for each different identity function. Ideally we would want the identity function to be polymorphic.

Exercise 9.2 If we think of vectors of n elements as *lists* then there are some standard list processing functions that we would like to apply, for example the *head* and *tail* functions, where $head(x_1, \ldots, x_n) = x_1$ and $tail(x_1, \ldots, x_n) = (x_2, \ldots, x_n)$. Give examples that show how we would benefit from a polymorphic approach here.

9.2 THE LAMBDA CALCULUS

The problems we identified in Sec. 9.1 were recognized in the 1930s by a logician called Church. He solved them by introducing a calculus, called the λ-calculus. This enables us to treat the many different types of functions, including higher order functions, and their arguments in a uniform manner. The λ-calculus, as a type-free theory about functions as rules, was originally studied as a foundation for logic and mathematics. The typed λ-calculus has provided many applications for program construction and verification and is the basis for a new programming language paradigm, called functional programming, which we shall study in more depth in Chapter 11.

The λ-calculus consists of a language, the λ-notation, whose wffs are called λ-expressions, together with rules for simplifying and manipulating λ-expressions. The λ-expressions turn out to be precisely the set of computable functions that we introduced briefly in Sec. 2.3. In this section we begin by explaining informally the principle of function application that is used in the λ-calculus. We then describe the language and its rules. We show how the λ-calculus is used for defining functions, and hence how it resolves the problems discussed in Sec. 9.1. Finally, we explain the role of the λ-calculus in defining partial and recursive functions.

9.2.1 Function application and currying

Suppose that $f : \mathbb{R} \to \mathbb{R}$ is the function defined by the rule $f(x) = (x+1)^2$ for each $x \in \mathbb{R}$. Then f is commonly said to be 'a function of a single variable x'. Indeed, the notation $f(x)$ is taken to mean precisely that. In such situations $f(a)$, for any specific a, may be obtained by substituting the value of a for each occurrence of x in f. To make this particular idea of function application more explicit we will write $f(x)\ a$. Thus

$$f(x)\ 3 = (3+1)^2 = 16$$

Now suppose $f : \mathbb{R} \times \mathbb{R} \to \mathbb{R}$. Then each argument of f is a pair of real numbers (x, y). For example, f might be defined by the rule $f(x, y) = x + y + (2 \times x \times y)$ for each pair (x, y). We normally say that 'f is a function of two variables x and y'. In such situations $f(a, b)$, for a specific pair (a, b), may be obtained by substituting each occurrence of x by a and each occurrence of y by b. We could write this as $f(x, y)\ a\ b$. Thus

$$f(x, y)\ 3\ 5 = 3 + 5 + (2 \times 3 \times 5) = 38$$

However, there is another way in which we can think of function application. Instead of computing $f(a, b)$ in one go we could:

1 First compute $f(x, y)\ a$ as in $f(x, y)\ 3 = 3 + y + (6 \times y)$. This gives a function $g(y)$ of one variable y.

2 Next compute $g(y)\ 5$ in the normal way: $g(y)\ 5 = 3 + 5 + (6 \times 5) = 38$.

Example 9.6 Let $f : \mathbb{R} \times \mathbb{R} \times \mathbb{R} \to \mathbb{R}$ be defined by the rule $f(x, y, z) = x + y + z$. To compute $f(2, 5, 4)$ (that is $f(x, y, z)\ 2\ 5\ 4$) we first substitute 2 for x in f, that is we compute $f(x, y, z)\ 2$. This results in a function of two variables, namely $2 + y + z$. Next we substitute 5 for y to get a function of 1 variable, namely $7 + z$. Finally we substitute 4 for z in this function to get 7+4 =11.

In general, we can always turn a function of n arguments into a function of $n - 1$ arguments by applying a value for one of the arguments. This important technique is known as *currying*, and is used in function application in the λ-calculus.

Exercise 9.3 Suppose $f : \mathbb{R} \times \mathbb{R} \times \mathbb{R} \times \mathbb{R} \to \mathbb{R}$ is the function of four variables defined by the rule $f(x, y, z, w) = (x \times y) + (x \times z) + (y \times w)$. Use currying four times to compute $f(4, 1, 5, 2)$ (that is $(f(x, y, z, w))\ 4\ 1\ 5\ 2)$.

9.2.2 The λ-notation

The λ-notation is a first-order language in the sense of Chapter 7. First we define an infinite set of variable names $V = \{x, y, z, x_1, y_1, \ldots\}$ and a set C of built-in constants. We shall assume that C contains numerical constants $0, 1, 2, \ldots$, logical constants T, F and character constants 'a', 'b', 'c', ..., as well as the standard arithmetic and logical operation function names $+, \times, \ldots$ and $\wedge, \vee, \ldots$ respectively.

Definition 9.1 Atom Every member of V and C is called an atom.

We may now define the wffs of the language of the λ-calculus by using the inductive style of definition in Chapter 7. We shall denote by Λ the set of λ-expressions.

Definition 9.2 The set of λ-expressions Λ The set λ-expressions, denoted Λ, is defined inductively by:

Basis clause. Every atom is in Λ.

Inductive clause.

(a) If $E_1, E_2 \in \Lambda$ then $(E_1\ E_2) \in \Lambda$. This is called the *rule of application*. We say that E_1 is the *operator* and E_2 is the *operand* of that application.

(b) If $E \in \Lambda$ and $v \in V$ then $(\lambda v.\ E) \in \Lambda$. This is called the rule of *λ-abstraction*.

Extremal clause. An expression is not a λ-expression unless it can be shown to belong to Λ by applying the basis and inductive clauses a finite number of times.

The BNF notation can be used to summarize the syntax of λ-expressions:

<exp>	::=	<constant>	
	|	<variable>	
	|	(<exp> <exp>)	application
	|	(λ <variable>. <exp>)	λ-abstraction

Example 9.7 x, z_2, 3 and + are all examples of λ-expressions that are atoms.

Example 9.8 Since x and 2 are λ-expressions then, by the rule of application, so is $(x\ 2)$, and hence so is $((x\ 2)\ 2)$, and also $(x\ (2\ 2))$.

So that we do not have too many brackets in λ-expressions we establish a convention that application associates to the left. Thus $E_1\ E_2\ E_3 = (E_1\ E_2\ E_3) = ((E_1\ E_2)\ E_3)$ but the expression $(E_1\ (E_2\ E_3))$ is different; it may be simplified to $E_1\ (E_2\ E_3)$ but $E_1\ (E_2\ E_3) \neq E_1\ E_2\ E_3$.

Example 9.9 The expression $((+\ x)\ y)$ simplifies to $+\ x\ y$.

Example 9.10 The expression $((x\ (3\ (z\ 5)))\ 4)$ simplifies to $x\ (3\ (z\ 5))\ 4$ but cannot be simplified further without changing it to a different expression.

Exercise 9.4 Simplify the expression $(x\ (((3\ z)\ 5)\ 4))$.

We can use the rule of application to generate all the standard arithmetic and logical expressions, but in pre-fix, as opposed to the more conventional infix, notation. Thus, the λ-expression $+\ x\ y$ corresponds to the normal in-fix arithmetic expression $(x + y)$. In this chapter we will use infix notation where appropriate for λ-expressions.

Example 9.11 Since $+, -, \times, x$, and y are all λ-expressions, then by several applications we get the λ-expression $\times\ (+\ x\ y)\ (-\ x\ y)$ which, in infix notation, is $(x + y) \times (x - y)$.

Exercise 9.5 Show how the pre-fix form of the expression $x + (2 \times y)$ can be generated from the rule of application applied four times.

The expressive power of the λ-calculus comes from those λ-expressions generated using the rule of λ-application.

Example 9.12 $(\lambda x.\ 2)$, $(\lambda x.\ (x{+}3))$ and $(\lambda x.\ x)$ are λ-expressions. So is $(\lambda x.\ (\lambda y.\ (x+ y)))$ since we can apply λ-abstraction as many times as we like.

Again, we use the convention that λ-abstraction associates to the left. Thus $\lambda x.\lambda y.\ E = \lambda x.(\lambda y.\ E) = (\lambda x.(\lambda y.\ E))$.

Example 9.13 The expression $\lambda x.\lambda y.\ (x + y)\ 2$ is equal to $(\lambda x.(\lambda y.\ (x + y)\ 2))$. This is a different expression from $(\lambda x.\lambda y.\ (x + y))\ 2$.

The variable v of a λ-abstraction $\lambda v.\ E$ is called the formal parameter. We say that λ *binds* the formal parameter. The expression E is called the *body* of the λ-expression. This notion of binding is exactly analogous to the notion of binding of variables by the predicate calculus quantifiers as described in Chapter 5. Thus we also talk about free and bound variables in the same way.

Example 9.14 The variable x is bound and the variable y is free in $\lambda x.\ (x + y)$.

Informally, the purpose of a λ-abstraction $\lambda v.\ E$ is to make a function of one argument, whose name is v, from a λ-expression E. The meaning of the function is in the body. We shall make this formal in Sec. 9.2.3.

Example 9.15 The λ-expression $\lambda x.\ (x + 3)$ will be thought of as 'that function of x which adds x to 3'.

Example 9.16 $\lambda x.\ \lambda y.\ (x+y)$ is 'that function of x which is that function of y which adds x to y'. Thus, it is that function of x and y which adds x to y. The formal link here to function currying, as described in Sec. 9.2.1, will be made precise in Sec. 9.2.3.

Consider again the λ-expression $\lambda x.\ (x + 3)$. If this is to be regarded as that function of x which adds x to 3, then we would expect that if we changed the name of the variable consistently we would get the same function, so $\lambda x.\ (x+3) = \lambda y.\ (y+3)$. Also, we would expect that if we applied it to the number 5 we would get the number 8. Thus we would expect that $(\lambda x.\ (x + 3))\ 5 = 8$. In each of these cases we need some rules of conversion that enable us to simplify λ-expressions and tell us when certain λ-expressions are equivalent.

9.2.3 Conversion rules in the calculus

First we present the rule that tells us when we can rename variables and still derive an equivalent λ-expression:

Rule 9.1 α-conversion A bound variable in a λ-expression may be consistently renamed, so long as no free occurrence of a variable, within the body of the expression, becomes bound.

Example 9.17 The expression $\lambda x.\ (x + y)$ may be renamed as $\lambda z.\ (z + y)$ but not as $\lambda y.\ (y + y)$ since the free variable y in the original expression becomes bound by the λ-abstraction.

Example 9.18 The expression $\lambda x.\lambda y.\ (x + y)$ may be renamed as $\lambda u.\lambda v.\ (u + v)$ by two applications of α-conversion.

The next rule determines how functions may be applied to arguments to get simplified expressions:

Rule 9.2 β-conversion The λ-expression $(\lambda x.\ E)\ E'$ may be reduced by substituting E' for every occurrence of x in the body of E provided that E' contains no free occurrences of variables that are bound in E.

Example 9.19 $(\lambda x.\ (x + 5))\ 3$ may be reduced to $3 + 5 = 8$. However, $(\lambda f.\lambda x.\ f\ x)\ x$ cannot be reduced to $\lambda x.\ x\ x$. However, by α-conversion, $(\lambda f.\lambda x.\ f\ x)\ x = (\lambda f.\lambda y.\ f\ y)\ x$, which can be reduced to $\lambda y.\ x\ y$ by β-conversion.

Example 9.20 Consider the expression $\lambda x.\lambda y.\ (x + y)$ which we said is supposed to represent 'that function of x and y which adds x to y'. We want to be sure that if we 'apply' this function to the arguments 3 and 5 we end up with something equivalent to 3+5. Indeed, we find:

$$(\lambda x.\lambda y.\ (x + y))\ 3\ 5\ = ((\lambda x.(\lambda y.\ (x + y)))\ 3)\ 5\ = (\lambda y.\ (3 + y))\ 5\ = 3 + 5$$

Our two applications of β-conversion have used the technique of currying.

From Example 9.20 we deduce that, in general, if we have an expression of the form $(\lambda x_1.\lambda x_2 \cdots \lambda x_n.\ E)\ a_1\ a_2\ \cdots\ a_n$ then we perform function application by substituting first a_1 for x_1 in E, then a_2 for x_2, etc. Thus we substitute arguments one at a time, moving from left to right of both the variable list and the argument list.

Exercise 9.6 Reduce the λ-expression $(\lambda x.\lambda y.\lambda z.\ (x \times y) + (y \times z))\ 4\ 1\ 6$.

Example 9.21 It is possible that there can be a non-terminating evaluation sequence. Consider the expression $(\lambda x.\ x\ x)\ (\lambda x.\ x\ x)$. When we substitute $(\lambda x.\ x\ x)$ for x in this expression we end up with the same expression we started with.

In all of the examples so far there has been only one possible order in which we could apply β-conversion. This is not always the case.

Example 9.22 Consider the expression $(\lambda x.\lambda y.\ (x+y+(\lambda z.(z+1))\ 3))\ 2\ 5$. We could apply β-conversion twice from the left to get $2+5+(\lambda z.(z+1))\ 3$ and then with another application we get $2+5+(3+1)=11$. However, there is no reason why we should not have first applied β-conversion to the expression $(\lambda z.(z+1))\ 3$. Then we would get $(\lambda x.\lambda y.\ (x+y+4))\ 2\ 5$. Now applying β-conversion again yields $2+5+4=11$.

Example 9.22 illustrates two important points:

1 There may be a number of different ways in which we could reduce a λ-expression. It is common to perform reduction by always selecting the left-most *redex* (reducible expression), as in the first approach in Example 9.22. Such a reduction results in an expression that is said to be in *normal form*.

2 Even though there may be different ways to perform the reduction it is often the case that we arrive at the same irreducible result, in which case the normal form is invariant.

The following theorem ensures that the order of reduction is unimportant as long as the different reduction sequences terminate in irreducible expressions.

Theorem 9.1 Church–Rosser If two different terminating evaluation sequences for a λ-expression result in irreducible expressions, then the two irreducible expressions are equivalent up to renaming of variables.

Exercise 9.7 Reduce the following λ-expressions:

(a) $(\lambda x.\lambda y.\ x)\ a\ b$

(b) $(\lambda x.\lambda y.\ y)\ a\ b$

(c) $(\lambda x.\lambda y.\lambda z.\ y\ (x\ y\ z))(\lambda x.\lambda y.\ x\ y)$

(d) $(\lambda x.\lambda y.\ y)((\lambda x.\ x\ x)(\lambda x.\ x\ x))$

9.2.4 Defining functions in the λ-calculus

We can now show that the λ-calculus provides an effective means of defining functions in such a way that we get round the problems discussed in Sec. 9.1. Specifically we can use the λ-calculus to define, name and refer to functions.

Example 9.23 The function f of Example 9.1, defined by the rule $f(x) = x^2$, may be defined using the λ-notation as $\lambda x.\ (x \times x)$. By β-conversion, we can assert that $(\lambda x.\ (x \times x))\ 2 = 2 \times 2 = 4$, which tells us precisely that the result of applying this function to 2 is 4. Since λ-expressions can be applied to any other λ-expression we have no limitations on the domain of this function. Thus we can assert that $(\lambda x.\ (x \times x))\ \frac{1}{2} = \frac{1}{2} \times \frac{1}{2} = \frac{1}{4}$. Hence we have a notion of polymorphic typing here. The function domain is any algebra that has a binary operation called $\times$.

Exercise 9.8 Write down the λ-expression for the function whose rule is to subtract 1 from its argument.

Example 9.24 Consider the problems identified in Example 9.3 on page 228. We now note that $\lambda r.\lambda h.\ (\pi \times r \times r \times h)$ expresses the rule for computing volumes of cylinders where both r, h are allowed to vary. If h is fixed, then we can use a different λ-expression to characterize precisely the necessary function, namely $\lambda r.\ (\pi \times r \times r \times h)$.

Exercise 9.9 Explain why the λ-notation for the function that returns a constant, say 3, is $\lambda x.\ 3$.

Example 9.25 Consider the problem of the identity function in Example 9.5 on page 229. The λ-expression $\lambda x.\ x$ describes the required general purpose identity function. For any argument y it will return y. Thus $(\lambda x.\ x)\ 2 = 2$, $(\lambda x.\ x)\ \pi = \pi$ and even

$$(\lambda x.\ x)\begin{pmatrix} 2 & 3 \\ 1 & 5 \end{pmatrix} = \begin{pmatrix} 2 & 3 \\ 1 & 5 \end{pmatrix}$$

We can also have functions as arguments: $(\lambda x.\ x)\ \lambda y.\ (y + 1) = \lambda y.\ (y + 1)$. In this case the result of applying the identity function is a function. It is now easy to formalize the assertion 'the result of applying the identity function to itself is the identity function'. This is just the equivalence $(\lambda x.x)\lambda x.x = \lambda x.x$ which follows from β-conversion. The free use of self-application led to paradoxes, however, and the awareness of the need for sound mathematical foundations for the λ-calculus. The semantic problems of the self-application of functions have been solved by Scott's calculus of type definitions (1976) and by the construction of the typed version of the λ-calculus, described in detail in Barendregt (1981).

Example 9.26 In the λ-expression $(\lambda y.\ y\ 3)\ (\lambda x.\ (x + 1))$ the function $\lambda x.\ (x + 1)$ is an argument of $(\lambda y.\ y\ 3)$. Using β-conversion the expression evaluates to $(\lambda x.\ (x + 1))\ 3 = 3 + 1 = 4$.

The fact that arguments of λ-expressions can themselves be functions gives us a convenient notation for describing new functions that are constructed from old ones.

Example 9.27 Let us define *plustwo* as $\lambda x.\ (x+2)$ and *plusthree* as $\lambda x.\ (x+3)$. Then

$$\textit{plusthree plustwo} = (\lambda x.\ (x + 3))\ \lambda x.\ (x + 2) = \lambda x.\ ((x + 2) + 3)$$

It follows that *plusthree plustwo* is the function that first adds 2 and then 3 to each argument, so that, for example, $(\textit{plusthree plustwo})\ 6 = (\lambda x.\ ((x + 2) + 3))\ 6 = (6 + 2) + 3 = 11$.

More significantly we can now describe conveniently higher order functions.

Example 9.28 The higher order function *square* of Example 9.4 may be defined as $\textit{square} = \lambda f.\lambda x.\ ((f\ x) \times (f\ x))$. If we want to define the function that is the square of the function *plusthree* we have: $\textit{square plusthree} = \lambda x.\ ((\textit{plusthree}\ x) \times (\textit{plusthree}\ x))$. To confirm that, when we apply this function to the number 5 we get the expected result 64:

$$\begin{aligned}(\lambda x.\ ((\textit{plusthree}\ x) \times (\textit{plusthree}\ x)))\ 5 &= (\textit{plusthree}\ 5) \times (\textit{plusthree}\ 5)\\ &= ((\lambda x.\ x + 3)\ 5)) \times ((\lambda x.\ x + 3)\ 5))\\ &= (5 + 3) \times (5 + 3) = 64\end{aligned}$$

Exercise 9.10 Use *square* to define the function that is the square of the function *plustwo*. Confirm that $\textit{square plustwo}\ 3 = 25$.

Example 9.29 We noted in Sec. 2.3 that the operation of function composition is a higher order function. In fact it is the λ-expression: $\lambda f.\lambda g.\lambda x.\ f\ (g\ x)$.

Exercise 9.11 Write down the λ-expression corresponding to the higher order function *multiply* of Exercise 9.1.

Example 9.30 In Sec. 2.3 we introduced a notation for expressing functions in conditional form. We can view this as the higher order function $\lambda p.\lambda f.\lambda g.\ (p \rightarrow f,\ g)$. This reads as 'that function of p, f and g such that if p is true then f else g'. As a specific example, we could define the function *absolute-value* as $\lambda x.\ (x \geq 0 \rightarrow x,\ -x)$.

Example 9.31 The function to compute the maximum of two numbers may be defined as $max_2 = \lambda x.\lambda y.(\ x \geq y \rightarrow x,\ y)$. We use this to define a function max_3, which computes the maximum of three numbers: $max_3 = \lambda x.\lambda y.\lambda z\ (x \geq (max_2)\ y\ z \rightarrow x,\ (max_2)\ y\ z)$.

Exercise 9.12 Define a function max_4, which computes the maximum of four numbers, in terms of max_3.

We can define arbitrarily complex functions in the λ-calculus by defining functions in terms of previously defined functions and by using functions as arguments of functions. In fact, as we shall see in Chapter 15, for every program that can be written in a language like Pascal, there is a λ-calculus expression that performs the same computation. Thus, in theory we could just as well define programs to be λ-calculus expressions, without altering our view of what problems could be solved by computers. In principle, a functional programming language is an implementation of the λ-calculus.

Example 9.32 To write a program that computes the square of an arbitrary number requires an implementation of the function $\lambda x.\ (x \times x)$. In the functional programming language LISP, this function is implemented as the statement `lambda x. x * x`. We can then name this function by writing `def f = lambda x. x * x`. Writing the statement `f 3` would produce the output 9. If we now write `def g = lambda x. ((f x) + 1)` then the statement `g 3` will produce the output 10, since this statement is implemented as the λ-expression $g\ 3 = (\lambda x.\ ((f\ x) + 1))3 = (f\ 3) + 1 = ((\lambda x.\ (x \times x))\ 3) + 1 = (3 \times 3) + 1 = 10$.

Example 9.33 A function f in conditional form $(p \rightarrow f_1, f_2)$ would be implemented in LISP as `def f = if p then f1 else f2`.

9.2.5 Partial functions

Suppose that $f : A \nrightarrow B$ is a partial function. Then we know that $f\ a$ may be undefined for some values $a \in A$. We saw in Sec. 2.3 that f can be made total by either:

(a) restricting the domain of f to that subset of A on which f is defined or

(b) extending the codomain B by adding an element $\perp$ called *undefined* (or *bottom*) and defining $f\ a = \perp$ for each $a \in A$ where a is undefined.

The problem with the first alternative is that we do not always know in advance which elements are undefined for f. This makes the second approach more attractive. However, it is also not a complete solution. For our extended notion of function we have to consider the possibility that an argument to the function may itself be an undefined object. In practical computing this is a very real problem since, for example, we cannot always guarantee that inputs to a function are within a specified domain. We would like to know how to respond to undefined inputs.

Example 9.34 Consider the function *reciprocal* defined by the rule that it returns $1/x$ for each number x. We know that this function is undefined for $x = 0$, and using the approach (b) above we might write $reciprocal = \lambda x.\ (x = 0 \rightarrow \perp,\ 1/x)$. What happens if the input argument is itself undefined? Then $reciprocal(\perp) = 1/\perp$, which does not make sense. Assuming that an undefined input should yield the value undefined, we see that we should have defined *reciprocal* as $\lambda x.(x = 0, \perp \rightarrow \perp,\ 1/x)$. This means that if x is either 0 or $\perp$ then the function returns the value $\perp$, otherwise it returns $1/x$.

In Example 9.34 we extended *both* the normal domain and codomain sets by adding the element $\perp$. Unfortunately it is not always obvious whether or not a function should yield an undefined value or not.

Example 9.35 Consider the function $f = \lambda x.\lambda y.\ (x = 0 \rightarrow 0,\ y)$. What is the value of $f\ 0\ h(0)$ where h is a partial function that is undefined for 0? Should the answer be 0 or undefined. It is not clear.

It is not good enough to abstain from a decision in cases like Example 9.35. In computing we are inevitably confronted with partial functions. We need to be able to return an unambiguous value for all arguments whether or not these are defined. We need a theory of partial functions to enable us to do this. Before describing what this theory is, we shall describe the other type of problem that we wish to solve, namely the problem of knowing which recursive functions are uniquely defined. This is also tackled using the theory of partial functions.

9.2.6 Defining recursive functions

The λ-calculus provides an elegant means of defining recursive functions which, as we saw in Sec. 2.3, are functions that are defined in terms of themselves.

Example 9.36 We could define multiplication of natural numbers recursively by the function $mult = \lambda x.\lambda y.(y = 0 \rightarrow 0,\ x + mult\ x\ (y - 1))$. Using this to compute $mult\ 5\ 3$ we get:

$$mult\ 5\ 3 = 5 + mult\ 5\ 2 = 5 + 5 + mult\ 5\ 1 = 5 + 5 + 5 + mult\ 5\ 0 = 5 + 5 + 5 + 0 = 15$$

This example is typical of recursively defined functions. The function is actually defined in terms of itself *and* a simpler function (in this case addition). The recursion must eventually terminate because, after a finite number of steps, $y = 0$.

Exercise 9.13 Assuming that we can add and subtract the number 1 from any natural number, write down a recursive definition of the function of addition of natural numbers.

Example 9.37 The factorial function for natural numbers may be defined recursively (using the multiplication function $\times$) as

$$factorial = \lambda n.(n = 0 \rightarrow 1,\ n \times factorial\ (n - 1))$$

It is crucial to note that the recursive functions *mult* and *factorial* each have the form $f = F\ f$ where F is some λ-expression:

Example 9.38 The factorial function has the form *factorial* = *F factorial* where

$$F = \lambda g.\lambda n.(n = 0 \rightarrow 1,\ n \times g\ (n-1))$$

Exercise 9.14 Write down the λ-expression F for which $mult = F\ mult$.

Given a recursive function defined in terms of an equation $f = F\ f$, our problem is to find a specific f that satisfies the equation. Such a solution is called a *fixed point* of the equation. We have already seen examples of fixed point solutions to equations in Chapters 7 and 8. A special λ-calculus expression, which we have not mentioned so far, is the symbol Y which represents the fixed point solution to a λ-expression F. We write $Y\ F$ to denote the fixed point of F. Thus in the case of *factorial* we can *define* this function in the λ-calculus as $factorial = Y\ \lambda g.\lambda n.\ (n = 0 \rightarrow 1,\ n \times g\ (n-1))$. Note that Y is a higher order function. Its argument is a function and the value it returns is a function.

Example 9.39 In the functional programming language LISP, the fixed point combinator Y is implemented as 'label'. To define the function f as the fixed point of F where F is some λ-calculus expression we write `def f = label F`.

When we considered examples of recursive equations in Chapters 7 and 8, we made the assumption that a fixed point solution must exist and that it was unique. Unfortunately, this is not always true. If, for example, we removed the terminating clause for $y = 0$ in our definition of multiplication, then the resulting equation has no solution. Even for the factorial example, the equation only has a solution over the domain $\mathbb{N}$. The next example shows that, where a fixed point solution does exist, there may be many different such solutions.

Example 9.40 Consider the recursively defined function $f = \lambda x.\ (x = 0 \rightarrow 1,\ f\ (x+1))$. In this case $f = F\ f$ where $F = \lambda g.\lambda x.\ (x = 0 \rightarrow 1,\ g\ (x+1))$. There are an infinite number of f's which are fixed points of F. For each n, consider the function $f_n = \lambda x.(x = 0 \rightarrow 1, n)$. It is easy to see that $f_n = F\ f_n$. The function $\lambda x.(x = 0 \rightarrow 1, \perp)$ is also a fixed point of F.

An elegant and powerful theory of fixed points, which includes a theory of partial functions, tells us when and how we can resolve these problems.

9.3 THE THEORY OF FIXED POINTS

We motivate the account of fixed point theory by using the simple example of the factorial function. We normally think of this as a (total) function $factorial : \mathbb{N} \rightarrow \mathbb{N}$. If we wanted to implement this function on a computer we know that memory limitations force us to restrict its domain. For example, we might only be able to compute the function for numbers that are less than 50. What we then have is not the factorial function but a partial function on the set $\mathbb{N}$ which is a crude approximation of it. We want to be able to construct the best possible approximation.

To formalize these ideas we first extend the set $\mathbb{N}$ by adding the undefined element $\perp$. We write $\mathbb{N}^{\perp} = \mathbb{N} \cup \{\perp\}$. We now have to think in terms of functions $f : \mathbb{N}^{\perp} \rightarrow \mathbb{N}^{\perp}$. First, it seems reasonable always to define $f(\perp) = \perp$; an undefined input has the value undefined. Now consider the sequence of functions $f^k : \mathbb{N}^{\perp} \rightarrow \mathbb{N}^{\perp}$ given by

$$f^k = \lambda n.\ (n = \perp \rightarrow \perp,\ n < k \rightarrow n!,\ \perp)$$

Table 9.1 Factorial function—increasingly accurate approximations

	0	1	2	3	4	5	6	7	...
f^0	$\perp$	$\perp$	$\perp$	$\perp$	$\perp$	$\perp$	$\perp$	$\perp$	...
f^1	1	$\perp$	$\perp$	$\perp$	$\perp$	$\perp$	$\perp$	$\perp$	...
f^2	1	1	$\perp$	$\perp$	$\perp$	$\perp$	$\perp$	$\perp$	...
f^3	1	1	2	$\perp$	$\perp$	$\perp$	$\perp$	$\perp$	...
f^4	1	1	2	6	$\perp$	$\perp$	$\perp$	$\perp$	...
f^5	1	1	2	6	24	$\perp$	$\perp$	$\perp$	...
f^6	1	1	2	6	24	120	$\perp$	$\perp$	...
f^7	1	1	2	6	24	120	840	$\perp$	...
...	...	...	...	...	...	...	...	...	

Table 9.1 shows what this sequence of functions looks like. Essentially f^k is the same as the factorial function for all inputs $< k$, but is otherwise undefined. The functions f^k are increasingly accurate approximations to the factorial function. Thus, intuitively it seems reasonable to conclude that *factorial* $= \lim_{k\to\infty} f^k$ and that this limit is unique. Before we give the formal justification for this we make one more important observation which should make the theory easier to follow.

In our definitions of the functions f^k we actually used the expression $n!$ which is a shorthand notation for precisely the function we are trying to define. Although this was an easy way of describing the required sequence of functions, we clearly cannot do this if we are trying to construct the factorial function from scratch. In fact, we can *construct* the sequence f^k by just using the λ-expression F in the recursive equation $f = F\ f$ for *factorial*, namely $F = \lambda g.\lambda n.\ (n = 0 \to 1,\ n \times g\ (n-1))$. What we do is first define the function $f^0 = \lambda x.\ \perp$. This is the constant function which returns $\perp$ for each argument $x \in \mathbb{N}^{\perp}$. So f^0 is everywhere undefined. Inductively, we now define

$$f^k = F\ f^{k-1} \text{ for each } k > 0$$

Thus, for example, let us see how this tells us what the function f^1 is. We know that $f^1 = F\ f^0$. Now for each x we can compute $f^1\ x = (F\ f^0)\ x$ using normal form β-conversion:

$$\begin{aligned} f^1\ 0 = (F\ f^0)\ 0 &= (\lambda g.\lambda n.(n = 0 \to 1,\ (n \times (g\ (n-1))\ f^0)))\ 0 \\ &= \lambda n.(n = 0 \to 1,\ (0 \times f^0\ (n-1)))\ 0 \\ &= (0 = 0 \to 1,\ 0 \times f^0(-1)) \\ &= 1 \end{aligned}$$

Similarly (but skipping some of the β-reductions):

$$\begin{aligned} &f^1\ 1 = (F\ f^0)\ 1 = \lambda n.(n = 0 \to 1,\ 1 \times (f^0\ 0))\ 1 = \perp \\ &f^1\ 2 = (F\ f^0)\ 2 = \lambda n.(n = 0 \to 1,\ 1 \times (f^0\ 0))\ 2 = \perp \\ &\ldots \end{aligned}$$

Thus we get the function f^1 defined in the second row of Table 9.1. Hence, next we can compute f^2:

$$\begin{aligned} &f^2\ 0 = (F\ f^1)\ 0 = \lambda n.(n = 0 \to 1,\ 0 \times (f^1\ -1))\ 0 = 1 \\ &f^2\ 1 = (F\ f^1)\ 1 = \lambda n.(n = 0 \to 1,\ 1 \times (f^1\ 0))\ 1 = 1 \\ &f^2\ 1 = (F\ f^1)\ 2 = \lambda n.(n = 0 \to 1,\ 1 \times (f^1\ 0))\ 2 = \perp \\ &\ldots \end{aligned}$$

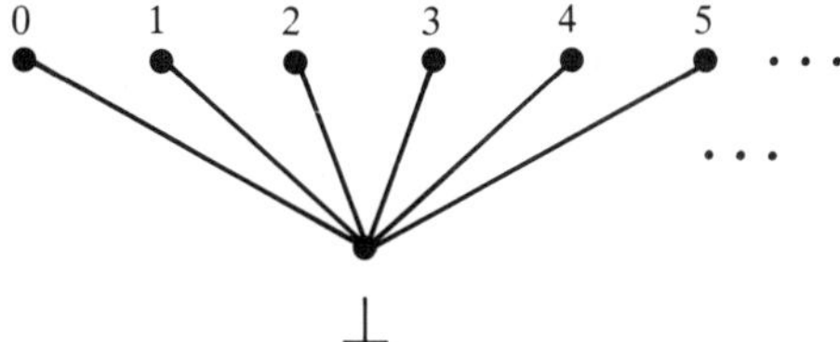

Figure 9.1 Order relation $\sqsubseteq$.

Thus we get the function f^2 defined in the third row of Table 9.1, etc.

In summary: we started with a recursive definition of a function f; we showed that this could be written as an equation of the form $f = F\ f$ where F is a λ-expression; by adding a new element $\perp$ to make all functions total, we have been able to construct from F (using β-conversion) a sequence of functions f^k that are increasingly accurate approximations of f. This sequence has a limit which is the unique fixed point of the equation $f = F\ f$.

We found a fixed point for the factorial function. That is a particularly simple function with only one argument, however. The question is whether the same approach will apply to other recursive functions. The answer is that it does apply to a very large class of functions, and the theory of fixed points tells us just what conditions have to hold. However, first we need to introduce the notion of a domain as a set to which some structure has been added.

9.3.1 Domain theory

We have already used the word domain in the context of the definition of a function. It is unfortunate that this word is also used to describe a different concept, namely a set with certain special properties. To distinguish the separate notions we shall write Domain (with a capital D) for this new concept. In the following definition, we use the notion of an order relation as defined in Sec. 2.2.

Definition 9.3 Domain Let D be a set with an order relation $\sqsubseteq$ satisfying the following three properties:

(a) $(D, \sqsubseteq)$ is a poset, as defined in Sec. 2.2.

(b) $(D, \sqsubseteq)$ contains a least element with respect to $\sqsubseteq$.

(c) Each chain in D has a least upper bound. This means that for any sequence $x_0 \sqsubseteq x_1 \sqsubseteq x_2 \sqsubseteq \cdots$ there is an $x \in D$ such that $x_n \sqsubseteq x$ for each n and if $x_n \sqsubseteq y$ for each n then $x \sqsubseteq y$. The least upper bound x is written as

$$\lim_{n\to\infty} x_n \text{ or } \bigsqcup_{n=0}^{\infty} x_n$$

Then D is called a Domain with respect to $\sqsubseteq$.

Example 9.41 If we take any set S and define $S^\perp = S \cup \{\perp\}$ then we can define an order relation $\sqsubseteq$ over $S^\perp$ by $x \sqsubseteq y$ if and only if $x = \perp$ or $y = x$. Thus, for each $x \in S^\perp$, $\perp \sqsubseteq x$ and $x \sqsubseteq x$. There are no other pairs in the order relation. Figure 9.1 is the Hasse diagram for this ordering on $\mathbb{N}^\perp$. It is easy to see that the

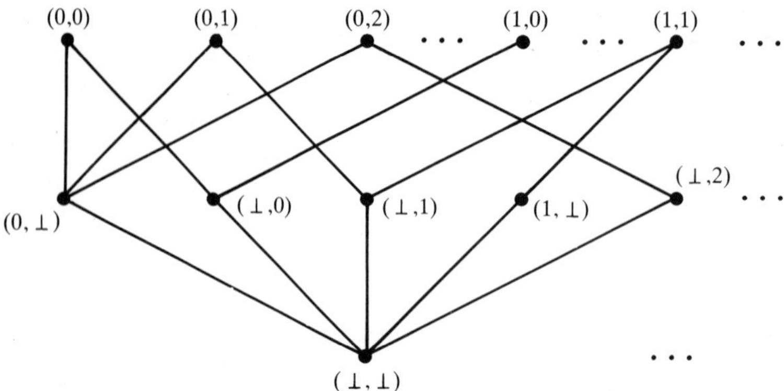

Figure 9.2 Order relation $\sqsubseteq_D$.

pair $(S^\perp, \sqsubseteq)$ satisfies the three properties of Def. 9.3. Property (a) follows from the way we have defined $\sqsubseteq$ and property (b) holds because $\perp$ is the least element. To see that property (c) holds we just note that the only chains possible are those of the form: $\perp \sqsubseteq \perp \cdots \sqsubseteq \perp \sqsubseteq x \sqsubseteq x \cdots$ where $x \in S^\perp$. In each case the least upper bound is x. It should now be clear that when we added the element $\perp$ to the set $\mathbb{N}$ on page 237 to form $\mathbb{N}^\perp$ we created a Domain with the ordering $\sqsubseteq$ given here.

Example 9.42 Consider the set $D = \mathbb{N}^\perp \times \mathbb{N}^\perp$. Let us define a relation $\sqsubseteq_D$ on D by $(x, y) \sqsubseteq_D (x', y')$ if and only if $x \sqsubseteq x'$ and $y \sqsubseteq y'$. The Hasse diagram for $\sqsubseteq_D$ is shown in Fig. 9.2. Thus, for example, $(\perp, \perp) \sqsubseteq_D (\perp, 3) \sqsubseteq_D (6, 3) \sqsubseteq_D (6, 3)$ is a chain with least upper bound $(6, 3)$. It is easy to see that $(D, \sqsubseteq_D)$ is a Domain whose least element is $(\perp, \perp)$.

For the factorial function we started with a function $\mathbb{N} \to \mathbb{N}$ and then had to consider approximation functions over the Domains $\mathbb{N}^\perp \to \mathbb{N}^\perp$. Now suppose $f : \mathbb{N} \times \mathbb{N} :\to \mathbb{N}$ is a function of two arguments. Then we can extend the set $\mathbb{N} \times \mathbb{N}$ to a Domain by *defining* $(\mathbb{N} \times \mathbb{N})^\perp$ to be the Domain $(\mathbb{N}^\perp \times \mathbb{N}^\perp, \sqsubseteq_D)$ of Example 9.42. This approach to defining direct product Domains extends to arbitrary numbers of arbitrary sets.

We need to construct another special class of Domains. Consider the functions f^k defined in Table 9.1. Each of these is a function from $\mathbb{N}^\perp$ to $\mathbb{N}^\perp$. It is not difficult to see that each of these functions has the property that, for each $x, y \in \mathbb{N}^\perp$, $x \sqsubseteq y$ implies $f^k\ x \sqsubseteq f^k\ y$. Any function from one Domain into another Domain that has this property is called *monotonic*. Monotonic functions conform to a natural computability requirement: the more an argument is defined, the more defined is the value.

In general, the set of all monotonic functions $f : D_1 \to D_2$, where D_1, D_2 are fixed Domains, is itself a Domain. The order relation required is a formalization of the notion of approximation that we have already seen above. Specifically, the relation $\sqsubseteq$ is defined by

$$f \sqsubseteq f' \text{ if, for each } x \in D_1,\ f\ x \sqsubseteq f'\ x$$

If $f \sqsubseteq f'$ we say that f approximates to f', f is weaker than f' or f' is stronger than f. It follows that with f^k defined as in Table 9.1, $f^0 \sqsubseteq f^1 \sqsubseteq f^2 \sqsubseteq \cdots$.

	$\perp$	0	1
f_0	$\perp$	$\perp$	$\perp$
f_1	$\perp$	$\perp$	0
f_2	$\perp$	$\perp$	1
f_3	$\perp$	0	$\perp$
f_4	$\perp$	0	0
f_5	$\perp$	0	1
f_6	$\perp$	1	$\perp$
f_7	$\perp$	1	0
f_8	$\perp$	1	1
f_9	0	0	0
f_{10}	1	1	1

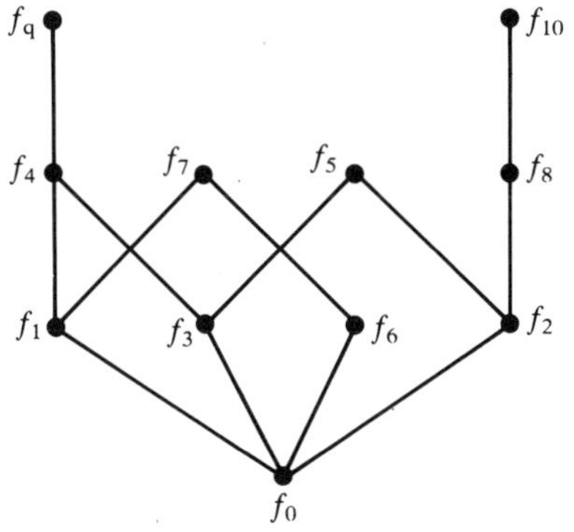

Figure 9.3 A function Domain.

Example 9.43 The set of all monotonic functions from $\mathbb{N}^\perp$ to $\mathbb{N}^\perp$ is a Domain. The least element of this Domain is the function that is everywhere undefined; this is the function f^0 of Table 9.1.

Example 9.44 If $D = \{0, 1\}$ then the set $D^\perp \to D^\perp$ is a Domain consisting of 11 monotonic functions as shown in Fig. 9.3.

We just need one final definition. Look at the functions f^k defined on $\mathbb{N}^\perp$. We noted that the only non-trivial chains in $\mathbb{N}^\perp$ have the form $\perp \sqsubseteq \cdots \sqsubseteq \perp \sqsubseteq n \sqsubseteq n \cdots$ where $n \in \mathbb{N}$. For example, $\perp \sqsubseteq 3 \sqsubseteq 3$ is one such chain. The least upper bound of this chain is 3. Let us apply any of the functions f^i, for example f^5, to each element of the chain. Then we get the chain $(f^5\ \perp) \sqsubseteq (f^5\ 3) \sqsubseteq (f^5\ 3)$, which is the same as the chain $\perp \sqsubseteq 6 \sqsubseteq 6$ and which has least upper bound 6. Since $f^5\ 3 = 6$ it is easy to extrapolate from this example that $f^5(\lim x_n) = \lim(f^5\ x_n)$ for every chain $x_0 \sqsubseteq x_1 \sqsubseteq \cdots$. Any monotonic function that has this property is called *continuous*.

Exercise 9.15 Provide a general definition of a continuous function $f : D_1 \to D_2$ (where D_1 and D_2 are Domains) based on the above informal description.

Exercise 9.16 Show that the function f^6 of Table 9.1 is continuous.

9.3.2 Fixed point theorem

Now consider the Domain in Example 9.43 above and recall our recursive definition of *factorial* on page 237. The λ-expression F is actually a function whose arguments are elements from this particular Domain; they are functions like f^k. It is thus perfectly reasonable to ask whether F is a continuous function over this Domain. It can be shown that it is. With this in mind we can now state Kleene's fixed point theorem which tells us precisely when we have a fixed point and how we can construct it.

Theorem 9.2 Kleene Suppose D is a Domain and $F : D \to D$ is a continuous function. Then F possesses a fixed point x (a solution to $x = F\ x$) given by

$$x = \lim_{n \to \infty} (F^n\ \perp)$$

where $\perp$ is the least element of D. Moreover, x is the least fixed point of F under the partial ordering.

Before proving the theorem let us see what it means for our factorial example. We have already noted that the λ-expression $F = \lambda g.\lambda n.\ (n = 0 \rightarrow 1,\ (n \times g\ (n - 1))$ may be viewed as a continuous function over the Domain of Example 9.43. This Domain has least element f^0. Thus F possesses a solution f to the equation $f = F\ f$, namely

$$f = \lim_{k\rightarrow\infty} (F^k\ f^0)$$

However, we have already seen that $F^k\ f^0 = f^k$ where the f^k are as defined in Table 9.1. It thus follows that $f = \lim_{k\rightarrow\infty} f^k$ is the factorial function that we were seeking to define. Being the *least* fixed point of F it follows from our definition of Domain that this solution is also unique.

PROOF OF THEOREM 9.2* We have to prove that:

(a) $x = \lim_{n\rightarrow\infty}(F^n\ \perp)$ is a well-defined element of D,

(b) $x = F\ x$,

(c) x is the *least* element of D satisfying the equation $x = F\ x$.

To prove (a) we note that, since F is continuous and hence monotonic, it follows that

$$\perp \sqsubseteq (F\ \perp) \sqsubseteq (F^2\ \perp) \sqsubseteq \cdots$$

is a chain in D. Hence its least upper bound, namely $x = \lim_{n\rightarrow\infty}(F^n\ \perp)$, is itself an element in D (this is from Def. 9.3).

To prove (b) we again use the continuity property of F to note that

$$F\ x = F(\lim_{n\rightarrow\infty} (F^n\ \perp)) = \lim_{n\rightarrow\infty} F\ (F^n\ \perp) = \lim_{n\rightarrow\infty} (F^{n+1}\ \perp) = \lim_{n\rightarrow\infty} (F^n\ \perp) = x$$

Finally, to prove (c), suppose that y is any other fixed point of F, so $y = F\ y$. Then we have to show $x \sqsubseteq y$. Since $x = \lim_{n\rightarrow\infty}(F^n\ \perp)$, it suffices to show that $(F^n\ \perp) \sqsubseteq y$ for each n. We can show this by induction on n. For $n = 0$ we have

$$(F^0\ \perp) \sqsubseteq \perp \sqsubseteq y \text{ since } \perp \text{ is least element of } D$$

Therefore, assume $(F^n\ \perp) \sqsubseteq y$. However, then by monotinicity of F:

$$(F^{n+1}\ \perp) = F\ (F^n\ \perp) \sqsubseteq F\ y = y$$

which completes the proof.

In summary, a recursively defined function may be thought of as the solution to an equation of the form $x = F\ x$, where F is a λ-expression. The fixed point theorem tells us when recursive functions are uniquely defined by specifying the properties that F must satisfy and shows us how to construct them when they are. Given the importance of recursion in computing, this result has great significance. Next, we shall use it to construct recursive *processes* rather than functions.

9.4 AN APPLICATION: DEFINING PROCESSES

In this section we describe an important application of the ideas presented in this chapter. We are concerned with the behaviour of systems that are made up of interacting subsystems. We begin by introducing the notion of process algebras for describing these systems, and then present a typical process algebra approach. Systems are identified as processes, and we describe some simple examples. Like functions, more complex processes can be defined recursively; it turns out that exactly the same theories we have seen so far, namely the λ-calculus, partial functions, Domains and fixed points, may be used to define and construct such processes. Finally, we show that processes may also be regarded as functions. As such, we show how we are able to implement them in a functional programming language.

9.4.1 Process algebras for specifying systems

A feature of any interesting system is the nature of its continual interaction with its environment. Most interesting systems may be decomposed into subsystems which must interact and communicate with each other as well as their common environment. Some subsystems must operate concurrently. A feature of most complex systems, for example a computer operating system, is the complexity of these interactions.

Defining and constructing such complex systems in such a way that we can reason formally about their behaviour is one of the most challenging tasks confronting modern systems engineers. Methods that seem to work well for simple sequential systems are inadequate when applied to systems with complex interactions between subsystems. Consequently, much recent effort has been devoted to notations and methods that deal with the special problems of communication and concurrency. Examples are Petri nets (which we shall describe in Chapter 13), CSP as described in Hoare (1985) and CCS as described in Milner (1980). The salient feature of approaches like the latter two is that systems are viewed as processes for which there are a number of operations for building new processes. For example, there are operations for concurrent execution of two processes and for various types of communication between two processes. Complex processes are constructed from simpler ones via the various operations. In the light of Chapter 8, it is clear that these approaches are concerned with the definition of particular algebras called *process algebras*.

The nature of the specific operations and their semantics often differ considerably between the various process algebra approaches. However, we can present a generic introduction to this work, using mainly the notation of CSP. Our primary objective is to show that, when it comes to the crucial definition of infinite processes, the theory of fixed points enables us to determine when these really exist and are unique.

9.4.2 Systems, processes and behaviours

Informally, associated with any system is a *process* that is the behaviour exhibited by the system. This process characterizes the system.

Example 9.45 Our system might be an anti-ballistic missile. The observed behaviour of this system up to any period of time may be any one of the four strings of events:

Λ, fire, fire hit, fire miss

The empty string, Λ, is included because initially no events have been observed.

Example 9.46 A slightly more complex example is a drinks machine DM_2 (labelled as such for reasons that will become clear later) which delivers a cup of tea or coffee upon insertion of a coin. This machine has the capacity to deliver two drinks. We may think of DM_2 as a process consisting of the set of possible strings:

Λ, coin, coin tea, coin coffee, coin tea coin, coin coffee coin, coin tea coin tea, coin tea coin coffee, coin coffee coin tea, coin coffee coin coffee

We can use the notation of Chapter 7 to formalize the ideas introduced in the examples. We start with an alphabet A of events, which represent the primitive actions. For example, in the case of missiles we might take $A = \{\text{fire, hit, miss}\}$ and in the case of drinks machines we might take $A = \{\text{coin, tea, coffee}\}$. A process P (over A) is simply a language over A, that is a set of strings. This corresponds to the set of strings of events in which P can participate if required. Normally this set of strings is called the *traces of P* and is written as *traces(P)*.

Example 9.47 Consider a clock that ticks up to three times before stopping. We can think of this as a process P over the alphabet $A = \{\text{tick}\}$ for which

$$\text{traces}(P) = \{\Lambda, \text{ tick, tick tick, tick tick tick}\} = (\text{tick})^*_3$$

where, using the notation of Chapter 7, E^*_n is the regular expression denoting the set of strings limited to a length of n instances of E. By convention we always include the empty string Λ as a trace of any process.

Example 9.48 Consider a deterministic drinks machine that can only deliver a cup of tea upon insertion of a coin, but has the capacity to deliver 25 cups. We can think of this as a process P over the alphabet $A = \{\text{coin, tea}\}$. We can use the notation of regular expressions to define the set of traces of P as $\text{traces}(P) = (\text{coin tea})^*_{25} + \text{coin}(\text{tea coin})^*_{25}$.

Exercise 9.17 Write down the set of traces for the process of a drinks machine that requires two coins before delivering a cup of coffee. You should assume that the machine has a capacity of 40 cups.

Example 9.49 We can construct a sequence of clocks, each of which is 'better' than the previous one. As above, think of the clocks as processes that can tick up to a certain number of times. Specifically $clock_n$ ticks up to n times. Thus

$$\begin{aligned}
&\text{traces}(clock)_0 = \{\Lambda\}\\
&\text{traces}(clock)_1 = \{\Lambda, \text{ tick}\}\\
&\text{traces}(clock)_2 = \{\Lambda, \text{ tick, tick tick}\}\\
&\ldots\\
&\text{traces}(clock)_n = \{\Lambda, \text{ tick, tick tick}, \ldots, \text{tick tick} \ldots \text{tick}\} = (\text{tick})^*_n\\
&\ldots
\end{aligned}$$

9.4.3 Recursively defined processes

Example 9.49 is particularly important for illustrating the application of fixed point theory to the definition and construction of processes. Up to now all the processes we have seen have been finite. What happens if we want to consider a drinks machine that never breaks down and is continually refilled? Or a perpetual clock which never stops ticking? Are such processes well defined? It turns out that the fixed point theorem answers this affirmatively.

Suppose *clock* is our perpetual clock. Then we can think of each of the processes $clock_n$ as being an approximation of *clock*. As n increases, this sequence of finite approximations becomes increasingly 'accurate'. This is analogous to the sequence of finite functions which we saw were increasingly accurate approximations of the factorial function. In exactly the same way, we want to be able to say that *clock* is the limit as $n \to \infty$ of the sequence $clock_n$. In fact, to apply the theory of fixed points, we want to show that *clock* is the solution to some recursive equation.

First we need to consider a simple operation for constructing new processes from old ones. Given a process P and an event a from the same alphabet, we can define a new process $a \to P$ as that process which first engages in the event a and then behaves exactly like P. This operation is referred to as the *prefix* operation. Using the notation for regular expressions defined in Chapter 7, we note that traces$(a \to P) = \Lambda + a$ traces(P).

Exercise 9.18 Explain why the prefix operation can be viewed as the function $\lambda P.\lambda a.\ (a \to P)$.

Example 9.50 $clock_4 = \text{tick} \to clock_3$

Example 9.51 Consider the drinks machine of Example 9.48 that is represented by the process P. Suppose we develop a modified machine represented by the process P' which, as a test, initially delivers a cup of tea without insertion of a coin. Then $P' = \text{tea} \to P$.

Returning to our perpetual clock, intuitively we feel that this may somehow be defined recursively as $clock = \text{tick} \to clock$. What does this mean? For a given a the prefix operation defined on processes can be expressed as the function

$$F_a = \lambda P.\ (a \to P)$$

In particular, for the function $F = F_{\text{tick}}$, we can ask whether there is a fixed point; that is can we solve the recursive equation $X = F\ X$ for X? Any such solution would then satisfy $X = \text{tick} \to X$.

The intuitive definition of *clock* amounts to the assertion that *clock* is the solution to the recursive equation $X = F\ X$. If we are to apply Theorem 9.2 to show that such a solution really exists, that it is equal to *clock* and that it is the limit of the sequence $clock_n$, then we need to show that the set of processes is a Domain. Therefore let $\mathscr{P}$ be the set of processes with alphabet A. We can define a partial order $\sqsubseteq$ over $\mathscr{P}$ by $P \sqsubseteq Q$ iff traces$(P) \subseteq$ traces(Q). For example, $clock_0 \sqsubseteq clock_1 \sqsubseteq clock_2 \sqsubseteq \cdots$. The set $\mathscr{P}$ contains a special process called *stop* which can never engage in any event, so traces$(stop) = \Lambda$ (note that in our example $clock_0 = stop$). Clearly *stop* is a least element of $\mathscr{P}$ with respect to $\sqsubseteq$. Thus to show that $(\mathscr{P}, \sqsubseteq)$ is a Domain we only have to show that each chain $P_1 \sqsubseteq P_2 \sqsubseteq P_3 \sqsubseteq \cdots$ in $\mathscr{P}$ has a least upper bound (denoted, as usual, by $\lim_{n\to\infty} P_n$) which is in $\mathscr{P}$. This is the case, for we just consider the process $\lim_{n\to\infty} P_n$ as that process $P \in \mathscr{P}$ for which

$$\text{traces}(P) = \bigcup_{n\geq 0} \text{traces}(P_n)$$

Exercise 9.19 For the function $F_a = \lambda P.\ (a \to P)$, show that

$$F_a\ (\lim_{n\to\infty} P_n) = \lim_{n\to\infty} (F_a\ P_n)$$

and hence deduce that F_a is a continuous function.

Now let F be any continuous function over $\mathscr{P}$. Then Theorem 9.2 tells us that the equation $X = F\ X$ has a unique solution, which is precisely the process

$$X = \lim_{n\to\infty} (F^n\ stop) \tag{9.1}$$

We can apply this in the case of our perpetual clock. We were looking for a solution to $X = F\ X$ where $F = F_{\text{tick}}$. By Exercise 9.19 the function F is continuous. Hence we deduce that a unique solution is (9.1). However,

$$\begin{aligned}
&F^0\ stop \doteq stop\\
&F^1\ stop = F\ stop = \text{tick} \rightarrow stop = clock_1\\
&F^2\ stop = F\ (F^1\ stop) = \text{tick} \rightarrow clock_1 = clock_2\\
&F^3\ stop = F\ (F^2\ stop) = \text{tick} \rightarrow clock_2 = clock_3\\
&\dots\\
&F^n\ stop = F\ (F^{n-1}\ stop) = \text{tick} \rightarrow clock_{n-1} = clock_n\\
&\dots
\end{aligned}$$

Thus indeed we deduce that $X = \lim_{n\to\infty} clock_n$. This proves our intuitive belief that the perpetual clock is the limit of the increasingly accurate finite approximations $clock_n$.

Exercise 9.20 Deduce that, in the notation of Chapter 7, our perpetual clock has the infinite set of traces given by the regular expression (tick)*.

Example 9.52 Consider a tea machine TM that never breaks down, which is defined recursively by TM = coin → tea → TM. Again the fixed point theorem ensures us that such a process is well defined. In this case TM is the unique solution to the recursive equation $X = F\ X$ where $F = \lambda P.\ (\text{coin} \rightarrow \text{tea} \rightarrow P)$. The traces of TM is the regular expression (coin tea)* + coin(tea coin)*.

9.4.4 Operations on processes

We have demonstrated that a range of infinite processes are well defined. However, the example processes seen so far can hardly be described as interesting or complex. The problem is that we have only really seen one way of building new processes from old ones, using the unary operation *prefix*. What we have defined is a very simple algebra, namely the set of processes together with a single function operation. General work in the area of process algebras is based around more extensive operations. For example, there are binary operations that correspond to intuitive notions, such as choice between two processes, and parallel execution of two processes. It turns out that the fixed point theorem again ensures well-definedness of infinite processes when we use these operations.

As a mere flavour of this work we consider a simple binary 'choice' operation which we denote by '|'. For two processes P, Q the process $P \mid Q$ is the process that can engage in the same events as either P or Q.

Example 9.53 Suppose that TM_1 is a simple tea machine that will deliver one cup of tea upon insertion of a coin (after which it never engages in any other event). Similarly CM_1 is a simple coffee machine that delivers one cup of coffee. Then $\text{TM}_1 \mid \text{CM}_1$ is the process DM_1 (drinks machine) that can deliver either a cup of tea or cup of coffee upon insertion of a coin. Thus traces(DM_1) = $\{\Lambda$, coin, coin tea, coin coffee$\}$.

Now suppose that TM_2 is a tea machine with a capacity of two cups and CM_2 is a coffee machine with a capacity of two cups. Then $\text{TM}_2 \mid \text{CM}_2$ is precisely the drinks machine DM_2 of Example 9.46. Analogously we could define $\text{DM}_n = \text{TM}_n \mid \text{CM}_n$ for each n. This is a machine that offers a choice of tea or coffee upon insertion of a coin. It has a capacity of n cups of tea and n cups of coffee.

Example 9.54 Now suppose we have the perfect tea machine TM of Example 9.52 and a perfect coffee machine CM. A general purpose drinks machine DM that offers either tea or coffee may be viewed as the process DM = TM | CM. Again we can ask if such a process is well defined. Using the λ-notation we see that we are looking for the solution of a recursive equation $X = F\ X$ where $F = \lambda X.((\text{coin} \rightarrow \text{tea} \rightarrow X) \mid (\text{coin} \rightarrow \text{coffee} \rightarrow X))$. We know that a unique solution is given by $\lim_{n\rightarrow\infty} F^n\ stop$, so we compute the sequence $F^n\ stop$. Now $F_1\ stop = F\ stop = (\text{coin} \rightarrow \text{tea} \rightarrow stop) \mid (\text{coin} \rightarrow \text{coffee} \rightarrow stop)$. By considering the traces of this process it is easy to see that $F_1\ stop = \text{DM}_1$. Similarly, $F_2\ stop = F(F_1\ stop) = F\ \text{DM}_1 = (\text{coin} \rightarrow \text{tea} \rightarrow \text{DM}_1) \mid (\text{coin} \rightarrow \text{coffee} \rightarrow \text{DM}_1) = \text{DM}_2$ and in general $F_n\ stop = \text{DM}_n$, where DM_n is defined as in Example 9.53.

9.4.5 Implementing processes

We are now going to show how we can view processes as functions, and hence show how to implement them.

Consider the process P of continually tossing a coin. We can think of P as the solution of the recursive equation $X = (\text{heads} \rightarrow X) \mid (\text{tails} \rightarrow X)$. Initially P can engage in either of two events, namely *heads* or *tails*. We can then think of the behaviour of P in terms of its behaviour if the first event is tails and its behaviour if the first event is heads. Thus we can think of P as a function f defined on the set $\{heads, tails\}$ that returns a set of traces. In this case,

$$\begin{aligned} f(heads) &= f(tails) \\ &= \{\Lambda, heads,\ tails,\ heads\ heads,\ heads\ tails, \ldots\} \\ &= traces(P) \end{aligned}$$

In general, every process may be regarded as a function whose domain B is the events in which the process can initially engage. This observation enables a direct implementation of processes into a functional programming language.

Example 9.55 The events in B, such as *heads* and *tails*, are represented as atoms. These represent the legal inputs to the function. For any other input the function returns the undefined symbol $\perp$. Thus, for example, the process *stop* may be viewed as the function $stop = \lambda x.\ \perp$, which is implemented in LISP as

```
def  Stop = lambda x. 'undefined'
```

Example 9.56 The process $(\text{tails} \rightarrow stop)$ is the function $\lambda x.(x = \text{tails} \rightarrow stop,\ \perp)$. This would be implemented in LISP as

```
lambda x. if  x = 'tails' then Stop
                          else 'undefined'
```

Example 9.57 The general prefix operation $(a \rightarrow P)$ may be implemented as

```
def Prefix = lambda a. lambda P. lambda x.
                 if x=a then P
                        else 'undefined'
```

Example 9.58 The general binary choice $(a \rightarrow P \mid b \rightarrow Q)$ would be implemented as

```
def Choice = lambda a. lambda b. lambda P. lambda Q
                                              . lambda x.
              if x=a then P
                     else if x=b then Q else 'undefined'
```

Example 9.59 Recursively defined processes would be implemented with the fixed point combinator. Therefore, to implement *new-clock* defined recursively by $X =$ tick $\rightarrow$ tock $\rightarrow X$ we would write `def new-clock = label X. (Prefix) ('tick' (Prefix) 'tock' X)`, where we are using the previously defined function *Prefix*.

Exercise 9.21 Write down an implementation for the process that is the solution of the recursive equation $X =$ (heads $\rightarrow X$) | (tails $\rightarrow X$).

9.5 SUMMARY

We have shown that the λ-calculus provides a notation for defining and naming functions in such a way that we can talk about them explicitly. Using the notation of the λ-calculus we have developed a theory that enables us to treat partial functions as approximations to total functions and to construct the solutions to recursive equations. There are programming languages, called functional languages, that are implementations of the λ-calculus. Hence we can implement functions defined within the λ-calculus on computers. Polymorphism in functional programming languages allows functions to have parameters of any type.

As an application, we have shown that the λ-calculus, together with the theory of fixed points and partial functions, is an important component of a formal approach to the specification and construction of interacting processes.

FURTHER READING

Much of the presentation of fixed points in this chapter was inspired by Chapter 7 of Bird (1976). For a more extensive treatment of the λ-calculus, see Revesz (1988) and Barendregt (1981), while Peyton-Jones (1987) describes in detail its implementation.

Part II

Theoretical Framework for Systems Construction

Chapter 10

FORMAL SPECIFICATION

In this chapter we identify both the mathematical structures and the logic that underpin the main approaches to the formal specification of systems. Our aim is to present a theoretical framework for system specification that is built on the mathematical foundations that we provided in the first part of the book. Being faced with the syntactic details of particular specification languages can be confusing for someone who lacks mathematical experience. We prefer to present the important concepts that underlie system construction in the familiar notation of logic and mathematics. Once understanding of these concepts is achieved, by working through the set exercises, the notations that are currently in use can be mastered without difficulty. We see an analogy with the need to understand the fundamental principles of programming before becoming too involved with the fussy, and often confusing, syntactic details of concrete mechanical codes. Understanding is best achieved when an *abstract* programming language is used.

In our view the activity of specification involves building theories and reasoning about them in a formal system. Formal languages for specification are designed over a formal deductive system and offer structuring mechanisms in order to gain power of expression. We present the concept of an abstract data type in Sec. 10.2 as a primitive object in a system and specify the behaviour of example abstract data types in a simple semi-formal language of sets and functions.

A many-sorted first-order theory of an abstract data type is then presented as a formal specification. First-order logic is a powerful and natural language for specification and has the advantage that it can be understood by the client who has acquired the development of the system. Specifications in the algebraic approach also present the properties of abstract data types as axioms, but use a restricted form of first-order logic, equational logic, for reasoning about these properties. The construction of an algebra as an explicit model for an algebraic specification is shown in Sec. 10.4 to be central to this approach. Because a minimal algebraic model can be constructed, a model-based semantics is used for algebraic specifications. The construction of this minimal, or initial, model is made explicitly as the specification is written—and this may be difficult for a client to understand.

In summary, the logic and algebraic approaches to specification take an abstract view of a system and specify the properties of its data structures by logical axioms. Although the abstract model approach is described as 'abstract', it produces specifications that come closer to describing the concrete representation of the data in a system. Specifications in the Vienna Development Method (VDM) and Z, currently the most popular specification languages, require the construction of an explicit model for the state of a software system. We explain in Sec. 10.5 how, in these notations, the state is modelled by mathematical objects such as sets, maps and sequences. The language of predicates expresses changes to the system state as pre-conditions and post-conditions. We describe specifications in VDM and Z as model-based. Clearly the difference between specification approaches are deeper than the notational variations that become obvious when they are used. The need to match the theoretical frameworks that are available for specification to the problems of system construction that exist is an urgent topic for research. We concentrate on comparing the theory underlying the different specification approaches and do not attempt to prescribe the suitability of a particular approach to the type of system that is to be constructed.

10.1 SPECIFICATION

The activity of specification is traditionally informal and has produced a textual description of system requirements, or an informal statement of what the system actually does. The formalization of this activity, by the use of formal languages for specification, introduces reasoning into the activity of system construction.

10.1.1 The activity of specification

The traditional waterfall model of the software life cycle, which we presented in Sec. 1.4, divides the production of a software system into distinct sequential stages. There are two problems with such a simple model, however. The first is a lack of control as production moves down the 'waterfall'; the second is a lack of communication between the client and the software engineer. A more useful model involves the integration of control into the software life cycle. By formalizing the activity of specification, the software engineer brings precision into the development process; by actively co-operating throughout a series of small development steps the customer brings understanding into the development process. The simple model which expresses the development of one large-scale system needs to be replaced by a model that breaks the development process into a series of small and well-defined steps. Each step should involve negotiation, with a clear contract entered into between the software engineer and the customer. Although we refer specifically to a software system, the ideas are applicable, in general, to the construction of any complex system.

The activity of specification takes place at each stage in the software life cycle. To specify means 'to give details of' or 'to indicate precisely'. Formal languages have been characterized in Chapter 7 and, as 'precisely defined unambiguous notations', are suitable for expressing system specifications. By making specification a formal activity, control is incorporated into the new software life cycle and verification becomes a parallel activity with construction. Each stage in the new life cycle for system development contains the following information:

- A specification of the problem
- A proposed solution
- A correctness argument

A further advantage of formalizing the activity of specification in order to provide a clear contract is the communication of information to *all* involved in the project. The requirement for precision and unambiguity may conflict with the requirement for ease of communication but in our view this is not an argument against formal specification in system development.

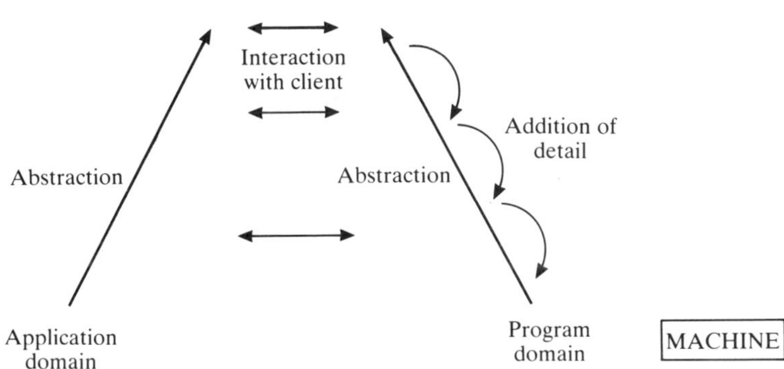

Figure 10.1 A specification as an abstract theory.

Building specifications has been described in Chapter 7 as an activity that is similar to the construction of theories. We build a specification by a process of abstraction in order to present our perception of an application domain. This process produces a theory that is given a name and expressed in some formal specification language. The specification is an abstraction of the final application system that is constructed, and, in the case of a software system, is finally implemented in a concrete programming language. The executable software belongs to a formal mathematical domain. We therefore express the specification as an abstraction of the two domains: one the informal application domain and the other the formal program domain in Fig. 10.1. The theoretical framework that is chosen for specification clearly influences the activity of specification. Within any formal framework, however, there are two main operations that produce the concrete executable code from the abstract theory of the application domain. These operations can be decomposed into several steps and may interleave at a more detailed level in system development.

1 *Structuring the specification.* The abstract theory of the application domain is expressed in a formal specification language and named. Either the specification is written as a monolithic (unstructured) piece of text or it is constructed by combining small specifications that describe parts of the application system. There is an increasing interest in the construction of specifications from reusable parts, which we shall call modules, as a bottom-up activity. We gave the traditional view of system construction in Sec. 1.4 as a top-down activity that involves writing a specification of the 'whole' system. Again it is the theoretical framework that influences the structuring of specifications.
2 *Implementation of the specification.* Detail must be added progressively to the abstract specification in order to implement the specification in a more concrete language. The addition of detail is made in stages and is completed when the abstract specification is expressed in a concrete mechanical code that can be executed by a computer. The stages of adding concrete detail are often called the *refinement* of the specification.

The operations of structuring and implementing specifications can be viewed inside

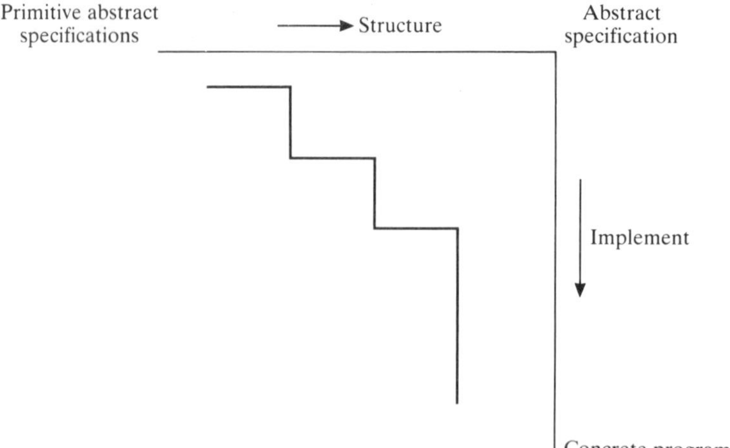

Figure 10.2 A two-dimensional development space.

a two-dimensional development space as shown in Fig. 10.2. Arbitrary movement is possible in the development space, but an optimal path could be one that uses the maximum number of 'prefabricated' objects in order to build the concrete program. The reusability of both specifications and programs is an important research area. The definition of the semantics of the structuring operations on the abstract specifications depends on the theoretical framework of mathematics and logic.

It is in the way that the two operations for constructing and implementing a specification are carried out that the formal approaches to specification vary. It is important to distinguish between the addition of information that is made by each of these two operations:

- Extra information may be required from the customer in order to complete the construction of the abstract specification.
- Extra detail is added by the software engineer, who develops the system, in order to complete the implementation of the specification.

Interaction with the client ensures that the final implementation is what the client really wants and should take place at each stage of system development, as shown in Fig. 10.1. Extra information from the client about the problem must be added to the specification and not to the code as a last minute fix. In contrast, the extra detail about the implementation is given in some chosen design language, before being further refined and expressed in some chosen programming language. The final implementation will express the algorithms and data structures in a concrete mechanical code that is directly computed by a machine.

We can illustrate the two ways of *extending* a specification by using an informal specification language.

Example 10.1 It is required that a program should sort a list of integers into increasing order. The specification states simply that 'the list of integers $a_1, a_2, \ldots, a_n$ where $n \geq 1$ will have the property that $\forall i\ a_{i-1} < a_i$ where $1 < i \leq n$'. The program is to read a list of integers from the terminal and to print them out into increasing order. The client forgot, however, that the user may repeat some of the integers in the list. In order to ensure that decisions are not made prematurely, the specification is extended only by the information that 'the integers are output in non-descending order so that $a_i \leq a_{i+1}$'. The specification is now 'tighter' in its description of the problem, but still permissive in allowing many possible design decisions about how the list is to be sorted and whether repeated integers are to be printed.

The extension of detail about implementation will depend on the choice of programming language. If Pascal is the choice, the following algorithmic detail could be given in the design:

```
read list (list,listlength);
sort list (list,listlength);
print list(list,listlength)
```

More detail must then be added to this design language in order to implement the procedures that these instructions represent. The list, as a data structure at the abstract level of the problem, could be implemented in Pascal by an array or by a linked list. The addition of detail is complete when the code is finally executable. We show in Chapter 12 how Pascal programs can be proved to be correct with respect to their specifications.

Exercise 10.1 Write an informal specification for a program that reads a list of integers from a file and outputs the largest integer in the list as well as the position at which this largest integer occurs. Consider any additions that you may need to make to the original specification, which should be permissive, and allow design decisions to be made later. Then write a design for your specification and implement the program in Pascal. Identify each refinement that you make to the abstract specification.

10.1.2 Formal languages for specifications

The most abstract formal languages are the first-order logic languages that are described in Chapter 7. The use of quantifiers provides power of expression for these languages, and a natural deduction system provides power of reasoning. Since complex systems involve operations on many different sorts of data, however, it is necessary to extend the simple first-order language of Chapter 7 to a *many-sorted* language with a set of symbols to represent each sort of data. Interpretation for a many-sorted theory involves dividing the domain of interpretation into subsets. This, of course, is exactly how many-sorted algebras were defined in Chapter 8. We shall present a many-sorted similarity type in a logical specification as the analogue of a many-sorted signature in an algebraic specification.

Designers of specification languages have aimed to provide expressive structuring mechanisms and to link the syntax of the language with our perceptions of the real world by the construction of models. The requirement for expression must be matched by a firm foundation for semantics when infinite data structures, which are recursive, and non-terminating processes are to be specified. One problem with modelling the structures in a system is that the resulting specification may not be sufficiently abstract because implementations are suggested by the structures that are used for modelling. The information that is given in a specification is more important than the notation used to describe the information.

10.2 ABSTRACT DATA TYPES

In this section we identify an *abstract data type* as a key concept for the construction of systems. We present specifications of abstract data types as the primitive specifications from which the specification for the whole system is built. The key concept of a *module* is identified as the reusable instance of the textual specification of an abstract data type. As simple examples, we specify the behaviour of both queues and tables in a semi-formal language of sets and functions.

The importance of writing specifications for parts of systems was recognized by Parnas in 1972. He specified modules in a new 'formal' notation by giving the user enough information for the module to be used without the user having any knowledge of the method of implementation. This idea has become the important design concept of *information hiding*. By specifying data abstractions, Liskov and Zilles (1974) extended information hiding to the users of data abstractions.

Definition 10.1 Abstract data type An abstract data type defines a class of abstract data objects that is completely characterized by the operations available on those objects.

The power of data abstraction is that the user is deprived of making use of implementation details. Objects can be described by their properties rather than by their representation in terms of concrete data structures such as arrays or pointers.

Example 10.2 A string, constructed as in Chapter 7 by a pre-fix operation or by concatenation, can be specified as an abstract data type. The operations that decompose strings are usually called *head* and *tail*.

Exercise 10.2 The list in the specification given in Example 10.1 can be specified as an abstract data type. The list can be constructed by adding elements to it and 'destructed' by deleting from a list or by using the *head* operation to remove the element at the head of the list. Try to identify relationships between these operations on a list and to express these relationships as equations.

10.2.1 Primitive objects in a system

Parnas' idea of an information-hiding module and Liskov's idea of specifying an abstract data type were major signposts for the formal specification of systems. They pointed along rather different routes, however, and we see these different routes reflected in the formal specification approaches that are currently popular. It seems today that the real importance of the concepts of a module and an abstract data type lies in the role that they can play as the reusable components in a system. Specifications of abstract data types form the primitive specifications in a system from which the specification for the whole system is built, as shown in Fig. 10.2. Modules can be seen as reusable instances of these textual specifications. The work of Parnas and Liskov has led to different views of the primitive objects in a system, and it seems now that both these views are useful if they are applied at different levels of abstraction.

1 *Objects with state.* Parnas thought of a module as an abstract machine with an explicit state. By operating on a module we cause the internal state of the module to change. We use this idea when we put a coin in a drinks machine and press a button to move the machine into a new state, which hopefully results in the output of our chosen drink. The notion of system state was presented in Sec. 2.4. The procedural style of programming that includes object-oriented programming is based on this

idea, as we shall see in Chapter 11. At the level of specification, some approaches define an explicit notion of state for a system and specify a change in state in terms of pre-conditions and post-conditions.

2 *Abstract data types with values.* Liskov's concept of data abstraction has been developed at a more abstract level within the logic and algebraic approaches to specification. Operations on abstract data types are specified by functions that return values. The relationships between the operations describe the meaning, or the semantics, of the abstract data type and there is no explicit notion of state. This view is mirrored by the declarative style of programming that we shall discuss in Chapter 11.

The concept of an abstract data type is clearly important for specification and we view abstract data types as the primitive objects in a system. A notion of state can be built in to primitive objects as they are refined and made more concrete. For the construction of a system specification from the primitive specifications of objects, a module can be constructed as a unique reusable instance of its textual specification. The construction of modules can be expressed in abstract category theory, introduced in Chapter 8, by the operation of taking a co-limit. The use of category theory to express the semantics of structuring specifications is an important area of research that was stimulated by Burstall and Goguen's work (1977) on structuring theories.

We are now ready to begin to use the framework of logic and mathematics that we have built in Part I to specify abstract data types. Recursively defined structures have already been defined by structural induction in Chapter 7; these structures have also been shown to be the least fixed point solutions of recursive function definitions in Chapter 9. The properties of recursive structures can be defined by axioms in the form of recursive equations. These axioms are similar to the production rules that defined the structure of formal languages in Chapter 7.

We begin by using a very simple language of sets and functions in order to describe the properties of some abstract types before we introduce the notation of formal specification languages. It is important to understand how the axioms specify the recursive structure of the objects before considering the formal interpretation of the language syntax by a mathematical model. It is also important to separate the behaviour of an abstract data type from its eventual implementation in some programming language.

10.2.2 Specification of a queue

Our first choice of an abstract data type is a common structure, at the problem level, but is not a concrete data type in a programming language. It is vital to consider structures with different disciplines of storage and retrieval when we specify systems. Unfortunately, however, the data structures of programming languages are inadequate when we work at an abstract level.

We specify the behaviour of a queue in terms of how we can use the queue for storing information. In particular we consider the relationship between the operations on the queue. First we give an intuitive definition of a queue:

1 Each queue holds items of information of the same type, or sort.

2 The queue is a general data type meaning that different queues may hold collections of items that are of different types. For example, one queue may hold a collection of

names, while another may hold a collection of people, and yet another a collection of integers.

3 The following operations may be performed on a queue:

(a) Add a new item to the tail of the queue.

(b) Delete the item at the head of the queue.

(c) Get a copy of the item at the head of the queue.

(d) Find out whether the queue is or is not empty.

In order to formally describe a queue in the problem domain rather than the program domain, we need to define a language that has a structure, or *syntax*, and also a *semantics* that gives a meaning to the specification. We use a simple language with a syntax defined by sets and functions and a semantics defined by equational axioms. Later we shall use formal languages, with more expressive notations, that are currently in use as specification languages.

The queue is represented as a general data type by passing the type *item* as a parameter to the type queue. The whole structure is queue[item] and a queue is said to be *generic* with respect to the type *item*. The definition of a queue forms a pattern for all queues, whatever the type of item that is stored in them. This demonstrates the power of specifying at the abstract level.

The syntax of the language We represent the sorts, or kinds, of objects involved by sets and the operations on these objects by functions. Let

$$\begin{aligned} Q &= \{\text{queues1, queues2,} \ldots\} \\ I &= \{\text{item1, item2,} \ldots\} \\ E &= \{\text{no-item}\} \\ B &= \{\text{true, false}\} \end{aligned}$$

The set E contains the only error condition. We shall avoid the use of error-values as much as possible in these early attempts at specification. Error-handling has proved to be very difficult in some formal specification approaches. As suggested for first-order languages in Chapter 7 and for the signature of algebras in Chapter 8, we define individual constants by functions and specify the empty queue as a 0-ary function. We specify the following argument and result sets for the functions:

$$\begin{aligned} &\text{create} &&: \ \to Q \\ &\text{add} &&: \ Q \times I \to Q \\ &\text{head} &&: \ Q \to I \cup E \\ &\text{delete} &&: \ Q \to Q \\ &\text{isempty} &&: \ Q \to B \end{aligned}$$

The semantics of the language We present rules that relate the functions and give meaning to the operations on the queue. The rules are arrived at by a process of intuition and represent the properties of the objects and the operations in the real world. As formal rules they are called *axioms* and we use them in an equational form. Our axioms are purely functional in that they only return values and do not have any side effects on a state. We saw in Chapter 2 how a function could be viewed as a machine without a state. We therefore do not have a notion of a *before object* as distinct from an *after object* in our specification. This means that we do not have a notion of pre-condition or post-condition as we do in a procedural programming language like Pascal. It is important to keep our set of basic axioms to a minimum; we can extend our specification later by adding more detail as we build and implement a system in the two-dimensional development space shown in Fig. 10.2.

We now define in a precise way the meaning of the operations that we may perform on the abstract data type queue. We describe the relationships between the functions that represent the operations by six axioms. Our axioms are expressed so that they apply to all possible queues by quantifying universally over the sets

$$\forall q \in Q,\ i \in I$$

Queue axiom 1. isempty(create) = true. This axiom formalizes our understanding that a newly created queue does not contain any elements.

Queue axiom 2. isempty(add(q, i)) = false. Once an item has been stored, the queue is no longer empty.

Queue axiom 3. head(create) = no-item. This axiom formalizes our understanding that we cannot get a copy of the item at the head of an empty queue. Note that *head* is a function that takes an argument that itself is a constant function. *Create*, as a constructor or constant function, is a representation of an empty queue.

Queue axiom 4. head(add(q, i)) = if isempty(q) then i else head(q).

Queue axiom 5. delete(create) = create. It is better not to over-specify with error conditions. For this reason, deleting from an empty queue merely results in an empty queue again.

Queue axiom 6. delete(add(q, i)) = if isempty(q) then create else add(delete(q), i). The axiomatic definitions for the *head* and *delete* as functions are recursive and the axioms for head and delete on the empty queue terminate the recursion. It is important to understand the way that recursion 'counts down' the structure until it terminates with an empty structure. This contrasts with the way that structural induction 'builds up' from the basis clause as the beginning of the induction. The axiom for *head* states that if an item has just been added to an empty queue, the *head* function on that queue will return a copy of that item. If the queue was not empty, however, before the item was added, then the *head* function is applied to the non-empty queue before the item was added.

The axiom for *delete* is more difficult to understand intuitively. If *delete* is performed on a queue that *was* empty before an item was added, then the resulting queue is empty. If the queue on which *delete* is performed has more than one item in it, however, then deleting from that queue is the same as adding the last item *after* deleting from the queue that contains all the previous items.

Exercise 10.3 Give an informal justification for the *delete* axiom by drawing diagrams to represent each side of the equational axioms for *delete*, and show that they represent the same queue. This should justify axioms 5 and 6 for a queue.

A formal specification should give just enough information to define the type, but not so much that the choice of implementation is limited. For example, the formal specification of the queue does not state that the items are added to the tail of the queue and deleted from the head of the queue. This is stated in the informal specification, but is really part of the implementation decision. The formal specification relates the functions implicitly and no explicit model is required. The diagrams that you have drawn in Exercise 10.3 provide an abstract model of a 'real' queue and make assumptions about *where* items are added and deleted from the queue.

We could use the following axioms for the *head* function. These are more algebraic and avoid the use of conditional expressions by using a rewrite rule with pattern matching on the terms.

Queue axiom 7. head(add(create, i)) $= i$.

Queue axiom 8. head(add(add(q, i), j)) $=$ head(add(q, i)).

All the functions that have been specified are total functions and defined for every argument.

Notice that the queue we have specified is unbounded and could be infinitely large. Only in the implementation of the queue may we need to bring in constraints about the size of the queue. If we wished to specify a bounded queue we would need the functions

$$\begin{array}{lll} \text{add} & : & Q \times I \rightarrow Q \cup E \\ \text{isfull} & : & Q \rightarrow B \end{array}$$

Our set of error conditions could then be $E = \{\text{no-item, overflow}\}$.

Exercise 10.4 Use our specification language for a queue to:

(a) Formally express the creation of an empty queue.

(b) Add Fred, Anne, Mary and Jill to the queue in stages, forming a new queue as each addition is made.

(c) Get a copy of the item at the head of the queue.

(d) Delete the item at the head of the queue.

10.2.3 Specification of a table

Again we are only concerned with the behaviour of a table as an abstract data type. The implementation of a table in some programming language is not our concern. It is useful initially to compare the table, as an abstract data type, with an array as a storage structure in a concrete programming language. A table contains information that can be stored or retrieved by the user of that table. Each item of data is stored with its key in order that the user has access to each item of data. Searching and sorting for data in tables is implemented through the set of keys, K, that are stored with the data that is in the set D.

Comparing a table with an array First we make the following informal comparison between a table and an array, as a concrete data type in a programming language:

1 In an array the set of index values, I, is fixed so that an index value cannot be deleted. In a table, however, it is often necessary to delete both a key and the item of data.

2 An array defines a relation on the Cartesian product $I \times V$ where V is the set of stored values in the array. Because the set I is fixed and each index value in an array is unique, the array defines a function from I to V.

A table defines a relation on the set $K \times D$ which is a mapping but not a function. This is because a key may be repeated to give a one-to-many mapping from K to D. Also a key may be deleted from the table with the result that there is no relationship in the table between that key (still in the set of keys) and any data in the set of data.

3 Tables can be viewed as being stored in arrays with the set $K \times D$ as the set of stored values in the array. At the level of implementation we often represent a table by an array in Pascal.

Now we write a formal specification of a table, beginning by defining the syntax and the semantics for the language. The table is represented as a general data type by passing the type *data* as a parameter to the type table. The whole structure is table[data] and a table is said to be *generic* with respect to the type *data*. The abstract definition of a table forms a pattern for all tables, whatever the type of data that is stored in them.

The syntax of the language As before we represent the sorts, or kinds, of objects involved by sets and the operations on these objects by functions. Let

$$\begin{aligned} T &= \{\text{table1, table2,} \ldots\} \\ K &= \{\text{key1, key2,} \ldots\} \\ D &= \{\text{data}\} \\ B &= \{\text{true, false}\} \\ E &= \{\text{not-found}\} \end{aligned}$$

The set K consists of all the keys that can be used to search the table. The set E contains the only error condition. Again we specify the argument and result sets for the functions that represent the operations on the table.

$$\begin{aligned} \text{create} &: \; \to T \\ \text{store} &: \; T \times K \times D \to T \\ \text{retrieve} &: \; T \times K \to D \cup E \\ \text{delete} &: \; T \times K \to T \cup E \\ \text{equal} &: \; K \times K \to B \end{aligned}$$

The semantics of the language We now define in a precise way the meaning of the operations that we may perform on the abstract data type table. We describe the relationships between the functions, which represent the operations, by four equational axioms:

$$\forall k,\ k' \in K,\ t \in T,\ d \in D$$

Table axiom 1. retrieve(create, k) = not-found.

Table axiom 2. retrieve(store(t, k, d), k') = if equal(k, k') then d else retrieve(t, k'). This is recursive until the keys are equal or the table is empty when the error 'not-found' results. The *retrieve* function works backwards through all the previous keys that have been stored in the table.

Table axiom 3. delete(create, k) = create. Deleting from an empty table merely results in an empty table again. This axiom stops the recursion in the next axiom, Axiom 4, and defines a non-erroneous delete on an empty key.

Table axiom 4. delete(store(t, k, d), k') = if equal(k, k') then t else store(delete(t, k'), k, d). *Delete* 'jumps over previous stores' until the right key is found or until the table is empty. The stored elements that are 'walked over' must not be deleted. In the last axiom, if $k \neq k'$ then k' is the key to be deleted whereas k is the key to be kept in the table. The recursion keeps on uncovering the previous store operations until it terminates.

Extra detail may be added as more decisions are made about the required operations on the table. The extra detail must not change the properties of our original specification, however. Safe extensions are described as *conservative extensions*. The additional detail is concrete detail that is needed for the implementation of the table.

We may implement the table so that more than one item of data can be stored for a given key. For example, the name Peter could be a key, and the names of Peter's five children could be entered as items of data. The second axiom for *delete* could be organized differently in order that a *delete* for a given key removes *all* the data for that key. We then have the extra axiom:

Table axiom 5. delete(store(t, k, d), k') $=$ if equal(k, k') then delete(t, k') else store(delete(t, k'), k, d). If the keys k and k' are equal, the *delete* function will be called recursively to delete all the previous items of data stored for the given key.

Notice that we began with only four axioms for the abstract data type table. It has been found that it is desirable not to overspecify, but to construct a loose, or permissive, specification initially. The early formal notations specified errors, but the implementation of these specifications led to some confusion. As an alternative we return an undefined value, a null value, or any constant value rather than an error at the abstract level. In engineering, for example, we often need to say 'there is no result' when we carry out an experiment. Decisions about what to do when there is no result are better left to the implementation stage. Here we distinguish, as we did in Chapter 2, between the notion of a *partial function*, with an undefined value for some argument, and a *partially defined* function, which is not defined for some value.

Exercise 10.5 Use our specification language for a table to:

(a) Store the following information in a table. Assume that names are the keys and ages are the data.

Fred is aged 42
Anne is aged 107
Mary is aged 49
Jill is aged 21

(b) Then use the table to find the age of Anne.

(c) Finally delete the key for Anne from the table because Anne has died.

Exercise 10.6 Simplify the following expressions:

(a) retrieve(store(store(store(create, k_1, d_1), k_2, d_2), k_3, d_3), k_2)

(b) delete(store(store(store(create,k_1, d_1), k_2, d_2), k_3, d_3), k_2)

(c) retrieve(store(store(create,k_1, d_1), k_3, d_3), k_1)

(d) retrieve(store(store(create,k_1, d_1), k_3, d_3), k_3)

(e) retrieve(store(store(create,k_1, d_1), k_3, d_3), k_2)

Exercise 10.7 This exercise requires you to write your own formal specification and then to use the defined operations on the abstract data type that is specified.

1. A stack is defined informally as follows:

(a) A stack holds items of information. All items of information within a particular stack are of the same sort, or type. In general, a stack is able to hold collections of information of any defined sort or type.

(b) The following operations may be performed on a stack:

- Push a new item on to the stack.
- Get a copy of the item at the top of the stack.
- Delete the item at the top of the stack.
- Find out whether the stack is or is not empty.

Think of stacking a pile of plates for washing up. The last plate put on the pile is the first to be washed up! We delete the plate in order to wash it up, but we can look at the plate on top. The concept of an empty stack is intrinsic to the concept of a stack. The concept of a full stack is not intrinsic to the abstract specification, however, but is a property of the implementation of a stack. In principle we have an infinite stack at the abstract level.

Write a formal specification of a stack. The operation *pop* returns the item at the top of the stack and leaves the stack with that item deleted. Define *pop* in terms of the operations provided in the formal specification. The reason for not using *pop* as a basic function is that it would give a product of sets as a result. It is preferable to build *pop* from the basic functions *top* and *delete*:

- *top* looks to see what is on the top of the stack but does not produce a new stack.
- *delete* removes an item from the *top* of the stack and produces a new stack (but not a new item) as a result.

If we define *pop* as a basic function, we must extend the basic specification later in order to define *top* and *delete* independently.

2. Using your formal specification of a stack, create a stack from the following items: Fred, Anne, Mary and Jill. Use the axioms in your specification to carry out the following operations on the stack that you have created:

   (a) Use the operation top once.

   (b) Use the operation delete once.

   (c) Repeatedly use the operation delete on the stack until the stack is empty.

   (d) Use the operation pop once on the original stack. You may find it helpful to draw diagrams to describe the state of the stack as you carry out these operations. These diagrams model the specification abstractly but are *not* part of the specification language.

10.3 SPECIFICATIONS IN FIRST-ORDER LOGIC

The languages of first-order logic were defined by induction in Chapter 7 where we gave examples of first-order theories in a formal system. First-order logic is simple and natural to use for specification and is becoming increasingly important as difficulties emerge with other more popular approaches. The simplicity of logic results from its power to abstract: specifications in logic are loose and descriptive with no explicit notion of state. Although model theory provides the notion of interpretation in a structure there is usually no need to build a model when we specify complex systems.

We take the view that the specifications of complex application systems are constructed by building many-sorted theories and naming them as textual specifications. The simple specifications of the primitive objects in a system are *combined* by structuring operations to form more structured specifications. A primitive operation on a specification is the *extension* of the specification by the addition of new symbols and properties. Extensions that are conservative play an important role in the refinement, or implementation, of specifications. The change of language that is required as one specification is implemented by another, more concrete, specification is made by the primitive operation of *interpretation* between theories. The refinement of specifications is expressed in Turski and Maibaum (1987) by the pair (interpretation, conservative extension), and successive refinements are shown to be composable within a logic framework.

As detail is added by refinement, specifications become less permissive. This is because refinement, and the eventual implementation of specifications by programs, requires the addition of further symbols for operations and constants to the language of the specification. An *extension* to a specification is the specification with the new symbols added. By extending safely, or conservatively, the need for complicated correctness arguments can be avoided. We introduce this style of specification in this section because it is directly based on the logical framework of Part I, and because it is becoming increasingly important as a powerful approach to specification.

A conservative extension is safe because every property in the specification that has been extended holds in the extension to the specification *and also* because in the extension no new property, in the language of the original specification, can be deduced that did not hold in the specification before the extension was made.

Example 10.3 If we extend a specification for the door of a house by adding a window we should extend conservatively. A basic door that is extended to have a window should possess all the properties of a basic door: it should, for example, still open and close. We should not add the new property that all doors can be seen through. Clearly, however, in the new language with symbols that refer to both a door and a window there will be extra properties about the new extended object. These will assert, for example, that a window lets light through.

Extensions that are made in the process of refinement to logical specifications should always be conservative. It is important to remember that specifications are loose and permissive because functions are partially defined rather than partial. Partially defined functions are under-determined not non-deterministic as relations are. For some values the results of partially defined functions are not stated; this does not require the assignment of error-values in an abstract specification.

The power of quantification is available for expressing the meaning of systems by first-order logic.

Example 10.4 We specify a simple program that forms the square of any number that is given as input. The domain of values that we quantify over is $D = \mathbb{N}$. We write $\forall x \exists y\ [y = x \times x]$ as an axiom. From this axiom we deduce as theorems the consequences that belong to the theory for this program:

$$\begin{array}{ccc} x = 2 & \rightarrow & y = 4 \\ x = 3 & \rightarrow & y = 9 \\ x = 4 & \rightarrow & y = 16 \\ \vdots & & \vdots \end{array}$$

10.3.1 Many-sorted theories

Our specification in Example 10.4 is simple because it expresses operations on only one sort of data, the set of numbers. A specification of an abstract data type such as a queue needs to describe elements that are queues as well as elements that are items. In fact, most specifications describe operations on many different sorts of data. We need to divide the domain of interpretation into subsets, according to the sorts of names that we need to quantify over. In our syntax we have a set S of many sorts, containing symbols that name each sort of object in the theory. Many-sorted theories are appropriate for expressing specifications of the varied sorts of objects in application systems. The many-sorted syntax of a logical specification is given by a many-sorted similarity type; for algebraic theory we have already presented a many-sorted signature in Chapter 8.

Definition 10.2 Many-sorted similarity type A many-sorted similarity type σ is defined as $\sigma = (S, ar_r, ar_f)$, where S is a non-empty set of sorts and the functions ar_r and ar_f are called arity functions. The elements in the domains of ar_r and ar_f are the function and relation symbols respectively. We write rel_σ for the set of relation symbols and func_σ for the set of function symbols.

We use the definition of a many-sorted similarity type to present a specification for a string as an abstract data type. As in Chapter 7 we build a string by a pre-fix operation that inserts a character at the beginning of a string. The operations of decomposing strings are *head* and *tail*. The *head* operation on a string removes the character at the *head* of the string which was the last character stored by the pre-fix operation, that is $head(abbb) = a$. The discipline of access on a string is therefore like that of a stack and is called a first-in-last-out property.

The specification is simply a renaming of the first-order theory for a string. The theory consists of the many-sorted similarity type for the string and the set of axioms, Γ, that express the properties of a string. The similarity type explicitly describes the arity of the function and relation symbols by the functions ar_f and ar_r respectively. The elements in the domains of ar_f and ar_r are given by the sets func σ_{string} and rel σ_{string}. We use a notation that gives the sort symbols explicitly as the arity for each name. This notation could be simplified when the sorts are obvious.

Example 10.5 The notation '$\text{head}^{s;c}$' explicitly describes the function that takes a string as its argument and produces a character as a result.

The axioms in the set Γ_{string} are grouped together to indicate whether they express the construction or the decomposition of the abstract data type. We describe $T_{\text{string}} = (\sigma_{\text{string}}, \Gamma_{\text{string}})$ as a theory, although it is also called a *theory presentation*, because it presents the axioms from which the properties of a string are derived. In our logical specifications, the symbol for equality between strings or between characters is a non-logical binary relation symbol.

spec string is string[character]

by renaming of $T_{\text{string}} = (\sigma_{\text{string}}, \Gamma_{\text{string}})$ where $\sigma_{\text{string}} = (S, ar_r, ar_f)$ and

$$S = \{s, c\}$$

$$\text{func } \sigma_{\text{string}} = \{\lambda^s, \text{prefix}^{s,c;s}, \text{tail}^{s;s}, \text{head}^{s;c}\}$$

$$\text{rel } \sigma_{\text{string}} = \{\text{string}^s, \text{character}^s\}$$

The formation axiom expresses the structure of a string of characters

$$\forall y^c\ [\text{character}^c(y^c) \rightarrow \exists x^s\ \text{string}^s(x^s[y^c])]$$

The introduction axioms define how strings are built as canonical elements, and also define equality between strings

$$\text{string}^s(\lambda^s)$$

$$\forall x^s \forall y^c\ \text{string}^s(\text{prefix}^{s,c;s}(x^s, y^c))$$

$$\forall x^s \forall y^c\ [\neg\text{prefix}^{s,c;s}(x^s, y^c) =_s \lambda^s]$$

$$\forall x_1^s \forall x_2^s \forall y_1^c \forall y_2^c\ [x_1^s =_s x_2^s \wedge y_1^c =_c y_2^c \rightarrow \text{prefix}^{s,c;s}(x_1^s, y_1^c) =_s \text{prefix}^{s,c;s}(x_2^s, y_2^c)]$$

The reduction axioms tell us that the first character stored is the last character removed

$\forall x^s \forall y^c\ [(\text{tail}^{s;s}(\text{prefix}^{s,c;s}(x^s, y^c)) =_s x^s) \wedge \text{string}^s(x^s)]$

$\forall x^s \forall y^c\ [(\text{head}^{s;c}(\text{prefix}^{s,c;s}(x^s, y^c)) =_s y^c) \wedge \text{character}^c(y^c)]$

The induction axiom schema is 'for each formula $\mathscr{F}(x^s)$ in the theory, T_{string}, the universal closure of the formula

$$[\mathscr{F}(\lambda^s) \wedge \forall x^s \forall y^c\ (\mathscr{F}(x^s) \rightarrow \mathscr{F}(\text{prefix}^{s,c;s}(x^s, y^c)))] \rightarrow \forall x^s\ \mathscr{F}(x^s)$$

where y^c does not occur free in $\mathscr{F}(x^s)$, is an axiom'.

endspec

An extension of the specification could be made to provide an additional operation of concatenation between strings. Concatenation would be defined in terms of the given function pre-fix. However, since strings are not nested, this concatenation operation would form a longer string of characters from two shorter strings rather than a string formed by pre-fixing a string as an element of another string.

If we use the informal specification for a stack given in Exercise 10.7 to write a theory for a stack, we find that $T_{\text{stack}} = (\sigma_{\text{stack}}, \Gamma_{\text{stack}})$ is exactly the same as T_{string} apart from the names that we choose for the sorts and operations. It is useful, therefore, to think of some more abstract theory that we could call $T_{\text{filo}} = (\sigma, \Gamma_{\text{filo}})$ as the basic theory for structures with the first-in-last-out discipline.

Exercise 10.8 Write a basic specification in first-order logic for the abstract data type list. A list is defined informally by the following operations:

(a) Add a new item to a list.

(b) Get a copy of the item at the head of a list using the operation *head*.

(c) Delete the item at the head of the list.

For example, the list $[A, B, C]$ is formed by adding the item A at the beginning of the list $[B, C]$. The list is decomposed by the *head* operation on the list $[A, B, C]$ to give a copy of the item A, although A has not been deleted from the list.

Although the specifications for first-in-last-out structures may differ only in their choice of names, specifications for structures that are used by a *first-in-first-out* property are based on a theory with a different set of axioms. The theory $T_{\text{fifo}} = (\sigma, \Gamma_{\text{fifo}})$ has a different reduction axiom from T_{filo}.

Exercise 10.9 Use the semi-formal specification that we gave in Sec. 10.2 to write a logical specification of a queue as an abstract data type.

10.3.2 Extending many-sorted theories

We have stressed that the *refinement* of logical specifications should be carried out by a process of conservative extension and is one that should involve a client in order to ensure that the evolving system meets its requirements. In order to define the conservative extension of a theory we first define the extension of a theory. We use the notation of Sec. 7.2.2 for describing theories of first-order languages.

A theory can be extended in different ways: by adding new function or predicate symbols to its language and also by adding new properties for the symbols of the language. It is important to ensure that when the language of a theory is extended, every non-logical symbol of the theory remains in the language of the extension. As well as ensuring that the language of the theory is contained in its extension, it is also necessary to ensure that every property of the theory is still a property of the extension.

Definition 10.3 Extension of a theory Let $T_1 = (\sigma_1, \Gamma_1)$ and $T_2 = (\sigma_2, \Gamma_2)$ be many-sorted theories. Let A be a sentence in L_{T_1}. Then T_2 extends T_1 if for all sentences A we have if $\Gamma_1 \vdash A$ then $\Gamma_2 \vdash A$; that is every theorem of T_1 is a theorem of T_2. We write $T_1 \subseteq T_2$ if T_2 extends T_1.

Although every non-logical axiom of T_1 must be a theorem of T_2, it is not necessary for it to be an axiom of T_2.

The following property of the conservativeness of an extension uses the converse of the property of extension between theories.

Definition 10.4 Conservative extension of a theory Let $T_1 = (\sigma_1, \Gamma_1)$ and $T_2 = (\sigma_2, \Gamma_2)$ be many-sorted theories. Let A be a sentence in L_{T_1}. An extension of a theory T_1 by another theory T_2 is a conservative extension iff the extended theory, T_2, does not allow the deduction of any more properties than T_1 in L_{T_1}. Then $T_1 \subseteq T_2$ is conservative if for all sentences A, in the language of T_1, we have if $\Gamma_2 \vdash A$ then $\Gamma_1 \vdash A$.

It is important to note that these definitions of extension between theories are syntactic and do not depend on the semantic notions of model theory. The advantage to the software engineer of using these logical specifications is that there is no need to construct a model of the software *before* it is developed. The construction of a model requires decision making at an early stage in the life cycle; this may be neither possible nor desirable.

Conservative extensions should be used as specifications are structured and refined because they preserve the consistency of specifications. A basic result in logic about theories, given in Shoenfield (1967) on page 42, tells us that if the extension $T_1 \subseteq T_2$ is conservative, then T_1 is consistent iff T_2 is consistent. This logical approach to the construction of specifications and their refinement is presented in detail in Turski and Maibaum (1987) and is an important research topic.

10.4 SPECIFICATIONS IN THE ALGEBRAIC APPROACH

In this section we bring together ideas and results from classical and universal algebraic theory, with the concept of abstract data types from computer science. An awareness of the need for the precise specification of complex systems led to the interest in discrete mathematics. Zilles was one of the first to use the theoretical framework of universal algebras to specify the abstract data types that Liskov had identified at the programming level. The abstract data type was specified by a syntactic presentation of an algebra by sorts and operation symbols together with a set of equational axioms.

The underlying logic for these specifications, called equational logic, was presented in Chapter 8. Although this logic lacks existential quantification and universal quantification is implicit only, it does offer the advantage that a minimal model can be constructed for a specification. This minimal model is useful for discussing the properties given by the equational axioms and has been chosen to provide an *initial* semantics for algebraic specifications. The name initial has been given to the semantics because, as we saw in Chapter 8, the initial algebra in the category of all algebras is the concrete model for an abstract data type. An alternative semantics for algebraic specifications is called a *loose* semantics.

The early use of algebraic specifications revealed their unsuitability (in a pure form) for expressing the properties of complex systems, however. Although they offered the advantages of a precise notation for specification, they showed the same disadvantages that large unstructured programs in low-level mechanical codes had at the programming level. Just as procedural abstraction and data structures had been used to structure programs, so efforts were made to structure the theories that algebraic specifications expressed. It is in the *structuring* of theories, pioneered by Burstall and Goguen (1979) in their work on Clear, that the algebraic approach to specification has made important contributions to the specification of complex systems.

10.4.1 A specification is a theory presentation

The algebraic framework that we require for specification has bccn constructed in Chapter 8. The syntactic presentation of an algebraic structure is used to specify an abstract data type. As in the logical approach to specification, we begin by defining an algebraic specification of an abstract data type as a named theory presentation. Our definition of a theory presentation in the algebraic approach is based on equational logic and the deduction of consequences that belong to the theory.

Definition 10.5 Theory presentation in equational logic A theory presentation is a pair (Σ, E) where Σ is a signature and E is a set of Σ-equational axioms.

Our definition of a theory presentation is therefore the same as Def. 8.12, where it was used to define an abstract algebraic structure. The algebra that *satisfies* a theory presentation (Σ, E) is the algebra defined by Def. 8.13. This algebra is called a *model* of the theory presentation. In order to define the theory that is derived from a theory presentation for a signature and set of equations, E, we need the concept of the closure of a set of equations, denoted by E^* in Def. 8.15.

Definition 10.6 Theory in equational logic A theory T for a signature Σ is called a Σ-theory and is a theory presentation (Σ, E) where E is closed. A theory is satisfiable if it has at least one model.

The theory, T, is therefore the same as its theory presentation when the set of equations is closed. We need the concept of a theory presentation as a *specification* for a theory. The words are used interchangeably, however. Within the algebraic approach the important idea is that a theory *specifies* a set of algebras which is the set of all its models.

Definition 10.7 Algebraic specification A specification in the algebraic approach is a theory presentation (Σ, E) where Σ is a signature and E is a set of Σ-equational axioms.

Example 10.6 The specification *Boolean* is a named theory presentation for the theory of truth-values. This is an initial specification that must be given an initial semantics. The importance of initiality is that it imposes a condition on the model for the specification, as we see in the next section.

Initial	*Boolean*
sorts	bool
constants	true: bool
	false: bool
opns	**not**: bool → bool
eqns	**not**(true) = false
	not(**not** (a)) =a
end	

10.4.2 A model for a specification

We saw in Chapter 8 how the elements in the models give values to, or name, the terms that are built from the signature. In this sense the model of a specification is more concrete than the specification, which is a named theory presentation. We also saw that the algebraic model for a specification can be easily characterized as the *initial* model for that specification, where the idea of initiality comes from category theory.

The existence of an initial model for a specification has contributed to the popularity of the algebraic approach. This is because it opens up the possibility of writing a specification in two different ways:

1 Specifying the properties of an abstract data type by directly giving the set of equations to form an 'abstract' specification.

2 First constructing a model for the abstract data type from some known properties and then deriving the 'constructive' specification.

The first way is close to that used for writing logical specifications in Sec. 10.3 but is restricted by the need to use equational logic instead of the full power of first-order logic. The restriction deprives the specifier of being able to write sentences that use quantification, negation and implication.

Example 10.7 Although there is an implicit universal quantifier around the equations of algebraic specifications, a definition such as $\mathscr{P}(x) \leftrightarrow \neg[\exists i\ \exists j\ i \neq 1 \wedge j \neq 1 \wedge i \times j = n]$, where $\mathscr{P}(x)$ denotes 'x is prime', cannot be written.

If algebraic specification languages are extended to permit axioms that use quantifiers then the existence of an initial model, as a minimal model, for an algebraic specification is not guaranteed. The advantage of using the restricted equational logic for specifying abstract data types is that the second way of writing a specification can be used to produce a 'constructive' specification by concentrating first on building an initial model of an abstract data type. We saw in Sec. 8.3.3 that the initial algebra always exists and satisfies the equational axioms E of an abstract algebraic structure (Σ, E), but that it does not satisfy any additional properties. This is why it is described as a minimal model. The other models of (Σ, E) are 'looser' models that satisfy additional properties. They are all related to the representative initial model because there is a homomorphism *from* the initial model *to* the other 'loose' models in the class of (Σ, E)-algebras. We saw in Sec. 8.3.3 that those models that are *finitely generated*, or null-generated, have the special property of being quotient structures of the initial model.

Now we need to explain the significance of the algebraic theory about the models of algebraic specifications that we have presented. First we recall that an algebraic specification of an abstract data type is a presentation of the theory that describes the data type. Then we recall the special properties of the initial model for the specification, (Σ, E):

1 Every element in the carrier set of the model is the value of some ground Σ term in the signature of the specification. This property holds for finitely generated algebras and is described by the slogan 'no junk', meaning that there must be no unnecessary (unnamed) elements in the model.

2 The model must not satisfy any ground equation that is not in E. This property is known as 'no confusion' and means that no two terms must be given the same value unless the equations in E say they should have the same value.

Clearly the initial model provides a semantics for a specification by giving values to the terms of the syntax of the specification. Intuitively this meaning is 'tight', or strict, and contrasts with the permissive style of specification we suggested in Sec. 10.3. The semantics provided by the rest of the models in the class of (Σ, E)-algebras provide a 'looser' and more permissive semantics. It is useful to view the semantics for algebraic specifications in terms of the closure of the set of equations E in the specification (Σ, E). An algebraic specification is either a loose or tight closure of a set of equations. The keywords *loose* and *initial* are often used to indicate which closure is used.

Definition 10.8 Initial algebraic specification A specification in the algebraic approach is initial if it tightens the closure on the set of equations in the specification. The tight closure is under the rules:

(a) of equational inference,

(b) of structural induction (to ensure there is no junk in the model),

(c) if equality between terms cannot be derived by the rules of equational inference and structural induction then the terms must be unequal (to ensure there is no confusion in the model).

Definition 10.9 Loose algebraic specification A specification in the algebraic approach is loose if it closes the equations of the specification under the rules of equational inference.

Example 10.8 A specification for natural numbers illustrates the different closures that result from a loose or tight semantics.

<u>Nat</u> =

sorts	nat
opns	0: $\rightarrow$ nat
	succ: nat $\rightarrow$ nat
equations	none

The loose closure with no equations in the specification is satisfied by many models, or representations, of the numbers that we use for counting. Each model is an association of a carrier set with the sort nat.

(a) $\mid$ Nat $\mid = \{0, 1, 2, 3, \ldots\}$ is an obvious possibility with succ interpreted by the successor function. Our counting numbers are modelled mathematically by the set $\mathbb{N}$.

(b) $\mid$ Nat$' \mid = \{0, I, II, III, \ldots\}$. This set is only a renaming of $\mathbb{N}$ and is within the same isomorphism class of models—essentially it is the same set of numbers.

(c) | Mod2 $|= \{0, 1\}$ is also a possible model with the following interpretation for the symbol succ:

$$\begin{aligned} \text{succ}(0) &= 1 \\ \text{succ}(1) &= 0 \end{aligned}$$

However, the constant symbol 0 is also represented by $0 \in$|Mod 2|. This interpretation for succ brings confusion by identifying both the terms 0 and succ(1) with the same element in the model. This is because the model itself satisfies a ground equation that is not given in the set of equations for the specification. Confusion is introduced by the unnecessary identification of terms, which is not satisfied by other models for the specification. Although |Mod 2| is allowed under the semantics of the loose closure it will not be allowed as a model under the third rule of the semantics for the tight closure.

(d) | Non-standard nat $|= \{0', 1', 2', \ldots, 0'', 1'', 2'', \ldots\}$ is another possible model under the loose semantics of the specification. The term 0 will be represented by $0'$, succ(0) by $1'$, and so on. However, $0''$ appears as 'junk' in the model: it is an element that is not 'named' by a term. This model will also be forbidden under the tight closure because elements such as $0'', 1'', \ldots$ are not generated by structural induction from 0 by the interpretation of the succ operation symbol.

Exercise 10.10 We gave Example 10.6 as an example of an initial specification. Explain why this specification would not allow a model with a carrier set $\{a, b, c\}$. Relate your answer to the closure of the equations in the specification.

Exercise 10.11 Explain why the initial specification in Example 10.6 would not allow a model with the carrier set $| A |= \{0\}$ and $\text{true}_A = \text{false}_A = 0$ as an equality that holds in the model.

10.4.3 Building theories for algebraic specification

Although the early use of algebraic specifications brought advantages for specifying simple abstract data types they were quite unsuitable for specifying large systems. We identified abstract data types as primitive objects in a system in Sec. 10.2.1. The view of an abstract data type with values is clearly expressed precisely by an algebraic specification. A major problem for specification approaches, however, is to provide a theoretical framework within which specifications can be structured from simple, or primitive, specifications. By joining simple specifications together we can work towards the specification of complex systems. We described the extension of algebras in Chapter 8 on page 212. The extension of specifications is one of the main ways of building more structured specifications.

The algebraic specification language Clear was the first to provide theory-building operations. The semantics of combining theories is an important topic for research. The important ideas in Clear were to build structured theories by extending theories (in different ways) and to allow parameterized theories. These ideas have been continued in the specification language OBJ which is described as a *functional logic* language that integrates a specification and a programming language. The integration of the logic and the algebraic approaches is illustrated in the language Eqlog which combines OBJ with logic programming.

We give two simple examples of specifications that are built by extending the even simpler specification for Boolean values. The notation is simple but explicitly states the extensions that are made.

Example 10.9 The following theory of lists is an extension of the theory of Boolean values:

List = the extension of *Boolean* by:

types	list of α
constants	nil: list of α
	cons: $\alpha \times$ list of $\alpha \rightarrow$ list of α
	head: list of $\alpha \rightarrow \alpha$
	tail: list of $\alpha \rightarrow$ list of α
	null: list of $\alpha \rightarrow$ bool
axioms	head(cons(x, l)) $= x$
	tail(cons(x, l)) $= l$
	null(cons(x, l)) = false
	null(nil) = true

The free variables are implicitly universally quantified. It is important to note that logical specifications use predicates rather than functions which have results in the set {true, false}.

Example 10.10 Stacks can also be built by extending the theory Boolean:

Stack = the extension of *Boolean* by:

types	stack of α
constants	nilstack: stack of α
	push: $\alpha \times$ stack of $\alpha \rightarrow$ stack of α
	top: stack of $\alpha \rightarrow \alpha$
	pop: stack of $\alpha \rightarrow$ stack of α
	isempty: stack of $\alpha \rightarrow$ bool
axioms	top(push(x, s)) $= x$
	pop(push(x, s)) $= s$
	isempty(push(x, s)) = false
	isempty(nilstack) = true

Exercise 10.12 Build a specification for a queue by extending the theory of Booleans.

We have identified the theory of Boolean values as a structural building block for the theory of lists. An alternative would be to build an abstract similarity type for first-in-last-out structures and extend this to theories for lists, stacks and strings by suitable renaming. An abstract similarity type would similarly be used to form a theory of a queue by simple renaming.

10.5 SPECIFICATIONS IN VDM AND Z

An alternative view of a primitive object as a building block for the construction of a system specification was suggested in Sec. 10.2.1. This view identified a primitive object, at a rather less abstract level, with its own internal *state* that is changed by the defined operations on that object. The incorporation of the notion of a state into system specifications is shown in this section to be a key characteristic of model-based specifications. In this section we consider the general principles of model-based specifications, and illustrate these using the notations VDM and Z. These are the most popular methods for specification and the methods that are most widespread in industrial use.

10.5.1 Construction of a mathematical model

Specifications in VDM and Z are described as *model-based*, or constructive, because they involve the explicit construction of a model of the system in terms of mathematical structures such as sets, lists, sequences and mappings. Specifying in VDM and Z can therefore be viewed as a less abstract activity than writing the axioms of a theory presentation within the logical and algebraic approaches to specification. The more concrete nature of model-based specifications may account for their greater popularity among programmers who work in software development as an industrial process.

In the abstract axiomatic approaches to specification, the relationships between operations on abstract data types are expressed by axioms, either in first-order logic or in the subset called equational logic. The behaviour of an abstract data type is therefore defined implicitly by the properties of the operations on the data type. Although no explicit model is constructed, we saw in Sec. 10.4 that the existence of a minimal algebraic model, the initial algebra, does provide a semantics for tight specifications. We also pointed out in some sense that the ability to construct this initial model during the activity of specification makes specification easier for programmers. However, the role of the initial model is essentially to model properties of the system by equational axioms and to give values to abstract data types by interpretation in the carrier sets.

By contrast, the mathematical model constructed in the model-based approaches to specification provides a semantics for the abstract data type and comes closer to suggesting an implementation for an abstract data type. It is because a *concrete* mathematical model is constructed for a specification in this approach that we avoid using the name 'abstract model approach' for specifications in VDM and Z.

Example 10.11 In the model-based approach a specification for a queue can be modelled by a sequence. The properties of a queue are, by definition, the properties of a sequence: an empty sequence represents the initial queue; the operation defined to concatenate sequences represents the addition of a new element to a queue. Since concatenation is only defined between sequences, the operation that adds to a queue must first create a sequence from the new element that is to be added to the queue. The sequence also models the property that the elements in a queue are ordered.

Exercise 10.13 Consider specifying a queue with a set as a model. Identify the set operations that would model the behaviour of a queue and any problems that this model may introduce. Use the queue by carrying out the operations suggested in Exercise 10.4.

VDM and Z are also described as *state-based* specification techniques because the notion of system state is central to the specification. The operations on an abstract data type are modelled by operations on mathematical structures that *process* objects by changing their values. This procedural view of a sequence of state changes, represented by a before state object and an after state object, is close to the way we think about programming in languages such as Pascal. In the specification, the abstract data type is represented by a mathematical object that *changes* when it is operated on. This contrasts with the algebraic approach in which a *new* value results from the application of a function to the set that represents the data type.

Example 10.12 In Exercise 10.4 a new queue was formed as each item of data was added to the queue. If we use a model-based approach and represent the queue by a sequence, we model the change of state in the queue as each new data item is added. The initial state of a newly created queue is that the queue is empty;

in our specifications we use the notation [ ] to represent the empty sequence. The after state of adding Fred to the queue is represented by $[\,]^\frown$ [Fred] to denote the *concatenation* of the empty sequence with the sequence containing Fred. However, this state is the before state for the operation that adds Anne to the sequence. For each operation on the queue we must describe the queue as it was *before* the operation *and* as it was *after* the operation.

Exercise 10.14 Draw diagrams to represent the before state and after state of the table that is used to store information in Exercise 10.5.

Model-based specification languages adopt conventions to describe state changes in a system, and usually give different names to the objects *before* the operation from the objects *after* the operation. This enables the operation itself to be described as a relation between the before and after objects. The predicate calculus is then used to define the relation formally. As specification languages, VDM and Z are closely related although they differ both in their theoretical foundations and in the facilities they offer for structuring specifications.

10.5.2 The Vienna development method (VDM)

VDM is a methodology for the systematic development of software, which was developed during the 1970s and has been applied to a variety of applications in industry. It is based on the denotational semantic approach to defining the meaning of formal languages. This is the same approach we used to define the language of binary numerals in Sec. 7.3. Offering more than a specification language, VDM provides rules and procedures for the stages of software development from abstract specification to implementation in a programming language. Support tools, management and training aspects are also provided within the methodology, which has been applied to the construction of medium-sized systems.

One reason for the acceptance of VDM in industry may be that it offers a flexible approach to the development of software within a formal system. By emphasizing a rigorous approach within a formal framework, it allows the use of intuition in the construction of correctness arguments, rather than demanding complete formality for the verification of all development steps.

The activity of specification in VDM is a top-down development from an abstract specification that expresses the functions that are required of the system at the top level. Development proceeds from the abstract specification by refining the data objects in the system to more concrete *reified types* and by modelling the operations at the abstract level by operations on the concrete types. The addition of more concrete detail is described as reification, rather than refinement, in Jones (1986). At each stage of reification *retrieve functions* are defined as mappings from the concrete type back to the abstract type, and an argument is constructed to show the *adequacy* of the development step. The *adequacy proof obligation* provides an argument for correctness and can be discharged by an informal constructive argument.

A VDM specification focuses on the functions of a system that define 'what' the system does. As development proceeds a transition is made, however, from mathematical functions to operations that are executed on a state. In effect operations are textually like procedures in programs. Although VDM is state-based, the ideas of the algebraic approach to specification are carried through into 'local' specifications of abstract data types. The semantics of VDM specifications is based on the theories for the mathematical modelling structures such as sets, sequences and mappings. Since all these theories rely on set theory for their foundation, VDM itself relies on set theory. In contrast with classical mathematics, VDM uses a much weaker logic than classical logic, called the *logic of partial functions*, LPF, for reasoning. There is no semantics for composing specifications in VDM, however, and the top-down approach leads to the construction of large monolithic specifications which, because of their lack of structure, are difficult to use on large systems.

VDM specifications The syntactic part of a VDM specification gives the names of the variables that define the state of the system. Each name *denotes* a set of possible values that is defined by the *type* of the mathematical structure in the model. Built-in types such as *Int* and *Nat*, denoting $\mathbb{Z}$ and $\mathbb{N}$, are provided and this part of the specification looks like a Pascal program. After the declaration of the state variables, the operations on the state are defined by their names, including any parameters. The syntactic specification is completed by predicates that express assumptions about the execution of each defined operation. Each predicate specifies the semantics of an operation in terms of pre-conditions and post-conditions for the operation.

The more abstract VDM specification is called an *implicit* specification; the concrete specification is called a *direct definition* and satisfies the implicit specification if a proof obligation can be discharged. The direct definition of a function uses the notation $\triangleq$ rather than the symbol for equality, =.

Example 10.13 An implicit specification for a simple function that gives as a result the larger of the two integers is

$max(i : \mathbb{Z}, j : \mathbb{Z}) \qquad r : \mathbb{Z}$
pre true
post $(r = i \vee r = j) \wedge i \leq r \wedge j \leq r$

The only assumption on the arguments to the function *max* concerns its type, so the pre-condition is explicitly stated to be true. The post-condition implicitly gives the meaning of the function, with the variable *r* denoting the maximum of the two integers. A direct definition for the function *max* is

$max\ (i, j) \triangleq$ if $i \leq j$ then j else i

The use of a pre-condition in an implicit specification implies that *partial* functions will be defined for non-trivial pre-conditions. Terms built from partial functions will then fail to denote values for certain arguments. The semantics for these functions is provided by the logic of partial functions, LPF, which extends the meaning of the logical connectives to belong to the set {true, false, $*$ } where $*$ denotes a 'non-value' or undefined value for a proposition. The logic LPF is weaker than classical logic but provides a firm logical foundation for VDM.

Implicit specifications of mathematical functions are extended by a notion of state in order to express programs in VDM. Any piece of program-like text is called an *operation*. The *state* of an operation is the collection of external variables that the operation can access and change. The input variables and their types are listed in brackets after the operation name. The VDM notation is extended to describe the access that an operation is allowed to variables as either read only (rd) or read and write (wr). It also marks the before object for an operation with a hook, $\overleftarrow{\ }$, to distinguish this object from the after object which is changed by the operation.

Example 10.14 The abstract data type stack is modelled by a sequence in the following VDM specification:

$Stack$ = seq of El

INITIALIZE-STACK( )
ext wr s : $Stack$
post $s_0 = [\,]$

PUSH(e : El)
ext wr s : $Stack$
post $s = [e]\overleftarrow{s}$

POP ( ) e : El
ext wr s : $Stack$
pre $s \neq [\,]$
post $\overleftarrow{s} = [e]^\frown s$

ISEMPTY ( ) r : $\mathbb{B}$
ext rd s : $Stack$
post $r \leftrightarrow s = [\,]$

This specification is for an unbounded stack. A bound on the length of a stack, to say 256, could be given by an invariant:

$BStack$ = seq of El where $inv\text{-}BStack(s) \triangleq lens \leq 256$

The invariant properties in a specification are defined on the state and specify the relationship that *must* hold between the values of the data objects in the system.

10.5.3 The Z notation

Specifications using the Z notation were developed by the Programming Research Group at Oxford University. The approach is similar to VDM and efforts are being made to extend the Z notation to a full development method. The readability of Z is emphasized by embedding the formal Z specifications in natural language documents. The *schema* has been developed as a syntactic unit that expresses the formal part of a specification, with the natural language document explaining the mathematical Z notation. Schemas can be extended and composed, although they originated as syntactic structures and have only recently been given a formal semantics based on set theory.

Basic types are the building blocks of the Z type system, which is constructed to avoid the paradoxes in set theory described in Sec. 2.1. The schema calculus provides the operations for constructing the parts of specifications that describe the types in a system. The specifications themselves describe the state of a system along with operations on the state. In describing the system state and its operations, a specification is structured by what is now a familiar pattern:

1 A declaration about the type of variables that represent the state

2 A predicate that constrains the values of these variables

This pattern, in two parts, is presented syntactically by a schema. A schema has a name and uses a box-like shape to divide the specification into its parts. The name of the schema is embedded in the top line of the box.

Example 10.15 The positive rational numbers, in the form p/q, can be expressed as a pair of integers with the constraint that q is not zero.

```
┌─ PositiveRationals ──────────────────────
│ a : ℤ;
│ b : ℤ
├──────────
│ a ≥ 0 ∧
│ b > 0
└──────────────────────────────────────────
```

In order to simplify the syntax, declarations are usually put on separate lines in a schema and the semi-colon is omitted. Similarly, by printing the conjuncts on separate lines, the conjunction symbol can be omitted.

Example 10.16 For any two sets A and B we specify the projection functions from the set $A \times B$ to the sets A and B. These functions project on to the first or second elements of a pair of elements.

```
╒═ [A, B] ═════════════════════════════════
│ first : (A × B) → A
│ second : (A × B) → B
├──────────
│ ∀ a : A; b : B
│ first (a, b) = a
│ second (a, b) = b
└──────────────────────────────────────────
```

The top of the box for this schema has a double line to indicate that the definition presented by the schema is *generic*. The name of the schema is given by the generic parameters A and B which are written inside square brackets. The replacement of the generic parameters by actual sets is by *instantiation*.

The projection functions can be applied to pairs of all types:

$$\begin{aligned} \text{first(`a', donkey)} &= \text{`a'} \\ \text{second(} \{1,2,3\}, aab\} &= aab \end{aligned}$$

Just as schemas can be constructed by parameterization so the name of one schema can be included among the declaration of another schema. The power of the schema is also illustrated by schema *decoration*, in which it is indicated at the schema level that all the state variables are constrained by being in the after state, following the effect of an operation on the state. The symbol Δ before the name of any schema S denotes a change in state just as δ denotes a change in the differential calculus. So ΔS means that to all the declarations of S are added the declaration of the changed variables of S. The changed variables of S are dashed variables and belong to the set of declarations, S'.

Example 10.17 A schema to define an operation to compute the square root of a positive rational number could be presented by the schema

$$\begin{array}{|l} \hline \textit{SquareRationals} \\ \textit{PositiveRationals} \\ \Delta\textit{PositiveRationals} \\ \hline (a')^2 = a \\ (b')^2 = b \\ \hline \end{array}$$

which is an abbreviation of the schema

$$\begin{array}{|l} \hline \textit{SquareRationals} \\ a, b, a', b' : \mathbb{Z} \\ \hline a \geq 0 \\ b > 0 \\ a' \geq 0 \\ b' > 0 \\ (a')^2 = a \\ (b')^2 = b \\ \hline \end{array}$$

A further decoration of schemas is by the Ξ-notation. This notation specifies that an operation does not cause any change of state, and will be illustrated in our example specification of an application system.

10.5.4 An application system specified in VDM and Z

We illustrate and compare the features of VDM and Z by using them to specify the same system. We specify a simple security database. A set of users is taken from a pre-defined population of users and assigned some level of security access. The database stores information about the users and also their security access level which is a number from 0 to 4, with 4 representing the most privileged access. Operations carried out by the database include: adding new users; finding the security level of a user; listing all privileged users; and changing security levels.

We now present both the VDM and Z specifications for this system, with the VDM specification first and the Z specification, as a schema, second. We start with the specification of the system state:

$$\begin{array}{ll} \textit{Security} :: & \textit{assigned} : \mathcal{P}(\textit{User}) \\ \textit{access}: & \textit{User} \nrightarrow \mathbb{N} \\ \text{where} & \\ \textit{inv-Security} = & \textit{assigned} = \text{dom}(\textit{access}) \wedge \\ & \text{range}(\textit{access}) = \{0, 1, 2, 3, 4\} \end{array}$$

$$\begin{array}{|l} \hline \textit{Security} \\ \textit{assigned} : \mathbb{P}\,\textit{user} \\ \textit{access} : \textit{user} \nrightarrow \mathbb{N} \\ \hline \textit{assigned} = \text{dom}\,\textit{access} \\ \text{ran}\,\textit{access} = \{0, 1, 2, 3, 4\} \\ \hline \end{array}$$

We see that in VDM and Z the declaration of the state variables is the same, with *access* declared as a partial function. The predicate constraining the value of the variables is split into two lines in Z, however, instead of being declared as an invariant and explicitly joined by a conjunction, as in VDM. The symbol we have used for the power set constructor is $\mathbb{P}X$ for some set X in Z and $\mathscr{P}(X)$ in VDM.

Example 10.18 A possible state of the system is: *assigned* = {bev, gillian, norman} and *access* = {bev ↦ 2, gillian ↦ 4, norman ↦ 4}.

Next we come to the operations. First we specify the operation to add a new user who is without security access:

ADDUSER$(name{:}User,\ level{:}\ \mathbb{N})$

$$
\begin{array}{lll}
\text{ext} & \text{wr} & assigned: \mathscr{P}(User) \\
 & \text{wr} & access: User \nrightarrow \mathbb{N} \\
\text{pre} & \multicolumn{2}{l}{(name \notin assigned) \land (level \leq 4)} \\
\text{post} & \multicolumn{2}{l}{access' = access \cup \{name \mapsto level\}}
\end{array}
$$

Adduser

$$
\begin{array}{l}
\Delta Security \\
name? : user \\
level? : \mathbb{N} \\
\hline
name? \notin assigned \\
level? \leq 4 \\
access' = access \cup \{name? \mapsto level?\}
\end{array}
$$

The arguments to the operations are expressed as parameters in VDM. The naming convention in Z is to end the names of input objects by '?' and the names of output objects by '!'. An after object has the same name as the before object but with a dash added. This is known as 'decoration' in Z. This convention is also often used in VDM, and we use it here to reduce confusion between the two notations.

In VDM both state variables have write and read access. The fact that the state is changed by the operation is shown in the Z notation by writing Δ *Security* under the name of the operation on all of the variables that represent the system state in the schema *Security*. The properties of the operation are described implicitly by pre- and post-conditions in both notations. In Z the predicate for the pre-condition is split into separate assertions on two lines, as usual, and the post-condition expresses the updating of the function *access*.

The importance of such a formal specification is that we can begin to prove things about the system that we expect should be true. As a simple example, we note that after the operation *Adduser*, the value of the variable *assigned* must also have changed. In fact, we would expect that $assigned' = assigned \cup \{name\}$. We can prove this as follows:

$$
\begin{array}{lll}
assigned' & = \text{dom}(access)' & \text{(state invariant property)} \\
 & = \text{dom}(access \cup \{name \mapsto level\}) & \text{(from the specification of } Adduser\text{)} \\
 & = assigned \cup \{name\} & \text{(definition of a function in Sec. 2.3)}
\end{array}
$$

The specification in VDM for the operation that finds the security access level of a user is:

FINDLEVEL(*name* : *User*) *level* : $\mathbb{N}$

ext	rd	*assigned* : $\mathscr{P}(User)$
	rd	*access* : $User \nrightarrow \mathbb{N}$
pre	($name \in assigned$)	
post	$level = access(name)$	

For this operation, the state does not get changed. This is reflected by the fact that, in VDM, both the state variables are specified as read only. In Z, this is specified by writing Ξ *Security* immediately underneath the operation name.

```
__Findlevel______________________________
| ΞSecurity
| name? : user
| level! : ℕ
|_______________
| name? ∈ assigned
| level! = access(name?)
|_________________________________________
```

The next operation we specify is to list all the most privileged users:

TOPLEVEL( ) *superusers* : $\mathscr{P}(User)$

ext	rd	*assigned* : $\mathscr{P}(User)$
	rd	*access* : $User \nrightarrow \mathbb{N}$
post	superusers $= \{x : assigned \mid access(x){=}4\}$	

```
__Toplevel_______________________________
| ΞSecurity
| superusers! : ℙ User
|_______________
| superusers! = {x : assigned | access(x) = 4}
|_________________________________________
```

The operation *Toplevel* has no inputs. It simply outputs the set of users (called *superusers* here) who have the top security level value 4. For the system state of Example 10.18, superusers = {gillian, norman}. Note that this operation has no explicit pre-condition but assumes the pre-condition *true*.

Finally, we need an operation to initialize the whole system:

INITSECURITY( )

ext	wr	*assigned* : $\mathscr{P}(User)$
	wr	*access* : $User \nrightarrow \mathbb{N}$
post	$assigned = \phi$	

```
__InitSecurity___________________________
| Security
|_______________
| assigned = φ
|_________________________________________
```

Thus we have initialized the system by defining the value of the variable *assigned* to be the empty set.

The use of the schema to provide reusability of parts of the Z specification is illustrated by the inclusion of the schema *Security* in the schemas *Adduser*, *Findlevel*, *Toplevel* and *InitSecurity*.

Exercise 10.15 Specify in both Z and VDM an operation *Changelevel* that enables the security level of a user, who already has security access, to be changed.

Exercise 10.16 Prove that, after the operation *InitSecurity*, the value of the state variable *access* must be the empty function.

10.6 SUMMARY

In this chapter we have presented the theoretical framework for the formal specification of systems. We have shown that the activity of specification involves building theories and reasoning about them within a formal framework. Formal languages provide different structuring facilities for describing systems and it is clearly important to match the theoretical framework to the type of application system that is to be constructed.

Abstract data types have been presented as the primitive objects in a system, and we specified them initially by a semi-formal language of sets and functions. The construction of a specification for a large system from the specification of its parts appears to be a promising technique for the future.

The most abstract specification approaches express the properties of abstract data types by axioms. First-order logic provides a powerful and natural language for writing loose and descriptive specifications of theories. In the algebraic approach the more restricted form of equational logic offers a less powerful language for expressing the axioms of an abstract data type. However, it does provide the possibility for a constructive approach to specification by guaranteeing that a model of the specification can be built. This is the initial algebra that realizes the specification as its minimal model.

The popularity of VDM and Z may be due to the fact that they both belong to the model-based approach of specification. By explicitly constructing a mathematical model based on set theory these specification methods are, in this sense, more concrete than the axiomatic approaches of first-order logic and equational logic. An explicit notion of state is declared in a specification, and operations that change the state are described by predicates. In Chapter 11 we shall identify the concept of state as a characteristic of the procedural model of programming. The abstract axiomatic approaches to specification can be linked, at a lower level in software development, with the declarative style of programming used by logical and functional programming languages. In Chapter 12 we use the axiomatic approach in a first-order language of logic to verify programs in the procedural paradigm.

The approaches to specification have emerged from different theoretical frameworks, and this is reflected in the different paradigms of programming. However, there is now an acceptance that advantages are to be gained by bringing together the different paradigms and matching the specification approach to the type of application system that is to be constructed. Within the algebraic approach there is an increasing use of first-order logic to gain greater power of expression: the language OBJ is a *functional logic* specification and programming language; *Eqlog* combines OBJ with logic programming; FOOPS unifies OBJ with object-oriented programming; and FOOPlog unifies the functional, logic and object-oriented paradigms and has a rigorous logical basis. The unification of specification paradigms is now being reflected by the unification of programming paradigms (Goguen and Meseguer, 1987).

FURTHER READING

The logical approach to specification is given in detail in Turski and Maibaum (1987) where specification is described as theory building. A classical treatment of model theory is given in Enderton (1972). The specification of complex systems is presented in Cohen, Harwood and Jackson's book (1986) with an emphasis on applications; this book gives specifications in the algebraic approach as well as in VDM. More detail on VDM is given in the book by Jones (1986), and for a deep treatment of the algebraic approach to specification we recommend the book by Ehrig and Mahr (1985). An introduction to formal specification using Z is to be found in Potter, Sinclair and Till's book (1991). Specifications in Z are also presented in the book by Woodcock and Loomes (1988).

The use of category theory for structuring specifications and modules in the algebraic approach is presented in detail in Ehrig and Mahr (1990). The necessary theoretical background of category theory for computer science can be found in Barr and Wells' book (1990). A constructive specification theory that uses categorical constructions is presented in detail in Ury and Gergely (1990).

Chapter 11

MODELS OF COMPUTATION FOR PROGRAMMING

In this chapter we classify the main approaches to programming and explain their relationships to the axiomatic and model-based approaches to specification.

The oldest style of programming is the *procedural style* (or the imperative style) and is the basis of most mechanical codes. It developed from the architectural model of the earliest computers and is based on the notion of changing the values of variables in the store of the computer. The model for this traditional style of programming is called the *von Neumann* model, and is named after John von Neumann who originally proposed the architecture. We will explain some of its disadvantages as a model for the construction and analysis of systems.

An emerging view of programming links the activity of designing a program to the mathematical activity of designing a computation. We show in Sec. 11.1 how the key notions of programming can be linked to the mathematical concepts that we presented in Part I of this book. The procedural style of programming is shown in Sec. 11.2 to be based on the von Neumann model, and we identify the more recent paradigms of programming that have emerged from this model. By contrast, declarative programming is without the concept of a changeable store that is fundamental to the von Neumann model. We show in Sec. 11.3 that two distinct models are used in the declarative style: the applicative model in which functions are applied to arguments and the logic model in which relations are defined between objects.

11.1 PROGRAMMING IS DESIGNING A COMPUTATION*

In this section we emphasize the mathematical view of programming and relate the models of computation for programming to the approaches to specification that we described in Chapter 10. Because programming is the activity of designing a computation, we then identify a computable function as one that can be defined both by a recursive function and by an expression in the λ-calculus. Finally we explain how the development of a constructive type theory offers a proof of correctness for a program as it is constructed. The importance of type theory is the link that it makes between programming, traditionally viewed as a craft, and the mature disciplines of mathematics and logic.

The earliest programming languages were low-level mechanical codes that could be read directly and executed by a machine. The advantage of high-level mechanical codes was that they could be understood by the human reader. An extension of the development from low-level to high-level programming languages has been the development of the *activity* of programming from one of writing a sequence of instructions to be executed by a machine to one of specifying in a precise way a solution to a problem as a computation.

Programming is a mathematical activity that has a lot in common with deducing and proving theorems in mathematics. This should not surprise us since we have defined a specification to be a named theory presentation in Chapter 10 and a program to be a concrete refinement of some abstract specification. The problem in presenting this idea is that programming began as an activity when the first computers were built; the activity of specification followed some fifty years later. Now we need to replace the emphasis of programming as a bottom-up development influenced by the hardware of the first computers. The emphasis should instead be on specification as a top-down development. This change of emphasis stems from the acceptance of the mathematical nature of specification, which we demonstrated in Chapter 10, and leads to an acceptance of the mathematical nature of programming. We can see a close relationship between the approaches to specification and the models of computation for programming:

- Specifications in first-order logic that belong to the axiomatic approach can be refined to logic programs.
- Algebraic specifications in equational logic can be refined to the recursive equations of functional programs.
- Model-based specifications can be refined to the languages of the von Neumann paradigm (Ada is known to be a suitable programming language for implementing VDM specifications).

As we saw in Chapter 10, it is likely that the future generation of programming languages will emerge from a unification of these programming paradigms to combine the advantages of each style into new languages that are best suited for each application area (Goguen and Meseguer, 1987).

11.1.1 Computable functions

Two of the most difficult problems in the construction of software systems are: the representation of infinite data objects and the representation of functions that are partial and not guaranteed to terminate. The concept of recursion is fundamental to computing because all the functions that are computable can also be defined recursively.

In Chapter 2 we introduced, informally, the notion of computable functions. These may be defined formally in terms of a special class of recursive functions, called μ-recursive functions, which are computable by a Turing machine, but are not guaranteed to terminate. It turns out that this is equivalent to being defined by an expression of the λ-calculus, as described in Chapter 9. Thus, every computable function is a λ-calculus expression. This explains the importance of the λ-calculus in programming theory, and will be exploited further in Chapter 15.

Achieving a precise definition for the semantics of non-terminating programs was a difficult theoretical problem, however. A way had to be found to describe infinite objects and the language of sets and functions was insufficient for this task. We explained the concepts of discrete and continuous in Sec. 1.2.3 as an introduction to this problem. The continuity of an infinite non-terminating program can be expressed if we can find a way of talking about the finite approximations to this infinite object. Figure 11.1 illustrates the discrete drops of water coming from a tap, on the left, as the finite approximations

Figure 11.1 Finite approximations to an infinite object.

of a continuous stream of water on the right. The solution to this problem can be found in the theory of Domains, as described in Chapter 9. Domain theory provides the foundation for the denotational semantics approach to defining the semantics of programming languages, and fixed point theory, also presented in Chapter 9, gives meaning to the recursive Domain equations that provide the denotational semantic definitions of programs.

Example 11.1 The *while-do* instruction in Pascal has a recursive definition, which we give as

while C do S = if C do S ; while C do S

Each while-do instruction therefore *approximates* to the intended meaning of the first occurrence of the while loop. Domain theory is required to provide a precise meaning for this instruction in Pascal; its meaning is modelled by a *lattice* with a partial ordering relation of 'approximates to'. By working with the sequential composition of programs in semantic Domains, instead of function composition on sets, the while-do can be shown to be the fixed point of a recursive definition in the form $A = FA$, using the theory of Chapter 9. A definition of the *while-do* instruction that is based on operational semantics will be given in Chapter 13.

11.1.2 Type theory

The notion of type originated in logic and now occupies a central position in programming theory. The distinction between an integer type and a floating-point type that was made in FORTRAN has been extended to the notions of data structure and data type in Pascal, and finally to the notion of an abstract data type at the level of specification. The theory of types developed by Martin-Löf (1984) now offers the opportunity of proving a program, written in the theory of types, formally at the same time as the program is being constructed.

The key idea of type theory is that the conceptual framework required for programming mirrors the framework of sets and functions that are established in Chapter 2—but to see this we must take a *constructive* view of mathematics. Both the proof of the

program, procedure, algorithm	function
input	argument
output, result	value
$x := e$	$x = e$
$S_1 ; S_2$	composition of functions
if B then S_1 else S_2	definition by cases
while B do S	definition by recursion
data structure	element, object
data type	set, type
value of a data type	element of a set, object of a type
$a : A$	$a \in A$
integer	$\mathbb{Z}$
real	$\mathbb{R}$
boolean	{true, false,}
$(c_1, \ldots, c_n)$	$\{c_1, \ldots, c_n\}$

Figure 11.2 Programming concepts with their corresponding mathematical concepts.

correctness of a program and the program itself must be *constructed* in order to be useful in programming. A classical view of the primitive notions of mathematics is unusable for programming because it rests on non-constructive rules such as the law of the excluded middle. We presented this law as a tautology in Chapter 3, and also gave a non-constructive proof by the method of contradiction in Sec. 6.2. We cannot go into the details of constructive mathematics here, but give in Fig. 11.2 some of the key notions of programming (using the notation of Pascal) on the left, with the corresponding notions of mathematics on the right.

In order to see how the programming notion of a type is mirrored by the concept of a set, it is necessary to lose the classical view of a set as defined by the elements that are related by *membership* of the set. Instead we read $a \in A$ as meaning 'a is an object of type A'; this is the same as the meaning of $a : A$. The significance of $a : A$ in programming is that the object a is defined by the *behaviour* of the type A.

11.2 PROCEDURAL PROGRAMMING

Procedural programming is the oldest of the programming styles, or paradigms, and is based on the earliest architectural model for computers, the von Neumann model. A computation is expressed by the informal concept of an *algorithm* which is executed *sequentially* with assignment as the basic action. The program state consists of both an *environment* and a *changeable store*. Recursion is expressed by recursive procedures and by unbounded repetition.

11.2.1 The von Neumann model

The von Neumann model gives rise to a 'bottleneck' that is known as the 'von Neumann bottleneck'. This is recognized as one of the factors that limit the power of the imperative model of programming (Backus, 1978). The bottleneck is the connecting tube between the CPU and the store in a von Neumann computer. The program changes the store by pumping words back and forth across this tube. Unfortunately this architectural bottleneck limits the power of the conventional computer. In this procedural paradigm for programming the current state is dependent on:

- the values of all the variables in the store,
- the point at which execution is taking place.

There is a sequential form of control, with *assignment statements*, or commands, having an irreversible effect on the program state. In contrast, declarations are definitions that establish a *binding* for the names in a program to their meaning. We saw in Sec. 5.3.4 that the *environment* is a record of all the identifier bindings and that in block-structured languages, such as Pascal, the *scope* of a binding is the *block* of text in which the declaration was made.

11.2.2 Extensions of the von Neumann model

The von Neumann model is also called the state transition model. The specification methods VDM and Z, discussed in Chapter 10, also belong to this model. Extensions, or variants, of the state transition model are:

- the object model which expresses the primitive objects in a system, as we suggested in Sec. 10.2.1, and the notion of classifying objects according to their attributes,
- the communication model for languages with modules such as Modula and Ada,
- concurrent models for languages such as Modula, Ada and Occam (based on the CSP model of Sec. 9.4).

The object model uses the classification paradigm that is based on inheritance. It provides a useful model for system construction and seems to be replacing the communication model which is based on passing parameters through interfaces between modules.

Programs based on the von Neumann model can be difficult to read. The effect of a program is described by 'what happens in the machine', and unexpected changes to the values of program variables occur as *side effects* of procedures if these variables are not passed as parameters. Denotational semantic descriptions of procedural languages are also complicated and, as we shall see in Chapter 12, proof of the correctness of procedural programs is more difficult to carry out. For these reasons computer scientists have turned towards different ways of thinking about programs.

Exercise 11.1 The computational state of a Pascal program consists of both a store and an environment. Give a simple example of a Pascal program and identify those statements in your program that change the store and those statements that change the environment. Differentiate between these two types of Pascal statement by explaining whether their effect on the program state is reversible or not.

11.3 DECLARATIVE PROGRAMMING

This most recent paradigm avoids the disadvantages of the von Neumann bottleneck because it is not based on a model with a changeable store. The program state consists solely of an environment involving binding, and the program itself consists solely of definitions or expressions. Two distinct models of computation have developed from the declarative paradigm: functional programming based on the applicative model and relational programming based on the logic model.

11.3.1 Functional programming based on the applicative model

This style of programming is based on the λ-calculus, described in Chapter 9, and the work of Peter Landin on the language ISWIM. Functional programming has now become fashionable: Miranda, Hope, ML, SASL, KRC and FP are all examples of functional languages. Of these languages Miranda, Hope and ML have strong typing. In contrast LISP, the earliest functional language, has no typing constraint and offers a general purpose storage location that produces insecurity. At present, however, implementations for well-designed functional languages and useful support tools are not widely available. Concepts such as real state-dependent behaviour and time are *not* as easy to express as in procedural languages. However, by passing the state as an argument to the function, it is possible to write operating systems and editors in functional languages.

In the applicative model, functions are *applied* to arguments and there is no sequence of executions, assignment or unlimited repetition. Functional languages use conditionals to define recursive expressions or equations. There is no concept from state transition; there are no control structures and no variables for assignment. Functions may return several values and there is no notion of the 'past history' of execution; for this reason functional languages are not context dependent. The composition of functions is simply defined in the applicative model so that more complex functions can be constructed.

Since most specification languages are functional the step from specification to program development is easier. In contrast the step from a functional specification language to a procedural programming language is a difficult one. Functional programs are elegant and usually shorter than the corresponding algorithms in the imperative style. They are free from side effects and there is no dependence on a notion of store. Because the functional model is closer to discrete mathematics, the proof of correctness of functional programs is easier than in the imperative style of programming, and the semantics of functional programming languages is simpler and therefore more clearly defined. The way forward would seem to be to integrate the best ideas in functional languages with those from the other programming paradigms.

Recursive equations We have seen that recursion is a compact and natural way of defining many functions. It is also powerful enough to describe *every* function that can be computed. Statements about the *correctness* or *equivalence* of programs which compute functions can therefore be written as statements about recursively defined functions.

In Chapter 9 we used the λ-notation to define new functions in terms of given functions and values. By building more complex functions we are able to compute more complex programs. We have seen that there are two ways of building functions: by function composition and by recursion. Because the theoretical framework of procedural languages is based on the concept of a machine with a state, however, we cannot compose functions in procedural languages. Instead we use a sequence of operations and make calls to procedures. Unless parameters are explicitly passed to procedures in order to record all changes to variables, side effects will occur in procedural languages, as *unexpected* changes are made to program variables.

Languages based on the applicative model follow the basic rules of discrete mathematics that we have established in Chapter 2. First, rules in mathematics are static and do not change. If a function f is given a value x, the value of $f(x)$ will always be the same if the value of x is the same. A procedure, based on the von Neumann model, often gives a different result each time it is called, however.

Example 11.2 In the following fragment of Pascal code, the procedure f changes the value of a variable without declaring that variable as a parameter. Even if the *same* variable is given as a parameter to f in consecutive procedure calls, the result will be different each time f is called.

```
y := 6 ;
  :
procedure f (var x) ;
begin
   y := y + 1
   x := x + y
end;
  :
f(x)
```

A second basic rule in mathematics is that the same expression always denotes the same value. For example, the expression $x^2 - 2x + 1$ has a solution $x = 1$ everywhere in the scope of x. Within this expression we would not expect x to have the value 1 in x^2 but the value 2 in $2x$. This basic rule is not always kept in languages that are based on the procedural model, however.

Example 11.3 In Pascal the value of x will change in the expression 'if $x > y$ then $x := x - 1$' according to the flow of control in the program. The assignment operation changes the value of a variable in the middle of its scope. An expression may not even be equal to itself.

Example 11.4 Even the expression 'if $x = x$', where x is the following function, may be false in Pascal:

```
function x : integer
begin
   y := y + 1 ;
   x := y ;
end;
```

Clearly the value of x, as a function, changes every time x is called.

Problems like this make it very difficult to reason about program correctness in the procedural model.

We showed in Exercise 9.32 how functions could be implemented in a functional programming language, which is itself an implementation of the λ-calculus. Now we see that in the applicative model we use languages that are based on higher-order recursive equations. This enables abstractions to be 'parcelled up', so that functions operate on functions and produce functions as a result.

Exercise 11.2 The following definition of a higher order function, called *twice*, is given in the language KRC:

```
twice f x = f (f x)
sq x = x × x
f = twice sq
```

Give the effect of the function f on 2 as an argument.

Recursive structures We have defined recursive structures by induction in Sec. 6.3 and have specified recursively defined abstract data types in Chapter 10. In the procedural paradigm abstract data types must be implemented by arrays of finite size or by programming with pointers. By contrast, in the applicative model operations on recursive structures are represented by recursive equations in programs that involve infinite data structures.

Example 11.5 In the programming language, ML, the function to return the length of a list can be defined recursively as

let rec *length list* =
    <u>if</u> *null list*
    <u>then</u> $\emptyset$
    <u>else</u> 1 + *length (tl list)*;

This says that the length of an empty list is zero and the length of a non-empty list is one greater than the length of its tail.

The keyword rec in the first line is necessary in all recursive declarations. This is the ML equivalent of the Y combinator of the λ-calculus discussed in Chapter 9. Recall that whereas induction counts *upwards* from a base case, recursion counts *downwards* to a base to ensure termination. The function *null* in the second line is a built-in function which tests whether a list is empty. For example, if $list = [2, \underbrace{5, 4, 3}_{\text{tail}}]$

then

$$\begin{aligned} length\ list &= 1 + length\ [5, 4, 3] \\ &= 1 + 1 + length\ [4, 3] \\ &= 1 + 1 + 1 + length\ [3] \\ &= 1 + 1 + 1 + 1 + length\ [\,] \\ &= 1 + 1 + 1 + 1 + 0 \\ &= 4 \end{aligned}$$

Exercise 11.3 Apply the recursive function that returns the length of a list to the list $[6, 2, 1, 1, 4]$.

Exercise 11.4 Write a Pascal procedure to return the length of list of numbers. You will need to use either recursion or unbounded repetition with a while-do or a repeat-until construct.

11.3.2 Relational programming based on the logic model

We saw in Chapter 10 that the most abstract approach to specification is based on a framework of first-order logic. The power of this logical approach is achieved by using the concept of a predicate to define relations between objects and allowing quantification over all the objects in the problem domain. First-order languages for specification were constructed in Chapter 7 by extending the pure language of predicates. In these languages, functions are defined on objects to represent operations on those objects. We saw how the addition of function symbols provides the power to express the internal structure of objects. Relationships between the functions are expressed as axioms in first-order logic.

By contrast, the algebraic approach to specification uses a subset of first-order logic and expresses equality between terms. Instead of relations between objects, the algebraic approach is based on the stricter rule of a function that requires a many-one or one-one relationship between objects. The flexibility of allowing quantification over objects that are related within a predicate is no longer available. Finally we have explained that neither the logical nor the algebraic approaches to specification are based on a concept of change of state that is central to the model-based or state-transition approaches.

These contrasting approaches to specification are reflected in the approaches to programming when it is viewed as 'designing a computation'. The mathematical and logical foundations for the procedural, applicative and logical styles of programming are quite different:

- A functional language specifies the solution to a given problem as a collection of many-to-one transformations.
- A relational language, based on first-order logic, will generate not just a single solution but a set of solutions to any given particular application and is a many-to-many transformation.

Although some parallel implementations of logic programming languages do produce the complete solution set automatically, the more traditional approach is, as in the popular language called Prolog (PROgramming in LOGic), to produce one solution and then to use 'back-tracking' if further solutions are required.

Prolog is based on logic programming just as functional languages in Sec. 11.3.1 are based on the λ-calculus. In Chapter 2 we presented a program as the formal description of an algorithm that can be executed on a machine. Then in Chapter 7 we defined programs as the wffs of some formal programming language. We build on this view of a program in order to define a logic program, and consider logic programming as the *process* of developing logic programs.

Logic programming languages We define a logic program to be a formula that describes an algorithm and can be executed on a machine. The execution of a formula in logic as a program will involve some system of logical deduction, and in order to express the solution to a given problem as a logical consequence a calculus is needed. A calculus can be given as an algorithm or as a set of inference rules. We presented a deductive calculus in Chapter 4 as a syntactic tool for deriving consequences by a set of inference rules for natural deduction. In logic programming if the calculus is given as a set of rules it must be organized to form an algorithm that can be implemented on a machine. The organization is provided by a *search strategy* which orders the executable rules and controls the process of generating the logical inferences.

> **Definition 11.1 A logic programming language** This is a proof procedure that consists of the triple (set of logic programs, calculus, search strategy). The implementation of the calculus and the search strategy provide an interpreter or compiler for the set of programs, which form the syntactic component of the triple.

The triple that is defined as forming a proof procedure is used by any theorem prover.

Instead of instructing a computer what to do, as in imperative programming, a logic programmer sets up a database of statements and inference rules and then asks questions which the computer answers by logical manipulation of the database. A logic program describes a set of individuals in a domain and the relations between them. Prolog makes many compromises with imperative programming, however. The development of a pure logic programming language has been achieved in the language LOBO, designed by Gergely and Szöts (1985). The ideal of achieving a pure logic language with a supporting implementation is an important goal for the future.

Example 11.6 A program in Prolog consists of questions, or goals, about relations between individuals in a domain, and these goals must be satisfied. A relation could be defined as the rule 'John likes X if X likes wine'. In Prolog this would be written as

```
likes (John, X) :- likes (X, wine)
```

A goal to be satisfied could be

```
? - likes (John, Mary)
```

By using recursive procedures, compact and elegant programs are produced. The procedural interpretation, suggested in Kowalski (1974), has given an operational character to logic programs and has brought credibility to logic as a programming language. Goals are viewed as sets of procedure calls and the semantics becomes similar to conventional procedural languages. Clearly, however, the underlying model is different from that of imperative programming which is based on the von Neumann model.

Example 11.7 In the notation of Prolog, the relation 'is a member of' can be defined recursively as

$$\text{mem } (X, [Y \mid Z]) \text{ :- } X = Y \text{ ; mem } (X, Z)$$

In the Prolog notation ',' denotes $\wedge$, ';' denotes $\vee$, and ':-' denotes 'is implied by'. The symbol '|' denotes that Y is the element at the head of the list and Z is the tail of the list. By contrast, in the first-order theory of lists we would write the definition of the binary predicate symbol $\in$ as $\forall x \ \forall y \ \forall z \ [x \in y \circ z \leftrightarrow x = y \vee x \in z]$, where x, y are atoms (or elements of lists) and z is a list. The symbol $\circ$ represents insertion in a list.

The *abstractness* of the logic model provides an increase in expressive power. The logic programming languages that are closer to predicate logic than Prolog are more elegant to use and produce clearer and better structured programs. Logic programs describe a logical solution to problems; there is no concept of 'pushing data around a store'! A logic program is a set of expressions in a restricted form of predicate logic. Relational database design and query languages such as QUEL are also based on this relational view of programming. These languages were discussed in Sec. 2.2.1.

Computable definitions As in the procedural paradigm the practice of programming has preceded the theory of programming. Logic programs are, however, objects of mathematical logic. According to mathematical criteria they consist of a series of definitions which are computable.

By Def. 11.1, a concrete programming language is a proof procedure with the set of wffs as the first component of the defining triple—the syntax. In order to be considered as a program, however, the formula must be *computable* in some sense, and in order to be useful the second component of the proof procedure must be *constructive*. This means that if a theorem $\exists y \ f(x, y)$ is proved, the calculus must also *construct* the solution for us by giving values for the output variables y. The proof then corresponds to the execution of a program, and the formula $\exists f(x, y)$ can be considered as a program. Each definition in a logic program is in the form:

$$\mathscr{P}(x_1, x_2, \ldots, x_n) \leftrightarrow \mathscr{P}'(x_1, x_2, \ldots, x_n)$$

In order to define a class of computable definitions, it is necessary to define a language that is a constructive sublanguage of the predicate calculus. We broaden our definition of a language to the triple $(F, \mathscr{A}, \models)$ where F is a set of formulae, $\mathscr{A}$ is a model and $\models$ is the validity relation. The following conditions must hold:

1 If a formula $\exists x \mathscr{P}(x)$ is true in $\mathscr{A}$ there is a term t such that $\mathscr{P}(t)$ is true in $\mathscr{A}$; that is the elements of the carrier set have to be *nameable*.

2 For any formula $\mathscr{P}(x)$, the set $\{a : \mathscr{A} \models \mathscr{P}(x)[a]\}$ is enumerable; that is we must be able to *decide* all those elements that satisfy a formula $\mathscr{P}$.

The set of formulae that can be used for logic programming are called *positive existential definitions*. These definitions have least fixed points, as required for a language that uses recursive techniques, and are never negated. The importance of the positive existential definitions is that their least fixed points are computable.

Definition 11.2 Positive existential definition A definition is positive existential, PE, if it is written in the form,

$$\mathscr{P}(x_1, x_2, \ldots, x_n) \leftrightarrow \mathscr{P}'(x_1, x_2, \ldots, x_n)$$

and none of the predicate symbols, $\mathscr{P}$, occur in the scope of the $\neg$ connective. No unbounded universal quantifier can occur in a positive existential definition. The only quantifiers allowed are bounded universal quantifiers or existential quantifiers, and unbounded existential quantifiers.

The whole set of PE definitions, without any restriction, are used for the pure logic programming language LOBO, the LOgic of BOunded quantifiers (Gergely and Szöts, 1985). Bounded quantifiers play a crucial role in LOBO; their function is to control the structure of the execution of a LOBO program. This control is also effected by applying the *rules* of the calculus $K1$, which are easily mechanized. The calculus controls the computation of the truth-values of the atomic and quantifier-free formulae. The search strategy for LOBO is built into the mechanization of $K1$, and determines the order of the evaluation of the formulae as well as enumerating the range of the bounding formulae.

Prolog is obtained by the use of a resolution calculus together with PE definitions. Only a subset of PE definitions that are in *clausal form* are used, however. The syntax of Prolog is the subset of PE definitions that are known as *Horn clauses*. The resolution calculus is designed for Horn clauses and the search strategy of Prolog is a form of linear input resolution. To obtain the clausal form of a PE definition it is necessary to carry out the following steps:

1 Transfer the definition to *prenex* form by moving any $\neg$ connective inwards so that negation is only applied to an atomic formulae. As the simplest form of expression, the atomic formulae and their negations are called *literals*. The transfer to prenex form is achieved by using the identities in Sec. 5.3. For example, $\neg\exists\ f(x, y) \equiv \forall x\ \neg f(x, y)$.

2 Create a *universal Skolem form* by removing all the existential quantifiers and introducing Skolem functions to replace the variables referred to by the existential quantifiers. Therefore, for the formula $\forall x \exists y\ \mathscr{P}(x, y)$ we substitute $\forall x\ \mathscr{P}(x, f(x))$, where the functional dependence of the second argument on the first is made explicit.

3 Rename the variables, if necessary, so that each universal quantifier binds a different variable. For example, replace $\forall x\ \mathscr{P}(x) \vee \forall x\ \mathscr{Q}(x)$ by $\forall x\ \mathscr{P}(x) \vee \forall y\ \mathscr{Q}(y)$.

4 Move all the universal quantifiers to the front, so that $\forall x\ \mathscr{P}(x) \vee \forall y\ \mathscr{Q}(y)$ becomes $\forall x\ \forall y\ [\mathscr{P}(x) \vee \mathscr{Q}(y)]$. The quantifiers at the outside of the formulae may now be dropped. We just need to remember that every variable that we use is introduced by an implicit quantifier.

5 Transform the formula to a *conjunctive normal form* by ensuring that no conjunction occurs within the scope of a disjunction. The rules given in Sec. 3.2.4 are used for this step. For example, $A \vee (B \wedge C) \equiv (A \vee B) \wedge (A \vee C)$.

6 The creation of a set of clauses in *clausal form*. In this step the conjunction of a set of clauses is formed, where each clause consists of the disjunction of a set of literals. Each of these disjunctions is therefore either an atomic formula or its negation.

For example, a formula in conjunctive normal form is a series of propositions $A \wedge B \wedge C \wedge D \wedge \cdots$ where each proposition is itself a series of literals joined together with disjunctions. Dropping the $\wedge$-connectives gives the set of propositions $\{A,\ B,\ C,\ D,\ldots\}$. Each member of this set is itself of the form $W \vee X \vee Y \vee Z$, and dropping the $\vee$-connective gives a *clause* $W,\ X,\ Y,\ Z$ that is implicitly disjointed. Here $W,\ X,\ Y,\ Z$ are all literals that are either positive or negative. For simplicity, a clause consisting of just one literal, called a *unit clause*, is written without braces.

Clausal form is concise because we do not have to write out conjunctions. For convenience, however, clauses are not usually left as the implicit disjunction of a set of literals. The literals are separated into those that are unnegated and those that are negated. Assuming that $A,\ B,\ldots$ are positive literals and $\neg X,\ \neg Y,\ldots$ are negated literals, then by the equivalences of Sec. 3.2.4, the clause $(A \vee B \vee \cdots) \vee (\neg X \vee \neg Y \vee \cdots)$ is equivalent to $(X \wedge Y \wedge \cdots) \rightarrow (A \vee B \vee \cdots)$. In the Prolog notation this is written as $A;B;\ldots$:- $X,Y\ldots$.

Definition 11.3 Horn clauses Horn clauses are formulae that are in clausal form, and are restricted to having at most one unnegated literal.

Example 11.8 The formulae $T,\ F,\ P,\ \neg P, \{\neg P,\ Q,\}$, $\{P,\ \neg Q,\ \neg R,\ \neg S\}$ are all Horn clauses. However, $\{P,\ Q\}$, $\{P,\ Q,\ \neg R\}$ and $\{P,\ Q,\ R,\ S,\ T\}$ are not Horn clauses.

There are two forms of Horn clause in Prolog: the headed type A :- $X,Y,\ldots$ and the headless type :- $X,Y,\ldots$.

Example 11.9 The Prolog translation of the clausal formula $A \vee B \vee C \vee \neg X \vee \neg Y \vee \neg Z$ is A :- X,Y,Z. B :- X,Y,Z. C :- X,Y,Z.

These Horn clauses are interpreted and implemented as procedures that reduce problems of the form A to a set of subproblems of the form $X,\ldots,\ Z$, for example. In Prolog this is carried out by the *resolution calculus*.

Exercise 11.5 Which of the following are Horn clauses?

$$\{\neg P,\ \neg Q,\ R\},\ \neg Q,\ \{\neg P,\ \neg Q,\ \neg R\},\ R,\ \{Q,\ R\}$$

Exercise 11.6 Obtain the Horn clause form of the definitions

$$\forall x\ \forall y\ [\neg\mathscr{P}(x) \vee \neg\mathscr{Q}(x,y) \vee \mathscr{R}(y)] \text{ and } \forall x\ [\neg\mathscr{P}(x) \vee \mathscr{Q}(x,a) \vee \mathscr{R}(x,a,f(x))]$$

Resolution calculus We now give a brief description of the single rule of inference that is used in the resolution calculus. The proof system for resolution differs from the natural deduction proof system used in Chapter 4. The single rule of inference is designed for formulae in clausal form.

Rule 11.1 Resolution inference rule For any clauses A, B and C,

$$\frac{\begin{array}{ccc} A & \vee & B \\ \neg B & \vee & C \end{array}}{\begin{array}{ccc} A & \vee & C \end{array}}$$

The clause $\{A,\ C\}$ is called the *resolvent* of the 'parent' pair of clauses $\{A,\ B\}$ and $\{\neg B,\ C\}$, and the process of obtaining the resolvent is called resolution. The resolution proof rule can be justified by the tautology

$$\models (A \vee B) \wedge (\neg B \vee C) \rightarrow (A \vee C)$$

Example 11.10 The formula $\forall x\ \forall y\ [\mathscr{P}(x) \vee \mathscr{R}(y)]$ is a logical consequence of the formulae $\forall x\ \forall y\ [\mathscr{P}(x) \vee \neg\mathscr{Q}(x, y)]$ and $\forall x\ \forall y\ [\mathscr{Q}(x, y) \vee \mathscr{R}(y)]$. By resolution, the clause $\{\mathscr{P}(x),\ \mathscr{R}(y)\}$ is the resolvent of the parent clauses $\{\mathscr{P}(x), \neg\mathscr{Q}(x, y)\}$ and $\{\mathscr{Q}(x, y), \mathscr{R}(y)\}$.

Exercise 11.7 Set up a domain of interpretation for the formulae in Example 11.10 and argue that the application of the resolution proof rule is justified.

Exercise 11.8 Assess the advantages for software development of using the following programming styles:

(a) Procedural programming

(b) Functional programming

(c) Logical programming

In your answer relate these programming styles to the models of computation that they are based on.

11.4 SUMMARY

We have considered programming as the activity of designing a computation and have shown how this activity is dependent on the mathematical framework we have established in the first part of this book. The approaches to programming have been shown to be closely linked to the approaches to specification. The procedural paradigm is dependent on the concept of a change of state and based on the von Neumann model of a computer; it is close to the model-based specification approach. Declarative programming is closer to the axiomatic approach to specification and is based on the applicative model, from which functional programs have been developed, and the logic model, which relational languages are based on. Functional languages specify the solution to a problem as a set of many-to-one transformations; in contrast, logic languages generate not just a single solution but a set of solutions by a many-to-many transformation. The choice of a model of computation affects many activities in the construction and analysis of systems. These activities include; programming language design; programming methods; specification methods; proof techniques; semantics of programming languages; programming style; and the understanding of programs.

FURTHER READING

An introduction to programming that is based on the principles of imperative programming languages is given in Bornat (1987). The denotational semantics of imperative programs is presented in Tennent (1981), with an informal introduction to the concepts of store and environment; in the book by Schmidt (1986) the denotational semantics of both imperative and applicative languages is given. A functional approach to knowledge processing and a general introduction to knowledge base systems is given in Frost (1986).

The principles of functional programming are presented in the book by Glazer, Hankin and Till (1984), and the paper by Turner (1982) views functional programming as programming with recursive equations. In Gordon (1988) the relationship between functional programming languages and the λ-calculus is given.

Prolog was first given a procedural interpretation in the paper by Kowalski (1974), and in Kowalski (1983) logic programming is compared with rule-based artificial intelligence languages and functional languages. The theory underlying the pure logic programming language, LOBO, is given in detail by Ury and Gergely (1990); Gergely and Ury (1991). We recommend the books by Bundy (1983) and Hogger (1984) for an introduction to logic programming and Lloyd (1987) for a deeper treatment of the foundations of logic programming. Recent research work in Goguen and Meseguer (1987) is interesting in the way it looks towards the unification of the programming paradigms.

Chapter 12

VERIFICATION OF ALGORITHM CORRECTNESS

In this chapter we present a classical method, based on a logical system of proof, for the verification of algorithms in the procedural model of computation. The axioms and inference rules of the logic provide the framework for the design of systems to automate the routine aspects of program verification.

In Sec. 12.1 we contrast the formal proof of algorithm correctness with informal methods of testing and debugging programs. The language of the logic is based on the Floyd–Hoare logic for reasoning about programs and is presented in Sec. 12.2.2. Assertions in the logic are made about the commands of the programming language. The axioms of the logic are specified by inference rules, in a system of deduction. In Sec. 12.3 we show how the instantiation of the inference rules by specific algorithms enables the assertion that the algorithm is partially correct to be deduced as a conclusion. Finally, in Sec. 12.4 we summarize the advantages and disadvantages of this classical system for verifying algorithm correctness, and indicate how the rules of Floyd–Hoare justify the mechanization of program correctness. We see the parallel activities of constructing and verifying programs as fundamental to software development.

12.1 FORMAL AND INFORMAL VERIFICATION

When an algorithm is designed during the construction of a system which has been specified to solve a given problem, consideration must be given to the properties of that algorithm. A specific problem may require that an algorithm is efficient, portable or easy to understand. We shall consider these properties of algorithms in detail in Chapters 13, 15 and 17. However, the property that an algorithm should be correct is a requirement for the construction of *any* system, and is of central importance now that software plays an increasing role in systems that have critical safety or financial implications. As the requirements for system construction become more complex, the need to tackle the issue of algorithm correctness at a formal level becomes more pressing.

The aim of the informal iterative process of testing a program and then changing it is to find errors and then remove them. We can never complete this process, however, because we can never be sure that we have discovered every error in a program. Although testing may successfully expose many errors, it cannot be *relied* on to show the presence of errors in a program. Unfortunately there may be only a very small chance of discovering certain errors, even though testing is carried out systematically. We therefore have to conclude that testing can establish reliably *neither* the correctness of a correct program *nor* the incorrectness of an incorrect program. The process of testing and changing a program is known as 'debugging' among programmers, who often devote many hours to it, and is unsuitable as a design methodology for system construction because it is itself unscientific and unreliable.

Testing is widely used, however, because formal methods for the verification of algorithms are still being brought to a level of development that is practically acceptable. The mechanization of program verification is likely to increase the acceptance of formal verification methods.

Most experience in the formal and informal verification of algorithms has been with the procedural model of computation, identified in Chapter 11. The Floyd–Hoare logic that we present in this chapter provides a framework for reasoning about procedural programs. Many people believe that it is easier to verify the correctness of declarative languages and that these languages will replace procedural languages for safety-critical applications. It has been necessary, however, to devise new logics such as LCF, the logic for computable functions, in order to reason about functional programs.

Floyd–Hoare logic belongs to the family of predicate logics that we described in Chapter 5. Its non-logical symbols and axioms provide a language and rules of inference for reasoning about procedural programs. These programs consist of a sequence of commands that change the state of a machine. The logic can be used to verify the correctness of existing programs or (even more usefully) to provide a foundation for a rigorous methodology in which programs are verified as they are constructed. There is little doubt that it is useful to think about the meaning of a program from the abstract axiomatic viewpoint of logic.

Floyd used logic for reasoning about flowgraphs, which we discuss in Chapter 13, before Hoare extended his work by introducing a logical notation for reasoning about programs. We have chosen to present the Floyd–Hoare logic close to its original form because it is simple, suitable for a first presentation of formal verification and is the basis for the mechanical verification of program correctness.

12.2 A LOGIC FOR REASONING ABOUT ALGORITHMS

Logic is a suitable framework for reasoning about algorithm correctness because it gains power from its level of abstraction. A logical view of a computation is more abstract than either a functional or operational view, because it is concerned solely with assertions *about* the program execution. This external or meta-level program logic must be distinguished from the internal logic of a program that determines the next action that is to be executed. For example, the action that follows a 'while C do S' command depends on the truth-value of the condition C. We begin this section by defining a programming language and then define the logical language that we can use for reasoning about the constructs in the programming language.

12.2.1 A simple programming language

We consider a simple procedural language that contains assignment commands that change the values of program variables. After an initial state is established by giving certain values to the variables, the algorithm is executed and transforms the initial state to some final state. The values of the variables in a final state should be those expected according to the specification of the algorithm.

We restrict out attention to those programs that represent algorithms constructed from simpler algorithms by the mechanisms of sequencing, choice and repetition. The following symbols are used for the syntax of the programming language:

- Arbitrary variable symbols $x, y, z, \ldots$
- Particular variable symbols i, n, *temp*, *product*, *fact*, ...
- Algorithm symbols $A, A_1, \ldots, A_n$
- Condition symbols $C, C_1, \ldots, C_n$
- Expression symbols $E, E_1, \ldots, E_n$

The condition symbols represent conditions such as $x \geq 0$ which are either true or false. We assume that our programs are without the side effects that are so confusing in the programs of procedural languages. Side effects are the *unexpected* changes to the program state that may occur when expressions are evaluated. They can be avoided by making all changes to the state explicit in a program. We give inference rules for the verification of the following types of algorithms:

- Sequences 'A; A_1; ...; A_n'
- Choice (or conditional) 'if C then A_1 else A_2'
- Unbounded repetition 'while C do A'

The inference rules relate the algebraic properties of the program data to the structured algorithms in the program.

12.2.2 The logical language

Floyd laid the foundations for the logic and Hoare extended the work by introducing a notation for expressing the behaviour of an algorithm as a proposition, in the logic, which is either true or false. The axioms of the logic are presented as inference rules. A statement in the logical language is used to make an assertion about the correctness of an algorithm. The inference rules allow the deduction from hypotheses of a conclusion that a particular algorithm structured in the programming language is correct.

The intended behaviour of an algorithm is specified by making an assertion about the values that the variables in the program will take *after* the execution of the algorithm. Our notion of algorithm correctness is relative to a given specification and will often depend on the initial values of the variables before the algorithm is executed. The specification is given in terms of:

- a pre-condition describing the properties of the data and
- a post-condition describing the effect of the algorithm.

Hoare introduced a notation similar to the following for specifying the behaviour of an algorithm:

$$\{P\}A\{Q\}$$

where $\{P\}$ describes the state before the algorithm A is executed and $\{Q\}$ describes the state after A is executed; that is $\{P\}$ is the initial condition and $\{Q\}$ is the final condition on the program variables used in the algorithm A.

The conditions P and Q are written as assertions in the predicate calculus, which we introduced in Chapter 5, using infix notation for the arithmetic predicates. The condition Q specifies the meaning of the algorithm in terms of its final effect.

Example 12.1 $\{x = 6\}x := x + 1\{x = 7\}$. Here P asserts that the value of x is 6, and Q is the condition that the value of x is 7. The algorithm assigns 'x to become $x + 1$'. The assertion $\{P\}A\{Q\}$ is clearly true, where P is the predicate '$x = 6$' and Q is '$x = 7$'. We appeal to the definition of the variable assignment $x := E$. The semantics of this command is that the state is changed by assigning the value of the expression E to the variable x.

The conditions P and Q represent predicates that express the values of variables in the program state. The predicates that belong to the logical calculus talk about the variables that belong to the programming language.

Definition 12.1 Specification of partial correctness The assertion $\{P\}A\,\{Q\}$ is called the specification of partial correctness, with P as its pre-condition and Q as its post-condition. We say that $\{P\}A\{Q\}$ is true if, whenever A is executed in a state that satisfies P and if the execution of A terminates, then the final state in which A terminates satisfies Q.

Exercise 12.1 Explain the meaning of the following specification of partial correctness and argue whether it is true or false: $\{x = 2 \wedge y = 3\}y := y + x\{y = 6\}$.

A stronger specification that requires the termination of the algorithm A is called a *total correctness specification*, but this is proved by first proving partial correctness and then proving termination.

Example 12.2 An algorithm *sum* that computes the sum of two numbers x and y has the pre-condition $\{x = x_1 \wedge y = y_1\}$ and the post-condition $\{z = x_1 + y_1\}$. Here x_1 and y_1 are 'ghost ' or auxiliary variables, which do not appear in the algorithm but name the initial values of the program variables x and y.

The algorithm *sum* is 'begin $z := x + y$ end'. This algorithm is correct because we can *prove* that the statement $\{x = x_1 \wedge y = y_1\}sum\{z = x_1 + y_1\}$ is true.

The statement in the logic asserts that 'if *sum* is executed in a state that satisfies the condition $x = x_1 \wedge y = y_1$ then, if execution terminates (as it does), the condition $z = x_1 + y_1$ will hold'. Clearly this specification is true.

Of course, in general algorithms will not be so short or so straightforward. We are concerned here with those that are structured by *sequences, conditionals* and *iterations*. In order to prove the correctness of such structured algorithms we shall use a system for deduction that is based on Hoare's rules of inference.

12.2.3 A system for deduction

The non-logical symbols in Hoare's notation, which represent the application of algorithm correctness, are part of the first-order predicate calculus that we presented in Chapter 5. We now add, to the logical language, a system for making formal proofs about the correctness of algorithms. In the natural deduction system that we introduced in Chapter 4 the logical axioms that define the propositional connective are presented as rules of inference. Similarly, in the Floyd–Hoare logic, the non-logical axioms that express the different ways of structuring algorithms are presented as inference rules.

In his deduction system Hoare directly relates the structure of proofs to the semantics of the algorithms. Because the axiomatic method for verifying program correctness is independent of *particular* input–output pairs, it is more powerful than testing. In fact, the Floyd–Hoare logic is the basis for the *axiomatic* approach to describing the semantics of programming languages by requiring that the languages satisfy the rules and axioms of a formal logic. It has also influenced the design of programming languages. As the most abstract approach, the axiomatic approach does not involve an explicit notion of the state of a machine.

12.3 PROOF OF CORRECTNESS

A proof of the partial correctness of an algorithm involves both propositions in the form of partial correctness specifications, $\{P\}A\{Q\}$, and mathematical statements which are proved for mathematical axioms. The inference rules of Floyd–Hoare logic look similar to the inference rules for the natural deduction system introduced in Chapter 4. The hypotheses are listed above a horizontal line and the conclusion is given below the line.

12.3.1 Inference rule for sequences

To establish the correctness of a *sequence* of algorithms A_1 and A_2, which form the compound algorithm $A_1;A_2$, we have the following inference rule:

$$\frac{\begin{array}{c}\{P\}A_1\{Q_1\}\\ \{Q_1\}A_2\{Q\}\end{array}}{\{P\}A_1;A_2\{Q\}}$$

This rule can be paraphrased as

> Suppose executing A_1 with pre-condition P guarantees post-condition Q_1 and executing A_2 with pre-condition Q_1 guarantees post-condition Q; then executing $A_1;A_2$ with pre-condition P guarantees post-condition Q.

Clearly the use of pre- and post-conditions is a way of defining the semantics of a sequence of algorithms. We are assuming that the semantics *are* defined in this manner. The post-condition for A_1 becomes the pre-condition for A_2. The inference rule for the sequence $A_1;A_2$ generalizes to n sequential algorithms. Therefore, if $A = A_1;A_2;\ldots;A_n$ then to prove $\{P\}A\{Q\}$ as a conclusion we must find *intermediate assertions* $Q_1, Q_2, \ldots, Q_{n-1}$ which prove that all the hypotheses $\{P\}A_1\{Q_1\}$, $\{Q_1\}A_2\{Q_2\}$, …,$\{Q_{n-1}\}A_n$ $\{Q\}$ hold.

Example 12.3 The following program is an algorithm to interchange the values of x and y. The pre-condition is $\{x = x_1 \wedge y = y_1\}$; the post-condition is $\{x = y_1 \wedge y = x_1\}$.

```
program swap
begin
  temp:= x;
  x := y;
  y := temp
end.
```

We prove the algorithm correct using the inference rule for sequences:

program *swap*
$\{x = x_1 \wedge y = y_1\}$
temp := x;
$\{\text{temp} = x_1 \wedge x = x_1 \wedge y = y_1\}$
$x := y$;
$\{\text{temp} = x_1 \wedge x = y_1 \wedge y = y_1\}$
y := temp;
$\{x = y_1 \wedge y = x_1\}$

Each assertion follows directly from the preceding assertion and the assignment statement. Hence, by the inference rule for sequences,

$$\{x = x_1 \wedge y = y_1\} swap \{x = y_1 \wedge y = x_1\}$$

is correct.

Exercise 12.2 Prove the following program is correct based on the stated pre- and post-conditions:

program *quadratic*
$\{x \in R\}$
begin
  $y := ax$;
  $y := (y + b)x$;
  $y := y + c$
end.
$\{y = ax^2 + bx + c\}$

Exercise 12.3 Use the axiomatic method to prove that the following program to compute the sum of two numbers x and y is incorrect:

program *sum*
begin
  $z := x$;
  $z := z + x + y$
end.

12.3.2 Inference rule for choice

To establish the correctness of the conditional algorithm 'if C then A_1 else A_2' where C is a predicate and A_1 and A_2 are algorithms, we use the following inference rule:

$$\frac{\{P \wedge C\}A_1\{Q\} \quad \{P \wedge \neg C\}A_2\{Q\}}{\{P\} \text{ if } C \text{ then } A_1 \text{ else } A_2\{Q\}}$$

In other words, in order to prove that the algorithm 'if C then A_1 else A_2', with pre- and post-conditions P and Q respectively, is correct we have to prove both $\{P \wedge C\}A_1\{Q\}$ and $\{P \wedge \neg C\}A_2\{Q\}$.

Example 12.4 We prove that the following *absolute value* algorithm is correct:

program *absolute value*
$\{x = x_1\}$
begin
  if $x < 0$
  then $y := -x$
  else $y := x$

end.
$\{y =| x_1 |\}$

To prove this we note that the post-condition $\{y =| x_1 |\}$ is equivalent to an implicit specification of absolute value

$$\{(x_1 \geq 0 \wedge y = x_1) \vee (x_1 < 0 \wedge y = -x_1)\} \tag{12.1}$$

We must first show $\{(x = x_1) \wedge (x < 0)\}\ \ y := -x\ \ \{y =| x_1 |\}$. The pre-condition and execution of the assignment permit us to conclude $(x_1 < 0) \wedge (y = -x_1)$, and Eq. (12.1) follows from the rule of $\vee$-introduction on page 126. We must next show that, similarly,

$$(x = x_1) \wedge (x \geq 0)\}\ y := x\ \{y =| x_1 |\}$$

The algorithm is then proved correct by Hoare's inference rule for conditional statements.

Exercise 12.4 Verify the following program for computing the maximum of a and b:

program *largest*
$\{a = a_1 \wedge b = b_1\}$
begin
  if $a > b$
  then $x := a$
  else $x := b$
end.
$\{(x = a_1 \wedge a_1 > b_1) \vee (x = b_1 \wedge b_1 \geq a_1)\}$

Exercise 12.5 The algorithm 'if C then A' is sometimes used to express choice. Richard Bornat (1987) explains, however, that this algorithm is not a good structuring mechanism for an algorithm involving choice, since it is incomplete and does not explicitly consider all alternatives. Its inference rule is

$$\frac{\begin{array}{l}\{P \wedge C\}A\ \{Q\} \\ \{P \wedge \neg C\} \rightarrow \{Q\}\end{array}}{\{P\}\text{ if } C \text{ then } A\ \{Q\}}$$

Paraphrase the inference rule for the 'if-then' algorithm in order to explain it.

Exercise 12.6 Attempt to carry out a correctness proof on the following program

$\{a = a_1\}$
begin
  $x := 5$;
  if $a > 10$
  then $x := a$
end.
$\{(x = a_1 \wedge a_1 > 10) \vee (x = 0 \wedge a_1 \leq 10)\}$

Your proof should fail!

12.3.3 Inference rules for repetition

Repetition that is bounded can be expressed by the algorithm 'for $x := E_1$ until E_2 do A'. However, because there are many different versions of this command in programming languages, the inference rules for bounded repetition in different languages vary. A particular problem with using the Floyd–Hoare logic for the verification of algorithms is that the inference rules are only easily applied to simple programming language constructs. The semantics of the 'for-do' construct is particularly hard to capture in the logic.

Repetition that is unbounded also brings problems for verification because it introduces the possibility that an algorithm may not terminate. The algorithm 'while C do A' has the meaning 'if C do A; while C do A' and is therefore recursively defined. An equivalent algorithm for unbounded repetition is 'repeat A until C'. In order to understand the meaning of these recursively defined algorithms we need to use the principle of mathematical induction presented in Chapter 6 and the theory of fixed points in Chapter 9.

Invariants A good way to understand an algorithm that repeatedly changes the program variables is to examine what is left *unchanged* by the iteration; this is called the *invariant* property of the iteration.

The inference rule of Floyd–Hoare logic for 'while C do A' is close to the principle of induction and uses the concept of an invariant to express the meaning of the unbounded repetition. Instead of using a post-condition Q, the rule states 'if the invariant is unchanged by A, it is unchanged by n iterations of A'.

An *invariant* is defined generally as something that is unchanging. It is a 'pattern' or 'rule' which, when recognized, provides understanding. By recognizing invariants we are often able to arrive at a surprisingly simple solution to a complex problem. We instinctively build an invariant when we talk in general about objects such as tables, houses and heads; we picture the property that is common to all the objects that go by that name.

Example 12.5 An invariant property of a house is that it has walls and a roof with some way of getting in and out of the house. Properties that change are the number of entrances and whether there are windows and chimneys.

Exercise 12.7 Describe an invariant property of a car.

Example 12.6 The following bounded repetition in Pascal sums the n elements in the array called 'table':

```
total := 0 ;
for i : = 1 to n
  do
  total : = total + table [ i ]
```

The invariant of this iteration is that, whatever the value of i, 'total' is the sum of the elements in table [1], table [2], ..., table [i] immediately before i is incremented.

Within this bounded repetition the value of i keeps changing over a sequence of values that represents the number of times the iteration is executed. The meaning of the repetition, which we represent by the invariant, is that the total held in the variable 'sum' is that of the first i elements in the array. The base of an inductive proof is that the total is the value of the first element when $i = 1$. Also, if the total is the sum of the first i elements for any i, then for $i + 1$ the total is the sum of the first $i + 1$ elements. Therefore, by the principle of induction, total is the sum of the first i elements for *all* values of i.

With practice it becomes easier to spot the invariant of an iteration. In an algorithm for unbounded repetition, the invariant will be true both before the algorithm is executed and after execution. The condition for termination will determine how many times the commands within the algorithm are repeated; the truth of the invariant is not dependent on this, however.

The rule for the while-do This rule requires that the invariant of the while-do construct is shown to be true after each iteration. If the invariant is unchanged by a single execution of A the rule states that the invariant is unchanged by the unbounded iteration 'while C do A'. Since A is only executed as long as C is true, C appears in the pre-condition for A. Since C is false when the iteration terminates, $\neg C$ appears in the post-condition for 'while C do A'.

With Q as the invariant assertion, the inference rule is

$$\frac{\{Q \wedge C\}A\ \{Q\}}{\{Q\}\text{while } C \text{ do } A\ \{\neg C \wedge Q\}}$$

Example 12.7 Consider the following algorithm:

```
procedure multiplication
{n ≥ 0 ∧ x = x1}
begin
    i := 0 ;
    product := 0 ;
    while i < n
    do
       begin
            product := product + x ;
            i := i + 1
       end
    end.
{ product = n.x1 }
```

We now prove correctness of this algorithm for multiplication with respect to the pre-condition $\{n \geq 0 \wedge x = x_1\}$ and the post-condition that describes the effect of the algorithm $\{\text{product} = n.x_1\}$. For example, for $n = 4, x_1 = 2$, the product = 8.

We need to find the invariant property for the iteration. Clearly the value of i *is* changed by the iteration, but it never exceeds the value of n. The actual value of product also changes as i is increased by each iteration. However, what does *not* change is the expression that denotes the changing value of product. This is the invariant.

Therefore Q is $\{\text{ product} = i.x \wedge i \leq n\ \}$ and C is $i < n$.

Now we produce the intermediate assertions up to the invariant assertion, Q.

```
{n ≥ 0 ∧ x = x1}
begin
    i := 0;
    {n ≥ 0 ∧ x = x1 ∧ i = 0}
    product := 0 ;
    { product = 0 ∧ n ≥ 0 ∧ x = x1 ∧ i = 0}
    { product = i.x ∧ i ≤ n } this is Q
end.
```

We now need to show that '$\{Q\}$ while C do A $\{\neg C \wedge Q\}$', the conclusion of Hoare's inference rule, is true.

$\{Q\}$	product $= i.x \wedge i \leq n\}$
while C do A	while $i < n$ do
	the statements representing A
$\{Q \wedge \neg C\}$	$\{$ product $= i.x \wedge i \leq n \wedge i \geq n\}$
	$= \{$ product $= i.x \wedge i = n\}$
	$= \{$ product $= n.x\}$
	which is our post-condition

To prove the conclusion of the inference rule, we must show that the hypothesis is correct; that is

$\{Q \wedge C\}$	$\{$product $= i.x \wedge i \leq n \wedge i < n\}$
	$= \{$product $= i.x \wedge i < n\}$
A	the statements representing A
$\{Q\}$	$\{$ product $= i.x \wedge i \leq n\}$

Therefore we have to show that Q is true before and after A is executed. We consider the sequence of statements representing A. The segment

$\{$product $= i.x \wedge i < n\}$
product $:=$ product $+ x$;
$\{$product $= i.x + x \wedge i < n\} = \{(i + 1).x \wedge i < n\}$

is correct since x is added to the value of the product.

If $\{$product $= (i + 1).x \wedge i < n\}$ is true before $i := i + 1$ is executed then $\{$product $= i.x \wedge i \leq n\}$ is true afterwards. Now this is Q, so we have shown that $\{Q \wedge C\}A\{Q\}$ is true when A is executed only once. Using Hoare's inference rule we can now conclude that the invariant Q is unchanged by n iterations of A. This is the conclusion of the inference rule. Therefore we deduce that

$\{Q\}$	$\{$ product $= i.x \wedge i \leq n\}$
	while $i < n$ do
while C do A	the statements representing A
$\{Q \wedge \neg C\}$	$\{$ product $= n.x \wedge i \geq n\}$

This proves that the algorithm is correct.

Exercise 12.8 Verify the following program which is intended to compute the factorial of a natural number that is greater than zero:

```
program factorial
{n = n1 ∧ n > 0}
begin
    i := 0;
    fact := 1;
    while i < n
    do
       begin
            i := i + 1 ;
            fact : = fact . i
       end
end.
{ fact = n1! }
```

Exercise 12.9 Verify the following algorithm which is intended to assign the quotient of x divided by 5 to q and the remainder to r. The method of successive subtraction is used in the algorithm.

```
program division
{x = x1}
begin
    r := x;
    q := 0;
    while 5 ≤ r
    do
        begin
            r := r − 5 ;
            q := q + 1
        end
end.
{x = r + 5 × q }
```

12.4 THE CONSTRUCTION AND VERIFICATION OF ALGORITHMS

We have presented the verification of algorithms as an activity that follows their construction. However, the construction of programs in parallel with their verification is a more powerful method for software development. By relating the proof of algorithm correctness to the semantics of the algorithm, the Floyd–Hoare logic provides a method whereby program verification is *possible*. This contrasts with the classical black box testing method of presenting specific values for input and then comparing the actual result of the program with the expected result. The drawback of this method of testing is that it depends on a finite set of pairs of input–output values.

A disciplined approach to constructing programs with formal verification is a scientific approach, but will only guarantee correctness if it is used properly. Because people tend to make mistakes it is useful to test programs and to debug them where necessary.

In our chosen axiomatic approach to verification the language constructs are defined by the axioms and rules of inference of the logic. Some languages are designed with complex structuring mechanisms, however, and for these languages the Floyd–Hoare logic is both incomplete and unsound. For languages with global variables, recursion and procedures as parameters, it is not always possible to prove that true conclusions follow from true premises by using the inference rules. Floyd–Hoare logic is *not sound* for these more complicated languages.

A further technical problem for Floyd–Hoare logic is that it is incomplete for some programming language constructs, because axioms and inference rules cannot be constructed to prove statements about the constructs. Although these problems indicate the need for simplicity in the design of programming languages, new languages such as Ada are exceptionally complex in their design. As a result it is difficult to verify programs in Ada.

You have probably found that proving the correctness of simple programs is tedious because of the need for detailed manipulations. Automating formal verification minimizes the possibility of human error by removing the boring and routine tasks. Simple proofs can be carried out mechanically and can also be checked. Unfortunately we cannot have everything proved automatically, because it is known in logic that there is no procedure for deciding automatically whether an arbitrary mathematical statement is true or false. We shall return to this point in Chapter 15.

In this chapter we have used a process of forward proof for algorithms by using inference rules to move from axioms to conclusions. An alternative way of proving, which can be mechanized, is to start with a goal and then generate subgoals, subsubgoals and so on until the problem is finally solved. This goal-oriented method of proof is used for mechanical theorem provers. An interactive system can be established with the user of the theorem prover directing the proof and being asked for advice by the mechanical program, which is able to deal with the routine aspects of the proof. The Floyd–Hoare logic that we have used provides the framework for mechanized verification.

12.5 SUMMARY

We have presented a logical framework for the formal verification of algorithm correctness. Formal verification can be used to establish the correctness of programs, whereas testing can only show the presence of errors in a program. Since testing cannot be exhaustive it cannot be relied upon to show *all* the errors in a program. A logical approach to verification does not rely on particular pairs of input–output values and is therefore more powerful than testing.

The language and deductive system that we have chosen for our logic for proving correctness is close to those in the classical logic introduced by Floyd for reasoning about flowgraphs and presented later, as a notation, by Hoare for reasoning about programs. Although Floyd–Hoare logic has been presented in many different forms, we have chosen the original version for its simplicity, believing it to be the best for an introduction to formal verification. The application of logic to algorithm correctness is an example of the power of a logical approach to the semantics of algorithms. We have only carried out verification for algorithms in the procedural model of computation that involves a change of state. For the declarative model verification is simpler.

The algorithms that are verified are written in a simple procedural programming language. Assertions are then made in the logical language about the partial correctness of these algorithms. Inference rules that belong to the deductive system of the logic are provided for each structuring mechanism in the programming language. Deductions are made about the partial correctness of algorithms by derivation from theorems in the logic that are presented as the hypotheses of the inference rules. The importance of Floyd–Hoare logic is in its application to the mechanized verification of programs.

12.6 FURTHER EXERCISES

Exercise 12.10 Prove that the following program is correct, based on the stated pre- and post-conditions:

$\{a = a_1\}$
begin
    $x := 5;$
    $y := 2;$
    if $a > 10$
    then $x := a$
    else $y := a$
end
$\{(x = a_1 \wedge a_1 > 10) \vee (y = a_1 \wedge a_1 \leq 10)\}$

Exercise 12.11 Prove that the following algorithm is correct:

```
program increment
{x = x1}
begin
    i := 0 ;
    while i < 5
    do
        begin
            x := x + 1 ;
            i := i + 1
        end
end
{ x = x1 + 5 }
```

In your proof explain why the assertion $\{x = x_1 + i \wedge i \leq 5\}$ is the *invariant* of the iteration.

FURTHER READING

The original paper on an axiomatic approach to program correctness is by Hoare (1969). A stimulating assertion of the importance of program verification is given in the book by Backhouse (1986). Program verification and the mechanization of program correctness is thoroughly treated in Gordon (1988).

Chapter 13

GRAPH MODELS FOR STRUCTURED PROGRAMMING

Almost everybody involved in technical work in information technology has at least some vague notion of what structured programming is and why it is important. Unfortunately many of these notions are quite different. In this chapter we use graph theory to explain and characterize some of the most important notions of structured programming in a formal and unifying way. We also explode a number of popular myths in doing so.

In Sec. 13.1 we provide an informal introduction to the basic ideas and problems of structured programming. We highlight a number of important issues that can be effectively resolved only by a formal treatment. The formal model proposed, the flowgraph, is described in Sec. 13.2. In Sec. 13.3 we show how flowgraphs enable us to characterize many popular interpretations of structured programming. We also show that, when using flowgraphs to model programs, there is a unique structural decomposition that enables us to answer almost any questions about the structural properties of a program. We describe the important applications of this decomposition to static analysis, reverse engineering and software measures. In Sec. 13.4 we describe the popular method of drawing structure diagrams as an aid to design and show how this is closely related to flowgraph decomposition. Finally, in Sec. 13.5, we describe a richer graphical model than the flowgraph: the Petri net, which enables us to model systems in which there may be concurrent processing.

13.1 BACKGROUND TO STRUCTURED PROGRAMMING

13.1.1 Flowcharts and structure

If you have ever seen a newspaper or magazine article that attempts to tell you what type of mortgage you should buy, then the chances are you will have seen a flowchart. A flowchart is a graphical description of an algorithm. It is a collection of special types of boxes and arrows. You follow the direction of the arrows, starting at an oblong box labelled 'start'. Sometimes you come to a rectangular box saying you have to do something, such as perform a specific calculation. Sometimes you come to a diamond shape box representing a decision. Depending on the outcome of the decision you may subsequently go in one or more different directions. In a mortgage flowchart you should eventually end at a box that tells you explicitly the type of mortgage to purchase that is most appropriate to your circumstances.

Flowcharts have been used for many years in systems design as an informal description of algorithms. They are informal in the sense that you can put any label that you

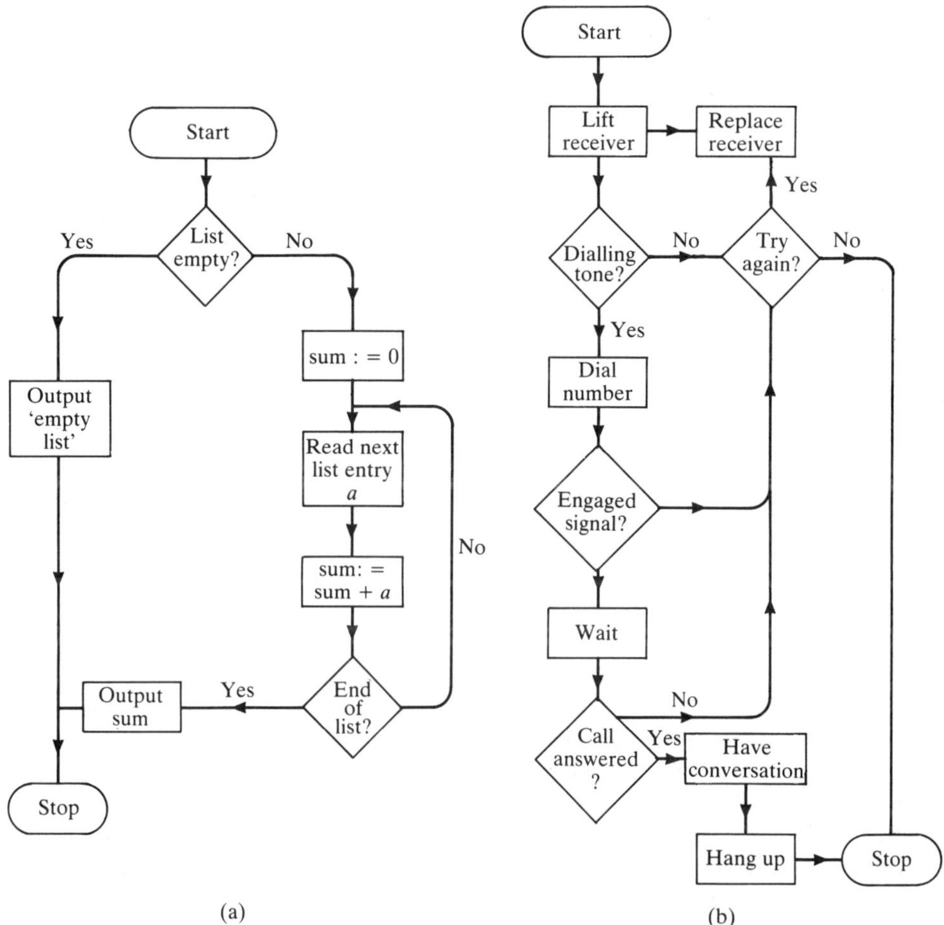

Figure 13.1 Flowcharts.

like inside a box. The expectation is that the label is sufficiently precise to explain the intended meaning to the target audience. Two typical flowcharts are shown in Fig. 13.1. Thus Fig. 13.1(a) describes an algorithm for summing a list of integers to anybody who might wish to implement such an algorithm in a procedural programming language like Pascal. Figure 13.1(b) describes an algorithm that explains the steps involved in making a telephone call. The target audience in this case is any reasonably intelligent English-speaking person who can recognize such objects as the telephone receiver and dialling pad.

Providing that the box labels are appropriately precise for the target audience, flowcharts are a useful documentation aid. They express the logic of a design. In the early days of computing, flowcharts were commonly used as a precursor for coding. The idea was that you could check that the logic was correct before coding and running the resulting program. Once checked, the transformation from a flowchart into code could be relatively straightforward (depending on the level of detail used).

Using a Pascal type pseudo-code we could encode the flowchart of Fig. 13.1(a) in a number of ways. Two possibilities are shown in Fig. 13.2 which allows us to highlight

VERSION A

```
begin
   if list is empty goto 20;
   sum := 0;
10 read next list entry a;
   sum:= sum + a;
   if not end of list goto 10;
   write(sum);
   goto end;
20 write("Empty list")
end.
```

VERSION B

```
begin
 if list is empty
  then write("empty list")
  else
   begin
    sum := 0;
    repeat
     read next list entry a;
     sum := sum + a;
    until end of list;
    write(sum)
   end
 end.
```

Figure 13.2 Two possible encodings of the flowchart of Fig. 13.1(a).

informally a number of principles underlying structured programming. In version A we have used *goto* statements to explicitly direct the flow of control at each point in the algorithm where there is more than one possible branching. We have not used *goto* statements in version B. The flow of control is implicit within the programming language structures being used, namely the *selection* structure 'if-then-else' and the *loop* structure 'repeat-until'.

When a program, like version B, is written in terms of the basic structures illustrated in Fig. 13.3 it is said to be *D-structured*, or, more simply, *structured*. The 'D' comes from the computer scientist Dijkstra, who proposed that all programs should be written only in this way. Since some programming languages have built-in constructs for implementing all of these basic structures, some people have said that a 'D-structured' program is one that contains no *goto* statements. This implies that version B is structured and version A is not. However, both version A and B represent the same algorithm. Should we not be more concerned about whether the underlying algorithm itself is structured? If so then we have to be a lot more careful about how we define structured programming.

Exercise 13.1 Write down a pseudo-code representation of the flowchart of Fig. 13.1(b). Is it possible to do this without *goto*'s?

For reasons that will be explained formally in Sec. 13.3, the flowchart of Fig. 13.1(b) cannot be represented in pseudo-code without *goto* statements, using only the structures of Fig. 13.3. There are a number of problems with this algorithm. In addition to a certain amount of tangled logic, it is not clear what is the difference between *replace receiver* and *hang up*, nor what happens if you want to make more than one call.

It would appear that the algorithm was poorly *designed*. A likely reason for this is that the designer was thinking in a 'bottom-up' manner. In many respects this is inevitable if you are using flowcharts as your primary *design* tool, for it is easy to just draw a number of boxes representing the detailed actions and decisions that you know have to be performed, rather than thinking abstractly about the whole problem. Once the boxes are drawn you might then be encouraged to draw arcs between them having decided that certain actions or decisions must precede others. With such an approach, you might end up with a flowchart that looks like a tangled mess of spaghetti. It is widely believed that, when implemented, such algorithms, with their tangled flow of logic, lead to incomprehensible and unmaintainable programs.

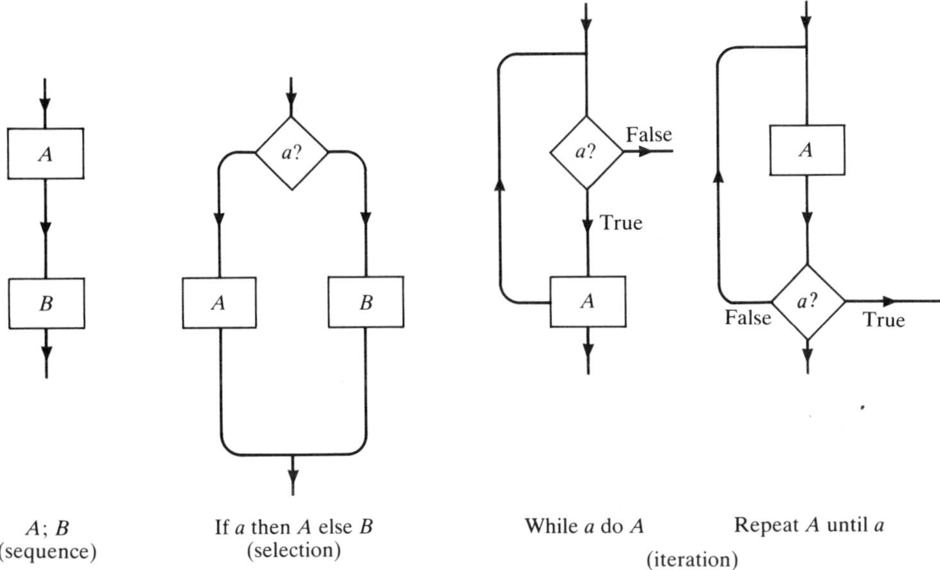

Figure 13.3 Some basic programming structures.

If we get rid of the design deficiencies already identified for the algorithm of Fig. 13.1 (b), we can restructure it in such a way that the resulting algorithm *is* D-structured and describes the same process as the original. This is shown in Fig. 13.4. The algorithm expresses zero or more attempts to make phone calls. A single phone call involves a nested sequence of selections. We have identified *replace receiver* and *hang up* as one and the same action, and so have simplified the algorithm.

In this specific example we have shown that we can turn an unstructured algorithm into a structured one. Remarkably, it turns out that we can similarly restructure any 'spaghetti-type' algorithm. This was proved in 1965 by Böhm and Jacopini, whose theorem can be stated informally as:

> **Theorem 13.1** Given any algorithm A there is an algorithm A' that is D-structured and performs the same computation as A in the sense that it produces the same outputs as A given the same inputs.

> **Example 13.1** Ashcroft and Manna (1972) provided a constructive proof of Theorem 13.1. The idea is to find every cycle in the flowgraph of A and to redirect the arc that completes the cycle to a single new node that has an arc back to the start node. The effect is to break up all the cycles and replace them with a single loop. Introduce Boolean flag variables on each of the redirected arcs and test the status of these at the new node. In this way it is possible to maintain the original flow of control. The resulting algorithm A' is a D-structured version of A in which cycles in A are replaced by new flag variables and extra tests.

13.1.2 Problems with structured programming

Theorem 13.1 provided the justification for Dijkstra's assertion that only D-structured programs should ever be written. However, although we know that *theoretically* the

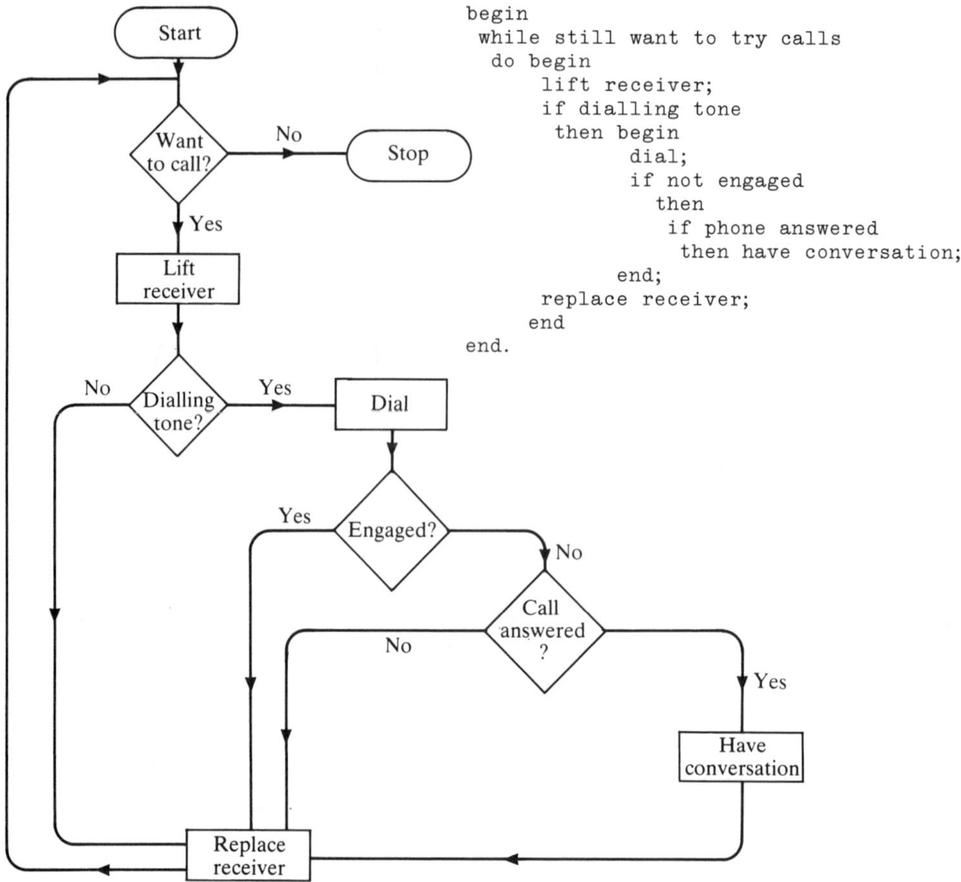

Figure 13.4 D-structured version of telephone algorithm.

structures in Fig. 13.3 are sufficient to describe any algorithm, they have proved to be very restrictive in practice. After all, the constructs available in machine language are also sufficient to describe any algorithm, but we would not dream of restricting ourselves to these. In fact, the restrictive definition gives rise to a number of questions:

- What happens if our programming language does not have built-in constructs for each of the D-structures of Fig. 13.3? For example, many versions of BASIC have no construct corresponding to the if-then-else structure. It can only be coded using a *goto* statement. Does this mean that a resulting program is inevitably unstructured?
- What is so special about the chosen constructs? Perhaps there are others just as natural as the chosen ones? Perhaps there is even a completely different set of natural constructs that is also sufficient to describe all algorithms.
- If you apply the Ashcroft–Manna algorithm of Example 13.1 to a non-D-structured algorithm A, the resulting D-structured algorithm A' may contain dozens of new flag variables and be totally incomprehensible as a result. If D-structured programming is synonymous with 'good' programming, is it justifiable to say that A' is always better than A?

- How can you tell whether an arbitrary algorithm is or is not structured?

We need a formal treatment to explain all of the above ideas properly, to answer the questions and to apply the results. Before doing so we finish this informal section with two further examples for you to ponder on, but will return to these later.

Example 13.2 The middle exit loop dilemma The two types of loops in Fig. 13.3, while-do and repeat-until, are examples of single-exit loops. The while-do may be thought of as an exit from the top of the loop and the repeat-until as an exit from the bottom of the loop. Unfortunately, in many situations it is more natural to solve a problem in terms of a different single exit loop, namely an exit from the middle loop. Consider, for example, the following simple programming problem: 'A set of numbers is to be read in sequentially, terminating with a special end of file character. The sum of the numbers is to be output.' A natural solution to this problem is to repeatedly read in the next file character, check for the end of file (eof) character and add the character to the cumulative sum. Thus we have an exit from the middle loop situation as described in Fig. 13.5(a). We have provided the associated pseudo-code using the construct 'loop-exit-when' to represent the middle exit loop structure. Although this is a perfectly natural and intuitively well-structured solution, most programming languages do not have such a built-in structure. Ada and Modula-2 are exceptions. This means that, in most languages, our natural algorithm cannot be directly implemented, and without the use of *goto* statements we are forced to restructure our solution as shown in Fig. 13.5(b). This D-structured version requires duplication of a statement—in this case *read(A)*—and slightly clouds the original logic. This cannot have been the intention of structured programming. Moreover, cognitive psychologists Soloway, Bonar and Ehrlich (1983) at Yale have shown that programmers who have not been subjected to any specific structured programming doctrine invariably consider the exit from the middle loop as a more natural construct than either of the others. One may conclude that the exclusion of this loop from the set of standard constructs is unjustified.

Example 13.3 A classic algorithm in computer science is the binary search algorithm. This is a divide and conquer approach to searching a sorted list for a specific item. We shall consider the details in Chapter 15. In one of the finest texts on algorithms, Harel (1987) describes binary search by the flowchart in Fig. 13.6. The algorithm is beautiful and clear. The flowchart consists of a loop with two exits. For reasons that will be made precise in the remaining sections, this algorithm is not D-structured. However, unlike the middle exit loop example, there is no simple restructuring that we can apply to make it D-structured. This means that the traditional definition of structured programming as synonymous with D-structuredness is extremely narrow. It implies that this most famous algorithm, simply described by one of the world's finest computer scientists, is not only unstructured, but requires major surgery. Again, this cannot have been the intention of those who advocated structured programming.

Exercise 13.2 How would you implement the exit from middle loop structure and the two-exit loop structure in Pascal?

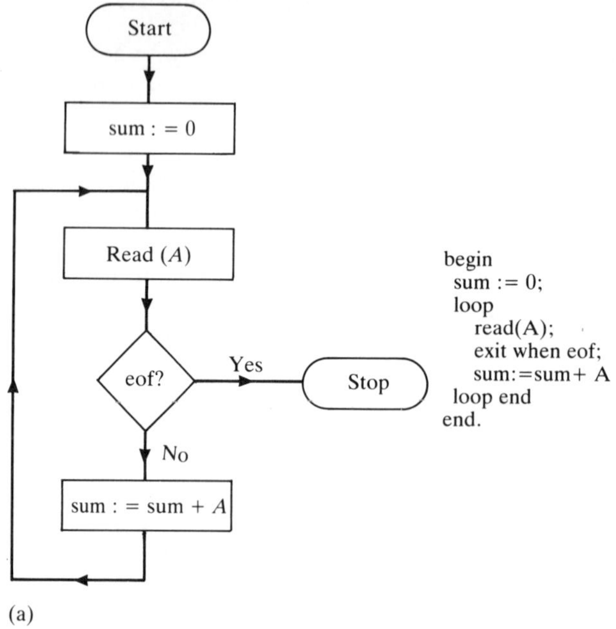

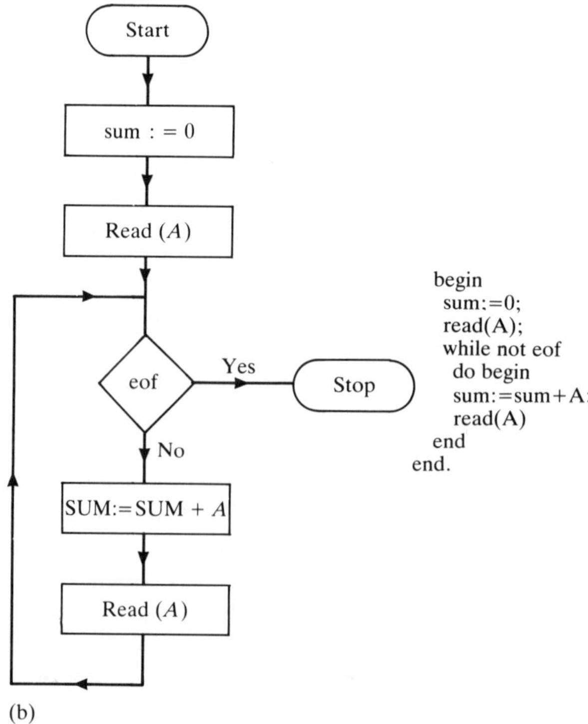

Figure 13.5 The middle exit loop dilemma.

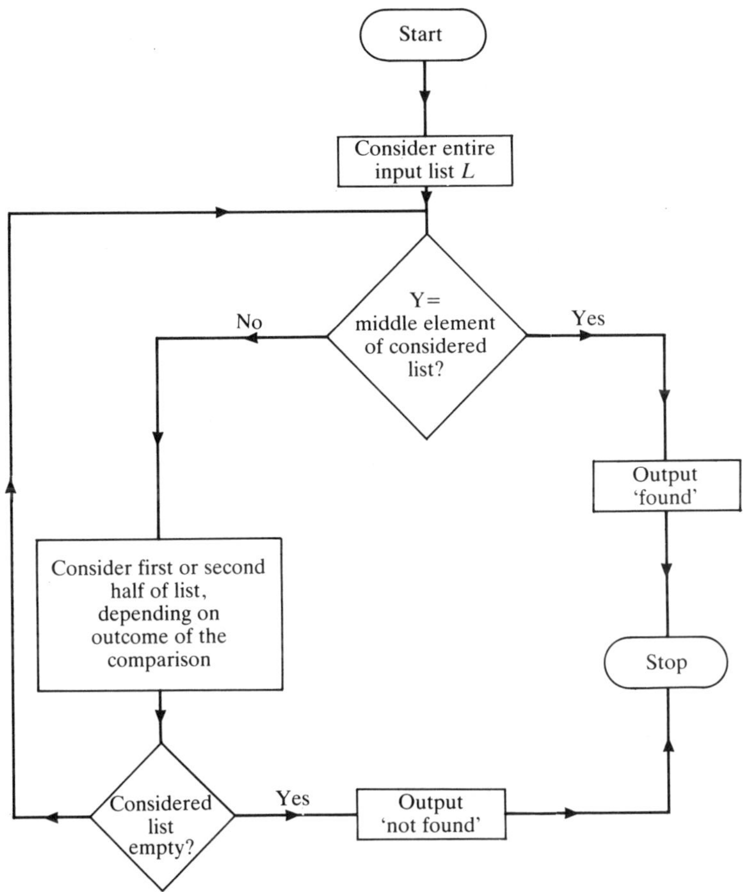

Figure 13.6 Binary search algorithm.

13.2 MODEL FOR STRUCTURED PROGRAMMING

In order to address the issues raised in Sec. 13.1, we now introduce a formal model of program control structure. This model, the flowgraph, is a special type of digraph. In Fig. 13.3, we used flowcharts to define informally the operational semantics of certain programming constructs. Using flowgraphs we will make these ideas quite formal. The notation and terminology of graph theory used in this and remaining sections of this chapter were used in Sec. 2.4.

13.2.1 The flowgraph model

The different shapes of boxes used in traditional flowcharts are purely cosmetic. Once we identify all boxes as being just nodes, it is clear that flowcharts may be viewed as a class of digraphs, in the sense of Chapter 2. Using this convention we shall speak about *flowgraphs* rather than flowcharts. Before giving a formal definition of flowgraphs we consider an example, and discuss the relationships between programs and flowgraphs.

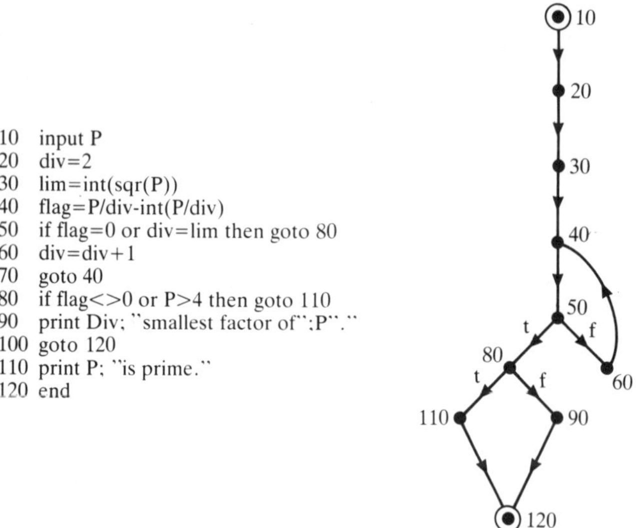

Figure 13.7 A program and corresponding flowgraph.

Example 13.4 The programming language BASIC is based on the von Neumann model and the concept of assignment, but does not distinguish between the symbol for equality of expressions and the symbol for the assignment command. Figure 13.7 provides a simple example program, which includes *goto* statements on the left and a reasonable interpretation of its corresponding flowgraph on the right. We say 'reasonable interpretation' because in many situations it is not at all obvious what the flowgraph should be.

The only special feature about flowgraphs that makes them different from any digraph is that we need to distinguish diagrammatically the two special nodes: the *start* node and the *stop* node. In both cases we encircle the node. It will always be clear which of the two is the stop node, because, as we shall see, this is the only node that has outdegree 0. Note that, unlike most flowcharts, the start node corresponds to the first actual instruction of the program. In fact, the stop node is the only node that does not correspond to an instruction in the program.

We may view a flowgraph as a model of program structure. Specifically we use it to model the flow of control in a program. This represents a subtle shift in emphasis from Sec. 13.1. We started there by looking at how we could find programs that implemented flowcharts so we mapped flowcharts to programs. Here we are more concerned with mapping programs to flowgraphs.

There are no universally agreed rules for modelling programs by flowgraphs. Many constructs in various languages cause difficulties: for loops, exception handling, recursion and assignment statements inside Boolean expressions. In many situations the approach to modelling will be determined by what you intend to do with the model. It is beyond the scope of this chapter to discuss this difficult issue. In all our examples the model will be self-evident.

Exercise 13.3 For each of the flowcharts in Sec. 13.1, draw the corresponding flowgraph.

Definition 13.1 Flowgraph A flowgraph $F = (G, a, z)$ consists of a digraph G together with distinguished nodes a, the start node, and z, the stop node, of G. The latter has outdegree 0. Every node must possess the 'walk property', meaning that it lies on some walk from a to z. Nodes of outdegree 1 are called procedure nodes. All other nodes except z are called predicate nodes.

Exercise 13.4 Recall from Sec. 2.4 that a *path* is a walk in which no nodes or edges are repeated. Show that there are valid flowgraphs in which not every node lies on a path from start to stop. (*Hint*: Look at one of the flowgraphs in Fig. 13.8.) What can you say about trails?

Certain flowgraphs occur sufficiently often when we model program control structure to merit special names. In particular, Fig. 13.8 describes the flowgraphs P_0, P_n, D_0, D_1, D_2, D_3, D_4, D_5, L_2, and the flowgraphs C_n (for $n \geq 3$), which will subsequently be referred to by name only. The flowgraphs P_0 and P_1 are referred to as the *trivial flowgraphs*. When we add labels to nodes and edges of flowgraphs, as we have done in Fig. 13.8, we may write down the corresponding programs that they may be considered to model. In general a flowgraph F, with m nodes labelled $A_1, \ldots, A_m$ respectively, is referred to as $F(A_1, \ldots, A_m)$.

Exercise 13.5 With any reasonable approach to modelling the control flow of programs as flowgraphs, it is possible to obtain the same flowgraph for different programs. Show that the following two programs both have the flowgraph D_2:

```
10 if not A then goto 40
20 X
30 goto 10
40 end
```

```
begin
 while A do X
end.
```

Definition 13.1 allows us to deduce a number of simple properties about flowgraphs. For example, it follows from the walk property that flowgraphs have no unreachable blocks of code, nor 'black holes' that we can enter but never exit. In reality, some programs do have these undesirable properties. These would be detected during the construction of the flowgraph. The assumption is that such programs should always be amended. Unreachable blocks of code must either be removed or provided with a means of entry. Black holes should either be removed or provided with an exit.

Exercise 13.6 Use Def. 13.1 to deduce that the node z is the only node of outdegree 0 and that the node a is the only node that *may* have indegree 0.

It follows from Def. 13.1 that we can have flowgraphs F, F' which are different even though their underlying digraphs G, G' are the same. This is because they can have different *start nodes*. An example of one such pair of flowgraphs is given in Fig. 13.9.

Exercise 13.7 The notion of flowgraphs being the same is formalized by a notion of flowgraph *isomorphism*. Specifically, we say that the flowgraphs $F = (G, a, z)$ and $F' = (G', a', z')$ are isomorphic if there is a digraph isomorphism $\phi : G \to G'$ in which $\phi(a) = a'$. Use this to prove that the flowgraphs in Fig. 13.9 are non-isomorphic. Also prove that in any flowgraph isomorphism $\phi(z) = z'$.

Exercise 13.8 Any flowgraph may be viewed as an *algebra*, in the sense of Chapter 8, whose signature consists of: two sorts V (corresponding to nodes) and E (corresponding to arcs), and two constants a and z that are of sort V. With this view of flowgraphs show that the notion of flowgraph isomorphism defined in the previous exercise is the same as an isomorphism between algebras as defined in Chapter 8.

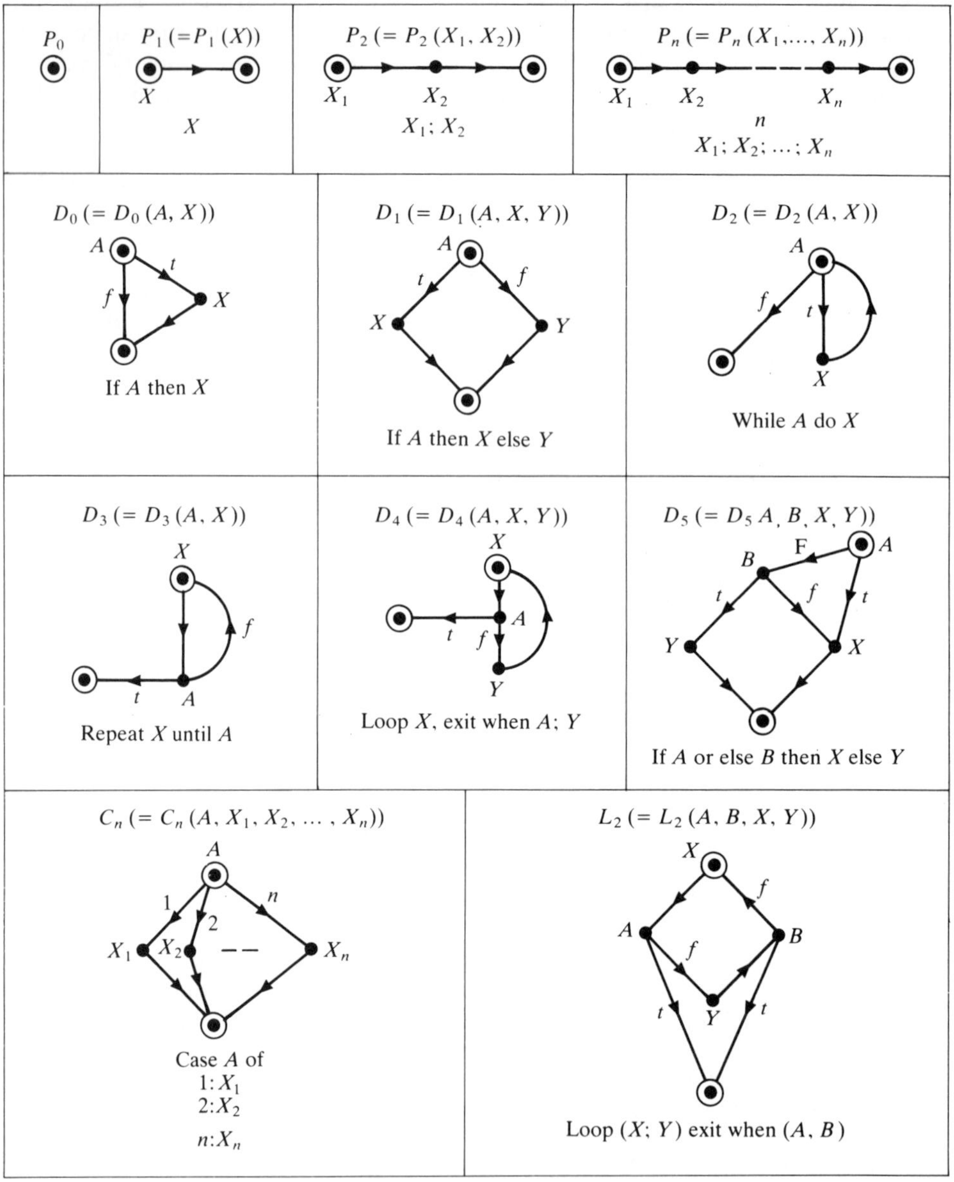

P_0
$P_1 (= P_1 (X))$
X
X
$P_2 (= P_2 (X_1, X_2))$
X_1 X_2
$X_1; X_2$
$P_n (= P_n (X_1, \ldots, X_n))$
X_1 X_2 X_n
n
$X_1; X_2; \ldots; X_n$
$D_0 (= D_0 (A, X))$
A t f X
If A then X
$D_1 (= D_1 (A, X, Y))$
A t f X Y
If A then X else Y
$D_2 (= D_2 (A, X))$
A f t X
While A do X
$D_3 (= D_3 (A, X))$
X f t A
Repeat X until A
$D_4 (= D_4 (A, X, Y))$
X A t f Y
Loop X, exit when A; Y
$D_5 (= D_5 A, B, X, Y))$
F A B t f t Y X
If A or else B then X else Y
$C_n (= C_n (A, X_1, X_2, \ldots, X_n))$
A 1 n 2 X_1 X_2 X_n
Case A of
$1{:}X_1$
$2{:}X_2$
$n{:}X_n$
$L_2 (= L_2 (A, B, X, Y))$
X f A B f t Y t
Loop (X; Y) exit when (A, B)

Figure 13.8 Some common flowgraphs.

D_2
D_3
Both D_2 and D_3 have same underlying digraph
G
but cannot be isomorphic, since the start node of D_2 has outdegree 2 and the start node of D_3 has outdegree 1

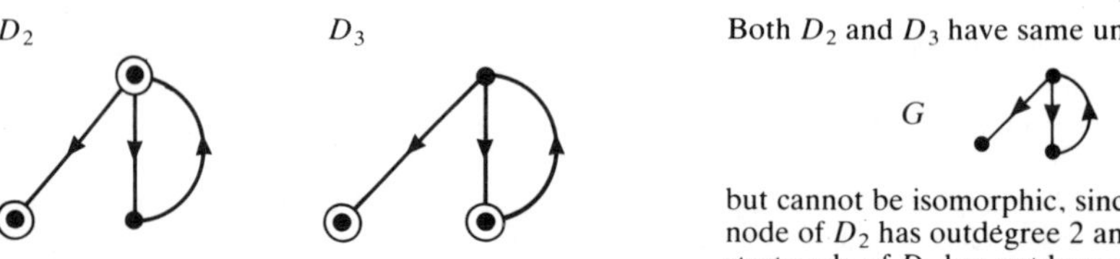

Figure 13.9 Two different flowgraphs with the same underlying directed graph.

13.2.2 Flowgraph 'language'

In Fig. 13.7 on page 318 the association between program and flowgraph was perfectly reasonable, because the flow of control in the program was quite explicit. However, what about the flowgraphs in Fig. 13.8 on page 320? Associated with each flowgraph we have written a program-like statement, some of which we introduced in Chapter 12. For example, 'while A do X' is associated with the flowgraph D_2. Certain types of control structure, like those in Fig. 13.8, occur so often and naturally in software design that we would like to have built-in programming language constructs to directly implement them. Otherwise we have to use the *goto* statement as shown for the D_2 construct in the program on the left-hand side of Exercise 13.5.

The constructs for D_0, D_1, D_2, D_3, in particular, are common to so many programming languages that we have come to think of these as defining their associated flowgraphs. It is our prior understanding of 'while A do X' that makes the link with the flowgraph D_2 intuitively obvious. What is really happening is that we are using the flowgraphs to define the special language constructs. Specifically the flowgraph provides an *operational semantics*; this means that the constructs are defined in terms of explicit sequences of computational operations, namely the set of all possible walks of the associated flowgraph.

Example 13.5 The flowgraph D_1 consists of just two possible walks, namely $AtXz$ and $AfYz$ (we include the arc labels t,f only for extra clarity). This means there are just two possible ways to execute D_1. In both we start with the test A. If A is true we execute X then stop. If A is false we execute Y then stop. By defining the construct 'if A then X else Y' to be the flowgraph $D_1(A, X, Y)$ we are then also defining its semantics operationally.

Example 13.6 The flowgraph D_2 consists of the infinite set of walks

$\{Afz, AtXAfz, AtXAtXAfz, AtXAtXAtXAfz, AtXAtXAtXAtXAfz, \ldots\}$

Example 13.7 The flowgraph L_2 is a generic version of the two-exit loop discussed in Example 13.3. It is a very natural construct and occurs in many control environments. Imagine that we wish to execute a process that is a loop. The loop consists of first performing X (for example this might be updating a specific variable) and then performing Y (which might be updating a different variable). After each execution of X and Y, we may need to check that the update has not caused some other system variable to take on an unsafe value. At any stage when such a check does reveal an unsafe value we immediately terminate the process. This is the structure of the binary search algorithm. Denoting the checks following X and Y as A and B respectively, it should be clear that L_2 is a model of this whole process. The set of walks is

$\{XAtz, XAfYBtz, XAfYBfXAtz, XAfYBfXAfYBtz, XAfYBfXAfYBfXAtz, \ldots\}$

Exercise 13.9 Write down the set of possible walks for the flowgraphs $P_4, D_0, D_3, D_4, D_5, C_4$.

We can use the notation of regular expressions in Chapter 7 to talk about the set of possible walks of a flowgraph F as the *language* $L(F)$. The alphabet of this language is the set of node labels of F.

Example 13.8

$$L(D_1) = AtXz + AfYz$$
$$L(D_2) = A(tXA)^*fz$$
$$L(L_2) = X(AfYBfX)^* + XAfY(BfXAfY)^*Btz$$

Exercise 13.10 Write down $L(P_4), L(D_0), L(D_3), L(D_4), L(D_5), L(C_4)$.

In general, if a program P is modelled by the flowgraph F, we can use $L(F)$ to define the operational semantics of P. This also allows us to formalize some of the earlier notions of program equivalence.

Definition 13.2 Two labelled flowgraphs F, F' are language equivalent (or more simply L-equivalent) if $L(F) = L(F')$. Two programs P, P' are L-equivalent if their corresponding flowgraphs are L-equivalent.

Example 13.9 Consider the two flowgraphs D_3, D_3':

These are L-equivalent, since $L(D_3) = L(D_3') = XA(fXA)^*tz$.

It follows from Example 13.9 that D_3 (the repeat-until loop) is L-equivalent to a flowgraph built up using a sequence statement and the D_2 (while-do) loop. Specifically, 'repeat A until X' is L-equivalent to 'X ; while A do X'. It follows that the repeat-until loop is technically redundant in the sense that we can always replace it by an L-equivalent structure built from the while-do loop. This has not stopped programming language designers from including both types of loop constructs in their languages. This is the right approach because, although L-equivalent, D_3' does not have the natural simplicity of D_3.

Now recall the discussion about the middle exit loop D_4 in Example 13.2. It follows that D_4 is L-equivalent to a flowgraph built using the sequence statement and the D_2 loop. Specifically 'loop X exit when A;Y' is L-equivalent to 'X ; while A do (Y ;X)'. Thus D_4, like D_3, is technically redundant. However, D_3 is included in programming languages like Pascal while D_4 is not. The normal argument used for the exclusion of D_4 is that it is redundant. We now see that this argument is valid but inconsistently applied.

Example 13.10 Consider the program statement 'if (A or B) then X else Y'. What does this statement mean? Ideally we might argue that the statement ought to have the semantics of the flowgraph D_5 of Fig. 13.8; technically this is said to be a *short-circuit* or *lazy evaluation* of the compound Boolean expression 'A or B'. This means that we do not always need to evaluate both A and B to determine the value of 'A or B'. When A is true, then no matter what the value of B, it follows that the expression 'A or B' is true. This could save us a lot of unnecessary processing, since we only need to evaluate B when we really have to. Unfortunately, most languages do not use this interpretation. In most versions of Pascal all compound Boolean expressions are evaluated fully. Thus the flowgraph D_5 does not define the semantics of 'if (A or B) then X else Y' in Pascal. The language Ada allows both lazy and non-lazy evaluation. To distinguish the lazy evaluation, the construct 'if A or else B then X else Y' is used. This *is* defined by D_5. The question remains: can we directly implement the structure D_5 in most versions of Pascal without using a *goto*. The answer is no, just as we cannot implement D_4 directly.

Exercise 13.11 Draw the flowgraph for the Pascal interpretation of 'if (A or B) then X else Y'.

Exercise 13.12 Show that D_5 is L-equivalent to a flowgraph built using just D_1 structures.

13.3 FLOWGRAPH DECOMPOSITION

In both Secs 13.1 and 13.2.1 we used the notion of structuredness without a formal definition. For example, we spoke about the D_5 structure being L-equivalent to a flowgraph structured in terms of D_2 flowgraphs alone. In this section we are going to use the flowgraph model to make these ideas absolutely precise. In doing so we can fill in many of the holes left so far.

We begin by describing two operations that can be performed on flowgraphs: sequencing and nesting. We use these operations to define the appropriate generalized notion of structuredness that we need to address the issues raised in Sec. 13.1. We then introduce the crucial notion of prime flowgraphs, which are flowgraphs that cannot be decomposed by sequencing and nesting. We show how every flowgraph has a unique decomposition into prime flowgraphs, and illustrate the importance of this result for structured programming. Finally, we show how the prime decomposition is usefully applied to the static analysis of software.

13.3.1 Operations on flowgraphs

Definition 13.3 Sequencing of flowgraphs Given two flowgraphs, F_1 and F_2, we can produce a new flowgraph called the sequence of F_1 and F_2, and written as $(F_1 \ ; F_2)$, by simply regarding the stop node of F_1 as identical with the start node of F_2.

This operation is illustrated in Fig. 13.10(a). If we think of flowgraphs as models of program control flow, then the sequencing operation of flowgraphs corresponds precisely to the sequence operation ';' in imperative language programming. Thus,

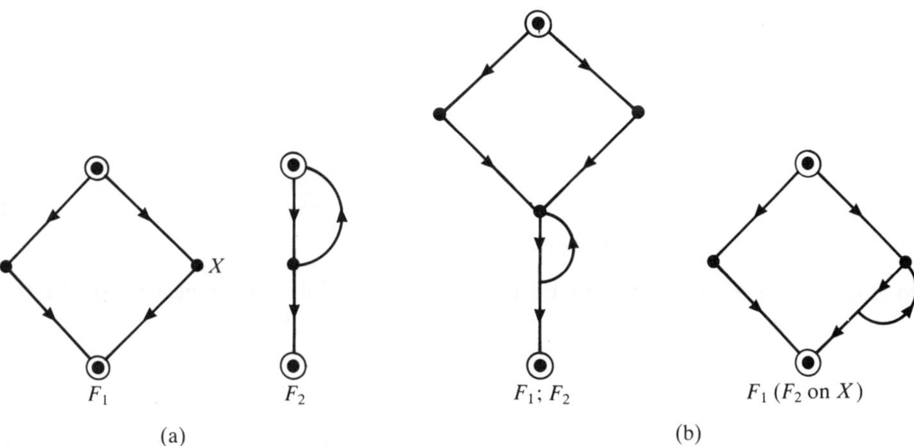

Figure 13.10 Sequencing and nesting.

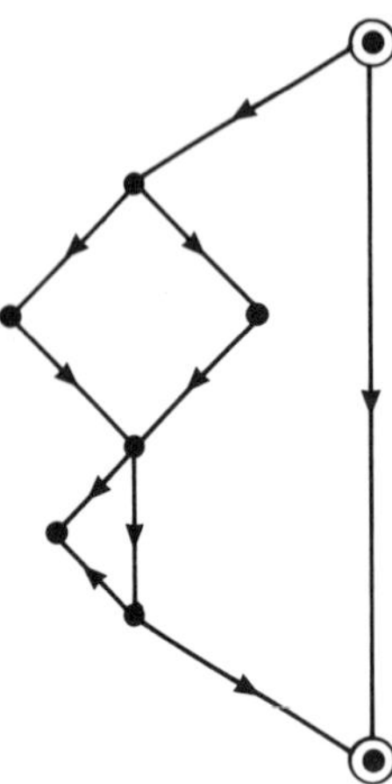

Figure 13.11 A flowgraph built from sequencing and nesting.

if A_1 and A_2 are programs, then $F(A_1;A_2)$, the flowgraph of $A_1;A_2$, is equal to $F(A_1);F(A_2)$, the sequence of $F(A_1)$ and $F(A_2)$.

Definition 13.4 Nesting of flowgraphs Suppose F_1 and F_2 are flowgraphs and that x is a procedure node of F_1. We may produce a new flowgraph called the nesting of F_2 on to F_1 at x, and written $F_1(F_2 \text{ on } x)$, by replacing the single edge leading from x by the whole flowgraph F_2. Thus, the start node of F_2 is identified with x and the stop node of F_2 is identified with the node of F_1 that x leads to.

The nesting operation is illustrated in Fig. 13.10(b). Suppose F_1 models a program A_1 in which the procedure A_2, modelled by F_2, is called by the parameter x. Then $F_1(F_2 \text{ on } x)$ is precisely the flowgraph that would result if we substituted A_2 for x in A_1. Thus nesting corresponds to the notion of procedure substitution in imperative language programming.

In general we may wish to nest n flowgraphs $F_1,\ldots,F_n$ on to n respective procedure nodes $x_1,\ldots,x_n$. The resulting flowgraph is written as

$$F(F_1 \text{ on } x_1, F_2 \text{ on } x_2, \ldots, F_n \text{ on } x_n)$$

In many of our examples the actual nodes nested on to is of no importance, and hence we would simply write this as $F(F_1,F_2,\ldots,F_n)$.

Example 13.11 The flowgraph F in Fig. 13.11 is made up from the sequence of the flowgraphs D_1 and D_4 which are in turn nested on to the single procedure node of the flowgraph D_0. Thus $F = D_0((D_1;D_4))$.

Sequencing of n flowgraphs can be viewed as a special case of nesting on to the flowgraph P_n. Specifically, $F_1;F_2;\ldots;F_n = P_n(F_1,F_2,\ldots,F_n)$.

13.3.2 Flowgraph families

Suppose we start with two flowgraphs, say D_1 and D_2. Then we can generate an infinite number of flowgraphs from these two by using just the operations of sequencing and nesting repeatedly. This is illustrated in Fig. 13.12. We now use this idea to give a

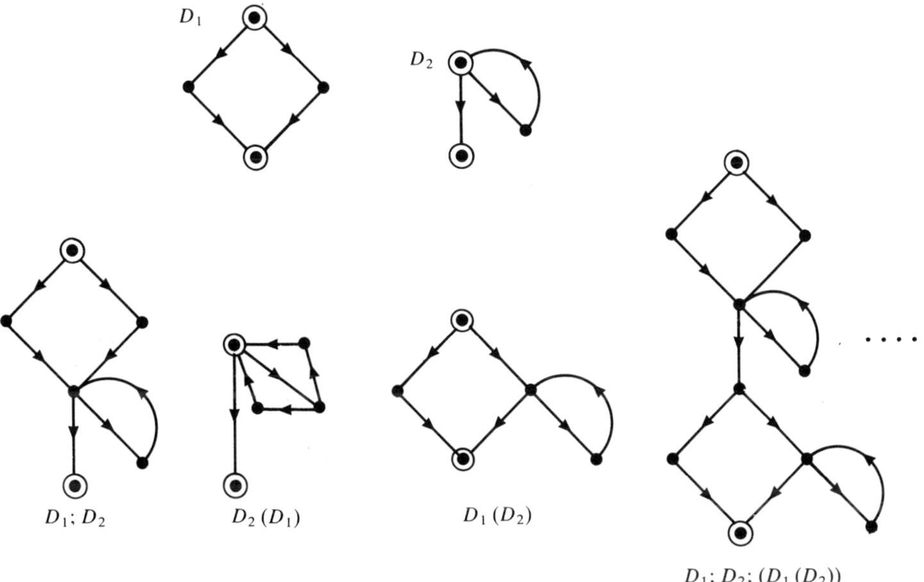

Figure 13.12 Generating flowgraphs from D_1 and D_2.

formal and generic definition of the notion of structured programming. We start with an arbitrary, but fixed, family S of flowgraphs. In our example we took $S = \{D_1, D_2\}$. In general S could be any family, either finite or infinite.

Definition 13.5 S**-structured graphs** The set of S-structured graphs is defined inductively as:

Basis clause. Each member of S is an S-structured graph and is called a basic S-graph.

Inductive clause. If F_1, F_2 are S-structured graphs then so are $F_1; F_2$ and $F_1(F_2)$.

Extremal clause. No flowgraph is an S-structured graph unless it can be constructed by applying the basis and the inductive clauses a finite number of times.

For simplicity we shall refer to the S-structured graphs as just S-graphs. We may use this definition to define arbitrary classes of structured programs. Structuredness is characterized by the family S.

Example 13.12 Let $S^D = \{P_1, D_0, D_1, D_2\}$. The traditional definition of D-structured programs discussed in Sec. 13.1.2 can now be seen formally to be the set of S^D-graphs. Theorem 13.1 on page 313 can be stated more formally as: for every algorithm A there is an algorithm A', whose flowgraph is an S^D-graph, which performs the same computation as A.

Example 13.13 When coding in Pascal, programmers are advised to stick to the built-in language constructs and not to use the *goto* statements. The built-in constructs consist of the family S^D of Example 13.12 and the *case* statement. The n-way *case* statement corresponds to C_n. Therefore, in theory, the 'structured' Pascal programs are those that are S^P-graphs where $S^P = S^D \cup \{C_n : n \geq 1\}$.

Exercise 13.13 Suppose $S = \{P_1\}$. Describe the set of S-graphs.

Exercise 13.14 Show that the set of S-graphs may be viewed as a many-sorted algebra whose signature is $(\{X, N\}, \{seq, nest\})$ where the functions have arity $seq : X \times X \to X$ and $nest : X \times X \times N \to X$.

It is easy to see informally that the flowgraphs D_3, D_4 and D_5 are *not* S^D-graphs (this will be explained formally in Sec. 13.3.3). However, we have shown that all of these are L-equivalent to S^D-graphs. In fact it follows from our arguments in Sec. 13.2.1 that, assuming appropriate node labellings:

1 D_3 is L-equivalent to the S^D-graph $P_1; D_2$.

2 D_4 is L-equivalent to the S^D-graph $P_1; D_2(P_1; P_1)$.

3 D_5 is L-equivalent to the S^D-graph $D_1(D_1, P_1)$.

So you may be thinking that all the constructs in Fig. 13.8 are L-equivalent to S^D-graphs and hence that the narrow, traditional definition of structured programming, that is a program is structured iff it is an S^D-graph, is satisfactory after all. This illusion is shattered by the following fundamental theorem.

Theorem 13.2 The flowgraph L_2 is not L-equivalent to any S^D-graph.

The theorem follows from a more general result of Kosaraju which asserts: a flowgraph is L-equivalent to an S^D-graph if and only if it contains no subgraph that is a loop having two paths to the stop node. Informally this means that a two-exit loop is a basic impediment to D-structured programming. If you wanted to implement a program with an L_2 structure without using a *goto* statement you would have to perform the kind of restructuring described by the Ashcroft–Manna algorithm in Example 13.1. We prefer to deduce that the traditional definition of structured programming is overly restrictive. As we have seen in examples like the binary search algorithm, the L_2 construct, and its generalization L_n the n-exit loop, is every bit as natural as D_2 or D_3. If your programming language does not contain a built-in construct for L_n then it has to be encoded using *goto* statements. This does *not* make the resulting program unstructured. The same goes for D_4, D_5 and the C_n flowgraphs. This suggests that the most appropriate set S for defining structured programming should contain the set $\{D_0, D_1, D_2, D_3, D_4, D_5, L_2, L_3, ..., C_2, C_3, ...\}$.

This does not mean that we have answered the question: which set S is best? Clearly much will depend on the context. It turns out that in order to perform various types of analyses on S-graphs, we must be very careful about which basic S-graphs can be allowed.

13.3.3 Prime flowgraphs and decomposition

All of the flowgraphs shown in Fig. 13.8 have a very important common property. In each case we cannot express the flowgraph as the sequence and nesting of smaller flowgraphs. This is in contrast with, say, the flowgraph F of Fig. 13.11 which can be decomposed as $F = D_0((D_1; D_4))$.

Definition 13.6 Prime flowgraph A flowgraph F is prime if it cannot be decomposed into smaller flowgraphs by sequencing and nesting.

Thus each of the flowgraphs P_1, D_0, D_1, D_2, D_3, D_4, D_5, C_n and L_2 is prime, whereas the flowgraph F of Example 13.11 is not. The definition we have given here is not the formal one. A strictly formal definition is based on the notion of *subflowgraph*, which is surprisingly tricky to describe. It is beyond the scope of this chapter to provide the definitions needed for this. In the formal definition, a prime flowgraph is one that contains no subflowgraphs of a certain type. We lose something by not using the formal definition, namely a deterministic procedure for deciding whether an arbitrary flowgraph is prime. However, in our examples this will always be reasonably clear anyway.

Exercise 13.15 The following sets of edges form flowgraphs on five nodes (1, ..., 5). Draw the flowgraphs using the conventions of Fig. 13.8. Which of the flowgraphs are primes? For those that are not, represent the flowgraphs by expressions using sequencing and nesting applied to the flowgraphs of Fig. 13.8.

(a) Edges (1, 2), (2, 3), (3, 4), (4, 3), (3, 5)

(b) Edges (1, 2), (2, 3), (1, 4), (3, 4), (4, 3), (3, 5)

(c) Edges (1, 2), (2, 3), (3, 2), (3, 4), (4, 3), (2, 5)

(d) Edges (1, 2), (2, 3), (2, 5), (3, 4), (4, 1)

The importance of prime flowgraphs as building blocks of structured programming is summarized by the following theorem.

Theorem 13.3 Prime decomposition Every flowgraph has a unique decomposition into a hierarchy of primes.

This theorem is analogous to the fundamental theorem of arithmetic described in Example 2.10 on page 26, and explains why prime flowgraphs are named after prime numbers. The proof of the theorem is dependent on the more formal definition of primes, and is based on the idea of recursively finding and decomposing *maximal* subflowgraphs until the flowgraph cannot be further decomposed. Figure 13.13 illustrates how the theorem produces the full *prime decomposition* of a flowgraph. It follows from the theorem that this is the only way in which F may be structured as a hierarchy of primes.

As Fig. 13.13 illustrates, the prime decomposition hierarchy of a flowgraph F is normally represented as a tree which we call the *prime decomposition tree of* F, written tree(F). We take advantage of the fact that the sequencing of n flowgraphs is the same as nesting the n flowgraphs onto the flowgraph P_n. Hence, each operation in the hierarchy is a nesting operation, and each node in the tree is labelled by the name of a prime flowgraph or the flowgraph P_n for some n. Figure 13.14 describes the prime decomposition tree of the restructured telephone algorithm of Fig. 13.4.

The prime decomposition theorem illustrates why it is important for our definition of structuredness to have only primes in S, our family of basic flowgraphs. This is the only way to ensure that an arbitrary S-structured graph can be uniquely decomposed.

Example 13.14 Suppose that $S = \{D_1, D_2, E\}$, where the basic S-graph E is the flowgraph $(D_1; D_2)$. Then E is, by definition, not prime. Now consider the flowgraph $F = D_2(E)$. This is certainly an S-graph. However, it has two distinct decompositions into basic S-graphs as shown in Fig. 13.15.

Suppose F is a flowgraph. If we select any family of primes S and look at the prime decomposition tree of F, then we have a simple means of determining whether F is S-structured or not. We just look at the node labels of tree(F). Only if every node is either a member of S or equal to P_n for some n is the flowgraph an S-graph. We also note that *every* flowgraph must be S-structured for some family S, namely the set S of distinct primes found in the decomposition tree; the question is whether there are members of S that are not allowed.

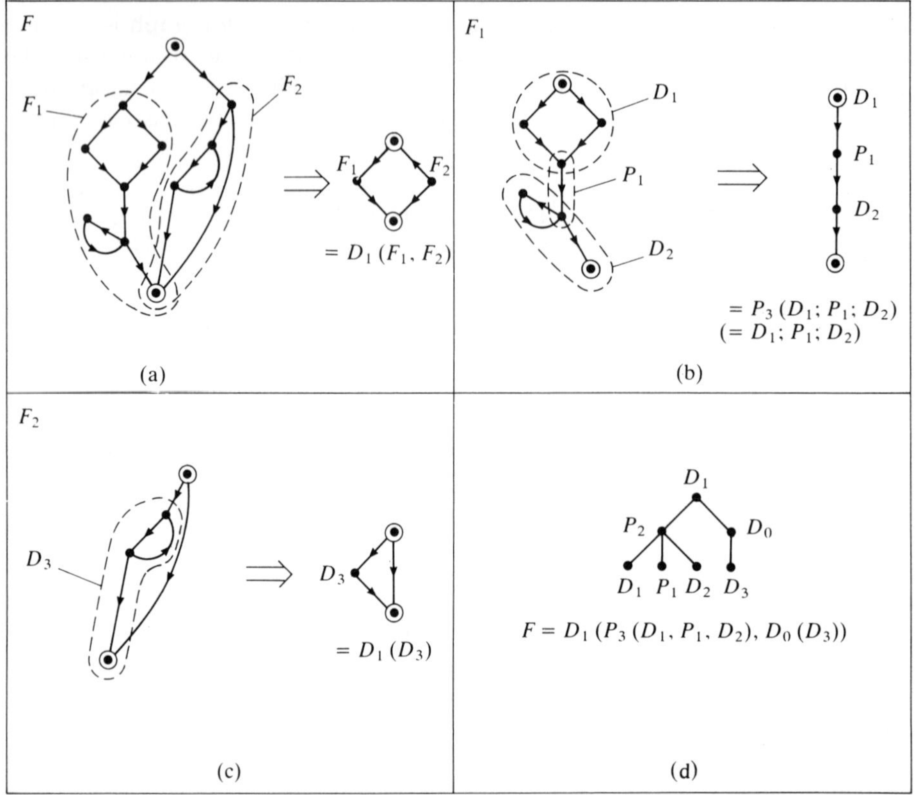

Figure 13.13 Prime decomposition.

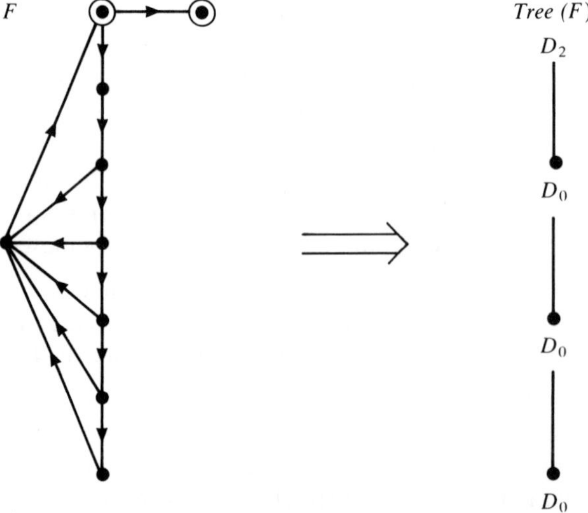

Figure 13.14 Flowgraph and decomposition tree of the structured telephone algorithm.

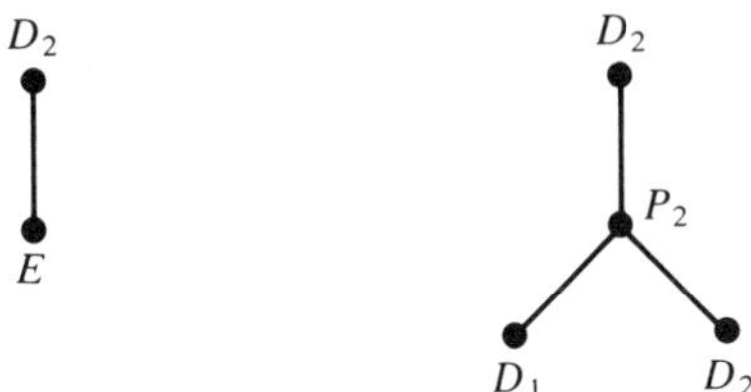

Figure 13.15 Two distinct decompositions.

Exercise 13.16 Now prove that the flowgraphs D_3, D_4 and D_5 are not S^D-graphs.

The decomposition theorem shows that every program has a quantifiable degree of structuredness characterized by its decomposition tree. The only structures that cannot be decomposed in any way at all are primes, so unless the whole flowgraph is prime even a large 'spaghetti' type structure can be decomposed to some extent. The proof of the theorem provides a constructive means of determining the decomposition tree, but for large flowgraphs it is impractical to perform this computation by hand. Fortunately, there are software tools, which are publicly available, to perform this computation.

In Fig. 13.16 we show an example of the use of the prime decomposition tree in analysing algorithm design. The algorithm is taken from Knuth (1969) and will calculate an approximation to $y = \log_b x$ for a number x, $1 \leq x < 2$. Note how the algorithm is written in an apparently unstructured manner using *goto*'s. It is relatively straightforward to derive a flowgraph that preserves all the features of the algorithm and to find the associated prime decomposition tree. The tree helps us to rewrite the algorithm in a manner that is easy to read and reveals the structure that was inherent, but not explicit, in the original.

This illustrates a powerful application of the decomposition theorem; it can be used to restructure code in an optimal manner. This is a form of *reverse engineering*. Restructuring will not turn spaghetti code into D-structured code; rather, it will identify those primes causing the 'spaghetti'. If these are truly unstructured then some genuine restructuring of these primes by the Ashcroft–Manna algorithm, for example, can be performed. We provide an elegant and general code restructuring approach.

13.3.4 Applications to static analysis and software measures

An enormous amount of research in recent years has been devoted to analysing software using a static representation such as the flowgraph model. We have shown how the flowgraph model and prime decomposition theorem provide an ideal basis for analysing and restructuring poorly written code. Many other types of code analysis depend on quantifying aspects of the code structure. Since the prime decomposition is a definitive description of the structure, it turns out that it has a major role to play in unifying this work.

Let us define informally a *structural measure* as a number defined on flowgraphs that characterizes some structural property of the program that the flowgraph models. There are numerous structural properties that we would like to characterize by such measures. For example, we would like to know: what maximum level of nesting is used in the flowgraph; how large is the flowgraph; and how many walks or paths of various types there are in the flowgraph. We might even want to have a number that

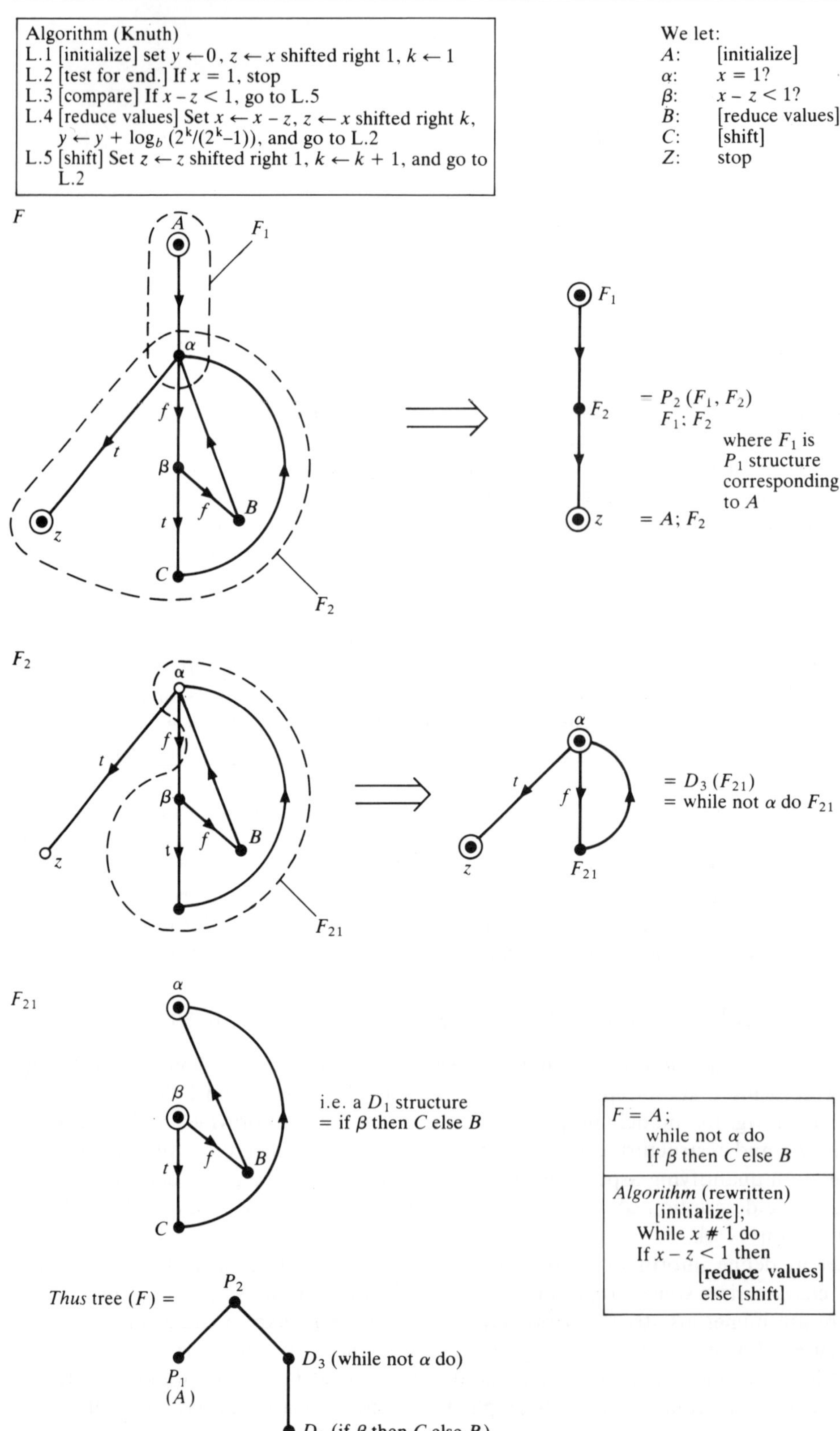

Figure 13.16 Decomposition used to 'restructure' Knuth's algorithm.

captures some composite views of the complexity of the flowgraph. Once we have such measures, we might, for example, be able to estimate how difficult the program will be to test using a specific strategy or how difficult it will be to maintain.

It turns out that a very wide range of structural measures can be described completely in terms of their effect on primes, and on the operations of sequence and nesting. Specifically, what we want to know for a given measure, m, is:

M1 (Primes). The value $m(F)$ for each prime F in our agreed family S.

M2 (Sequence). The sequence function g such that $m(F_1;\dots;F_n)=g(m(F_1),\dots,m(F_n))$.

M3 (Nesting). The nesting functions h_F for each prime F such that $m(F(F_1,\dots,F_n) = h_F(m(F_1),\dots,m(F_n))$.

Measures that can be defined in this way are called *hierarchical*.

Example 13.15 Consider the intuitive notion of *depth of nesting* within a program, modelled by a flowgraph F. An intuitively accurate measure α of depth of nesting can be completely described in terms of its effect on primes, sequence and nesting:

M1. The depth of nesting of the prime P_1 is zero, and the depth of nesting of any other prime F is equal to one. Formally, $\alpha(P_1) = 0$ and if F is a prime $\neq P_1$ then $\alpha(F) = 1$.

M2. The depth of nesting of the sequence $F_1,\dots,F_n$ is precisely the maximum of the depth of nesting of the F_i's. Formally, $\alpha(F_1;\dots;F_n) = \max(\alpha(F_1),\dots,\alpha(F_n))$.

M3. The depth of nesting of the flowgraph $F(F_1,\dots,F_n)$ is equal to the maximum of the depth of nesting of the F_i's *plus one* because of the extra nesting level in F. Formally, $\alpha(F(F_1,\dots,F_n)) = 1+\max(\alpha(F_1),\dots,\alpha(F_n))$.

Thus α is a hierarchical measure. We can use this information to compute the value of α for an arbitrary flowgraph F. Consider, for example, F in Fig. 13.13 on page 328. We know that $F = D_1(D_1;P_1;D_2), D_0(D_3))$. Thus we may compute:

$$\begin{aligned}
\alpha(F) &= 1+max\,(\alpha(D_1;P_1;D_2),\alpha(D_0(D_3))) && \text{(by M3)}\\
&= 1+max\,(max\,(\alpha(D_1),\alpha(P_1),\alpha(D_2)),1+\alpha(D_3)) && \text{(by M2 and M3)}\\
&= 1+max\,(max\,(1,0,1),2) && \text{(by M1)}\\
&= 1+max\,(1,2)\\
&= 3
\end{aligned}$$

Exercise 13.17 We wish to define a *length* measure, v, which provides a formal measure corresponding to the intuitively defined 'number of statements' in a program when the latter is modelled by a flowgraph. Using the example of F in Fig. 13.13 compute $v(F)$, where v is defined hierarchically as:

M1. $v(P_1) = 1$, and for each prime $F \neq P_1$, $v(F) = p+1$ where p is the number of *procedure* nodes in F.

M2. $v(F_1;\dots;F_n) = \sum_{i=1}^{n} v(F_i)$

M3. $v(F(F_1,\dots,F_n)) = 1+\sum_{i=1}^{n} v(F_i)$ for each prime $F \neq P_1$

Do you think this is a reasonable measure of program length?

Once a hierarchical measure m has been characterized in terms of the conditions M1, M2 and M3 we have the minimum information that we need in order to be able to calculate m for each S-graph F. Using this information, together with the prime decomposition tree of F, we have a constructive procedure for calculating $m(F)$. The tools referred to in Sec. 13.3.3 compute software measures in this way.

The most useful hierarchical measures are those that measure the maximum number of test cases required to satisfy particular 'white-box' testing strategies. For example, it has been proposed in McCabe (1976) that a good testing strategy is to choose test data in such a way that you traverse every one of a maximal set of linearly independent paths through a flowgraph. It is useful to know what this maximum number of paths is so that we know how big our testing task is. The well-known measure for this is called the *cyclomatic complexity measure*. It can be shown to be equal to $e - n + 2$, where e is the number of edges and n the number of nodes in the flowgraph. This and a whole range of testing measures are described formally in the book by Fenton (1991), along with their hierarchical definition. The following example provides merely a flavour of this work.

Example 13.16 The most demanding white box test strategy is to select test cases that traverse *every* possible walk in the flowgraph. Howcvcr, if the flowgraph contains even one loop then there are an infinite number of walks, and so the test strategy cannot be completely satisfied. On the other hand, a very simple strategy would be to select test cases such that every arc of the flowgraph is traversed at least once. This test strategy is called *branch testing*.

The minimum number of test cases required to satisfy branch testing of F is just the number μ which is the minimum number of walks in F that contain each arc of F. Suppose our family of primes is $S = \{P_1, D_0, D_1, D_2, D_3, D_4, L_2\}$. Then μ is defined hierarchically as:

M1. The value of $\mu(P)$ for each $P \in S$ is given by the following table:

Prime P	P_1	D_0	D_1	D_2	D_3	D_4	L_2
$\mu(P)$	1	2	2	1	1	1	2

M2. The sequence function for μ is: $\mu(F_1; F_2; \ldots; F_n) = \max(\mu(F_1), \mu(F_2), \ldots, \mu(F_n))$

M3. The nesting functions for each prime is given by the table:

Flowgraph F	$D_0(F_1)$	$D_1(F_1, F_2)$	$D_2(F_1, F_2)$	$D_3(F_1)$	$D_4(F_1, F_2)$	$L_2(F_1, F_2)$
$\mu(F)$	$\mu(F_1) + 1$	$\mu(F_1) + \mu(F_2)$	1	1	1	2

Again we consider the flowgraph F of Fig. 13.13, but to clarify the above ideas, we have labelled each arc as shown in Fig. 13.17. We know that $F = D_1((D_1; P_1; D_2), D_0(D_3))$ from the decomposition tree. Now we can compute μ by referring to M1, M2 and M3:

$$\begin{aligned}
\mu(F) &= \mu((D_1; P_1; D_2)) + \mu(D_0(D_3)) && \text{(by M3)}\\
&= \max(\mu(D_1), \mu(P_1), \mu(D_2)) + \mu(D_3) + 1 && \text{(by M2 and M3)}\\
&= \max(2, 1, 1) + 1 + 1 && \text{(by M1)}\\
&= 4
\end{aligned}$$

Thus a complete set of walks for this strategy is:
(1,3,5,7,8,9,10), (1,4,6,7,10), (2,11,13,14,13,15), (2,12)

Exercise 13.18 A testing strategy called *statement coverage* aims to select enough test cases to pass through each node of the flowgraph. Let $m(F)$ be the minimum number of walks required to pass through each node of F at least once. Then m is the number of test cases required for statement coverage. With the family S described in Example 13.16, define the measure m in terms of M1, M2

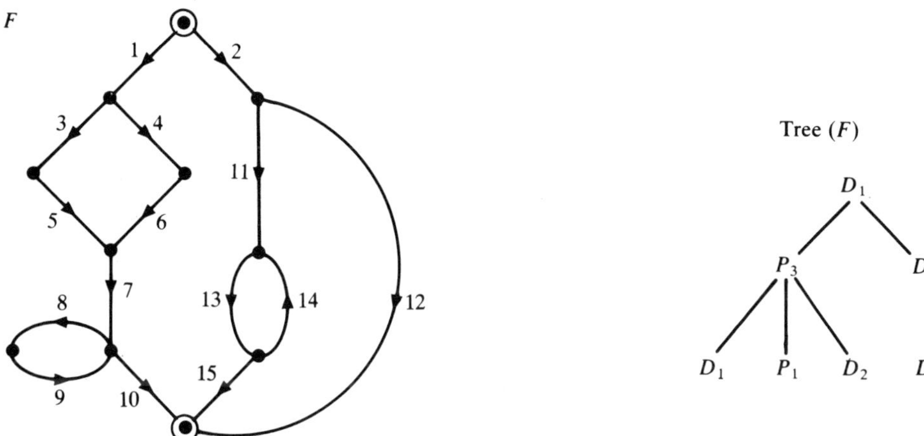

Figure 13.17 Flowgraph with arcs labelled.

and M3, and hence determine $m(F)$ for the flowgraph of that example. List a complete set of walks for this strategy.

13.4 SOFTWARE DESIGN REVISITED

We remarked in Sec. 13.1 that the use of flowcharts for designing algorithms encouraged an unstructured, bottom-up, approach. The resulting algorithms could potentially be a spaghetti-like tangle, whose decomposition trees contain very large esoteric primes, so that structured coding becomes impossible.

The popular solution to this problem was to propose that flowcharts never be used as a design aid. An alternative, and now widely used, diagrammatic notation to aid algorithm design is a structure diagram notation originally developed by Jackson (1975). This notation, which is described in Fig. 13.18(a), enforces the very principles at the heart of traditional structured programming. Thus all designs are constrained to the three basic structures of sequence, selection and iteration.

Documenting the design of an algorithm by this notation encourages the use of abstraction and a more top-down approach. This can be seen in the comparison between the flowchart and structure diagram descriptions of the algorithm for computing roots of quadratic equations in Fig. 13.18(b).

Example 13.17 If a procedure A is composed of a sequence of subprocedures $A_1, \ldots, A_n$, then we can think of A as an abstraction of this sequence. For example, *make coffee* is an abstraction of the sequence

put coffee in cup;
pour boiling water in cup;
add milk and sugar if required

In the structure diagram representation of sequence the abstraction is explicit—there is a box labelled A. However, in the flowchart description, only the most detailed instructions are explicit. The abstraction A simply vanishes.

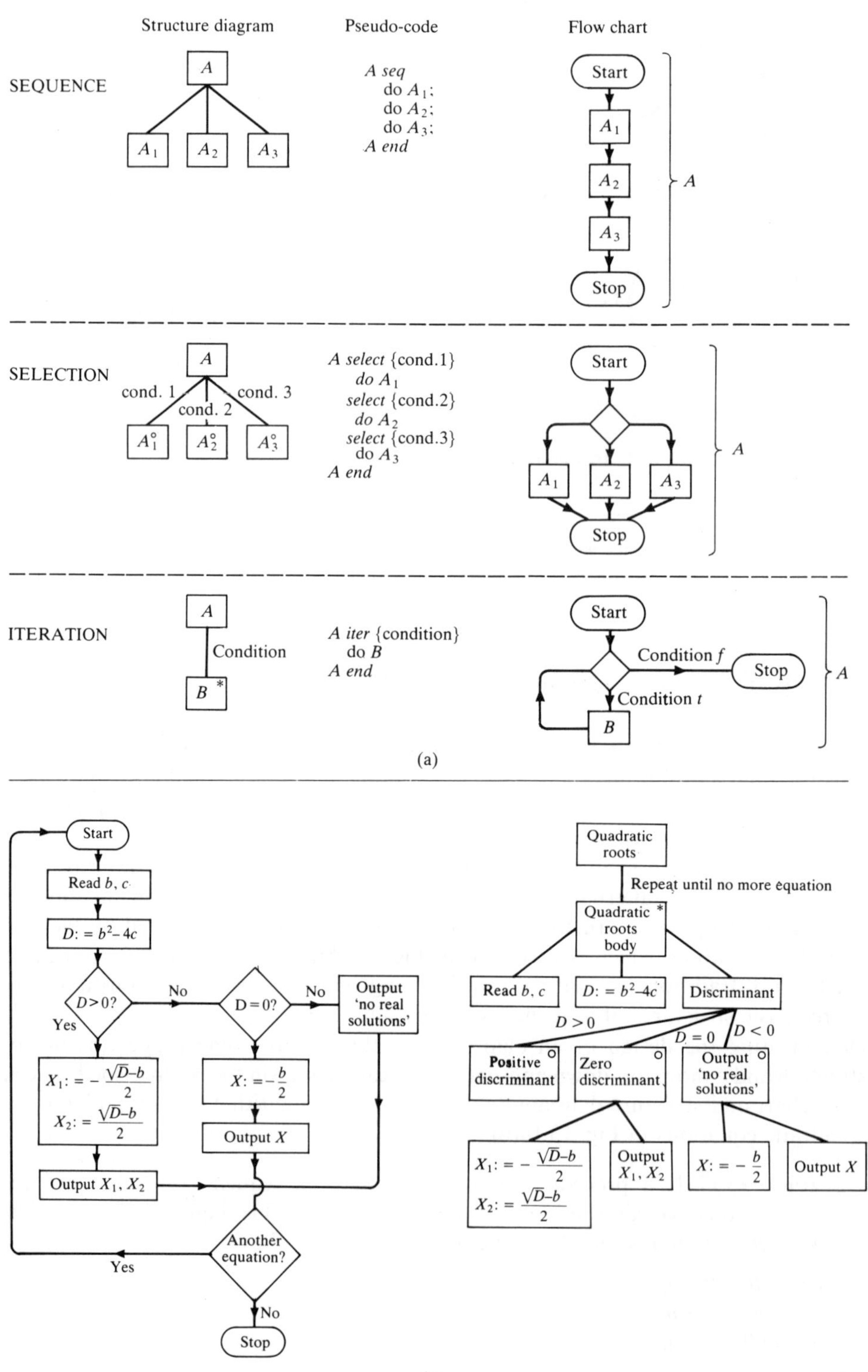

Figure 13.18 Structure diagram notation.

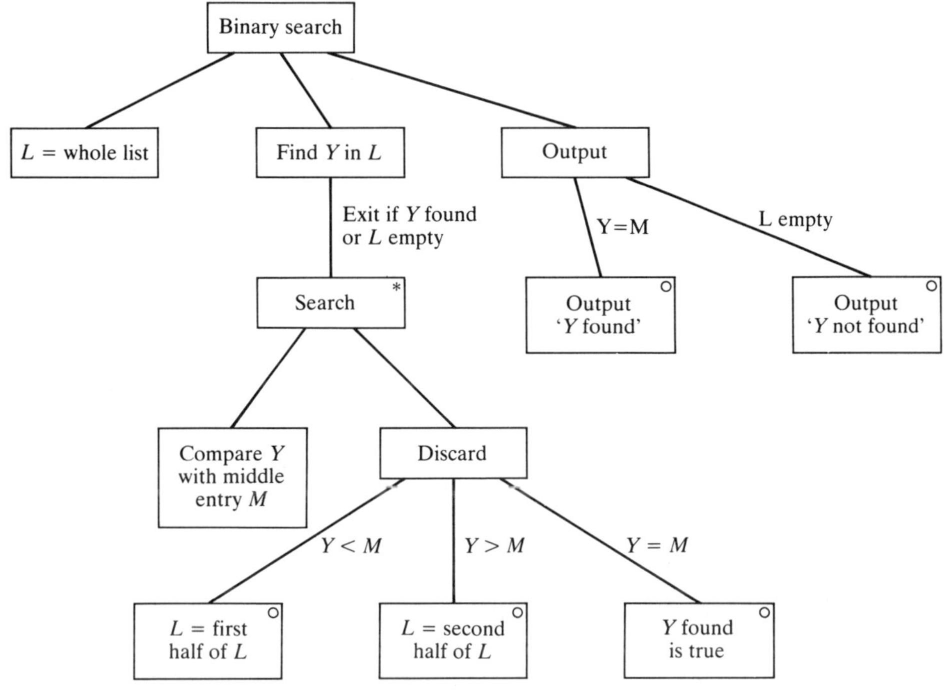

Figure 13.19 Structure diagram version of binary search algorithm.

At first glance it may seem that the structure diagram notation, with its insistence on just three basic constructs, suffers from the same limitations that we have already identified for D-structured programming. Indeed, we could ask the question: 'What is the set of primes S for which all programs implemented from structure diagrams are S-graphs?' It might appear that the answer is $S = \{P_1, D_0, D_1, D_2\}$. That this is not the case is due to a liberal interpretation of what is meant by selection and iteration. We assume that selection includes not just two-way conditional statements but also n-way conditionals. This is analogous to adding all the C_n's to the set S. Additionally there is nothing to stop us interpreting a compound Boolean expression by either lazy or non-lazy evaluation. This is analogous to allowing us to add primes like D_5 to S.

However, it is our interpretation of iteration that really enables the structured diagram approach to apply the true (generalized) spirit of structured programming. There is no reason to restrict ourselves to the single-exit loops D_2 and/or D_3. As long as we clearly describe the loop termination conditions on the diagram, then we can include not only D_4 but also all the families of multiexit loops that we have argued need to be allowed within structured programming. Thus, for example, Fig. 13.19 shows the structure diagram description of the binary search algorithm incorporating the two-exit loop.

In studying the examples, the astute reader will no doubt realize that there is a very close relationship between structure diagrams and decomposition trees. In fact, we can describe the relationship quite formally. Suppose a structure diagram T describes some procedure or algorithm. Encode this diagram into some programming language and

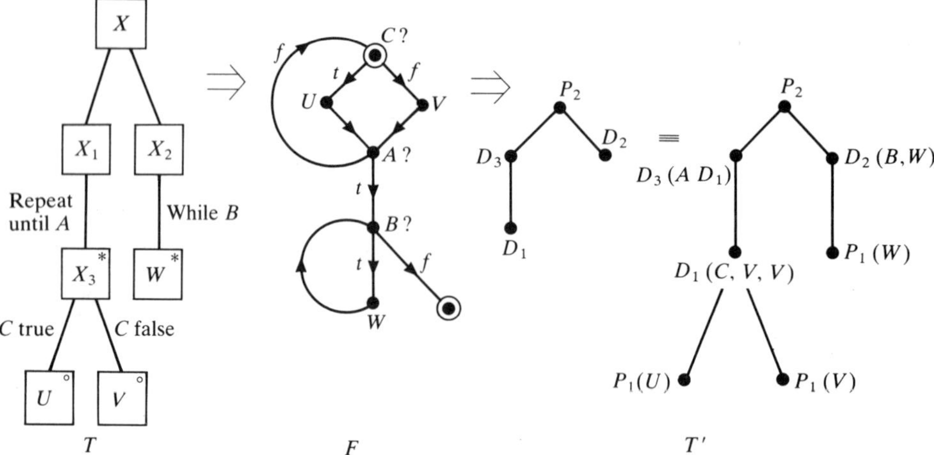

Figure 13.20 Structure diagram and decomposition tree are isomorphic.

compute the flowgraph F of the resulting program. Construct the decomposition tree, adding the specific P_1 structures associated with each prime at the leaf nodes.

Because of the constraints of the original design it turns out that the resulting tree T' is isomorphic to T. The node labels of T' are just the primes that are implicitly used in the structure diagram notation. This whole relationship is described in Fig. 13.20.

Exercise 13.19 Consider the flowcharts and flowgraphs in Figs 13.1 and 13.7. Determine the structure diagrams that would give rise to these.

13.5 PETRI NETS

The flowgraph and structure diagram are fine for describing processes that are sequential. The finite state machine model, which we described in Sec. 2.4, is fine for describing systems that can never be in more than one state at any one time. However, a richer model is available for capturing the idea of *concurrent* processing and *concurrent* states, as well as the necessary notion of synchronization. This is the Petri net model, which may be viewed as a generalization of both the flowgraph and finite state machine. We first provide an example that introduces the key concepts.

Example 13.18 Figure 13.21 shows a Petri net model of a very simple parallel algorithm for summing four numbers. The algorithm exploits a possible implementation in a system with two parallel processors. A Petri net is a special type of digraph. The round nodes represent *conditions* and the square nodes represent *events* or processes. At any instance the *state* of the system is represented by the collection of conditions that contain a black dot, called a *token*. Thus, initially at time t_0 four conditions hold. These correspond to the conditions of 'having available the four input numbers a, b, c, d'. Process 1 adds a to b and can occur when the first two of these conditions hold. Similarly, process 2 adds c to d and can occur when the last two of these conditions hold. Processes 1 and 2 can

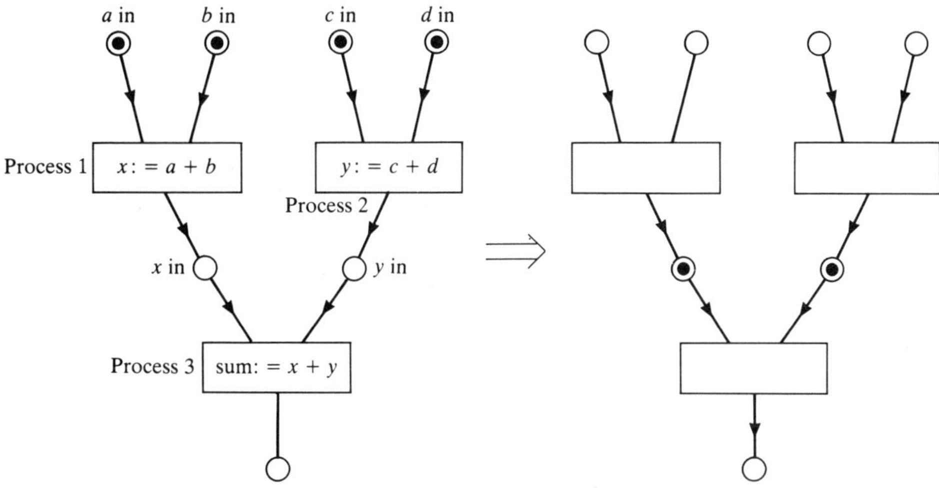

Figure 13.21 Modelling a simple parallel algorithm using a Petri net.

occur concurrently—they only require that their two respective input conditions hold first. Hence we could exploit the two parallel processors here. After these two processes are performed two new conditions hold; this is represented by the moving of tokens in a manner that is called a *firing* of the Petri net. Process 3 adds x to y and requires both of its input conditions to hold before it can occur.

Definition 13.7 Petri net A Petri net is a digraph $G = (V, E)$ where the set of vertices V is partitioned into two sets: S, corresponding to conditions, and T, corresponding to events. Each edge of E is incident with one member of S and one member of T. A marking of a Petri net assigns to each S-vertex a number, called its token, which is either 0 or 1.

The S-vertices of a Petri net are drawn as round nodes and the T-vertices are drawn as square nodes. The marking is represented by drawing a black dot, the token, in those nodes assigned the number 1.

Definition 13.8 Input and output conditions Suppose $t \in T$. Then if s is a predecessor node of t, that is $(s, t) \in E$, we say that s is an input condition for t. If s is a successor node of t, that is $(t, s) \in E$, we say that s is an output condition.

Strictly speaking, what we have defined are *condition-event Petri nets*. There are more general types of Petri nets that, for example, allow arbitrary numbers of tokens in each node, or even individually identified tokens.

Definition 13.9 Petri net firing rule If every input condition of an event node t contains a token, then t is said to be enabled. Providing that none of t's output conditions contains a token, then we say that the event t can occur. This is represented by a firing of the Petri net in which the tokens are removed from each input condition of t and added to each output condition of t.

The firing rule for Petri nets is illustrated in Fig. 13.22. Petri nets may be used to model many kinds of systems and procedures in which concurrency and information flows play a role. The most important application of Petri nets is in analysing certain types of properties of these systems, notably *deadlock* and *liveness*.

Figure 13.22 Petri net firing.

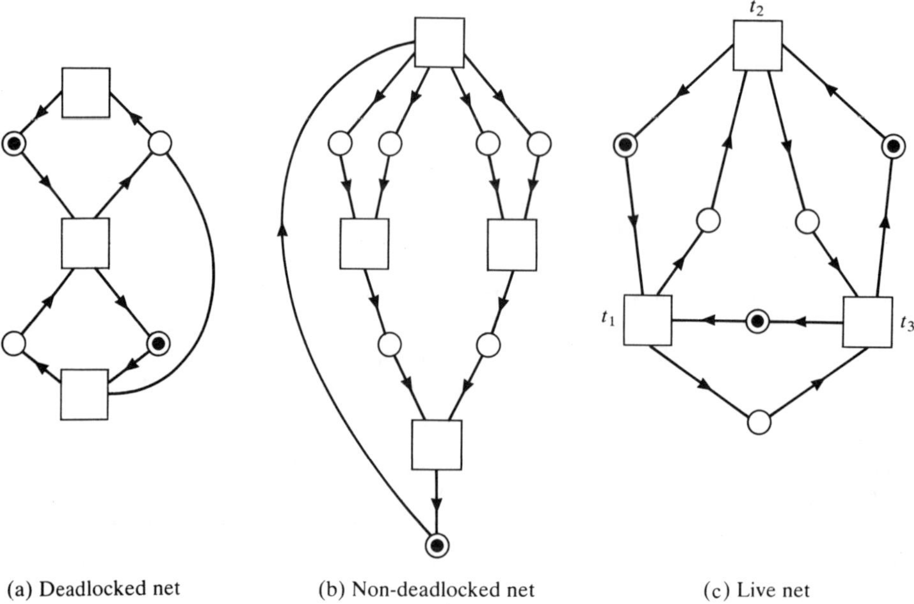

Figure 13.23 Deadlock and liveness.

A net is *deadlocked* if no event can occur, so that it is impossible to fire any event. Figure 13.23(a) illustrates a deadlocked Petri net. Obviously, for any given net, we are interested in knowing if there is a potentially deadlocked state that can be reached from the initial state. The net of Fig. 13.21 reaches a deadlocked state once process 3 occurs. However, if we modify the net as shown in Fig. 13.23(b), then it can never be deadlocked from the initial state described in Fig. 13.21.

A Petri net is *live* if every event can eventually occur. This is a much stronger condition than not being deadlocked, which only asserts that some event can always occur after each possible firing. Figure 13.23(c) shows a live net. In this case t_1 must occur first (since there is no other option) followed by t_2, and then t_3, which returns us to the initial state of the system.

Exercise 13.20 Show that Fig. 13.23(b) is a live net (not just non-deadlocked). Draw a Petri net that is non-deadlocked, but not live.

Much of the extensive theory of Petri nets concerns conditions for determining liveness and potential deadlock. Petri nets may also be used to model and analyse safety aspects of systems. In this case we are concerned with determining that certain events can never be enabled. Although the Petri net firing rules encompass a notion of discrete time intervals, the model is unable to capture real-time system properties. However, recent extensions of the theory are attempting to deal with this very problem.

Exercise 13.21 Draw the Petri net of Fig. 13.21 at instance t_2, after process 3 has occurred.

Exercise 13.22 Using a Petri net, describe a parallel algorithm for summing six numbers. You can assume that it is to be implemented on a system that has up to three parallel processors.

13.6 SUMMARY

We have shown that informal approaches and definitions of structured programming lead to unanswered questions and inconsistencies. These can be resolved by taking a formal approach. One such approach is based on the flowgraph model.

Prime flowgraphs are those that cannot be built up from other flowgraphs by the operations of sequence and nesting alone. Every flowgraph has a unique decomposition in terms of sequence and nesting of prime flowgraphs. We can always compute this decomposition. It enables us to perform various types of static analysis. It is useful for reverse engineering and for computing a wide range of software measures. The prime flowgraphs are the building blocks of a generalized approach to structured programming. For any family of primes S the programs structured with respect to S are defined recursively using the operations of sequence and nesting.

A classical result of structured programming asserts that sequence, selection and iteration are sufficient structures for constructing any algorithm. This theoretical result has been used to preach that the set of primes $S^D = \{P_1, D_1, D_2\}$ is the only reasonable set to use in structured programming. However, this is artificially restrictive. There are many naturally occurring control structures that correspond to primes but are not S^D-structured. These include certain more general types of conditional and looping constructs which would have to be rewritten if we were restricted to S^D alone. The generalized approach to structured programming asserts that a number of extra primes such as these be added to the set of basic primes.

The Jackson structure diagram notation is a useful aid to software design which is consistent with the more general view of structured programming. Flowgraphs and structure diagrams can only model algorithms and systems that are sequential in nature, however. Where concurrency is a feature, a richer graph model, namely the Petri net, is more appropriate. Petri nets can be used to analyse the properties of deadlock and liveness in concurrent systems.

FURTHER READING

To find out more about the history of, and context for, structured programming we recommend the book by Dahl, Dijkstra and Hoare (1972) and the paper by Whitty, Fenton and Kaposi (1985). For a complete, and formal, account of prime decomposition see the papers by Fenton and Kaposi (1989) and Prather and Giulieri (1981). A detailed description of its application to structural analysis and software measurement is given in Chapter 10 of Fenton's book (1991). The use of prime decomposition to support program correctness proofs is described in Linger, Mills and Witt (1979). For a more thorough account of structural testing, see Beizer (1990). The Jackson approach to structured programming appears in Jackson (1975), while a subsequent book by Jackson (1983), which describes a system development methodology, is also strongly recommended. For an intriguing empirical study comparing the merits of different structured programming documentation methods see the paper by Scanlan (1989). We only provided a brief overview of Petri nets; a thorough account may be found in Reisig (1985). For an excellent alternative diagrammatic-based approach to concurrent system specification and analysis, we recommend the statechart method of Harel, which is introduced in Harel (1987).

Part III

Theoretical Framework for Systems Analysis

Chapter 14

PROBABILITY THEORY

In this chapter we analyse systems for pattern and predictability. Our work involves the construction of an axiomatic calculus that describes the probability of an event and provides a set of rules for building probabilities. Uncertainty is unavoidable in the construction of complex systems. The tools of analysis should therefore include methods and concepts for evaluating the significance of any uncertainty about the performance of a system. Our axiomatic calculus models uncertainty and therefore enables its effects to be analysed.

We are concerned with the notion of *experiment*—doing something or observing something happen under certain conditions that result in some final state of affairs or *outcome*. The experiments may be physical, chemical, social, industrial or medical. Occasionally an experiment is of such a nature that the outcome is uniquely determined by the conditions under which it is performed: it is exactly *predictable*. In practice this is rare—experiments are not precisely repeatable even under identical conditions since there are usually factors beyond our control. Because the outcome is unpredictable in the sense that it involves chance, the deterministic mathematical model of a function applied to a set is inadequate for analysing such experiments.

We need a model for each experiment that represents some kind of list of the possible outcomes—this is the *sample space* of the experiment, which we study in Sec. 14.1. The notion of an event formalizes the different outcomes of an experiment. The notion of *probability* formalizes the observation that some outcomes may be more or less likely than others. In Sec. 14.2 we build an axiomatic calculus of probabilities that is interpreted in a model by sets. The rules enable us to calculate the probability that some event will occur. We define conditional probability and the notion of independence between events in Sec. 14.3. Finally, in Sec. 14.4, we study *statistical inference* in which inferences about certain unknown aspects of the mathematical model are made on the basis of results of one or more trials of the experiment under consideration. The new mathematical models that we build are *probability distribution* models. We describe two discrete models: the binomial and Poisson distributions.

14.1 SAMPLE SPACES

Experiments whose results cannot be predicted exactly are difficult to analyse. We are particularly interested in *trials*, which are experiments whose outcome need not be the same every time they are repeated. In this section we consider experiments that consist of repeated individual trials, but whose results appear to lack pattern and and to be unpredictable. We describe a result that we have no means of predicting as *random*.

One way to begin the analysis of such experiments is to identify, at an intuitive level, the possible outcomes of each trial.

Definition 14.1 Sample space of an experiment The sample space of an experiment is the set of all possible outcomes of the experiment.

14.1.1 Single trials

The simplest sample space will be for an experiment that consists of only one trial.

Example 14.1 Consider an experiment in which an ordinary coin is tossed. The usual sample space in this case is {coin is head, coin is tail}, abbreviated to $\{H, T\}$.

Note, however, that the same experiment may yield different sample spaces depending on different interests and circumstances. In Example 14.1 an additional outcome could be 'coin lands on its edge' if the experiment is conducted on a muddy pitch. If the experiment is not clearly specified, there may be problems in defining the sample space. The outcome of Example 14.1 could have been interpreted as 'the height above ground level achieved in the toss'. In this case the sample space would be the continuous set which is represented by an interval of the real line $(0, \infty)$.

We usually use the set, Ω, to denote the sample space of an experiment. Now we consider some obvious sample spaces.

Example 14.2 For the experiment of tossing an ordinary coin, $\Omega = \{H, T\}$.

Example 14.3 For an experiment in which a six-faced die is thrown,

$$\Omega = \{1, 2, 3, 4, 5, 6\}$$

We may be interested in only one individual outcome or a set of several outcomes from the sample space.

Example 14.4 An experiment to measure the height in centimetres of a person chosen at random. Again the sample is a continuous set representing intervals of the real line. It seems reasonable to take $\Omega = (0, 1000)$, but strictly we should take $\Omega = (0, \infty)$.

Example 14.5 An experiment to record the number of telephone calls received at a telephone exchange in one day. The sample space is clearly a set of natural numbers. It would be tempting to assume a *finite* set $\{0, 1, 2, \ldots, n\}$ for some fixed large n. Rapid technological developments could mean that we keep having to make n larger, however. Thus it is best to assume that $\Omega = \mathbb{N}$.

Exercise 14.1 For each of the previous example sample spaces, identify whether they are

(a) discrete or continuous,

(b) finite or infinite.

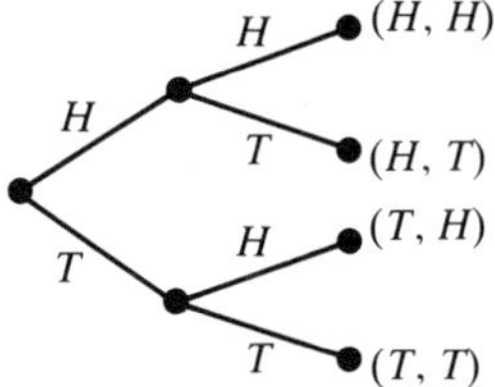

Figure 14.1 Tree diagram for a sample space.

14.1.2 Compound trials

Where an experiment consists of repeated trials, the sample space for the complete experiment will consist of outcomes that are built from the product of the outcomes of single trials.

Example 14.6 An experiment in which a coin is tossed twice. We have

$$\Omega = \{(H,H),(T,T),(H,T),(T,H)\}$$

Here $\Omega = \Omega_1 \times \Omega_1$ where $\Omega_1 = \{H,T\}$. We represent the sample space by the tree diagram in Figure 14.1. The leaves of the tree represent the sample points.

Definition 14.2 Compound trial If a trial has two or more parts and the sample space of the complete trial is the Cartesian product of the sample spaces of each of the parts, the trial is called a compound trial.

Example 14.7 An experiment in which two dice are thrown and the results are recorded in the order they occur. We have $\Omega = \Omega_1 \times \Omega_1$ where $\Omega_1 = \{1,2,3,4,5,6\}$. So

$$\Omega = \{(1,1),(1,2),\ldots,(1,6),(2,6),\ldots,(6,1),(6,2),\ldots,(6,6)\}$$

There are 36 possible outcomes since $|\,\Omega\,|=|\,\Omega_1 \times \Omega_1\,|=|\,\Omega_1\,|\times|\,\Omega_1\,|$.

Exercise 14.2 Draw the tree diagram that represents the sample space for the experiment in Example 14.7.

Example 14.8 In an experiment, two dice are thrown at the same time. The order in which the dice are read is not important—the tree diagram for the previous example gives the compound sample space in which each outcome is a permutation. In this experiment the outcome $(1,2)$ is the same as the outcome $(2,1)$ since the order of the pair is not important. The sample space consists of *all combinations* of two members from the set $\{1,2,3,4,5,6\}$.

Exercise 14.3 Calculate the cardinality of the sample space for the experiment in the previous example.

14.1.3 Events

We now consider experiments in which we are only interested in *some* of the possible outcomes in the sample space. We may be interested in only one individual outcome or a set of several outcomes from the sample space.

Example 14.9 The experiment of tossing a coin three times has, as its sample space, $\Omega = \Omega_1 \times \Omega_1 \times \Omega_1$ where $\Omega_1 = \{H, T\}$. Explicitly we have

$$\Omega = \{(H,H,H),(H,H,T),(H,T,H),(T,H,H),\\ (T,T,H),(T,H,T),(H,T,T),(T,T,T)\}$$

Suppose we are only interested in those outcomes where there are at least as many heads as tails. There are four such outcomes,

$$(H,H,H),(H,H,T),(H,T,H) \text{ and } (T,H,H)$$

and as a collection they comprise a subset of Ω.

Definition 14.3 Event Any subset of a sample space is called an event.

In the previous example we considered the event where there are at least as many heads as tails. The event $\{(H,H,T),(H,T,H),(T,H,H)\}$ is the event that exactly one tail occurs, whereas $\{(T,T,T)\}$ is the event that exactly three tails occur.

Events, the elements in events and the outcomes that they represent are not usually distinguished. Strictly, however, the outcomes in a sample space are represented by *sample points*. For the sample space $\{1,2,3,4,5,6\}$ we identify

- The singleton set $\{1\}$ as an elementary event
- The element 6 as a sample point
- The set $\{4,2,3\}$ as an event

From our examples it will be clear in general that for a sample space Ω an event may be defined by:

1 Listing the sample points that it contains; or

2 Giving some property that characterizes the set of sample points. The property may be a predicate and there may be many such characterizing properties.

If Ω is finite, there are $2^{|\Omega|}$ different events—one for each subset of Ω. In particular, every singleton set $\{x\}$, where $x \in \Omega$, the complete sample space Ω and the empty set $\{\}$ are all examples of events.

Example 14.10 Consider an experiment of selecting a card from a fair pack of 52 cards. In this case $\Omega = \{A\clubsuit, 2\clubsuit, \ldots, K\clubsuit, A\diamondsuit, 2\diamondsuit, \ldots, K\diamondsuit, \ldots, K\spadesuit\}$. The event E characterized by 'the card is a spade' is given explicitly by $E = \{A\spadesuit, 2\spadesuit, \ldots, K\spadesuit\}$ and $|E| = 13$.

Example 14.11 Consider the experiment of throwing two dice, one after the other, for which we have previously described the sample space. We name the following events:

E_1: 'the first die is a 3' defines the set $\{(3,1),(3,2),(3,3),(3,4),(3,5),(3,6)\}$
E_2: 'the sum of the results is 12' (inclusive) defines the set $\{(6,6)\}$
E_3: 'the sum is between 2 and 12 ' defines the set Ω
E_4: 'the sum is 13' defines the set $\{\}$.

Exercise 14.4 Determine the sample space in an experiment to toss three coins and record the number of 'heads'.

The urn model The process of mathematical modelling can be applied to capture the common properties of many problems in the real world that involve the calculation of probabilities. By first capturing the essential ingredients of these problems, in a simple model, and calculating the solution in this simple model, the pattern of solving the problem can then be translated back to the more detailed applications in the real world. A useful discrete model for determining the outcomes of various types of experiments is the *urn model*. The sample space for the single trial of throwing a die or choosing a ball from six balls in an urn is clearly identical. For a compound trial the selection of balls from the urn can be made either with replacement or without replacement. The selection can be specified as *ordered* selection by noting the labels of the balls in the order in which they are chosen by someone who cannot see inside the urn. If each ball is replaced after it has been selected then the choice of each ball is made independently. We present the next exercise in terms of the urn model.

Exercise 14.5 Determine the sample space in an experiment to place four balls in a jar and pick two at random:

(a) without replacement,

(b) with replacement.

Draw a tree diagram to represent the sample space. The order in which the balls are selected is important and the labels of the balls are noted as they are withdrawn. Give both the explicit definition of the sample space and its cardinality.

Exercise 14.6 Determine the sample space in an experiment to toss three coins and record the set of possible outcomes. Assume that the coins are marked and that it is noted in some order whether the result is H or T.

14.1.4 Constructing new events from old

We have identified events as the primitive objects in our calculus but have yet to define the probability of an event. Since we want our calculus to provide rules for building probabilities, we first tackle the task of building events and interpreting the building operations in our mathematical model of sets. We define the semantics of constructing events by operations on sets. Look back now at Chapter 3 to recall the way that we modelled the construction of compound propositions by lines in the truth tables. These give the values true or false to the new propositions, depending on the interpretation of the more primitive propositions. In this chapter we set up the model for our theory about probability and deduce theorems from the non-logical axioms.

Since events are just subsets of the set Ω, we interpret the construction of events by the standard set operations.

Example 14.12 Union of events If E_1 and E_2 are two events then the event $E_1 \cup E_2$ is simply the event E_1 `or` E_2. In Example 14.11, $E_1 \cup E_2$ is the event 'the first die is a 3 or the dice sum to 12'. Then

$$E_1 \cup E_2 = \{(3,1),(3,2),(3,3),(3,4),(3,5),(3,6),(6,6)\}$$

Example 14.13 Intersection of events The event $E_1 \cap E_2$ is the event E_1 **and** E_2. In Example 14.11, $E_1 \cap E_2$ is the event 'the first die is a 3 and the dice sum to 12', which is $\{\}$.

Example 14.14 If we take E_5 to be the event 'the sum of the results is 8', then $E_5 = \{(2,6),(3,5),(4,4),(5,3),(6,2)\}$ and $E_1 \cap E_5 = \{(3,5)\}$ is the event 'the first die is a 3 and the dice sum to 8'.

Definition 14.4 Complement of an event For a given event, E, the event $\overline{E}$ (or strictly $\Omega \setminus E$) is the complement of E and therefore the event 'not E'.

Example 14.15 In Example 14.11, $\overline{E_1}$ is the event 'the first die is not a 3' and has 30 elementary outcomes.

Definition 14.5 Exclusive events If E_1 and E_2 are events in a sample space, Ω, and $E_1 \cap E_2 = \{\}$, then E_1 and E_2 are exclusive events because they do not share any sample points. In general the set of events $E_1, E_2, \ldots$ are mutually exclusive if $E_i \cap E_j = \{\}$, for each i and j where $i \neq j$.

14.2 DEFINING PROBABILITY

Just like gamblers who lay odds (and bet money) on any experiment whose outcome is uncertain, so too must scientists assess the relative likelihood of various outcomes of an experiment. *Probability* is defined as a numerical measure of this likelihood. We first present an intuitive definition of probability as a long-range relative frequency. Motivated by this intuitive approach, we then present an axiomatic theory of probability which enables us to reason formally about probabilities of events.

14.2.1 Relative frequency approach

In a sequence of trials of a given experiment, the number of times a particular event occurs is called its *frequency*.

Definition 14.6 Relative frequency The relative frequency of an event in a sequence of trials is the ratio

$$\frac{\text{Number of occurrences of the event}}{\text{Total number of trials}}$$

Example 14.16 In an experiment a die is thrown eight times and on two throws the outcome is 6. The relative frequency for the event $\{6\}$ is $2/8 = \frac{1}{4}$.

It is an observable phenomenon that as n, the number of trials, increases the relative frequency of each event stabilizes or approaches some *limit*.

Example 14.17 If we tossed a fair coin and took as the event 'the coin is H', our graph of the relative frequency against n would be similar to the graph shown in Figure 14.2 where the limit is $\frac{1}{2}$.

If the coin were *not* fair, we might find that after 1000 tosses there were 560 heads, giving a relative frequency of 0.56. It is likely that even after 10 000 tosses the relative frequency will remain more or less the same, so that in this case the limit is 0.56 rather than 0.5.

The crucial point is that whatever the experiment and whatever the chosen event E, the relative frequency of E will eventually approach some limit. It is this limit, $P(E)$, which is normally taken to be the *probability* that the event will occur. This relative frequency notion of probability leads us to deduce the following properties for sample spaces that contain a finite number of sample points:

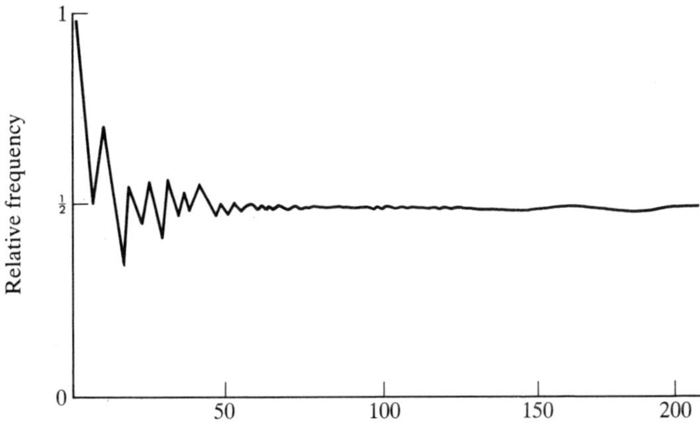

Figure 14.2 Graph of relative frequency.

1 For any event E, we know that its relative frequency must be between the values 0 and 1 inclusive; that is $0 \leq P(E) \leq 1$.

2 For the complete sample space every trial, in a sequence of n trials, will lead to some outcome that is represented by a sample point. The relative frequency of occurrences of the complete sample space is therefore $n/n = 1$; that is $P(\Omega) = 1$.

3 The relative frequency of the event $\{\}$, that of *no* outcome occurring in n trials, is $0/n = 0$; that is $P(\{\}) = 0$. This property can be deduced from the previous two properties.

4 Suppose that in a sequence of n trials an event E_1 occurs m_1 times and another event E_2 occurs m_2 times. If E_1 and E_2 are exclusive events, the m_1 occasions must be different from the m_2 occasions. It follows that the number of occasions when either E_1 or E_2 occurs must be $m_1 + m_2$. The relative frequency of the event $E_1 \cup E_2$ is therefore

$$\frac{m_1 + m_2}{n} = \frac{m_1}{n} + \frac{m_2}{n}$$

This is, as we would expect, the sum of the relative frequencies of E_1 and E_2. Thus formally we have

$$P(E_1 \cup E_2) = P(E_1) + P(E_2)$$

if E_1 and E_2 are exclusive events.

Unfortunately there is no practical way of calculating the relative frequency of an event every time we wish to find its probability. There is a further reason, however, for losing confidence in a model of probability that is based on long-range relative frequency. The model is based on a definition of probability as a limit to a sequence and assumes a definition of *randomness*. We say that a random sequence is one that is unpredictable and without pattern—this is difficult to define without using the notion of probability. We are in a *circular* situation! We break the circularity by axiomatizing the notion of probability. By employing an appropriate theory of the real world and expressing real world properties formally as axioms we are able to calculate the probabilities of various combinations of events.

14.2.2 Axiomatic model approach

Now that we have constructed a language for our calculus of probabilities we need to set up the mathematical model for interpreting the probability of an event. We define the non-logical axioms that characterize the construction of probabilities and deduce theorems that are valid in the model. The non-logical axioms and the theorems that we deduce together form our theory of probability.

This formal approach enables us to calculate the probability of a particular event in an experiment by representing it within a mathematical model that is based on set theory. We formalize the foundations of the subject but keep the intuitive roots that are based on the notion of relative frequency. Following the mathematical modelling process described in Fig. 1.8 we set up a mathematical model of the real world situation. In our model we represent the outcomes of a trial by sample points in a sample space, and events by subsets of the sample space. The probability of each event is then represented by a function on the appropriate set. The rules for building the probabilities of several events are represented by axioms described in the language of our calculus. The axioms are valid in our mathematical model and are therefore consistent.

We have already introduced the language to represent outcomes by events (themselves represented by sets in the model) and all possible outcomes by the example sample space (itself represented by the set Ω). The definition of a probability space that we now give will apply to the mathematical model rather than the real world experiments being modelled. We can only tell that the model is accurate by measuring probability in the real world. To do this we measure relative frequency using a *large* number of trials—even then we will not obtain complete accuracy. Our choice is either to use a mathematical definition or to accept that there is no formal definition at all for probability.

We allow the intuitions of relative frequency to suggest the axioms for the structure that we build for our model of probability. This very general structure is called a *probability space*, and may usefully be viewed as an instance of creating an algebra of two sorts, 'event' and 'number', and a single function such as is described in Chapter 8. To a given sample space Ω, we assign a number $P(E)$ to *each* event E in such a way that the following axioms hold:

Axiom 14.1 $0 \leq P(E) \leq 1$ for each event $E \subseteq \Omega$

Axiom 14.2 $P(\Omega) = 1$

Axiom 14.3 $P(\bigcup_{i=1}^{n} E_i) = P(E_1) + \cdots + P(E_n) = \sum_{i=1}^{n} P(E_i)$ for any pairwise disjoint sets $E_1, \ldots, E_n$. This axiom can be extended to infinite unions.

Definition 14.7 Probability space Any set Ω together with the function $P : \mathscr{P}(\Omega) \to [0, 1]$, where $\mathscr{P}(\Omega)$ is the power-set of Ω, that satisfies Axioms 14.1 to 14.3 is said to be a probability space. The function P is called the probability function.

Example 14.18 Let $\Omega = \{\text{H, T}\}$. There are four events: $\{\}, \{H\}, \{T\}, \Omega$. If we define $P(\{\}) = 0, P(\{H\}) = \frac{1}{2}, P(\{T\}) = \frac{1}{2}, P(\Omega) = 1$ then it is easy to check that (Ω, P) is a probability space. Similarly, if we define $P'(\{\}) = 0, P'(\{H\}) = \frac{2}{3}, P'(\{T\}) = \frac{1}{3}, P'(\Omega) = 1$ then (Ω, P') is also a probability space. Note that $P(\{\}) = 0, P(\{H\}) = \frac{2}{3}, P(\{T\}) = \frac{2}{3}, P(\Omega) = 1$ does *not* define a probability space since Axiom 14.3 is violated. We have $\{H\} \cup \{T\} = \Omega$ but $1 = P(\Omega) = P(\{H\} \cup \{T\}) \neq P(\{H\}) + P(\{T\}) = 1\frac{1}{3}$.

Example 14.19 Let $\Omega = \{(H,H),(H,T),(T,H),(T,T)\}$. There are 16 events in $P(\Omega)$:

$$\{\},\{(H,H)\},\{(H,T)\},\{(T,H)\},\{(T,T)\},\{(H,H),(H,T)\},\{(H,H),(T,H)\},$$
$$\{(H,H),(T,T)\},\{(H,T),(T,H)\},\{(H,T),(T,T)\},\{(T,H),(T,T)\},$$
$$\{(H,H),(H,T),(T,H)\},\ldots,\Omega$$

We define a probability function on Ω as follows: take $P(\{\}) = 0$ and $P(\Omega) = 1$. For each elementary event,

$$P(\{(H,H)\}) = P(\{(H,T)\}) = P(\{(T,H)\}) = P(\{(T,T)\}) = 1/4$$

For the events containing two elements,

$$P(\{(H,H),(H,T)\}) = P(\{(H,H),(T,H)\}) = \cdots P(\{(T,H),(T,T)\}) = 1/2$$

For the events containing three elements,

$$\begin{aligned} P(\{(H,H),(H,T),(T,H)\}) &= P(\{(H,H),(H,T),(T,T)\}) \\ &= P(\{(H,T),(T,H),(T,T)\}) = \tfrac{3}{4} \end{aligned}$$

The function P together with Ω is then a probability space.

Exercise 14.7 Using the theoretical framework of Chapter 8, specify the algebra that represents a probability space.

The task of turning a sample space into a probability space, by defining the function P so that it satisfies the axioms, may at first sight appear daunting. Example 14.19 may indicate to you, however, that we can cut down on the work we have to do. We call on the axioms to help us. In particular, it is a direct consequence of the axioms that we only need to define $P(e)$ for the elementary events, e, the singleton subsets of Ω. This is because in general, if E is any event,

$$E = \bigcup e_i \text{ where } e_i \text{ is an elementary event in } E$$

Therefore from Axiom 14.3 we deduce the following theorem.

Theorem 14.1 Sum of probabilities For any event E, $P(E)$ must be the sum of the probabilities of the elementary outcomes that make up E; that is

$$P(E) = \sum_{e \in E} P(e)$$

It is enough just to define the probabilities for the elementary events, since the other probabilities must follow immediately by Theorem 14.1. We showed this in Example 14.19. In fact, this observation allows us to define, very simply, an important class of probability spaces called *equiprobable spaces*.

Definition 14.8 Equiprobable space An equiprobable space is a probability space for which the elementary events have the same probability.

Suppose $|\,\Omega\,| = n$ and $\Omega = \{e_1,\ldots,e_n\}$. For each e_i, we define $P(e_i) = 1/n$. Then P extended to the whole of $P(\Omega)$ by Theorem 14.1 determines an equiprobable probability space.

Theorem 14.2 Probabilities in an equiprobable space For any event E, in an equiprobable space of cardinality n $P(E) = |\,E\,|\,/n$.

Equiprobable spaces are the most appropriate probability models for experiments where we assume that each elementary outcome is equally likely.

Example 14.20 The following spaces are equiprobable:

(a) Tossing a fair coin where $\Omega = \{H, T\}$ and $P(\{H\}) = P(\{T\}) = \frac{1}{2}$.

(b) Throwing a fair die where $\Omega = \{1, \ldots, 6\}$ and $P(\{1\}) = \cdots = P(\{6\}) = \frac{1}{6}$.

(c) Throwing 2 dice and recording the results in order, where $\Omega = \{1, \ldots, 6\}$ and

$$P(\{(1,1)\}) = \cdots = P(\{(6,6)\}) = 1/36$$

(d) Tossing a coin twice where $\Omega = \{(H,H), (H,T), (T,H), (T,T)\}$ and

$$P(\{(H,H)\}) = \cdots = P(\{(T,T)\}) = 1/4$$

Example 14.21 If Ω is the sample space for an experiment to select a card from a fair pack of 52 cards then it is reasonable to assume equiprobability. The selection of each card is an elementary event in the sample space. Therefore, $P(e) = 1/52$, where e is the elementary event 'the card is chosen'.

Let E_1 name the event 'the card is an ace'. Then E_1 defines the set

$$\{A\clubsuit, A\diamondsuit, A\heartsuit, A\spadesuit\}$$

and we deduce that $P(E_1) = 4/52 = 1/13$. Similarly, if E_2 names the event 'the card is a king', then $P(E_2) = 1/13$. Since E_1 and E_2 are exclusive events, we also deduce from Axiom 14.3 that the event E_3 which is 'the card is an ace or king' is equal to $E_1 \cup E_2$. Therefore, $P(E_3) = 1/13 + 1/13 = 2/13$.

The model of an equiprobable space is of course inappropriate for any *infinite* sample space (discrete or continuous), and will not be appropriate for many finite sample spaces.

Example 14.22 The following experiments are *not* appropriately modelled by an equiprobable space:

(a) Any of the above experiments where the coin or the dice are 'loaded'.

(b) Tossing a fair coin twice and counting the number of heads. In this case $\Omega = \{0, 1, 2\}$. It is certainly unrealistic to assume equally likely outcomes here, since it is clear that 1 is more likely to occur than either 0 or 2.

We have shown how to define P for an equiprobable space in such a way that the axioms are satisfied. Before dealing with other cases, we shall look at some consequences of the axioms which tell us some very useful things about probability. We can then apply these results to our equiprobable spaces.

14.2.3 Theorems of the axiomatic calculus

From the axioms, or rules, given in the previous section we can deduce theorems that will help us to calculate probabilities. We have already deduced Theorem 14.1 from Axiom 14.3.

Theorem 14.3 For any event E, $P(\overline{E}) = 1 - P(E)$.

PROOF By Def. 14.4, $\overline{E} = \Omega / E$, giving $\Omega = E \cup \overline{E}$. By Axiom 14.3, since E and $\overline{E}$ are disjoint sets, $P(\Omega) = P(E) + P(\overline{E})$. By Axiom 14.1, $P(\overline{E}) = 1 - P(E)$.

Example 14.23 We extend Example 14.21.

Let E_1 name the event 'the card is an ace' as before.
Let E_2 name the event 'the card is not an ace'.

Since $E_2 = \overline{E_1}$, we have $P(E_2) = P(\overline{E_1}) = 1 - P(E_1) = 12/13$.

This theorem is useful because it is often easier to calculate $P(\overline{E})$ than $P(E)$ for some event E.

Corollary 14.1 $P(\{\}) = 1 - P(\Omega) = 0$.

Theorem 14.4 Rule of addition For any events E_1 and E_2,

$$P(E_1 \cup E_2) = P(E_1) + P(E_2) - P(E_1 \cap E_2)$$

It is important to compare this theorem with Axiom 14.3 which gave a rule for the sum of the probabilities of mutually exclusive events. We now ask you to prove Theorem 14.4.

Exercise 14.8 Draw a Venn diagram for *any* two sets E_1 and E_2. The sets should intersect since the case when they are disjoint is covered when $E_1 \cap E_2 = \{\}$. Mark on your diagram $E_1 \cap \overline{E_2}$ and $E_1 \cap E_2$. The sets E_1 and E_2 represent events in a sample space, Ω. Write E_1 as a disjoint union of sets. Use the axioms for a probability space to assign a probability to E_1 in terms of exclusive events. Hence prove Theorem 14.4 by applying Axiom 14.3.

Exercise 14.9 Use Theorem 14.4 to show that

$$P(E_1 \cup E_2 \cup E_3) = P(E_1) + P(E_2) + P(E_3) - P(E_1 \cap E_2) - P(E_1 \cap E_3) - P(E_2 \cap E_3) \\ + P(E_1 \cap E_2 \cap E_3)$$

Example 14.24 We calculate the probability that either an ace or a red ace is drawn in a random selection from a pack of 52 cards. First we assume an equiprobable space and identify the following events:

E_1 : 'the card is an ace'
E_2 : 'the card is red'
E_3 : 'the card is either an ace or a red card'

We want to find $P(E_3)$ and we note that $E_3 = E_1 \cup E_2$. Therefore,

$$\begin{aligned} P(E_3) &= P(E_1 \cup E_2) \\ &= P(E_1) + P(E_2) - P(E_1 \cap E_2) \text{ by Theorem 14.4} \end{aligned}$$

Now $E_1 \cap E_2$: 'the card is a red ace'. There are only two red cards in the pack, so $P(E_1 \cap E_2) = 2/52$, giving $P(E_3) = 4/52 + 26/52 - 2/52 = 28/52$.

Example 14.25 The probability that a man watches a film in any one evening is 0.6; the probability that he watches the news is 0.3; and the probability that he does both is 0.15. We wish to find the probability that he neither watches a film nor watches the news.

This is typical of many probability problems in the sense that a certain probability space is implied but is not made explicit. The first step in the solution is to define the probability space. We are then able to calculate the required probability from the axiomatic model. We identify sample points in the sample space and represent them by the elementary events

e_1 : 'watches a film only'
e_2 : 'watches the news only'
e_3 : 'both watches a film and watches the news'
e_4 : 'neither watches a film nor watches the news'

We therefore have $\Omega = \{e_1, e_2, e_3, e_4\}$ and we are only given the probability of the elementary event e_3. Now we define the events for which we do have probabilities:

E_1 : 'watches a film'
E_2 : 'watches the news'
$E_1 = \{e_1, e_3\}$ and $P(E_1) = 0.6$
$E_2 = \{e_2, e_3\}$ and $P(E_2) = 0.3$
$E_1 \cap E_2 = \{e_3\}$ and $P(E_1 \cap E_2) = 0.15$

Now $P(e_4) = P(\overline{E_1 \cup E_2}) = 1 - P(E_1 \cup E_2)$ and $P(E_1 \cup E_2) = P(E_1) + P(E_2) - P(E_1 \cap E_2) = 0.75$. Therefore $P(e_4) = 0.25$.

Exercise 14.10 Consider an experiment in which two dice are thrown. Write out the following events explicitly:

E_1: 'the sum of the dice is 7'
E_2: 'the second die is a 3'
E_3: 'the difference between the dice is ≤ 1'

Calculate $P(E_1), P(E_2)$ and $P(E_3)$. Give an explicit description of the events $E_1 \cap E_2$, $E_2 \cap E_3$, $E_2 \cup E_3$ and calculate their respective probabilities.

By working within an equiprobable space we are now able to calculate the probabilities of events that occur within compound trials.

Example 14.26 From a shuffled pack of cards, the top two cards are drawn without replacement. We want to calculate the probability that we draw a pair of kings. First we use the framework set up in Sec. 2.6.2 to identify the sample space, Ω, as the set of all permutations of size 2 from the 52 cards in the pack. Therefore, $|\Omega| = P(52, 2) = 52 \times 51$. Alternatively we can consider Ω, as in Sec. 14.1.2, as the Cartesian product, $\Omega = \Omega_1 \times \Omega_2$, where Ω_2 has one less sample point than Ω_1 because the first card has already been withdrawn. We then have $|\Omega| = |\Omega_1| \times |\Omega_2| = 52 \times 51$, as before.

Next we establish how many ordered pairs in Ω consist of two kings. This, of course, is the number of ways of choosing two kings from four kings and is $P(4, 2) = 4 \times 3$. Let E be the event 'both cards are kings'. By Theorem 14.2, the probability that E occurs is

$$P(4, 2)/P(52, 2) = (4 \times 3)/(52 \times 51)$$

We can check our result by ignoring the order of the cards that are selected. The sample space will then contain all the combinations of two cards from a pack, giving

$$|\Omega| = C(52, 2) \text{ or } \binom{52}{2} = (52 \times 51)/2!$$

The number of ways of choosing a pair of kings is, $\binom{4}{2} = (4 \times 3)/2! = 6$. Again by Theorem 14.2 we get the same result. The probability that E occurs is

$$\frac{\binom{4}{2}}{\binom{52}{2}} = (4 \times 3)/2! \times 2!/(52 \times 51)$$

It is more useful for checking purposes to leave any factorizing of expressions until the final expression for the probability is obtained.

Exercise 14.11 Jane tosses two pennies and John tosses three pennies. The number of heads is recorded in some order for each of the tosses. What is the probability that John gets more heads than Jane? First consider the sample space for the complete experiment as compounded of two trials. Then calculate the number of outcomes for which John gets more heads than Jane. Finally calculate the required probability. Next think of a *different* sample space for the experiment that provides the same answer with far less work.

Exercise 14.12 Five cards are selected at random from a standard deck of 52 cards. Determine the probabilities of the following events:

(a) The hand contains exactly one pair.

(b) The hand contains two pairs (and one odd card).

(c) The hand contains two cards of one suit and three of another suit.

(d) The hand contains three cards of one suit, but the other two do not form a pair.

(e) The hand consists of five cards, all of the same suit.

This exercise is an extension of Exercise 2.89 in Chapter 2 where you were asked in how many ways the hands of cards could be chosen. Give your answers as expressions rather than calculating the final values. This exercise can be worked out by using either permutations or combinations. Use both methods in order to obtain a way of checking your results.

14.3 CONDITIONAL PROBABILITY

14.3.1 Defining conditional probability

We have used our theory of probability, modelled by the simple structure of a probability space, to provide a framework for the assignment of probabilities to events within the sample space of an experiment. In Example 14.26 we calculated the probability of drawing two kings from a pack of cards without replacing the first card before the second card was drawn. We calculated this result over a compound sample space,

$$|\Omega| = |\Omega_1| \times |\Omega_2|$$

and adjusted Ω_2 as a result of the first trial that had Ω_1 as its sample space. Only 51 cards remained in the pack for the second trial. Now we take a different viewpoint from that of Example 14.26.

Example 14.27 By viewing the compound event of drawing two kings as a *sequence* of two different events,

E_1: 'the first card is a king'
E_2: 'the second card is a king'

we see that in Example 14.26 we calculated the probability of the event $E_1 \cap E_2$. The compound event $E_1 \cap E_2$ is interesting because the second event E_2 is *conditional* on whether the first event E_1 occurred.

Taking this viewpoint of a compound experiment leads us to define a *conditional* probability for an event, and provides us with an alternative solution to Example 14.26. A conditional probability is an ordinary probability for an event, but one that involves a change in the sample space for the compound event.

Definition 14.9 Conditional probability The probability of an event E_2, given that event E_1 has already occurred, is the conditional probability of E_2 given E_1, and is written as $P(E_2/E_1)$.

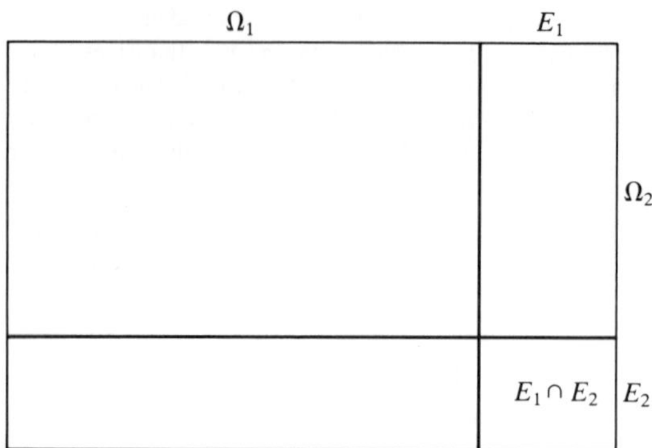

Figure 14.3 A two-dimensional sample space.

We build on Examples 14.26 and 14.27 in order to explore the intuitions underlying conditional probabilities.

Example 14.28 In a compound trial in which two cards are drawn, without replacement, from a shuffled pack, we have the events

E_1: 'the first card is a king'
E_2: 'the second card is a king'
$E_1 \cap E_2$: 'both cards are kings'

The following elementary events are in $\Omega = \Omega_1 \times \Omega_2$:

$$\{(K\spadesuit, K\diamondsuit)\} \in E_1 \cap E_2$$
$$\{(K\spadesuit, 3\diamondsuit)\} \in E_1$$
$$\{(4\spadesuit, K\heartsuit)\} \in E_2$$

From Example 14.26 we know that $P(E_1 \cap E_2) = 4 \times 3/52 \times 51$. We know from Chapter 2 that the number of ways of choosing first a king and then any other card is 4×51 by the product rule.

This is $| E_1 |$. Therefore by Axiom 14.2, $P(E_1) = (4 \times 51)/(52 \times 51) = 4/52$. The conditional probability, E_2/E_1, is the probability of selecting a second king given that one king has already been drawn from the pack. All we have to consider is the simpler problem of selecting a king from a pack of only 51 cards that has only three kings. We obtain

$$P(E_2/E_1) = 3/51$$

You may have noticed a relationship between our three probabilities:

$$P(E_1 \cap E_2) = \frac{4 \times 3}{52 \times 51} = \frac{4}{52} \times \frac{3}{51} = P(E_1) \times P(E_2/E_1)$$

We shall investigate this observation at a more general level.

First, however, we continue with our example using Theorem 14.2 to guide us. We work within an equiprobable space with $\Omega = \Omega_1 \times \Omega_2$. It is helpful to represent Ω by Figure 14.3 of a two-dimensional sample space in which the events E_1 and E_2 intersect.

By Axiom 14.2 we know that

$$P(E_1 \cap E_2) = \frac{| E_1 \cap E_2 |}{| \Omega_1 \times \Omega_2 |} \text{ and } P(E_1) = \frac{| E_1 |}{| \Omega_1 \times \Omega_2 |}$$

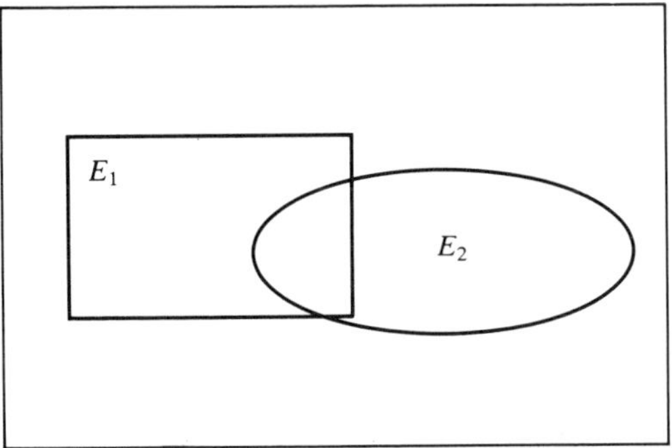

Figure 14.4 Venn diagram for conditional probability.

Now $P(E_2/E_1)$ measures the conditional probability of both E_1 and E_2 occurring in the *reduced* sample space $E_1 \times \Omega_2$. Any elementary event *must* have a king as the first card of the pair; we exclude any other elementary event in Ω_1. Again, by Axiom 14.2,

$$\begin{aligned} P(E_2/E_1) &= \frac{\text{number of ways } E_1 \text{ and } E_2 \text{ can occur}}{\text{number of ways } E_1 \text{ can occur}} \\ &= \frac{\mid E_1 \cap E_2 \mid}{\mid E_1 \times \Omega_2 \mid} = \frac{\mid E_1 \cap E_2 \mid}{\mid E_1 \mid \times \mid \Omega_2 \mid} \\ &= \frac{4 \times 3}{4 \times 51} = \frac{3}{51} \end{aligned}$$

as before. This time we have found that

$$P(E_2/E_1) = \frac{P(E_2 \cap E_1)}{P(E_1)} = \frac{4 \times 3}{52 \times 51} \times \frac{52}{4} = \frac{3}{51}$$

The example has provided a result that fits our intuitive understanding of $P(E_2/E_1)$ as an ordinary probability that is calculated over a changed sample space.

14.3.2 Calculating conditional probability

From our definition of conditional probability and from Axiom 14.2 we have arrived at a rule for calculating conditional probabilities. We now state this rule generally as another axiom within our axiomatic system for probability.

Axiom 14.4 Conditional probability Let E_1 and E_2 be arbitrary events with $P(E_1) \neq 0$; then $P(E_2/E_1) = P(E_2 \cap E_1)/P(E_1)$.

We can also use Axiom 14.4 to calculate $P(E_2 \cap E_1)$ if we know $P(E_2/E_1)$ and $P(E_1)$. In this case we do not have to assume $P(E_1) \neq 0$; when $P(E_1) = 0$ we know that $P(E_2 \cap E_1) = 0$. Figure 14.4 shows a Venn diagram for the general case, where $P(E_2/E_1)$ measures the probability of E_2 with respect to the reduced sample space E_1.

Example 14.29 The probability that it rains in London on 15 July is 0.6. The probability that it rains in London on 15 July *and* on 16 July is 0.35. If we know it has rained in London on 15 July then the probability of rain the following day is $0.35/0.6 = 7/12$.

Exercise 14.13 Two dice are thrown. Calculate the probability of the total score exceeding 8, given that the first die shows the values 6, 4 and 2 in successive throws.

Exercise 14.14 A pair of fair dice are thrown and the sum is 6. Calculate the probability that one of the dice shows 2.

Exercise 14.15 Use Exercise 14.14 to show that $P(E_2/E_1) \neq P(E_1/E_2)$.

We now state some theorems for conditional probability.

Theorem 14.5 $P(E/E) = 1$

Theorem 14.6 $0 \leq P(E_2/E_1) \leq 1$

Exercise 14.16 Deduce Theorems 14.5 and 14.6 from the axioms for conditional probability.

Theorem 14.7 If $A \cap B = \{\}$ then A and B are exclusive events, and $P((A \cup B)/E) = P(A/E) + P(B/E)$.

Exercise 14.17 A babysitter arrives at a house to look after two children. A little boy opens the front door. Calculate the probability that the other child is also a boy if:

(a) The other child is known to be younger.

(b) Nothing is known about the other child.

Exercise 14.18 Two cards are drawn without replacement from a pack. Draw a Venn diagram to represent the sample space and use the axiom for conditional probability to calculate the probability that:

(a) Both cards are jacks.

(b) One is a king and one is an ace.

Check your results by using, as an alternative method, the axioms for probability and events that are:

(a) ordered and

(b) unordered.

14.3.3 Bayes theorem

We now generalize the concept of the conditional probability of an event, given that some other event has occurred, to the conditional probability of *several exclusive* events, given that some other event has occurred. We first present the intuitions as an example.

Example 14.30 In an experiment two black balls and one white ball are placed in one bag, and two white balls and one black ball are placed in a second bag. In the first stages of the experiment a ball is transferred, without looking, from the first bag to the second bag. This random selection and transference of a ball from the first bag is then followed by the random selection of a ball from the second bag. We first calculate the probability that a black ball is selected from the second bag. We identify the following events:

A: 'a white ball is transferred from bag1 to bag2'
B: 'a black ball is transferred from bag1 to bag2'
E: 'a black ball is selected from bag2'

The events A and B are mutually exclusive events. The sample space of all the transfers is $A \cup B$. We say that the events A and B are *collectively exhaustive* events over Ω, since their union is the entire sample space. We consider the intersection of the event E with the exclusive events, A and B. The events $E \cap A$ and $E \cap B$ are both exclusive and $E = (E \cap A) \cup (E \cap B)$.

By Axiom 14.3, $P(E) = P(E \cap A) + P(E \cap B)$. We use Axiom 14.4 to substitute for $P(E \cap A)$ and $P(E \cap B)$, giving

$$P(E) = P(A)P(E/A) + P(B)P(E/B) = 1/3 \times 1/4 + 2/3 \times 2/4 = 5/12$$

Now we assume that a black ball was picked in the second stage and calculate the probability that a black ball was transferred in the first stage. This is $P(B/E)$. Similarly we could require $P(A/E)$, since the event A can also be considered as conditional on the knowledge that a black ball was picked in the second stage of the experiment.

This example points to the need for some general formula, to calculate the probability of one of several events, which are exclusive but fill a sample space, when it is already known that some other event has occurred. We use the formula given by Bayes theorem to calculate this general form of conditional probability.

Theorem 14.8 Bayes theorem Suppose there are k events, $A_i, \ldots, A_k$, such that

(a) $P(A_i) \neq 0$ for any i.

(b) The events A_i are mutually exclusive, so that $A_i \cap A_j = \{\}\ \forall i,j$ where $i \neq j$.

(c) The events A_i are exhaustive, so that $A_1 \cup A_2 \cup \cdots \cup A_k = \Omega$.

Let E be another event such that $P(E) \neq 0$; then, for each j,

$$P(A_j/E) = \frac{P(A_j)P(E/A_j)}{\sum_{i=1}^{k} P(A_i)P(E/A_i)}$$

Example 14.31 Using Bayes theorem we can now complete Example 14.30 by calculating

$$\begin{aligned} P(B/E) &= \frac{P(B)P(E/B)}{P(A)P(E/A) + P(B)P(E/B)} \\ &= \frac{2/3 \times 2/4}{1/3 \times 1/4 + 2/3 \times 2/4} = \frac{4}{5} \end{aligned}$$

Exercise 14.19 Using Example 14.30, draw a general diagram of the sample space and provide a proof for Bayes theorem.

Exercise 14.20 Suppose that the probability that a jury at the Old Bailey returns a correct verdict is 0.95. Suppose also that if someone is on trial, the probability that the person is guilty is 0.99. Mary Smith has been found not guilty of treason by the jury. Calculate the probability that she is *not* guilty.

Exercise 14.21 Given four mutually exclusive, collectively exhaustive events B_i where $i = 1, 2, 3, 4$ and the information below, find $P(A)$ where A is some other event. Describe a suitable discrete sample space by drawing a Venn diagram, and also identify the sample points in each event. Decide whether A is pairwise disjoint with each of the events, B_i.

1/24	1/3	1/4	3/8	$P(B_i)$
1	1/4	0	1/3	$P(A/B_i)$
B_1	B_2	B_3	B_4	—

14.3.4 Independent events

Having considered conditional probability as a modification of the probability of one event by the occurrence of another event, we now consider events that are not linked by dependence on each other.

Example 14.32 An experiment consists of first tossing a coin and then drawing a card from a pack. The sample space is $\Omega = \Omega_1 \times \Omega_2$ where $\Omega_1 = \{H, T\}$ and $\Omega_2 = \{A\clubsuit, K\clubsuit, Q\clubsuit, \ldots, 4\spadesuit, \ldots, K\heartsuit, \ldots, 1\diamondsuit\}$. Let

E_1: 'the coin is a head'
E_2: 'the card is an ace'

There is unlikely to be any interaction between the two events. We would expect the probability of drawing an ace to be unaffected by whether or not the toss of the coin was a head; that is $P(E_2) = P(E_2/E_1) = 4/52$.

Definition 14.10 Independent events Let E_1 be an event such that $P(E_1) \neq 0$. Then another event E_2 is independent of E_1 if $P(E_2) = P(E_2/E_1)$. Otherwise E_2 is dependent on E_1.

We can obtain three important theorems about independent events that have non-zero probabilities.

Theorem 14.9 Let E_2 be an event that is independent of another event E_1 such that $P(E_2) = P(E_2/E_1)$, $P(E_1) \neq 0$ and $P(E_2) \neq 0$. Then $P(E_1) = P(E_1/E_2)$ also.

PROOF We use Axiom 14.4 to deduce this theorem.

We have	$P(E_2) = P(E_2/E_1)$
and by Axiom 14.4	$P(E_1 \cap E_2) = P(E_1) \times P(E_2/E_1)$
Since $\cap$ is commutative	
and by Axiom 14.4	$P(E_2 \cap E_1) = P(E_2) \times P(E_1/E_2)$
This gives	$P(E_1) \times P(E_2/E_1) = P(E_2) \times P(E_1/E_2)$
Substituting for $P(E_2/E_1)$ gives	$P(E_1) \times P(E_2) = P(E_2) \times P(E_1/E_2)$
and since $P(E_2) \neq 0$ we have	$P(E_1) = P(E_1/E_2)$

Theorem 14.10 $P(E_2) = P(E_2/E_1) \Leftrightarrow P(E_1) = P(E_1/E_2)$ where $P(E_1) \neq 0$ and $P(E_2) \neq 0$.

PROOF From Theorem 14.9 we have both

$$P(E_2) = P(E_2/E_1) \Rightarrow P(E_1) = P(E_1/E_2)$$

and

$$P(E_1) = P(E_1/E_2) \Rightarrow P(E_2) = P(E_2/E_1)$$

We see that independence is a symmetric relationship: if E_2 is independent of E_1 then E_1 is independent of E_2.

Theorem 14.11 If E_1 and E_2 are independent events then $P(E_1 \cap E_2) = P(E_1) \times P(E_2)$.

PROOF We know from Axiom 14.4 that $P(E_1 \cap E_2) = P(E_1) \times P(E_2/E_1)$ for all events. Substituting for $P(E_2/E_1)$ we get $P(E_1 \cap E_2) = P(E_1) \times P(E_2)$.

All of the last three theorems are equivalent but the last theorem is useful in showing a symmetrical relationship for independence.

Our next example demonstrates the difference between events that are independent and events that necessarily follow other events. Note that events may be non-independent even if there is no causal relationship between them.

Example 14.33 Consider the experiment in which a dice is thrown. We record the number on the dice and are interested in the following events:

E_1: 'a 4 or a 5 is thrown' so $E_1 = \{4, 5\}$
E_2: 'a 3, 4 or 5 is thrown' so $E_2 = \{3, 4, 5\}$
E_3: 'a 2, 3 or 4 is thrown' so $E_3 = \{2, 3, 4\}$

We have $P(E_2) = 1/6 + 1/6 + 1/6 = 1/2$. By Axiom 14.4, $P(E_1 \cap E_2) = P(E_1) \times P(E_2/E_1)$. Since $E_1 \cap E_2 = E_1$, $P(E_2/E_1) = 1$. Intuitively, therefore, the event E_1 *must* affect the probability of the event E_2. Clearly E_1 and E_2 are not independent events and $P(E_2) \neq P(E_2/E_1)$.

Now we consider $P(E_3/E_1)$, noting that $P(E_3) = P(E_2) = \frac{1}{2}$. Intuitively, $P(E_3/E_1)$ is a measure of the probability that 2, 3 or 4 are thrown, *given* that a 4 or a 5 is thrown. Clearly only a throw of a 4 affects the probability of the event $\{2, 3, 4\}$. We consider the event E_3 over the restricted sample space $E_1 = \{4, 5\}$. If the event E_1 occurs either a 4 or 5 is thrown, and since the dice is fair these two possibilities are equally likely. Therefore knowing that E_1 has occurred, we see that in the restricted sample space $P(\{4\}) = \frac{1}{2}$. However, E_3 will occur as well as E_1 *only* if a 4 is thrown. From this we deduce that $P(E_3/E_1) = \frac{1}{2}$. Since $P(E_3) = P(E_3/E_1)$, we infer that the event E_3 is *independent* of E_1.

Example 14.34 A circuit consists of three components in parallel. The probability of one of them failing is 0.05. We assume that the components fail independently of each other and that the circuit will work providing at least one component is working. Calculate the probability that the circuit will work.

Let E_1, E_2, E_3 be the events that the first, second and third components fail respectively. The probability that all the components fail is $(0.05)^3$ by Theorem 14.11 applied to pairs of components, and also by the assumption that $P(E_1 \cap E_2 \cap E_3) = P(E_1) \times P(E_2) \times P(E_3)$. The probability that the circuit will work is $1 - (0.05)^3 = 0.1999875$.

This example demonstrates that physical independence implies statistical independence. It also *assumes* independence between three events, which may not follow from pairwise independent events.

Definition 14.11 Independence of three events Three events A, B, C are independent if:

(a) $P(A \cap B) = P(A)P(B)$, $P(A \cap C) = P(A)P(C)$ and $P(B \cap C) = P(B)P(C)$, that is the events are pairwise independent, and

(b) $P(A \cap B \cap C) = P(A)P(B)P(C)$.

Clearly the second condition for independence does not follow from the first condition.

Exercise 14.22 In an experiment a pair of coins is tossed. Consider whether the following events are independent:

E_1: 'the first toss gives heads'
E_2: 'the second toss gives heads'
E_3: 'exactly one head is tossed'

Exercise 14.23 A circuit consists of three independent components a, b, c in series. Consider the following events:

A: 'component a is defective'
B: 'component b is defective'
C: 'component c is defective'

Then $P(A) = 0.03$, $P(B) = 0.15$, $P(C) = 0.01$. The circuit fails if *any* component is defective. Calculate the probability that:

(a) the circuit fails,

(b) component b alone fails.

Exercise 14.24 Consider the following events in an experiment to toss a coin and then throw a die. Draw a tree diagram to represent the sample space. Then show that the following events are independent:

E_1: 'the first toss is a head'
E_2: 'a 6 is thrown'

Exercise 14.25 Two cards are selected without replacement from a deck of 52 cards.

(a) Describe as concisely as possible the sample space of this experiment.

(b) Construct a sample space for this experiment.

(c) Describe explicitly the event E: 'both cards are aces'. Calculate the probability of E stating any assumptions you are making.

(d) Assume the following events:

E_1: 'first card is a heart'
E_2: 'second card is a spade'

Calculate the probability of E_2 given E_1. What does this result mean in terms of the dependence or independence of the events E_1 and E_2?

Exercise 14.26 This exercise is based on the urn model, presented on page 347. A jar contains four white balls and eight black balls. Calculate the probability that if two balls are picked out at random without replacement,

(a) both balls are white,

(b) the second ball is white.

14.4 PROBABILITY DISTRIBUTIONS

In this section the concept of a random variable is introduced, and we use this to construct probability distributions as models for probability. We discuss the binomial and Poisson distributions in detail.

14.4.1 Random variables and distributions

We introduce two important ideas that concern the deduction of information from the outcomes of experiments. For a single experiment, with a numerical sample space, we shall consider, at an abstract level, some *possible* value from the sample space. This unknown value will be represented by a *random variable*. Our next idea concerns the repeated selection, by *sampling*, that is often necessary in order to deduce useful information about complicated real world experiments. Clearly our second idea differs from the first because it involves *choosing* a sample space and conducting an experiment several times. Sampling lies behind the idea of a random variable, however, because it involves the construction of a manageable sample space for an experiment.

Choosing a sample space The concept of a sample space whose sample points represent all the possible outcomes of an experiment is fundamental to a study of probability and statistics. However, this simple idea is inadequate for many problems that need to be solved in the real world. The *selection* of an appropriate sample space for a particular experiment may itself pose problems. The sample space that is appropriate will depend on the purpose of the experiment as well as on the possible outcomes of the experiment. Some possible sample spaces will be so large that they are unmanageable. It is, therefore, necessary to consider ways in which large sample spaces can be controlled and simplified so that the probability inherent to the problem can be meaningfully expressed.

Our first example shows how a sample space can be chosen for a particular problem that in some way depends on some other more general problem. The chosen sample space is a smaller sample space and is numerical.

Example 14.35 Consider the experiment of tossing a coin three times. The sample space has eight elementary outcomes. The purpose of this experiment is, however, to find the number of heads that are thrown in the compound trial. Clearly the sample space that is appropriate is $\Omega_H = \{0, 1, 2, 3\}$, which in some way *depends* on Ω. Whereas Ω has eight sample points which are all ordered 3-tuples, Ω_H has only four sample points which are numbers.

Random variables We now abstract over the sample space for an experiment in order to represent a *possible* value from the set of outcomes by a variable. Once we have identified this variable, we are able to calculate the *actual* values of the probabilities for each of the outcomes in the experiment. This mapping from the outcomes of an experiment to their probabilities will be made by a probability distribution function.

We shall generalize from particular examples to consider any trial whose possible outcomes are numbers $a_1, a_2, \ldots$. Then we select a general element from this set.

Definition 14.12 Random variable We denote by X any number whose value is given by the outcome of some experiment whose results cannot be predicted exactly, and call X a random variable.

Example 14.36 In Example 14.35 the number of heads when a coin is tossed three times is a random variable, X. The variable takes any value in the set $\{0, 1, 2, 3\}$.

Example 14.37 A die has already been thrown twice and is to be thrown once more. The value on the third throw is unknown but will belong to the set $\{1, 2, 3, 4, 5, 6\}$. The random variable, X, can represent this unknown value. If a 6 is thrown in the third throw, then 6 is the *realization* of the random variable in this single trial.

Definition 14.13 Realization of a random variable A realization of a random variable, X, is the numerical value that is taken by X in a particular trial.

In general we can think of a random variable, X, as a function on a set of outcomes that assigns a number to each elementary outcome. We define the real-valued function $X : \Omega \to \mathbb{R}$.

Example 14.38 In Example 14.35 the random variable contracts the complex sample space of 3-tuples, Ω, to the simpler numerical sample space. We have $X : \Omega \to \{0, 1, 2, 3\}$ as a function where $X((H, H, T)) = 2$ and $X((T, T, T)) = 0$.

Probability distributions For a random variable X, we want to know the probability of the realization of each of the sample points in the new sample space. These probabilities will not in general be equal so we would not expect to build an equiprobable space. If the set of possible outcomes of a trial is $\{a_1, a_2, \ldots\}$ then $P(X = a_r)$, where $r = 1, 2, \ldots$, denotes the probability that X has realization a_r.

Example 14.39 The realization $X = 1$ is the result of mapping three equiprobable events from the complete sample space, Ω, in Example 14.35. We have

$$\begin{aligned} X((H,T,T)) &= 1 \\ X((T,H,T)) &= 1 \\ X((T,T,H)) &= 1 \end{aligned}$$

In this case the probability function is not one-to-one and we have

$$P(X = 1) = P(\{(H,T,T)\}) + P(\{(T,H,T)\}) + P(\{(T,T,H)\}) = \tfrac{1}{8} + \tfrac{1}{8} + \tfrac{1}{8}$$

In general, if $E_1, E_2, \ldots, E_n$ are the events that are mapped to a_r, where $r = 1, 2, \ldots, n$, then $P(X = a_r) = P(E_1) + P(E_2) + \cdots + P(E_n)$.

From the numerical outcomes of a trial and the probability of those outcomes, we define a function to express how the total probability, of value one, is *distributed* over all the numerical outcomes.

Definition 14.14 Probability distribution function If the set of outcomes for a trial is $\{a_1, a_2, \ldots\}$ then the function $P(X = a_r)$ is called the probability distribution function of X. If the outcome a_r has probability p_r we write $P(X = a_r) = p_r$. This function is also called the probability mass function.

This function is also called the probability mass function.

Because we are interested in a distribution it is useful to consider the domain $\{a_1, \ldots\}$ and range $\{p_1, \ldots\}$ of the functions as sequences rather than sets.

Example 14.40 In Example 14.39 we have the distribution

$$\begin{aligned} P(X = 0) &= 3/8 \\ P(X = 1) &= 1/8 \\ P(X = 2) &= 3/8 \\ P(X = 3) &= 1/8 \end{aligned}$$

Exercise 14.27 The random variable X can take values $0, 1, 2, 3, 4, 5, 6$ with respective probabilities $0.3, 0.14, 0.07, 0.08, 0.13, 0.18$ and 0.1.

(a) Verify that this is a description of a probability distribution function.

(b) Calculate $P(X \geq 3)$ and $P(X < 2)$.

(c) Display the distribution on a graph.

We have begun with a trial that has numerical outcomes and have calculated the probability distribution function of the random variable X that will be realized by some values in the sample space. Alternatively, for any numerical sample space with probabilities p_r such that $\sum_{r=1}^{n} p_r = 1$, we can identify a random variable X satisfying $P(X = a_r) = p_r$.

14.4.2 Expectation

If a trial is repeated a large number of times and the sample space is numerical, the results of the trial will be a large list of numbers. An analysis of the data can then be made by applying statistical measurements such as the *mean of the distribution* and the *variance of the distribution*. We begin by defining the *expected value* of a random variable. From now on all random variables are assumed to be discrete.

We first recall that the precise definition of the probability of an event, given in Sec. 14.2, was based on the relative frequency of occurrences of that event over many trials. We defined probability to formalize the notion that some outcomes are more likely to occur than others. When a large list of observed values, or realizations of a random variable X, collected it is useful to have some idea of 'the most likely value' for X. Clearly the observed values will be the *actual* sample points of the experiment. A calculation to provide an *average* realization for X will not necessarily provide a value that is equal to, or even close to, an actual sample point. It is no more than an approximation of the average in the long run, as the number of trials increases and the relative frequency of occurrences approximates to a limit. The value of measuring a distribution by its mean is that we may gain a useful single measure for comparing two distributions and choosing between them.

Example 14.41 We calculated in Example 14.39 the probabilities that X will have each of the values in this numerical sample space. To find the average of the values taken by X, we add together the products of each sample point with its individual probability. We obtain

$$\begin{aligned}\text{Average value for } X &= 0\times 1/8+1\times 3/8+2\times 3/8+3\times 1/8\\ &= 3/8+6/8+3/8=12/8=1.5\end{aligned}$$

Therefore our average value, as expected, is in the middle of the sample space! If the observed average after a large number of trials was very different from 1.5, this would bring into question the assumption of equiprobability and suggest that the coin was not fair.

The average value for the random variable of an experiment is called the *expected value* of X or the *expectation* of X. We do not expect (in the everyday meaning of the word) that a variable X will take this value, however, or even be very close to it. For some distributions the *expected* value of X may be the value that is least expected in the everyday sense.

Definition 14.15 Expected value of X The expected value of X, denoted by $E(X)$, is defined as $E(X) = \sum_{i=1}^{\infty} p_i a_i$ where X takes values $a_1,\ldots$ with probabilities $p_1,\ldots$.

Yet another way of referring to the expected value of X is as the *mean* of the distribution which is associated with X. These identical measures are also denoted by μ.

Exercise 14.28 Calculate the expected value for the random variable of an experiment to throw a die.

Exercise 14.29 Calculate the mean of the distribution for an experiment to toss a fair coin.

Exercise 14.30 A game consists of drawing a ball from a bag containing six white and four blue balls. If the ball is white you win 40p; if it is blue you lose 80p. A ball is replaced once chosen and the bag is shaken, ready for another ball to be drawn. What are your expected winnings from each play of this game?

We have introduced the definition of $E(X)$ by discussing the expected value of a single random variable X. In fact the definition is more powerful and presents an operator that possesses the property of linearity that was introduced in Sec. 2.5. This means that if $Y = aX + b$ where X and Y are random variables, and a and b are constants, we can find $E(Y) = \mu_Y$ in terms of μ_X.

Definition 14.16 Variance of X The variance of X, denoted by Var(X), is defined as $E[(X - E(X))^2]$.

It is often easier to calculate the variance by using the following result:

$$E[(X - \mu)^2] = E(X^2) - \mu^2$$

Example 14.42 In order to calculate the variance for the same distribution as in Example 14.41, we first calculate

$$\begin{aligned} E(X^2) &= 0 \times 1/8 + 1 \times 3/8 + 4 \times 3/8 + 9 \times 1/8 \\ &= 3/8 + 12/8 + 9/8 = 24/8 = 3 \end{aligned}$$

Therefore $E(X^2) - \mu^2 = 3 - 144/64 = 3/4$.

Exercise 14.31 Demonstrate the linearity of the operator for the expected value of a random variable by showing that $E(aX_1 + bX_2) = aE(X_1) + bE(X_2)$.

14.4.3 Parametric models

The concept of a random variable has been used to simplify large sample spaces so that the probability inherent to the problem can be meaningfully expressed. The probability distribution function has then been defined to express how the total probability of an experiment is distributed over all the values of the sample space. In constructing simple sample spaces for an experiment we no longer assume that our probability space is equiprobable. Measurement of the mean of a probability distribution may provide us with a useful comparison between distributions.

Classifying probability distributions and constructing models to represent distributions is a further way of analysing the appropriateness of distributions for specific experiments. Models of situations do not have to be correct in every detail and they are most useful if the amount of detail they present is reduced.

Example 14.43 Consider an experiment of tossing a coin. If we do not assume that the coin is fair, we only need to represent within our model that the random variable for the sample space satisfies

$P(X = H) = p_1$, $P(X = T) = p_2$, where $0 \leq p_1, p_2 \leq 1$ and $\sum_{r=1}^{2} p_r = 1$

For any experiment in which a coin is tossed the variables p_1 and p_2 are constants in the model, although their actual values will depend on the physical state of the coin and how it is thrown. In this model p_1 and p_2 are *parameters* that express the property that there are two sample points in the sample space.

Definition 14.17 Parameter of a probability distribution A parameter of a probability distribution is an arbitrary constant, which provides actual properties about an experiment and occurs in the expression of the probability distribution.

The problem of choosing an appropriate model is one that requires an understanding about the physical properties of the experiment.

Exercise 14.32 In an experiment a die is thrown which is thought to be biased. Over many trials the number of 4's has not occurred with a frequency of one in six times, although the other numbers have appeared equally as often as each other. Assuming that the probability of throwing a 4 is p, construct an appropriate model, with a single parameter, to represent the throwing of a biased die.

Certain models of probability distributions are sufficiently important to warrant an identification by name and a systematic study of some of their properties and applications. Specific names are usually assigned to classes of distributions rather than to particular ones. We have already seen one family of parametric distributions.

Example 14.44 Equiprobable distribution The equiprobable distribution, $\mathscr{E}(n)$, has a single parameter n and refers to sample spaces of n equally likely outcomes, where $n \in \mathbb{N}$. The probability of each outcome is therefore $1/n$.

Example 14.45 For an experiment in which a fair coin is tossed, $\Omega = \{H, T\}$ and $P(X = H) = \frac{1}{2}, P(X = T) = \frac{1}{2}$, we use the distribution $\mathscr{E}(2)$.

Example 14.46 For an experiment in which a die is thrown we use the model $\mathscr{E}(6)$.

The distributions in a class have properties in common and these are represented by the parameters of the distribution. In the case of equiprobable distribution, $\mathscr{E}(n)$, there is only one parameter, n, so once n is known the distribution is known. It does not matter—from a probability viewpoint—whether the n equiprobable outcomes represent dice throws, balls drawn or people selected. The next probability distribution we shall consider also has a single parameter, but is more interesting.

14.4.4 The Bernouilli sequence and the binomial distribution

When we analyse systems for pattern and predictability, we are often concerned with whether an event does or does not happen. Problems of this type may be modelled by a *Bernouilli sequence*. We consider experiments, which are in the form of a sequence of repeated trials, and whose outcomes are denoted by 'success' or 'failure'. Such experiments are called Bernouilli trials; the repetition of n trials is represented by the binomial distribution.

Definition 14.18 Bernoulli trial A Bernouilli trial has only the two outcomes of success or failure. In a single trial $P(\text{success}) = p$ and $P(\text{failure}) = q = 1 - p$. In a sequence of n independent trials we are interested in the probability of r successes.

Definition 14.19 Bernoulli random variable Let X be the Bernouilli random variable corresponding to the number of successes in a single Bernouilli trial. Then the probability distribution of X is given by

$$P(X = 1) = p$$
$$P(X = 0) = 1 - p$$

In a sequence of n independent trials we have n Bernouilli random variables, X_i, where $1 \leq i \leq n$.

Example 14.47 The prediction of whether a new-born baby is a boy is based on the probability distribution $P(X = 1) = p = 0.517$. The probability that the baby is a girl is $P(X = 0) = q = 0.483$.

Example 14.48 A component out of a large consignment is tested. On average the consignment contains a proportion of 1 in 100 faulty components. If we judge success to be that a component is faulty, we have the distribution

$$P(X = 1) = p = 1/100$$
$$P(X = 0) = q = 99/100$$

Example 14.49 In a trial a marksman fires a shot at a target. Success is the event that a bulls-eye is scored. If the marksman fires 10 rounds at the target we might reasonably assume the chance of his scoring a bulls-eye remains constant, providing no sudden change in the light occurs. In that case we have a Bernouilli trial as a sequence of 10 trials. However, this may not be the case if he fires 100 rounds in quick succession. There is then the strong probability of fatigue setting in. Because the probability of success varies we no longer have a sequence of *identical* trials.

Exercise 14.33 In a Bernouilli trial a coin is tossed. Give the probability distribution of the Bernouilli random variable.

Although the model for repeated Bernouilli trials is a sequence, the trials themselves may be simultaneous.

Example 14.50 A group of patients in hospital may all be treated with a drug. Success is the event that a patient recovers. The patients are all treated at the same time, so that the trials take place simultaneously.

We see from Example 14.49 that it is necessary to define certain conditions that we would expect to hold in a model that represents experiments in which Bernouilli trials are repeated a fixed number of times. We identify four conditions that must hold if we define an experiment to be a *binomial experiment*. The conditions form the assumptions of a *binomial model*.

Definition 14.20 Binomial model The binomial model, denoted by $\mathscr{B}(n, p)$, represents the repetition of a Bernouilli trial a fixed number of times, n. The probability of success in each trial is p, and the trials are independent of each other.

There are four assumptions in a binomial model:

1 Each trial has only two outcomes: success or failure.

2 The number of trials is fixed.

3 The probability of success is the same for all trials.

4 The trials are independent.

Example 14.51 In an experiment to toss a coin five times, success is the event that a head is tossed. We could reasonably expect all the assumptions to hold.

Example 14.52 If we test components from our consignment and *replace* them after testing, then our four assumptions hold. If we do not replace them (which is a more reasonable way to test) the probability of success changes from trial to trial. However, if we are testing without replacement 5 out of, say, 1 000 000, then the four assumptions nearly hold and we may approximate our experiment with this model.

The random variable for the binomial model represents the number of successes in the sequence of Bernouilli trials and can therefore be defined in terms of the Bernouilli random variable.

Definition 14.21 Binomial random variable Let T_n be the binomial random variable corresponding to the number of successes in n Bernouilli trials. Then $T_n = \sum_{i=1}^{n} X_i$, where X_i is the Bernouilli random variable for the ith trial.

Deriving the binomial distribution Given a binomial model consisting of n Bernoulli trials with probability of success p, we now derive the probability distribution function of the binomial random variable T_n. We motivate the derivation of the distribution by an example.

Example 14.53 In Example 14.47 we considered a single Bernouilli trial with sample space $\{S, F\}$ that models the prediction of whether a new-born baby is a boy or a girl. The prediction of whether a family of three children in a family will be boys or girls can be based on the binomial model. The random variable T_3 takes values in the sample space $\{0, 1, 2, 3\}$. Clearly this is not an equiprobable sample space. The realizations of T_3 for the events in the sample space for the sequence of three Bernouilli trials are

$$\begin{array}{lll} T_3 = 0 & \text{for the event} & (F, F, F) \\ T_3 = 1 & \text{for the event} & (S, F, F)(F, S, F)(F, F, S) \\ T_3 = 2 & \text{for the event} & (S, S, F)(F, S, S)(S, F, S) \\ T_3 = 3 & \text{for the event} & (S, S, S) \end{array}$$

Since the trials are independent, the probabilities that T_3 has these realizations are

$$\begin{array}{lllll} P(T_3 = 0) & = & q^3 & = & (0.483)^3 \\ P(T_3 = 1) & = & 3pq^2 & = & 3 \times 0.517 \times (0.483)^2 \\ P(T_3 = 2) & = & 3p^2q & \fallingdotseq & 3 \times (0.517)^2 \times 0.483 \\ P(T_3 = 3) & = & p^3 & = & (0.517)^3 \end{array}$$

As expected, the probabilities for this distribution sum to 1. According to our model the probability of having only sons in a family of three children is higher than the probability of having only daughters. It is most probable, however, that the children will be a *combination* of one son and two daughters, in three possible *permutations*.

When we generalize to n repeated trials in a binomial experiment we obtain events that are sequences of length n and in the form $SFSFFSS, \ldots, SFSFF$ where the letter in the ith position denotes the outcome of the ith trial. Since we want to find the probability $P(T_n = r)$ of observing r successes in the n trials, we need to sum the probabilities of all the events that consist of r S's and $(n - r)$ F's. The order of the S's and F's in the sequence is not important. We can represent these events as

$$\overbrace{SSSS \ldots S}^{r}\overbrace{FF \ldots F}^{(n-r)}$$

or some different permutation of S's and F's.

It follows that in order to find the *number* of events that contain r S's and $(n-r)$ F's we need to calculate the number of combinations of r objects from n.

Therefore, in general, for a sequence of n trials the *number* of sequences which represent r successes is $\binom{n}{r}$. The *probability* of a single sequence that represents r successes and $n - r$ failures is $p^r(1 - p)^{n-r}$ by Theorem 14.11, since each of the n trials is independent. Therefore, the probability of getting r successes is the probability of getting *any one* of the $\binom{n}{r}$ possible sequences each of probability $p^r(1-p)^{n-r}$. This is $\binom{n}{r}p^r(1-p)^{n-r}$. The *distribution* for the binomial random variable is therefore

$$P(T_n = r) = \binom{n}{r}p^r(1-p)^{n-r} \text{ where } r = 0, 1, 2, \ldots, n$$

Example 14.54 In an experiment to throw a die where success is the number '6' and failure is 'any number other than 6', the probability distribution is

$$\begin{aligned} P(X=1) &= p = 1/6 \\ P(X=0) &= q = 5/6 \end{aligned}$$

We now want to calculate the probability distribution for a single experiment to find the probability distribution of the sampling statistic over a sequence of three identical and independent trials. We use the binomial model $\mathscr{B}(3, \frac{1}{6})$, since $n = 3$ and $p = \frac{1}{6}$, as the parameters in this experiment. The complete binomial distribution is

$$\begin{aligned} P(T_3 = 0) &= \binom{3}{0}\left(\frac{1}{6}\right)^0\left(\frac{5}{6}\right)^3 = \left(\frac{5}{6}\right)^3 = \frac{125}{216} \\ P(T_3 = 1) &= \binom{3}{1}\left(\frac{1}{6}\right)^1\left(\frac{5}{6}\right)^2 = \frac{1}{6} \times \frac{25}{36} = \frac{75}{216} \\ P(T_3 = 2) &= \binom{3}{2}\left(\frac{1}{6}\right)^2\left(\frac{5}{6}\right)^1 = \frac{1}{6} \times \frac{25}{36} = \frac{15}{216} \\ P(T_3 = 3) &= \binom{3}{3}\left(\frac{1}{6}\right)^3\left(\frac{5}{6}\right)^3 = \frac{1}{6} \times \frac{25}{36} = \frac{1}{216} \end{aligned}$$

The sum of these four probabilities is 1, as we would expect.

We have seen that the probabilities for the realization of T_n, the binomial random variable, in the sampling distribution add up to 1. We give the following proof that the sum of the probabilities in $\mathscr{B}(n, p)$ is always equal to 1, as required by the axioms for probability.

We sum the probabilities of the realizations of the random variable, T_n, and then represent $1 - p$ by q. We have

$$\sum_{r=0}^{n} P(T_n = r) = \sum_{r=0}^{n}\binom{n}{r}p^r(1-p)^{n-r} = \sum_{r=0}^{n}\binom{n}{r}p^r q^{n-r} = (p+q)^n$$

by the binomial theorem on page 78. Now since $q = 1 - p$, we have $(p+q)^n = 1^n = 1$.

Exercise 14.34 In Example 14.33 we gave the distribution for an experiment on which a coin is tossed and success is 'coin is a head'. Find the complete distribution over five independent trials and show that the probabilities sum to 1.

The expectation of the binomial random variable The expected value of the random variable X for a single trial is given by Def. 14.15. For the probability distribution of a single Bernouilli trial, the *expectation*, or mean of the distribution, is $E(X) = 1 \times p + 0 \times (1-p) = p$. We have defined the binomial random variable to be

$T_n = X_1 + X_2 + \cdots + X_n$, where $X_1, X_2, \ldots, X_n$ are the Bernouilli random variables for each of the n trials.

In order to calculate $E(T_n)$ we use again the linearity of expectation from Exercise 14.31. We have

$$E(T_n) = E(X_1) + E(X_2) + \cdots + E(X_n) = np$$

Alternatively we can calculate $E(T_n)$ directly from Def. 14.15 for the binomial model $\mathscr{B}(n,p)$. The main steps in the calculation are

$$\begin{aligned} E(T_n) &= \textstyle\sum_{r=0}^{n} r\ P(T_r = r) \\ &= \textstyle\sum_{r=0}^{n} r \binom{n}{r} p^r (1-p)^{n-r} \\ &= np(p + (1-p))^{n-1} \\ &= np \end{aligned}$$

Exercise 14.35 Give the detailed steps in the calculation that $E(T_n) = np$.

Example 14.55 In an experiment a coin is tossed 100 times. We assume the binomial model, $\mathscr{B}(100, \frac{1}{2})$. The expected number of heads is 50 since $E(T_{100}) = 100 \times \frac{1}{2} = 50$.

Example 14.56 A die is thrown 10 times. Calculate the probability of obtaining

(a) exactly two sixes,

(b) at most three sixes,

(c) at least four sixes.

PROOF In all cases we have the model $\mathscr{B}(10, 1/6)$.

(a) We require $P(T_{10} = 2) = \binom{1}{0}2\,(1/6)^2\,(5/6)^8$

(b) We require

$$\begin{aligned} P(T_{10} \le 3) &= P(T_{10} = 0) + P(T_{10} = 1) + P(T_{10} = 2) + P(T_{10} = 3) \\ &= \binom{10}{0}(1/6)^0(5/6)^{10} + \binom{10}{1}(1/6)^1(5/6)^9 \\ &\quad + \binom{10}{2}(1/6)^2(5/6)^8 + \binom{10}{3}(1/6)^3(5/6)^7 \end{aligned}$$

(c) We require

$$P(T_{10} \ge 4) = 1 - P(T_{10} \le 3)$$

If n is large in the model $\mathscr{B}(n,p)$, calculating a probability such as $P(T_n \le 20)$ is difficult. Fortunately, there are tables to do the calculations for us. The cumulative binomial probabilities table calculates $P(T_n \ge r)$ for various values of r ranging over a number of binomial distributions $\mathscr{B}(n,p)$.

Example 14.57 In a manufacturing process it is found that on average 5 per cent of the articles produced are defective. The articles are packed in cases of 100.

(a) Calculate the probability that a case has no defective articles.

(b) Reliable sources inform you that the manufacturer has been trying to push through a number of substandard cases, which have more than the average number of defective articles. Make deductions about the likelihood that this has been happening if a sample case has at least 12 defective articles.

PROOF We use the $\mathscr{B}(100, 0.05)$ model.

(a) $P(T_{100} = 0) = \binom{100}{0}(0.05)^0(0.95)^{100} = (0.95)^{100} = 0.0059$ by using logarithms.

(b) From the tables for $n = 100$ and $p = 0.05$ we discover $P(T_{100} \geq 12) = 0.00427$. It would seem that there is some foundation for the rumours about the unscrupulous manufacturer. The probability that a normal case could contain at least 12 defective articles, and therefore be substandard, is 0.00427. The probability is small, but is it small enough to give the manufacturer the benefit of the doubt?

We now give a rule that is useful when we calculate probabilities from tables. In the general case, we have T_n as the binomial random variable. Then T_n is realized by any number r where $r = 0, 1, \ldots, n$. Although the tables help us to calculate $P(T_n \geq r)$, we often need to calculate $P(T_n = r)$ or $P(T_n \leq r)$. Since $\{r\} \cup \{r+1, \ldots, n\} = \{r, r+1, \ldots, n\}$, we have $P(T_n \geq r) = P(T_n = r) + P(T_n \geq r+1)$.

Rule 14.1 $P(T_n = r) = P(T_n \geq r) - P(T_n \geq r + 1)$ where T_n is the random variable.

Example 14.58 Quality control procedures are carried out on large consignments of a certain component by selecting 20 components at random and checking these. It is known on average that 1 in every 25 components is faulty. Calculate the probability that there are:

(a) more than three faulty components,

(b) exactly two faulty components.

PROOF The assumptions for the binomial model hold. We use the tables for $\mathscr{B}(20, 0.04)$.

(a) $P(T_{20} \geq 4) = 0.00741$

(b) $P(T_{20} = 2) = P(T_{20} \geq 2) - P(T_{20} \geq 3) = 0.18966 - 0.04386 = 0.14580$

A consignment is rejected if more than four faulty components are found in the sample of 20. We calculate the probability that an entirely normal consignment is erroneously rejected under the criteria. The consignment is erroneously rejected if $\mathscr{B}(20, 0.04)$ *is* the correct distribution. Thus we need only find $P(T_{20} \geq 5) = 0.00096$, which is very small.

Exercise 14.36 In planning a family of four children, find the probability distribution of:

(a) the number of boys,

(b) the number of changes in sex sequence.

State the assumptions that you make and the model that you use. You may assume that the probability of having a boy is $\frac{1}{2}$. Find the expected value for each of these distributions.

Exercise 14.37 An examination consists of four multiple choice questions, each with a choice of three answers. Consider the number of correct answers that are given when the student has to resort to pure guessing for each question. Find the complete distribution and the expectation for this distribution.

Exercise 14.38 A person attempts to predict the fall of a coin in each of several successive trials. If the person really is only guessing, what is the probability that the prediction will be correct in:

(a) four out of four successive trials,

(b) in at most two out of ten trials,

(c) in eight or more out of ten successive trials?

Exercise 14.39 The binomial random variable of a distribution is found to have an expected value of 3 and variance 2. Calculate the probability that the realization of the random variable is 7.

14.4.5 The Poisson process and the Poisson distribution

It is reasonable to ask what happens to the binomial distribution when n is very large and p is very small. Many practical binomial experiments are of this nature. It turns out that as $n \to \infty$ and $p \to 0$, $P(X = r) = \lambda^r e^{-\lambda}/r!$ for $r = 0, 1, 2, \ldots$ and where $\lambda = np$.

Definition 14.22 Poisson distribution A random variable X which has a probability distribution function

$$P(X = r) = (\lambda^r e^{-\lambda})/r! \text{ for } r = 0, 1, 2, \ldots \text{ and where } \lambda > 0$$

is called a Poisson distribution function.

The Poisson distribution has only one parameter, λ, so we denote it by $\mathscr{P}(\lambda)$.

This distribution provides a model for a wide variety of phenomena that share certain characteristics. These are physical processes in which some kind of rare event takes place sporadically over a given period of time, or in a given area or volume, in a manner that is commonly thought to be at random. Examples of such processes are:

1 Telephone calls received at an exchange

2 Arrivals at a service counter

3 Flaws in a long wire that has been manufactured

4 Breakdowns or failures in equipment

5 Goals scored by Arsenal (very rare events)

We are, of course, particularly interested in the probability distribution of the random variable X which is the number of events in some unit interval. For our examples the intervals could be: a day, an hour, a metre, a year, a minute and a game respectively. Ideally we want a distribution that involves only an average rate, λ, of events in some specified interval. The distribution is only a satisfactory model if four assumptions, called the Poisson postulates, hold. A physical process that is characterized by the Poisson postulates is called the *Poisson process*.

Definition 14.23 Poisson postulates The Poisson postulates are the following assumptions:

1 The number of events that occur in one unit of time, area or volume is independent of the number that occur in other units.

2 The probability structure of the distribution is time invariant over the interval.

3 The probability of exactly one event in a small interval of time is approximately proportional to the size of the interval.

4 The probability of more than one event in a (sufficiently) small interval is negligible in comparison with the probability of one event in that interval.

Example 14.59 We consider the number of goals scored in 500 football league games. The frequency of the number of goals scored throughout the 500 games is compared to a Poisson distribution.

Goals per game	0	1	2	3	4	5	6	7	8
Frequency of scores	52	121	129	90	42	45	18	1	2
Poisson predictions of scores	48	113	132	103	60	28	11	4	1

We take the unit of time to be 1 game of football. It is reasonable to assume that the Poisson postulates hold. We ignore higher scores than 8 even though their probability is non-zero. The mean number of goals per game is

$$((52 \times 0) + (121 \times 1) + (129 \times 2) + (90 \times 3) + (42 \times 4) + (45 \times 5) + (18 \times 6) \\ +(1 \times 7) + (2 \times 8))/500 = 2.346$$

We take this as the value for λ, the average number of events in the specified interval. By the definition of the Poisson distribution,

$$P(X = r) = \frac{(2.346)^r \mathrm{e}^{-2.346}}{r!}$$

For example,

$$P(X = 0) = \frac{(2.346)^0 \times 0.09575}{0!} = 0.09575$$

This explains the first column entry of the table, since if the probability of a 0 goal game is 0.09575 we would *expect* the number of 0 goal games in 500 to be $500 \times 0.09575 = 48$. The table shows that the expected frequencies compare quite favourably with the actual frequencies of scores. Suppose that in a following year a change in the rules results in an average of three goals per game. If 1000 games are played, in how many games can we expect to have more than four goals? We assume a Poisson distribution with $\lambda = 3$. We have to find $P(X \geq 5)$ in this case. Again we have tables to determine $P(X \geq r)$ for given λ. Now $P(X \geq 5) = 0.18474$, so in 1000 games we expect around 185 to have more than four goals.

The expectation of the Poisson random variable We calculate the mean of the Poisson distribution, $\mathscr{P}(\lambda)$, as follows:

$$\begin{aligned} E(X) &= \sum_{i=0}^{\infty} i \times P(X = i) = \sum_{i=0}^{\infty} i\lambda^i \mathrm{e}^{-\lambda}/\mathrm{i}! = \mathrm{e}^{-\lambda} \sum_{\mathrm{i}=1}^{\infty} \lambda^{\mathrm{i}}/(\mathrm{i}-1)! \\ &= \mathrm{e}^{-\lambda}\lambda \sum_{\mathrm{i}=1}^{\infty} \lambda^{\mathrm{i}-1}/(\mathrm{i}-1)! = \mathrm{e}^{-\lambda}\lambda \sum_{\mathrm{i}=1}^{\infty} \lambda^{\mathrm{i}}/\mathrm{i}! = \mathrm{e}^{-\lambda}\lambda\mathrm{e}^{\lambda} = \lambda \times 1 \end{aligned}$$

using the exponential expansion $\mathrm{e}^{\mathrm{x}} = \sum \mathrm{x}^{\mathrm{i}}/\mathrm{i}!$

So the expected value of the random variable converges to λ.

Exercise 14.40 Show that the Poisson distribution of $\mathscr{P}(\lambda)$ satisfies the axioms for probability; that is, show that $\sum_{i=0}^{\infty} P(X = i) = 1$.

Example 14.60 The average rate of telephone calls received at a manual exchange where eight operators work is 6 per minute. A caller is unable to make a connection if all the operators are engaged. We assume that a call lasts on average one minute. We calculate the probability that a caller is unable to make a connection. We assume a Poisson distribution and take the unit interval to be 1 minute. Hence $\lambda = 6$ and $P(X = r) = 6^r e^{-6}/r!$ We therefore find $P(X \geq 8) = 0.15276$.

Exercise 14.41 In a system requirements document, it is discovered that only 13.5 per cent of the pages are free from typing errors. Assuming that the number of errors per page is a random variable with the Poisson distribution, find the percentage of pages that have exactly one error.

Exercise 14.42 A random variable X has a Poisson distribution in which $P(X = 1) = P(X = 2)$. Find $P(X = 3)$. Use the formula for the Poisson distribution as well as tables to obtain your result.

Exercise 14.43 Weak spots occur in a certain manufactured tape. On average there is one weak spot per 1000 metres. Assuming a Poisson distribution for the number of weak spots in a given length of tape, find the probability that:

(a) a 2400-metre roll will have at most two defects,

(b) a 1200-metre roll will have no defects,

(c) in a box of five 1200-metre rolls two have just one defect and the other three have none.

14.5 SUMMARY

In this chapter we have constructed an axiomatic calculus of probabilities, within which the notion of an event formalizes the different outcomes of an experiment. The semantics of building events is interpreted within a mathematical model of sets and operations on sets. The axioms for the calculus are based on the intuitive notion of relative frequency. From the axioms for an equiprobable space we deduced theorems that enable us to calculate the probability that some event will occur. We then gave further axioms of the conditional probability of events that occur in a reduced sample space and defined a notion of independence between events. Bayes theorem generalizes the concept of conditional probability.

The deduction of information from statistics is based on the concept of a random variable and a probability distribution function. Using the notion of the expected value of a random variable and the concept of a random sample, we constructed the binomial and Poisson models to represent probability distributions.

14.6 FURTHER EXERCISES

Exercise 14.44 An electronic system consists of three components, and the probability of failure of each component is 0.05, 0.06, 0.03 respectively. Given that the system will not function properly unless at least two components perform satisfactorily, calculate the probability that the system will function properly assuming that component failure occurs independently.

Exercise 14.45 Two cards are selected without replacement from a deck of 52 cards.

(a) Describe as concisely as possible the sample space of this experiment.

(b) How can this sample space be most reasonably turned into a probability space?

(c) Describe explicitly the event E: 'both cards are aces'. Calculate the probability of E, stating carefully any assumptions you are making.

(d) Let

E_1: 'first card is a heart'
E_2: 'second card is a spade'

Calculate the probability of E_2, given that E_1 has occurred.

(e) What does this mean in terms of the dependence or independence of the events E_1 and E_2?

Exercise 14.46 From the integers 1,2,3,4 and 5, first one integer is chosen and then a second from the remaining four. Using the axiomatic model approach, describe as concisely as possible the sample space for this compound experiment as a set and deduce its cardinality. Show how this sample space can be turned into a probability space. Define the following events:

E_1: 'first integer is even'
E_2: 'second integer is even'
O_1: 'first integer is odd'
O_1: 'second integer is odd'

(a) Use a Venn diagram of the compound experiment to write down an expression for E_2 as the non-trivial union of two sets.

(b) Assuming that each outcome has an equal probability, find the probability that the second integer chosen is even. Use this to deduce the probability that at least one even integer is chosen. (*Hint*: Use the rule of addition of probabilities of events.)

(c) Calculate the probability of E_2/E_1. Are E_1 and E_2 independent?

Exercise 14.47 Five cards are marked consecutively with the numbers 1 to 5, and then placed in a box. On three occasions a card is chosen at random and its number written down, before the card is put in a pile beside the box. The three numbers, recorded in the order they were chosen, then form a three-digit number at the end of the experiment.

What is the probability that the three-digit number formed is a multiple of three?

You should explain how you use the axioms of the probability space. You may also need to use the fact that if a number written to the base 10 is a multiple of three then the sum of the digits is also a multiple of three.

Exercise 14.48 An electronic system consists of three components in parallel. The system functions properly providing that at least two of the components function properly. Assuming that each component has a probability of failure of 0.1 and that any failures occur independently of each other, calculate the probability that the system functions properly.

Exercise 14.49 Let E_1 be the event that the first card is a heart and E_2 be the event that the second card is a spade. Calculate the probability of E_2 given E_1. What does this result mean in terms of dependence or independence of E_1 and E_2?

Exercise 14.50 On average 240 students log into a certain computer per hour. If more than three students attempt to log in during a minute then a queue is formed. Calculate the probability that a queue will form in any given minute and state any assumptions that you make.

Exercise 14.51 A man buys a lottery ticket. Out of 100 000 tickets sold there is 1 ticket that wins £1 000 and 50 tickets that win £100. What is a fair price to pay for the ticket?

FURTHER READING

The importance of the concepts of probability in engineering planning and design and the analytical models of random phenomena are presented from an engineering viewpoint in the book by Tang and Tang (1975). Applications in computer science are presented in Mendenhall and Sincich (1988). Further work on distributions constructed for statistical inference is given in Hogg and Craig (1978).

Chapter 15

ALGORITHMIC AND COMPUTATIONAL COMPLEXITY

Many of the earlier chapters of this book have been concerned with the problem of building a system that is correct with respect to its specification. We have mainly been concerned with specifying, and ensuring the correctness of, the *functional* requirements. In practice, however, there are many non-functional requirements that are often forgotten or ignored in the specification. These additional requirements must be met in order to ensure that the system can be used satisfactorily.

Here we are concerned with one particular class of non-functional requirements for software systems, namely efficiency of resource usage. For example, we are concerned with requirements like 'the system must perform x number of transactions per second' or 'the system must use no more than y bytes of main memory'. There are two broad aspects of efficiency that we consider in this chapter. On the one hand we must know how to predict and assess the efficiency of the algorithms that are implemented. The techniques for doing this are described in Sec. 15.1. On the other hand, we need to know if there are inherent complexities in the system requirements which inevitably constrain the efficiency of any solution. This is the issue of problem complexity. The techniques for measuring and classifying problem complexity are described in Sec. 15.2. This section contains some of the most fundamental and important topics in computability. For example, we reveal that many important problems, for which people have attempted for many years to find efficient programming solutions, are now believed to be infeasible.

15.1 EFFICIENCY OF ALGORITHMS

This section is concerned with the definition and measurement of algorithmic efficiency. We discuss the meaning of algorithmic efficiency and explain why it is commonly referred to as algorithmic *complexity*. One especially important aspect of efficiency of algorithms is their time efficiency: how fast they will run for various inputs. We show how to compute time efficiency as a function of the size of input. It turns out that we are most interested in knowing what happens to these functions as the input size increases. Hence, we examine the asymptotic behaviour of these time efficiency functions.

15.1.1 The meaning of algorithmic efficiency

When we talk about efficiency of algorithms we mean, informally, the efficient use they make of machine resources. There are two types of efficiency:

Time efficiency. How much time is consumed by the algorithm.

Space efficiency. How much memory space is used by the algorithm.

For historical reasons, this notion of efficiency of algorithms is commonly referred to as *complexity* by computer scientists. This stems from the limitations of early computers, which meant that much of the complexity of software design was concentrated on the implementation of the algorithm. Early pioneers found that saving a few bytes of memory or a few machine instructions could make the difference between an algorithm that ran and one that did not. Hence complexity became synonymous with poor efficiency. This view of complexity of algorithms has nothing to do with, and is probably orthogonal to, other views of complexity like cognitive complexity (which is concerned with the difficulty of understanding an algorithm) or structural complexity (which is concerned with an algorithm's structure in the sense of Chapter 13).

Everybody is aware that the last 20 years have seen a massive increase in the speed and power of computers and memory devices, accompanied by rapidly decreasing costs. This has led to a widely held illusion that even cheap personal computers are so fast and their memory, or potential memory, so vast that we no longer have to worry about the resources that algorithms use. It is now accepted that you should not compromise a clearly structured algorithmic solution in order to save a few bytes of memory or a few machine instructions. The reason is that such resource savings will rarely be unnoticeable. However, you should not be lulled into a false sense of security. In many circumstances it is still the case that both correctness and structuredness count for nothing if the algorithm is genuinely 'inefficient'.

Example 15.1 Travelling salesman problem There are n cities labelled $1,\ldots, n$ for which the distance $d_{i,j}$ between any two cities i,j is known. Our problem is to compute the shortest route, starting and ending at city 1, which includes each city. In Example 2.94 on page 76 we showed that the number of different possible routes which start and end at city 1 is $(n-1)!$ Each of these routes corresponds to a permutation $(\sigma(2)\cdots\sigma(n))$ of $2\cdots n$, as illustrated in Fig. 15.1. For each such route, R say, the total distance travelled is

$$d_{1,\sigma(2)} + \left(\sum_{i=2}^{n-1} d_{\sigma(i),\sigma(i+1)}\right) + d_{\sigma(n),1}$$

A simple algorithmic solution is given in Fig. 15.2. This algorithm is a *provably* correct solution to the problem. It has a simple structure. However, it is almost totally useless because of its inefficiency. To see this, we note that computing the total distance of each route involves n additions. Since there are $(n-1)!$ such routes to compute, the algorithm requires $n!$ additions. Suppose that $n = 30$. This is the sort of input size that would be considered quite small for such a problem. Now $30! \sim 10^{20}$. The fastest parallel computers can perform around 10^9 addition operations per second. Therefore, even if we forget about all the other computations that have to be performed, such as generating the permutations, doing the comparisons and assigning values to variables, it will take 10^{11} seconds to terminate. It would therefore take several thousand years to perform just the additions. When $n = 100$ the time needed is much longer than the expected life-span of the universe, even if we could increase the machine speed by a factor of millions. Thus we cannot argue that only current machine limitations stop this algorithm from being practically useful. There will never be a computer

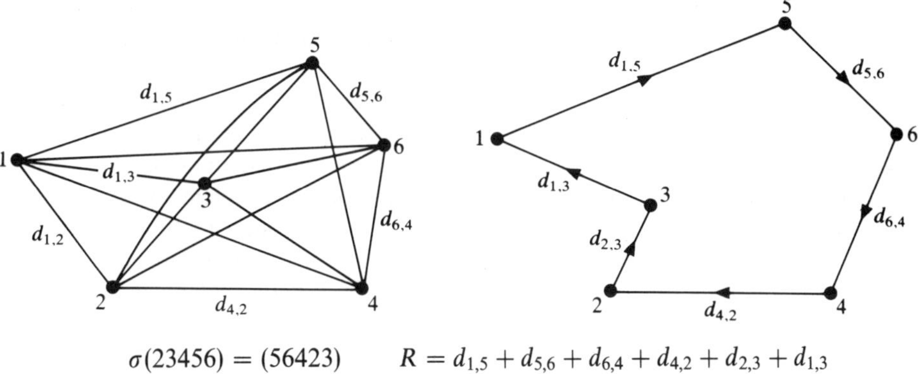

Figure 15.1 Travelling salesman problem.

```
begin
   min_dist := total distance of any one route;
   for each of the (n-1)! different routes R
       do begin
          compute total distance D of R;
             if D <  min_dist
                then min_dist := D
          end
end.
```

Figure 15.2 Algorithmic solution to the travelling salesman problem.

sufficiently fast to run this algorithm for even moderate size inputs. Improvements in technology will just not help.

We have argued that the simple algorithm is no good. Unfortunately, it turns out that the best-known algorithms for this problem are not really much better. It is believed that for this apparently simple problem there is no possible efficient solution. We shall return to this problem in Sec. 15.2.

15.1.2 Computing time efficiency

Example 15.1 illustrates a number of basic principles that underpin a more formal definition of efficiency measurement than so far discussed. Any solution to this problem requires the input of the n cities and their pairwise distances. In a sense, n characterizes the size of the problem in any given instance. In computing the output, there are certain primitive machine operations, in this case *additions*, that have to be performed. The number of these additions is a function $T(n)$ of the input size, and this seems to be the main factor in determining how fast the algorithm can run. In Example 15.1, $T(n)$ is the function $n!$

Many problems for which people try to find computer solutions have a similar property. We shall always assume that the input size for such problems is characterized by the integer n. For any algorithmic solution A, we define the function $T_A(n)$ as the maximum number of relevant primitive operations that have to be performed by A on a problem of size n. The function $T_A(n)$ is called the *time complexity function of the algorithm A*. Strictly speaking this is the *worst case time complexity* function, since we considered the maximum number of operations. Equally we could consider the minimum or average number of operations, and hence derive *best case* and *average case complexity functions*. We restrict our discussion to worst case time complexity.

The time complexity function is a commonly used measure of time efficiency. An analogous measure of efficiency is the memory space complexity function $M(n)$, which is the number of basic units of memory required to solve a problem of size n. Since the analyses in either case are similar, we restrict the discussion to time complexity. For both simplicity and conformance to other texts we make one important abuse of terminology throughout this chapter when referring to functions defined on $\mathbb{N}$. The rule $f(n)$ that defines the function will be used to refer to the function itself. Thus we shall speak about the function '$n + 1$' rather than using the more accurate function name '$\lambda n.\ n + 1$' which we described in Chapter 9.

The following examples illustrate how we might compute $T(n)$ for specific algorithms and compare different algorithms with respect to this function.

Example 15.2 Suppose we have a class of n students whose exam marks are stored in an array X. We wish to compute these marks as percentages. Suppose, for example, that the marks were out of 70. Then two possible algorithms are:

```
ALGORITHM A

total := 70;
for i:=1 to n do
    X(i) := X(i) * (100/total)
```

```
ALGORITHM B

factor := 100/70
for i:=1 to n do
    X(i) := X(i) * factor
```

The important primitive operations are *multiplication* and *division*. In algorithm A, two operations are executed each time through the loop: one multiplication and one division. Thus in total there are $2n$ operations, whence $T_A(n) = 2n$. In algorithm B there is one division performed before the loop and one multiplication for each loop iteration. Thus $T_B(n) = n + 1$. An optimizing compiler would automatically transform algorithm A into algorithm B, since it would move constant operations, such as $(100/total)$, outside the loop.

Example 15.3 Consider the following simple algorithm for searching *list*, an ordered list of objects, for an element Y. We use the general loop structure introduced in Chapter 13:

```
    ALGORITHM A (LINEAR SEARCH)

loop  exit when (Y is found) or (end of list)
  begin {loop}
   read next element X of list;
   if X=Y then Y is found
  end {loop}
```

The important primitive operation here is *comparison*, the test for equality of X and Y. The input size is n, where n is the number of elements in *list*. If we are lucky, Y could be the first element of *list*, and the number of comparisons required is just one. However, in the worst case Y could either be the last element of *list* or not in *list* at all. Either way, we would go through the loop n times, making n comparisons in all. We conclude that $T_A(n) = n$.

In Fig. 13.6 on page 317 we described a different algorithm, the binary search algorithm, for solving the same problem. Analysing its time complexity, we find that again each time through the loop we make one comparison. However, in this case we note that every time we go through the loop we reduce the size of *list* by at least half. In the worst case Y is not in *list* and we have to continue looping until *list* is empty. How many iterations is this in all? Think about the case where $n = 16$. After one iteration the list size is reduced to at most eight. After two iterations the list size is reduced to at most four. After three iterations the list size is reduced to at most two. After four iterations the list size is reduced to at most one. After five iterations the list must be empty. Thus for $n = 16$, the maximum number of comparisons required is 5. In fact, by extending this argument, it is not difficult to see that if $n = 2^m$, then the maximum number of comparisons required is $m + 1$. This is the same as $\log_2 n + 1$. In general, if n is any integer then the time complexity function $T(n)$ for binary search is equal to the (integer part) of $\log_2 n + 1$.

Suppose *list* contains one million names, so $n = 10^6$. Then the execution of the linear search algorithm requires, in the worst case, one million comparisons. However, the integer part of $\log_2 10^6$ equals 19. It follows that executing the binary search algorithm requires only 20 comparisons in the worst case. This is a major efficiency improvement.

Exercise 15.1 Some programming languages, such as Pascal, have no built-in function to compute the result of raising a number to a power. Thus if we want to compute x^n for a real number x and an integer n we have to write our own algorithm and code it. Since we may need to use this function many times, and with large values of n, it is important that we make the algorithm as efficient as possible. The following two algorithms both compute x^n for a positive integer n. Algorithm B contains a 'divide and conquer' approach similar to that of binary search:

```
ALGORITHM A

power := 1;
for i:=1 to n  do
  power := power * x
```

```
ALGORITHM B

power := 1;
while n > 0 do
 begin {while}
   if n is odd then power:= power * x;
   x := x * x;
   n := n div 2
 end {while}
```

In each case compute, as a function of n, the number of loop iterations required in the worst case. Assuming that the primitive operations are $*$ and *div* (integer part after division), deduce the time complexity functions in each case and compare their values when $n = 1000$.

Exercise 15.2 On the basis of the examples and exercises seen so far, what can you say about the relationship between algorithmic complexity and structural complexity, where the latter is interpreted in the sense of Chapter 13?

Exercise 15.3 Suppose algorithms A and B require respectively n^2 and 2^n operations for an input of size n. For a machine that can perform 10^9 operations per second, calculate the largest input which A and B can compute within 1 second, 1 hour, 1 year, 1 century, etc. ($2^{10} \approx 10^3$; 1 day $\approx 8 \times 10^4$ seconds; 1 year $\approx 3 \times 10^7$ seconds; the age of the universe is approximately 13 billion years).

15.1.3 Asymptotic behaviour of functions

Our crude algorithm for solving the travelling salesman problem had a time complexity of $n!$ We argued that this was unreasonable because, for all but the smallest values of n, it would take far too long to perform the computation. In subsequent examples we have seen algorithms whose time complexity functions are $\log n + 1$, n, $n + 1$, $2n$, n^2. It was assumed that these were all reasonable. Intuitively, what seems to make a function $T(n)$ reasonable or not is its growth rate, that is its behaviour as $n \to \infty$. Informally,

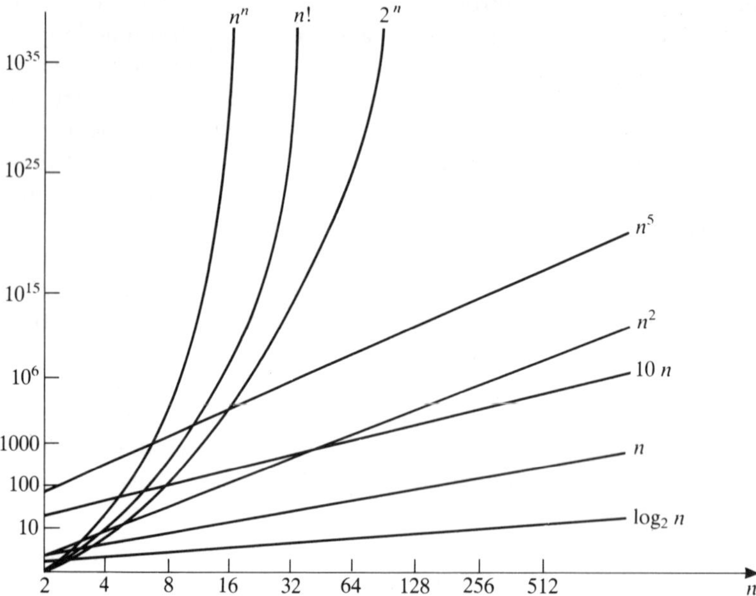

Figure 15.3 Growth rates of some common functions of n.

the asymptotic behaviour of a function is this growth rate. Figure 15.3 describes the growth rates of various functions, while Table 15.1 describes the actual execution time required for algorithms of various time complexities and a range of input sizes. If $f(n) > g(n)$, we say that the function f *dominates* the function g for the value n. Note that, in Fig. 15.3, some functions dominate others for *all* values of n. For example, n^5 always dominates n^2 and n always dominates $\log n$. Some functions dominate others only after reaching a certain value of n. For example, 2^n dominates $100n$ for all values of $n > 9$. In this case we say that $100n$ is bounded from above by 2^n. Formally:

Definition 15.1 Bounded functions A function $f(n)$ is bounded from above by the function $g(n)$ if, for some $k, f(n) \leq g(n)$ for all $n > k$.

The following definition enables us to formalize the intuitive distinction between time complexity functions that are reasonable and those that are unreasonable.

Definition 15.2 Polynomial and superpolynomial functions A function $f(n)$ is a polynomial function if it is bounded above by n^k for some k. All other functions are superpolynomial.

The polynomial functions are considered to be the reasonable functions, while the superpolynomial functions are considered to be unreasonable.

Example 15.4 The functions $\log n + 1$, n, $25n$ and $n^{10} + n^5 + 6$ are all polynomial functions.

Example 15.5 Exponential functions All functions that have the form a^n for some constant $a > 1$ are superpolynomial. These special superpolynomial functions are called *exponential*. Thus 2^n and 1.01^n are exponential functions. The function $n^{\log n}$ is superpolynomial but not exponential. Some functions, such as $n!$ and n^n

Table 15.1 Execution time of different algorithms

	Time complexity $T(n)$ of algorithm					
Size n of input	$\log_2 n$	n	n^2	2^n	$n!$	n^n
10	0.000 003 seconds	0.000 01 seconds	0.0001 seconds	0.001 seconds	3.6 seconds	2.8 hours
100	0.000 007 seconds	0.0001 seconds	0.01 seconds	10^{14} centuries	10^{146} centuries	10^{185} centuries
1000	0.000 01 seconds	0.001 seconds	1 second	—	—	—
10 000	0.000 013 seconds	0.01 seconds	1.7 minutes	—	—	—
100 000	0.000 017 seconds	0.01 seconds	2.8 hours	—	—	—

Entries with '—' represent astronomical figures, far greater than the expected life-span of the universe. Note that the universe is reckoned to be less than 10^9 centuries old. We assume one instruction per microsecond.

are worse than exponential, in the sense that they strictly bound an exponential function, but it has become common to refer to all such superpolynomial functions as exponential.

Exercise 15.4 Explain why the function $n^2 \log n$ is polynomial.

Definition 15.3 Feasible and infeasible algorithms An algorithm whose time complexity function is polynomial is said to be feasible, while one whose time complexity function is superpolynomial is said to be infeasible.

Definition 15.3 enables us to deduce the nice properties that we would expect intuitively of the notion of feasibility. For example, the sequence and nesting of two feasible algorithms (as discussed in Chapter 13) is again feasible. Also, the property of feasibility is not dependent on particular machines. Although the time function is ultimately dependent on the speed of the primitive operations in question, it turns out that, no matter what speeds are achieved for these operations, an algorithm that runs in polynomial time on one sequential machine will run in polynomial time on any other sequential machine. Conversely, an algorithm that is exponential on one machine is exponential on any other machine. This is the *sequential computation thesis*.

Big O notation Although the time complexity function $T(n)$ is a reasonable measure of algorithmic efficiency there are times when we want a more coarse-grained measure. Consider the two algorithms in Example 15.2 on page 380 for computing student marks. Algorithm A has time complexity $2n$ while algorithm B has time complexity $n + 1$. Although we assert that algorithm B is more efficient because $2n$ dominates $n + 1$, there are two senses in which these two time functions are not 'very' different:

1 Algorithm A will always run faster than an algorithm B if we run it on a machine whose primitive operations execute over twice as fast.

2 If we execute the algorithms on the same machine, then although algorithm B is always faster, for large input n the *rate* at which it is faster is constant.

Contrast this state of affairs with the two searching algorithms discussed in Example 15.3. Binary search has time complexity $1 + \log n$ while linear search has time complexity n. Even if you run linear search on a machine whose primitive operations are 1000 times as fast, binary search will still outperform it for all inputs above about 15 000. In fact, no matter how much we speed up the machine time, binary search will always perform better for sufficiently large n. What we have is the informal notion that there is an *order of magnitude* difference between $\log n$ and n that does not exist between n and $2n$ (or indeed any constant multiple of n). By a similar argument there is an order of magnitude difference between n and n^2, and between n^2 and $n!$, etc.

In an intuitive sense we want to be able to say that 'a $\log n$ algorithm is really more efficient than an n algorithm' and 'an n algorithm is really more efficient than an n^2 algorithm' but that 'in the limiting case there is not really much to choose between an n and a $2n$ algorithm'. The precise formalism that allows us to characterize efficiency in this way is called the *big O* notation. Before defining the notation we explain the idea behind it. For every function $f(n)$ there is a *dominating* term $g(n)$ of $f(n)$ for which

$$f(n) = cg(n) + h(n)$$

where c is a constant and $g(n)$ increases much more quickly than $h(n)$ as $n \to \infty$. We can think of $h(n)$ as containing the slower growing terms of $f(n)$. As $n \to \infty$ we can effectively ignore all terms except $g(n)$.

Example 15.6 If $f(n) = 3n^2 + 2n + 26$, then the dominating term of $f(n)$ is n^2, because the growth rate of this term quickly outstrips the rest. The constant term, c, is 3, while the function $h(n)$ of slower growing terms is $2n + 26$.

Definition 15.4 Asymptotic domination and big O notation Let f, g be functions defined on $\mathbb{N}$. Then g asymptotically dominates f if there is a positive constant C and a natural number k such that $f(n) \leq Cg(n)$ for all $n \geq k$. The set of all functions that are asymptotically dominated by g is denoted by $O(g(n))$. If $f(n) \in O(g(n))$ then f is said to be 'big O $g(n)$' or, alternatively, 'of the order $g(n)$'. This is written as $O(g(n))$.

The *big O* value of a function $f(n)$ is computed by finding the dominating term of $f(n)$. Specifically, if $g(n)$ is the dominating term, then f is $O(g(n))$. Thus, in Example 15.6, $f(n)$ is $O(n^2)$.

Example 15.7 If $f = 2n + 5$ then f is $O(n)$. If $f = \log n + 1$ then f is $O(\log n)$.

Example 15.8 The functions n and $2n$ asymptotically dominate each other. Hence $2n \in O(n)$ and also $n \in O(2n)$. The function n does not asymptotically dominate n^2. Thus $n \in O(n) \subset O(n^2)$ and $n^2 \notin O(n)$.

Example 15.9 We know by our informal discussion that, since the dominating term in the function $2n + 3$ is n, the function is $O(n)$. In fact, we can prove this using Def. 15.4. Take $C = 4$ and $k = 2$. Then $2n + 3 \leq 4n$ for all $n \geq 2$.

Exercise 15.5 Prove that the function $3n^2 + n + 5$ is $O(n^2)$.

Example 15.10 It can be shown that the following strict containments hold, where c denotes any constant:

$$O(1) \subset O(\log n) \subset O(n) \subset O(n \log n) \subset O(n^2) \subset O(c^n) \subset O(n!)$$

$$O(n^i) \subset O(n^j) \text{ for all } i < j$$

$$O(n^i) \subset O(c^n) \text{ for all integers } i$$

Some of the *big O* sets are sufficiently common and important to merit special names. For example, if

f is $O(1)$, then we say f has *constant complexity*
f is $O(logn)$, then we say f has *logarithmic complexity*
f is $O(n)$, then we say f has *linear complexity*
f is $O(n^2)$, then we say f has *quadratic complexity*
f is $O(n^k)$ for some k, then we say f has *polynomial complexity*
f is $O(c^n)$, where $c > 1$, then we say f has *exponential complexity*.

Advantages of the big O notation When we introduced the idea of computing the time complexity function $T(n)$ on page 377, we suggested that it was always enough to restrict attention to the number of executions of certain primitive operations. This meant that we ignored other operations and fixed instructions in the algorithm, such as initializing variables and formatting inputs and outputs. If we use $O(T(n))$ as our measure of algorithmic efficiency, then this simplification is totally justified. This is because the contribution in time for performing primitive operations dominates that of the others. It is this *robustness* that makes the big O notation so important. Thus, when computing professionals consider specific problems, like that of searching or sorting lists, they compare algorithms in terms of their big O values.

Example 15.11 Searching lists It can be proved that any algorithm to search a sorted list requires, in the worst case, at least $O(\log n)$ comparisons. Thus $O(\log n)$ represents a lower bound on all searching algorithms. Since $1 + \log n = O(\log n)$, it follows that the binary search algorithm is an *optimal* solution for searching. Linear search is not optimal.

Example 15.12 Sorting lists There are many well-known algorithms for sorting lists of n elements as described, for example in Knuth(1969). The *bubblesort* algorithm is $O(n^2)$ in the worst case, so for a list on n elements the algorithm will require at most $O(n^2)$ comparison operations to sort the list. The *quicksort* algorithm also has a worst case complexity of $O(n^2)$, but it has an average case complexity of $O(n \log n)$. Both the *mergesort* and *heapsort* are superior in the sense that the algorithms are $O(n \log n)$ in the worst case. It has been proved that $O(n \log n)$ solutions are optimal for the sorting problem.

15.2 COMPLEXITY OF PROBLEMS

In Sec. 15.1 we concentrated on measuring the complexity, in the sense of time efficiency, of *algorithms*. However, the last two examples have also touched on a closely related issue, namely the complexity of *problems*. The problems in question were those of searching and sorting lists. We hinted that there may be ways to measure the

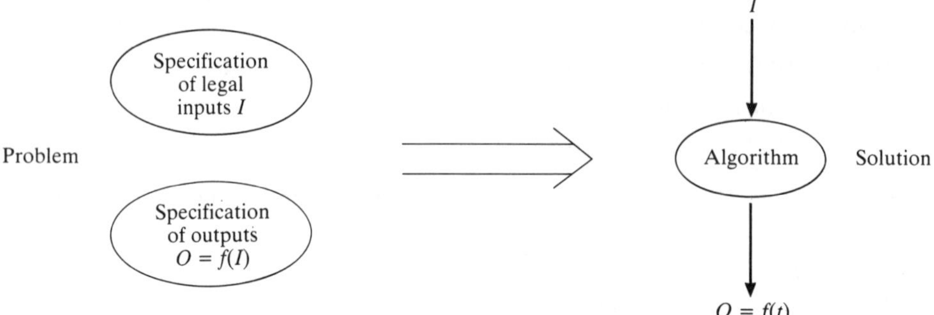

Figure 15.4 The formal problem and its solution.

computational complexity of such problems by considering the efficiency of the best algorithms that solve them. In this section we will formalize this notion.

First, we show why we have to be careful to restrict our scope to a class of problems that we shall call *formal*. We then show that many formal problems are not solvable at all. We show that we can restrict our discussion of problem complexity to the complexity of a class of problems that only have a yes or no answer. This leads to an important classification of problem complexity, and includes the notion of $\mathcal{NP}$-completeness. It transpires that many important problems, although solvable, do not appear to admit a feasible solution. We describe pragmatic ways to handle such problems.

15.2.1 Formal problems

Some people believe that computers can solve any problem. To all but those whose knowledge of computers is restricted to the Hollywood image of the 1950s, this myth is immediately dismissed by considering examples of well-known problems:

- The problem of determining the existence of God
- The problem of world hunger
- The Middle East problem
- The problem of nuclear disarmament

In order to pursue a formal discussion we must first define the class of relevant problems that lie within the scope of a computerized solution. Hence we define:

> **Definition 15.5 Formal problem** A formal problem is one that can be specified by a precise definition of the legal inputs, and a precise definition of the required outputs as a function of those inputs; that is a specification can be made of each output in terms of the input. A formal problem has been solved when an appropriate algorithm has been found for transforming any legal inputs into the correct outputs.

The idea of a formal problem is illustrated in Fig. 15.4. The inputs of a formal problem may be viewed as the problem's *parameters*. When we give these parameters specific values we talk about a specific *instance* of the problem. Thus, when we say that an algorithmic solution has been found, we mean that the algorithm will solve the problem for all instances.

Example 15.13 The travelling salesman problem of Example 15.1 is clearly an example of a formal problem. One instance of this problem is when $n = 4$ and the four cities are London, Glasgow, Manchester and Edinburgh, with the pairwise distances given as in the AA Handbook. The algorithm described in Example 15.1 is a solution to the problem, which in this instance might yield the route London–Manchester–Glasgow–Edinburgh–London.

Example 15.14 Consider the problem of searching an ordered list L of n items for a given item Y. An instance of this problem is when $n = 4$, $L = (2, 34, 45, 46)$ and $Y = 37$. Both binary search and linear search are examples of algorithmic solutions for this problem, because for each instance of the problem they will correctly determine whether or not Y is in L.

Some other examples of well-known formal problems are:

Halting problem. For a given program P, determine whether P terminates for all inputs.

Sorting problem. For a given list L, find another list L' whose elements are a permutation of the elements of L such that for any $i < j$, $L'[i] \leq L'[j]$.

Factorization problem. Given an n digit composite number a, compute numbers b and c such that $a = bc$.

Maximum problem. Given a list L of n numbers, compute the maximum number in L.

Timetable problem. Given a list of subjects and students enrolled on them together with a number of available time slots, construct a timetable with the minimum number of clashes.

Suppose that an algorithm for solving all instances of a problem has time complexity $T(n)$. Then $T(n)$ is said to be *asymptotically optimal* if, for every other algorithm with complexity $f(n)$ that solves the problem, $T(n)$ is $O(f(n))$. Consequently, we define:

Definition 15.6 Complexity of a formal problem The complexity of a formal problem is big O of the asymptotically optimal algorithm for the problem's solution.

Definition 15.7 Feasible problem A feasible problem is one whose complexity is polynomial.

Example 15.15 It follows immediately from Example 15.12 that the complexity of the sorting problem is $O(n \log n)$. Hence this problem is feasible.

Exercise 15.6 Show that the complexity of the searching problem is $O(\log n)$. (*Hint*: Consider Example 15.11.) Deduce that this problem is feasible.

Exercise 15.7 Compute the complexity of the maximum problem and deduce that it is feasible.

Do not let the previous definition and subsequent exercises lull you into a false sense of security. You may think that it is always easy to determine the computational complexity of a formal problem. In fact, for many important problems nobody knows what the computational complexity is. For each of the travelling salesman, factorization and timetabling problems, the best-known algorithms are exponential; but nobody knows if these are optimal. Hence we do not know if these problems are feasible or not. So things look pretty grim. But worse is to come. Although all known solutions to these particular problems are infeasible (and hence practically useless), at least solutions exist. It turns out that most formal problems, including the halting problem, have no solution at all — let alone a feasible one.

15.2.2 Non-solvable problems

Before we can tackle the question of non-solvable formal problems we need to concentrate on a crucial definition that we have thus far skimmed over, which is the definition of an *algorithm*. Our definition has assumed a model of a computer based on the von Neumann architecture, as discussed in Chapter 11. Underlying this we have assumed, for our measures of algorithmic efficiency and problem complexity, that our computer performed certain primitive operations and that the number of these was invariant.

Unfortunately, there are other apparently radically different definitions of algorithm, for which the notion of (sequential) machine operations is either different or not relevant at all. For example, the following have all been proposed as definitions of algorithm:

- An expression in the λ-calculus (Church's definition)
- A simple hypothetical machine with an infinite tape and a movable read–write head for scanning it together with a state transition diagram (Turing's definition)
- A syntactically correct and terminating FORTRAN program
- A syntactically correct and terminating Prolog program

It would thus appear that our measures are dependent on our definition of algorithm. In fact it has been proposed that this is not the case.

Church–Turing thesis

1 All reasonable definitions of algorithm known so far are equivalent.
2 Any reasonable definitions of algorithm anyone is likely to make in the future are equivalent to the existing definitions.

What this thesis really asserts is that no matter how you define algorithm, whether or not a problem is solvable or not is invariant. Thus a problem is solvable by some algorithm according to one definition if and only if it is solvable by some algorithm according to any other definition. Regarding the complexity measures, the sequential computation thesis saves us again, at least to the extent of invariance of feasible and infeasible solutions. If we implement binary search in LISP, Pascal or on a Turing machine, it will always have polynomial complexity.

Until comparatively recently people believed that there were no non-solvable formal problems. It was Hilbert (1862–1943) who unwittingly discovered the first known non-solvable problem. He suggested that every well-formed formula of mathematics was either true or false. This was the so-called *Entscheidungsproblem*. His idea was to find an algorithm that, given any wff, would determine whether or not it was true. In 1931 Gödel, with his *incompleteness theorem*, proved Hilbert wrong. Soon after, Church, Kleene, Post and Turing all discovered well-defined mathematical problems with no algorithmic solution. Although different definitions of algorithm were used, the Church–Turing thesis ensures that their examples were universally relevant.

The classic example of a non-computable problem is the halting problem. It should be of special interest to programmers. Anybody who has ever written a program is likely to have written one that, due to a design error, enters an infinite loop under certain conditions, and so fails to terminate. This can be very frustrating because it might mean we have to re-boot the system and even lose data. It would be very nice if there was a standard program, called, say, *Halt*, that would take as input any program P and would tell us whether or not P terminates. This seems reasonable, since *Halt* is something like a compiler; in fact, whereas a compiler examines a program and constructs executable code for it, *Halt* simply has to examine the program and give us a yes or no answer. Unfortunately, no such program can possibly exist.

Theorem 15.1 The halting problem is non-computable.

PROOF This is based on the proof presented in Goldschlager and Lister's book (1981). We argue by contradiction. Let us assume that there *is* an algorithm to solve the halting problem. Then this can be encoded as a program called *Halt* which performs the function described above. Thus *Halt* (P) will output *yes* if program P terminates and will output *no* otherwise.

Now since *Halt* works for any program P that is input then it will certainly work for the following recursive program *Silly*:

```
program Silly
 begin
  while Halt(Silly) = "yes" do writeln('Spurs')
 end.
```

Let us look at the behaviour of *Silly*. Whether or not the program terminates is given by the output of *Halt(Silly)*. If *Silly* terminates then we know that *Halt(Silly)* must output 'yes', and if it does not terminate then *Halt(Silly)* must output 'no'. Exactly one of these must be the case. Suppose then that *Silly* terminates. Then since *Halt(Silly)* is always 'yes', the loop in *Silly* is never exited. This means that *Silly* does not terminate. Thus we have a contradiction: *Silly* terminates implies *Silly* does not terminate.

Let us assume that *Silly* does not terminate. Then *Halt(Silly)* outputs 'no', in which case *Silly* terminates after execution of one line. Thus we have another contradiction: *Silly* does not terminate implies that *Silly* terminates.

The fact that we arrive at a contradiction in either case means that our original hypothesis must have been incorrect. Thus there is no algorithm that can determine whether an arbitrary program terminates, and the halting problem is unsolvable.

Example 15.16 Although it follows that there is no general purpose algorithm for determining whether or not an arbitrary program terminates, this does not mean that we cannot determine whether specific algorithms terminate or not. For example, it can be proved that the binary search algorithm always terminates for all inputs, and that the program

```
read(x);
while x=6 do writeln('Spurs')
```

does not terminate when we input $x = 6$. However, even in specific cases it may be very difficult to determine whether a given algorithm terminates.

Exercise 15.8 One of the most famous theorems in number theory is *Fermat's last theorem*, which asserts that there are no positive integers a, b and c such that $a^n + b^n = c^n$ when $n > 2$. Unfortunately, although the theorem is known to hold for many values of n, nobody has proved it for *every* value of $n > 2$. Use this information to explain why we cannot yet determine whether or not the following program terminates:

Program Fermat
  for $n = 3, 4, 5, \ldots$ do
    for $a = 1, 2, 3, \ldots$ do
      for $b = 1, 2, 3, \ldots, a$ do
        for $c = 2, 3, 4, \ldots, a + b$ do

if $a^n + b^n = c^n$
then output a, b, c and n, and halt

We have seen that some problems, which people believed could be solved algorithmically, are not solvable at all. In fact, it turns out that there are many more unsolvable problems than solvable ones. Moreover, most of the solvable problems do not have *feasible* solutions. Fortunately, the relatively small class of feasible problems is still sufficiently large and interesting to make computing a useful topic.

15.2.3 Decision problems

We now wish to return to the problem of classifying the complexity of problems. We restrict the class of formal problems to so-called *decision problems*.

Definition 15.8 Decision problem A decision problem is one whose outputs are just yes or no.

We have already seen two examples of decision problems: the halting problem and the searching problem. The halting problem is non-computable, while the searching problem is computable and feasible, with complexity $O(\log n)$.

Most classical problems have a decision problem associated with them which is equally as complex as the original problem. Thus, from the theoretical viewpoint, we can restrict our attention to decision problems. The following are some well known examples of decision problems:

Travelling salesman decision problem. Given n cities, the pairwise distances between them and a number $K > 0$, is it possible to complete a round trip in less than K miles?

Timetabling decision problem. Given a list of subjects and students enrolled in them, as well as the number of time slots available, is it possible to timetable the subjects so that no student has a clash?

Bin packing problem. Given n crates of different weights, are t trucks, each of which can carry a load w, sufficient to transport the weights?

Linear programming problem. Given an $m \times n$ integer matrix $\mathbf{M}$, vectors $\boldsymbol{d} = (d_1, \ldots, d_m)$ and $\boldsymbol{c} = (c_1, \ldots, c_n)$, and an integer b, is there a vector $\boldsymbol{x} = (x_1, \ldots, x_n)$ of rational numbers such that $\mathbf{M}\boldsymbol{x} \leq \boldsymbol{d}$ and $\boldsymbol{c} \cdot \boldsymbol{x} \geq b$?

Knapsack problem. Given a knapsack and a set of objects of known size, can we find a subset of the objects that exactly fill the knapsack?

Primality problem. Given an n digit number, is the number prime?

Compositeness problem. Given an n-digit integer a, can we find integers b, c such that $a = bc$?

n-Dimensional chess problem. Given any position in a game of $(n \times n)$ chess, is there a winning strategy for one player?

In Sec. 15.2.4 we shall consider the complexity of each of these problems.

Exercise 15.9 Write down the natural decision problem associated with the maximum problem described in Sec. 15.2.1. Compute the complexity of this problem.

15.2.4 Complexity classes

The class of decision problems whose complexity is polynomial is written $\mathscr{P}$. Thus $\mathscr{P}$ is precisely the class of feasible decision problems and hence, for example, the searching problem is in $\mathscr{P}$. On the other hand, it is known that the n-dimensional chess problem is not in $\mathscr{P}$ since the fastest possible algorithms must be exponential (the proof is beyond the scope of this chapter, however).

As far as practical computing is concerned, we are restricted to problems that are in $\mathscr{P}$. However, there is a huge class of important decision problems for which it is not known whether or not they lie in P. This includes the travelling salesman decision, timetabling decision, bin packing, primality and compositeness problems. In each case the fastest *known* solutions are exponential, but nobody has yet proved that no polynomial solution exists. However, each of these examples has another interesting property in common. Although they seem to admit no feasible solution, in each case it is easy (meaning there is a polynomial algorithm) to *check* whether a proposed 'yes' solution is correct.

Example 15.17 Consider the compositeness problem. Although this has no known feasible solution, it is easy to check in general whether a proposed solution of the form $a = bc$ is correct or not; we simply multiply b and c together. Even a 'slow' multiplication algorithm, like the high school method, is polynomial with complexity $O(n^2)$, where a and b are n-digit numbers.

Example 15.18 In the case of the travelling salesman decision problem, there is no known polynomial algorithm that will always determine if the shortest route is less than some threshold figure K. However, it is easy to determine in general whether a proposed route is less than the threshold figure. We just sum the $n - 1$ distances in the proposed route and compare the answer with K. This requires just $O(n)$ additions and comparisons.

Definition 15.9 $\mathscr{NP}$ problems The class of decision problems for which it is feasible to check whether a proposed solution is correct is called $\mathscr{NP}$.

Thus the compositeness problem and the travelling salesman decision problem are both in $\mathscr{NP}$.

Exercise 15.10 Show that the bin packing, knapsack and timetabling decision problems are in $\mathscr{NP}$.

It can also be shown that the primality problem is in $\mathscr{NP}$ but this is by no means obvious. The same is true for the normal, (8×8), game of chess. Now $\mathscr{P} \subseteq \mathscr{NP}$, since if it is possible to construct a polynomial solution then we can use the same algorithm to check any proposed solution.

What makes the set $\mathscr{NP}$ interesting is that, as well as containing all the feasible problems, it contains many of the open problems that different disciplines have been trying to solve for many years. What is remarkable is that, despite numerous attempts by some of the world's greatest mathematicians, it is not known whether or not $\mathscr{P} = \mathscr{NP}$. In 1971 Cook discovered that a number of open problems were among the hardest in $\mathscr{NP}$ in the following sense: if a polynomial time algorithm were ever found for one of these problems then there would be a polynomial time algorithm for every problem in $\mathscr{NP}$. Any problem that is one of these hardest problems is said to be *$\mathscr{NP}$-complete*. Thus, if any $\mathscr{NP}$-complete problem is ever shown to have a polynomial algorithm then we would know that $\mathscr{P} = \mathscr{NP}$. In fact, it is strongly conjectured that

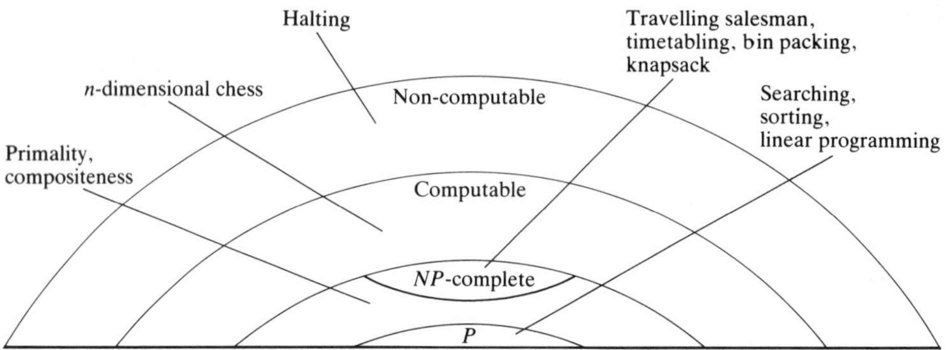

Figure 15.5 Schematic summary of our current state of knowledge of complexity classes.

$\mathscr{P} \neq \mathscr{NP}$. A schematic summary of our current state of knowledge of complexity classes is shown in Fig. 15.5.

The travelling salesman, knapsack, bin packing and timetabling problems have all been proved to be $\mathscr{NP}$-complete. Hundreds of important problems from different disciplines have also been shown to be $\mathscr{NP}$-complete and hence computationally equivalent. Because of the strong $\mathscr{P} \neq \mathscr{NP}$ conjecture, a proof that any specific problem is $\mathscr{NP}$-complete is considered to be sufficient evidence that the problem is practically infeasible. If $\mathscr{P} \neq \mathscr{NP}$ were true, it is reasonable to ask if there are any problems that are in $\mathscr{NP} \setminus \mathscr{P}$ but are not in $\mathscr{NP}$-complete. It is strongly conjectured that the primality problem and its dual, compositeness, are examples of such problems. This belief is based on the fact that there are polynomial algorithms that, in a sense to be made precise in Sec. 15.2.5, almost always correctly solve these problems. Interestingly, until quite recently, it was conjectured that the linear programming problem was another example of a problem in $\mathscr{NP} \setminus \mathscr{P}$, but not in $\mathscr{NP}$-complete. This was because the Simplex algorithm, which everybody used to solve the problem, although known to be exponential, runs in polynomial time for almost all inputs. However, in the late 1970s a correct polynomial solution for the linear programming problem was discovered, hence proving that linear programming is in $\mathscr{P}$. This should act as a warning to you not to believe all mathematicians' conjectures.

15.2.5 Confronting difficult problems

Proving that a problem is $\mathscr{NP}$-complete might seem at first glance to be a rather negative and purely theoretical activity. In fact, such knowledge can be used to practical effect. In Chapter 16 we shall explain the relevance of this to cryptography. Also, knowing that a problem is $\mathscr{NP}$-complete can save much unnecessary work in attempting to find a polynomial solution. That is the good news. The bad news is that $\mathscr{NP}$-complete problems seem to crop up all over the place. They just will not go away, and in many situations we desperately need to find some kind of feasible solution. Since we know it is pointless to seek a correct polynomial solution, we need to lower our sights and attempt to find some pragmatic, imperfect or partial solution. In fact, there are a number of possibilities:

1 *Find a probabilistic polynomial algorithm.* This is the next best thing to a correct algorithm. A probabilistic algorithm is one that is correct for all but a very small number of cases. Unfortunately there are not many hard problems that admit such an algorithm. One of the few that does, however, is particularly important, as we shall see in Chapter 16. This is the primality problem. The details of the algorithm may be found in Harel (1987). It is based on the selection of k random numbers between 1 and $a - 1$ where a is the n-digit number to be tested for primality. It turns out that if a is prime then the algorithm always correctly answers 'yes'; if a is not prime, then there is a small probability that the algorithm will erroneously answer 'yes' rather than 'no'. However, this probability is less than $1/2^k$. By choosing a reasonably large number k of random numbers, like 100, this probability of error is less than the probability of the hardware failing. Because such a good probabilistic polynomial algorithm exists, we think of the primality problem, and its dual compositeness, as being effectively feasible. This compares starkly with the related factorization problem.

2 *Restrict the problem somehow to suit our needs and then see if this is in $\mathscr{P}$.* For example, consider the bin packing problem. If the capacity w of each truck is the same then the problem is solvable in polynomial time by exhaustive search. In the case of the timetabling problem there are polynomial solutions in the restricted case where there are less than three subjects.

3 *Find an approximate solution which is in $\mathscr{P}$.* There are two types of approximate solutions. On the one hand we can have a solution that, although not always the optimal answer, will not be too far away in every case. For example, there are polynomial algorithms that, although not solving the travelling salesman problem, will always compute a route that is never more than 60 per cent longer than the optimal route. This may be satisfactory in certain cases. Alternatively, we can have a solution that might in very rare cases be wildly wrong, but otherwise comes very close to an optimal solution.

4 *Introduce parallelism.* This means using more than one independent processor. This can certainly help to speed up certain algorithms. For example, when n^2 processors are used, there is a parallel algorithm for multiplication of n-digit numbers which is $O(\log n)$. This is much better than can be achieved sequentially. Unfortunately, it has been proved that parallelism cannot really help with infeasible problems. This is because we can only turn an exponential algorithm into a polynomial time parallel algorithm by introducing an exponential number of processors. Thus we merely trade off infeasible time for infeasible hardware resources.

15.3 SUMMARY

The popular notion of complexity of algorithms generally refers to the algorithms' efficiency in terms of machine resource usage. We introduced the notion of a formal problem and showed that algorithms are just solutions to such problems. Many formal problems have a size associated with each instance of the problem. For example, the size of the problem of sorting lists is the number of elements in the list. The time complexity function of an algorithm is the number of primitive machine operations required to run the algorithm for a given size. Algorithmic efficiency can be characterized by the asymptotic value of this function. There is a notation, the big O notation, that is a robust measure of the asymptotic value of functions.

Feasible algorithms are those whose big O value is polynomial. The sequential time thesis asserts that the property of feasibility is machine independent. The complexity of a formal problem is the big O value of an optimal solution of the problem. For example, the sorting problem is $O(n \log n)$. Unfortunately, most formal problems have no solution at all. A classic example of one such problem is the halting problem. For many other important problems we do not know the complexity. One major class of problems has the strange property that while it is easy to check a proposed solution, it appears to be very difficult to construct a complete algorithmic solution. These problems are called $\mathcal{NP}$ problems. The most difficult problems in this class, which includes the travelling salesman problem and the timetabling problem, are called $\mathcal{NP}$-complete. It is strongly conjectured that these problems are not feasible. In the absence of a complete solution to problems like those in $\mathcal{NP}$-complete we may need to find imperfect, or partial, solutions.

FURTHER READING

For a definitive overview of the theory of algorithms Harel (1987) is highly recommended, while Goldschlager and Lister's book (1981) provides a good introduction. For an extensive and formal treatment of computational complexity, see the book by Garey and Johnson (1979); this includes an exhaustive appendix detailing current knowledge about the complexity of hundreds of problems classified by subject area.

Chapter 16

CODING THEORY

This chapter is concerned with how to communicate information accurately and securely. In Sec. 16.1 we explain the two major types of problems that can jeopardize these requirements. A noisy channel over which we transmit our information can cause a loss of *accuracy* in the sense that the receiver receives something other than the message sent. An eavesdropper on the channel can cause a loss of *security*, meaning that the contents of the message become known to an unauthorized third party. To counter the problem of a noisy channel we use *error correcting codes*, described in Sec. 16.2. To counter the problem of the eavesdropper we use *cryptographic codes*, described in Sec. 16.3. In both these sections we explain techniques for encoding and decoding. We shall explain the advantages and disadvantages of various specific codes, and how and where these are used in practice. In Sec. 16.3 we explain how certain cryptographic codes can be easily adapted to solve other, related, security problems like that of creating and verifying digital signatures.

Coding theory provides some of the most important and exciting applications of discrete mathematics. The best coding techniques are based on a deep understanding of various branches of abstract algebra (notably linear algebra, group theory, finite fields), probability theory, combinatorics, computational and algorithmic complexity, plus all the introductory topics described in Chapter 2. Although it is beyond our scope to explore in detail all these dependencies, we aim to provide a thorough overview.

16.1 MESSAGE COMMUNICATION SYSTEMS

The problem of communication is a common theme in the various branches of coding theory.

Definition 16.1 Communication Communication is the transmission of information through some channel.

In this context, information is the general term for any kind of message. It could be a telephone conversation, an instruction at a cash point machine to your bank, a command to a computer, a computer program stored on disk or an electronic transfer of funds. The *channel* is the general term for any communicating medium. This could,

Figure 16.1 Conceptual view of communication.

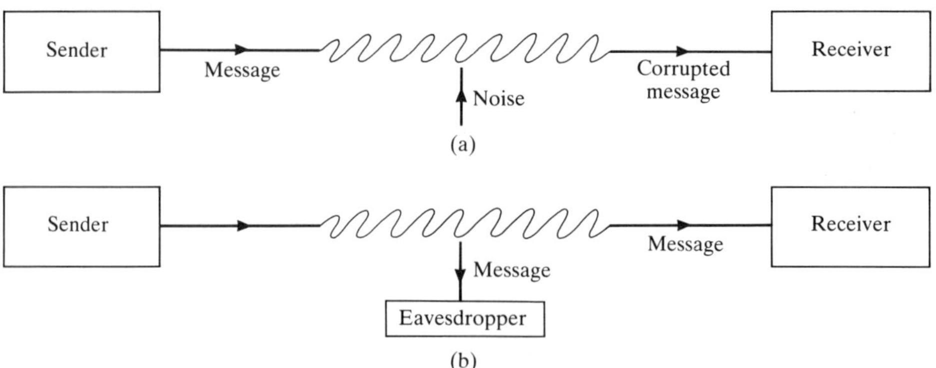

Figure 16.2 Possible problems in communication.

Figure 16.3 Message encoding and decoding.

for example, be an optical fibre or copper cable, the UK post office mail system, a computer bus or simply the air. A conceptual view of communication is given in Fig. 16.1. There are two major problems that can occur when we communicate in this way:

1 *Noise problem.* The message that the sender sends might not be the one that the receiver receives; it could be corrupted either accidentally or deliberately (Fig.16.2(a)).
2 *Interception problem.* During transmission, the message could be intercepted by somebody other than the receiver, either by accident or deliberately (Fig. 16.2(b)).

Example 16.1 Consider a telephone conversation. Noise on the channel can easily ensure that a sender's message is not the one that the receiver receives; this is accidental corruption. Deliberate corruption could occur by a third party creating unnecessary noise on the channel. A cross-line is an example of accidental message interception by a third party, while a wire-tap is an example of deliberate third party interception.

The way we counter both the noise and interception problems is to send an encoded version of the message instead of sending the original message. The encoded version must be decoded by the receiver. This is illustrated in Fig. 16.3. The two different types of problems give rise to different classes of codes:

1 For the noise problem, the encoded message must provide sufficient *redundancy* to counter the effect of noise and enable the receiver to decode the original message. Codes in this class are called *error correcting, and detecting, codes*.
2 For the interception problem we have to encode the message in such a way that it cannot be understood by a possible interceptor, but *can* still be decoded by the receiver. Codes in this class are called *cryptographic codes*.

Strictly speaking, there is one other class of codes that we need to consider separately. These are codes that are simply alternative, but equivalent, representations of the original message. As a very simple example, suppose the only messages we ever need to send are 'yes' and 'no'. Then representing 'yes' and 'no' by '1' and '0' respectively is an alternative but equivalent representation. Nevertheless, it is still common to call this an encoding. Codes like this are relevant when the equivalent representation is in a notation that is simpler to use or easier to analyse. A classic example is the ASCII binary encoding of the normal character set:

... ...
a 1000001
b 1000010
c 1000011
... ...

When you type a message *print* on your computer keyboard, the ASCII coded version

1010000 1010010 1001001 1001110 1010100

is the message that is actually sent to the CPU. The ASCII encoding actually takes place before transmission of the resulting instruction.

Although these types of codes cannot help us with either of our communication problems, they are a useful precursor for our solutions. They allow us to simplify the communication model. Instead of considering messages as arbitrary strings in arbitrary languages (natural or otherwise), we can assume an equivalent binary string such as the ASCII representation. Thus we restrict our attention to messages that are strings over the alphabet $\{0, 1\}$. In this way we assume that we have already performed a transformation that is itself an encoding, namely into an equivalent representation. This assumption is made acceptable by the impact of digital technology.

16.2 ERROR CORRECTING CODES

In this section we look at how we can tolerate errors that are introduced because of noise on the channel. We begin by describing a simple model of a noisy channel. We then consider families of error correcting codes that have varying properties. We look at the repetition codes, which are good at correcting errors but can be prohibitively slow to transmit. We look at the parity check codes, which are fast to transmit but not very good at error correcting. In order to get the right balance between speed of transmission and error correction capability, we then look at some examples of specific families of codes that achieve this balance. All the example codes discussed in the section turn out to be *groups* in the sense of Chapter 8. Such codes have some very nice properties and can be encoded and decoded easily.

16.2.1 Binary symmetric channels

If we send a 1 we usually expect the receiver to receive a 1, and if we send a 0 we usually expect the receiver to receive a 0. However, occasionally an error is introduced due to noise on the channel. The only type of error we are interested in is when $0 \mapsto 1$ or $1 \mapsto 0$. For simplicity we ignore the other possibilities, namely $0 \mapsto ?$ and $1 \mapsto ?$, because in many realistic situations a decision to send a 0 or a 1 is made by the medium. We shall also assume that there are fixed probabilities of error associated with the channel. Specifically, we assume that there is fixed probability p of sending a

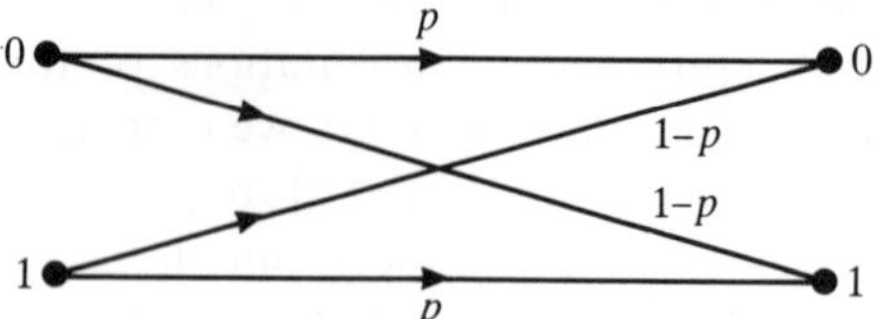

Figure 16.4 Binary symmetric channel.

0 as a 1, or a 1 as a 0. Thus we speak about a *binary symmetric channel* as illustrated in Fig. 16.4. We also treat successive transmissions as independent events. Thus, it follows from Theorem 14.9 on page 360 that the probability of two successive errors is p^2.

Example 16.2 Consider a binary symmetric channel in which $p = 0.1$. We wish to compute the probability P that the message 1010 is received as 1100 over this channel. First we note that, by our independence assumption,

$$P(1 \mapsto 1, 0 \mapsto 1, 1 \mapsto 0, 1 \mapsto 1) = P(1 \mapsto 1).P(0 \mapsto 1).P(1 \mapsto 0).P(1 \mapsto 1)$$

However, $P(1 \mapsto 1).P(0 \mapsto 1).P(1 \mapsto 0).P(1 \mapsto 1) = (0.9)(0.1)(0.1)(0.9) = 0.0081$ and so the solution is 0.0081.

Exercise 16.1 In a binary symmetric channel in which $p = 0.2$, compute the probability that the message 11001 is received as 10101.

Example 16.3 Suppose we use the ASCII representation discussed in Sec. 16.1, and that we transmit across a binary symmetric channel in which $p = 0.1$. If we transmit the letter b (= 1000010), then the probability that a single error occurs on the last digit is 0.053 (specifically $P(1000010 \mapsto 1000011) = 0.053$). However, the received string 1000011 corresponds to the letter c. Thus over 1 out of 20 times the message b is erroneously received as a c. In special circumstances this probability of error may be acceptable. However, if the letters represented exam grades and your future depended on getting a b rather than a c, then you may not be too happy about this situation.

In Example 16.3 a single bit of erroneous information leads to the *wrong* (as opposed to just a corrupted) message being received. In virtually all communication problems this is unacceptable. So how can we guard against it? The obvious thing to do is to add some *redundancy* to the original message which will allow us to tolerate some corrupted bits of information. It is redundancy in natural language that enables us, more often than not, to correctly understand a message across a crackling telephone line. It is precisely the same principle that is embodied in error correcting codes.

Exercise 16.2 The probability of error in a binary symmetric channel is p. If the transmitted message has n bits, where $n > 6$, calculate the following probabilities. You should assume that occurrences of errors are binomially distributed in the sense of Sec.14.4.5.

(a) That the sixth bit is transmitted correctly.

(b) That no errors occur at all.

(c) That the number of errors is at most two.

16.2.2 Repetition codes

Since we have restricted our messages to strings of 0's and 1's, the simplest way to build redundancy into our message is to replace each occurrence of 0 by a string of 0's and each occurrence of 1 by a string of 1's. Let us suppose that each occurrence of 0 is encoded as 000 and that each occurrence of 1 is encoded as 111. The strings 000 and 111 are called *codewords*. The set of codewords, in this case the two-element set $\{000, 111\}$, is called a *code*; specifically it is the *repetition code of length 3*. More generally, the set

$$\{\overbrace{000...000}^{n}, \overbrace{111...111}^{n}\}$$

is called the *repetition code of length n*.

Exercise 16.3 Suppose that the probability of error in the channel is 0.1. Show that the probability that the message 000 is received as either 011, 110, 101 or 111 is 0.028. For the repetition code of length 3, deduce that the probability of receiving a codeword in which at most one bit is in error is 0.972.

Suppose now that we use the repetition code of length 3 to send our messages 0 and 1. We encode 0 as 000 and 1 as 111. Imagine yourself as the intended receiver of the message 0. You know that the message is encoded as one of the two codewords 000 or 111. You will receive a 3-bit string. Assuming that the probability of error in the channel is small, then if we receive the message as either 000, 100, 010 or 001, the sent encoded message would be more likely to be 000 than 111.

Example 16.4 Suppose $p = 0.1$ and that E is the event 'string received is 000'. Let A_1 be the event 'message sent is 000', and let A_2 be the event 'message sent is 111'. Using conditional probabilities, as in Axiom 14.4 on page 357, we wish to show that $P(A_1/E) > P(A_2/E)$; that is if we know that 000 is received then it is more likely that 000 was sent than it is that 111 was sent. The events E, A_1 and A_2 satisfy the conditions stated in Theorem 14.12. Consequently, by Theorem 14.12, we compute

$$\begin{aligned} P(A_1/E) &= \frac{P(A_1)P(E/A_1)}{P(A_1)P(E/A_1) + P(A_2)P(E/A_2)} \\ &= \frac{\frac{1}{2}(0.9)(0.9)(0.9)}{\frac{1}{2}(0.9)(0.9)(0.9) + \frac{1}{2}(0.1)(0.1)(0.1)} = 0.9986 \end{aligned}$$

So the probability that 000 was sent given that 000 is received is 0.9986, compared with a probability of 0.0014 that 111 was sent if 000 is received.

Exercise 16.4 With the same assumptions as in Example 16.4, show that the probability that 000 was sent given that 100 is received is 0.9, compared with a probability of 0.1 that 111 was sent if 100 is received.

Definition 16.2 Decoding procedure for repetition code of length 3 If any of the strings 000, 100, 010 or 001 are received then decode the message as the codeword 000. If any of the strings 111, 110, 101 or 011 are received then decode the message as the codeword 111.

With this procedure we improve our chances of receiving the correct message sent.

Example 16.5 Suppose that the probability of error in the channel is 0.1 and that the message 0, coded as 000, is sent. The probability that this message is received as one of 000, 001, 010 or 100 is 0.972, by Exercise 16.3. Hence, using the decoding procedure, the probability of receiving the correct message is 0.972. This compares favourably with what happens when we use no encoding. If we just send 0 as 0, the probability of receiving 0 is only 0.9.

By using redundancy that is implicit in the repetition code of length 3, our decoding procedure will always *tolerate* up to one error in transmission. This means that, provided at most one of the bits is corrupted during transmission, we will still decode the correct message. Of course, if two or three of the bits are corrupted (which is unlikely) then our decoding procedure will decode the wrong message. To tolerate more errors in transmission and get an even higher probability of successfully decoding the original message, we need to use repetition codes of longer length than 3.

Definition 16.3 Decoding procedure for repetition code of length *n* Decode a received string of length *n* as the codeword:

00...0 if x contains less than $n/2$ 1's and
11...1 if x contains more than $n/2$ 1's.

Example 16.6 Suppose we are using the repetition code of length 5. If we receive 01010 then we decode it as 00000. If we receive 11010 then we decode it as 11111. If at most two errors occur in transmission of a codeword then the codeword will still be correctly decoded. If the probability of error on the channel is 0.1, then it follows from the binomial distribution that the probability of decoding the correct codeword is

$$(0.9)^5 + \binom{5}{1}(0.9)^4(0.1) + \binom{5}{2}(0.9)^3(0.1)^2 = 0.99$$

Example 16.7 When n is even, Def. 16.3 does not specify how to decode strings that have exactly $n/2$ 1's. This is because the codewords 00...0 and 11...1 were equally likely to have been sent. Consider the repetition code of length 6. If we receive the message 010101, then we *know* that at least three errors have occurred. Hence, we say the code can *detect* up to three errors. Assuming that exactly three errors have occurred, which is the most likely outcome since the probability of channel error is assumed to be small, we cannot choose between which of the codewords 000000 or 111111 was most likely to have been sent. The safest thing to do might be to ask for the message to be re-sent since there were so many errors. If there were two errors, say 000000 is sent as 010010, then we can not only detect these two errors but correct them as well.

Theorem 16.1 Let $m \in \mathbb{N}^+$. Then the repetition code of length $2m + 1$ can correct up to m errors. If we have a repetition code of even length $2m$ then we can detect up to m errors and correct up to $m - 1$ errors.

Example 16.8 The repetition code of length 7 is three-error correcting. This code cannot correct four errors since if 000000 is received as 110101 it will be decoded wrongly as 111111. The repetition code of length 8 is four-error detecting and three-error correcting.

Exercise 16.5 Show that the repetition code of length 13 can correct up to six errors in each codeword. In what sense is the repetition code of length 14 superior?

In theory it would appear that the repetition codes can solve all our requirements for error correcting codes. Assuming that the probability of error in the channel is small (in fact we need only assume it is less than 0.5), then we can satisfy any requirements for error correction. We just choose a repetition code of sufficiently large n. If, for example, we want a seven-error correcting code then we just use the repetition code of length 15. Unfortunately there is a drawback. All our messages, in the form of binary strings, must expand by a factor of 15 when we encode them. For example, the message 011 has to be encoded as: 000000000000000 111111111111111 111111111111111.

Thus, the cost of high error correction capability is that we must transmit very long messages that yield comparatively little information. Formally, we define:

Definition 16.4 Information rate of a code For any code C,

$$\text{Information rate of } C = \frac{\text{length of message}}{\text{length of codeword}}$$

Hence, the repetition code of length n has information rate $1/n$. There is a trade-off between error correction capability and the information rate: as the length of the codeword increases, the probability of an error in decoding decreases, but so does the information rate. A code with a high error correction capability is said to be *reliable*, while a code with a high information rate is said to be *fast*. By choosing n sufficiently large, we get repetition codes that are as reliable as we want, but very slow to transmit.

16.2.3 Parity check codes

In this section we describe a family of codes that are very fast to transmit but have low reliability. We assume that any message we wish to encode is made up of fixed length binary strings, which we shall refer to as *blocks*. For example, all textual messages are viewed as being made up from blocks corresponding to ASCII codewords, and all messages that are computer files are made up of computer words. These words are binary strings of fixed length such as 8, 16 or 32. We can restrict our discussion to encoding just the primitive blocks since, once these are known, we can then encode arbitrary messages made up from these.

Suppose that our blocks have fixed length j. Then there are 2^j different possible blocks, since there are 2^j binary strings of length j. A very simple encoding for this set of blocks is to add a single *parity* bit to the end of each block. Specifically, we add a 1 to the block x if there are an odd number of 1's in x, and a 0 otherwise. The resulting codewords all have length $k = j + 1$.

Example 16.9 For $j = 3$, and hence $k = 4$, we have the parity bit encoding:

$$\begin{array}{lcl} 000 & \mapsto & 0000 \\ 100 & \mapsto & 1001 \\ 010 & \mapsto & 0101 \\ 001 & \mapsto & 0011 \\ 110 & \mapsto & 1100 \\ 011 & \mapsto & 0110 \\ 101 & \mapsto & 1010 \\ 111 & \mapsto & 1111 \end{array}$$

In general, there are 2^{k-1} codewords in the set of codewords that is called *the parity check code of length k*.

Exercise 16.6 Show that the parity check code of length k consists of the 2^{k-1} binary strings of length k that have an even number of 1's. Write out in full the encoding procedure used in the parity check code of length 5.

The decoding procedure for parity check codes is very simple. Suppose the string x is received. If x is a codeword then we decode x as the codeword x. If x is not a codeword, then we know that at least one error in transmission has occurred, but we do not know how to correct it.

Example 16.10 Using the parity check code of length 4, the message 011 is encoded as 0110. If this is erroneously transmitted as 0100 then the receiver knows that an error has occurred because the received message is not a valid parity check codeword. The receiver assumes the most likely scenario that a single error has occurred. However, each of the messages 0000 (from 000), 1100 (from 110), 0101 (from 010) or 0110 (from 011) is then equally likely to have been sent.

The information rate of the parity check code of length k is $(k-1)/k$. This means that we can get it is as close as we like to the optimum, 1, by choosing k sufficiently large. Unfortunately, these codes are useless at error correction, because they only *detect* a single error.

Exercise 16.7 Suppose the message 0111 is received. How would you decode this?

Thus the parity check codes are one-error detecting, but zero-error correcting codes. These codes cannot even detect two errors. Suppose 0110 is transmitted with two errors as 1010. Then the received message is itself a valid codeword, and hence would be erroneously decoded as 1010.

16.2.4 General principles of error correcting codes

We now formalize some of the notions we have seen so far.

Definition 16.5 Code A code C of length n is a subset of $\mathbb{Z}_2^n$, the set of n-dimensional binary vectors. The elements of C are called the codewords.

Definition 16.6 Size and weight of a code The size of a code C is just the number of codewords. The weight of a codeword is just the number of 1's in it.

Example 16.11

(a) For any n, the set P_n of n-bit binary strings of even weight is precisely the parity check code of length n. Its size is 2^{n-1}.

(b) For any n, the set R_n of n-bit binary strings of weight 0 or n is precisely the repetition code of length n. It has two codewords 00...0 and 11...1, so its size is 2.

Definition 16.7 Encoding Encoding is a function $E: M \to C$ where M is a subset of $\mathbb{Z}_2^m$ (called the set of messages) and C is a code of length $n \geq m$.

Example 16.12 For the repetition code R_5 of length 5, the encoding function E maps 0 to 00000 and 1 to 11111. For the parity check code P_3 of length 3, $E(00) = 000$, $E(01) = 011$, $E(10) = 101$ and $E(11) = 110$. Now suppose we have the message string 001001 to transmit. If we use the code P_3, we need to break the message into blocks of length 2; that is we treat 001001 as 00 10 01, which we would encode as 000 101 011. Using R_5 we would encode 001001 in blocks of length 1; that is we would encode it as 00000 11111 00000 11111.

Exercise 16.8 Consider the message string 101101101101010. By subdivision of the string into suitable blocks as necessary, encode this string using:

(a) repetition code of length 3,

(b) parity check code of length 6.

Definition 16.8 Decoding Suppose C is a code of length n. Then decoding is a function $D : \mathbb{Z}_2^n \to C \cup \{\perp\}$ where $\perp$ represents an undefined element.

To provide a formal generalization of the specific decoding procedures we have seen so far, we need to define the notion of *difference* between binary strings.

Definition 16.9 Hamming distance If x and y are two binary strings of length n, then the Hamming distance, written $d(x, y)$, between x and y is the number of positions in which x and y differ.

Example 16.13 If $x = 0010011$ and $y = 1011001$ then $d(x, y) = 3$ since x and y differ in their first, fourth and sixth positions.

Definition 16.10 Maximum likelihood decoding Suppose C is a code of length n. Then the maximum likelihood decoding is the function $D : \mathbb{Z}_2^n \to C \cup \{\perp\}$ defined by $D(x) = y$ if there is a unique codeword y for which $d(x, y)$ is minimal. If there is no unique codeword at minimal distance from x then $D(x) = \perp$.

Example 16.14 Maximum likelihood decoding is precisely the decoding procedure that we used for both the repetition codes and the parity check codes. For the repetition code R_n, where n is odd, the decoding procedure D will always return a valid codeword. When n is even, $D(x) = \perp$ for each x containing $n/2$ 0's. This is because x has an equal Hamming distance of $n/2$ from each of the two codewords 00...0 and 11...1.

For the parity check codes of length $n > 2$, $D(x) = \perp$ for any x containing an odd number of 1's, since it will have an equal Hamming distance from n different codewords. For example, when $n = 3$ the codeword 101 has Hamming distance 2 from each of the codewords 110, 011 and 000. For each codeword x containing an even number of 1's, $D(x) = x$ since x is the unique codeword whose Hamming distance from x is 0.

Definition 16.11 Hamming distance of a code Let C be any code. The Hamming distance of C, written $d(C)$, is the minimum Hamming distance between distinct codewords of C. Thus $d(C) = \min d(x, y)$ where $x, y \in C$ and $x \neq y$.

Example 16.15 The repetition code of length n has Hamming distance n. This is because it contains just two codewords 00...0 and 11...1, and the Hamming distance between these is n.

Example 16.16 The parity check code of length $n \geq 2$ has Hamming distance 2. This is because, by Exercise 16.6, the code is the set E_n of binary strings of length n that have an even number of 1's. Suppose $x, y \in E_n$, with $x \neq y$. We cannot have $d(x, y) = 1$ for this could only happen if one of x and y has an odd number of 1's. Hence $d(E_n) \geq 2$. For any codeword x we can find a codeword y for which $d(x, y)=2$; we just change the parity of exactly two bits in x. Hence $d(E_n) = 2$.

Exercise 16.9 Compute the Hamming distance of the code $C = \{0000, 1100, 0011, 1111\}$.

In Example 16.15 we showed that the repetition code of length n has Hamming distance n. From Theorem 16.1, this code is an e-error correcting code where e is the largest integer $\leq (n-1)/2$. This is a special case of the following theorem which shows that the Hamming distance of any code determines its error correcting capability:

Message				Codeword						
0	0	0	↦	0	0	0	0	0	0	0
1	0	0	↦	1	0	0	1	0	1	1
0	1	0	↦	0	1	0	1	1	1	0
0	0	1	↦	0	0	1	0	1	1	1
1	1	0	↦	1	1	0	0	1	0	1
0	1	1	↦	0	1	1	1	0	0	1
1	0	1	↦	1	0	1	1	1	0	0
1	1	1	↦	1	1	1	0	0	1	0

Figure 16.5 Hamming code of length 7.

Theorem 16.2 A code C of Hamming distance d is an e-error correcting code where e is the largest integer $\leq (d-1)/2$.

Example 16.17 Consider the code $C = \{(001000), (100101), (011110), (111011)\}$. It is easy to see that $d(C) = 3$. It follows from Theorem 16.2 that this set of words could be used as a one-error correcting code. We can use it to encode messages of length 2 by the encoding procedure $00 \mapsto 001000$, $10 \mapsto 100101$, $01 \mapsto 011110$, $11 \mapsto 111011$. The information rate of C is $\frac{1}{3}$.

Exercise 16.10 Use Theorem 16.2 to deduce that the parity check codes are zero-error correcting.

Exercise 16.11 Encode the message 0101100011 using the code of Example 16.17, by subdivision of the string into suitable blocks.

Exercise 16.12 Write down in full the following codes:

(a) The repetition codes of length 2,3,4,5 and 6 respectively

(b) The parity check codes of length 3,4 and 5 respectively

In each case calculate the information rate, minimum distance and error correcting capacity.

16.2.5 Codes that are reliable and fast

We have seen that the repetition codes have high reliability but a low information rate. The parity check codes have a high information rate but low reliability. Ideally we want to strike a balance between the two. We would like codes that have high reliability, but not at the expense of a low information rate which results in slow and costly encoding and decoding.

Hamming codes A family of codes that have a reasonable balance between error correction capability and information rate are the *Hamming codes*. The simplest code in this family, the Hamming code of length 7, is shown in Fig. 16.5. The easiest way to think of this code is that it encodes all 3-bit strings by adding four extra bits of information. These extra bits may be thought of as a generalized version of the parity check digits we saw for the parity check codes.

It is easy to see that this Hamming code has minimum distance 4, so, by Theorem 16.2, it is one-error correcting. Since it encodes all messages of length 3, this code has an information rate of $\frac{3}{7}$. This is an improvement on the best one-error correcting code we have seen so far, namely the repetition code of length 3, whose information rate is $\frac{1}{3}$.

Example 16.18 To use the Hamming code of length 7 to encode the message $M = 101000110$, we break M into blocks of length 3. These are 101, 000 and 110 respectively. They are encoded respectively as 1011100, 0000000 and 1100101. The message sent is a 21-bit string. Suppose that errors in the ninth and twentieth positions cause the receiver to receive the string 1011100 0100000 1100111. Using maximum likelihood decoding the receiver can correctly decode the original message.

Exercise 16.13 Consider the message string 101101101101010. By subdivision of the string into suitable blocks as necessary, encode this string using the Hamming code of length 7.

Exercise 16.14 Suppose that the following message string is received after transmission:

11010110010111101010010000100111001

(a) If it is known that the repetition code of length 5 was used, what was the original message? State carefully any assumptions you are making in your decoding procedure and also what might go wrong if these assumptions are incorrect.

(b) Decode the message given that the Hamming code of length 7 was used, again stating any assumptions you make.

Reed Müller codes There are a number of interesting and useful families of error correcting codes that achieve a better balance between reliability and speed than is possible with the Hamming codes. The Reed Müller codes is one such family. It is beyond the scope of this chapter to describe these in any detail but the following example illustrates their properties and applications.

Example 16.19 The Mariner 9 spacecraft to Mars had to transmit colour photographs of the planet's landscape back to Earth. Each photograph consisted of a grid of tiny pixels—several hundreds of thousands in all. Each pixel could be one of several thousand colour codes, corresponding to colour spectrum and light intensity. Thus each message, transmitted as a photograph, consisted of several million binary bits of information. An acceptably clear photograph would be received if up to seven errors could be corrected per 32 bits of coded message. A repetition code of length at least 15 would satisfy this requirement. This is because 30 bits of coded information consists of two codewords, and at worst all seven errors could occur in one of the two codewords; these would be corrected. Unfortunately, the repetition code of length 15 has an information rate $1/15$, which was unacceptably low for this real-time application; it would simply take too long for the message to be received back on Earth. The problem was solved by using a Reed Müller code, which has length 32, is seven-error correcting and has an information rate of $6/32$.

Exercise 16.15 Why would a repetition code of length < 15 not satisfy the error correction requirement of the Mariner 9?

Goppa codes The Goppa family of codes also achieves a better balance than the Hamming codes between reliability and speed. For each m and t for which $2^m \geq mt$, there is a Goppa code which has length $n = 2^m$ and which is t-error correcting. The number of codewords is at least 2^{n-mt}, so the message strings have length at least $n - mt$. Therefore, if we take $m = 4$ and $t = 3$ this means that there is a three-error correcting Goppa code of length 16 that encodes message strings of length 4. Thus, the code has information rate $1/4$. This compares very favourably with the best three-error correcting repetition code R_7 whose information rate is $1/7$.

16.2.6 Group codes

All of the examples of codes considered so far have a special property in common. They are commutative groups as defined in Sec. 8.1.1. In fact, they are all subgroups of the group $(\mathbb{Z}_2^n, \oplus)$ for some n where $\oplus$ is the operation of component-wise modulo 2 addition. This means that the addition modulo 2 of any two codewords in C yields another codeword in C, that C contains the zero vector and also that every codeword has an inverse (with respect to $\oplus$) in C.

Example 16.20 Consider the parity check code $E_3 = \{000, 101, 110, 011\}$. The zero vector $000 \in E_3$. It is easily checked that adding codewords always results in another codeword: $101 \oplus 110 = 011 \in E_3$, $101 \oplus 011 = 101$, ... Finally, each codeword c has an inverse in C, namely c itself. For example, $101 \oplus 101 = 000$ ....

Exercise 16.16 Show that the repetition codes R_n, the parity check codes E_n and the Hamming code of length 7 are all group codes.

Exercise 16.17 Show that the code $C = \{0000, 1100, 0110, 0011, 1010, 1001, 0101\}$ is not a group code.

Exercise 16.18 Show that in a group code C, the Hamming distance $d(C)$ is always equal to the minimum weight of the non-zero codewords. Deduce that the Hamming distance of the Hamming code of length 7 is 4.

The group codes are most used in practice. They have a number of nice properties, but above all they are easy to encode and decode. This is because such codes can be characterized by a *generator matrix* and a *parity check matrix*.

Example 16.21 Consider the Hamming code C of length 7. This maps any 3-bit string into an encoded 7-bit string. The matrix

$$\mathbf{G} = \begin{pmatrix} 1 & 0 & 0 \\ 0 & 1 & 0 \\ 0 & 0 & 1 \\ 1 & 1 & 0 \\ 0 & 1 & 1 \\ 1 & 1 & 1 \\ 1 & 0 & 1 \end{pmatrix}$$

is a generator matrix for C. This means that for any 3-bit string $\boldsymbol{x}$, we can automatically determine how to encode $\boldsymbol{x}$ by computing $\mathbf{G}\boldsymbol{x}$ as defined in Sec. 2.5. If $\boldsymbol{x} = 011$ then

$$Gx = \begin{pmatrix} 1 & 0 & 0 \\ 0 & 1 & 0 \\ 0 & 0 & 1 \\ 1 & 1 & 0 \\ 0 & 1 & 1 \\ 1 & 1 & 1 \\ 1 & 0 & 1 \end{pmatrix} \begin{pmatrix} 0 \\ 1 \\ 1 \end{pmatrix} = \begin{pmatrix} 0 \\ 1 \\ 1 \\ 1 \\ 0 \\ 0 \\ 1 \end{pmatrix}$$

Thus 011 is encoded as 0111001. In general, any 3-bit string $\boldsymbol{x}$ is encoded as $\mathbf{G}\boldsymbol{x}$.

The parity check matrix $\mathbf{H}$ is a matrix for which $\mathbf{H}\boldsymbol{x} = \boldsymbol{0}$ for each $\boldsymbol{x} \in C$. Readers who are comfortable with linear algebra should be able to show a relationship between **G** and **H**. In this case,

$$\mathbf{H} = \begin{pmatrix} 1 & 1 & 0 & 1 & 0 & 0 & 0 \\ 0 & 1 & 1 & 0 & 1 & 0 & 0 \\ 1 & 1 & 1 & 0 & 0 & 1 & 0 \\ 1 & 0 & 1 & 0 & 0 & 0 & 1 \end{pmatrix}$$

This matrix is formed from the 'parity check bits' of the non-zero codewords. Therefore, if we take a codeword, say 1001011, we see that

$$H = \begin{pmatrix} 1 & 1 & 0 & 1 & 0 & 0 & 0 \\ 0 & 1 & 1 & 0 & 1 & 0 & 0 \\ 1 & 1 & 1 & 0 & 0 & 1 & 0 \\ 1 & 0 & 1 & 0 & 0 & 0 & 1 \end{pmatrix} \begin{pmatrix} 1 \\ 0 \\ 0 \\ 1 \\ 0 \\ 1 \\ 1 \end{pmatrix} = \begin{pmatrix} 0 \\ 0 \\ 0 \\ 0 \end{pmatrix}$$

It also follows easily that **HG** is the zero matrix.

Thus, while the generator matrix describes the encoding procedure, the parity check matrix helps with decoding. Suppose our received word is $\boldsymbol{x}$. Then $\boldsymbol{x}$ is a codeword if and only if $\mathbf{H}\boldsymbol{x} = \boldsymbol{0}$. If $\mathbf{H}\boldsymbol{x} \neq \boldsymbol{0}$ then we know that $\boldsymbol{x}$ is not a codeword. Suppose $\boldsymbol{e}$ is the n-tuple with 1's in those positions in which there were errors and 0's elsewhere. We think of $\boldsymbol{e}$ as the *error vector*. Then it follows that we should decode $\boldsymbol{x}$ as $\boldsymbol{c} = \boldsymbol{x} \oplus \boldsymbol{e}$.

Example 16.22 In the case of the Hamming code, if the codeword $\boldsymbol{c} = 1011100$ is transmitted with two errors in the third and seventh positions then $\boldsymbol{x} = 1001101$ is received. Clearly $\boldsymbol{c} = \boldsymbol{x} \oplus \boldsymbol{e}$ where $\boldsymbol{e} = 0010001$.

Thus if we could find $\boldsymbol{e}$ we could compute $\boldsymbol{c}$. Group theory provides a very nice way of finding $\boldsymbol{e}$. Suppose that our code C is, like the Hamming code, one-error correcting. Since C is a subgroup of the group $\mathbb{Z}_2^n$ of all binary n-tuples, for any binary n-tuple $\boldsymbol{x}$ we can form the coset $\boldsymbol{x} \oplus C$ as described in Sec. 8.1.1. In particular, for each $\boldsymbol{e}$ having zero or one 1 (that is the error vectors denoting one or fewer errors) we list the cosets $\boldsymbol{e} \oplus C$.

Example 16.23 For the Hamming code of length 7, there are eight cosets of interest corresponding to the $\boldsymbol{e}$'s 0000000, 1000000, 0100000, 001000, 0001000, 0000100, 0000010, 0000001. The first four of these are shown in Fig. 16.6. The entries in the top row are the $\boldsymbol{e}$'s, and the columns underneath these are the corresponding cosets. For example, the coset $1000000 \oplus C$ consists of the eight column entries underneath 1000000.

Exercise 16.19 Complete all the entries in the table of Fig. 16.6.

If we know that a received word $\boldsymbol{x}$ has fewer than two errors (this is the only sort we can decode anyway) then we simply locate $\boldsymbol{x}$ in the table. To decode $\boldsymbol{x}$ we just take the codeword at the left of the row in which $\boldsymbol{x}$ appears.

Example 16.24 Suppose that we receive 1101110. This entry appears in the second column, third row. Thus, assuming there was one error, this comes from the codeword 0101110 and hence from the original message 010.

Codewords	Cosets				
	0000000	1000000	0100000	0010000	...
0000000	0000000	1000000	0100000	0010000	...
1001011	1001011	0001011	1101011	1000011	...
0101110	0101110	1101110	0001110	0111110	...
0010111	0010111	1010111	0110111	0000111	...
1100101	1100101	0100101	1000101	1110101	...
0111001	0111001	1111001	0011001	0101001	...
1011100	1011100	0011100	1111100	1001100	...
1110010	1110010	0110010	1010010	1100010	...

Figure 16.6 Hamming code cosets.

Exercise 16.20 Consider the code C resulting from the encoding

$$\begin{array}{lcl} 00 & \mapsto & 0000 \\ 01 & \mapsto & 0101 \\ 10 & \mapsto & 1010 \\ 11 & \mapsto & 1111 \end{array}$$

Show that C is a group code. Determine all the cosets of C of the form $\boldsymbol{x} \oplus C$ where $\boldsymbol{x}$ has Hamming distance 1 from a codeword.

Exercise 16.21 The two most common telephone dialling errors are:

(a) a single mis-dialled digit,

(b) the interchange of two digits.

A proposed telephone numbering system is to use those 10-digit numbers $(a_1, a_2, \ldots, a_{10})$ that satisfy the two constraints: (1) $\sum_{i=1}^{10} a_i = 0 \bmod 11$, (2) $\sum_{i=1}^{10} ia_i = 0 \bmod 11$. Show that the type 1 errors can be corrected and the type 2 errors detected.

16.3 CRYPTOGRAPHIC CODES

In this section we are no longer concerned with noise on the channel causing the receiver to receive the wrong message. We are concerned with an eavesdropper who might understand our message. Whether this message is a sensitive military or intelligence command, a major financial transaction, contains details of the Spurs' tactics in a forthcoming cup final or is a party invitation is not important to us. All that matters is that we have a message to send which we do not want to be intercepted and understood by an unauthorized third party. We attempt to do this by sending an encoded version of the message rather than the message itself. The encoded message is meant to be meaningless to everyone except the receiver, who knows how to decode the message. The collection of techniques concerned with such encoding and decoding is called *cryptography*. To make clear the distinction between cryptographic codes and error correcting codes we speak henceforth about *encryption* and *decryption* rather than encoding and decoding respectively. If accidental noise on the channel is also a problem, then we can apply an error correcting code after encryption and before decryption. However, with regard to the eavesdropper, we assume the worse case scenario. This is that such a person receives the transmitted message without any errors.

We introduce many of the fundamental ideas in cryptography via a simple, classical example, namely the Caesar codes. Unfortunately, these codes are almost useless in

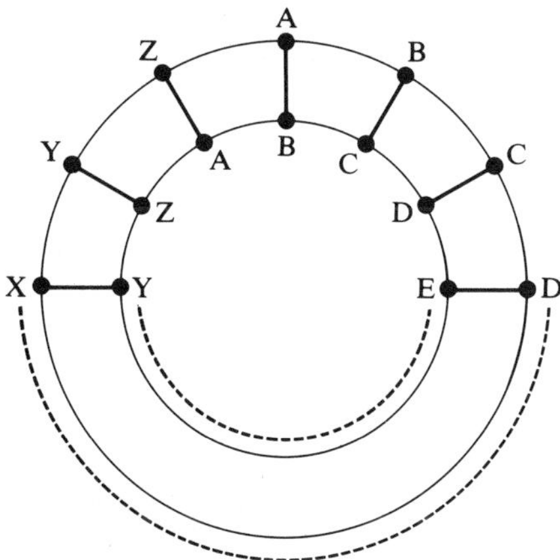

Figure 16.7 Caesar codes.

practice because they are too easy to break. Thus we introduce a code, the *one-time pad*, that is theoretically impossible to break. The practical problem with this code is that we have to store *keys* that are impractically long. Hence we consider codes that attempt to simulate the one-time pad using shorter keys. We then consider codes in which the keys, as well as the coding procedures, are made public. We show how such codes can be used for digital signatures and their authentication.

16.3.1 Caesar codes and fundamentals of cryptography

For purposes of illustration, let us temporarily relax our insistence that all messages consist only of strings of 0's and 1's. Suppose we are trying to send a message in English. The message M might be

SPURS WILL PLAY SWEEPER SYSTEM

A very simple encryption procedure is to replace each letter by its successor in the alphabet, with Z being mapped to A. Thus we encrypt M as

TQVST XJMM QMBZ TXFFQFS TZTUFN

The receiver can decrypt this message by replacing each letter with its predecessor in the alphabet. If we think of the letters of the alphabet arranged in a circle as in Fig. 16.7, this encryption procedure consists of shifting each letter one place to the right. Equally good would be a procedure in which we shift each letter two to the right, or a procedure in which we shift each letter three to the right, etc. As long as the receiver knows which shift has been chosen, decryption is straightforward. In fact, what we have is a general encryption procedure that gives rise to 25 different codes.

Example 16.25 When the shift is 8, we encode A as I, B as K, C as L, ..., R as Z, S as A, T as B, ..., Z as H.

Definition 16.12 Caesar code encryption with shift k For $i = 1, \ldots, 26$ encrypt the ith letter of the alphabet as the jth letter, where $j = (i + k) \bmod 26$.

Definition 16.13 Caesar code decryption with shift k For $i = 1, \ldots, 26$ decrypt the ith letter of the alphabet as the jth letter, where $j = (i - k) \bmod 26$.

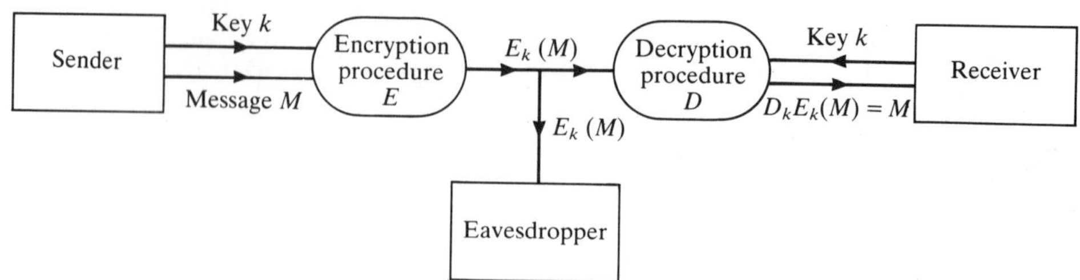

Figure 16.8 The classic encryption problem and solution.

Example 16.26 Suppose the shift is 4. Then A gets decrypted as W since $1 - 4 \bmod 26 = -3 \bmod 26 = 23 \bmod 26$. Note that $0 = 26 \bmod 26$, whence D gets mapped to Z because $4 - 4 \bmod 26 = 0 \bmod 26 = 26 \bmod 26$.

For each $k = 1, \ldots, 25$ we have a different code. We call the number k the *key*. The resulting codes are called the *Caesar codes*.

The general cryptography problem and solution is summarized in Fig. 16.8. The sender and receiver agree on an encryption procedure E, which is also called a *cipher*. This cipher may be public information, like 'the Caesar code cipher'. What is generally secret is the key k which is known only to the sender and receiver. Applying the key to the cipher results in a specific means of encryption E_k and decryption D_k. In the case of the Caesar cipher the key is a number between 1 and 25.

Example 16.27 When the key for the Casear cipher is 5, E_k maps the letter A to F, the letter B to G, ..., Z to E.

While the Caesar cipher illustrates all the fundamental notions in cryptography, it does not happen to be a particularly good cipher. Essentially, this is because there are not enough keys. Assuming, which we normally do, that the eavesdropper knows which cipher is being used, it is not too difficult to apply each possible key in turn. In fact, if we have sufficient text, we can do something even simpler. For example, we could just count the most commonly occurring letter. In the English language this is likely to be the letter on to which E is mapped. Suppose, for example, that N is the most frequently occurring letter in the intercepted text. Then it is likely that the relevant key was 9. For these reasons we do not think of the Caesar cipher as being particularly *secure*. We can do much better.

Exercise 16.22 Suppose you 'tap' the following message which has been encrypted by a Caesar code: EPMVMDMZBPMGMIZMVLAQVWVMAXCZAEQVBPMKCX. Try to find the key (without exhaustive search through the 25 keys) and hence decrypt the message.

16.3.2 One-time pad cipher

From considering messages in English we now return to the case where all messages are binary strings. Suppose we have a message M, say $M = 011001$. This message has length 6. Suppose a random 6-bit string K is known to both sender and receiver. For example, suppose $K = 101101$. If the sender encrypts M by adding to M the string K, using component-wise addition mod 2, then we get the encrypted message

$E(M) = M \oplus K = 110100$:

$$\begin{array}{rl} M & 011001 \quad \oplus \\ K & 101101 \\ \hline E(M) & 110100 \end{array}$$

If the receiver now adds K to the received message $E(M)$ it will be decrypted as 011001. This is the original message M:

$$\begin{array}{rl} E(M) & 110100 \quad \oplus \\ K & 101101 \\ \hline M & 011001 \end{array}$$

What we have described is an instance of a general encryption procedure E called the *one-time pad cipher*. For a given message M we add (using component-wise mod 2 addition) another fixed binary string K of the same length as the message string M. The string K is the key to this cipher; it is known only to the sender and receiver. The encryption procedure is: add the key string K to the message M. Thus $E(M) = M \oplus K$. The decryption procedure is: add the key string K to the received string $E(M)$. Clearly $K \oplus E(M) = K \oplus M \oplus K = M \oplus 2K = M \oplus \mathbf{0} = M$, the original message.

Example 16.28 Suppose our message string is $M = 1001000111001$. If $K = 0010100101000$, then $E(M) = M \oplus K = 10011100010001$. Now we decrypt as $E(M) \oplus K = 1001000111001 = M$.

Exercise 16.23 Suppose $K = 011011001010110$ and you receive the string 111001101101001. What was the original message?

The secret key string K is assumed to have been randomly generated. For example, it could have been generated by tossing a coin, with 0 representing heads and 1 representing tails. The key K is never used more than once.

The one-time pad cipher is theoretically unbreakable. To see this, suppose that an eavesdropper picks up the encrypted message $E(M) = M \oplus K$. To decrypt this, the eavesdropper has to know the string K. However, this string is completely random. The task of discovering this string is no easier than that of discovering the original message string. Thus the eavesdropper has not gained anything by installing the wire-tap. This one-time pad cipher is used extensively for very sensitive messages. Its drawback is that both the sender and receiver have to keep secret a key string that is as long as any message they will ever send. This means that the key cannot be stored in their heads, as in the case of the Caesar ciphers. It must be stored somewhere else, probably with copies in at least two places. Thus we have a serious *key management problem*. It could be argued that the task of keeping such a string secret is just as difficult as that of keeping secret the message to be sent.

16.3.3 Stream ciphers

One way round the key management problem of one-time pad ciphers is as follows: generate long key strings, which look like purely random binary strings, from short key strings. We can then mimic the one-time pad cipher with the long key string. The real key, which is the short string, should be sufficiently short that it can be remembered by both the receiver and sender. This procedure is illustrated in Fig. 16.9, and is precisely the principle that is used in *stream ciphers*.

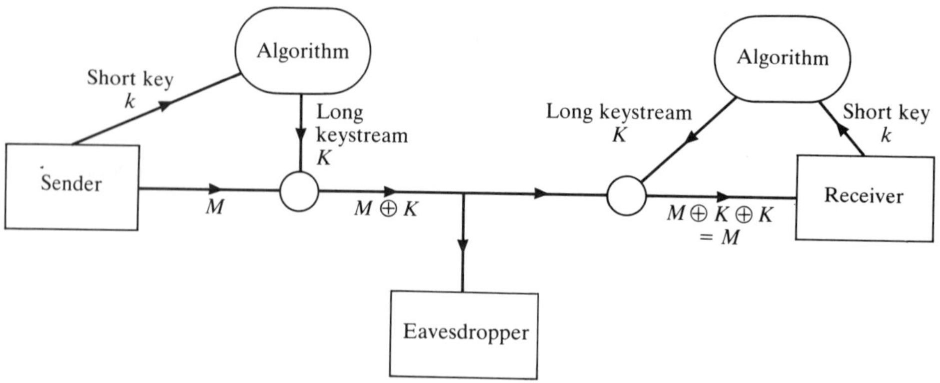

Figure 16.9 Stream ciphers.

Example 16.29 Suppose that we have a short string k, say $k = 00101$, which is known only to the sender and receiver. We want to use this to generate a long string K, which we shall call a *keystream sequence*. For example, we could use the following algorithm:

> First extend the string by duplicating it. Next map each 0 in the resulting string to 0110010, and map each 1 to 110101.

Thus $k = 00101$ is first mapped to 0010100101 and then to the string K where

$K = 0110010\ 0110010\ 110101\ 0110010\ 110101\ 0110010\ 0110010\ 110101\ 0110010\ 110101$

Assuming that both the sender and receiver use the same algorithm, they can both generate the same long keystream K from the short key k.

Since the keystream K in Example 16.29 is generated by an algorithm, we know that it is certainly not random as in the case of the real one-time pad. The problem with this particular algorithm is that to the discerning eye (which can in fact be automated) the keystream K does not even look random. We want algorithms that generate keystreams that are *pseudo-random* sequences; informally this means that they look as though they are randomly generated.

Linear feedback shift registers A common, and more structured, approach is to use an algorithm that is described by a *linear feedback shift register*. Consider, for example, a register with four locations l_1, l_2, l_3, l_4, as shown in Fig. 16.10, whose respective contents are x_1, x_2, x_3 and x_4. Initially, at time t_0, these locations contain the 4 bits of a 4-bit key k. Here $k = 0010$. Thus, at t_0, we have $x_1 = 0$, $x_2 = 0$, $x_3 = 1$ and $x_4 = 0$. At discrete time intervals the register outputs the contents of l_4 and the remaining x_i's get shifted to the right. Thus, at time t_1, the content of l_4, which is $x_4 = 0$, is output. The contents of l_2, l_3, l_4 become respectively 0,0 and 1. The content of l_1 at time t_{i+1} is determined by the values of the x_i's at time t_i. Specifically, it is replaced by the value of the linear function

$$x_1 \oplus x_3 \oplus x_4$$

at time t_i where addition is mod 2. In the physical register this is easily implemented using an AND gate as shown in Fig. 16.10. Thus, at time t_1 the content x_1 of l_1 is $0 \oplus 1 \oplus 0 = 1$.

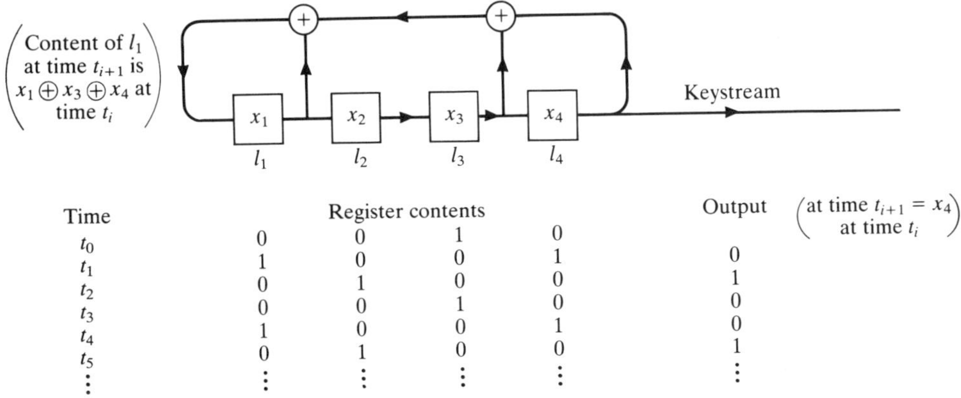

Time	Register contents				Output
t_0	0	0	1	0	0
t_1	1	0	0	1	1
t_2	0	1	0	0	0
t_3	0	0	1	0	0
t_4	1	0	0	1	1
t_5	0	1	0	0	
⋮	⋮	⋮	⋮	⋮	⋮

Figure 16.10 Linear feedback shift register.

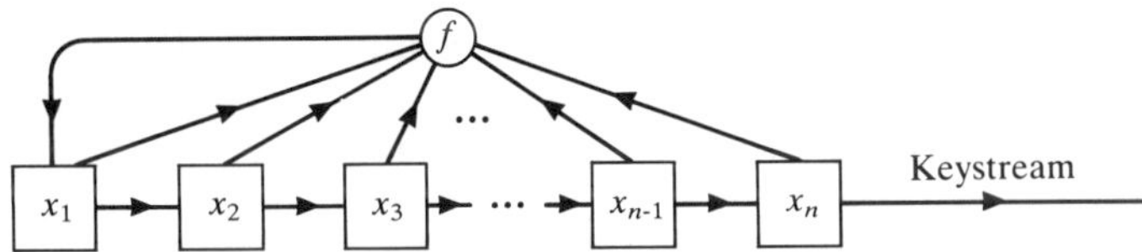

Figure 16.11 Feedback shift register—general case.

Exercise 16.24 Compute the first 40 bits output from the shift register of Fig. 16.10.

By computing the first few dozen bits from the output string, you can see that the string repeats itself every 15 bits. We say that the string has *period* 15.

In general, a linear feedback shift register consists of n locations and an equation to compute the contents y of the first location after each shift. The equation is a linear function f (in the sense of a linear combination defined in Sec. 2.5) of the contents of the locations $l_1, \ldots, l_n$. Denoting the contents by $x_1, \ldots, x_n$ respectively, this means:

$$y = f(x_1, \ldots, x_n) = a_1x_1 \oplus a_2x_2 \oplus \ldots a_nx_n$$

where each a_i is either 0 or 1. This is illustrated in Fig. 16.11.

If the a_i are chosen well, then the output string will only start to repeat itself after $2^n - 1$ bits, so the period will be $2^n - 1$. When n is quite large, say 50, this period is likely to be longer than any message we are ever likely to send. Thus it would appear that we have simulated the one-time pad using a small key string. Indeed, this type of cipher is very popular because it is very easy to implement, either digitally or electronically. Unfortunately it is quite easy to break. The proof of this is left to Exercise 16.26. We have to assume that the eavesdropper knows the equation f, since we always assume that the full encryption procedure is known—only the key is secret.

Exercise 16.25 Suppose the secret four-digit key of a linear feedback shift register is 1100. If this is used as the initial contents of the register, calculate the output sequence, and hence use it to encrypt the message: 11010100110101000101111110 01.

Exercise 16.26 Suppose that the eavesdropper can obtain any n successive bits of matching message text and encrypted text. Show that you can recover the key, namely the original contents of the n register locations, and hence break the code. You should base your solution on the following argument:

if x is the n-bit part of the message text, with corresponding encryption y, compute $z = x \oplus y$ and let the register run with the content z.

Non-linear feedback shift registers and their extensions Except for ease of practical implementation, there is no reason to restrict ourselves to linear functions $f(x_1, \ldots, x_n)$ in shift registers. In fact, if we use complicated non-linear functions of the x_i, we can get ciphers that are much more secure. Some of the most important ciphers are based on extensions of non-linear feedback shift registers. They are made particularly secure if, before outputting the contents of the register, we apply the non-linear function $f(x_1, \ldots, x_n)$ and then *permute* the contents of the locations l_i. If we repeated this procedure a number of times, each time being called a *round*, we would get a very well scrambled message. It is normal in such cases to divide the message into blocks of, say, 64 bits, rather than treat it as one stream. In such cases we talk about a *block cipher* rather than a stream cipher.

The best-known cipher of this type is the *Data Encryption Standard (DES)*. This cipher has 16 rounds and its block size is 64. The details of the encryption algorithm are contained in a public ANSI standard. Many major financial institutions use DES, and although it has been criticized, exhaustive key search is still the best way of breaking the cipher. Interestingly, the DES has a 56-bit key, which means there are 2^{56} possible keys in all. Given the importance of the use of this cipher and the sophisticated hardware that could be brought to bear in an attempt to break it, this number is considered by some to be worryingly small.

16.3.4 Public key cryptosystems

It may have come as a surprise to you to learn that encryption procedures are generally made public. If so then you may be astonished to learn that an important new trend in cryptography is to use ciphers in which the keys as well as the encryption procedures are made public. This radical, but surprisingly simple and effective, idea was first devised by Diffie and Hellman (1976). To explain the principle, we use the locked-box metaphor described in Harel (1987):

> **Example 16.30 Locked box metaphor** Everybody who wants to send a secret message does so by locking a box with the message in. Everybody has their own padlock and key, which are assumed to be different. The nice thing about padlocks is that anybody can lock anybody else's padlock, but only the owner who has the key can open it. Everybody now writes their own name on their padlock, and puts their padlocks in a public place. Suppose that Terry wants to send a message to Paul. Then Terry puts his message in a box, and locks it with Paul's padlock. Only Paul can now open this box, because only Paul can unlock Paul's padlock. Thus only Paul can read Terry's secret message. Anybody who buys a padlock and key can join in. They can immediately start sending and receiving messages to people without having to set up any prior communication with them.

To use this idea in cryptography, we need a functional analogy of a padlock and key. Specifically, we need a function that is easy to compute but is difficult to invert. Applying the function is like locking the padlock—anyone can do it. Inverting the function must be analogous to opening the padlock without the key. For many functions it is more difficult to compute the inverse than the function itself. For example, it is easier to square a number than to compute a number's square root.

Unfortunately, the latter computation is not difficult enough for our purposes. A better example is:

Example 16.31 Multiply two large numbers together. This is feasible in the sense of Chapter 15; there are very fast algorithms for doing this. However, if we are told that the number x is formed by multiplying together two large numbers, then it is very difficult to find the two factors of x. This is the factorization problem of Chapter 15 which is believed to be infeasible.

Functions like *multiply* of Example 16.31 are called *one-way functions*. To carry the padlock and key analogy through it is not enough to have just a one-way function. We need to have the key that enables the receiver to unlock the padlock. The functional analogy of the key is called a *trapdoor*. The trapdoor is some technique known only to the receiver which makes it easy to reverse the function. Really satisfactory one-way trapdoor functions are notoriously difficult to construct. The following famous example is due to Rivest, Shamir, and Adleman (1978).

Example 16.32 RSA one-way trapdoor function* Take any two prime numbers, say $p = 3$ and $q = 11$. Compute $(p - 1)(q - 1)$. In our case this is 20. Choose any number h that is relatively prime to this, for example $h = 3$. Then (by an elementary theorem of number theory) we can always find another number d such that $hd = 1 \bmod (p - 1)(q - 1)$. In our case we can take $d = 7$ since $hd = (3)(7) = 21 = 1 \bmod 20$. Now let f be the function defined on integers by the rule $f(m) = m^h \bmod n$ where $n = pq$. For example, if $m = 9$, then in our case $f(9) = 9^3 = 729 = 3 \bmod 33$. We now use the results of Chapter 15 to show that f is a one-way function. Since the primality problem is effectively solvable (page 392), we know we can easily generate large prime numbers. Therefore, we can easily compute f even if we have to choose the primes p, q to be very large. However, because the factorization problem is believed to be infeasible (page 392), we can safely assume that it would then be very difficult to compute the inverse of f; to do so means that we would have to be able to factor the large number n.

Thus f is a one-way function when p and q are large. Moreover, there is a trapdoor for f if you know the numbers p and q, and hence d. To invert f we simply have to raise $f(m)$ to the power d, since it turns out that $f(m)^d = (m^h \bmod n)^d = m^{hd} \bmod n = m \bmod n$ holds for any number m (this is also an elementary theorem of number theory). To see this in our example, we note that: $f(9)^7 = (3 \bmod 33)^7 = 3^7 \bmod 33 = 2187 \bmod 33 = 9 \bmod 33$.

Given that one-way trapdoor functions really do exist, we can now explain how these functions (defined on message strings) are used for public key cryptosystems. The analogy of each person buying their own padlock and key is that each person X chooses their own one-way trapdoor function E_X as their encryption procedure. Since E_X is the padlock it is made public—anyone can use it to send messages to X. The key to the padlock E_X is E_X's inverse function D_X. This is known only to X via the trapdoor technique. Now suppose person Y decides to send a secret message m to X. Then Y looks up X's public encryption procedure E_X and transmits the message $m' = E_X(m)$. Like the locked boxes containing messages, it is assumed that any eavesdropper can see this encrypted message. However, only X can decrypt it since only X knows the inverse function D_X. Hence only X can determine

$$D_X(m') = D_X(E_X(m)) = m$$

which is the original message.

RSA and other specific public key cryptosystems Now that we have explained the principle of public key cryptosystems, we can briefly look at some specific examples. The best known is the RSA cryptosystem of Rivest, Shamir and Adleman (1978). This is based on the one-way trapdoor function of Example 16.32. Any person X who wants to participate chooses numbers p, q, h, d as in Example 16.32. Then X publishes the numbers n to denote pq and h, but keeps p, q, d secret. For simplicity we can assume that the messages to be sent are integers because any binary strings can be mapped to a unique integer. The encryption procedure E_X for sending the message m to X is

$$E_X(m) = m^h \bmod n = m'$$

The decryption procedure D_X is

$$D_X(m') = m'^d \bmod n = m$$

From Example 16.32, we know that E_X is a one-way function with inverse D_X which is really a trapdoor. Knowledge of n will not enable an eavesdropper to compute p, q which is needed for D_X. Although most experts accept that the RSA cipher is more elegant and likely to be more secure than a conventional cipher like DES, it has the drawback of being slower to implement. Where large amounts of data have to be encrypted quickly, as in the case of many financial systems, DES is justifiably still preferred.

The RSA approach inspired other attempts to find one-way trapdoor functions as the basis for public key cryptosystems. The work on $\mathcal{NP}$-completeness, described in Chapter 15, really comes to the fore here. Any function for which the computation of the inverse is an $\mathcal{NP}$-complete problem can reasonably be called a one-way function. A number of $\mathcal{NP}$-complete problems can be phrased in a form where they also have a trapdoor. One well-publicized example is the Knapsack problem, which Merkle and Hellman (1978) showed could be used as the basis for a public key cryptosystem.

16.3.5 Signing messages and authentication

Conventional cryptography is concerned with ensuring that an eavesdropper cannot decrypt a secret message. We have shown we can solve this problem reasonably well, but we still have another important problem. Cryptographic codes are used to send messages, like bank transfers of funds, digitally. In order to be sure that the encrypted message was sent by the person who said they sent it, we need a digital analogy of a signature, which itself can be verified digitally.

Example 16.33 Suppose that an encrypted message in a bank system asserts that Irving's account should be credited with £1 million from Bob's account. The message says it comes from Bob. There is no problem if it really was authorized by Bob, but what happens if he knows nothing about it and in fact it comes from Irving? Then we have a serious case of fraud. Indeed, it is known that much computer fraud is of precisely this nature.

It turns out that the public key cryptosystems can provide a wonderfully simple solution to this problem. We know that the encryption functions E_X and decryption functions D_X satisfy

$$D_X(E_X(m)) = m \tag{16.1}$$

for any message m. However, if we examine these functions in the case of the RSA cipher, we find *additionally* that, for every m,

$$E_X(D_X(m)) = m \tag{16.2}$$

This enables us to solve the signature problem. Suppose X wants to send a signed message m to Y. Normally X would just look up Y's public encryption procedure E_Y and send the message $E_Y(m)$, which Y would encrypt by applying $D_Y(E_Y(m)) = m$. Anybody claiming to be X could have sent the message m to Y because E_Y is public. So instead of applying E_Y directly to the message m, X first applies the *private* decoding procedure D_X before using E_Y. Thus X transmits $m' = E_Y(D_X(m))$. On receiving this Y first applies D_Y, so Y computes

$$D_Y(m') = D_Y(E_Y(D_X(m))) = D_X(m) \text{ from (16.1)}$$

Finally, Y applies X's public E_X to get

$$E_X(D_X(m)) = m \text{ from (16.2)}$$

Now Y has decrypted the original message m and Y knows that X must have sent this because only X knows D_X.

With the above assumptions, we can use a public key cryptosystem to solve another closely related problem. Suppose Bob wants to send a message asserting that £1 million is to be transferred from his own account to his son Kevin's account. Irving might be able to change the name Kevin to Irving on this message. The problem of detecting such a change is known as the *authentication problem*.

Exercise 16.27 Show how a public key cryptosystem like RSA can be used to solve the message authentication problem. You should base your solution on the following argument: if X wants to send the message m, X could send both m and $D_X(m)$.

16.4 SUMMARY

We have discussed the two major classes of codes required in communicating messages across a channel. Error correcting codes enable messages to tolerate a certain amount of corruption due to random noise on the channel. Cryptographic codes, or ciphers, enable messages to be sent securely over a channel even if an eavesdropper on the channel can intercept encrypted messages perfectly.

There are two competing requirements for good error correcting codes. On the one hand we want reliability, meaning good error correction and detection capability. On the other hand we want a high information rate. This means that encoded messages should not be so much longer than the original message that the speed or cost of transmission become unacceptably high. While the repetition codes achieve an arbitrarily high reliability and the parity check codes achieve arbitrarily high information rate, we have to be more careful in finding codes that strike the right balance. Hamming codes and Goppa codes are examples of families of codes that attain reasonable levels of both reliability and information rate. Most interesting error correcting codes turn out to be groups in the sense of Chapter 7. The group properties facilitate efficient encoding and decoding procedures.

Conventional ciphers involve both the sender and receiver keeping secret keys that enable encryption and decryption. The encryption and decryption algorithms are assumed to be public. A 'perfect' cipher, meaning one that is theoretically unbreakable, is the one-time pad cipher. It has the disadvantage of very long keys that have to be kept secret. Thus many ciphers, including the famous DES cipher used by financial institutions, attempt to simulate the one-time pad using a relatively small key. There are ciphers, called public key encryption systems, for which only the receiver has a secret key. The sender's key is public, and is used by anybody wishing to send that person a message. The theory of computational complexity is central to these ciphers since they are based on the fact that discovering the secret decryption algorithm is equivalent to solving problems that are believed to be infeasible. These ciphers can also be used to solve the problems of digital signatures and message authentication. The most famous public key cipher, the RSA cipher, is being used increasingly for these important purposes.

FURTHER READING

One of the few books that covers both error correcting codes and cryptographic codes in any depth is Welsh (1988). A thorough account of error correcting codes may be found in the book by McWilliams and Stone (1975), while Beker and Piper's book (1982) is highly recommended for cryptographic codes.

Chapter 17

MEASUREMENT THEORY

Measurement lies at the heart of many systems that govern our lives. In economic systems it is used to determine price and pay increases, while in radar systems it enables us to detect aircraft through clouds. Measurement in medical systems enables the diagnosis of specific illnesses, while in atmospheric systems it is the basis for weather prediction. Yet for all its obvious importance, measurement is a poorly understood subject, even in classical engineering disciplines. In novel engineering disciplines, like software engineering, there is little agreement on what can be measured and how. Much confusion and misunderstanding about measurement can be avoided by using a body of knowledge known as *measurement theory*. This is now acknowledged as the necessary scientific basis for developing and reasoning about all kinds of measurement. This includes measurement in the social sciences as well as the physical sciences.

In its purest form measurement theory is a sophisticated application of many of the topics described earlier in this book. In our presentation of it we shall be dependent on: relations, and in particular order relations as described in Sec. 2.2; logic as presented in Chapters 3, 4 and 5; theories, models and interpretations as presented in Chapter 7; homomorphisms as described in Chapter 8; and similarity types as presented in Chapter 10. The important role of probability theory in measurement (notably to formalize the notion of measurement error) is unfortunately beyond the scope of this chapter.

Section 17.1 provides an introduction to measurement, in which many of the key terms are introduced informally. In Sec. 17.2 we describe the formal, *representational* theory of measurement. This approach enables us to provide a rigorous definition of both measurement scales and the related notion of meaningfulness for measurement which are described in Sec. 17.3. In Sec. 17.4 we extend the earlier ideas to indirect measurement.

17.1 WHAT IS MEASUREMENT?

It is not only professional technologists who use measurement. We all use it in everyday life. We can calculate the total bill in a shop to make sure we are given the correct change. We can measure the height of our children to make sure we buy the correct size of clothes. When we go on a journey by car, we can work out how far we will be travelling by using a map. By using a speedometer, we can then use this to predict how long the journey will take or how much petrol we need to buy. All the examples we have given make up a varied collection of measurement activities. What is it that these activities all have in common?

Definition 17.1 Measurement Measurement is the process by which numbers or symbols are assigned to attributes of entities in the real world in such a way as to describe them according to clearly defined rules.

Measurement is concerned with capturing information about *attributes* of *entities*:

An entity may be an object, such as a person or a room, or an event, such as a journey or the testing phase of a software project.

An attribute is a feature or property of the entity that we are interested in, such as the height or blood pressure (of a person), the area or colour (of a room), the cost (of a journey) or the time (of the testing phase).

Thus it is wrong to say that we 'measure things' or that we 'measure attributes'. We measure attributes of things. It is ambiguous to say that we 'measure a room', since we could measure its length, area or temperature. Equally it is ambiguous to say that we 'measure the temperature', since we measure the temperature of a specific geographical location under specific conditions.

Measurement assigns *numbers* or *symbols* to these attributes of entities in order to *describe* them. Hence when we are measuring the heights of people we will always assign bigger numbers to the taller people, although the numbers themselves will differ according to whether we use metres, inches or feet. The number is a useful and important abstraction. If we have never met Frankie but are told that he is 7 feet tall, then we can imagine how tall Frankie is in relation to ourselves, and we will know that he will have to stoop when he enters the door of our house.

We intend to use measurement theory to answer the following questions:

1 How much do we need to know about some attribute before it is reasonable to consider measuring it? For example, do we know enough about the *complexity* of programs to be able to measure it?

2 How do we know if we have really measured the attribute we wanted to measure? For example, does a count of the number of bugs found in a system during integration testing measure the *reliability* of the system? If not, then what does it measure?

3 Using measurement, what kind of statements can we make about an attribute, and the entities that possess it, that are *meaningful*? For example, is it meaningful to talk about a 20 per cent increase in the *quality* of a design?

4 What kind of operations can we perform on measures that are meaningful? For example, can we meaningfully compute the average level of complexity of a group of software modules?

The framework for answering the first two questions is provided by the *representation condition* for measurement in Sec. 17.2. The answers to the last two questions come out of an understanding of the notion of *scales* of measurement in Secs 17.3 and 17.4. We need to know what the different scale types are, and if and when we are measuring on an appropriate scale.

Exercise 17.1 Explain the role of measurement in determining the following:

(a) the 'best' bowlers and batsmen over a cricket season,

(b) the 'best' all-round athlete in the *decathlon* event.

Exercise 17.2 How would you begin to measure the 'quality' of a software product?

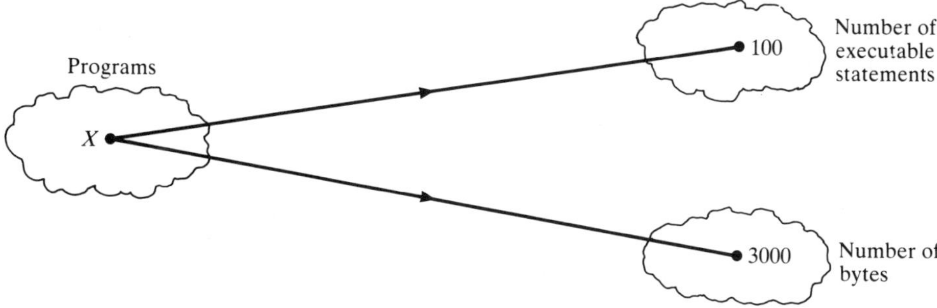

Figure 17.1 Different measures of length.

Exercise 17.3 Consider some everyday measurements. What entities and attributes of these are being measured? What can you say about error margins in the measurements? Also explain how the measuring process may affect the entity being measured.

Based on our definition of measurement we now define a *measure*:

Definition 17.2 Measure A measure is an empirical objective assignment of a number (or symbol) to an entity to characterize a specific attribute of that entity.

The notion of 'characterizing a specific attribute' will be made precise in Sec. 17.2. The assignment in Def. 17.2 is also referred to as the *measurement mapping*; it can be thought of as a modelling procedure for the entity and attribute. Thus, a measure is not a number, as is commonly assumed, but a function $M : C \rightarrow A$ where C is the set of entities in question and A the appropriate set of numbers (or symbols). However, measurement theorists sometimes deliberately relax the distinction between the function and its results.

Example 17.1 Suppose we wish to measure the attribute of *length* for computer programs. Then two possible candidate measures are $M, M' : \{\text{programs}\} \rightarrow \mathbb{R}$, where

$$\begin{aligned} M(X) &= \text{number of executable source statements in } X \\ M'(X) &= \text{number of bytes of computer storage of } X \end{aligned}$$

These are illustrated in Fig. 17.1. We clearly cannot say, without ambiguity, that 'the length measure of program X is 100'. However, we do normally relax the terminology and say 'the length measure of X is 100 executable source statements'. If the only choice was between the two mappings M and M' then it is unambiguous which measure we were referring to. However, there may be a number of alternative ways to define the mapping onto executable source statements and in such situations we cannot simply talk about X having 100 executable statements without reference to the chosen mapping.

To measure something we must know what entities are being measured and we must have some idea of the attribute (property) of the entity that we are attempting to capture numerically. Although this point seems obvious, it is ignored surprisingly often in many data collection activities. Once we have identified an attribute and a means of measuring it, we can begin to accumulate data. Analysing the results of this process normally leads to the clarification and re-evaluation of the attribute. This in turn leads to improvements in the accuracy of measurement and, as we shall see, an improved *scale*. This is, for example, how the modern thermodynamic definition of temperature evolved from simple devices and concepts.

We can measure some attributes such as mass and length without reference to any other attribute. On the other hand, measuring attributes such as density involves measuring other attributes, namely mass and length. To make clear these distinctive types of measurement we define:

> **Definition 17.3 Direct and indirect measurement** Direct measurement of an attribute is measurement that does not depend on the measurement of any other attribute. Indirect measurement of an attribute is measurement that involves the measurement of one or more other attributes.

> **Example 17.2** Some attributes can be measured in terms of just one other attribute. For example, temperature can be measured by the *length* of a mercury column. Note, however, that such measurement is still indirect.

The representational theory of measurement, as described in the remainder of this chapter, is initially concerned with direct measurement of attributes. Where no previous measurement has been performed, this constitutes a natural process of understanding the attribute and the entities that possess it. It does not preclude the possibility that more accurate measurement will subsequently be achieved indirectly.

17.2 ATTRIBUTES AND MEASURES

In this section we make more precise the notion of an attribute and the notion of a numerical characterization of an attribute. Hence, we make more precise the notion of a measure as defined informally in Def. 17.2. No attribute of any real-world entity can ever be completely formalized. However, we show how to model an attribute in such a way that, with respect to the model, we can determine formally when we have a measure for it. There is a close link here with the formal modelling of any real-world system: we know that the most difficult task, of turning the informal system requirements into a formal specificaton, cannot itself be formalized.

To make precise the notion of a real-world attribute Q, we assume that our intuition gives rise to a theory about Q, in the sense of Chapter 10. The theory contains predicate symbols, which are interpreted as relations in the real world, and axioms, which must be satisfied in any interpretation. For example, the attribute of heat of liquids leads to an empirically observed binary relation 'hotter than' of liquids. This relation intuitively satisfies the axiom of transitivity: if liquid A is hotter than liquid B, which is in turn hotter than liquid C, then we may infer that A is hotter than C. Consequently, we introduce the notion of an *empirical structure* which, in the sense of Chapters 7 and 10, is a real-world structure that is a model of the theory about Q.

To make precise the notion of a numerical characterization of Q, we have to find a certain type of interpretation, called a *representation*, of the empirical structure in a more concrete model, called a *numerical structure*. A representation must preserve the relations. For example, suppose A and B are two liquids that are mapped to the numbers x and y respectively. Then, provided that the relation 'hotter than' is mapped to the relation '>', we must have 'A hotter than B' if and only if $x > y$. This necessary and sufficient condition, imposed on the interpretation of all the empirical relations, is called the *representation condition* for measurement. Only when we have found such a representation for Q do we say that we have found a measure for Q.

17.2.1 Empirical structures

Before we can measure we must have a clear concept of an attribute and a set of entities to be measured that possess this attribute. Thus, whether we are measuring length of steel rods, heat of liquids, intelligence of humans or complexity of software systems, the concept in each case precedes the measurement. In what follows we shall assume that we have identified an attribute Q and sets of entities that possess Q. Our intuition about Q is expressed as a theory (σ, Γ), in the sense of Chapter 10. Specifically, the similarity type σ consists of: a single sort, denoting the name of a set of entities possessing Q; and a set of predicate symbols denoting the names of various intuitive relations that Q imposes on the set of entities. The axioms, Γ, express the intuitive properties about Q.

Our first step towards measurement of Q for a specific set, C, of real-world entities is to find an empirical model of Q in C. This means finding an interpretation of the theory in which C is the carrier set and in which the predicate symbols are interpreted as empirically observed relations over C.

Example 17.3 Consider the attribute Q of *height*, or more specifically *tallness*, which is possessed by people. A theory about Q may include a number of predicate symbols which are interpreted by empirical relations over a set of people C. Examples of such relations were given in Fig. 2.8 on page 34. Specifically, the relations we considered there were:

$R_1 \subset C \times C$: where $(x, y) \in R_1$ if 'x is taller than y'
$R_2 \subset C$: where $x \in R_2$ if 'x is tall'
$R_3 \subset C \times C$: where $(x, y) \in R_3$ if 'x is much taller than y'
$R_4 \subset C \times C \times C$: where (x, y, z) if 'x is higher than y when sitting on z's shoulders'

What is most important to note is that, by observation, we can determine membership of the sets that express the relations *without measurement*. This is the sense in which we assert that intuition about an attribute precedes its measurement. There will, of course, be some dispute about membership of the sets that express the relations, which will lead to many different interpretations of the relation symbols. For example, while most of us would agree that Frankie $\in R_2$ and that Peter $\notin R_2$, there may be some disagreement that Wonderman $\in R_2$. This is what we mean when we say that the relations are *empirical*. To reach a reasonable consensus we may need to set down certain standards and definitions, such as whether or not we include hair height or set criteria for posture. This essentially amounts to agreeing on some kind of model for the objects being measured.

Once we have interpreted the predicates by specific empirical relations, we have to check that all the axioms of the theory for Q are satisfied. For example, the observation that 'Frankie is much taller than Peter implies that Frankie is taller than Peter' confirms that, in this instance, the axiom '$(x, y) \in R_3 \rightarrow (x, y) \in R_1$' is satisfied. Another axiom would express transitivity of the relation R_1, as defined in Sec. 2.2.

Definition 17.4 Empirical structure for Q An empirical structure $\mathscr{C}$ for an attribute Q is a model for the theory of Q.

It follows from Def. 17.4 that an empirical structure $\mathscr{C}$ is a pair $(C, \mathscr{R})$ where C is a set of entities and $\mathscr{R}$ is a set of relations over C. In the measurement theory literature, $\mathscr{C}$ is also referred to as an *empirical relation system*.

Over a period of time, our increased understanding of Q is reflected in the fact that we may gradually extend the theory of Q by adding new predicate symbols and axioms. In turn, we will need to find increasingly rich empirical structures for each such theory extensions.

Example 17.4 Consider the attribute of *criticality* defined on a set of *software failures*.

(a) We start with a simple theory of criticality, which captures an intuition that criticality imposes a *classification* of failures into named classes. This means that the predicate symbols of the theory are just the unary predicate symbols denoting the names of the failure classes. To make the example as simple as possible, let us assume that there are just three classes of failures named *syntactic, semantic* and *system.* The theory asserts that every failure lies in exactly one of these named classes. A structure $\mathscr{C} = (C, \mathscr{R})$ for this attribute consists of a set of observed software failures C and a set of unary relations $\mathscr{R} = \{R_1, R_2, R_3\}$ where:

$x \in R_1$ iff x is observed as a syntactic failure
$x \in R_2$ iff x is observed as a semantic failure
$x \in R_3$ iff x is observed as a system failure

The notion of classification means there is an axiom in the theory that asserts that, for every $x \in C$, x is in exactly one of R_1, R_2 or R_3. At this point we have no value judgement about the relative criticality of these types of failures; we merely know that these are the classes and that they are different.

(b) Now suppose we reflect our deeper understanding of failure criticality by adding to the theory a new predicate symbol denoting 'more critical than'. Then we have to find a new binary relation R_4 over C where $(x, y) \in R_4$ if 'x is observed to be more critical than y'. Our understanding of this relation is that all system failures are more critical than all semantic and syntactic failures, and all semantic failures are more critical than all syntactic failures. Formally, this means that we have also added the following axiom to the theory:

$$(x, y) \in R_4 \text{ iff } (x \in R_3 \wedge (y \in R_2 \vee y \in R_1)) \vee (x \in R_2 \wedge y \in R_1)$$

The new structure for failure criticality is $\mathscr{C}' = (C, \mathscr{R}')$ where $\mathscr{R}' = \{R_1, R_2, R_3, R_4\}$.

We will show quite formally that the extension of the theory about an attribute Q is what we mean when we speak about more accurate measurements for Q. Thus, when we speak about measuring an attribute Q it must always be with respect to a particular theory about Q.

The idea of enriching relation structures should not be confused with the idea of *changing* previously observed relations. Relations such as those identified in Example 17.3 will vary over time. Thus whether 'J.R. Ewing is taller than J.R. Ewing Jnr' is true or not will depend on the time of the observation. This appears to suggest that each relation is only well-defined with respect to a particular point in time, whereas our intuitive understanding of height is independent of time. Therefore, we assume that entity x at time t is a distinct entity from x at time t'. The fact that entity x at time t'' may not even exist is then also accounted for.

Example 17.5 J.R. Ewing Jnr on 18.5.90 is considered to be a distinct entity from J.R. Ewing Jnr on 18.5.99. The entity J.R. Ewing Jnr on 18.5.60 does not exist.

Example 17.6 A pertinent example from software measurement is the case where our set of entities is the set of programmers, and the attribute of programmers that we wish to capture is *productivity*. Clearly, a programmer's productivity will change over time, given increased experience, new tools, etc. Suppose Fred Hacker is an entity whose productivity we wish to characterize numerically. Then as an entity we have to consider Fred Hacker working during time t as distinct from Fred Hacker working during time t'.

17.2.2 Representations

Finding an empirical structure $(C, \mathscr{R})$ for an attribute Q does not constitute measurement of Q. We need to find a more concrete model for $(C, \mathscr{R})$, such as a structure whose carrier set is the set of real numbers $\mathbb{R}$. This could enable us to interpret the real-world objects in C objectively as numbers and the empirical relations in $\mathscr{R}$ as numerical relations such as '>'. This would bring us close to the informal notion of measurement described in Sec. 17.1. Consequently, we need a *numerical structure for* Q. Like an empirical structure, this is a pair $\mathscr{A} = (A, \mathscr{P})$ where A is a set and $\mathscr{P}$ is a set of relations $\{P_1, P_2, \ldots, P_n\}$ defined on A. An empirical structure and a numerical structure for the same attribute Q must have the same similarity type. The difference is that the carrier set A is assumed to be a set of numbers.

Example 17.7 In Example 17.3 on page 423 we noted four empirical relations R_1, R_2, R_3 and R_4 for the attribute height. Suppose the set of people is $C = \{\text{Frankie, Wonderman, Peter}\}$, as shown in Fig. 2.8 on page 34. Then our empirical structure for height is $\mathscr{C} = (C, \{R_1, R_2, R_3, R_4\})$. A numerical structure that is a concrete model for $\mathscr{C}$ is the structure $(\mathbb{R}, \{P_1, P_2, P_3, P_4\})$ where the relations are defined by:

$P_1 \subset \mathbb{R} \times \mathbb{R}$: given by '$(x, y) \in P_1$ if $x > y$'
$P_2 \subset \mathbb{R}$: given by '$x \in P_2$ if $x > 70$'
$P_3 \subset \mathbb{R} \times \mathbb{R}$: given by '$(x, y) \in P_4$ if $x > y + 15$'
$P_4 \subset \mathbb{R} \times \mathbb{R} \times \mathbb{R}$: given by '$(x, y, z) \in P_3$ if $0.7x + 0.8z > y$'

and the interpretation M maps people to numbers as shown in Fig. 17.2. For example, $M(\text{Wonderman}) = 72$. For each $i = 1, \ldots, 4$, the interpretation of R_i under M is P_i. Now M is defined in such a way that the relation R_i holds if and only if the relation P_i holds.

When $i = 1$, this means that for each $x, y \in C$, $(x, y) \in R_1$ iff $(M(x), M(y)) \in P_1$. As an example, we observed that (Frankie, Wonderman)$\in R_1$. Under the mapping M we have $M(\text{Frankie}) = 84 > 72 = M(\text{Wonderman})$ and so indeed $(M(\text{Frankie}), M(\text{Wonderman})) \in P_1$.

When $i = 2$, we must check that, for each $x \in C$, $x \in R_2$ iff $M(x) \in P_2$. For example, we observed that Wonderman $\in R_2$. Now $M(\text{Wonderman}) = 72$, and since $72 > 70$ it follows that $M(\text{Wonderman}) \in P_2$.

When $i = 4$, we must check that, for each $x, y, z \in C$, $(x, y, z) \in R_4$ iff $(M(x), M(y), M(z)) \in P_4$. For example, we observed that Peter is higher than

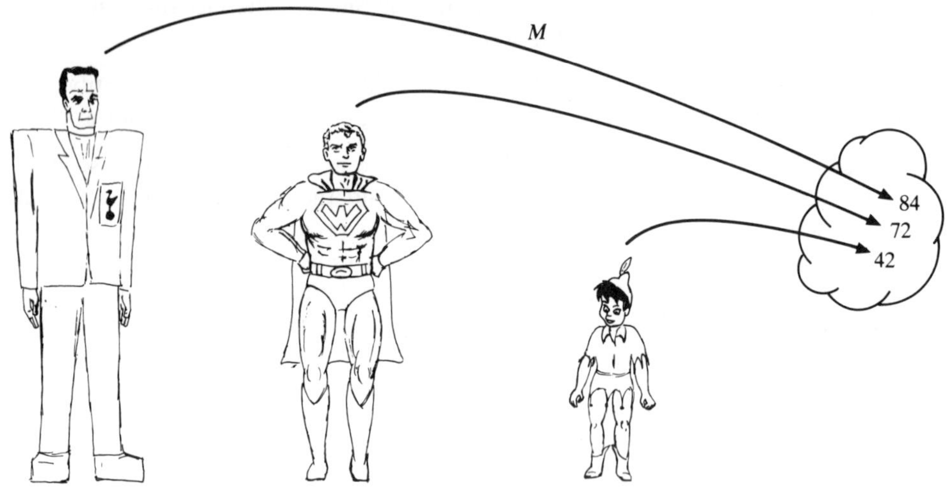

Figure 17.2 Interpretation mapping M.

Frankie when sitting on Wonderman's shoulders, so (Peter, Frankie, Wonderman) $\in R_4$. Now (M (Peter), M (Frankie), M (Wonderman)) $= (42, 84, 72) \in P_4$ since $(0.7)(42) + (0.8)(72) = 87 > 84$.

Exercise 17.4 Consider the empirical structure and interpretation of Example 17.7. With the help of Fig. 2.8 on page 34 write out in full the relations R_1, R_2, R_3, R_4. Hence complete the checks that, for each $i = 1, \ldots, 4$, R_i holds if and only if the relation P_i holds.

In Example 17.7, M preserves all the relations in such a way that we define M as a *measure* for Q, or more formally a *representation* for the empirical structure $\mathscr{C}$.

Definition 17.5 Representation Suppose $(C, \mathscr{R})$ is an empirical structure for an attribute Q and that $(A, \mathscr{P})$ is a numerical structure of the same similarity type. A representation is a homomorphism $M : (C, \mathscr{R}) \rightarrow (A, \mathscr{P})$. Assuming that $\mathscr{R} = \{R_1, \ldots, R_n\}$ and $\mathscr{P} = \{P_1, \ldots, P_n\}$, this means that for each $i = 1, \ldots, n$:

(a) $M(R_i) = P_i$, with P_i having the same arity as R_i, and

(b) $R_i(x_1, \ldots, x_k)$ if and only if $P_i(M(x_1), \ldots, M(x_k))$.

Condition (b) in Def. 17.5 is called the *representation condition*. This determines whether or not we have genuinely captured the attribute in question.

Example 17.8 Suppose that, in Example 17.7, we add Frankie's brother Hulk to the set C. Suppose that we are genuinely indifferent about which of Frankie and Hulk is the taller. Then neither (Frankie,Hulk) $\in R_2$ nor (Hulk,Frankie) $\in R_2$. Suppose we extend the interpretation M by defining M(Hulk)=85. It is still the case that, under M, the numerical structure $(\mathbb{R}, P_1, P_2, P_3, P_4)$ is a concrete model for the new empirical structure. However, it is *not* a representation. This is because (M(Hulk),M(Frankie)) $\in P_2$ but (Hulk,Frankie) $\notin R_2$. If, instead, we define M(Hulk)=84, then M is still a representation.

Example 17.9 In Example 17.4 on page 424 we considered two increasingly rich views for the attribute of criticality of software failures. Let us consider examples of representations for both of the resulting empirical structures:

(a) To find a representation M for $(C, \mathscr{R})$, take any three distinct numbers, say 6,2 and 69. We can then define

$M(x) = 6$ for each $x \in R_1$ (syntactic failures)
$M(x) = 2$ for each $x \in R_2$ (semantic failures)
$M(x) = 69$ for each $x \in R_3$ (system failures)

The relations R_1, R_2, R_3 are mapped to relations P_1, P_2, P_3 on $\mathbb{R}$. The relation P_1 is defined by $x \in P_1$ iff $x = 6$. Similarly, $x \in P_2$ iff $x = 2$ and $x \in P_3$ iff $x = 69$. If we had chosen to map syntactic failures and semantic failures to the same number 2 then we would not have got a representation. This is because if x is a semantic failure then $R_1(x)$ is false but $P_1(M(x))$ is true, since $M(x) = 2$.

(b) To find a representation for $(C, \mathscr{R}')$ we have to be much more careful with our assignment of numbers. In $\mathscr{R}'$ we added the relation R_4 to denote 'more critical than'. We therefore need a relation P_4 to interpret R_4. It is reasonable to take P_4 to be the binary relation '>'. It is not enough, as in (a), to simply map system failures, semantic failures and syntactic failures on to any three distinct numbers. In order to preserve R_4 with respect to $>$ we have to ensure that system failures are mapped into a higher number than semantic failures, which in turn are mapped to a higher number than syntactic failures. One acceptable representation is the mapping: syntactic $\mapsto$ 1, semantic $\mapsto$ 6, system $\mapsto$ 7. Note that the mapping defined in (a) would *not* be a representation for $\mathscr{R}'$. This is because '>' does not preserve R_4 under that mapping. Instead, semantic failures are mapped to a lower, rather than higher, number than syntactic failures: if x is a semantic y is syntactic, then $(x, y) \in R_4$ but $(M(x), M(y)) \notin P_4$, since $M(x) = 2 < 6 = M(y)$.

It is normal, but by no means mandatory, that the concrete numerical structure in a representation has, as its carrier set, the set $\mathbb{R}$ and includes the relation $>$. However, examples of the use of the complex numbers in electrical engineering should dispel the notion that the real numbers are the only useful number system for measurement. Moreover, we will show that classification of a set of entities is a special form of measurement, and we will certainly wish to use many types of symbols other than numbers for this purpose. An example of measurement in a numerical structure that is not, and indeed cannot be, the real numbers is given in Fig. 17.3.

Example 17.10 The big O notation of Chapter 15 is a measure of algorithmic efficiency in which the carrier set of the numerical structure consists of symbols like $O(f(n))$.

Exercise 17.5 In this exercise we refer to Example 17.9.

(a) For the empirical structure $(C, \mathscr{R})$ show that the mapping

syntactic $\mapsto$ 6, semantic $\mapsto$ 6, system crash $\mapsto$ 69

is *not* a representation. If we now change this by mapping semantic $\mapsto$ 10, show that we *do* get a representation.

(b) For the empirical structure $(C, \mathscr{R}')$ show that the mapping

syntactic $\mapsto$ 6, semantic $\mapsto$ 7, system crash $\mapsto$ 3

is *not* a representation. If we now change this by mapping semantic $\mapsto$ 10, show that we *do* get a representation.

Exercise 17.6 Consider Fig. 17.3. Find a different representation from the one described.

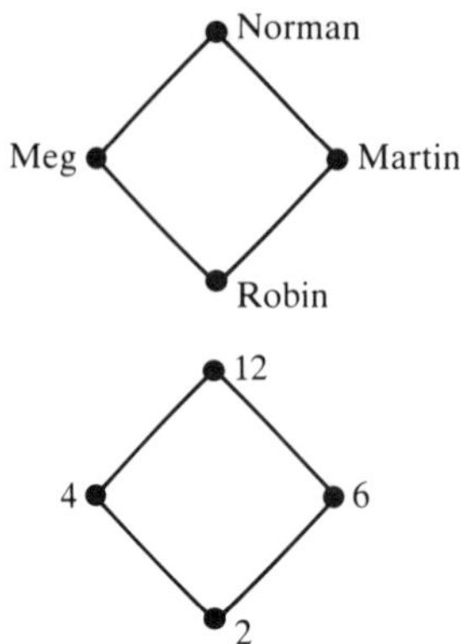

We are interested in the attribute of 'seniority' of members of staff in a company C. Suppose $C = \{$Norman, Meg, Martin, Robin$\}$ and R is the order relation 'more-senior' defined by the Hasse diagram on the left. Thus:

(Norman, Meg) $\in R$
(Martin, Robin) $\in R$, etc.

The attribute of seniority is characterized by the empirical structure $(C, \{R\})$. Note that neither (Meg, Martin) nor (Martin, Meg) are in R. This means that Meg and Martin are *incomparable* with respect to the relation R.

It follows that there can be no representation into the numerical structure $(\mathbb{R}, \leq)$, because otherwise this would *force* a relationship between Martin and Meg. However, we do have a representation into the numerical structure $(\mathbb{N}, |)$ where '|' is the relation divides. As shown, this maps Norman into 12, Meg to 4, Martin to 6 and Robin to 2.

Figure 17.3 Measurement in a non-conventional numerical structure.

17.3 MEASUREMENT SCALES

Having made formal the notion of measuring an attribute, we now wish to formalize the notion of measurement scales and scale types. We all know that if we want to measure length of physical objects we can do so using a tape measure calibrated in inches, centimetres or metres. Informally, we speak of the results of such measurement as being on different *scales*. You may also have heard people say that the *scale type* for measuring length is *ratio*. Since a *scale* is just a particular representation of an attribute in the sense of Sec. 17.2, it is easy to formalize. However, the crucial notion of scale type is rather difficult to formalize and is one of the most misunderstood concepts in measurement. This is very unfortunate, because only by knowing the relevant scale type for a measure do we know what meaningful analysis can be applied to the results of measurement data.

It turns out that attempts to produce an informal definition of scale type, without using the kind of theory we have presented, do not seem to work. To define scale types formally we introduce the notion of uniqueness of representations. Essentially, we have to characterize the relationships that exist between different representations. For example, each two of the above representations of length are related by a scalar multiple. In this case, multiplication by a scalar is said to be an *admissible transformation* from one representation into another. It is the class of admissible transformations that determines the scale type. Having defined the notion of scale type we are then able to define formally the notion of meaningful statements involving measurement, which in turn leads us to determine what kinds of manipulations we can meaningfully apply to the results of measurement data. The cost of failing to understand these notions can be seen in the results of many published experiments which can be shown to be flawed because of meaningless analyses of data.

17.3.1 Uniqueness

From Sec. 17.2 we know that direct measurement of an attribute Q has been performed if we can assign a representation mapping M from an observed empirical structure $\mathscr{C}$ for Q to some numerical structure $\mathscr{A}$.

Definition 17.6 Scale If $M : \mathscr{C} \rightarrow \mathscr{A}$ is a representation for an attribute Q, then the triple $(\mathscr{C}, \mathscr{A}, M)$ is called a scale.

Where $\mathscr{C}$ and $\mathscr{A}$ are obvious from the context, we sometimes refer to M alone as the scale.

Example 17.11 Consider Example 17.9. For the empirical structure $\mathscr{C} = (C, \mathscr{R})$ both of the following are scales:

(a) $M : \mathscr{C} \rightarrow (\mathbb{R}, \mathscr{P})$ defined by

$M(x) = 6$ for each $x \in R_1$ (syntactic failures)
$M(x) = 2$ for each $x \in R_2$ (semantic failures)
$M(x) = 69$ for each $x \in R_3$ (system failures)

(b) $M' : \mathscr{C} \rightarrow (\mathbb{R}, \mathscr{P}')$ defined by

$M'(x) = 1$ for each $x \in R_1$ (syntactic failures)
$M'(x) = 5$ for each $x \in R_2$ (semantic failures)
$M'(x) = 2$ for each $x \in R_3$ (system failures)

In fact, any mapping in which syntactic, semantic and system failures are mapped into distinct numbers is an acceptable representation. Thus, there are an infinite number of different possible representations. For $\mathscr{C} = (C, \mathscr{R}')$, the empirical structure in which we add the relation 'more critical', we have to be more selective. However, any assignment in which system is mapped to a higher number than semantic, which in turn is mapped to a higher number than syntactic, will be an acceptable representation. This is still an infinite number of different representations.

In Example 17.11, it is interesting that, although for each empirical structure there is an infinite number of different representations, it can be shown that, in each case, any two representations are related in a very simple way.

For $\mathscr{C}$, if M and M' are any two representations then M' can always be derived from M (and vice versa) by a *one-to-one mapping*. Conversely, if we apply any one-to-one mapping to a representation M we arrive at another representation M' for $\mathscr{C}$. We say that M' is a *rescaling* of M.

For $\mathscr{C}'$, if M and M' are any two representations then M' can always be derived from M (and vice versa) by a *monotonic increasing function*. Conversely, if we apply any monotonic increasing function to a representation M we arrive at another representation M' for $\mathscr{C}'$. Again we say that M' is a rescaling of M.

Example 17.12 Let M be any representation of length of physical objects. For example, M may measure length in inches. Then, for any positive real number α, it must be the case that αM is also a measure for length, since any relations that hold for M must surely hold for αM. Again we say that αM is a rescaling of M.

Definition 17.7 Admissible transformation Any mapping that transforms one representation M into another representation M' is called an admissible transformation. We also say that M' is a rescaling of M.

Example 17.13 In the case of $\mathscr{C}$ in Example 17.9, the admissible transformations are all the one-to-one mappings. For $\mathscr{C}'$, the admissible transformations are all the monotonic increasing functions. For length, the admissible transformations are all the positive scalar multiples.

17.3.2 Scale types

The class of admissible transformations for a given empirical structure defines how unique each scale is, and is used to define *scale type*. This means that scale type is dependent on the kinds of rescaling that are allowed. The fewer possible rescalings for a given structure, the more restrictive, and hence more accurate, will be the scale type. For example, the scale type for $\mathscr{C}'$ in Example 17.4 is more restrictive than the scale type for $\mathscr{C}$.

In order to give definitions of specific scale types that really work, we must restrict ourselves strictly to representations that are called *regular*. It turns out that every example representation seen so far is regular. Non-regular representations are genuinely bizarre and do not tend to occur in practice. For completeness, we next provide a formal description of regular scales. If you are happy to assume that regular means normal and that you will only ever be concerned with normal representations then you can skip the discussion on regular scales.

Regular scales* To motivate the definition of regular scales we begin with an example.

Example 17.14 Suppose that $\mathscr{C} = (\mathbb{N}, <)$ (which is a standard abbreviation for $(\mathbb{N}, \{<\})$) and $\mathscr{A} = (\mathbb{R}, <)$. Let M be the representation that maps the relation $<$ onto the relation $<$ and each natural number n onto the real number $2n$. Now consider another representation M' that maps n onto $5n + 3$. Can we find an admissible transformation φ for which $\varphi \circ M = M'$? The answer is 'yes', for we may define $\varphi(x) = 5/2x + 3$ so that

$$(\varphi \circ M)(x) = \varphi \circ (M(x)) = \varphi(2x) = 5x + 3 = M'(x)$$

Now let us consider yet another representation M'' defined by

$$M''(x) = \begin{cases} x & \text{for } n < 100 \\ x + 27 & \text{for } n \geq 100 \end{cases}$$

Clearly M'' is a representation because it is a strictly monotonically increasing function, whence $x > y$ if and only if $M''(x) > M''(y)$ (which is precisely the representation condition in this case). Yet again we are able to find an admissible transformation φ for which $\varphi \circ M = M''$, namely

$$\varphi(x) = \begin{cases} x/2 & \text{if } x < 100 \\ x/2 + 27 & \text{if } x \geq 100 \end{cases}$$

It is not difficult to see that the representation M, and hence the scale $(\mathscr{C}, \mathscr{A}, M)$ in Example 17.14, is always transformable by an admissible transformation into any other representation M' (scale $(\mathscr{C}, \mathscr{A}, M')$). This property of M is very desirable for a scale and is what we mean by regularity. Before giving the formal definition we need one more piece of terminology: since there may in general be many representations $M : \mathscr{C} \to \mathscr{A}$, we often refer to the set of all such representation as *the representation* $\mathscr{C} \to \mathscr{A}$.

Definition 17.8 Regular representation If $(\mathscr{C}, \mathscr{A}, M)$ is a scale such that for every scale $(\mathscr{C}, \mathscr{A}, M')$ there is a transformation $\varphi : M(C) \to N$ for which $M' = \varphi \circ M$, then the scale $(\mathscr{C}, \mathscr{A}, M)$ is called regular. If every representation M from $\mathscr{C}$ into $\mathscr{A}$ is regular, we call the representation $\mathscr{C} \to \mathscr{A}$ regular.

Thus a representation $\mathscr{C} \to \mathscr{A}$ is regular if, given any two scales M and M', each can be mapped into the other by an admissible transformation. It follows that in Example 17.14 not only is the scale $(\mathscr{C}, \mathscr{A}, M)$ regular but it can be shown that *every* scale $(\mathscr{C}, \mathscr{A}, M')$ is regular, and hence the representation $\mathscr{C} \to \mathscr{A}$ is regular. It is instructive to consider the following examples of non-regular scales.

Example 17.15 We consider a subtle change to the previous example. In this case consider the representation $(\mathbb{N}, \leq) \to (\mathbb{R}, \leq)$. It is not difficult to see that the mapping M defined by

$$M(x) = \begin{cases} x & \text{if } x < 100 \\ 100 & \text{if } x \geq 100 \end{cases}$$

is a representation. So too is the identity function M' where $M'(x) = x$ for all x. There is no admissible transformation φ for which $\varphi \circ M = M'$. If there were, then, since $M(100) = M'(100)$, it would follow that we must have $\varphi(100) = 100$. Let us see how φ maps any other number above 100, say 101. Now since $M(101) = 100$ we have $\varphi(100) = \varphi \circ M(101)$. However, $\varphi(100) = \varphi \circ M(101) = M'(101) = 101$, which leads to a contradiction. Thus M is not a regular scale. However, there *is* an admissible transformation φ for which $\varphi \circ M' = M$: we simply take $\varphi = M$. It follows from a generalization of this argument that the scale M' is regular.

Example 17.16 Suppose $C = \{a, b, c\}$ is a set of three software systems for which there is a binary relation R intended to represent the empirical relation $(x, y) \in R$ if and only if 'x is significantly more difficult to maintain than y'. Suppose that $R = \{(a, b), (a, c)\}$, so a is significantly more difficult to maintain than both b and c. The pair (C, R) is an empirical structure. Consider the numerical system $\mathscr{A} = (\mathbb{R}, P)$ where P is the binary relation defined by $(x, y) \in P$ if and only if $x > y + 1$. Let

$$\begin{array}{lll} M(a) = 2 & M(b) = 0 & M(c) = 0 \\ M'(a) = 2 & M'(b) = 0.5 & M'(c) = 0 \end{array}$$

Clearly M and M' are both representations $\mathscr{C} \to \mathscr{A}$. However, M is not regular because there is no function $\varphi : M(C) \to \mathbb{R}$ for which $M' = \varphi \circ M$. The problem is created by the fact that b and c are mapped to the same number under M but a different number under M'. This means that $\varphi(0)$ is ill-defined, since on the one hand,

$$\varphi(0) = \varphi M(c) = M'(c) = 0$$

but on the other hand,

$$\varphi(0) = \varphi M(b) = M'(b) = 0.5$$

These examples give an intuitive justification for the following theorem.

Theorem 17.1 The scale $(\mathscr{C}, \mathscr{A}, M)$ is regular if and only if for every other representation $M' : \mathscr{C} \to \mathscr{A}$ and for all $x, y \in C$, $M(x) = M(y)$ implies $M'(x) = M'(y)$.

Classification of scale types Assuming henceforth that all representations are regular, we summarize the most important scale types in Table 17.1. Since scale types are defined with respect to the set of admissible transformations, examples of attributes really ought to specify the relevant theories for the attribute. We have seen in Example 17.9 that as we extend the theory for an attribute by adding new predicate symbols and axioms, so

Table 17.1 Scales of measurement

Admissible transformations	Scale types	Examples
$M' = F(M)$ (F one-to-one mapping)	Nominal	Labelling/classifying entities
$M' = F(M)$ (F monotonic increasing i.e. $M(x) \geq M(y) \Rightarrow M'(x) \geq M'(y)$)	Ordinal	Preference, hardness, air quality intelligence tests (raw scores)
$M' = \alpha M + \beta$ $(\alpha > 0)$	Interval	Time (calendar) Temperature (Fahrenheit, Celsius) Intelligence tests ('standard scores')
$M' = \alpha M$ $(\alpha > 0)$	Ratio	Time interval, length, temperature (absolute)
$M' = M$	Absolute	Counting entities

we arrive at a more restrictive (and hence different) scale type. Thus, when Table 17.1 says that the attributes length, time interval and absolute temperature are *ratio* scale measures, what it really means is that we have developed sufficiently refined theories about the attributes to facilitate ratio scale measures for them.

Example 17.17 Consider again the empirical structures $\mathscr{C}$ and $\mathscr{C}'$ for the two theories for the attribute of criticality of software failures given in Example 17.4.

(a) We have already noted that the set of admissible transformations for $\mathscr{C}$ is just the set of one-to-one mappings. Thus, the scale type for this structure for criticality is *nominal*.

(b) We have already noted that the set of admissible transformations for $\mathscr{C}'$ is just the set of monotonic increasing functions. Thus, the scale type for this structure for criticality is *ordinal*.

Broadly speaking, any attribute that imposes only a classification on a set of entities has nominal scale type, and any attribute that imposes only a linear ordering has ordinal scale type. If, in addition to a linear ordering, there is a notion of relative distance between entities, then the scale type is interval. If there is also a 'zeroness' relation, containing entities that possess *nothing* of the attribute, then the scale type is ratio since the zeroness relation must be mapped to 0.

Example 17.18 It follows from Example 17.12 on page 429 that the scale type for the normal intuitive understanding of the attribute of length of objects is ratio.

Absolute scales arise out of attributes that amount to simple counts of entities.

Example 17.19 The 'number of known bugs' is an attribute of software systems. The empirical structure is rather trivial; for each number n there is a corresponding relation R_n: 'n known bugs'. A software system belongs to exactly one of these relations; if the system called UNOX has 29 known bugs then UNOX $\in R_{29}$. The obvious representation for this structure is to map each system in R_n on to the number n. Thus UNOX is mapped to 29. There is no (non-identity) admissible transformation of this representation. Hence its scale type is absolute. Note, however, that if we use the count of number of known bugs to measure a different attribute, namely quality of software systems, then we cannot say that the measure is absolute. Depending on what kind of relations we can observe empirically for this attribute, the measure 'number of known bugs' will at best be a ratio scale measure (if it is indeed a representation at all) for quality.

We cannot over-emphasize the importance of the notion of regular representations in the definition of scale types. Using the notation introduced on page 430, if a representation $\mathscr{C} \rightarrow \mathscr{A}$ is not regular then it follows from Def. 17.8 that the notion of a scale type for the representation $\mathscr{C} \rightarrow \mathscr{A}$ is not well defined. That this sorry state of affairs cannot happen for regular representations is made explicit by the following theorem.

Theorem 17.2 If the representation $\mathscr{C} \rightarrow \mathscr{A}$ is regular and M, M' are representations from $\mathscr{C}$ into $\mathscr{A}$ then M is an absolute, ratio, interval, ordinal or nominal scale if and only if M' is, respectively, an absolute, ratio, interval, ordinal or nominal scale.

The representation problem An important question that we have not yet addressed is whether we can determine, in advance of measurement, the scale type for a given empirical structure. More specifically, given a particular numerical structure $\mathscr{A}$, we would like to find conditions on an empirical structure $\mathscr{C}$ necessary and sufficient for the existence of a representation from $\mathscr{C}$ into $\mathscr{A}$. This is a central topic in measurement theory, known as the *representation problem*.

In the height example on page 425 we seemed to conjure the relations P_i out of thin air. There are many different relations that we could have used, but the axioms of the theory, such as transitivity, constrain our choice. Any theorem stating the necessary and sufficient conditions for the existence of a particular class of representations is called a *representation theorem*. There are numerous representation theorems that solve the representation problem for various types of structures. A typical example of such a theorem, due to Cantor, gives necessary and sufficient conditions for ordinal measurement in an important class of structures over a countable set. It relies on the notion of *strict weak order* defined in Sec. 2.2.

Theorem 17.3 Cantor Suppose C is a countable set and R is a binary relation on C. Then there is a real-valued function $M : C \rightarrow \mathbb{R}$ satisfying $xRy \leftrightarrow M(x) > M(y)$ if and only if (C, R) is a strict weak order. Moreover, if there is such an M, then $\mathscr{C} \rightarrow \mathscr{A}$, where $\mathscr{C} = (C, R)$ and $\mathscr{A} = (\mathbb{R}, >)$, is a regular representation and $(\mathscr{C}, \mathscr{A}, M)$ is an ordinal scale.

Theorem 17.3 has important ramifications for a popular topic in software measurement, namely so-called 'complexity measures' of programs.

Example 17.20 Many attempts have been made to find a (single) real-valued function to characterize program complexity. In this case our set C is the set of all flowgraph models of programs as defined in Chapter 13. It is claimed that the notion of 'complexity' leads to an intuitive order relation R on program flowgraphs. Specifically, two programs x, y are in the relation R precisely when 'x is more complex than y'. Now complexity functions are mappings of flowgraphs

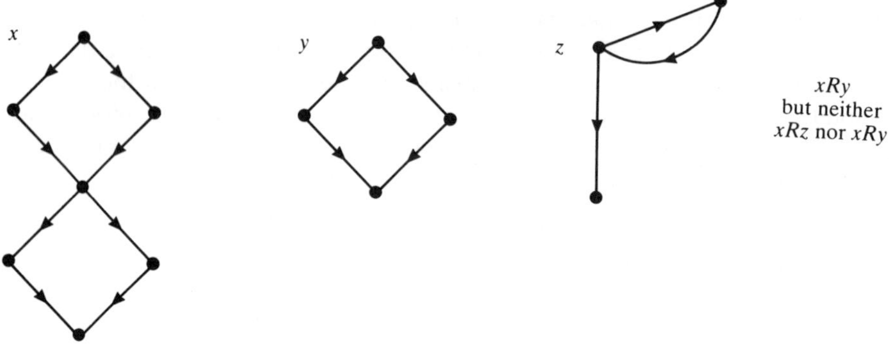

Figure 17.4 Complexity relation not negatively transitive?

into real numbers which are supposed to preserve the relation R. It follows from Theorem 17.3 that these are ordinal measures of 'complexity' if and only if the relation R is a strict weak order. It is our contention that no general notion of complexity can give rise to such an order because negative transitivity is not a reasonable expectation. In Fig. 17.4 it seems plausible that xRy but that neither xRz nor zRy. However, let us take a well-known 'complexity measure', namely McCabe's cyclomatic number M which we defined in Sec. 13.3.4. Then $M(x) = 3$ and $M(y) = M(z) = 2$. Now if M really was a measure of 'complexity', then it follows that xRz, so the definition of M *forces* x to be more 'complex' than z, which does not concur with our intuitive understanding of R.

Although Cantor's theorem appears to suggest that single, real-valued, measures of general software complexity are not feasible, it can be used positively to construct ordinal scale measures of specific complexity attributes (such as those discussed on page 432) that do reasonably lead to strict weak orders. Note how the real task is to first establish the relation (the flowgraph ordering), since the ordinal measure then follows naturally.

Exercise 17.7

(a) Consider the attribute of 'length' of programs. Show that 'number of lines of code' is a reasonable ratio scale measure for this attribute.

(b) Some people have said that 'number of lines of code' is an *absolute* scale measure of program length. Explain why this cannot be the case. Of what is it an absolute scale measure?

Exercise 17.8 Consider the attribute of 'number of bugs found' for software testing processes. Define an absolute scale measure for this attribute. Why is 'number of bugs found' not an absolute scale measure of the attribute of *program correctness*?

17.3.3 The notion of meaningfulness

Now that we have established a theory of scale types, we can use it to describe the notion of meaningfulness. This provides a formal mechanism for reasoning about when statements involving measurement make sense. This will also tell us about the limitations on the kind of mathematical operations that can be performed on numbers arising as scale values. We can always perform operations like adding, averaging and taking logarithms of real numbers. However, the key question is whether, after having done so, we can still deduce meaningful statements about the entities being measured. Consider the following statements:

1 The number of errors discovered during integration testing of program X was at least 100.

2 The cost of fixing each error in program X is at least 100.

3 A semantic error takes twice as long to fix as a syntactic error.

4 A semantic error is twice as complex as a syntactic error.

Arguing at a purely intuitive level, statement 1 seems to make sense but statement 2 does not, for the number of errors may be specified without reference to a particular scale, whereas the cost of fixing an error cannot. Statement 3 seems to make sense (even if we think it cannot possibly be true) whereas statement 4 does not; this is because the ratio of time taken is the same regardless of the scale of measurement used (if a semantic error takes twice as many minutes to repair as a syntactic error, it also takes twice as many hours, seconds, years, etc.), whereas the ratio of 'complexity' (which is ambiguous anyway in this statement) is not necessarily the same. Our intuitive notion of meaningfulness of statements involving measurement is quite distinct from the notion of *truth* of the statements in the sense of Chapter 3; the statement 'the Prime Minister of England is 125 years old' is meaningful even though it is clearly false.

Measurement accounts for these kinds of observations by considering the uniqueness of the representations. We have seen that it is quite possible for there to be many different representations of an empirical structure. Thus, any statement about measurement should specify which scale (representation) is being used or should make sense independent of scale.

Definition 17.9 Meaningfulness A statement involving numerical scales is meaningful if its truth (or falsity) remains unchanged if every scale M involved is replaced by an acceptable rescaling M'.

When we say that M' is an acceptable rescaling we mean that it may be derived from M by an admissible transformation.

Example 17.21 Suppose that we have a crude notion of 'strength', characterized by the simple empirical structure $\mathscr{C} = (C, \mathscr{R})$ where $C = \{\text{Frankie, Peter, Wonderman}\}$ and $\mathscr{R}$ consists of the single binary relation R: 'is stronger than'. Suppose that, explicitly,

$$R = \{(\text{Wonderman,Frankie}), (\text{Frankie, Peter}), (\text{Wonderman, Peter})\}$$

Then, the mapping $M : \mathscr{C} \rightarrow \{\mathbb{R}, >\}$ given by

$$M\,(\text{Peter}) = 1,\ M\,(\text{Wonderman}) = 2,\ M\,(\text{Frankie}) = 3$$

is clearly a representation. Moreover, any mapping M' into $\mathbb{R}$ in which

$$M'(\text{Peter}) < M'(\text{Wonderman}) < M'(\text{Frankie})$$

is also an acceptable scale, as the scale type is ordinal. Thus, consider the statement: 'Wonderman is stronger than both Peter and Frankie'. This statement is true since

$$(\text{Wonderman,Peter}) \in R \wedge (\text{Wonderman, Frankie}) \in R$$

It is also meaningful, for under the scale M it corresponds to the statement

$$(M\,(\text{Wonderman}) > M\,(\text{Peter})) \wedge (M\,(\text{Wonderman}) > M\,(\text{Frankie}))$$

which is equal to $(3 > 1) \wedge (3 > 2)$. This assertion is true, and if we replace M by another acceptable scale M', it is clear that the corresponding statement will also be true. By a similar argument we can show that the statement 'Peter is stronger than both Frankie and Wonderman' is meaningful even though it is false. However, the statement 'Frankie is more than twice as strong as Peter' is not meaningful, for under M this corresponds to the assertion:

$$M\,(\text{Frankie}) > 2 \times M\,(\text{Peter})$$

which is equal to '$3 > 2 \times 1$', which is true. However, consider a new scale M' which is the same as M except that $M'(\text{Peter}) = 1.5$. Then M' is still an acceptable scale, but under M' the statement corresponds to '$3 > 2 \times 1.5$', which is false.

Exercise 17.9 Consider the structure $\mathscr{C}'$ in Example 17.4. Determine the meaningfulness or otherwise of the following statements with respect to this structure for criticality of software failures:

(a) A system crash is more critical than either a semantic or a syntactic failure.

(b) A semantic failure is twice as critical as a syntactic failure.

17.3.4 Operations on measures

One of the most powerful applications of the theory of scale types and meaningfulness is in determining which types of operations or statistical analyses can be sensibly applied to particular types of measures. A summary of the necessary information is shown in Table 17.2, which is derived from Siegel and Castellan (1988). Rather than presenting a comprehensive explanation of each table entry, we select the important case of the *average*. For each scale type we want to show which statistical operations we can use to compute a meaningful average of a set of numbers that represent the results of measurement of that type.

Example 17.22 Our general problem is that we have a measure M and a set of entities $X = \{x_1, \ldots, x_n\}$ for which we know each of $M\,(x_1), \ldots, M\,(x_n)$. The question is how do we compute the average value of the $M\,(x_i)$'s. To tackle this problem formally it is best to think of another set $Y = \{y_1, \ldots, y_m\}$ for which we also know $M\,(y_j)$ in each case. For example, X and Y may be respectively the sets of modules appearing in two different programs, and M may be a size measure. We want to be able to determine whether the average module size in X is higher than the average module size in Y. In general, for whatever the measure M represents, we want to define average in such a way that the statement

The average of the $M\,(x_i)$'s is greater than the average of the $M\,(y_j)$'s

is meaningful (whether or not it is true). One possible way to compute averages is to use the arithmetic mean. In this case we would want the statement

$$\frac{1}{n}\sum_{i=1}^{n} M\,(x_i) > \frac{1}{m}\sum_{i=1}^{m} M\,(y_j) \qquad (17.1)$$

Table 17.2 Summary of statistics relevant to measurement scales

Scale	Defining relations	Examples of appropriate statistics	Appropriate statistical tests
Nominal	1. Equivalence	Mode Frequency Contingency coefficient	
Ordinal	1. Equivalence 2. Greater than	Median Percentile Kendall τ Spearman r_S Kendall W	Non-parametric statistical tests
Interval	1. Equivalence 2. Greater than 3. Known ratio of any intervals	Mean Standard deviation Pearson product-moment correlation Multiple product-moment correlation	Non-parametric and parametric statistical tests
Ratio	1. Equivalence 2. Greater than 3. Known ratio of any two intervals 4. Known ratio of any two scale values	Geometric mean Coefficient of variation	

to be meaningful. For this to be the case, for any other measure M' (resulting from an admissible transformation of M), Eq. (17.1) holds if and only if the following holds:

$$\frac{1}{n}\sum_{i=1}^{n} M'(x_i) > \frac{1}{m}\sum_{i=1}^{m} M'(y_j) \tag{17.2}$$

If M is a ratio scale measure then we know that $M' = \alpha M$ for some positive α. In this case it is easy to see that Eq. (17.1) holds if and only if (17.2) holds. Similarly, if M is an interval scale measure then $M = \alpha M + \beta$ (with $\alpha > 0$) and again Eq. (17.1) holds if and only if Eq. (17.2) holds.

Thus we can meaningfully take the arithmetic mean of measures that are defined on a ratio or interval scale. However, Eq. (17.1) is not meaningful if the scale of M is ordinal. To see this suppose that we have an ordinal scale for software complexity which is a ranking of five different classes of complexity:

	M	M'
Trivial	1	1
Simple	2	2
Moderate	3	3
Complex	4	4
Incomprehensible	5	10

The last two columns represent two perfectly acceptable ordinal scales of measurement M and M'. There is an admissible transformation mapping M on to M', namely the monotonic mapping: $\{1 \mapsto 1, 2 \mapsto 2, 3 \mapsto 3, 4 \mapsto 4, 5 \mapsto 10\}$. Now suppose X_1, X_2, X_3 and Y_1, Y_2, Y_3 are software systems for which X_1 is 'moderate', X_2 is 'complex', X_3 is 'simple', Y_1 is 'trivial', Y_2 is 'incomprehensible' and Y_3 is 'simple'. We hope to be able to say which of the sets $\{X_1, X_2, X_3\}$ and $\{Y_1, Y_2, Y_3\}$ has the greatest average complexity; however, taking the *arithmetic mean* is not meaningful because

$$1/2(M(X_1) + M(X_2) + M(X_3)) = 4.5 > 4 = 1/2(M(Y_1) + M(Y_2) + M(Y_3))$$

whereas

$$1/2(M'(X_1) + M'(X_2) + M'(X_3)) = 4.5 < 6.5 = 1/2(M'(Y_1) + M'(Y_2) + M'(Y_3))$$

All is not lost because there is a measure of 'average' value which *is* meaningful for ordinal scale measures. This is the *median* value: the value of the middle ranked item. In our example, under both M and M' the median of the X_i's is 3, while the median of the Y_i's is 2.

Exercise 17.10 Prove that the median is a meaningful notion of average for ordinal scale measures.

Exercise 17.11 Show that for nominal scale measures the median is not a meaningful notion of average, but the *mode* (most commonly occurring class of item) is meaningful.

17.4 INDIRECT MEASUREMENT*

Although most attributes can be measured directly in the manner discussed so far, it is normally the case that more accurate measurement may be achieved *indirectly*. This is done by defining new scales in terms of old ones.

Example 17.23 The attribute *speed* of moving objects can be shown to be measured directly, but only on an ordinal scale; however, when measured indirectly in terms of *time* and *distance*, we arrive at the generally used ratio scale of measurement for speed.

Definition 17.10 Indirect scale A function M is an indirect scale if it is defined in terms of some functions $M_1, M_2, \ldots, M_n$ where $n > 0$.

This is a very broad definition. Mass divided by volume and mass plus volume are equally good indirect measures according to this definition. In general, M and the M_i will satisfy a certain condition $E(M_1, M_2, \ldots, M_n, M')$. Normally, E will be a predicate relating M to $M_1, M_2, \ldots, M_n$.

Example 17.24 Consider density d measured indirectly in terms of mass m and volume V. In this case $E(m, V, d)$ is the equation $d = m/V$.

Example 17.25 It has been argued that in software production, effort e in person months is an indirect measure of program size s in thousands of lines of code. For example, Walston and Felix (1979) claim that $E(s, e)$ is an empirical equation: $e = 5.2s^{0.91}$.

The notion of scale types for indirect scales can be approached in an analogous manner as for direct measurement. This means we have to find the 'admissible transformations' (rescalings) of M that preserve the condition E.

Definition 17.11 Rescaling Suppose $E(M_1, M_2, \ldots, M_n, M)$ holds for the indirect scale M. We say that M' is a rescaling of M if there are rescalings $M_1', M_2', \ldots, M_n'$ of $M_1, M_2, \ldots, M_n$ respectively, such that $E(M_1', M_2', \ldots, M_n', M')$ holds.

Thus the condition E holds for M' when the values of the M_i's are substituted by other acceptable scales.

Example 17.26 Consider the example of density where $E(m, V, d)$ is the equation $d = m/V$. We claim that the rescalings of d are all of the form $d' = \alpha d$ (for $\alpha > 0$). To show this formally we have to show two things: (a) that these are rescalings and (b) that every rescaling has this form.

We note that both m and V are ratio scale measures and hence all their rescalings have the form αm and αV respectively. Now we show (a). We have to find rescalings m', V' of m, V respectively such that $E(m', V', \alpha d)$ holds. Certainly αm and V are acceptable rescalings of α and V respectively. Therefore, it is enough to show that $E(\alpha m, V, \alpha d)$ holds. However, this is the equation $\alpha d = (\alpha m)/V$ which reduces to $d = m/V$, and this is just the condition $E(d, m, V)$ which we know holds. This demonstrates (a). We leave (b) as an exercise.

We can now define scale types for indirect scales in exactly the same way as for direct scales. From Example 17.26 we can assert that the scale for density d is ratio, because all the admissible transformations have the form $d \to \alpha d$. It can be shown that the scale type for an indirect measure M will generally be no stronger than the 'weakest' of the scale types of the M_i's. Thus if the M_i's contain a mixture of ratio, interval and nominal scale types, then the scale type for M will at best be nominal, since this is weakest.

Example 17.27 If the Walston–Felix equation in Example 17.25 really did measure effort then it would be a ratio scale measure. To see this we have to show that the rescalings of e are of the form αe for $\alpha > 0$. Thus first we have to find a rescaling s' of s for which $\alpha e = 5.2(s')^{0.91}$ holds (assuming that the equation for effort holds). The trick is to take s' to be the rescaling $\alpha^{1/0.91}s$. This is admissible because s is itself a ratio scale. Since we then have $s = \alpha^{-1/0.91}s'$, it follows that

$$\alpha e = \alpha(5.2s^{0.91}) = 5.2\alpha s^{0.91} = 5.2\alpha(\alpha^{-1/0.91}s')^{0.91} = 5.2(s')^{0.91}$$

Conversely, we have to show that every rescaling e' of e is of the form αe. To see this we note that because s is ratio, its only rescalings are those of the form βs. Thus we have to find an α such that $\alpha e = 5.2(\beta s)^{0.91}$. In fact this will work if we take $\alpha = \beta^{0.91}$. Although we have shown that the scale is ratio, it is highly unlikely that it really measures *effort*, but a full explanation of this is beyond the scope of this chapter.

Example 17.28 The equation $e = 2.7v + 121w + 26x + 12y + 22z - 497$ has also been proposed as a measure of software effort where e is supposed to represent person months, v is the number of program instructions, w is a subjective complexity rating, x the number of internal documents, y the number of external documents and z the size in words. Unfortunately, the equation is meaningless. If effort is measured in person months as suggested, then the scale type would have to be ratio. However, here it is only ordinal because w is only ordinal.

Exercise 17.12 Show that condition (b) in Example 17.26 holds.

Exercise 17.13 On page 420 we posed four questions that we said we were going to answer. Write down your own answers to these questions on the basis of what you have learnt.

17.5 SUMMARY

Measurement requires the identification of intuitively understood attributes possessed by clearly defined entities. Measurement is then the assignment of numbers or symbols to the entities in a way that captures our intuitive understanding about the attribute.

Direct measurement of a particular attribute must be preceded by intuitive understanding of that attribute. This intuitive understanding leads to the identification of relations between entities. Thus height of people gives rise to relations like 'is tall', 'taller than' and 'much taller than'. To measure the attribute we need to have corresponding relations in some number system; then measurement is the assignment of numbers to the entities in such a way that these relations are preserved. This is the so-called *representation condition*.

There may in general be many ways of assigning numbers which satisfy the representation condition. In general, the nature of these different types of assignments determines the *scale type* for the attribute. There are five well-known scale types, *nominal, ordinal, interval, ratio* and *absolute*. The scale type for a measure determines what kind of statements we can meaningfully make using the measure. In particular, this extends to what kind of operations we can perform on them. For example, we can compute *means* for ratio scale measures, but not for ordinal measures, and we can compute *medians* for ordinal scale measures, but not for nominal scale measures. Indirect measures are normally equations relating one or more measures, and we define scale types for these in a similar way to direct measures.

FURTHER READING

Much of the work in this chapter was inspired by Roberts' book (1979), the paper by Finkelstein (1984) and the book by Krantz, Luce, Suppes and Tversk (1971). These are all well worth reading for more details about measurement theory. For its detailed application to software measurement, see Fenton (1991). For a formal theory of measurement that accommodates the notion of measurement error, see Kyburg (1984). To find about the statistical techniques available for analysing measurement data, see the book by Siegel and Castellan (1988).

SOLUTIONS TO SELECTED EXERCISES

1.2 The radio may be viewed as a concrete model of the set of requirements, while the set of requirements may be viewed as an abstract model of the radio.

1.5 Purpose: to produce a machine executable version of a syntactically correct program. Key inputs: text file (intended to be a syntactically correct program); compiler directives (e.g. 'set debugger ON'). Key outputs: file of executable code; error messages.

2.1 Division = {Spurs, Arsenal, Liverpool} is a valid variable assignment.

2.4 Equal as sets, not equal as multisets.

2.8 Any even number $m \neq 2$ is divisible by both 2 and $m/2$.

2.9 $240 = 2^4.3.5$

2.10 The set contains 16 elements including $\{\}$, $\{1\}$, $\{1,2\}$, $\{1,2,3\}$ and $\{1,2,3,4\}$.

2.15 $\mathscr{P}(S) \notin S$ because $\mathscr{P}(S)$ always contains elements not in S. If S contains every set then it must contain the set $\mathscr{P}(S)$. Hence $\mathscr{P}(S) \in S$.

2.21 Let U be a set whose elements are all sets under consideration. Then $\cup \subseteq U \times U \times U$ where $(A, B, C) \in \cup$ if $A \cup B = C$. The operation $-$, which for a number x returns the value $-x$, is a unary operation over $\mathbb{R}$.

2.23 Transitive, antisymmetric, asymmetric and irreflexive.

2.25 $\{0, \pm 3, \pm 6, \pm 9, \ldots\}$, $\{1, 4, -2, 7, -5, \ldots\}$, $\{2, 5, -1, 8, -4, \ldots\}$

2.32 The element 1 is minimal and 4,5 and 6 are all maximal.

2.38 $a \times b = (b = 0 \rightarrow 0,\ a + (a \times (\textit{minus-one}(b))$

2.39 Product rule is a function $D^* : F \times F \rightarrow F$ (where F is the set of differentiable functions) which asserts that $D^*(fg) = D(f)g + fD(g)$.

2.47 Each edge has two endpoints. Hence each edge contributes 2 to the sum of the vertex degrees.

2.49 (a, b, e, d), (b, c, e), (c, f), (b, c, f, g)

2.57 $y = \frac{2}{3}x + \frac{2}{3}z$.

2.58 Suppose that $x_1, \ldots, x_n$ is a linearly independent set. If some subset, say $x_1, \ldots, x_k$ $(k < n)$, was linearly dependent then we could find a_i's not all zero such that $a_1x_1 + \cdots + a_kx_k = 0$. However, $a_1x_1 + \cdots + a_kx_k + 0x_{k+1} + \cdots + 0x_n = 0$, which contradicts the fact that the original set is linearly independent.

2.62 $\begin{pmatrix} 1 & 0 & 0 \\ 0 & 1 & 0 \\ 4 & 5 & 1 \end{pmatrix}$, $\begin{pmatrix} 1/\sqrt{2} & 1/\sqrt{2} & 0 \\ -1/\sqrt{2} & 1/\sqrt{2} & 0 \\ 0 & 0 & 1 \end{pmatrix}$

2.64 $1 \times 4 \times 4 \times 2 = 32$, since the first position may be filled in 1 way (by a), the second and third positions in 4 ways (by a, b, c, or d), and the fourth position in 2 ways (a or d).

2.67 Total number of variables = 3-character variables + 2-character variables + 1-character variables. Number of 3-character variables = $26 \times (26 + 10) \times 10 = 9360$ (by rules of sum and product). Number of 2-character variables = $26 \times 10 = 260$. Number of 3-character variables = 26. Thus the total number is 9646.

2.88

(a) Each of the 5 students must have a different number. For each group of 5 students with the same coloured jumper there are 4 colours to choose from. Choose the numbers for the students in $C(6,5) = 6$ ways and choose the colours for the students in $C(4,1) = 4$ ways. By the product rule, choose the group in 24 ways.

(b) The 2 students must share the number but belong to different groups. Choose the number in $C(6,1) = 6$ ways and choose the colour in $C(4,2) = 6$ ways. By the product rule, choose the 2 students in 36 ways. The remaining 3 students have numbers chosen from the remaining 5 numbers. Each of these students can be chosen from any of the 4 groups, possibly the same. Choose the number in $C(5,3) = 10$ ways; choose the colour in $C(4,1) \times C(4,1) \times C(4,1) = 64$ ways. By the product rule, choose the 3 students in 640 ways. By the product rule, choose the group in 36×640 ways.

3.19 (a) The man does not have grey eyes (as an English sentence). The proposition is $\neg$ the man has grey eyes.

3.23

(a) F because there is no King of Japan.

(b) F because there is no King of Japan.

(c) T as the negation of the first sentence.

3.73 'No one likes applied mathematics' is the negation so (b) is correct.

4.19 The truth of a conclusion does not imply the truth of the hypotheses from which the conclusion was deduced.

5.1

(a) '____ is a divisor of 10' y (no truth-value), 2 (is T), 3 (is F), a constant symbol naming '2' (is T)

(b) '____ is prime' x, z (no truth-value), 1 (is true), 52 (is F), a representing '5' (is T)

(c) '____ writes books' Jill, x, y (all could be T)

(d) 'Everybody likes ____ ' Neil, x, y (all could be T)

(e) 'No one finds ____ difficult' logic, maths, swimming (could be T or F)

5.2

(a) '$x = 3$' '____ $= 3$' 3 (is T), 2 (is F), y (not known)

(b) '$x = y$' '____ $=$ ____ ' 3,3 (is T), 2,3 (is F), r, s (not known)

(c) '$x + y = z$' '____ $+$ ____ $=$ ____ ' 5,2,7 (is T), 4,6,2 (is F)

(d) 'She lives in a city' '____ lives in ...' Sally, London (may be T), Sarah, Hull (may be F)

5.3

(a) '$2 = 5$' is expressed by $\mathscr{E}(2,5)$

(b) 'Sam is a female' is expressed by $\mathscr{F}$(Sam)

(c) 'The sum of 0 added to 4 is 4' is expressed by $\mathscr{S}(0,4,4)$

(d) '$2 + 5 = 9$' is expressed by $\mathscr{S}(2,5,9)$

(e) 'Sam hates the female Liz' is expressed by $\mathscr{H}$(Sam, Liz)$\wedge\mathscr{F}$(Liz)

5.4

(a) $\mathscr{L}$: 'x lives in y'. Satisfied by (Sam,Hull) and (Norman,London) in $D = D_1 \times D_2$ where D_1 ={inhabitants of England} and D_2={towns in England}. Valid in $D = D_1 \times D_2$ where D_1={inhabitants of London} and D_2={London}.

(b) $\mathscr{P}$: 'x is prime'. Satisfied by 5 and 11 in $D = \mathbb{N}$. Valid in D = {primes}.

(c) $\mathscr{T}$: 'x is taller than y'. Satisfied by (Bob,Sue) in D ={people} ×{people}. Valid in $D = D_1 \times D_2$ where D_1={people over 5 feet tall } and D_2={people under 5 feet tall}.

(d) $\mathscr{D}$: 'x divides y'. Satisfied by $(2,10)$ in $D = \mathbb{Z} \times \mathbb{Z}$. Valid in $D = D_1 \times D_2$ where $D_1 = \{2\}$ and D_2={multiples of 2}.

(e) $\mathscr{V}$: 'x voted for y'. Satisfied by (Sam,John Major) and (Brenda, Neil Kinnock) in $D = D_1 \times D_2$ where D_1={inhabitants of England} and D_2={candidates for Parliament in England}. Valid in $D = D_1 \times D_2$ where D_1={members of the Labour party} and D_2={leader of the Labour party}.

5.5 If y is assigned the value 10 the predicate $\mathscr{C}'(x)$ denotes '$x + 10 = 10 + x$'.

5.7 In $\mathscr{V}(x, y)$ assign Margaret $\in$ {adults} to y to form $\mathscr{V}'(x)$ denoting 'x voted for Margaret'. $\mathscr{V}'$(Dennis) is a possible instantiation for x.

5.8

$$\forall \mathscr{M}(\underline{\quad\quad}) \wedge \forall \mathscr{P}(\underline{\quad\quad}, \ldots)$$

The x in $\forall y\ \mathscr{P}(x, y)$ is free.

5.9 $\forall x\ \mathscr{V}(x,$ Donald Duck).

5.11 $\exists x\ \mathscr{L}(x,$ Charlie Chaplin).

5.13 Let $\mathscr{M}(x, y)$ denote 'x is married to y' over the domain {men} $\times$ {women}. The assertion is $\exists! y\ \mathscr{M}($Bill, $y)$.

5.16 Let D={people} and define

$\mathscr{K}(x)$: x is the King of Japan
$\mathscr{B}(x)$: x is bald

Then $\exists x\ \mathscr{K}(x)$ is false so $\exists x\ [\mathscr{K}(x) \wedge \mathscr{B}(x)]$ is true as before.

5.18

(a) Meaning of i is 2. Meaning of 'age' is any integer between 10 and 100. Meaning of 'personsage' is given by the meaning of 'age'.

(b) Commands are 'personsage := 10' and 'personsage := personsage + i'.

(c) A command has an irreversible effect on the computational state of a Pascal program. The effect of a definition is normally undone later; it only lasts within a program block. When control leaves the block, the effect of the definition is undone; some previously defined meaning of the identifier may be restored.

(d) Scope. The scope of the definition is that block of text.

(e) Expressions yield a value (also a new store if side effects take place). The expression 'personsage + i' has a value. Commands yield a new store. The command 'personsage :=10' puts the value 10 in the location called personsage. Definitions yield a new environment; $i = 2$ changes the binding for i.

5.19 i, 'tableindex', x, y are free, 'temp' is bound.

5.21 Let D={people} and

$\mathscr{F}(x)$: 'x is a father'
$\mathscr{M}(x)$: 'x is a male'
$\mathscr{W}(x)$: 'x is a woman'
$\mathscr{S}(x)$: 'x is a sister'

'All fathers are male' is $\forall x\ [\mathscr{F}(x) \rightarrow \mathscr{M}(x)]$ and 'Some women are sisters' is $\exists x\ [\mathscr{W}(x) \wedge S(x)]$.

5.22 Let D={people} and

$\mathscr{S}(x)$: 'x is a father'
$\mathscr{L}(x)$: 'x is a lecturer'
$\mathscr{L}(x, y)$: 'x likes y'(the arity is different from that of $\mathscr{L}(x)$)

We rephrase the assertion to mean 'there is at least one person who is a student and that person likes every lecturer'. This translates to $\exists x\ (\mathscr{S}(x) \wedge [\forall y\ \mathscr{L}(y) \rightarrow \mathscr{L}(x, y)])$.

5.24

$\forall x\ \exists y\ \mathscr{F}(x, y)$ means 'no matter what person is chosen there is another person who is that person's father', and is true.

$\exists y\ \forall x\ \mathscr{F}(x, y)$ means 'there is at least one person such that, regardless of which other person we choose, the first person is the father of the second person', and is false.

5.25 'There is some integer so that whichever integer we choose the product of the two integers is the same as the first integer'. This is true.

5.27 $\neg\forall x\ [\neg(\neg(S(x) \rightarrow (\neg\mathscr{P}(x))))]$

5.28 By the equivalences for compound quantified assertions:

$$\begin{aligned}\neg\forall x\ [\mathscr{P}(x) \rightarrow \mathscr{Q}(x)] &\equiv \exists x\ \neg[\mathscr{P}(x) \rightarrow \mathscr{Q}(x)] \\ &\equiv \exists x\ \neg[\neg\mathscr{P}(x) \vee \mathscr{Q}(x)] \\ &\equiv \exists x\ [\mathscr{P}(x) \wedge \neg\mathscr{Q}(x)]\end{aligned}$$

6.11 It can be proved that $\exists x\ [\mathscr{P}(x) \wedge \mathscr{Q}(x)] \vdash [\exists x\ \mathscr{P}(x) \wedge \exists x\ \mathscr{Q}(x)]$. However, we cannot prove $[\exists x\ \mathscr{P}(x) \wedge \exists x\ \mathscr{Q}(x)] \vdash \exists x\ [\mathscr{P}(x) \wedge \mathscr{Q}(x)]$. We cannot use formal inference rules to *disprove* something. Therefore we cannot prove that the equivalence does not hold.

6.17 Show that 'If $A = B$ then $A \subseteq B$ and $B \subseteq A$' and also that 'If $A \subseteq B$ and $B \subseteq A$ then $A = B$'.

6.19 If $\neg B \rightarrow F$ is T then $\neg B$ is F. If $\neg B$ is F then B is T. If B is T then $A \rightarrow B$ is T.

7.1 L uses $\{a, b, c\}$. A rule is 'The only strings permitted are those that are finite strings of zero or more a's followed by between one and five b's and then a string of one or more c's with other symbols following'.

7.2 $A^* = \{\Lambda, 0, 1, 00, 01, 10, 11, 000, \ldots\}$.

7.3

Basis clause. $\forall x\ [x \in A \rightarrow x \in A^+]$

Inductive clause. $x, y \in A^+ \rightarrow xy \in A^+$

Extremal clause. Unless a string can be shown to be a member of A^+ by applying the basis clause and the inductive clause a finite number of times then that string is not in A^+.

7.4 $ab * (bc * cd) = abbccd = (ab * bc) * cd$ so $*$ is associative.
$ab * bc = abbc \neq bcab = bc * ab$ so $*$ is not commutative.

7.5 The terms $f(f(c))$ and $f(m(c))$ represent the paternal and maternal grandfathers. The terms $m(f(c))$ and $m(m(c))$ represent the two grandmothers.

7.6 $\{a, s(a), s(s(a)), s(s(s(a))), s(s(s(s(a)))), \ldots\}$

7.7

(a) Is a wff

(b) Is not a wff because q is binary

(c) Is not a wff because $\neg$ is unary

(d) Is a wff

(e) Is not a wff because a right-hand bracket is missing (7 left hand, 6 right hand)

7.10 $u, v, w, 0$ are the only terms since there are no functions. Atomic formulae are $\in (u, v), = (u, w)$. Some wffs are $\neg(\in (v, u)), u = w$. The wff that expresses the assertion is $\forall u\ \neg(\in (u, u))$.

7.11 $(\neg(\neg\forall v\ (\neg\forall w\ \in (w, v))))$.

7.12 The interpretation is $0 < 1 \wedge (1 + 1) < 1$. The wff is false in the structure.

7.13

(a) 'There is a natural number that is smaller than or equal to any natural number'. This is true.

(b) 'There is a giraffe that has a longer neck than any other giraffe'. This is false in this interpretation.

8.3 $f \circ g(1) = 3$, but $g \circ f(1) = 2$.

8.6 It is easy to show it does not preserve the identity elements (the zero matrix is not mapped to the zero vector).

8.9 $(\mathbb{Q}, +)$ is a group with identity 0, while $(\mathbb{Q}, \times)$ is a monoid with identity 1. The function $\times$ distributes over $+$ since $a \times (b + c) = (a \times b) + (a \times c)$. Finally every $a \in \mathbb{Q}$ not equal to 0 has an inverse with respect to $\times$, namely $1/a$.

8.12 The isomorphism maps $\{\}$ to F and X to T.

8.17 -2

8.19 Clearly $\mathbb{Z}$ is commutative and associative with respect to $+$ (hence the first two axioms are OK). For the third axiom we have to show $x + (-x) = 0$ which is true for each $x \in \mathbb{Z}$ and for the fourth that $x + 0 = x$ for each x. $(\mathbb{Z}, \{+, -, 27\})$ is not a (Σ_1, E)-algebra since Axioms 8.3 and 8.4 are not satisfied; clearly $x + (-x) \neq 27$ for any $x \in \mathbb{Z}$.

8.20 $inv(e'\Box(e'\Box(e'\Box e')))$

9.1 $multiply(f, g) = h$ where $h(x) = f(x) \times g(x)$

9.4 x ((3 z 5) 4)

9.7

(a) $= (\lambda x.(\lambda y.\ x)\ a)\ b = (\lambda y.\ a)\ b = a$

(b) $=(\lambda x.(\lambda y.\ y)\ a)\ b = (\lambda y.\ y)\ b = b$

(c) $= \lambda x.(\lambda y.\lambda z.\ y\ (x\ y\ z))(\lambda x.\lambda y.\ x\ y) = \lambda x.(\lambda y.\lambda z.\ y\ (x\ y\ z))(\lambda x'.\lambda y'.\ x'\ y')$ (by α-reduction) $= \lambda y.\lambda z.\ y\ ((\lambda x'.\lambda y'\ x'\ y')\ y\ z)) = \lambda y.\lambda z.\ y\ (y\ z)$

(d) If we perform β-reduction from the left, that is we substitute $((\lambda x.x\ x)(\lambda x.\ x\ x))$ for x in $(\lambda x.\lambda y.\ y)$, then we get the solution $\lambda y.\ y$. However, if we perform β-reduction from the right, that is we substitute $((\lambda x.x\ x)$ for x in $(\lambda x.\ x\ x))$ we get the original expression; this is a non-terminating reduction sequence.

9.11 $\lambda f.\lambda g.\lambda x.\ (f\ x) \times (g\ x)$

9.13 $add = \lambda x.\lambda y.(y = 0 \rightarrow x,\ add\,(x + 1)(y - 1))$

9.15 A monotonic function $f : D_1 \rightarrow D_2$ is continuous if for every chain $x_0 \sqsubseteq x_1 \sqsubseteq \cdots$ in D_1

$$f(\lim_{n\to\infty} x_n) = \lim_{n\to\infty} (f\ x_n)$$

9.17 (coin coin coffee)$^*_{40}$ + coin(coin coffee coin)$^*_{40}$ + coin coin(coffee coin coin)$^*_{40}$

10.7 Let

$$\begin{aligned} S &= \{\text{stacks}\} \\ I &= \{\text{items}\} \\ E &= \{\text{no-item}\} \\ B &= \{\text{true, false}\} \end{aligned}$$

The set E contains the only error condition. We specify the argument and result sets for the functions that represent the operations on the stack:

create	:	$\rightarrow S$
push	:	$S \times I \rightarrow S$
top	:	$S \rightarrow I \cup E$
delete	:	$S \rightarrow S$
isempty	:	$S \rightarrow B$

The semantics is expressed by axioms:

$$\forall s \in S,\ i \in I$$

Stack axiom 1. isempty(create) = true.

Stack axiom 2. isempty(push(s, i)) = false.

Stack axiom 3. top(create) = no-item.

Stack axiom 4. top(push(s, i)) = i.

Stack axiom 5. delete(create) = create.

Stack axiom 6. delete(push(s, i)) = s

The definition of *pop* is that it removes a new item from the stack and produces a new stack:
pop: $s \rightarrow I \cup E \times S$
pop(s) = (top(s), delete(s)))

10.10 If $\{a, b, c\}$ were the carrier set, one of these elements would be 'junk' and not represented by a term. This would block the closure under structural induction.

10.11 The equality added in the model is not derived by the equations in the specification. This would give confusion in the model.

11.2 $f = sq\ (sq\ x)$ so that $f(2) = 16$.

11.6 $\{\neg\mathscr{P}(x),\ \neg\mathscr{Q}(x, y),\ \mathscr{R}(x, y)\}$ and $\{\neg\mathscr{P}(x),\ \mathscr{Q}(x, a),\ \mathscr{R}(x, a, f(x))\}$

12.5 If it can be proved that

(a) if P and C describe the state before A is executed then Q will describe the state afterwards, and also that

(b) if P and not C describe the state then it can be deduced that Q holds,

then it can be inferred that if P describes the state before 'if P then A' is executed then Q will describe the state afterwards.

13.6 If a node $x \neq z$ had outdegree 0 then it would be impossible to find a walk from x to z. If a node $x \neq a$ has indegree 0 then it would be impossible to find a walk from a to x.

13.10 $L(D_4) = X\,(AfYX)^{*}Atz$

13.13 The set $\{P_n : n \geq 1\}$

13.15 Only (b) is prime.

13.17

$$\begin{aligned} v(F) &= 1 + v(D_1; P_1; D_2) + v(D_0(D_3)) \\ &= 1 + (v(D_1) + v(P_1) + v(D_2)) + (1 + v(D_3)) \\ &= 1 + (2 + 1 + 1) + 1 + 1 = 7 \end{aligned}$$

Condition M1 asserts that the length of a statement containing no control flow is 1 and that the length of a prime with n procedure nodes (which will correspond to a control statement involving n non-control statements) is $n + 1$. This corresponds to our intuitive notion of length and is a formalization of the usual lines of code count. The sequence and nesting functions M2 and M3 are equally non-controversial.

14.8 Consider that $E_1 \cup E_2$ consists of the disjoint sets E_2 and $E_1 \cap \overline{E_2}$; that is $E_1 \cup E_2 = (E_1 \cap \overline{E_2}) \cup E_2$. By Axiom 14.3, $P(E_1 \cup E_2) = P((E_1 \cap \overline{E_2}) \cup E_2) = P(E_1 \cap \overline{E_2}) + P(E_2)$. Now since E_1 and E_2 are any events, we know that $E_1 \subseteq \Omega$ and $E_2 \cup \overline{E_2} = \Omega$. Therefore,

$$\begin{aligned} E_1 &= E_1 \cap \Omega \\ &= E_1 \cap (E_2 \cup \overline{E_2}) \\ &= (E_1 \cap E_2) \cup (E_1 \cap \overline{E_2}) \end{aligned}$$

by the distributive rule. Since these sets are disjoint, by Axiom 14.3,

$$P(E_1) = P(E_1 \cap E_2) + P(E_1 \cap \overline{E_2})$$

which gives Theorem 14.4.

14.13 2/3, 1/3 and 0.

14.16 $P(E/E) = P(E \cap E)/P(E) = 1$. $P(E_2/E_1) = P(E_2 \cap E_1)/P(E_1)$. We show $P(E_2 \cap E_1) \leq P(E_1)$. Now $E_1 = (E_1 \cap E_2) \cup (E_1 \cap \overline{E_2})$ which are exclusive events. By Axiom 14.3, $P(E_1) = P(E_1 \cap E_2) + P(E_1 \cap \overline{E_2})$ so $P(E_1 \cap E_2) \leq P(E_1)$ and $P(E_2/E_1) \leq 1$.

14.18 (a) 4/52.17 and (b) 32/52.51.1

14.22 Ω is the equiprobable space, $\{(H,H), (H,T), (T,H), (T,T)\}$. Identify the following events:

E_1: 'the first toss gives heads' so $E_1 = \{(H,H), (H,T)\}$
E_2: 'the second toss gives heads' so $E_2 = \{(H,H), (T,H)\}$
E_3: 'exactly one head is tossed' so $E_3 = \{(H,T), (T,H)\}$

Then $P(E_1) = P(E_2) = P(E_3) = 2/4 = 1/2$ and $P(E_1 \cap E_2) = 1/4$, $P(E_1 \cap E_3) = 1/4$, $P(E_2 \cap E_3) = 1/4$. Therefore the first condition for independence is satisfied. However, $E_1 \cap E_2 \cap E_3 = \{\}$ and so $P(E_1 \cap E_2 \cap E_3) = P(\{\}) = 0$ and $P(E_1 \cap E_2 \cap E_3) \neq P(E_1)P(E_2)P(E_3)$. Therefore the second condition is not satisfied and so the three events are not independent.

14.23

(a) $P(\text{circuit fails}) = 1 - P(\text{all components work}) = 1 - P(\overline{A} \cap \overline{B} \cap \overline{C}) = 1 - P(\overline{A})P(\overline{B})P(\overline{C}) = 1 - (0.97)(0.85)(0.99) = 0.184$

(b) $P(\text{alone fails}) = P(a \text{ works}, b \text{ fails}, c \text{ works}) = P(\overline{A} \cap B \cap \overline{C}) = P(\overline{A})P(B)P(\overline{C}) = (0.97)(0.15)(0.98) = 0.144$

14.26

E_1: 'the first ball is white'
E_2: 'the second ball is white'

(a) We require $P(E_1 \cap E_2)$. Now $P(E_1 \cap E_2) = P(E_2)P(E_1/E_2)$. Since $P(E_2) = 4/12$ and $P(E_1/E_2) = 3/11$, $P(E_1 \cap E_2) = 4/12 \times 3/11 = 1/11$. Note that if we replace the ball after the first choice, the choices are independent.

(b) We require $P(E_1)$. Now $E_1 = (E_1 \cap E_2) \cup (E_1 \cap \overline{E_2})$ where events $(E_1 \cap E_2)$ and $(E_1 \cap \overline{E_2})$ are exclusive since $(E_1 \cap E_2) \cap (E_1 \cap \overline{E_2}) = (E_1 \cap E_1) \cap (E_2 \cap \overline{E_2}) = E_1 \cap \{\} = \{\}$, so $P(E_1) = P(E_1 \cap E_2) + P(E_1 \cap \overline{E_2})$.
Now find $P(E_1 \cap \overline{E_2})$. $P(E_1 \cap \overline{E_2}) = P(\overline{E_2}) = P(E_1/\overline{E_2})$, where $P(\overline{E_2}) = 8/12$, $P(E_1/\overline{E_2}) = 4/11$ so $P(E_1 \cap \overline{E_2}) = 8/12 \times 4/11 = 8/33$. So $P(E_1) = P(E_1 \cap E_2) + P(E_1 \cap \overline{E_2}) = 1/11 + 8/33 = 11/33 = 1/3$.

14.28 We have seen that $\Omega = \{1, 2, 3, 4, 5, 6\}$ and $P(X = a_i) = 1/6$ for $i = 1, \ldots, 6$, since we have assumed an equiprobable space:

$$E(X) = 1/6 \times 1 + 1/6 \times 2 + 1/6 \times 3 + 1/6 \times 4 + 1/6 \times 5 + 1/6 \times 6 = 21/6 = 3.5$$

14.29 $\Omega = \{H, T\}$ and $X : \Omega \to \{0, 1\}$. The assumption of fairness indicates an equiprobable space. Therefore $P(X = 0) = P(X = 1) = 1/2$ and $E(X) = 1/2 \times 0 + 1/2 \times 1 = 1/2$. Note that $E(X)$ is not a value in the numerical sample space.

14.30 We assume the game is only played once. Then $\Omega = \{+40, -80\}$. Now

$$\begin{aligned} P(X = +40) &= 6/10 \quad \text{when a white ball is drawn} \\ P(X = -80) &= 4/10 \quad \text{when a blue ball is drawn} \end{aligned}$$

Therefore $E(X) = 6/10 \times 40 + 4/10 \times (-80) = 24 - 32 = -8$ and on average we expect to *lose* 8p.

14.32 This model contains a single parameter, p. The numerical sample space for the experiment is $\{1, 2, \ldots, 6\}$. The distribution is

$$\begin{aligned} &P(X = 4) = p \\ &P(X = r) = (1 - p)/5 \ (r = 1, 2, 3, 5, 6) \end{aligned}$$

14.40 $\sum_{i=0}^{\infty} P(X = i) = \sum_{i=0}^{\infty} \lambda^i e^{-\lambda}/i! = e^{-\lambda} \sum_{i=0}^{\infty} \lambda^i/i! = e^{-\lambda} e^{\lambda} = 1$.

14.44 The binomial model is not suitable because the probability of failure for each component is *not* the same. Let

W_i : component i works, where $i = 1, 2, 3$
F_i : component i fails, where $i = 1, 2, 3$

Then $P(W_1) = 0.95$, $P(W_2) = 0.94$, $P(W_3) = 0.97$, $P(F_1) = 0.05$, $P(F_2) = 0.06$, $P(F_3) = 0.03$.

$$\begin{aligned} &P(\text{at least two components work}) = P(\text{exactly two work}) + P(\text{all three work}) \\ &= P(W_1 \cap W_2 \cap F_3) + P(W_1 \cap F_2 \cap W_3) + P(F_1 \cap W_2 \cap W_3) + P(W_1 \cap W_2 \cap W_3) \\ &= P(W_1)P(W_2)P(F_3) + P(W_1)P(F_2)P(W_3) + P(F_1)P(W_2)P(W_3) + P(W_1)P(W_2)P(W_3) \\ &= 0.99388 \end{aligned}$$

14.48 The binomial model is suitable because the probability of failure for each component is the same. Let $p = 0.9$ (the same for each component) and $1 - p = 0.1$. Then P(at least 2 components function)$=P$(3 components work) + P(2 components work) $=P(X = 3) + P(X = 2)$ where X is the number of working components.

Now $P(X = 2) = \binom{3}{2} p^2(1 - p)^1$ and $P(X = 3) = p^3$ so required probability $= (0.9)^3 + (0.9)^2(0.1) = 0.972$.

15.1 $T_A(n) = n$ since the loop is entered n times. But $T_B(n) = 3(\log_2 n + 1)$ since the loop is entered at most $\log_2 n$ times, and each time there are at most 3 primitive operations. When $n = 1000$ we have $T_A(n) = 1000$, whereas $T_B(n) = 30$ (in fact, the actual number of operations for algorithm B when $n = 1000$ is only 25).

15.4 It is bounded above by n^3.

15.7 Complexity is at least $O(n)$ since every element in the list must be compared with some other element. However, it is easy to find an actual algorithm to solve the problem which has complexity $O(n)$ (you should write down such an algorithm). Hence the complexity of the maximal problem is $O(n)$.

15.8 The program only terminates if we can find integers $n > 2, a, b$ and c for which $a^n + b^n = c^n$. Thus, if we could show that this program terminates then we would have proved Fermat's theorem to be false. On the other hand, if we could show that the program does not terminate then it follows that we would have proved Fermat's theorem. Since the theorem has neither been proved nor disproved we conclude that we cannot determine yet whether this program terminates.

16.1 $0.8 \times 0.2 \times 0.2 \times 0.8 \times 0.8 = 0.020\,408$

16.2

(a) $1 - p$

(b) $(1 - p)^n$

(c) $(1 - p)^n + \binom{n}{1} p(1 - p)^{n-1} + \binom{n}{2} p^2(1 - p)^{n-2}$

16.4 Let E be the event '100 is received'. Then

$$P(A_1/E) = \frac{P(A_1)P(E/A_1)}{P(A_1)P(E/A_1) + P(A_2)P(E/A_2)} = \frac{\frac{1}{2}(0.1)(0.9)(0.9)}{\frac{1}{2}(0.1)(0.9)(0.9) + \frac{1}{2}(0.9)(0.9)(0.1)} = 0.9$$

16.7 You cannot decode it, but you know an error has occurred.

16.9 For each of the 6 pairs of codewords x, y compute $d(x, y)$. For example, $d(0000, 1100) = 2$, $d(1100, 0011) = 4$. The smallest distance is 2, hence $d(C) = 2$.

16.14

(a) 1110001

(b) 100 001 101 000 011

16.17 The code is not closed with respect to $\oplus$, since $1100 \oplus 0011 = 1111 \notin C$.

16.22 The most frequently occurring letter in the text is M. Therefore try out the shift that takes E to M. This would be the key 8. Decrypting with key 8 yields the message:

WHENEVERTHEYEARENDSINONESPURSWINTHECUP

which, when we insert spaces sensibly, yields the valid message.

17.5

(a) Syntactic and semantic failures cannot be mapped to the same number in any representation. For suppose x is a syntactic failure. Then $R_2(x)$ is false, but $M(P_2(x))$ is true since $M(x) = 6$.

(b) System crashes must be mapped to a higher number than both syntactic and semantic failures in $\mathscr{R}'$. For suppose x is system crash and y is semantic failure. Then $(x, y) \in R_4$ but $(M(x), M(y)) \notin P_4$, since $M(x) < M(y)$.

17.10 Suppose that $x_1, \ldots, x_n$ and $y_1, \ldots, y_m$ are two sets of objects measured for some property on an ordinal scale by M. It is enough to prove that the statement 1:'the median of the $M(x_i)$'s is greater than the median of the $M(y_i)$'s' is meaningful. We can assume that the x_i's are ordered so that $M(x_1) \leq M(x_2) \leq \cdots \leq M(x_n)$ and similarly the y_i's. Let M' be an admissible transformation of M and let statement 2 be the same as statement 1 except that M' replaces M. By definition, the mapping M' preserves the ordering of the x_i's and y_i's. It follows that if x_k is the middle ranked item from the $M(x_i)$'s, then x_k is also the middle ranked item from the $M'(x_i)$'s, irrespective of the values of M and M'. Similarly, if y_l is the middle ranked item from the $M(y_i)$'s, then it is also the middle ranked item from the $M'(y_i)$'s. This statement 1 is true iff statement 2 is true, which means the former is meaningful.

Bibliography

Ashcroft, E. and Manna, Z. (1972), 'The translation of goto programs to while programs', in *Information Processing 71*, volume 1, Friedman, C. V. (ed.), pp. 250–255, North-Holland.

Backhouse, R. C. (1986), *Program Construction and Validation*, Prentice Hall.

Backus, J. (1978), 'Can programming be liberated from the von Neumann style? A functional style and its algebra of programs', *Communications of the ACM*, **21**(8):613–641.

Barendregt, H. P. (1981), *The Lambda Calculus: Its Syntax and Semantics*, North-Holland.

Barr, M. and Wells, C. (1990), *Category Theory for Computing Science*, Prentice-Hall International.

Bauer, F. L. and Wossner, H. (1982), *Algorithmic Language and Program Development*, Texts and Monographs in Computer Science, Springer-Verlag.

Beeson, M. J. (1984), *Foundations of Constructive Mathematics: Metamathematical Studies*, Springer-Verlag.

Beizer, B. (1990), *Software Testing Techniques*, 2nd edn, Van Nostrand Rheinhold.

Beker, H. and Piper, F. (1982), *Cipher Systems: The Protection of Communications*, Northwood Books.

Bird, R. (1976), *Programs and Machines: An Introduction to the Theory of Computation*, John Wiley.

Birkhoff, G. and Lipton, J. D. (1974), 'Universal algebra and automata', in *Proc. XXV Symp. on Pure Maths*, pp. 41–51, American Mathematical Society.

Bornat, R. (1987), *Programming from First Principles*, Prentice-Hall International.

Bundy, A. (1983), *Computer Modelling of Mathematical Reasoning*, Academic Press.

Burstall, R. M. and Goguen, J. A. (1977), 'Putting theories together to make specifications', in *Proceedings of the 5th International Joint Conference on Artificial Intelligence*, pp. 1045–1058, Cambridge, Mass.

Burstall, R. M. and Goguen, J. A. (1979), 'The semantics of Clear, a specification language', in *Abstract Software Specifications, LNCS 86*, Springer-Verlag.

Cohen, B., Harwood, W. T. and Jackson, M. I. (1986), *The Specification of Complex Systems*, Addison-Wesley.

Cohn, P. M. (1974), *Algebra*, volume 1, John Wiley.

Cook, S. A. (1971), 'The complexity of theorem-proving procedures', in *Proc. 3rd Ann. ACM Symp. on Theory of Computing*, pp. 151–158, Ass. Computing Machinery, New York.

Dahl, O. J., Dijkstra, E. W. and Hoare, C. A. R. (1972), *Structured Programming*, Academic Press, London.

Diffie, W. and Hellman, M. E. (1976), 'New directions in cryptography', *IEEE Trans. Information Theory*, **22**:644–654.

Dummett, M. (1980), *Elements of Intuitionism*, Oxford University Press, Oxford. First published in 1977.

Ehrig, H. and Mahr, B. (1985), *Fundamentals of Algebraic Specification 1: Equations and Initial Semantics*, Springer-Verlag.

Ehrig, H. and Mahr, B. (1990), *Fundamentals of Algebraic Specification 2: Module Specifications and Constraints*, Springer-Verlag.

Enderton, H. B. (1972), *A Mathematical Introduction to Logic*, Academic Press.

Fenton, N. E. (1991), *Software Metrics: A Rigorous Approach*, Chapman and Hall.

Fenton, N. E. and Kaposi A. A. (1989), 'Metrics and software structure', *J. of Information and Software Technology*, July, pp. 298–320.

Finkelstein, L. (1984), 'A review of the fundamental concepts of measurement', *Measurement*, **2**(1):25–34.

Frost, R. A. (1986), *Introduction to Knowledge Base Systems*, Collins.

Galton, A. (1990), *Logic for Information Technology*, John Wiley.

Garey, M. R. and Johnson, D. S. (1979), *Computers and Intractability: A Guide to the Theory of NP-Completeness*, W. H. Freeman, San Francisco.

Gergely, T. and Szöts, M. (1985), 'Logical foundations of logic programming', Technical report, Applied Logic Laboratory, SZÁMALK, Budapest.

Gergely, T. and Ury, L. (1991), *First Order Programming Theory*, Springer-Verlag.

Glazer, H., Hankin, C. and Till, D. (1984), *Principles of Functional Programming*, Prentice-Hall.

Goguen, J. A. and Meseguer, J. (1987), 'Unifying functional, object-oriented and relational programming with logical semantics', in *Research Directions in Object-Oriented Programming*, pp. 417–477, MIT Press.

Goldschlager, L. and Lister, A. (1981), *Computer Science: A Modern Introduction*, Prentice-Hall.

Gordon, M. J. (1988), *Programming Language Theory and Its Implementation*, Prentice-Hall.

Grimaldi, R. P. (1985), *Discrete and Combinatorial Mathematics*, Addison-Wesley.

Harel, D. (1987), *Algorithmics*, Addison-Wesley.

Hoare, C. A. R. (1969), 'An axiomatic basis to computer programming', *Communications of the ACM*, **12**(10):570–583, October.

Hoare, C. A. R. (1985), *Communicating Sequential Processes*, Prentice-Hall International.

Hodges, W. (1977), *Logic*, Penguin.

Hogg, R. V. and Craig, A. T. (1978), *Introduction to Mathematical Statistics*, 3rd edn, Collier MacMillan.

Hogger, C. (1984), *Introduction to Logic Programming*, Academic Press.

Hopcroft, J. E. and Ullman, J. D. (1979), *Introduction to Automata Theory, Languages and Computation*, Addison-Wesley.

Ince, D. C. (1988), *An Introduction to Discrete Mathematics and Formal System Specification*, Clarendon.

Jackson, M. A. (1975), *Principles of Program Design*, Academic Press, London.

Jackson, M. A. (1983), *System Development*, Prentice-Hall, London.

Jones, C. (1986), *Systematic Software Development Using VDM*, Prentice-Hall International.

Kalmanson, K. (1986), *An Introduction to Discrete Mathematics and Its Applications*, Addison-Wesley.

Knuth, D. E. (1969), *The Art of Computer Programming, volume 1, Fundamental Algorithms*, Addison-Wesley.

Kolman, B. and Busby, R. C. (1987), *Discrete Mathematical Structures for Computer Science*, Prentice-Hall.

Kowalski, R. (1974), 'Predicate logic as a programming language', in *Information Processing 74*, pp. 569–574, North-Holland.

Kowalski, R. (1983), 'Logic programming', in *Information Processing 83*, pp. 133–145, North-Holland.

Krantz, D. H., Luce, R. D., Suppes, P. and Tversky, A. (1971), *Foundations of Measurement*, volume 1, Academic Press.

Kyburg, H. E. (1984), *Theory and Measurement*, Cambridge University Press.

Levy, L. S. (1980), *Discrete Structures of Computer Science*, John Wiley.

Linger, R. C., Mills, H. D. and Witt, R. L. (1979), *Structured Programming: Theory and Practice*, Addison-Wesley.

Lipschutz, S. (1974), *Theory and Problems of Linear Algebra*, Schaum's Outline Series, McGraw-Hill.

Liskov, B. H. and Zilles, S. N. (1974), 'Programming with abstract data types', in *Proc. ACM SIGPLAN Conf. on Very High Level Languages*, April, pp. 50–59.

Lloyd, J. W. (1987), 'Foundations of logic programming', in *Symbolic Computation*, pp. 7–39, Springer-Verlag.

Martin-Löf, P. (1984), 'Constructive mathematics and computer programming', *Phil. Trans. R. Soc. London*, **A312**:501–518.

McCabe, T. J. (1976), 'A complexity measure', *IEEE Trans. Software Eng.*, **2**(4):308–320.

McWilliams, F. J. and Stone, N. J. A. (1975), *The Theory of Error Correcting Codes*, Elsevier–North-Holland.

Mendenhall, W. and Sincich, T. (1988), *Statistics for the Engineering and Computer Sciences*, 2nd edn, Dellen and MacMillan.

Merkle, R. C. and Hellman, M. E. (1978), 'Hiding information and signatures in trapdoor knapsacks', *IEEE Trans. Information Theory*, **24**:525–530.

Milner, R. (1980), *A Calculus of Communicating Systems*, volume 92 of *Lecture Notes in Computer Science*, Springer-Verlag, New York.

Parnas, D. (1972), 'A technique for software module specification with examples', *Communications of the ACM*, **15**(5):330–336.

Peyton-Jones, S. L. (1987), *The Implementation of Functional Programming Languages*, Prentice-Hall International Series in Computer Science, Prentice-Hall International.

Potter, B., Sinclair, J. and Till, D. (1991), *An Introduction to Formal Specification Using Z*, Prentice-Hall.

Prather, R. E. (1976), *Discrete Mathematical Structures for Computer Science*, Houghton-Mifflin.

Prather, R. E. and Giulieri, S. G. (1981), 'Decomposition of flowchart schemata', *Computer Journal*, **24**(3):258–262.

Pressman, R. S. (1988), *Software Engineering: A Practitioner's Approach*, McGraw-Hill.

Reisig, W. (1985), *Petri Nets: An Introduction*, Springer-Verlag, Berlin.

Revesz, G. E. (1988), *Lambda-Calculus, Combinators, and Functional Programming*, Cambridge University Press.

Rivest, R. L., Shamir, A and Adleman, L. (1978), 'A method for obtaining digital signatures and public-key cryptosystems', *Communications of the ACM*, **21**:120–126.

Roberts, F. S. (1979), *Measurement Theory with Applications to Decision Making, Utility, and the Social Sciences*, Addison-Wesley.

Scanlan, D. A. (1989), 'Structured flowcharts outperform pseudocode: an experimental comparison', *IEEE Software*, September, pp. 28–36.

Schmidt, D. (1986), *Denotational Semantics: A Model for Language Development*, Prentice-Hall.

Scott, D. (1976), 'Data types as lattices', *SIAM J. Computing*, **5**(3):522–578.

Shoenfield, J. R. (1967), *Mathematical Logic*, Addison-Wesley.

Siegel, S. and Castellan, N. J. (1988), *Nonparametric Statistics for the Behavioural Sciences*, 2nd edn, McGraw-Hill, New York.

Skvarcius, R. and Robinson, W. B. (1986), *Discrete Mathematics with Computer Science Applications*, Benjamin Cummins.

Soloway, E., Bonar, J. and Ehrlich, K. (1983), 'Cognitive strategies and looping constructs: an empirical survey', *Communications of the ACM*, **26**(11):853–860.

Stanat, D. F. and McAllister, D. F. (1977), *Discrete Mathematics in Computer Science*, Prentice-Hall.

Stewart, I. and Tall, D. O. (1977), *The Foundations of Mathematics*, Oxford University Press.

Tang, A. H. S. and Tang, W. H. (1975), *Probability Concepts in Engineering Planning and Design*, volume 1, *Basic Principles*, John Wiley.

Tennent, R. D. (1981), *Principles of Programming Languages*, Prentice-Hall.

Tremblay, J. P. and Manohar, R. (1975), *Discrete Mathematical Structures with Applications to Computer Science*, McGraw-Hill.

Turner, D. A. (1982), 'Recursion equations as a programming language', in *Functional Programming and Its Applications*, Darlington *et al*. (eds), Cambridge University Press.

Turski, W. M. and Maibaum, T. S. E. (1987), *The Specification of Computer Programs*, International Computer Science Series, Addison Wesley.

Ury, L. and Gergely, T. (1990), 'A constructive specification theory', in *Declarative Systems*, David, G., Boute, R. T. and Shriver, B. D. (eds), Elsevier Science Publishers B. V. (North-Holland) IFIP, SZÁMALK, Budapest, 1015 Csalogány utca 30-32, Hungary.

Walker, D. W. (1988), *Computer Based Information Systems*, Pergamon Press.

Walston, C. E. and Felix, C. P. (1979), 'A method of programming effort and estimation', *IBM Systems J*., **16**(1):54–73.

Welsh, D. (1988), *Codes and Cryptography*, Clarendon.

Whitty, R. W., Fenton, N. E. and Kaposi, A. A. (1985), 'Structured programming: a tutorial guide', *IEE Software and Microsystems*, **3**(3):54–65.

Wilson, R. and Watkins, J. (1990), *Graphs: An Introductory Approach*, John Wiley.

Woodcock, J. and Loomes, M. (1988), *Software Engineering Mathematics: Formal Methods Demystified*, Pitman.

Index

Sections

1. Chapters 2 — 4 Geometry

2 (a) 2, 4

(b) 3 — 6

(c) Time allowing: 8, 10, 11, 16, 9, 15

Core